Fodor's **2nd Edition**

W9-BZS-196

Venice and
the Veneto

Fodor's Travel Publications • New York, Toronto, London, Sydney, Auckland
www.fodors.com

CONTENTS

MAPS

Circled letters in text correspond to letters on the photographs. For more information on the sights pictured, turn to the indicated page number Ⓐ on each photograph.

DESTINATION VENICE AND THE VENETO

The most useful piece of gear you can bring to this part of the world is a lively imagination. Rising from the sea, shimmering in the sun or wrapped in mist, Venice might be mistaken for a mirage, and its combination of Renaissance splendor and Eastern exoticism can be fully appreciated only if you leave rational, quotidian concerns behind at the gondola launch. Even when you depart the lagoon and venture inland, a sense of the extraordinary prevails—you'll find it in the coolly perfect symmetry of Palladian villas, the rugged majesty of the Dolomites' jagged peaks, and the refined decadence of Trieste's elegant cafés.

Ⓐ▷ 38

VENICE

Ⓑ▷ 39

Clichés come to be reborn in Venice, where the unique combination of the splendid and the bizarre can turn the most worldly traveler into an unbridled sentimentalist. Witness dawn breaking across the Ⓐ**Piazzetta San Marco**— the city's grand "front door," where trading ships once landed after voyages to the Orient—and you may feel as though you're straddling the

Ⓒ▷ 21

axis of the Eastern and Western worlds. A few steps away at the Ⓔ**Basilica di San Marco,** 43,000 square feet of gold-laden mosaics provide proof that no excess was too great for the mighty Republic of Venice. Another few steps and you're at the Ⓓ**Ponte dei Sospiri,** known to romantics as the place prisoners of the Republic took their parting glance at the outside world, breathed a sigh, then proceeded to their execution. Famous sights like these fill Venice, but you really fall under its spell when you spend time away from such tourist attractions. Explore Ⓑ**Dorsoduro** (or another of the city's six districts), wandering narrow streets that seem at once quaint and mysterious, and you're likely to have the quintessential Venetian experience of getting lost.

Ⓓ▷**37**

Nowhere else can you be so blissfully disoriented. Finally, seek out the sentimental heart of Venice in its people, whose outward aplomb disappears during events like the Ⓒ**Regata Storica,** where oarsmen race down the Grand Canal in boats of 14th-century design while onlookers cheer passionately from shore.

Ⓔ▷**32**

For all its air of fantasy, Venice remains a workaday place, too, though perhaps it's not surprising that many of the trades practiced here strike outsiders as rather extraordinary. In its illustrious past the city was home to some of the world's great artists—men who spent most of their lives bedecking their hometown in splendor. The results of this labor often remain in their original settings; stroll into one of the city's churches and you'll likely encounter a work of genius, such as Bellini's altarpiece at ⓘ**San Zaccaria,** Veronese's frescoes at San Sebastiano, or Titian's *Assumption* at Santa Maria Gloriosa dei Frari. The most ubiquitous artisans of present-day Venice are the glassblowers, who have been practicing their craft on the outer islands of Ⓕ**Murano** since the 13th century (when glassworks were removed from the city center because of the fire hazard). You can visit the glassblowers' workshops, and you'll find their creations, ranging from simple beads to sophisticated chandeliers, virtually anywhere you turn in the city. Elsewhere, housepainters have left ⓙ**Burano** awash in color, but it's the lace makers

Ⓕ 80

who have gained that island its greatest fame. They uphold a tradition of painstaking needlework that one generation has handed down to the next through the centuries. A 10-inch-square doily can cost in the thousands of euros, and the limited supply makes the pieces difficult to come by at any price; almost all the lace in Venetian shops is made elsewhere. Ⓗ**Carnevale,** the two weeks of revelry preceding Lent, was discontinued after the fall of the Republic in 1797 but was revived with great success in the 1970s. Its return has brought with it the reemergence of mask making as a trademark Venetian craft. Masks are de rigueur at many of Carnevale's lavish balls, and they now rival glass as a popular souvenir. Like glass, they come in wide varieties of price and quality. Venice has its share of unusual trades, but here even the most universal of vocations is a spectacular show: the Ⓖ**Rialto Fish Market,** in operation since the 11th century, is a daily wonder of exotic, colorful catches—often sold by equally colorful vendors.

Ⓘ▷ 69

Ⓙ▷ 79

SOUTHERN VENETO

Ⓐ> 181

Although it's called *La Serenissima* (the Most Serene), Venice can be hectic. For the perfect calming antidote, follow the Venetians and head inland. That they've always enjoyed a good *villeggiatura* (country vacation), is evidenced by the more than 100 stately retreats that line the Brenta River west of the city. The grandest of them, Ⓔ**Villa Pisani** at Stra, is reminiscent of Versailles, which no doubt explains its appeal to Napoléon, once a resident there. But for sheer beauty, the most note-

©⟩ 172

worthy villas are those designed by Renaissance architect Andrea Palladio, and the most renowned of those is Ⓐ**Villa La Rotonda,** outside Vicenza. Its symmetrical proportions and clean lines are distinguishing characteristics of the Palladian style, which architects the world over emulate to this day. While the villas of the Veneto skillfully accommodated a lavish lifestyle, the ©**Cappella degli Scrovegni** in Padua, lined with Giotto frescoes (including a depiction of the Seven Deadly Sins), was built to *atone* for such a life. Farther west, the magnificent Ⓓ**Arena di Verona** hosted public events in the days of the Roman Empire, and today people still flock to its marble terraces for concerts and elaborate opera productions.

Another of Verona's pleasures is Ⓑ**Giardino Giusti,** a formal garden overlooking the city that was a preferred retreat of Goethe's. Chances are you'll find it a tranquil spot to unwind as well.

Ⓓ⟩ 184

Ⓔ⟩ 202

11

NORTHERN VENETO

As you travel north from Venice across the marshland, the outline of an entirely different landscape appears before you. The road rises through gentle hills covered by vineyards that run right up to the walls of medieval towns such as Treviso and Ⓑ**Asolo.** Next come lush meadows laced with rushing rivers and backed dramatically by the ©**Dolomites,** one of Italy's grandest mountain ranges and a favorite of both hikers and skiers. At the end of the road, in Alpine-style resort towns such as the jet-set haven Ⓐ**Cortina d'Ampezzo,** gondolas of a different sort from those in Venice soar high into the mountains.

FRIULI-VENEZIA  Ⓐ▷ 244

GIULIA

The northeastern spur of Italy is a mix of green mountains and ragged coast, and it's an intriguing cultural patchwork as well. The largest city, Ⓐ**Trieste,** once served as the primary port of the Habsburg Empire, and the Austrian influence remains in its coffeehouses, famously popular with literary clientele such as James Joyce and Rainers Maria Rilke. Like Trieste, Gorizia, on the Slovenian border, didn't become part of the Italian republic until 1918; its Ⓑ**Castello** is testament to centuries of conflict. One of the region's most pleasant towns is Cividale del Friuli, where northern influences date to 568, when it became the first Lombard duchy in Italy. The Altar of Ratchis, a masterpiece of Lombard sculpture, graces Cividale's Ⓒ**Museo Cristiano.**

Ⓑ▷257

Ⓒ▷261

FODOR'S CHOICE

Even with so many special places in Venice and the Veneto, Fodor's writers and editors have their favorites. Here are a few that stand out.

ARCHITECTURAL WONDERS

Ⓔ **Basilica di San Marco, Venice.** If you had to choose one building that best defined the character of Venice, this Byzantine-Romanesque treasure would be it. ☞ p.32

Ca' d'Oro, Venice. The most regal of the palaces lining the Grand Canal houses a fine art museum. ☞ p.28

Cappella degli Scrovegni, Padua. Brilliant frescoes by Giotto decorate Italy's second most famous chapel (after the Sistine). ☞ p.172

Ⓓ **Cattedrale di San Giusto, Trieste.** Here you'll encounter architectural styles from throughout the ages, with mosaics and frescoes aglow in dusky candlelight. ☞ p.247

Santa Maria dei Miracoli, Venice. This Renaissance gem by master builder Pietro Lombardo is Venice's most important shrine to the Virgin Mary. ☞ p.68

Teatro Olimpico, Vicenza. Palladio's final work is arguably his most inspired. ☞ p.180

DINING

Osteria Da Fiore, Venice. Come here for classic Venetian cuisine in an elegant setting. $$$$ ☞ p.97

Harry's Grill, Trieste. It's the most sophisticated restaurant in Trieste, and even unusual dishes beg to be sampled. $$$–$$$$ ☞ p.249

Il Sole sulla Vecia Cavana, Venice. This former boathouse is a star on the Venetian dining scene. $$$–$$$$ ☞ p.84

Bancogiro, Venice. This Venetian wine bar in the Rialto market serves inspired cuisine. $–$$ ☞ p.99

Toni del Spin, Treviso. Old-fashioned charm and hearty yet carefully prepared meals make this a local favorite. $–$$ ☞ p.219

Altanella, Venice. The canal-side terrace with a view of the Zattere is the perfect place to escape the city's buzz and sample its exotic fish. $ ☞ p.93

LODGING

Ⓕ **Gritti Palace, Venice.** This legendary hotel in a Gothic palace feels like an aristocratic private home. $$$$ ☞ p.118

Ⓐ **Villa Cortine Palace, Sirmione.** Beautiful grounds border Lake Garda at this oasis of luxury. $$$$ ☞ p.200

Gabbia d'Oro, Verona. Cupids, antiques, and sumptuous fabrics fill this hotel in the heart of ancient Verona. $$$–$$$$ ☞ p.189

San Cassiano–Ca'Favretto, Venice. The draw of an impeccably kept historic building, with real antiques and wonderful views of the Grand Canal, keeps Ca' Favretto booked months in advance. $$$ ☞ p.121

Ⓑ **Belvedere, Bassano del Grappa.** Venetian furnishings, an excellent restaurant, a fireplace in the lounge, and a garden outside all make this a choice spot in central Veneto. $$–$$$ ☞ p.228

La Calcina, Venice. Ruskin loved it here, and the serene, understated atmosphere still earns raves today. $$ ☞ p.114

PERFECT PIAZZAS

Campo San Giacomo dall'Orio, Venice. This low-key square has trees, benches, and a fountain—perfect for relaxing in an idle moment. ☞ p.49

Piazza delle Erbe, Verona. Legions of merchants under grand umbrellas create an explosion of colors, sounds, and flavors, against a background of medieval buildings. ☞ p.187

Piazza San Marco, Venice. The "world's most beautiful drawing room" is always a pleasure, in spite of the crowds it attracts—and because of them. ☞ p.37

Piazza Unita d'Italia, Trieste. This city's answer to Piazza San Marco has the cafés, the grand palazzo, and the waterfront—but fewer tourists and pigeons. ☞ p.248

SPECIAL MEMORIES

Altarpieces, Santa Maria Gloriosa dei Frari, Venice. Bellini's *Madonna with Child and Saints* and Titian's *Madonna di Ca' Pesaro* and *Assumption* rank among Venice's greatest artistic treasures. ☞ p.53

Ⓒ **Cocoa during Carnevale, Caffè Florian, Venice.** Sipping cocoa with your mask on is a bit like eating spaghetti without staining your bib, but you'll feel part of the show. ☞ p.134

Glassblowing demonstration, Murano. It's awesome to watch incandescent balls of mud transformed into gracefully sculpted glass. ☞ p.80

Ⓖ **Gondola ride at dawn, Venice.** Make arrangements with a sympathetic gondolier for a tour of the sleeping city. ☞ p.20

Summer opera at Arena di Verona. There may be no more stunning setting for Italian opera than this 2,000-year-old marble amphitheater surrounded by red roofs, Renaissance palaces, and verdant hilltops. ☞ p.191

Sunset on the Dolomites. Whether you're here when the slopes are thick with snow or when the valleys are a riot of flowers, the view of the Dolomites at the golden hour is no less than breathtaking. ☞ p.233

Torre Campanaria, Cittadella. From the top of this fortified city's bell tower the view encompasses Roman tiled roofs and huge outer walls that are a masterpiece of military engineering. ☞ p.225

1   EXPLORING VENICE

A miracle born from the mud, Venice captures your eyes and seduces your soul with a courtesan's guile. Nothing comes cheap in this city that has always lived for gold, except for its greatest treasures—the colors and shapes, the sounds and smells, all unlike anything else in the world. Go to see the Basilica and the Palazzo Ducale, but set aside time to get lost as well. Deceptive, mysterious Venice has a soft spot for wanderers, and to them it will open its heart.

By Carla
Lionello

T WAS CALLED LA SERENISSIMA REPUBBLICA, "the most serene republic," a name suggesting the power and majesty of the city that was for centuries the unrivaled mistress of trade between Europe and the Orient and the staunch bulwark of Christendom against the tides of Turkish expansion.

No matter how many times you've seen it in movies or TV commercials, the real thing is more surreal and dreamlike than you had ever imagined. Its landmarks—the Basilica di San Marco, the Palazzo Ducale—hardly seem Italian. Delightfully idiosyncratic, they are exotic mélanges of Byzantine and Gothic styles. Sunlight shimmers and silvery mist softens every perspective. It is full of secrets, ineffably romantic, and, at times, given over entirely to pleasure.

Venice was founded in the 5th century when the Veneti, inhabitants of the region roughly corresponding to today's Veneto, fled their home to escape invading barbarians. The city rose from the waters to dominate the Adriatic and hold the gorgeous East in fee. Early in its history the city called in Byzantine artists to decorate its churches with brilliant mosaics, still glittering today. From the 13th to 15th century, the influence of Gothic architecture produced the characteristic type of palace in the Florid Gothic style, with ogival windows and finely wrought facades for which the town is famous the world over. The Renaissance arrived in Venice relatively late, at a time when the city had peaked in power and prosperity. In its early phase the style is referred to as Lombardesque, after the Lombardo family of masons and sculptors, who created distinctive intertwined discs, roundels, and crosses made of red, green, and dark yellow marble. The city's greatest Renaissance artists—the Bellini brothers, Carpaccio, and Giorgione—were all active between the late 15th and early 16th centuries. Along with the stars of the next generation—Veronese, Titian, and Tintoretto—they played a decisive role in the development of Western art, and their work still covers walls and ceilings all over the city.

Venice's participatory democracy, established in the 7th century, featured a ruler, the doge, who was elected to a lifetime term. However, from the 12th century on the doge's power was increasingly limited by a growing number of councils, commissions, and magistrates, and in 1268 a complicated procedure for his election was established to prevent nepotism. By this point, power really rested with the Great Council, originally an elected body but from 1297 onward an aristocratic stronghold, with members inheriting their seats from their noble forebears. Laws were passed by the Senate, a group of 200 elected from the Great Council (which could have as many as 1,700 members). Executive powers belonged to the College, a committee of 25 leaders. In 1310, the Council of Ten was formed to deal with emergency situations. Under such circumstances as war or internal conflict endangering the Republic's democracy, the doge would consult only the Council of Ten, thus allowing for rapid decisions and greater secrecy. In order to avoid too great a concentration of power, members could only serve for one year and had to be chosen from different families.

Another Venice institution that you'll hear frequent reference to is the *scuola* (plural *scuole*). The scuole were not schools, as the present-day Italian word would imply, but instead an important network of institutions that were established by different social groups—enclaves of foreigners, tradesmen, followers of a particular saint, and parishioners. For the most part secular despite their devotional activities, the scuole had their own bylaws and elected leaders and by the 13th century had created a sort of administrative system parallel to that of the Republic. By 1500 there were more than 200 of them in Venice, divided into major and minor scuole and those dedicated to the arts and crafts guilds. The Republic actually favored their existence, in that the scuole kept strict records on the names and professions of contributors to the brotherhood, which helped when it came time for the Republic to collect taxes.

The decline of Venice came slowly. For 400 years the powerful maritime city-republic held sway, but after the 16th century the tide changed. The Ottoman Empire blocked Venice's Mediterranean trade routes, and newly emerging sea powers such as Britain and the Netherlands ended Venice's monopoly by opening oceanic trading routes.

You must walk everywhere in Venice, and where you cannot walk you go by water. Occasionally, from fall to spring, you have to walk *in* water, when extraordinarily high tides known as *acqua alta* invade the lower parts of the city, flooding Piazza San Marco for a few hours. The problem of protecting Venice and its lagoon from dangerously high tides has generated extravagant plans and so many committee reports that the city may sink as much under the weight of the paper. Progress is being made, however. For centuries Venice's canals were regularly dredged to keep them clean and navigable. After 30 years of neglect, the dredging of canals was finally resumed in 1993; over half the city area has so far been treated, and the unpleasant odors caused by exceptionally low tides will eventually be a thing of the past.

It's almost a given that at some point you'll find yourself lost in Venice. The narrow streets make it difficult to navigate by way of a fixed point of reference such as a church dome or bell tower, and the winding paths tend to leave you without any sense of which way north is, much less where your restaurant might be. Dead ends are common, and streets and canals look deceptively familiar. Consider that on a detailed map you'll able to count more than 100 separate islands, divided by a network of roughly 150 canals and crossed by about 400 bridges. The city poses a considerable challenge even to natives unfamiliar with a particular part of town.

To help combat the confusion, signs all over town indicate the way to the train station, the Rialto Bridge, and Piazza San Marco, and place-names are neatly hand-painted at nearly every corner and bridge. The names, however, look nothing like those you may have grown familiar with while visiting other Italian towns. Here, a street is called a *calle* or a *riva* or *fondamenta* if it runs alongside a canal, and a street with shops is often called a *ruga* or *salizzada*. A small canal is called a *rio* (*rii* plural); a *rio terà* is a street created when a canal was filled in with earth. San Marco is the only square called a piazza in Venice—all the rest are called *campo, campiello,* or *corte* (field, little field, or yard), harking back to a time when they were used to grow vegetables and raise poultry.

Don't depend on addresses to clarify things. In 1170 the government divided central Venice into six *sestieri* (neighborhoods): San Marco, Castello, Dorsoduro, Cannaregio, San Polo, and Santa Croce. What began as a rather artificial dissection of the city now seems almost as natural a feature of Venice as its hundreds of man-made islands and canals; over the course of time, each neighborhood developed its own distinctive atmosphere and layout. In 1841, to simplify the address system, houses were numbered by sestiere rather than by street. Except for churches, which go just by their saint's name, all Venetian addresses are consequently made up of the name of the sestiere and a number.

PLANNING YOUR DAYS IN VENICE

YOU COULD EASILY SPEND 10 days visiting Venice's monuments, wandering in the less-central neighborhoods, taking trips to the islands of the lagoon, shopping, and eating good fish. But Venice is also a popular weekend destination, and it fills two days to the brim with sights, walks, and wonder.

If You Have 2 Days

The best introduction to the city is an early morning cruise along the **Grand Canal** from Piazzale Roma to San Zaccaria. You'll treasure seeing **Piazza San Marco** for the first time from the water as travelers before you have for hundreds of years. Spend the morning visiting the **Basilica** and **Palazzo Ducale,** allowing time to climb the **Campanile.** After lunch, take Salizzada San Moisè and Calle Larga XXII Marzo—lined with fashionable shops—to reach the *traghetto* (gondola ferry) in Campo Santa Maria del Giglio. Once across the Grand Canal, bear left and walk to the Baroque **Chiesa della Madonna della Salute,** with several paintings by Titian. The Punta della Dogana, to the right as you come out of the church, opens to one of the best panoramas in town. Head for the **Collezione Peggy Guggenheim,** home of first-rate 20th-century art, and then stretch your legs on the Zattere promenade while having a gelato. After dinner, splurge on a romantic gondola ride.

On day two, start early to beat the crowds at the **Rialto Bridge** and market. Don't miss the lively pescheria, where fish have been sold for more than 1,000 years. Follow the main drag to Campo San Polo and the **Chiesa dei Frari,** with two important works by Titian. Visit the **Scuola Grande di San Rocco,** famous for a series of more than 50 paintings by Tintoretto—Venice's answer to the Sistine Chapel. After lunch, jump into 18th-century Venice at Ca' Rezzonico, home of the **Museo del Settecento Veneziano.** Finish your day with a quick visit to the **Gallerie dell'Accademia,** with masterpieces of Western painting dating from the 14th to 19th century, or stroll to the center along the Ponte dell'Accademia for late-afternoon shopping.

If You Have 4 Days

Start day three at the **Museo Correr,** dedicated to the art and history of Venice, before exploring the sestiere of Castello. On a clear morning, an alternative to the museum is the **Isola di San Giorgio,** with breathtaking views of the lagoon and the city. From Piazza San Marco, go to the church of **San Zaccaria,** with a famous altarpiece by Giovanni Bellini. Then visit the Greek church of **San Giorgio dei Greci,** lined with Byzantine icons. Time your walk to hit the **Scuola di San Giorgio degli Schiavoni** before it closes at midday. Head to the graceful **Santa Maria Formosa,** and then take Calle del Paradiso via Campo Santa Marina toward a miracle born of marble, **Santa Maria dei Miracoli.** After a late lunch, visit **Campo Santi Giovanni e Paolo** and its Gothic abbey; then take Barbaria delle Tole to the **Campo dell'Arsenale,** only a short walk from the picturesque island of **San Pietro di Castello.** Take vaporetto Line 82 from the Giardini della Biennale to the **Giudecca,** where you can have dinner, or return to Piazza San Marco along the Riva degli Schiavoni, particularly beautiful at sunset.

On your final morning, take a guided tour of the **Jewish Ghetto.** Board vaporetto Line 42 (Ponte delle Guglie landing) by 11 AM, cruising to the islands of the lagoon: **Murano** and its glass museum, where you should stop for lunch; **Burano** and its lace museum, where you should have a *merenda* (afternoon tea) with the local cookies called *buranelli*; and romantic **Torcello,** wrapped in the mists of the lagoon. Unless you are dining at Locanda Cipriani, plan for dinner in central Venice.

The hitch is that the numbers don't go in any sequential order, so San Marco 3672 and 3673 might well be several narrow winding streets away from one another. Therefore, addresses, when necessary, give the nearest campo, bridge, or calle.

Unlike in other Italian towns, streets and squares in Venice are rarely dedicated to places or historical figures. Many streets take the name of the type of establishments that once characterized them, such as Calle del Cafetier (Street of the Coffeeshop) or Ponte Tette (Bridge of the Breasts, named for a nearby brothel). Others take the names of saints or noble families, such as Corner, Morosini, and Tron. Still others are references to now-obscure local legends or stories: no one can say with certainty how Ponte delle Maravegie (Bridge of the Wonders) or Ponte della Donna Onesta (Bridge of the Honest Woman) earned their names.

Although the smaller canals are often spanned by several bridges, the Grand Canal can only be crossed on foot at three points: Ponte degli Scalzi, near the train station (Ferrovia); Ponte di Rialto, at the Rialto; and at Ponte dell'Accademia, between Campo Santo Stefano and the Gallerie dell'Accademia. It's supremely maddening to find yourself on the wrong bank of the big canal with no bridge in sight, but more often than not you won't be far from one of the eight stops of the *traghetti*, essentially gondolas that ferry between opposite banks of the canal. The ride lasts a minute or two, and at €0.40 each way, it's much cheaper than a *vaporetto* (water bus).

The vaporetti that circulate through the city on set routes are best used to cover long distances. However, if you plan on jumping on and off vaporetti frequently, you can save a considerable amount of money by purchasing a three-day or weekly pass. Pick up a map of vaporetto routes, available with a complete schedule, from ACTV ticket booths in front of most stops.

In 1997, a group of parish priests founded Chorus, a nonprofit organization to raise money to maintain Venetian churches and protect them from further deterioration. The group instituted an admission charge (€1.55) for visits during fixed hours that do not interfere with church services. Free leaflets are provided (available in English), and postcards and booklets are on sale. The following churches belong to Chorus: Santa Maria del Giglio, Santo Stefano, Santa Maria Formosa, Santa Maria dei Miracoli, Santa Maria Gloriosa dei Frari, San Polo, San Giacomo dall'Orio, San Stae, Sant'Alvise, Madonna dell'Orto, San Pietro di Castello, SS. Redentore, and San Sebastiano. If you plan to visit more than a few, consider a pass (€7.55) good for one visit to each church within two months. The artwork in all Chorus churches is clearly labeled, and free lighting systems (ask the staff to point out switches) enable you to get a better look. You will need coins to turn on the art illumination in other churches. Priests are rarely available to pick up the phone in churches, so if you're seeking information the best bet is to call Chorus (☎ 041/2750462) during office hours, Monday–Friday 9–1 and 2–6, or check their Web site, WEB www.chorus-ve.org.

THE GRAND CANAL

One of the best initiations to Venice is a trip down the Grand Canal. The name "Grand Canal" couldn't be more to the point. Venice's main thoroughfare competes with the Piazza San Marco for the honor of being the city's most famous landmark, and it is without a doubt one of the world's great "avenues": for 3 km (2 mi) it winds its way through Venice in a backward "S," lined with nearly 200 stupendous 12th- to 18th-century palaces built by the city's richest families. A hand-

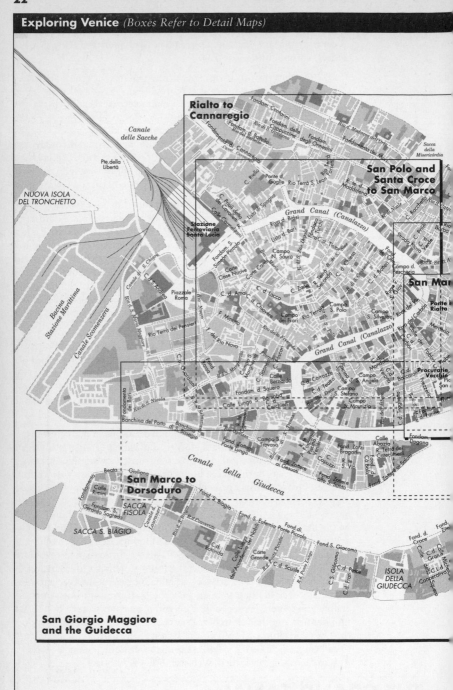

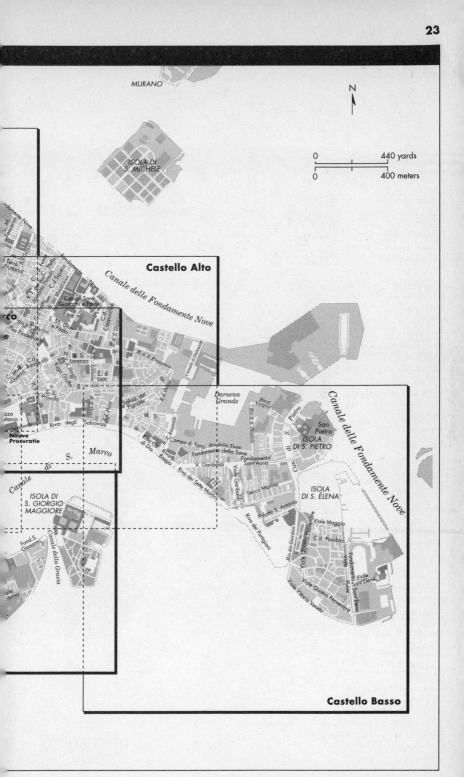

MURANO

N

ISOLA DI
S. MICHELE

| 0 | | 440 yards |
| 0 | | 400 meters |

Castello Alto

Canale delle Fondamente Nove

Campo Santi
Giovanni e Paolo

B. S.
Lorenzo

C. d.
Lion

Riva degli Schiavoni

*Nuove
Procuratie*

S. Marco

Darsena
Grande

Rio d.
Vergini

S.
Pietro

San
Pietro
**ISOLA
DI S. PIETRO**

Canale delle Fondamente Nove

N. Campo d. Tana Rio della Tana
Fondamenta della Tana

V. Garibaldi

Fondamenta
Sant'Anna

Riva dei Sette Martiri

Viale Garibaldi

Secco Marina

**ISOLA
DI S. ELENA**

Paludo S. Antonio

Riva dei Partigiani

Canale di

**ISOLA DI
S. GIORGIO
MAGGIORE**

Fond. S.
Giovanni

Canale della Grazia

Rio dei Giardini

Viale Maggio

Viale Quattro Novembre

C. d. Pasubio

Viale Quattro Novembre

Viale Vittorio Veneto

Viale
Sant'Elena

Fondamenta Sant'Elena

Viale Sant'Elena

Castello Basso

24

Grand Canal

ful still belong to the descendants of those who built them, but many have been converted to other uses. A dozen museums, several five-star hotels, a few modest inns, government and city offices, courts, university departments, a post office, a TV station, and even a casino are housed in Renaissance studios and in Baroque ballrooms that often lie behind the Byzantine and Gothic facades.

There is a definite theatrical quality to the Grand Canal, something particularly noticeable as you pass in a vaporetto or a gondola. It's as if each facade had been designed to steal your attention from its rival across the way. But there is no hurry here, and although today most see the canal from a vaporetto rather than a gondola, this promenade along the water still unfolds gently, its magnificence washing over you—only metaphorically, of course: the canal is just 9 ft deep on average, but it's no longer safe to swim.

The most romantic way to see the canal is from inside a gondola. Take a ride from Rialto to San Marco an hour or so before sunset, or at the break of dawn when dreamlike scenery will be there just for you. The next best thing is to enjoy the view from vaporetto Line 1, especially if you manage to sit in one of the coveted seats at the prow, which offers a clear view of both banks. Although you can board a vaporetto at any of the 16 stops along the canal, it makes sense to begin your voyage from Piazzale Roma or the train station (Ferrovia) and end at San Marco or San Zaccaria. Don't leave Venice until you have seen it by night from the water—but bring a warm scarf in winter and mosquito repellent in summer. Once off the vaporetto, keep in mind that traghetti at many points along the Grand Canal will ferry you from one bank to the other for just €0.40.

Vaporetto landings are well marked with huge yellow signs, but perhaps the best way to enjoy yourself and learn about the town is just to lean back in your seat, take in the view, and marvel at the history steeped in the grand past of this Grand Canal. Below is a description of what you'll see. For more detailed information about the major sights, see the neighborhood tours that follow.

Numbers in the text correspond to numbers on the Grand Canal map.

Timing

From Piazzale Roma to San Zaccaria, vaporetto Line 1 takes exactly 41 minutes; service runs between 5 AM and midnight, with departures every 10 minutes during the day, and about every 20 minutes early in the morning and after 9:30 PM. There is *servizio notturno* (night service) from midnight to 5 AM, with N boats running between Piazzale Roma and San Zaccaria every 40 minutes (to and from Rialto every 20 minutes). A trip down the Grand Canal by gondola takes about an hour and a half. Never let a gondolier help you climb down into his gondola without having discussed the duration and cost of the ride.

From Piazzale Roma to Rialto

If you arrive in Venice by train or car, you'll immediately encounter this first tract of the Grand Canal, which flows between the Cannaregio and Santa Croce sestieri. Highlights include the Baroque San Stae church, Venice's fabulous casino, and the sensational Ca' d'Oro.

Vaporetto Line 1 starts at Piazzale Roma landing. The first stop is **Ferrovia** ① (the train station, officially "Stazione Ferroviaria Santa Lucia"), which, along with Piazzale Roma, is the least "Venetian" spot in the city: it's modern in design and situated back from the water. Near the stop is the Baroque **Chiesa degli Scalzi** ②. The church was partially re-

DISNEY IN A GONDOLA

PLASTIC CARILLONS in the shape of a gondola with a swirling dancer, silver gondola brooches, striped gondolier's T-shirts, and hats with a nylon ribbon saying "Venezia" in a dozen languages are only some of the Disneyesque souvenirs that rob an ingenious piece of craftsmanship of its history and pride. Originally, gondolas were much less refined than they are today, both aesthetically and from an engineering point of view. The last substantial improvements were made as late as the 19th century, and only two features have survived through the centuries: the flat bottom and the slender shape, which allow for deft maneuvering in the shallow and narrow canals. In the heyday of the Renaissance, some 14,000 gondolas clogged Venice's waterways: they served as private "carriages," ferries, public taxis, and vessels for hauling light goods. Most came with a cabin for privacy (like the one Casanova used to woo the ladies). Gondolas were not painted black until 1562, when sumptuary laws curtailed lavish decoration.

Gondolas are made and sold in workshops called *squeri*, of which only a few remain. From start to finish it takes more than three years to build one, as the different kinds of wood must be shaped, bent, and cured by hand. The finishing touch comes with the addition of the *dolfin* (prow). S-shape like the Grand Canal, its six prongs represent the town's six quarters, the longest one jutting out in the opposite direction from the rest representing the Giudecca. Inserted between the six prongs are three leafy decorations that signify Murano, Burano, and Torcello. Last but not least, the round top of the dolfin stands for the doge's hat. To arrange a tour of a squero, contact **Roberto Tramontin** (✉ 1542 Dorsoduro, ☎ 041/5237762); don't expect fluent English, but you can get by fine without it. While there, you can inquire about ordering your own gondola. Prices start at €26,000.

— Carla Lionello

built after being struck by an Austrian bomb in World War I that destroyed two ceiling frescoes by Tiepolo. Inside is the tomb of the last, rather inept doge, Ludovico Manin, aptly buried at the edge of town. You'll pass under **Ponte degli Scalzi** ③, named after the order of barefoot friars who founded the similarly named church. It dates from the 1930s, which makes it the newest bridge straddling the Grand Canal.

Opposite the landing of **Riva di Biasio** ④ (stop 3), a plaque on the wall of the adjoining church of **San Geremia** ⑤ recalls the demolition of the Church of Santa Lucia to make room for the train station. The reliquary of the patron saint of eyesight (according to Catholics, Lucia tore her eyes out after being complemented on their beauty by one of her pagan jailers) was moved to San Geremia, and the train station took the name "Santa Lucia." The imposing palace half-hidden behind the bell tower is the famous **Palazzo Labia** ⑥ (☞ Rialto to Cannaregio, *below*), with magnificent frescoes by Tiepolo. A left turn into the Canale di Cannaregio would bring you to the north side of the lagoon facing the industrial complex of Marghera.

Looking at the uncompleted facade of the church of **San Marcuola** ⑦
(stop 4), you get a chance to see what's behind the marble decorations
of similar 18th-century churches. More compelling is the lovely *altana*
(a wooden platform supported by poles, often seen on Venetian roofs)
of neighboring 18th-century **Ca' Gatti** ⑧. Noblewomen would climb
up here wearing hats with a hole in the center and a large brim, upon
which they would arrange their hair, treated with herbs, for it to dry
in the sun. On the other riva, flanked by two *torricelle* (side wings in
the shape of small towers) and a triangular *merlatura* (crenellation),
is the **Fondaco dei Turchi** ⑨, a great-looking Byzantine merchant's
house that is now home to the local Museo di Storia Naturale (☞ San
Polo and Santa Croce to San Marco, *below*). Next comes the plain brick
Fondaco del Megio ⑩, which served as the city's millet silo; a lion marks
it as the Serenissima's property. Baldassare Longhena, who invented
the *orecchioni* (spirals in the shape of big ears) used on the facade of
Santa Maria della Salute, is responsible for the obelisqued **Ca' Belloni-
Battagia** ⑪ on your right, which is overshadowed by the extraordinary
Palazzo Vendramin-Calergi ⑫ on the other bank. Charismatic Leonardo
Loredan was the doge who led Venice to victory against the League of
Cambrai, which was formed in 1508 by the pope, the Holy Roman
Emperor, and the kings of France and Spain with the intention of de-
stroying the Republic. He commissioned this Renaissance gem from
Mauro Codussi (1440–1504) in the 1480s, at a time when the late-
Gothic style was still fashionable. In 1883, the German composer
Wagner died in a room he had rented in the new wing following the
success of his *Parsifal*. As stated in gilded letters on a banner hanging
from the first floor, the palace is now the winter home of Venice's casino.

Stop 5 corresponds to the white, whimsical church of **San Stae** ⑬, which,
like a well-wrapped gift with a dull present inside, is best left un-
opened. Farther down the bank another Baroque creation comes into
view. **Ca' Pesaro** ⑭ houses a gallery of contemporary paintings and a
collection of Oriental art; here once lived the man who declared war
against Napoléon (☞ San Polo and Santa Croce to San Marco, *below*).
One block and two *rii* (small canals) ahead stands a tall, attractive palace
with a balcony and an intriguing name: **Ca' Corner della Regina** ⑮ (of
the Queen). In 1468, Caterina Cornaro, the "daughter of the Republic," was married at age 13 to the King of Cyprus in order to support
the foreign policy of the Serenissima. Although the queen's birthplace
was demolished by her descendants when they built Ca' Corner in the
1720s, the old name stuck. In the 1970s it was turned into a library
and *cineteca* (film archive) for the Biennale.

The **Ca' d'Oro** ⑯ (stop 6), or "Golden House," takes its name from
the gilding that once accentuated the marble carvings of its facade. One
of the most striking palazzi on the Canal, it holds a good collection of
antiquities and paintings (☞ Rialto to Cannaregio, *below*). Boat traffic increases as you approach the Rialto district, a commercial hub with
a concentration of souvenir booths and inexpensive retail stores. As
the canal narrows, you pass one of the oldest outdoor food markets
in the world. The neo-Gothic, loggia-like shelter to the right, the
pescheria, marks the spot where fish from the lagoon and the Dalmatian coast have been sold for the last 1,000 years. Fruit and vegetable
stalls fill the spacious fondamenta, and cheese shops and butchers are
hidden behind the buildings in the background. Next is the porticoed
edifice built by Sansovino in 1555 to house the Republic's equivalent
of a stock exchange and chamber of commerce. Today it contains
Venice's Tribunal and Court of Justice. On the opposite bank is picturesque **Ca' da Mosto** ⑰, with a water porch, a lovely balcony, and a
well-preserved 13th-century Byzantine house, which in the 18th cen-

tury came to be known as the most fashionable hotel in town, the Leon Bianco. Farther down the bank, just before Rialto Bridge, is the white-washed central post office, once frescoed with alluring female figures by Giorgione and Titian. It's an apt decoration for what was then the busiest trading center of the Republic—the **Fondaco dei Tedeschi** ⑱— where merchants from Germany, Austria, Bohemia, and Hungary had their warehouses, shops, and sleeping quarters. Opposite stands the curiously angled **Ca' dei Camerlenghi** ⑲, built in 1525 to accommodate the powerful State Treasury. Tax evaders were thrown in a jail on the ground floor. The **Rialto Bridge** ⑳ (stop 7), arched enough to allow a galley to pass beneath it, dates from the late 16th century (☞ Rialto to Cannaregio, *below*).

From Rialto to the Ponte dell'Accademia

Heading toward more noble quarters, the Grand Canal continues its run across the southern part of town, circling the San Marco sestiere. Mansions of the many families that provided the Republic with doges line the San Polo and Dorsoduro side, vying for the glance of those passing by with those built on the San Marco side. The murky green water, with its wavering reflection, seems to demand the question of the witch in *Snow White*: Who's the fairest one of all . . .

On the left, just past the Rialto stop, is **Ca' Dolfin-Manin** ㉑, which served as the residence of the last doge. Designed by Sansovino in the 1560s, today it is headquarters of the Banca d'Italia. This is the only point in the Grand Canal where the buildings do not have principle entrances on the water, a consequence of the two long and spacious *rive* (streets), which had been used for the unloading of two vital staples: coal and wine. On the Riva del Carbon, to the left, where a suspended double passageway unites them, are **Ca' Loredan** ㉒ and **Ca' Farsetti** ㉓, 13th-century Byzantine structures that house the city's town hall. A bit farther down is the stern, rather intimidating **Ca' Grimani** ㉔, perhaps an appropriate site for the Court of Appeals. On the opposite Riva del Vin, just before the landing of **San Silvestro** ㉕ (stop 8), a deep-red building with pointed windows and arches sticks out—an example of early 20th-century architecture mocking the Gothic style. Right after Ca' Grimani, the tiny, white-and-red-striped Casetta Tron is squeezed between the 15th-century **Ca' Corner-Contarini dei Cavalli** ㉖, with horse heads to the sides of the balconies, and the huge **Ca' Martinengo** ㉗, known for having been the residence of Conte Volpi, the man who modernized the city during the first half of the 20th century. Venice has him to thank for innovations such as electricity, the nearby industrial zone in Porto Marghera, the foundation of Mestre, the chain of five-star CIGA hotels, and the now-famous Biennale film festival.

Lord Byron was a passionate admirer of the owner of **Ca' Benzon** ㉘ (just after a plain-looking block of houses), a fair-haired Venetian countess who inspired the gondoliers' hit song, "La Biondina in Gondoleta" (The Fair Maiden in the Little Gondola). As you approach **Sant' Angelo** ㉙ (stop 9), the beautiful **Ca' Corner-Spinelli** ㉚ comes into view, built by Codussi while he was attending the construction of Palazzo Vendramin-Calergi (identical windows grace each facade). At the corner of the next rio, the four-story Gothic **Ca' Garzoni** ㉛ is now part of the Università di Venezia Ca' Foscari, and the crowds of students coming from the main university building across the Canal line up for the *traghetto* (gondola ferry) of **San Tomà** ㉜ (stop 10), running more or less daily since 1354. A plaque on the wall of squat **Ca' Mocenigo** ㉝ (opposite San Tomà) recalls that Lord Byron lived here from 1818 to 1819, but neglects to mention that he shared the apartment with two monkeys one bear, two parrots, and one fox, and had 14 servants, a butler, and a gondolier at his service. The vaporetto makes a sharp turn, and on the right bank stands perhaps the tallest Gothic palace in town, with no fewer than 40 windows, commanding a splendid view of the Grand Canal. Built in 1437 for Doge Francesco Foscari—under whose reign La Serenissima reached its greatest extent—**Ca' Foscari** ㉞ has been home to Venice's university since the 1870s. Next door, in one wing of **Ca' Giustinian** ㉟ (1452), Wagner composed the second act of *Tristan and Isolde*. The so-called "House of the Thirteen Windows," on the other bank, is believed to have been the mansion of the historical character upon whom Shakespeare (who never saw Italy) modeled Othello, although the jealous Venetian who killed his wife, Desdemona, actually wasn't a Moor, simply a member of the Moro family.

The landing of **Ca' Rezzonico** ㊱ (stop 11) marks the spot where Longhena in 1649 began the construction of the conspicuous Baroque palace that now houses the Museo del Settecento Veneziano (☞ San Marco to Dorsoduro, *below*). Opposite stands **Palazzo Grassi** ㊲, the Grand Canal's youngest noble mansion, commissioned in 1749 by a Bolognese tycoon from the architect Giorgio Massari—who also completed Ca' Rezzonico after the death of Longhena. Italian car manufacturer Fiat acquired it in 1984, and since then some of the country's most prestigious exhibitions have been hosted in its rococo rooms, with frescoes by a follower of Alessandro Longhi, Jacopo Guarana, and others. Past **Campo San Samuele** ㊳ and its little church, the first house past the garden has an apartment that was once Titian's studio.

Among the scores of churches that Napoléon mercilessly demolished or deconsecrated was the brick Gothic Chiesa di Santa Maria della Carità. In its place the **Accademia di Belle Arti** ㊴ (whose first director had been Tiepolo in the 1750s) was installed here in 1807. Its original collection of paintings quickly grew with private donations and the works from suppressed *scuole* (confraternities) and churches. Today the **Gallerie dell'Accademia** ㊵ (☞ San Marco to Dorsoduro, *below*) also occupy the adjoining convent and *scuola*. As with the Eiffel Tower, with which it shares a certain structural grace, the Ponte dell'Accademia was not intended to be permanent. Built in 1933 as a quick alternative to a rusting iron bridge built by the Austrians, it was so well liked by Venetians that a perfect replica with steel bracing was created in 1986.

From the Ponte dell'Accademia to San Zaccaria

You're only three stops from the end of the line, but this last tract of the Grand Canal is like a rich dessert after a delicious meal: a baroque creation resembling a wedding cake topped with meringue and whipped cream marks the end of what Charles VIII's ambassador to Venice called the *"plus belle rue en tout le monde"* (the most beautiful street in all the world).

Lovely **Ca' Franchetti** ㊶, with a central balcony made in the style of Palazzo Ducale's loggia, dates from the late Gothic period, but its gardens are no older than the cedar tree that stands at their center—until the late 19th century, this was the *squero,* where gondolas were made and repaired. Next door **Ca' Barbaro** ㊷ was the residence of the illustrious family who rebuilt the church of Santa Maria del Giglio (☞ San Marco to Dorsoduro, *below*). In more recent times it hosted guests such as Monet, Henry James, and Cole Porter, who eventually moved to a boat anchored in the Giudecca Canal. Past Campo San Vio, the bright 19th-century mosaics of **Ca' Barbarigo** ㊸ will give you a general idea of how the frescoed facades of many Venetian palaces must have looked in their heyday. Farther down the bank, the lush garden growing behind the **Palazzo Venier dei Leoni** ㊹ adds a romantic touch to what looks more like a well-kept ruin than the unfinished building it is. A small-scale model of the palace inside the Museo Correr gives some credit to the theory that its construction had been somehow sabotaged by the family living in Sansovino's **Ca' Granda** ㊺ across the canal, who didn't want the Veniers' house to obstruct their view of the lagoon. In 1951 the site was bought by American heiress and art collector Peggy Guggenheim, who kept her private gondola parked at the doorway and left her ever-present dogs to stand guard in place of roaring lions (☞ Collezione Peggy Guggenheim *in* San Marco to Dorsoduro, *below*). Had it been up for sale, perhaps Guggenheim would have preferred the fascinating **Ca' Dario** ㊻ instead. Narrow and tilted, yet inexplicably graceful and full of character, this little Lombardesque miracle of colored marbles and arched windows will make you want to ask the driver to stop the boat. Past the landing of Santa Maria del Giglio (stop 13) stands the 15th-century **Ca' Pisani-Gritti** ㊼, best known as the Gritti Palace Hotel. On the other bank, the small Palazzo Salviati, with a harsh 20th-century mosaic on the facade, is the only surviving glass factory in Venice outside of Murano. As you approach the cupola of **Santa Maria della Salute** ㊽ (☞ San Marco to Dorsoduro, *below*), save a glance or two for the picturesque Rio di San Gregorio, and what's left of the namesake Gothic abbey, now converted to private apartments.

Leaving the **Punta della Dogana** ㊾ and its golden Palla della Fortuna (Golden Ball, with a figure representing Fortune) shining against the sky, the vaporetto stops in front of the world-famous Harry's Bar and the **Giardinetti Reali** ㊿—planted by Napoléon where the Republic's grain warehouses once stood—before proceeding to **San Zaccaria** ㋕ (last stop). The last great view is of the **Piazzetta San Marco** ㋖, the **Basilica di San Marco** ㋗, and **Palazzo Ducale** ㋘ (☞ Piazza San Marco, *below*), which moved Thomas Mann to claim that to arrive in Venice from the mainland (he had taken the train) was like entering the house of a beautiful woman through the service entrance.

PIAZZA SAN MARCO

One of the most engaging squares in the world, Piazza San Marco is the heart of Venice, a vast open space enclosed by an orderly procession of arcades marching toward the fairy-tale cupolas and marble lacework of the Basilica di San Marco. Perpetually animated during the day, when it's filled with people and crowds of fluttering pigeons, it can be magical at night, especially in the winter, when melancholy mists swirl around the lampposts and bell tower.

Numbers in the text correspond to numbers in the margin and on the San Marco map.

A Good Walk

The areas around **Piazza San Marco** ① offer enough interesting sights to fill up the better part of a day. Begin with a morning visit to the **Basilica di San Marco** ②, home of the Pala d'Oro and the Museo Marciano. Next, get a bird's-eye view of the piazza and city from the top of the **Campanile** ③. Move on to the adjacent **Piazzetta San Marco** ④ for a visit to the glorious **Palazzo Ducale** ⑤ and a look at the Ponte dei Sospiri. Return to Piazza San Marco, and cross to the side opposite the Basilica, the Ala Napoleonica—so named because it was Napoléon who closed off the piazza. Inside is the **Museo Correr** ⑥.

Allow some time between sights to browse in the shops under the arcades of the Procuratie and the adjoining streets, particularly in the Mercerie district, reachable through the passage under the **Torre**

dell'Orologio ⑦. The Frezzeria and Salizzada San Moisè, which both begin at the Museum Correr (the former is to the right; the latter is straight ahead and after the campo is called Via XXII Marzo), also make for good shopping strolls.

You'll need a full day to visit all sights thoroughly. If you have limited time, give priority to the Palazzo Ducale over the Museo Correr. Plan on 1½ hours to see the Basilica di San Marco and its Pala d'Oro, Galleria, and Museo Marciano. It takes about two hours to do justice to Palazzo Ducale. On a reasonably clear and warm day, the view from the Campanile is enchanting (unless the bells are ringing, on the hour); allow at least 40 minutes.

Sights to See

★ ❷ **Basilica di San Marco.** An opulent synthesis of Byzantine and Romanesque architectural styles, Venice's gem is laid out in a Greek-cross floor plan and topped with five plump domes. The Basilica did not actually become the cathedral of Venice until 1807, but its role as the church of the doge placed it at the center of Venetian life long before then. Begun in 1063, it was inaugurated in 1094 as the resting place of St. Mark the Evangelist, after two agents of the doge stole his remains from Alexandria two centuries earlier by hiding them in a barrel under layers of pickled pork to get them past the Muslim guards. The escapade is illustrated in a 13th-century mosaic in the semicircular lunette over the far left door, the earliest image on this heavily decorated facade. Look closely to see a picture of the church as it appeared at that time. Over the years the basilica stood as a symbol of Venetian wealth and power, and it was endowed with all the riches the Republic's admirals and merchants could carry off from the Orient, earning it the nickname Chiesa d'Oro (Golden Church). The four bronze horses that prance and snort over the central doorway are copies of sculptures that victorious Venetians took from Constantinople in 1204 (the originals are in the Museo Marciano). Look for a medallion of red porphyry set in the floor of the porch, just inside the central doorway. It marks the spot of one of Venice's political coups: the reconciliation between Barbarossa, the Holy Roman Emperor, and Pope Alexander III, brought about by Doge Sebastiano Ziani in 1177.

The basilica is famous for its 43,055 square ft of stunning mosaics, made possible by an innovative roof constructed with brick vaulting rather than wood. Many of the original windows were filled in to make room for even more mosaics, resulting in an interior so dark that candlelight is necessary even in the daytime. The soft light shimmering against the tiny gold tiles, each mounted at a slight angle to enhance the effect, is nothing short of magical. The earliest mosaics date from the 11th and 12th centuries; the last were added in the 16th century, including the *Last Judgment* on the arch between the porch and the nave, said to be based on drawings by Tintoretto (1518–94). The matroneum (women's galleries high above the nave), the iconostasis (altar screen), the massive Byzantine chandelier, and even the Greek-cross floor plan add to San Marco's exotic feel.

To the right, just off the porch, is the **Cappella Zen** (Zen Chapel), named after a local cardinal, with 13th-century mosaics that tell the story of the life of St. Mark. Next to it, the **Battistero** (baptistery) contains a bronze baptismal font cover by Jacopo Sansovino (1486–1570) and the tomb of Doge Andrea Dandolo (1307–54), a friend of Petrarch (1304–74) and a writer himself. Several early doges were buried here, while later ones were interred in the Chiesa dei Santi Giovanni e Paolo.

Two more chapels, both in the left transept, are worthy of special notice: the **Cappella della Madonna di Nicopeia** (Chapel of the Madonna of Nicopeia), which takes its name from a precious icon that many consider Venice's most powerful protector. The nearby **Cappella della Madonna dei Mascoli** (Chapel of Madonna of the Males) has fine 15th-century mosaics depicting the life of the Virgin, possibly based on drawings by Jacopo Bellini (circa 1400–70).

The basilica's **sanctuary** contains the main altar, with its green marble canopy lifted high on carved alabaster columns, built over the tomb of St. Mark. Much more impressive is the extraordinary **Pala d'Oro** (Golden Altarpiece), a dazzling gilded silver screen encrusted with 1,927 precious gems and 255 enameled panels. Made in Constantinople in the 11th century, it was continually embellished over the following three centuries by Byzantine and Venetian master craftsmen. The bronze door leading from the sanctuary back into the sacristy is another work by Sansovino; look for his self-portrait in the top left corner and, above that, a picture of his friend and fellow artist Titian (circa 1488–1576). Tickets for the sanctuary also include admission to the **Tesoro** (treasury), entered from the right transept. Many of its exotic treasures were brought from Constantinople and other vanquished lands.

From the atrium, climb the steep stairway to the **Galleria** and the **Museo Marciano** for a look at the interior of the church from the organ gallery and a sweeping view of Piazza San Marco and the Piazzetta dei Leoncini from the outdoor gallery. The highlight of the museum is the opportunity for a close-up look at the four magnificent gilded bronze horses that once stood outside on the Galleria. The originals were probably cast in Imperial Rome and later transported to Constantinople. Napoléon hauled them off to Paris after he conquered Venice in 1797, but they were returned "blind" after the fall of the French Empire: their big ruby eyes had been sold.

Be warned: guards at the door turn away any visitors wearing shorts, short skirts, tank tops, and other attire considered inappropriate (no bare shoulders or knees). If you want to take a free guided tour in English during summer months (with less certainty in winter, as the guides are volunteers), wait on the left in the porch for a group to form. You can also arrange for free tours by appointment. ⊠ *Piazza San Marco,* ☎ *041/5225697.* ▧ *Basilica free. Free guided tours of basilica by appointment (at least 2 days' notice, though there are occasional last-minute vacancies); contact Alata Point, Bacino Orseolo (near the Piazza),* ☎ *041/2770659,* WEB *www.alata.it.* ⊙ *May–Oct., Mon.–Sat. 9:45–5:30, Sun. 2–5:30; Nov.–Apr., Mon.–Sat. 9:45–4:30, Sun. 1–4:30 (last entry ½ hr before closing). Pala d'Oro* ▧ *€1.55. Tesoro* ▧ *€2.00. Galleria and Museo Marciano,* ☎ *041/5225205,* ▧ *€1.55.*

Biblioteca Marciana (Marciana Library). The Libreria Sansoviniana, designed by Renaissance architect Sansovino and located on the Piazzetta, on the south side of Piazza San Marco, now houses this collection of antique books and illuminated manuscripts. It also is the site of temporary exhibits related to Venetian history. ⊠ *Piazza San Marco (entrance through Museo Correr),* ☎ *041/5224951.* ▧ *€9.30 combined ticket also gives admission to Museo Archeologico, Museo Correr, and Palazzo Ducale; €15.50 combined ticket, besides the museums listed above, includes Ca' Rezzonico, Museo Vetrario, Museo del Merletto, and Palazzo Mocenigo.* ⊙ *Apr.–Oct., daily 9–7; Nov.–Mar., daily 9–5 (last entry 1½ hrs before closing).*

Ⓒ ★ ❸ **Campanile.** Venice's famous brick bell tower (325 ft tall, plus the angel) stood here for 1,000 years before it collapsed one morning in

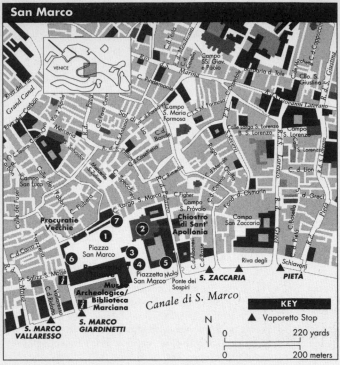

1912, practically without warning. It was swiftly rebuilt according to the old plan. Jacopo Sansovino's pretty marble loggia below, dating from the early 16th century, was crushed and also promptly restored. Miraculously no other building suffered serious damage and there were no casualties. In the 15th century, clerics found guilty of immoral behavior were suspended in wooden cages from the tower, sometimes forced to subsist on bread and water for as long as a year, other times left to starve. The stunning view from the tower on a clear day includes the Lido, the lagoon, and the mainland as far as the Alps but, strangely enough, none of the myriad canals that snake through the city. ⊠ *Piazza San Marco,* ☎ *041/5224064.* 🎟 *€5.15.* ☉ *Last Sun. in Mar.– last Sat. in Oct., daily 9:30–sunset; last Sun. in Oct.–last Sat. in Mar., daily 9:30–4:30 (last entry ½ hr before closing). Closed 2 wks in Jan.*

Chiostro di Sant'Apollonia. Behind the Basilica, down Ponte della Canonica at the end of the short fondamenta to the right, is the unassuming entrance to the cloister and the **Museo Diocesano** (upstairs). Despite later additions, the 12th-century cloister, which originally belonged to a Benedictine monastery, is a little gem of Romanesque architecture, the only surviving example of this style in Venice. The brick pavement is original, and the many inscriptions and fragments (some dating from the 9th century) are all that survive from the first Basilica di San Marco. The museum contains an array of sacred vestments, reliquaries, crucifixes, ex-votos, and paintings from various Venetian churches. ⊠ *Ponte della Canonica, 4312 Castello,* ☎ *041/5229166.* 🎟 *Free (donations accepted).* ☉ *Mon.–Sat. 10:30–12:30. Ring bell.*

Museo Archeologico. This museum was first conceived in 1523, when Cardinal Domenico Grimani, a noted humanist, left his collection of original Greek (5th–1st centuries BC) and Roman (mostly from the imperial era) marbles to the Republic, which enriched the collection with many other pieces. Highlights include an Attic original, the statue of Kore, known as Abbondanza Grimani (420 BC); the 1st-century BC Ara Grimani, an elaborate Hellenistic altar stone with a bacchanalian scene; a refined 1st-century BC crystal woman's head, which some claim is a portrait of Cleopatra; and a remarkable gallery of Roman busts. Don't miss the small collection of Egyptian and Assiro-Babylonian relics, including two mummies and a brick bearing the name of King Nebuchadnezzar. ⊠ *Piazza San Marco, 52 San Marco, entrance through Museo Correr,* ☎ *041/5225978.* ⊡ *€4.15; €9.30 combined ticket also gives admission to Biblioteca Marciana, Museo Correr, and Palazzo Ducale; €15.50 combined ticket, besides the museums listed above, includes Ca' Rezzonico, Museo Vetrario, Museo del Merletto, and Palazzo Mocenigo. Contact the museum for information about free guided tours in English.* ⊙ *Daily 9–8 (last entry at 6:30).*

★ ❻ **Museo Correr.** The museum of the art and history of Venice, the Correr is probably best visited after you've seen a bit of the town as it looks today—so much the better to appreciate the glorious past of La Serenissima. In 1830 the aristocrat Teodoro Correr donated his private collection—a fascinating, diverse mix of historical items and old master paintings—to the city. Exhibits range from the absurdly high-soled shoes worn by 16th-century Venetian ladies (who walked with the aid of a servant on either side) to fine Venetian paintings and the so-called **Museo del Risorgimento,** made up of 11 rooms illustrating the period from the Napoleonic and Austrian occupation through the unification of Italy. Map buffs should not miss the huge, exceptionally detailed *Grande Pianta Prospettica* by Jacopo de' Barberi (about 1440–1515), which faithfully portrays every inch of 16th-century Venice. You can see the older version of the Rialto Bridge, a topless campanile on Piazza San Marco (the roof had been destroyed in a fire), and the many churches, convents, and hostels that stood in the area that is now the Giardini della Biennale before being demolished by Napoléon. Four rooms are dedicated to Admiral Francesco Morosini (doge from 1688 to 1694) and intriguing displays of objects and garments used by the doges. The **Quadreria** (Picture Gallery) on the second floor features stunning Gothic works by the *madoneri,* a group of Greek-Venetian artists who specialized in the painting of glittering gold Madonnas. Room 30 houses a small but evocative Pietà by Ferrarese Cosmè Tura (1430–95). Room 36 is entirely devoted to the talented Bellini family of Renaissance painters: Jacopo and his sons, the more-famous Giovanni (1430–1516) and Gentile (1429–1507), who was responsible for the wonderful *teleri* (large narrative canvases of legendary and religious scenes) depicting the history of the cross at the Gallerie dell'Accademia. If you've already been to the Scuola di San Giorgio degli Schiavoni, you'll recognize Carpaccio's (circa 1465–1525) hand in his *Two Venetian Ladies, Young Man Wearing a Beret,* and *Visitation* (Rooms 38 and 39). ⊠ *Piazza San Marco, Ala Napoleonica,* ☎ *041/5224951.* ⊡ *€9.30 combined ticket also gives admission to Biblioteca Marciana, Museo Archeologico, and Palazzo Ducale; €15.50 combined ticket, besides the museums listed above, includes Ca' Rezzonico, Museo Vetrario, Museo del Merletto, and Palazzo Mocenigo.* ⊙ *Apr.–Oct., daily 9–7; Nov.–Mar., daily 9–5 (last entry 1½ hrs before closing).*

★ ❺ **Palazzo Ducale** (Doge's Palace). Part governor's residence and capitol building, part torture chamber and prison, Palazzo Ducale has for centuries served as the majestic expression of the prosperity and power attained by Venice during its most glorious period. Rising above Piazzetta San Marco and once the first building seen by visitors arriving from the lagoon, it dominates the city's formal entrance. A Gothic-Renaissance fantasy of pink-and-white marble, its top-heavy design—the

TO LIVE LIKE A DOGE

IT WASN'T EASY BEING DOGE. Called the Serenissimo (Most Serene), his existence was anything but. In the 1,100 years of the Republic (697–1797), 121 men became doge for life through a convoluted election process. Forty-one electors, chosen by random drawing and secret vote, were sequestered in the Palazzo Ducale until 25 concurred, something that could take months. When a doge was chosen, city bells rang and cannon were fired from the Bacino di San Marco. On Coronation Day, 80 arsenal workers carried the doge through Piazza San Marco as crowds cheered and pocketed silver coins he tossed to them.

Severe measures were taken to ensure the doge didn't abuse his office. He couldn't send notes (not even to his wife), accept gifts other than flowers and rosewater, or go to theaters or cafés. He paid his own bills but couldn't earn money. And the splendid dogal garments were worn according to strict etiquette for state occasions only. The doge led Venice into battle, literally, regardless of health or age. Blind, 90-year-old Enrico Dandolo laid siege to Constantinople in 1203–04, making off with the four horses that now adorn the Basilica. Even in death, doges followed a rigid protocol: they were mummified and put on display in the Chiesa dei SS. Giovanni e Paolo. But Venetian taxonomists were not so expert as the Egyptians; after centuries of unpleasant odors, "symbolic" mummies replaced the real ones, which were interred in family chapels.

— Carla Lionello

dense upper floors rest on the graceful ground-floor colonnade—has always confounded architectural purists, who contend that buildings should be built the other way around.

A fortress for the doge existed on this spot in the early 9th century, but the building you see today was begun in the 12th century and, like the basilica next door, was continually added to and transformed for hundreds of years. The ornate Gothic **Porta della Carta** (Gate of the Paper), where official decrees were traditionally posted, opens onto an immense courtyard. Ahead is the **Scala dei Giganti** (Stairway of the Giants), guarded by Jacopo Sansovino's huge statues of Mars and Neptune. Ordinary mortals do not get to climb these stairs, however. After paying your entrance fee, walk along the arcade to reach the central interior staircase. The lavishly gilded upper portion, called the **Scala d'Oro** (Golden Staircase), was also designed by Sansovino. The arduous climb must have intimidated a fair number of foreign emissaries.

Visitors must also have been overwhelmed by the sumptuous decoration of the apartments, their walls and ceilings covered with works by Venice's greatest artists. Among the grand rooms you can visit are the **Anticollegio** (an antechamber to the Sala del Maggior Consiglio) with two fine paintings, Tintoretto's *Bacchus* and *Ariadne Crowned by Venus* and Veronese's (1528–88) *Rape of Europa*; the **Sala del Collegio** (College Chamber), its ceiling magnificently painted by Veronese; and the **Sala del Senato** (Senate Chamber), with Tintoretto's *Triumph* *of Venice* on the ceiling. The dark, dynamic *Paradise* on the end wall of the **Sala del Maggior Consiglio** (Great Council Hall) is Jacopo Tintoretto's masterpiece and the world's largest oil painting (23 ft by 79 ft). The towering carved and gilded ceiling is breathtaking, even dizzying, as you wheel around searching for the best vantage point from which to admire Veronese's majestic *Apotheosis of Venice* filling one of the center panels. Look at the frieze of portraits of the first 76 doges around the upper part of the walls. One picture is missing: a black painted curtain near the left-hand corner of the wall opposite Tintoretto's painting marks the spot where the portrait of Doge Marin Falier should be. A Latin inscription bluntly explains that Falier was executed for treason in 1355, when, at age 71 and less than a year into his reign, he was accused of planning a coup to establish a tyranny.

A guided tour of the palace's secret rooms takes you to the doge's private apartments, up into the attic and the Piombi prison, and through hidden passageways to the torture chambers, where prisoners were interrogated. The 18th-century writer and libertine Giacomo Casanova (1725–98), a native of Venice, was imprisoned here in 1755, having somehow offended someone in power (he was officially accused of being a Freemason). He made a daring escape 15 months later and fled to France, where he continued his career of intrigue and scandal. Casanova was the only prisoner ever to escape, and his guard was condemned to serve 10 years.

From the east wing of the Palazzo Ducale, the enclosed marble **Ponte dei Sospiri** (Bridge of Sighs) arches over a narrow canal to the cramped, gloomy cell blocks of the so-called Nuova Prigione (New Prison). The bridge's melancholy history made it one of the prized sights for 19th-century tourists. Its name comes from the sighs of those being led to execution. Take a look out its windows to see the last glimpse of the outside world many of these prisoners had. ⊠ *Palazzo Ducale, Piazzetta San Marco,* ☎ *041/5224951.* ▣ *€9.30 combined ticket also gives admission to Biblioteca Marciana, Museo Correr, and Museo Archeologico; €15.50 combined ticket, besides the museums listed above, includes Ca' Rezzonico, Museo Vetrario, Museo del Merletto, and Palazzo Mocenigo; "Secret Itineraries" tour €12.40.* ☉ *Apr.–Oct., daily 9–7; Nov.–Mar., daily 9–5 (last entry 1½ hrs before closing). English tours daily 10:30; reservations essential.*

❶ **Piazza San Marco.** If you stand at the far end of the piazza (facing the basilica), you'll notice that rather than being a strict rectangle, it becomes wider at the basilica end, distorting the perspective and creating the illusion that the basilica is even larger than it is. The long arcaded building to the left is the **Procuratie Vecchie,** built in the early 16th century as offices and residences for the powerful procurators—the only Venetian magistrates, besides the doge, to be elected for life (perhaps because they didn't receive a salary), their main job was to administer the funds for the basilica and to supervise the doge's chaplains. To the right is the **Procuratie Nuove,** built half a century later in a more grandiose classical style, having been planned by Venice's great Renaissance architect Sansovino. Sansovino died before the Procuratie Nuove were begun, and his design was executed by Vincenzo Scamozzi (circa 1552–1616), a pupil of Andrea Palladio (1508–80) and a devout neoclassicist. Later sections were completed by Baldassare Longhena (1598–1682), Venice's other great architect, who belonged firmly to the Baroque tradition.

When Napoléon (1769–1821) entered Venice with his troops in 1797, he called Piazza San Marco "the world's most beautiful drawing room"—and promptly gave orders to redecorate it. His architects demolished a church with a facade designed by Sansovino to build the Ala Napoleonica (Napoleonic Wing), or Fabbrica Nuova (New Building), which closed off the square and linked the two 16th-century buildings on either side.

NEED A
BREAK?

Coffee, which by the end of the 16th century had become a popular drink in the Muslim countries to the east, owes its diffusion in the Western world to Venetian merchants and traders, who started importing the beans in the early 17th century, and who also founded the first European coffee shop in Venice in 1640. The prestigious **Caffè Florian** (☎ 041/5205641; closed Wed. Nov.–Mar. except during Carnevale and Christmas holidays), on the Procuratie Nuove side of Piazza San Marco, dates back to 1720, making it the world's oldest café. Casanova, Wagner, and Proust were regulars here, but it must be said that the quality of the coffee today isn't what it used to be. On the Procuratie Vecchie side of Piazza San Marco, **Caffè Quadri** (☎ 041/5289299; closed Mon. Nov.–Mar. except during Carnevale and Christmas holidays) exudes almost as much history as the Florian across the way. It was shunned by Venetians during the 19th century, when the occupying Austrians made it their gathering place. Note that both places are very expensive; it's a good idea to inquire about prices in advance. However, taking a seat at the Florian's counter is a more affordable experience.

★ ❹ **Piazzetta San Marco.** This "little piazza" on the edge of what is known as the Bacino di San Marco (St. Mark's Basin) offers great views of the basilica and island of San Giorgio and the long Giudecca island, as well as a breath of sea air. Now crowded with excursion boats, the landing once served as the grand entrance to the Republic, the two tall columns near the waterfront forming a kind of open doorway to the larger piazza behind. One bears a statue of San Todaro—St. Theodore, the first patron saint of Venice—and his dragon. Atop the other column is the winged lion, a traditional emblem of St. Mark and by extension the symbol of Venice. These two pieces are also emblematic of the architectural and artistic growth of the city, which was in large part driven by art imported from the Near East. In this case, the lion was likely to have once been a 4th-century BC chimera (a mythological creature with a lion's head and body, goat's head attached to its back, and serpent's tail) to which the Venetians attached the wings, which are thought to be of obscure Etruscan, Persian, or even Chinese origin. Theodore is no less a patchwork, having been assembled from a beautiful statue of King Mithridates mounted on a later Roman trunk, with "new" 15th-century legs. Despite the fact that a third column was lost when it fell in the lagoon while being unloaded, the architect in charge of the operations was paid with the only gambling license in Venice, to be used "between the Lion and St. Theodore." A stage was also set up here for public executions.

★ ❼ **Torre dell'Orologio.** Erected between 1496 and 1499, the Clock Tower has an enameled timepiece and animated Moorish figures that strike the hour (HORAS NON NUMERO NISI SERENAS—"I only count happy hours"—declares the inscription on the tower). During Ascension Week (40 days after Easter) and on Epiphany (January 6), an angel and three wise men go in and out of the doors and bow to the Virgin Mary. Inside, you can catch a glimpse of the complicated clock mechanism, which also indicates the phase of the moon and the path of the sun across the signs of the zodiac. The tower has been closed for renovation but is scheduled to reopen in 2002. ✉ *Northern side of Piazza San Marco.*

SAN MARCO TO DORSODURO

The sestiere known as Dorsoduro, literally "hardback," owes its name to the hard geological substrate that rises out of the lagoon on the southern side of town. It includes the Punta della Dogana, which served as a maritime customs station during Republican times; the *arzere* (shore) of Santa Marta, once a poor neighborhood of fishermen and now part of the harbor; and Giudecca island (☞ San Giorgio Maggiore and the Giudecca, *below*), a long strip that parallels the southern side of the city. Stretched between the noble east end of the Grand Canal and the wide, somewhat lagoonlike Giudecca Canal, this part of the city is prone to great changes in color: extremely blue and warm under the sun, it becomes creamy white and icy when the fog falls; hazy gray under a summer storm; tinged with golden orange on a spring evening. Crossed by winds, it is the place to come to smell the briny perfume of the sea and peek into secret gardens.

The long Fondamenta delle Zattere plays the role of Venice's gigantic public terrace: with its bustling bars and gelaterias, it is the ideal place to stroll, read in the open air, go for a run, or play hooky from sightseeing. The call of the seagulls or the whistle of the boats on their way to port recall days gone by. This vaguely intellectual and cosmopolitan part of town is home to the Università degli Studi di Venezia and the Accademia di Belle Arti. At the border of the small sestiere of Santa Croce is the prestigious institute of architecture, frequented by students from all over Europe. Campo Santa Margherita, the largest square in Dorsoduro, is the scene of what's left of the city's nightlife.

Numbers in the text correspond to numbers in the margin and on the San Marco to Dorsoduro map.

A Good Tour

Leave Piazza San Marco from the Museo Correr side, taking upscale Salizzada San Moisè and Calle Larga XXII Marzo—home to some of the most fashionable shops in town—to reach **Santa Maria del Giglio** ⑧, with a *Madonna* by Rubens and a spruced-up collection of silver reliquaries. From here, the traghetto to Dorsoduro crosses the Grand Canal at one of its most spectacular points—between St. Mark's Basin and the Accademia Bridge—so play Venetian and jump in the gondola for a quick ride. Once across the canal, bear left and walk past the Abbazia di San Gregorio (closed) and down the bridge to **Santa Maria della Salute** ⑨, with several paintings by Titian in the sacristy. The golden ball with a statue of Fortune, known as the Palla della Fortuna, at the tip of the Zattere is just a few steps to the right as you exit the church. It marks the Punta della Dogana, Venice's maritime customs office, where goods leaving or arriving were once inspected. This is one of the windiest spots in town—a fresh spot even on humid summer days and a good place to sit down and feed the seagulls some stale bread. From the Zattere promenade, turn onto the Fondamenta Ca' Balà, cross the rio, and walk toward Campiello Barbaro, a delightful little square with a view of the back of Ca' Dario. Climb down the bridge, and after a few steps you'll spot the artistic entrance of the **Collezione Peggy Guggenheim** ⑩, a small but first-rate collection of 20th-century paintings and sculpture. From the museum, follow the Fondamenta Venier and Calle della Chiesa to Campo San Vio, where you can rest on a bench facing the Grand Canal. Return to the Zattere on pretty Fondamenta Bragadin, head right, and stop in for a look at the **Chiesa dei Gesuati** ⑪. Up ahead at the next rio, tucked away in one of Venice's most picturesque corners, is the *squero* of San Trovaso (best seen from Fondamenta Nani), the workshop where gondolas are still being made and repaired. On top of the Ponte Lungo, take in the view of the Giudecca, and then follow the twisted Calle del Magazzen to reach Campo San Trovaso, a grassy square evocative of a time when grass covered all Venetian campi. The church here is worth a brief stop for the *Adoration of the Magi* by Tintoretto's son, Domenico (1565–1637).

Follow Fondamenta Ognissanti to Fondamenta San Basilio and the church of **San Sebastiano** ⑫ across the rio, with a number of astounding paintings by Veronese. From Campo Angelo Raffaele, turn left onto Fondamenta di Pescheria, and then make a right over the bridge to the church of **San Nicolò dei Mendicoli** ⑬, isolated on a little square surrounded by water. Leave the square from the south end and look for Fondamenta Barbarigo. Cross the rio at Ponte del Soccorso to reach **Santa Maria del Carmelo** ⑭ and **Scuola Grande dei Carmini** ⑮, not to be missed for Tiepolo's famous paintings inside. To the right is Campo Santa Margherita, the only large square in town without a church to visit. If you look at the pavement, you'll see that the *masegni* (gray stones used exclusively for paving) are laid in different directions, which gives away the fact that this campo was once traversed by several canals.

Head toward **Ca' Rezzonico** ⑯ on the zigzag mesh of alleys that leads to pretty Campiello Squellini, with the handwoven fabrics shop Arras. While on Calle Pedrocchi, you can visit one of the city's few authentic mask workshops, Ca' Macana. After visiting the Museo del Settecento Veneziano, you can hop on vaporetto Line 1 (the Ca' Rezzonico landing is at the end of Calle del Traghetto, across Campo San Barnaba), or walk straight to the Accademia Bridge to finish your day with an aperitivo in Campo Santo Stefano. As you make up your mind, you can stop for a taste of good wine at the *enoteca* (wineshop) in Campo San Barnaba, or buy some fruit from the boat anchored in the rio— one of the few surviving examples of a Venetian itinerant shop. The bridge here is called Ponte dei Pugni (of the Blows), as this was one of the battlegrounds of the Nicolotti and Castellani, two factions of the poor citizens who lived on the outer limits of the city (San Pietro di Castello and San Nicolò dei Mendicoli). The bridge's "footprints" in Istrian stone mark the place where the combatants placed their feet— the winner was he who succeeded in tossing his opponent into the water below. The **Gallerie dell'Accademia** ⑰ is a sight unto itself in this neighborhood. Decide when to dedicate some time to its collections, maybe on a rainy morning or when the Quadreria is open.

TIMING

This walk takes about two hours without stops, or a full day covering all the sites and excluding the Gallerie dell'Accademia. A few hours will allow you to see a good sampling of what's on view in the Gallerie dell'Accademia and its often overlooked Quadreria; if you have little time, trust the very selective acoustic guide, which covers just the highlights in about an hour. Give yourself at least 1½ hours for the Collezione Peggy Guggenheim—although the gardens, gift shop, café, and air-conditioning might tempt you to linger. The churches on this itinerary are not large, and unless you are captured by a particular element, 20 minutes or so should be enough for each one. Ca' Rezzonico deserves a couple of hours, and a bit more if you stay to see whatever is on temporary exhibition. The Scuola dei Carmini is less demanding of your time: 30 to 40 minutes should do the trick.

Sights to See

★ ⑯ **Ca' Rezzonico.** Begun by Longhena in the 1660s and completed by Giorgio Massari (1686–1766) a century later, this imposing building lacks the subtle charm of its Byzantine and Gothic neighbors. English critic John Ruskin (1819–1900) called Ca' Rezzonico "the silliest palace" on the Grand Canal; he thought the pillars looked like wheels of cheese piled atop one another and that the oval windows in the attic resembled portholes. It was bought and sold frequently over the centuries and for a time belonged to the son of the English poet Robert Browning, who came to visit, caught a bad cold on the Lido, and died here. His epitaph-like quip, "Open my heart and you will see graven inside of it Italy," is still visible on the facade. Ca' Rezzonico was acquired by the city in 1930, and today its gilded salons house the **Museo del Settecento Veneziano** (Museum of 18th-Century Venice). With its stuccowork, colored marble fixtures, brocade tapestry, fine furniture, Murano glass chandeliers, and valuable frescoes, this impressive Baroque mansion shows just how elegant Venetian lifestyle was in spite of the declining times. The sumptuous ballroom calls to mind the parties of the era. The lovely bedroom with alcove on the second floor would have been a likely place for Casanova and his intrigues. The carefully reconstructed 18th-century *Farmacia ai Do San Marchi* (Pharmacy at the Two St. Marks), with its jars full of magic powders and herbs, gives you some sense of how people once dealt with health and medicine. A worthwhile art gallery includes several portraits by Rosalba Carriera (1675–1757), one of Venice's few female painters, and several cityscapes by Francesco Guardi (1712–93), a great landscape painter who had the misfortune of being a contemporary of the more popular Canaletto. The delightful genre pictures by Pietro Longhi (1702–85) open a window onto the most intriguing aspects of 18th-century Venice: the daily life of the nobles and the common people, family intimacy, leisure, masquerades, and gentlemen, ladies, and cavaliers. ✉ *Fondamenta Pedrocco, 3136 Dorsoduro,* ☎ *041/2410100.* ✉ *€6.70; or €15.50 combined ticket gives admission to Biblioteca Marciana, Museo Correr, Museo Vetrario, Museo del Merletto, Palazzo Mocenigo, Museo Archeologico, and Palazzo Ducale.* ☉ *Wed.–Mon. 10–6 (last entrance at 5).*

⓫ **Chiesa dei Gesuati.** The first thing the Dominicans did when they took the place of the suppressed fraternal order of the poor Gesuati was to commission a brand-new church from the greatest Venetian architect of the time, Giorgio Massari, well known for having said: "An architect who doesn't want to starve must by necessity adapt himself to see and think according to classical norms and models." What else could be done? This was the era in which only those who observed and copied Vitruvius (circa 1st century BC) and Palladio merited the label of true artist. Not surprisingly, the decoration inside is a triumph of 18th-century neoclassical painting. Expect a score of saints in Dominican attire signed by the "trinity": Tiepolo (1669–1770), Piazzetta (1683–1754), and Ricci (1659–1734). Sadly, the priest keeps the beautiful 15th-century *Madonna delle Grazie* by Stefano di Sant'Agnese locked away—perhaps because it wouldn't fit with the decor?—except during holidays dedicated to the Virgin. ✉ *Zattere, Dorsoduro,* ☎ *041/5230625.* ✉ *Free.* ☉ *Daily 8–noon and 5–7:30.*

★ ⓾ **Collezione Peggy Guggenheim.** Extremely rich, provocative, and extravagant, Peggy Guggenheim (1898–1979)—wife of Max Ernst and niece of Solomon Guggenheim, founder of New York's well-known museum—was among the 20th century's greatest collectors of modern art. On display in Palazzo Venier dei Leoni, her residence for 30 years, are works representing the most important artistic movements from the early 20th century through the postwar period: Cubism (Picasso and Braque); Futurism (Balla, Severini, and Boccioni); metaphysical painting (*The Red Tower* by De Chirico); abstract painting (Kandinsky); and a large group of Surrealist masterpieces, including Magritte's *Empire of Light,* Max Ernst's outstanding large Dada canvases *The Kiss, The Attirement of the Bride,* and *The Anti-Pope* (he gave the last two to

Ca' Rezzonico **16**

Chiesa dei
Gesuati **11**

Collezione Peggy
Guggenheim **10**

Gallerie
dell'Accademia ...**17**

San Nicolò
dei Mendicoli **13**

San Sebastiano ...**12**

Santa Maria
del Carmelo **14**

Santa Maria
del Giglio **8**

Santa Maria
della Salute **9**

Scuola Grande
dei Carmini **15**

KEY

▲ Vaporetto Stop

Guggenheim as a wedding present), and Miroac:'s *Dutch Interior II* and *Seated Woman II*. The modernist generation of painters is represented by Rothko, Motherwell, Pollock, and Bacon. A room is dedicated to the lively little pictures made by the heiress's daughter Pegeen, who disappeared under mysterious circumstances. Scattered around the two beautiful gardens of the villa are sculptures ranging from Giacometti's ethereal bronze figures to the obscene giant phallus pointing out to the Grand Canal. In a tiny family cemetery, several tombstones indicate the resting place of Guggenheim herself and her beloved dogs. Don't miss the gift shop, with large black-and-white pictures (not for sale) of the young heiress living her dazzling life, and an array of thematic gifts such as mugs and neckties designed by architect Frank Lloyd Wright, Mondrianesque umbrellas, and Modigliani pins. ☒ *Palazzo Venier dei Leoni, entrance on Calle San Cristoforo, 701 Dorsoduro,* ☏ *041/5206288,* WEB *www.peggyguggenheim.com.* ☒ *€6.20.* ☉ *Wed.–Fri. and Sun.–Mon. 10–6, Sat. 10–10.*

★ ⑰ **Gallerie dell'Accademia** (Accademia Galleries). Since 1807 the Accademia has held the most complete collection of 14th- to 18th-century Venetian painting, as well as masterpieces of Italian figurative sculpture. Its exhibits come largely from churches, convents, and scuole that were either suppressed or judged unsuitable to house such treasures. It also holds numerous nonreligious works, mostly portraits.

Two elements central to Venetian art are Byzantium and color. Venice's close ties to Eastern art and culture forestalled the arrival of the Florentine Renaissance. Moreover, the gold, enamel color, and the unreal, schematic narrative structure of Byzantine art were thriving elements of Gothic style, as seen in the outstanding 14th-century polyptychs by Paolo Veneziano (circa 1290–1360) and Lorenzo Veneziano (active 1356–72)—no relation—which show the influences of both the purely Byzantine Pala d'Oro and the art of the following century. In Room 1 are the masters of 15th-century Gothic style: Jacobello del Fiore (circa 1370–1439) and Antonio Vivarini (circa 1415–1476/84).

Although he was born in the era of the so-called *madoneri* (Gothic painters of Madonnas), Jacopo Bellini, the father of Giovanni, had the good fortune to study in the Perugia workshop of Gentile da Fabriano (circa 1370–1426), where apprentices practiced perspective drawing and sketching from life. When he opened his own workshop in Venice, Jacopo Bellini availed himself of these new techniques, and for this reason he is credited as the father of Venetian Renaissance. Study his harmonious *Sacred Conversation* and compare it to the touching *Madonna of the Orange Tree* by Cima da Conegliano or the narrative *Ten Thousand Martyrs of Mt. Ararat* by Carpaccio to understand what local painters did with Jacopo's seeds. These large altarpieces, all housed in Room 2, belong to the early Renaissance period.

Now a few words about color: under the light reflected by the lagoon, contour blurs and colors seem to melt together. Venetian painters, having broken away from medieval and Byzantine models, learned to use color to bring figures together and give a unity of composition to representative scenes. On the other hand, the Renaissance painters in Florence and elsewhere in Italy sought to reproduce human bodies and landscapes by means of perfect drawing, balanced arrangement, and perspective, relegating color to incidental, decorative status. In the best works by Jacopo's son Giovanni (circa 1430–1516), it is the mellowness and richness of color, rather than the subject matter, that catches the observer's attention.

For the painter known as Giorgione (circa 1478–1510), color was often all that counted. In his enigmatic *Tempest* (Room 5) it's difficult to tell just what he intended by the content: a mother nursing a baby in the wilderness, a soldier observing, and a city under storm in the background. But it's not the mysterious content that qualifies the *Tempest* as exceptional. The 20th-century art historian E. H. Gombrich found that the strength of the picture lies in the way the artist managed to render a powerful sense of reality through the use of color: "Though the figures are not particularly carefully drawn, and the composition is somewhat artless, the picture is clearly blended into a whole simply by the light and air that permeates it all . . . ; for the first time, it seems, the landscape is not just a background . . ." Next door in Room 7 is perhaps the most compelling portrait in the Galleries, Lorenzo Lotto's *Young Man in his Study,* noted for its intensity of expression.

Giorgione's heir was Titian. Born in the early 1480s in the Alps near Venice, Titian was one of Venice's great stars; only Michelangelo was more famous in the 16th century. The official painter of the Republic, he traveled widely, often at the invitation of the royal courts throughout Europe, including to Rome and Pope Paul III. The Galleries feature his *Presentation of the Virgin* (Room 24) and the *Pietà* (Room 10), his last masterpiece, a large canvas on which glowing colors are applied against dark shadows. He was in the midst of finishing it for his tomb, which had been planned for the Frari, when he fell victim to the plague in 1576, having lived nearly a century.

In Room 10 are paintings by Venice's two other giants of the Renaissance: Jacopo Tintoretto, with several canvases from his celebrated cycle of the *Life of San Marco,* and Paolo Veronese, with *Feast in the House of Levi.* Giorgio Vasari, in his famous *Lives of the Painters* (1550), reproaches Tintoretto for having a touch "so crude that his pencil strokes show more force than judgment and seem to have been made by chance," while other contemporaries found his works marred by careless execution and a taste for eccentric composition. But Tintoretto, like all great innovators, was at odds with convention. He sought emotions and tension; he felt that the incomparable beauty of Titian's works rendered them more pleasing than moving. So, perhaps, Tintoretto started to consider technical excellence and careful "finish" as impediments to his own goal of highly dramatic painting. Veronese, on the other hand, wanted to make his paintings as attractive, pleasing, and varied as possible. His *Feast* shows the Venetian high Renaissance in all its richness and glamour. The friars of San Zanipolo, who had commissioned Veronese to paint a *Last Supper,* rejected the painting and reported the artist to the Inquisition, which predictably took issue with his inclusion of jesters, dogs, and German (therefore Protestant) soldiers in the painting. Veronese cleverly avoided the charges of profanity by changing the painting's title to the *Feast of Levi,* representing a bawdy but nonetheless biblical event.

Rooms 20 and 21 have several cycles of teleri by two masters of Renaissance narrative painting: Gentile Bellini, brother of Giovanni, and Carpaccio. The teleri are an exceptional source of historical information. Replete with fascinating details ranging from the design of shoes to boat shapes and hairdos, they also reveal how little (or how much) the city has changed since the 15th century. For instance, the *Procession of the Relic of the Cross,* painted for the Scuola Grande di San Giovanni Evangelista, serves as a snapshot of Piazza San Marco, circa 1496; the *Healing of a Lunatic* shows the old wooden version of the Rialto Bridge, which opened for large passing boats. The people who populate the paintings are particularly realistic, as monks or 15th-century nobles often sat for the artist, including Caterina Cornaro, the Queen of Cyprus (first lady on the left) in the *Recovery of the Relic from the Canal of San Lorenzo,* or the red-haired Patriarca di Grado in the scene of the *Miracle at Rialto.*

The 1700s were the years of the decorators (whose works in fresco and stucco are not represented in the Galleries) and an important novelty: landscape painting. Travelers often wanted souvenirs of their trip to Venice, and a school of specialized painters rose to the occasion. The two greatest among them had their destinies written in their names: Antonio Canal, called Canaletto (literally, "Small Canal"), and Francesco Guardi ("You Look"). Compare the style of the former, the official landscape painter of the Republic, admired and courted all over Europe for the precision of his renderings, with that of the latter, who left the eye to imagine that which was not revealed in paint. Canaletto's remarkable verisimilitude and Flemish details become marks of color in Guardi's painting, his gondoliers in the *Island of St. George* made up of a few deftly placed colored patches.

More works by Giovanni Bellini, Cima da Conegliano, Carpaccio, Titian, Tintoretto, and Veronese are housed in the **Quadreria** on the top floor, which can be visited, at no extra charge, every Tuesday afternoon by reservation (☎ 041/5222247; tours leave at 3 and 4), or any day of the week by appointment with an authorized guide (☎ 041/713498); it is essential to agree on the guide's fee in advance.

The acoustic guide to the Gallerie is good, but quite selective, and should be considered only if you have limited time, as it doesn't add anything to the excellent annotation (in English) in each room. Neither an acoustic guide nor annotation is available for the Quadreria, but there's an English-language booklet about it available in the bookshop. ⊠ *Campo della Carità, Accademia, Dorsoduro,* ☎ *041/5222247.* ▨ *€6.20; €9.30 combined ticket includes Museo d'Arte Orientale and Galleria Franchetti.* ☉ *Tues.–Sun. 8:15–7:15, Mon. 8:15–2.*

★ ⑬ **San Nicolò dei Mendicoli.** This church takes its name (San Nicolò of the Beggars) from the many beggars who congregated in the humble fishermen's neighborhood at the west end of town, home to the Nicolotti, one of the two popular factions into which the city was historically divided. A community unto itself, it had its own flag, column, and winged lion (still standing on the campo), and even a leader called the Doge of the Nicolotti. San Nicolò was founded as early as the 7th century, and subsequent partial renovations have made its astounding combination of styles its greatest charm. It takes the form of a typical Veneto-Byzantine three-aisled basilica. The oldest surviving parts are the small mullion windows on the facade, the apse, and the detached 12th-century bell tower. The columns, the arches of the sanctuary, and the wooden beams date from the early Gothic period. The Gothic-style porch was added in the 15th century. Front porches like this were once a common feature of Venetian churches and served as a shelter for the *pinzocchere* (female beggars). The gilded wood paneling, along with the arches in front of the sanctuary, is Renaissance in style. The side facade leans more toward the Baroque, and the Chapel of the Sacrament flows into the rococo. San Nicolò is also worth a visit for some good mid-16th-century paintings by Alvise Dal Friso (1554–1608) and other pupils of Veronese. ⊠ *Campo San Nicolò dei Mendicoli, 1907 Dorsoduro,* ☎ *041/2750382.* ▨ *Free.* ☉ *Daily 10–noon and 4–6.*

★ ⑫ **San Sebastiano.** The dull facade of this church hides an example of what you could miss in Venice if you were to trust first impressions—in this case your loss would be the extraordinary pictorial cycle by Paolo

Caliari, better known as Veronese, who as a young painter in his early twenties was called to Venice from his hometown of Verona (hence the nickname). A grand-scale decorator and contemporary of Tintoretto, he was famous for glowing colors. The first frescoes he painted, in the church of San Sebastiano, launched an intense and celebrated career. Veronese lived in the salizzada nearby and embellished this, his parish church, during three distinct periods: 1555–56 (Old Testament scenes in the Sacristy; episodes from the Book of Esther in the coffered ceiling), 1558–59 (upper part of the nave, choir, organ doors, and frontispiece), and 1565–70 (*Madonna in Glory with St. Sebastian, Sts. Mark and Marcellino Led to their Martyrdom,* and the *Martyrdom of St. Sebastian*). The artist, not surprisingly, was buried here; his tomb is to the left of the sanctuary. ⊠ *Campo San Sebastiano, Dorsoduro,* ☎ 041/5282487; 041/2750462 Chorus. 🎫 €1.55, €7.75 Chorus ticket. ☉ Mon.–Sat. 10–5.

⑭ Santa Maria del Carmelo. This rather simple Gothic redbrick basilica has two remarkable altarpieces: the *Nativity,* by Cima da Conegliano, and *Sts. Nicholas, John the Baptist, and Lucy,* by Lorenzo Lotto. The titular saint, Santa Maria del Carmelo, was left for several centuries without even a painting in her honor, but her followers finally managed to build the scuola nearby. ⊠ *Campo dei Carmini, Dorsoduro,* ☎ 041/5226553. 🎫 *Free.* ☉ *Mon.–Sat. 8–noon and 2:30–6:30, Sun. 4:30–6.*

❽ Santa Maria del Giglio. This white, airy church is one of the most remarkable examples of Venetian Baroque: step back and turn your eyes to the angel on the upper-left corner, which seems about to take off into the blue sky. Also called Santa Maria Zobenigo after the family that originally built it in the 9th century, the present church, dedicated to the "Virgin with the Lily" (in the iconography of the Annunciation, the angel offers Mary a white lily, a symbol of purity), forms one large monument to the five Barbaro brothers, who financed the reconstruction. Their statues decorate the facade, and the maps of Zara, Candia, Padua, Rome, Corfu, and Spalato refer to the towns where Antonio Barbaro spent his life in the service of the Republic. The interior has more the feeling of an art gallery than a place of worship, as the walls and ceiling are packed with paintings of all sizes and shapes, including a good stations-of-the-cross series, and, behind the fine main altar, *Four Evangelists,* by Tintoretto, next to a moving *Annunciation,* by Salviati (died 1575). The cozy Cappella Molin is full of exquisite gold and silver reliquaries containing everything from bones to fragments of fingernails. The easel holds a valuable *Madonna and Child* with the young St. John, the only work by Rubens in Venice. ⊠ *Campo Santa Maria del Giglio, San Marco,* ☎ 041/5225739; 041/2750462 Chorus. 🎫 €1.55, €7.75 Chorus ticket. ☉ Mon.–Sat. 10–5, Sun. 1–5.

★ ❾ Santa Maria della Salute. The view of "La Salute," as Venetians affectionately call it, from the Riva degli Schiavoni at sunset or from the Accademia Bridge under the moonlight is simply unforgettable. Early birds should also go for a walk to the Piazzetta at the break of dawn to see the lines of the temple's dome slowly emerge from the morning mist. The architect Baldassare Longhena was only 32 years old when, together with 10 colleagues, he participated in the design competition to build a great shrine in Venice dedicated to the Virgin Mary in gratitude for liberation from a terrible plague that from 1630 to 1631 killed 47,000 people in Venice alone. Presenting his project, Longhena spoke of it as an "unprecedented work which had never been even imagined in total or in part by other churches in this city." His plan for a classically inspired white octagonal temple covered by a colossal cupola, with a Palladian-style facade and bizarre Baroque decorations, effortlessly conquered the avant-garde judges of the competition.

The grandiose temple is made of *marmorino* (brick covered with marble dust) and Istrian stone, an inexpensive material used in Venice for framing windows and lining steps on bridges. Building it was no easy task: about 100,000 trunks of oak were used to reinforce the muddy terrain. The luminous interior features six chapels with one altar each and a beautiful polychrome marble floor. Look for Titian's *Pentecost* across the aisle to the left. Since it was brought from Crete by Francesco Morosini in 1672, the Byzantine icon above the main altar has been venerated as the Madonna della Salute (of Health). (A small-scale silver replica still hangs in many Venetian bedrooms.) To its side is a remarkable sculpture group showing Venice on bended knee, asking the Virgin for protection from the plague, represented as a fleeing old woman. The **Sacrestia Maggiore** contains a wealth of art, including five works by Titian, the best of which are the *Five Saints* altarpiece; a large *Nozze di Canaan* by Tintoretto; and a precious 15th-century *paliotto* (tapestry), made from a drawing in the style of Mantegna (1431–1506) and Bellini on wool, silk, and silver thread that represents the Pentecost against a naturalistic background. A traditional thanksgiving pilgrimage during November's Festa della Madonna della Salute is one of the most evocative Venetian festivals. ⊠ *Punta della Dogana, Dorsoduro,* ☎ *041/5225558.* 🎫 *Church free, sacristy €1.00.* ☉ *June–Sept., daily 9:30–5:30; Oct.–May, daily 9:30–11:30 and 3–5:30.*

★ ⓲ **Scuola Grande dei Carmini.** By the time Longhena completed this scuola in the 1670s, the brotherhood of Santa Maria del Carmelo had grown to 75,000 members, becoming the largest fraternal order of the period. It was also one of the wealthiest, so little expense was spared in the decoration of its brand-new scuola: stuccoed ceilings, Baroque ebony paneling, and choice paintings served the basic, predictable decor. The real show started when the nine great canvases that adorn the vault of the **Sala Capitolare** was entrusted to the internationally famous Giambattista Tiepolo in 1739. These works are considered the artist's masterpiece: Tiepolo's vivid techniques transformed some unpromising religious themes into flamboyant displays of color and movement. ⊠ *Campo dei Carmini, Dorsoduro,* ☎ *041/5289420.* 🎫 *€4.15.* ☉ *Nov.–Mar., daily 9–4; Apr.–Oct., Mon.–Sat. 9–6, Sun. 9–4.*

SAN POLO AND SANTA CROCE TO SAN MARCO

The smallest of Venice's six sestieri, San Polo and Santa Croce are named after their main churches, although the Chiesa di Santa Croce was demolished in 1810. San Polo, with the Rialto market and the lively shopping streets nearby, is more fun to explore than Santa Croce, which, especially near Piazzale Roma, feels removed from the swing of things. The sestiere of San Marco, contained between the south bend of the Grand Canal and the rio that flows below the Ponte dei Sospiri, is the most fashionable part of town and the most expensive place to sleep, eat, and shop. Its fairly straight main drag runs between Campo San Bartolomio, at the foot of the Rialto Bridge, which reaches over the Grand Canal to San Polo and Santa Croce, and Campo Santo Stefano. Both squares are popular meeting places, with bars and monuments where young Venetians break for an espresso and the inevitable chat on the *telefonino* (cell phone) while waiting for their friends. Between this last campo and Calle Larga XXII Marzo are the burned ruins of the Teatro La Fenice and the gloomy network of decadent alleys where Visconti's *Death in Venice* was shot.

After a day spent looking at the sights of San Polo and Santa Croce, which include big attractions like the Frari and the Scuola Grande di San Rocco, and worthwhile but little-known churches and museums such as San Pantalon and Palazzo Mocenigo, it's nice to stroll back to the busy center, stopping along the way for an aperitivo. In Venice ask for a "spritz" (white wine, Aperol or Campari, and soda), Campari (served with soda and a green olive), or *prosecchino*, the Venetian word for a glass of prosecco, either *dolce* (sweet), or *secco* (dry). By request a prosecchino is also prepared with a third of fresh fruit juice.

Numbers in the text correspond to numbers in the margin and on the San Polo and Santa Croce to San Marco map.

A Good Walk

If you are planning to visit Ca' Pesaro or Palazzo Mocenigo, it's probably best to start your day with a vaporetto trip to the San Stae landing (Line 1). As you land, **Ca' Pesaro** ⑱ is two alleys and bridges to the left, and **Palazzo Mocenigo** ⑲ stands 150 ft ahead, its entrance on Salizzada San Stae. You can also visit the church of San Stae, but you pay an entry fee and see very little. From Palazzo Mocenigo, head toward Campo San Zandegolà via Calle del Tintor and Calle dello Spezier; note that the church in the campo, **San Zandegolà** ⑳, is only open Monday through Saturday 10 to noon. Follow the red sign to the **Fondaco dei Turchi** ㉑, home to the Museo di Storia Naturale (closed for restoration until 2003), or traverse the rio to reach **Campo San Giacomo dall'Orio** ㉒ and its church, **San Giacomo dall'Orio** ㉓, through Calle dello Spezier and Calle Larga. This large and quiet square is a good place to rest. Take Calle del Tintor to Ponte del Parrucchetta, which offers a picturesque view of Campo San Boldo, its ruined bell tower discreetly converted into a block of apartments. Continue down the bridge and make a right onto Calle della Chiesa, which leads to Campo San Stin. The superb Renaissance entrance to the **Scuola Grande di San Giovanni Evangelista** ㉔ is to the right of the Campo. Follow long Calle della Lacca to a large bridge; from here, turn left onto Fondamenta delle Sacchere toward the Fondamenta and tiny Campo dei Tolentini, filled with the seemingly out-of-place church of **San Nicola da Tolentino** ㉕. Follow Fondamenta Minotto and Salizzada San Pantalon to Calle Crosera, then left onto Calle della Scuola to get to the **Scuola Grande di San Rocco** ㉖, lavishly decorated by Tintoretto. From here, you can already see the walls of the imposing Franciscan church of **Santa Maria Gloriosa dei Frari** ㉗, with two famous paintings by Titian. Retrace your steps back to the Calle Crosera and the surprising **San Pantalon** ㉘ in the campo of the same name. Back on the Crosera, go right and follow the street until you come to the Rio della Frescada. Down the bridge, to the left, is pretty Campo San Tomà, with the Scuola dei Calegheri (of the shoemakers) on one side and antiques shops on the other. Past the neoclassical church, over the Ponte di San Tomà, is the birthplace (with plaque and open to the public) of Carlo Goldoni, the great 18th-century Venetian comedy writer. Not far are **Campo San Polo** ㉙ and the **San Polo** ㉚ church, with a remarkable roof and cycle of paintings depicting the stations of the cross From Campo San Tomà, a sign points to the traghetto landing. Cross the Grand Canal and take narrow Calle del Traghetto to the Campiello Novo o dei Morti (of the Dead, because a cemetery was once here) and the church of **Santo Stefano** ㉛ in **Campo Santo Stefano** ㉜. This is a good place for a sweet fix: the campo is home to two good gelaterie, and one of the best pastry shops in town is on nearby Calle dello Spezier. After paying homage to Doge Francesco Mo-

HOW TO USE THIS GUIDE

Great trips begin with great planning, and this guide makes planning easy. It's packed with everything you need—insider advice on hotels and restaurants, cool tools, practical tips, essential maps, and much more.

COOL TOOLS

Fodor's Choice Top picks are marked throughout with a star.

Great Itineraries These tours, planned by Fodor's experts, give you the skinny on what you can see and do in the time you have.

Smart Travel Tips A to Z This special section is packed with important contacts and advice on everything from how to get around to what to pack.

Good Walks You won't miss a thing if you follow the numbered bullets on our maps.

Need a Break? Looking for a quick bite to eat or a spot to rest? These sure bets are along the way.

Off the Beaten Path Some lesser-known sights are worth a detour. We've marked those you should make time for.

POST-IT® FLAGS
Dog-ear no more!

"Post-it" is a registered trademark of 3M.

Favorite restaurants • Essential maps • Frequently used numbers • Walking tours • Can't-miss sights • Smart Travel Tips • Web sites • Top shops • Hot nightclubs • Addresses • Smart contacts • Events • Off-the-beaten-path spots • Favorite restaurants • Essential maps • Frequently used numbers • Walking tours • Can't-miss sights • Smart Travel Tips • Web sites • Top shops • Hot nightclubs • Addresses • Smart contacts • Events • Off-the-beaten-path spots • Favorite restaurants • Essential maps • Frequently used numbers • Walking tours •

ICONS AND SYMBOLS

Watch for these symbols throughout:

★ Our special recommendations

✕ Restaurant

🏠 Lodging establishment

✕🏠 Lodging establishment whose restaurant warrants a special trip

🐣 Good for kids

☞ Sends you to another section of the guide for more information

✉ Address

☎ Telephone number

FAX Fax number

WEB Web site

🎟 Admission price

🕐 Opening hours

$-$$$$ Lodging and dining price categories, keyed to strategically sited price charts. Check the index for locations.

①❶ Numbers in white and black circles on the maps, in the margins, and within tours correspond to one another.

ON THE WEB

Continue your planning with these useful tools found at **www.fodors.com**, the Web's best source for travel information.

"Rich with resources." —*New York Times*

"Navigation is a cinch." —*Forbes* "Best of the Web" list

"Put together by people bursting with know-how."
—*Sunday Times* (London)

Create a Miniguide Pinpoint hotels, restaurants, and attractions that have what you want at the price you want to pay.

Rants and Raves Find out what readers say about Fodor's picks—or write your own reviews of hotels and restaurants you've just visited.

Travel Talk Post your questions and get answers from fellow travelers, or share your own experiences.

On-Line Booking Find the best prices on airline tickets, rental cars, cruises, or vacations, and book them on the spot.

About our Books Learn about other Fodor's guides to your destination and many others.

Expert Advice and Trip Ideas From what to tip to how to take great photos, from the national parks to Nepal, Fodors.com has suggestions that'll make your trip a breeze. Log on and get informed and inspired.

Smart Resources Check the weather in your destination or convert your currency. Learn the local language or link to the latest event listings. Or consult hundreds of detailed maps—all in one place.

rosini (buried inside the church), turn right and cross Campo Sant'Angelo. From here, find your way to Campo San Beneto and **Palazzo Fortuny** ㉝, a great-looking Gothic building with a unique museum. Finish your day by climbing the **Scala Contarini del Bovolo** ㉞.

TIMING

The first part of the itinerary includes a number of minor sights that can slow down your walk. If you are willing to skip Ca' Pesaro, San Zandegolà, the Fondaco dei Turchi, San Nicola da Tolentino, and the interior of the Scuola di San Giovanni Evangelista, you can start this tour at midday (Palazzo Mocenigo closes at 1:30). In any case, you need to begin the second leg by at least 2, or you'll miss some of the churches. Allow at least 40 minutes for the Scuola Grande di San Rocco, more if you are a real Tintoretto fan. The Frari will take another 30 to 40 minutes, and the rest of the churches will need an average of 20 minutes each, with San Pantalon being the most engaging and San Polo the least time-consuming of the group. Palazzo Fortuny won't require more than 30 to 40 minutes, unless a temporary exhibition on the ground floor catches your eye.

Sights to See

㉒ **Campo San Giacomo dall'Orio.** The several streets that lead to this square all approach it laterally, giving no sense of its pleasantly odd shape. Trees, benches, a public fountain—so rare on Venetian campi—and a church nicely set among the houses (rather than towering above them) make this a low-key campo. Perhaps it is fitting that the name of the titular saint, San Giacomo dall'Orio, refers not to a cruel way of martyrdom nor a far-off homeland but to a laurel tree that once gave shade to the church. More intriguing is the name of the bridge on the south side of the campo: dell'Anatomia, which recalls the anatomy theater established here in 1507—some 87 years before the more famous one at the Università di Padua—to bring an end to what had been until then itinerant anatomical experiments.

㉙ **Campo San Polo.** At its worst Campo San Polo today conveys a sense of bleak wasteland. Only Piazza San Marco is larger than this square, where not even the pigeons manage to look cozy, and the echo of the children's voices, bouncing against the surrounding palaces, makes the space seem even emptier. But not so long ago this campo was a throbbing center of activity, animated by shows, bull races, fairs, military parades, and packed markets. A bit of this returns in the summer months, when an outdoor cinema is set up. A stone's throw from the Grand Canal, this neighborhood was colonized by some of the richest families of the city. The early 15th-century Palazzo Soranzo (at No. 2170–1) was entirely decorated with frescoes by Giorgione; the Baroque building at Number 1957 took the place of the Gothic mansion of the Bernardo family, covered with frescoes by Salviati. The facade of the Renaissance **Palazzo Corner Mocenigo** is best seen from Ponte San Polo, on the way to the Frari, to the right, or take the Sotoportego dei Cavalli to reach Campiello Albrizzi, with the famous 17th-century palazzo of the same name, Palazzo Albrizzi, occasionally open to the public for temporary exhibits.

㉜ **Campo Santo Stefano.** How many men are born and die in a square named in their honor, never to have called it home while they were alive? Although Venetians steadfastly refer to this campo by its old saint designation, on maps and on walls it bears the name of Francesco Morosini (1618–92). He came from a family that had already given the Republic four doges; at age 23 he was the captain of a galley, at 39 supreme commander of the Venetian navy, and at almost 70 was still at the helm. With a cannon shot he nearly destroyed the Parthenon in

50

Athens, which the Turks had seized and transformed into a mosque. He was elected doge while he was taking the Peloponnese. Upon his return he was welcomed by a 125-ft-tall triumphal arch that spanned Piazzetta San Marco; wine flowed through two enormous fountains, and the Republic placed a bronze bust of him inside Palazzo Ducale (previously considered strictly a posthumous honor). The family palace, **Ca' Morosini** (at No. 2802–3), was sold after the death of the last Morosini heir in 1884, but the city acquired the records and personal effects of the family (now in Museo Correr). To the right stands the massive **Palazzo Pisani,** the largest private home in Venice until it became a conservatory in 1897 (closed to the public). History apart, this is one of the nicest squares in town, and a favorite meeting point for Venetians who these days are more likely to associate Santo Stefano with the good gelato from Paolin than with their heroic ancestor.

NEED A
BREAK?

Caffè Paolin (⊠ 3464 Campo Santo Stefano, ☎ 041/5220710) makes some of the best gelato in Venice and is a pleasant spot from which to watch the passing parade. It's closed Saturday.

🔞 **Ca' Pesaro.** Designed by Baldassare Longhena in grand Baroque style, this impressive mansion was completed only in 1710, when both the commissioner and the architect had already been dead for many years. After having been sold to several families, the palace was turned over to the city on the condition that it be used as a venue to exhibit the works by young Venetian artists. This is why the museum, called the **Galleria Internazionale d'Arte Moderna,** was initially made up of paintings and sculpture shown at the Biennale, the big international art event that, with few interruptions, has regularly taken place in Venice every two years since 1895. But numerous new acquisitions and donations have made it one of Italy's most varied collections of modern art. Ca' Pesaro also houses the **Museo d'Arte Orientale**, a mix of art, garments, armor, and musical instruments from China and Japan. ⊠ *San Stae, Santa Croce,* ☎ *041/5241173.* 🎫 *€2.00, €4.15 combined ticket with Galleria Franchetti.* ⊘ *Museo d'Arte Orientale Tues.–Sun. 8:15–2. Galleria closed for restoration, scheduled to reopen in 2002; call 041/5240695 for current status.*

㉑ Fondaco dei Turchi. Built in 1225 by an immigrant from Pesaro, this palace was so beautiful that in 1381 it was bought by the Republic, which loaned it to the Duke of Ferrara (from whom it was periodically confiscated in conflicts), and at the same time used it as a hotel for visiting emissaries. Perhaps because of its ruined interior, in 1621 the building was rented as a warehouse to Turkish merchants, who took up residence and installed a mosque and bathhouse.

The great state of repair of the Fondaco dei Turchi is due to its total restoration in the late 19th century as the first location of the Museo Correr. It now contains the city's **Museo di Storia Naturale,** with interesting collections of flora and fauna native to the lagoon and the skeletons of two prehistoric reptiles. ⊠ *Salizzada del Fontego dei Turchi, 1730 Santa Croce,* ☎ *041/5240885.* ⊘ *Museum closed for restoration until 2003.*

㉝ Palazzo Fortuny. The facade of this outstanding palace dominates little Campo San Beneto (marked San Benedetto on most maps). The home of the Pesaro family until they moved to the Ca' Pesaro on the Grand Canal, the building later served as a concert and dance venue, and then a print shop. It was then purchased by Mariano Fortuny y Madrazo, a genial, eclectic artist from Granada, friend of Proust, and protagonist of Venice's worldly cultural scene during the Belle Epoque. Besides hosting temporary exhibitions, the **Museo Fortuny** houses the works and inventions left by this singular aficionado of theater, photography, and textiles. Fortuny had rediscovered the dyes used in the 16th century, the same shades that young Tintoretto used when playing in his father's dyer shop, and reinvented the technique of Venetian fabric decoration that made use of gold and silver thread. Eleonora Duse, Sarah Bernhardt, and Isadora Duncan were among those who wore his creations, and his name remains linked to the factory he opened on the Giudecca next to the Molino Stucky, where precious fabrics are made according to a procedure so secret that the workers are trained to perform only their particular phase of the process. A tiny shop on Campo San Maurizio called Trois sells these wonders for about $250 a meter, but you can browse through the catalog samples for free. ⊠ *Campo San Beneto, 3780 San Marco,* ☎ *041/5200995.* 🎫 *€4.15.* ⊘ *Tues.– Sun. 10–6 (last entrance at 5:30).*

★ **⑲ Palazzo Mocenigo.** So well preserved it looks like a movie set, this palazzo gives a sense of what private architecture was like in the last years of the Republic, with outstanding floors and glass chandeliers from Murano. The *portego* (entry hall) at the center of the apartment is an ample room with few furnishings and portraits of the seven Mocenigo doges and other notables. It occupied about one-third of the total space of the apartment and could also be used as a dance hall. The portego is lined with bedrooms and salons, where visitors were received in the early morning hours with a cup of hot chocolate after a night typically spent at parties, immersed in conversation, or seated at the gambling table. The furniture and paintings are all original and constitute a sort of permanent exhibit. The suits, lace, fabrics, and accessories on display come from the collection of the **Center for the History of Textiles and Costumes** (housed in a wing of the palace), which organizes thematic exhibits spanning from the 15th to the 18th century. ⊠ *Saliz-*

zada San Stae, 1992 San Stae, ☎ *041/721798.* 🎫 *€4.15; €15.50 combined ticket also gives admission to Ca' Rezzonico, Biblioteca Marciana, Museo Correr, Museo Vetrario, Museo del Merletto, Museo Archeologico, and Palazzo Ducale.* ☉ *Tues.–Sun. 10–5 (last entrance at 4:30).*

★ ㉓ **San Giacomo dall'Orio.** Founded according to legend in the 9th century on an island still populated by wolves, the church as it presently stands was built in 1225 and modified in the Renaissance, but it still retains a distinctly archaic atmosphere. Perhaps it's the low, monumental, unmatched Byzantine columns that make this place seem more like an old pagan temple set beneath a beautiful 15th-century ship's keel roof. In the sanctuary, the large, mystical Lombardesque crosses in marble and gilded wood restore a religious sense to the space, surrounded by a bevy of small medieval Madonnas. Above the main altar is one of the few works by Lorenzo Lotto in Venice, *Madonna and Four Saints,* but it falls short of the artist's *Young Man* at the Gallerie dell'Accademia. Don't let the bare brick walls mislead you: by now you know better than to leave without first asking the custodian about special chapels or the like—in this case a pair of sacristies with works by Palma il Giovane (circa 1544–1628) and Veronese. ✉ *Campo San Giacomo dall'Orio, Santa Croce,* ☎ *041/5240672; 041/2750462 Chorus.* 🎫 *€1.55, €7.75 Chorus ticket.* ☉ *Mon.–Sat. 10–5, Sun. 1–5.*

㉕ **San Nicola da Tolentino.** A Corinthian portico with very tall columns gives some character to this otherwise unremarkable church, made up of just the kind of "stones" Ruskin would probably have liked to toss into the lagoon. So why come here at all? Because this building makes a bizarre sight against the Venetian sky, and it might offer that necessary break in the litany of Romanesque and Gothic magic—come here for a break from Venice. The architect responsible for the main structure is Vincenzo Scamozzi (1552–1616), a bit surprising in light of some of his other projects in town, which include the Libreria Sansoviniana in Piazzetta San Marco and the Procuratie Nuove in the Piazza itself. Expect a great deal of stuccowork and second-rate paintings, with a couple of exceptions: the *Charity of St. Lawrence* by Bernardo Strozzi (1581–1644) on the external walls of the third chapel in the left transept, and *St. Jerome Visited by an Angel* by Giovanni Lys (circa 1597–1630) in the right transept. The interior is too dark to be seen after sundown. ✉ *Santa Croce 265,* ☎ *041/5222160.* 🎫 *Free.* ☉ *Mon.–Sat. 8–noon and 5–6:30, Sun. 5–6:30.*

★ ㉘ **San Pantalon.** The name Pantalon is not so common anymore, probably because it's the name of one of the most popular characters in the Venetian Masquerade: a greedy old merchant with a hooked nose, notoriously difficult personality, and a weakness for "*le bele putte*" (the good-looking girls) who teased him—anything but a saint. But the church was named after a different Pantalon, a poor doctor martyred under the Roman Emperor Diocletian, and it makes a very serious stop among the great Venetian scuole, abbeys, and churches. Put some coins in the slot in the right nave marked *illuminazione soffitto* (ceiling illumination), and out of the darkness emerges the *Martyrdom of St. Pantaleo,* a colossal masterpiece by Gian Antonio Fumiani (1643/50–1710). The little-known artist spent the last 24 years of his life on this ceiling, which is actually made up of 40 separate canvases joined together to look like one large fresco. This technique was not unheard of, but the enormity of the work demanded tremendous mastery of perspective. Perhaps in the end it was too much for him—he fell to his death while applying the finishing touches. The **Cappellina del Sacro Chiodo** (Little Chapel of the Holy Nail) holds a splendid *Coronation* *of the Virgin* by Antonio Vivarini. Sorting out who's who in its dense world of Gothic symbols takes some doing (the custodian sells a book that can help). There are also three less-intense works by Paolo Veneziano: a *Madonna with Child,* an *Annunciation,* and the *Presentation to the Temple.* Next to the small chapel is the 18th-century reconstruction of the Virgin Mary's house in Nazareth, with the wooden statue of the Madonna di Loreto in the niche at the back. According to Catholic legend, the house was miraculously "flown" from the Holy Land to a hill in Loreto, a town in Italy's Marche region, and it has since become an internationally known pilgrimage site. One of the last works by Veronese, *St. Pantalon Healing a Child,* is in the second chapel to the right. ⊠ *Campo San Pantalon, Santa Croce,* ☎ *041/ 5235893.* ▱ *Free.* ☉ *Mon.–Sat. 4–6.*

③⓪ **San Polo.** Founded in the 9th century, the church of St. Paul underwent a major reconstruction in the late Gothic period and a neoclassical makeover in the early 1800s. Extensive restoration in the 1930s brought back the wonderful wooden ship's keel roof, as well as the earlier Byzantine window on the facade. The artwork inside is not particularly engaging, as the 19th-century alterations were so costly that the friars had to sell the best paintings in order to pay the bills. The *Stations of the Cross* in the oratory to the left of the entrance is the remaining gem: painted by Giambattista Tiepolo's son Giandomenico (1727–1804), the 14 scenes are remarkably expressive and theatrical. With the help of the free guide available at the entrance, find your way to the less-exciting works by Tiepolo's father, Tintoretto, and Veronese, which survived the auction. The sturdy bell tower, guarded by two lions playing with a detached human head and a serpent, has remained unchanged through the centuries. ⊠ *Campo San Polo, San Polo,* ☎ *041/ 5237631; 041/2750462 Chorus.* ▱ *€1.55, €7.75 Chorus ticket.* ☉ *Mon.–Sat. 10–5, Sun. 1–5.*

★ **②⑦** **Santa Maria Gloriosa dei Frari.** St. Francis was still alive when a group of friars from his order arrived in Venice in 1222. They remained without a fixed residence for about 30 years, until the Doge Tiepolo gave them a vast tract of land in the San Polo sestiere. The small original church was built in just a few years and remained in use until this huge Gothic temple, begun in 1340, was finished a century later. It is thought that the architect responsible for this spiritual fortress—which has come to be known simply as I Frari—was the Franciscan friar Scipione Bon or Beato Pacifico, whose portrait is in the right transept beneath his funeral monument. Striking for the relative absence of art (except for the sumptuous choir stalls), the church has in recent times lost some of the austerity befitting the Franciscans, for whom abstinence and poverty were key tenets. A number of pompous and bombastic 19th-century mausoleums contrast stridently with the russet-color walls, which close-up reveal themselves to be disappointingly restored and painted in a faux-brick pattern. In particular, the spooky pyramid-shape tomb of 19th-century sculptor Antonio Canova, with a sleepy lion (perhaps hinting at Venice's captivity under the Austrians), stands opposite an equally ungainly monument to Titian, who was so important to Venetians that his body was exhumed from a communal grave where those killed by the plague had been indiscriminately buried.

This church contains Titian's famous *Assumption,* considered his finest painting by most art historians for its revolutionary use of space and movement. It hangs above the altar, recognizable from a distance for its gaudy colors, especially the glowing reds. Back in the 1970s the Frari became the first church in Italy to charge admission, a policy that caused almost as much talk as the picture itself. When it was unveiled in 1518, the *Assumption* caused a real sensation, as it put Venetian painting on a level with the art being made for the pope. If the Apostles look a bit like those of Michelangelo, or the figure of the Virgin seems to share something with that of Raphael, keep in mind that Titian hadn't yet been to Rome. His main achievement wasn't so much to come up with his own style as it was to break with the still rather Byzantine tradition of positioning the primary subject in the center of the composition, facing straight out of the painting. In this context, the beautiful so-called *Madonna di Ca' Pesaro* (left nave) is an even more revolutionary painting. Begun immediately after the delivery of *Assumption*, this altarpiece took almost 10 years to complete and was made for nobleman Jacopo Pesaro as a token of thanks for a Venetian victory over the Turks. Looking at the patron (Pesaro) kneeling before the Madonna (modeled on the artist's wife), it's hard to perceive Titian's total disregard for the conventions of his time, but to move the Virgin out of the center of the picture and to portray the interceding saints as active participants in the scene was unheard of at the time. Giovanni Bellini's cool and collected triptych *Madonna with Child and Saints* in the **Sacristy** (1488) will help you appreciate how rapidly Venetian Renaissance painting developed after Titian. Conclude your visit to the Frari with a look at an arrestingly realistic wooden sculpture of *St. John the Baptist*, which Donatello made for the Florentine community in 1438. ⊠ *Campo dei Frari, San Polo,* ☎ *041/5222637; 041/2750462 Chorus.* 🔁 *€1.55, €7.75 Chorus ticket.* ⊙ *Mon.–Sat. 9–6, Sun. 1–6.*

❸❶ Santo Stefano. The third-largest convent building in Venice after the Frari and San Zanipolo, the church of Santo Stefano was founded by Augustinian hermits in the 13th century. Perhaps there was something wrong from the very beginning—the church had to be entirely rebuilt in the 14th century, and the story goes that it was reconsecrated six times because of bloodstains that appeared on the ceiling. Nevertheless, the church developed into an excellent example of Florid Gothic style, with a great-looking doorway and tall pillars inside. More than in a smaller church, here you appreciate the Venetian ingenuity in lightening structures that otherwise would have sunk into their muddy foundations: in place of the typically heavy roofs that bore down on static walls, the master shipbuilders of the lagoon envisioned and created a roof shaped like a ship's keel. The most valuable artwork, including three paintings by Tintoretto and a cross by Paolo Veneziano, is kept in the **Sacristy.** Don't miss the pretty **Cloister,** and on the way out look for the tomb of Doge Francesco Morosini. ⊠ *Campo Santo Stefano, San Marco,* ☎ *041/5225061; 041/2750462 Chorus.* 🔁 *€1.55, € 7.75 Chorus ticket.* ⊙ *Mon.–Sat. 10–5, Sun. 1–5.*

❷⓿ San Zandegolà. This little old church, also known as San Giovanni Decollato, is dedicated to St. John the "Beheaded." Several Byzantine frescoes, poorly preserved, were discovered inside during restoration work in the late 1940s. ⊠ *Campo di San Zandegolà, Santa Croce.* 🔁 *Free.* ⊙ *Mon.–Sat. 10–noon.*

🐚 ★ **❸❹ Scala Contarini del Bovolo.** Easy to miss despite its vicinity to Piazza San Marco, this Renaissance-Gothic beauty is accessible only through a narrow, smelly shortcut that connects Campo Manin with Calle dei Fuseri. Structurally unstable and closed to the public for decades, the stairway was finally restored in 1995, and it's now possible to climb six floors to the top, in a spiral of amazement at what Venetian architects were quietly accomplishing when America had just been "discovered." One of Venice's oldest patrician families, the Contarini provided the Republic with doges for about six centuries—eight doges in all, the first elected in 1043, the last in 1676—and built so many magnificent palaces that the locals used nicknames to tell them apart, often inspired by some particular decorative detail. *Bovolo* is the word for "snail" in Venetian dialect. ⊠ *Corte dei Risi o del Bovolo, 4299 San Marco,* ☎ *Contact Ufficio Beni Culturali, 041/2702464.* 🎫 €2.00. ⊙ *Apr.–Oct., daily 10–6; open during Carnevale daily 11–5 and Christmas daily 11–3:30.*

★ ㉔ **Scuola Grande di San Giovanni Evangelista.** Starting from Campo San Stin, two turns bring you to a rather magical Lombardesque marble wall; the great intimidating eagle perched on top signals the sacred territory of the apostle St. John. Founded in 1349 by the powerful brotherhood of St. John the Evangelist, the Scuola Grande was closed by Napóleon and then bought from the Austrian government in 1857 by the Guild of Arti Edificatorie (Guild of Building Arts), which still runs the place. Its lovely facade and front yard are captivating examples of Lombardesque-Renaissance style, and since 1998 the Guild—for the first time in its long history—has opened its doors to the public (for very limited hours, by appointment only). The layout inside suits the standard requirements of any Venetian scuola, whose primary function was to host crowds of petitioners as well as the wealthier members of the fraternal order. The plain, spacious entry hall was meant to welcome the needy. It now contains architectural fragments and sculptures from around town, which were dumped here "for storage" after the suppression of the brotherhood in the 1800s. Note a rare 14th-century sculpture of the beloved *Madonna della Misericordia,* with the faithful gathered beneath her ample mantel; and the Gothic capitals with the pastoral symbol of St. John in Ephesus inserted between the portraits of different praying brothers to signify the intercession of the Apostle. The double flight of stairs, skillfully designed by Codussi, takes care of the narrow space with a simple perspective trick, in which the steps incrementally increase in height, creating the illusion of depth. The engravings on the marble threshold representing the tools of the guild were added in the 20th century. The richer scuole would typically commission the decoration of their main meeting hall, called the **Sala del Capitolo,** from the best available artists. But here, Tintoretto painted only some of the episodes from the *Life of St. John* that cover the walls. Although Tiepolo had discussed redoing the ceiling with the famous architect Massari, the painter left for Spain (where he ultimately died) and the job was eventually given to a group of minor artists. The addition of several extra rooms, the Albergo (sort of a deluxe hostel for pilgrims), and a small chapel for prayer increased the efficiency, comfort, and prestige of the larger scuole. Here, the chapel is dedicated to nothing less than the relics of the Holy Cross. Perhaps you'll recognize the carved wooden pole to the left of the altar as the same pole used to carry the relics across town in the paintings relating to the Miracles of the Holy Cross in the Gallerie dell'Accademia. A small-scale model of the room shows the original disposition of the stupendous teleri by Gentile Bellini and Carpaccio. Titian's ceiling painting for the Albergo was robbed by Napóleon; the only high-quality piece currently on exhibit is a 14th-century *Madonna with Child and the Sts. Peter, John the Baptist, and John*—perhaps you'll notice a "missing head": St. John has been sawed off. ⊠ *Campiello della Scuola, 2454 San Polo,* ☎ *041/718234.* 🎫 *Free (donation).* ⊙ *Upon request.*

★ ㉖ **Scuola Grande di San Rocco.** The Brotherhood of San Rocco, recognized by the Republic since 1475, came together around the figure of one of the greatest natural fund-raisers who ever appeared on the Venetian scene: a French-born former student of medicine who in his early twenties renounced a career and wealth and made a pilgrimage to Italy, where he dedicated himself to curing those struck with the plague.

Having become infected himself, he hid in a forest and was miraculously healed with the help of a dog that brought him bread each day. Upon return to France, he was not recognized by his family and died in prison at age 32. The cult of St. Rocco, invoked against the plagues that decimated Europe, was particularly strong in Venice, and after the grave epidemic of 1576, the saint was made co-patron of the city. Generous donations to the brotherhood led to the construction of a church and one of the most sumptuous scuole in the city.

Apart from being a great example of Venetian Renaissance architecture, the Scuola Grande di San Rocco is famous for a series of more than 50 paintings by Tintoretto that did for Venice what Michelangelo's Sistine Chapel did for Rome. More mystical and devout than his sophisticated contemporaries, Tintoretto sought pathos and emotional tension rather than a good "finish" and carried Titian's love of motion and unusual composition to highly dramatic effects: his wall-size *Crucifixion* scene left such a tough-skinned critic as Ruskin speechless. The story goes that in 1564 Tintoretto won the competition to decorate the Albergo of the scuola by submitting a finished work—*St. Rocco in Glory* at the center of the ceiling—instead of a sketch. He offered the painting for free "not to win, but to honor St. Rocco" and spent the next 23 years on the cycle of paintings. Start from the **Albergo** on the first floor, which also houses two intense works on easels attributed to Giorgione and Titian. Then return to the large adjoining hall, where Tintoretto worked from 1576 to 1581, after the scuola agreed to pay him an annual pension for life. On the ceiling are episodes from the Old Testament: the three larger, central subjects (*Moses Striking Water from the Rock to Quench the People's Thirst; Moses Erecting the Brazen Serpents to Save Those Bitten by Snakes;* and *The Fall of Manna*) were specifically selected to solemnly represent the three bodily sufferings of humanity—thirst, disease, and hunger—which San Rocco and later his brotherhood sought to eliminate. The walls feature scenes from the New Testament and some conspicuous wood carvings by 17th-century sculptor Francesco Pianta. The mildly satirical, bizarre figures are allegories of the sentiments, such as Fury (the winged youth with the blindfold, flask of wine, and cannon); of activities like Espionage (the man wrapped in a large scarf); and of the arts—bad-tempered Tintoretto, with a bunch of brushes, symbolizes Painting. The eight canvases on the ground floor, conceived when Tintoretto was in his sixties, show his innovative use of light and shadow, which play a key role in the economy of his masterpiece *Flight into Egypt.* ✉ *Campo di San Rocco, San Polo,* ☎ *041/5234864.* ✉ *€5.15.* ☉ *Nov. 3–Mar., daily 10–4; Apr.–Nov. 2, daily 9–5:30 (last entry ½ hr before closing).*

RIALTO TO CANNAREGIO

Cannaregio's main drag, which is also the longest street in Venice, winds its way parallel to the Grand Canal. Lined with fruit and vegetable stalls near Ponte delle Guglie, quiet shops, gelaterias, and bakeries, the Strada Nova (literally, "New Street," as it was opened in 1871) serves as a pedestrian expressway from the train station to Ca' d'Oro. A number of nightspots, including Venice's only disco, have cropped up along this paved ribbon, which, although bereft of sights itself, is a convenient point of reference while exploring Cannaregio. Seen from above, this part of town seems like a wide field plowed by several long, straight canals that are linked by intersecting straight streets—not typical of Venice, where the shape of the islands usually defines the shape of the canals. But these canals were cut through a vast bed of reeds (hence the name Cannaregio, which means "Reed Place"), and not even the Venetians could overlook such an opportunity to make long, straight thoroughfares. What also sets Cannaregio apart from the rest of the town are its relatively clean canals and a distinct absence of odors you sometimes encounter in other parts of Venice. The daylight reflected off the bright-green canals, wooden boats painted vivid red or blue, and the big sky visible from the fondamente make this a particularly luminous area of town. It's no surprise, perhaps, that Titian and Tintoretto had houses nearby.

The noble palaces of the Cannaregio district were built along the Grand Canal. The northern part of the sestiere is more typical of a working-class neighborhood, where many *bacari* (wine bars) fill up with old card players every afternoon. The Jewish Ghetto, isolated by a moat-like rio, and several striking churches built for the poor hold the primary architectural interest, and the Ca' d'Oro's Galleria Franchetti and the Tiepolo Ballroom in Palazzo Labia add some color to your walk.

Numbers in the text correspond to numbers in the margin and on the Rialto to Cannaregio map.

A Good Walk

Start your day at Campo San Bartolomio, guarded by a statue of the good-natured, witty Venetian playwright Carlo Goldoni, responsible for resurrecting the commedia dell'arte, and browse through the lively stalls on the **Ponte di Rialto** ㉟ as visitors to Venice have done for centuries. Half-hidden behind the heaps of fruit and vegetables in the market area beyond stands **San Giacometto** ㊱ church. Don't miss the arcade that runs parallel to it, with well-restored but faded 16th-century ceiling frescoes and more jewelry shops. Straight ahead is Campo delle Beccarie, once the butchers' quarter, with the adjoining—and still thriving—*pescheria* (fish market) on Campo della Pescheria. Have a look at the nearby produce stalls facing the Grand Canal. Not long ago, the area between the Rialto Bridge and the pescheria was entirely devoted to food, but as the local population sunk from 300,000 at the end of World War II to 200,000 in the late '50s, and finally to 60,000 today, the market has in part been taken over by souvenir and mask shops. Take the traghetto from the pescheria to Campo Santa Sofia (Venetians call this the Strada Nova) to reach the **Ca' d'Oro** ㊲, with the interesting collection of antiques and paintings in the Galleria Franchetti.

Follow Strada Nova to the train station, stopping on the way at Campo della Maddalena (down Ponte Sant'Antonio), where you'll see the only round church in town, Chiesa della Maddalena, a fine Renaissance well, and an impressive block of medieval houses with towering chimney pots. From the top of Ponte delle Guglie you'll catch a side glimpse of **Palazzo Labia** ㊳, with Tiepolo's celebrated ballroom inside (entrance in Campo San Geremia). Stroll along breezy Fondamenta Venier until you come to the church of **San Giobbe** ㊴. You might want to explore this odd neighborhood, with a view of the bridge connecting Venice to the mainland, before heading toward the **Jewish Ghetto** ㊵ via the Ponte dei Tre Archi—so tall because the canal below was once the most trafficked waterway to town from the lagoon. Make a left onto Calle del Ghetto Vecchio, with a (non-kosher) Jewish bakery, leading to the Campiello delle Scuole (also called Campiello del Ghetto Vecchio) and to Campo del Ghetto Nuovo, home to some of the world's oldest synagogues. Here, to the right, is the entrance to the Museo Ebraico. Go over Ponte del Ghetto Nuovo, and bear left along Fondamenta degli Ormesini. At the first bridge, make a left onto Calle Turlona to Calle dei Riformati, which leads to the Fondamenta dei Riformati, where, to the right, stands the church of **Sant'Alvise** ㊶.

Take the bridge opposite the church, and make a left at the end of the calle onto Fondamenta della Sensa; this goes straight to pretty Campo dei Mori, which takes its name from an Arab warehouse that once stood in the square. Tintoretto once lived a few steps farther down the fondamenta at No. 3399. He kept his family awake at night to study how to reproduce candlelight effects. Some of the painter's best works can be admired in his parish church, the **Madonna dell'Orto** ㊷, which stands across the rio on the other side of Campo dei Mori. As you leave the church, turn left toward the expanse of water and reach the Campo dell'Abbazia via Corte Vecchia and the porticoed Fondamenta dell' Abbazia. Night people and honeymooners should make a point of returning after dark to this mysteriously romantic place. Take a left to reach Fondamenta San Felice, where an old bridge without parapets survives. It's hard to imagine now, but until the 11th century, Venetians preferred riding horses to walking or rowing, so they built their first bridges flat. Bridges were then rebuilt so that boats could pass underneath. For centuries they were left without railings, which appeared only in the final period of the Republic. Go over Ponte Racchetta and turn left onto Calle Racchetta, which then becomes Calle Lunga Santa Caterina. Here Titian had his house, with a large garden facing the lagoon. From the Fondamente Nuove, you can clearly see the islands of Murano, with its lighthouse, and San Michele with cypress trees; in the distance float Burano and tiny Torcello. Turn into the Salizzada degli Specchieri to visit the Baroque **Chiesa dei Gesuiti** ㊸; then bear right to approach the Strada Nova via Fondamenta Zen, Ruga Do Pozzi, and Ponte Priuli. From Campo Santi Apostoli, follow the main drag to the church of San Giovanni Grisostomo, with two remarkable paintings by Sebastiano dal Piombo and Giovanni Bellini. Past the church, take the Sotoportego to the left leading to Corte del Milion—Marco Polo was born here in 1254, although nobody is sure in which of the three houses. The courtyard takes its name from his nickname, "Milion," because he told a million different stories about his travels to China. Taken as a prisoner of war by the rival city of Genoa, he dictated some of these stories to his literate cell mate, and the resulting book—which is actually a serious historical document—became famous as *Il Milione*. Go over Ponte Storto to Calle Scaletta and turn right toward central Campo San Lio, from where you can easily reach the Rialto landing or the Piazza San Marco in time for sunset.

TIMING

Make an early start to beat the crowds that clog the Rialto Bridge and market for most of the day, and try to make it to the Ca' d'Oro around mid-morning. Allow about one hour to see the Galleria Franchetti, so that you can visit San Giobbe before getting an early lunch. If you want to take the guided tour of the Jewish Ghetto's synagogues, make sure you'll be done by 4 o'clock—the churches of Sant'Alvise and the Madonna dell'Orto close at 5. If you are late, the latter is a more engaging site and should be given priority. The rest of the walk, including a visit to the Chiesa dei Gesuiti, will take about an hour. If you are counting on seeing the Tiepolo Ballroom in Palazzo Labia, call ahead to make sure it's open.

Sights to See

★ ㊲ **Ca' d'Oro.** This exquisite Gothic palace was once literally a "Golden House," when its marble traceries and ornaments were embellished with pure gold. Created in 1434 by the rich and enamored patrician Marino Contarini for his wife, the Ca' d'Oro served as a demonstration of love a second time in the 19th century, when a Russian prince offered it to the celebrated classical dancer Maria Taglioni, who collected palaces along the Grand Canal. The last proprietor, perhaps more taken with

---

Close-Up

ODES TO VENICE

SINCE THE EARLY 19TH CENTURY, Venice has been a stop on the writer's Grand Tour, and the result has been a long serenade sung by some of literature's greats. Lord Byron, for one, was so enchanted that he moved to Venice in 1817, to be followed by Percy Shelley. Charles Dickens visited in 1844 and wrote to a friend, "the gorgeous and wonderful reality of Venice is beyond the fancy of the wildest dreamer . . . it is a thing you would shed tears to see." Mark Twain, visiting in 1867, refused to be seduced, dismissing the gondola and gondolier as "the one an inky, rusty old canoe with a sable hearse-body clapped on to the middle of it, and the other a mangy, barefooted gutter-snipe . . ." Marcel Proust, on the other hand, arrived on a visit with his mother and refused to leave. Such varied talents as Henry James, Ernest Hemingway, Erica Jong, and Ezra Pound (who is buried on San Michele) all adored the place; Thomas Mann's *Death in Venice* is the city's most bittersweet love song.

Venice's literati have for the most part been tourists, inspired by the traveler's Venice that you can see every day. James praised the monuments but also the typical "sunny, shabby square." Pound was moved by nothing greater than the play of light on an evening gondola ride. Centuries before any of them, Shakespeare set two plays in Venice (*Othello* and *The Merchant of Venice*) without setting foot there—proof that for some, the Venice of the imagination is inspiration enough.

— Valerie Hamilton

Venice than with any of his lovers, left the Ca' d'Oro to the city, after having had it carefully restored and filled with a fine collection of antiquities, sculptures, and paintings that today make up the **Galleria Franchetti.** Besides Mantegna's celebrated *St. Sebastian* and other first-rate Venetian works of art, the Galleria Franchetti contains the only surviving example of the type of fresco that once adorned the exteriors of Venetian buildings (commissioned by those who could not afford a marble facade). The detached fresco fragments on exhibit were made by Giorgione and a young Titian for the (now grayish-white) facade of the Fondaco dei Tedeschi, which today houses the main post office. ✉ *Calle della Ca' d'Oro, 3933 Cannaregio,* ☎ *041/5238790.* 💶 *€3.10; € 4.15 combined ticket with Museo d'Arte Orientale; €9.30 combined ticket with Museo d'Arte Orientale and the Gallerie dell'Accademia.* ☉ *Tues.–Sun. 8.15–7:15, Mon. 8:15–2.*

㊸ Chiesa dei Gesuiti. The classical arches and straight lines of the Renaissance were abandoned in favor of flowing, twisting forms in this extravagantly Baroque 18th-century church, which dominates its campo. Inside, gray-and-white marble is used like brocade, carved into swags and drapes. Titian's *Martyrdom of St. Lawrence,* over the first altar on the left, is a dramatic example of the great artist's feel for light and movement. ✉ *Campo dei Gesuiti,* ☎ *041/5231610.* 💶 *Free.* ☉ *Daily 10–noon and 5–7.*

★ **㊵ Jewish Ghetto.** The neighborhood that gave the world the word "ghetto" is today a quiet warren of streets off the main arteries, away

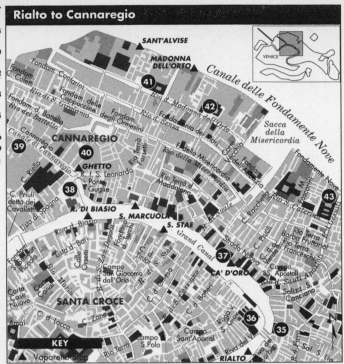

Rialto to Cannaregio

from the tourist flow, and still home to Jewish religious and administrative institutions, a kosher restaurant, a rabbinical school, and five synagogues. The first Jews probably came to Venice in the early 11th century, although they were not granted resident status. Through the Middle Ages, the Rialto commercial district was dependent upon itinerant Jewish merchants and moneylenders to finance ship cargoes, as vividly recounted in Shakespeare's *Merchant of Venice*. It was an extremely expensive war against nearby Chioggia in 1385 that convinced the Republic to allow Jews to live in the city, selling them a sort of temporary entry visa that could be repurchased every 5 or 10 years under certain conditions. In return for the right to live and work in Venice, protection in case of war, and religious freedom, the Jews were asked to pay increasingly heavier taxes and lend money at low interest.

In 1516, a prominent patrician attacked the Jews, asking the Senate to confine them to the periphery of town. The island of Cannaregio was selected, then named for its foundry ("*geto*" in Venetian), which produced the cannons for the Republican fleet before the Arsenale had been built. Gates at the entrance to the neighborhood were locked at night, and two boats patrolled the canals around the island. The first settlers were Central European Jews who spoke with a German accent, and "geto" came to be pronounced as "ghetto." They were allowed only to lend money, operate pawnshops controlled by the government, trade in textiles, and practice medicine. Jewish doctors were highly respected for their skills and could leave the ghetto at any hour when on duty. All men were required to wear a yellow circle stitched on the left shoulder of their coats and women had to wear a yellow scarf. Jews were nevertheless safe in Venice, and in the 16th century the community grew considerably, with refugees from the Near East, southern and central Italy, Spain, and Portugal. The Eastern European Jews (Ashkenazim) situated their two synagogues, the **Schola Grande Todesca** (1528) and the **Schola Canton** (1531), on the top floors of two adjacent houses. The Levantine Jews, who came next, were wealthy enough to purchase some land on the island across the rio and in 1541 built the sumptuous **Schola Levantina,** currently used for worship in winter. A third atticlike synagogue was built by the poor Italian Jews in the 1570s: the tentative dome is barely visible from the Campo below. Finally, in 1589, the ghetto accommodated a batch of Sephardic Jews fleeing from Spain. Their **Schola Spagnola** is used for religious services in the summer and stands just across the Schola Levantina in the Campiello delle Scuole. In the first half of the 17th century, the ghetto housed about 5,000 Jews; notice the narrow, slanting buildings that remain on Campo del Ghetto Nuovo.

Jews were subsequently "ghettoed" in other cities in Italy. Although the gates were pulled down during Napoleonic rule, Jews realized freedom only in the late 19th century with the founding of the Italian state. On the eve of World War II there were about 1,500 Jews left in the ghetto: 289 were deported by the Nazis. Eight returned.

Centuries of Jewish culture fill the tiny but well-arranged **Museo Ebraico,** which contains splendid silver Hanukkah lamps and torahs, Passover plates, brocade torah sheaths, and handwritten, beautifully decorated wedding contracts in Hebrew. Guided synagogue tours in Italian and English leave hourly from the museum. You might complete your tour of Jewish Venice with a visit to the **Antico Cimitero Ebraico** (Ancient Jewish Cemetery) on the Lido, full of fascinating old tombstones half-hidden by ivy and grass. The Jewish community was granted this burial ground in 1348, probably under the emergency of the terrible plague that in the years 1347–49 killed over half of the city's inhabitants. The cemetery was in use until the end of the 18th century. ✉ *Museo Ebraico: Campo del Ghetto Nuovo, 2902/b Cannaregio,* ☎ *041/715359.* ☞ *€2.60, guided tours €6.20 (includes museum entry).* ☺ *Oct.–May, Sun.–Fri. 10–5:30; June–Sept., Sun.–Fri. 10–7. Tours Oct.– May, Sun.–Fri. hourly from 10:30 to 4:30; June–Sept., Sun.–Fri. hourly 10:30–5:30. Cemetery:* ✉ *Via Cipro, Lido (vaporetto stop S. Maria Elisabetta),* ☎ *041/715359.* ☺ *Oct.–May, tour Sun. at 2:30; June–Sept., tour Sun. at 2:30, Fri. at 10:30.* ☞ *€6.20.*

★ ㊷ **Madonna dell'Orto.** A magical sight as you approach it in the thick silence of the night, with the white statues of the 12 Apostles floating above the cozy darkness of the little square, this church is also impressive in the daytime for its Oriental-style bell tower and handsome facade rising from its front yard of brick and Istrian stone parquet. Built in the Gothic style with some residual Romanesque squatness and a pre-Renaissance doorway, the church is dedicated to St. Christopher. It became known as the Madonna dell'Orto after a large statue of the Madonna, reputed to perform miracles (in the **Cappella di San Mauro**), was abandoned in an orchard nearby. This was Tintoretto's parish church, and he decorated it with two large and awe-inspiring canvases: *Jewish People Adoring the Golden Calf while Moses Receives the Ten Commandments* and the even more powerful *Last Judgment.* The painting draws your glance upward, toward the convergence of the celestial court of the Redeemer, which, with the strong use of chiaroscuro, contrasts sharply with the damned, who are being violently pulled by a gushing river into the trenches of hell below. The river, descending through the valley in a torrent, uproots trees and sweeps away the wicked, who pile up in mounds at the shores, where Charon's boat appears against a background of flames. More works by Tintoretto (all well labeled) are visible in the apse, and a simple plaque in the chapel to the right indicates the grave of the artist, who asked to be buried here together with his family.

Of a totally different texture and scope than Tintoretto's paintings is the fresh and luminous masterpiece by Cima da Conegliano, *St. John the Baptist and Saints,* which seems to be a concentrated effort to represent peace, both at the level of one's own soul and in the surrounding world. Finally, the first chapel to the left displays a photographic reproduction of a precious *Madonna with Child* by Giovanni Bellini. The original was stolen one night in March 1993. ⊠ *Campo della Madonna dell'Orto, Cannaregio,* ☎ *041/719933; 041/2750462 Chorus.* ☞ €*1.55,* €*7.75 Chorus ticket.* ◷ *Mon.–Sat. 10–5, Sun. 1–5.*

③⑧ **Palazzo Labia.** This palace was once the stomping grounds of Venice's showiest 18th-century family, famous for serving dinner on golden plates that were thrown out of the window at the cry: "*L'abia o no l'abia, sarò sempre Labia*" ("With or without it, I'll always be a Labia")— although it seems that a net strung across the bottom of the canal caught the dishes, which were recovered in time for the next dinner party. The palace today is the regional headquarters of the RAI, the Italian national radio and television network. However apt in Italy, it is hard to imagine a broadcasting company in such opulent Baroque splendor. The gorgeous **Tiepolo Ballroom,** which after the decline of the Labias was turned into a school and then a laundry room, exhibits the final flowering of Venetian painting: Giambattista Tiepolo's (1696–1770) frescoes of *Anthony and Cleopatra,* dressed like noble Venetians of the time, teeming with dwarfs, Barbary pirates, and toy dogs. ⊠ *Campo San Geremia, Cannaregio,* ☎ *041/52781277 or 041/781203.* ☞ *Free.* ◷ *Wed.–Fri. 11–noon by appointment only.*

★ ③⑤ **Ponte di Rialto** (Rialto Bridge). It is rather startling to consider that Venice, which by the end of the 12th century had already produced its first version of Palazzo Ducale and most of Basilica di San Marco, didn't build a permanent stone bridge across the Grand Canal until the late 1500s. It was not as if there hadn't been a need: earlier there had been an inconvenient toll bridge, replaced in the 13th century by a rickety wooden bridge (which collapsed twice). In the 15th century a larger bridge was built, this time with shops and an open central corridor, but a century later it had deteriorated to such an extent that the Republic finally decided to give up on wood and stage a competition for the best design in stone. The commission attracted the best architects of the period, including Michelangelo, Palladio, and Sansovino, but the job went to the appropriately named Antonio da Ponte. His plan focused on structure rather than elaborate decoration and kept costs down at a time when the Republic's coffers were low due to the opening of oceanic trade routes and continual wars against the Turks. A single arcade, more than 91 ft in length, supports two rows of shops selling jewelry, clothing, shoes, leather, tablecloths, and perfumes, with windows that open onto the often crowded central passage. The side paths offer a prime look at one of the city's most captured views: the Grand Canal full of gondolas and boats.

③⑥ **San Giacometto.** The church, according to legend, was founded in the 5th century by the first refugees (settlers who came from Torcello) from the lagoon. It was more likely built for the merchants who had businesses in the Rialto district in the 11th century: look for the inscription in the shape of a cross (on the external apse), which invokes the Holy Father and recommends that merchants be honest, weights and measures be exact, and contracts be honored. The church is rarely open, and inside there's nothing noteworthy. ⊠ *Rialto Market.*

39 **San Giobbe.** Like San Pietro di Castello, Sant'Elena, and San Francesco della Vigna, this church once marked the edge of town. You can see tiny orchards on the other side of the bridge. Even in this remote place you can find the remains of a doge. Cristoforo Moro had San Giobbe built for the poor residents of a nearby hospice, testimony to just how far the social fabric of the Venetian Republic extended and how the Republic protected even the poorest in the population. Begun in Gothic style (note the brick bell tower, the well, and what survives of the cloister) and finished by Pietro Lombardo in the early 1470s, this church is the first example of Renaissance church architecture in Venice. Especially fine are the **Sanctuary,** with a triptych by Antonio Vivarini and Giovanni d'Alemagna, and the **Cappella Martini,** with pretty blue and yellow majolica decorations commissioned from the Della Robbia workshop by a Tuscan family. Jacopo Bellini's *Madonna with Saints* (better known as the *Pala di San Giobbe*) and Carpaccio's *Presentation to the Temple* once hung here. Attempts in the late 1990s to claim them back from the Gallerie dell'Accademia ultimately proved unsuccessful but revived a long-standing controversy in Italy about the display of artistic masterpieces out of the context for which they were created. In their absence, the best Renaissance picture here is a Nativity scene by Gian Girolamo Savoldo (circa 1485–after 1548). ⊠ *Campo di San Giobbe, Cannaregio,* ☏ *041/5241889.* ▣ *Free.* ☉ *Mon.–Sat. 3:30–6, Sun. 8–noon.*

41 **Sant'Alvise.** Founded by young patrician Antonia Venier in the late 14th century after St. John, the Bishop of Tolosa, had appeared to her in a dream, the church of Sant'Alvise took its name from another, more popular Venetian saint, whose statue decorates the brick facade. Together with the Scuola Grande dei Carmini and Palazzo Labia, this is the third Venetian "Tiepolesque" building: in the sanctuary is Tiepolo's famous *Road to Calvary,* painted after the Scuola dei Carmini but before Palazzo Labia, and two of his juvenile works hang on the right wall. Note the nuns' *barco,* or choir stall, which was supported by pillars and leads directly to the convent. Below the barco are eight tempera paintings with biblical scenes that Ruskin had enthusiastically called "baby Carpaccios." They are now attributed to an older, unknown painter from Carpaccio's master's workshop—Carpaccio was six or seven years old at the time of their execution. A careful restoration of the church was completed by Chorus in 1999. ⊠ *Campo Sant'Alvise, Cannaregio,* ☏ *041/5244664; 041/2750462 Chorus.* ▣ *€ 1.55, €7.75 Chorus ticket.* ☉ *Mon.–Sat. 10–5, Sun. 1–5.*

CASTELLO ALTO

Venice's largest *sestiere,* Castello covers the area east of Piazza San Marco, extending from Campo Santa Maria Formosa and Campo Santi Giovanni e Paolo to the Arsenale and Sant'Elena. Its name probably comes from a fortress that once stood on the far east side of town facing the Lido. Venetians divide it into *alto* (high) and *basso* (low) sections. Roughly speaking, Castello Basso covers the area between the Rio dei Greci at the Chiesa della Pietà to the west, the Scuola di San Giorgio degli Schiavoni and the Arsenal to the north, and Sant'Elena to the east. Castello Alto is delimited by the Sestiere di San Marco to the west, stretching to the Fondamenta Nove to the north, with the Arsenal serving as its eastern border.

Not every well-off Venetian family could afford to build a palazzo on the Grand Canal. Many that couldn't instead settled in Castello Alto, taking advantage of its proximity to the Rialto and San Marco, and built the noble palazzi that today distinguish this neighborhood from the fishermen's enclave in the adjacent streets of Castello Basso. Castello Alto has a colorful history: in the early 15th century, large Greek and Dalmatian communities moved into the area along the Riva degli Schiavoni, where many of them sold dried fish and meat; the Confraternity of San Marco, based in what is now the hospital on Campo Santi Giovanni e Paolo, was patronized by Venetian high society in the 16th to 18th centuries; and nearby Campo Santa Maria Formosa served as a popular open-air theater for shows of various kinds, some involving bulls, until Napoléon conquered the Republic. Nonetheless, today many of the gracious palazzi look rather neglected, except for those bordering the sestiere di San Marco. Despite the reassuring presence of bars and osterias—more vital to Venetian daily survival than bread—the various tourist shops that illuminate the streets and small campi are not enough to bring a sense of vitality back to these streets.

Numbers in the text correspond to numbers in the margin and on the Castello Alto map.

A Good Walk

Combining a visit to all the sights with a leisurely walk and a couple of breaks, you should keep an eye on your watch every so often or you might find some closed doors. Start from Campo San Zaccaria and head toward the church of **San Giorgio dei Greci** ㊹ and the **Museo dei Dipinti Sacri Bizantini** ㊺ by way of pretty Fondamenta dell'Osmarin. On the opposite side of the rio stands the 14th-century Palazzo Priuli, with striking Gothic corner windows. On the way out of the museum, turn right onto Salizzada dei Greci, cross the Rio della Pietà, and make a left to the **Scuola di San Giorgio degli Schiavoni** ㊻ to admire nine remarkable works by Carpaccio, whose shades of red gave the owner of Harry's Bar the name for his famous *carpaccio* (marinated, thinly sliced raw beef). After your visit, take the shortest route (Calle dei Furlani, Campo and Salizzada delle Gatte, and Ramo San Francesco) to the church of **San Francesco della Vigna** ㊼, with its stern classical Palladian facade. Calle San Francesco will lead you to the Fondamenta Santa Giustina. Climb over the only bridge in sight, from the top of which you can see the island of San Michele. Follow the long Barbaria delle Tole—after the pastry shop to the right is one of the oldest mask workshops in Venice, opened up by a group of young artisans in the early 1970s, years before the city government officially revived the tradition of Carnevale celebrations. Walk past the Ospedaletto and enter one of Venice's grandest campi—**Campo Santi Giovanni e Paolo** ㊽, site of the gigantic Dominican church of **Santi Giovanni e Paolo** ㊾, San Zanipolo in Venetian, and of the Scuola Grande di San Marco, now the city hospital (closed to the public). If the church is closed, have an *aperitivo* (aperitif) at one of the three bars facing the powerful equestrian monument of Bartolomeo Colleoni. Hold your appetite until after you visit the fairy-tale **Santa Maria dei Miracoli** ㊿ (best approached from Calle Larga Gallina), a sight you might want to return to under the moonlight. After lunch, retrace your steps to San Zanipolo for a second chance to go inside the church and perhaps also to see the **Ospedaletto** ⑤ and its Sala della Musica (open Thursday through Saturday only). Follow Calle dell'Ospedaletto, which between bridges narrows into the most cramped alley in town, and bear right to Calle Lunga Santa Maria Formosa, at the end of which stands the white marble church of **Santa Maria Formosa** ㊾. Walk along the Rio di Santa Maria Formosa and cross it at Calle del Paradiso (of Heaven). The name of this street, lined with some of the oldest houses in Venice, refers to the splendid *luminarie* (decorative lights) once displayed here on Good Friday. Note the Gothic arch over the bridge, and the well-preserved wooden *barbacani* (buttresses) running along the walls of the building, a common strategy used by local architects to enlarge living rooms. Turn left onto Salizzada San Lio, right at the dead end, and cross the canal over Ponte della Guerra (of the War), like Ponte dei Pugni near San Barnaba, a site of civic rivalry. There should be enough time left to end your walk where it began, with a visit to the unusual half-Gothic, half-Renaissance **San Zaccaria** ⑤ church, which features a 10th-century, waterlogged crypt with the bones of eight early doges as well as a masterpiece by Giovanni Bellini. The nearby **Pinacoteca Querini-Stampalia** ⑤ would perhaps be best appreciated with fresher eyes on a slower day, or after an early dinner on the days in which the gallery stays open late.

TIMING

You will need an early start and a full day to make the most of this itinerary, although the actual walking time is no more than 1½ hours. The church of San Giorgio dei Greci and the nine paintings by Carpaccio at the Scuola di San Giorgio degli Schiavoni are worth a long look. The Church of San Francesco della Vigna is a 30-minute stop. It is a good idea to visit Santa Maria dei Miracoli just before or just after lunch, and then plan to be at the church of Santi Giovanni e Paolo when it reopens at 3:30. If you are still on schedule, hit Campo Santa Maria Formosa with its church around 4 or 4:30, so as to make it to San Zaccaria by 6. Finally, allow about one hour for the Pinacoteca Querini-Stampalia. If you wish, you can split the itinerary into two days, bearing in mind that only the churches of Santa Maria Formosa and the Miracoli are open at lunchtime; all the other sights close between noon or 12:30 and 3:30 or even 4 o'clock.

Sights to See

❹ **Campo Santi Giovanni e Paolo.** This large, attractive square is the site of three city landmarks: the imposing namesake Gothic church; the **Scuola Grande di San Marco,** with one of the loveliest Renaissance facades in Italy; and the only equestrian monument ever approved of by La Serenissima. The lucky rider, Bartolomeo Colleoni, had served Venice well as a *condottiere,* or mercenary commander. (The Venetians preferred to pay others to fight for them on land.) When he died in 1475, he left his fortune to the city on the condition that a statue be erected in his honor "in the piazza before San Marco." The republic's shrewd administrators coveted Colleoni's ducats but had no intention of honoring anyone, no matter how valorous, with a statue in Piazza San Marco. So they collected the loot, commissioned the statue, and put it up before the Scuola Grande di San Marco, which, before being incorporated by the city hospital, was headquarters of a powerful fraternal order. The statue, by Florentine sculptor Andrea del Verrocchio (1435–88), is believed to make eye contact with another famous bronze condottiere: Donatello's *Gattamelata* in Piazza del Santo in Padova, dating from 1453. Step closer to the scuola to admire the polychromatic trompe l'oeil panels and sculptures by Pietro Lombardo (1438–1515) and his sons.

❹ **Museo dei Dipinti Sacri Bizantini** (Museum of Sacred Byzantine Painting). This museum, housed on the first floor of Longhena's Scuola di San Nicola dei Greci, is one of a kind in Europe: a rich collection of remarkable post-Byzantine works. Even if at first glance the icons seem to be identical in color and style, a more attentive look reveals a great variety of subjects: Madonnas and saints of the Orthodox tradition; exquisitely literal representations of Biblical verse, as in the *Vine by Victor*; and the extremely crowded *Last Judgment.* ⊠ *Scuola di San Nicola dei Greci, Ponte dei Greci, 3412 Castello,* ☎ *041/5226581.* 🖼 *€3.60.* ☉ *Mon.–Sat. 9–12:30 and 1:30–4:30, Sun. 9–5.*

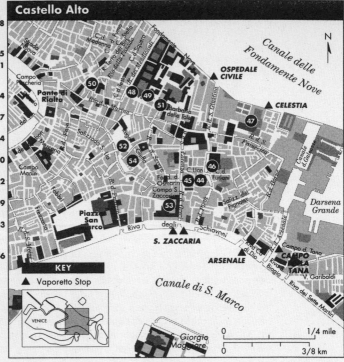

Castello Alto

KEY

▲ Vaporetto Stop

🔟 **Ospedaletto.** The "little hospital" (as its name translates) was founded in the 16th century and served as one of four Venetian orphanages where little girls were given a musical education. The church of **Santa Maria dei Derelitti** (St. Mary of the Destitute) is next door; note the large gallery above the Derelitti altar, built to accommodate the young musicians. The orphanage is now a convalescent home, but the beautiful 18th-century **Sala della Musica** (Music Room), where rehearsals took place and patrons and honored guests were received, has been magnificently restored. On the Music Room's end wall is a lovely fresco by Jacopo Guarana depicting Apollo, the God of Music, surrounded by the orphan musicians conducted by their music master, Pasquale Anfossi. ⊠ *Barbaria delle Tole, Castello,* ☎ *contact Ufficio Beni Culturali, 041/ 2702464.* 💶 *Sala della Musica €1.55.* 🕙 *Church and Sala della Musica Thurs.–Sat. 3:30–6:30.*

★ 🔟 **Pinacoteca Querini-Stampalia.** This art collection, housed on the second floor of a beautiful Renaissance palace that is now home to a student library, is a fine mix of paintings from the 13th to the 18th century. Highlights include Giovanni Bellini's *Presentation in the Temple* and Palma Il Vecchio's (circa 1480–1528) intense portraits of newlyweds Francesco Querini and Paola Priuli; the artist died before finishing the bride and the right hand of Francesco. The well-preserved, original 18th-century furniture and stuccoworks, along with Pietro Longhi's vivacious family portraits and nearly 60 lovely scenes of Venetian festivals and ceremonies by the painter Gabriele Bella (1730–99), portray the final years of the Republic. ⊠ *Campiello Querini-Stampalia, 4778 Castello,* ☎ *041/2711411.* 💶 *€6.20.* 🕙 *Tues.–Thurs. and Sun. 10–1 and 3–6, Fri.–Sat. 10–1 and 3–10.*

★ 🔟 **San Francesco della Vigna** (St. Francis of the Vineyard). A vineyard here once surrounded a small, early Christian church dedicated to St.

Mark. It was built on the spot where the Evangelist, according to legend, was awakened by an angel with the famous words "Pax tibi Marce Evangelista meus" (Peace to you Mark, my Evangelist), which later became the motto of the Venetian Republic. The land was given to the Franciscans in 1253. They kept the vineyard but replaced the church with a new one dedicated to St. Francis. Another three centuries passed before the Franciscan church was enlarged and rebuilt by Sansovino in 1534. Don't come all the way without a pocket full of coins—you'll need them to turn on the lights, which bring to life the surprising artwork inside. All labeled paintings are worth at least a look, especially Antonio Vivarini's triptych with the saints Girolamo, Bernardino da Siena, and Ludovico (on the wall to the left of the main door) and Giovanni Bellini's *Madonna with Saints and Patron* (down the steps to the left, inside the Cappella Santa). The highlight is the glittering gold *Madonna Adoring the Child* by Antonio da Negroponte, an inspiring work that invites contemplation. Painted in the second half of the 15th century, this masterpiece marks the transition from Gothic style, of which it preserves a certain formal rigidity, to the Renaissance style revealed in its elaborately detailed decoration and naturalistic subjects. The sweet features of the Virgin suggest several of Antonio Vivarini's Madonnas at the Gallerie dell'Accademia. Two pretty cloisters open out from the left nave, their pavement constructed entirely of tombstones of patricians, admirals, and cardinals, a testimony to the fact that San Francesco della Vigna was once favored by noble Venetian circles. ✉ *Campo di San Francesco della Vigna, Castello,* ☎ *041/5206102.* 🎟 *Free.* 🕐 *Mon.–Sat. 8–12:30 and 3–7, Sun. 3–6:30.*

★ ㊹ **San Giorgio dei Greci.** The small Greek Orthodox community that had been in Venice for centuries grew dramatically with the influx of Greeks fleeing the Turks after the fall of the Byzantine Empire in 1453. La Serenissima allowed them to join together in a fraternal order and form a scuola (charitable confraternity), and a papal bull entitled them to build a church to celebrate their own rites. Over the centuries, the scuola became the richest and most important center of Greek Orthodoxy in the Western world. The church, built in the 16th century by the noted architect Sante Lombardo, cost 15,000 gold ducats, an exorbitant sum in those days. The property of the Greek Orthodox community was confiscated when Napoléon conquered Venice. Today most members of the brotherhood live in Padua and join together here for Sunday Mass (sung in Alessandrine Greek) and during major religious holidays. Because the Orthodox rite concentrates on the significance of Christ's resurrection rather than his crucifixion, Easter celebrations continue for days in an atmosphere of joyful rebirth. Traditional Easter dishes are on offer.

The interior of San Giorgio is second only to San Marco for its glittering gold and Byzantine accents. The walls are covered by notably intense icons, mosaics, and nearly 100 silver reliefs, mostly the work of little-known 17th-century artists from Crete, whose figurative style has been passed down to the workshops of the monks of Mt. Athos. Among the images of saints, madonnas, and prophets, it is the extremely rich yet subtle iconostasis with a large *Annunciation* mosaic that draws your attention. The second focal point of this jewelry box of a church is the stunning ceiling fresco by 16th-century artist Giovanni di Cipro representing a tidy *Last Judgment* with Christ the Pantocrator at the center surrounded by scenes of *Preparation of the Throne* (first ring), *Apostles and Angels* (second ring), and *Prophets* (third and largest ring). ✉ *Ponte dei Greci, 3412 Castello,* ☎ *041/5226581.* 🎟 *Free.* 🕐 *Mon. and Wed.–Sat. 9–12:30, Sun. open for Mass only.*

★ **㊿ Santa Maria dei Miracoli.** Built in the 1480s to house an image of the Madonna that was said to perform miracles and heal the sick, the Miracoli was Venice's most important shrine to the cult of the Virgin Mary, where once more than 40 masses were celebrated every day and the walls were covered floor to ceiling with ex-votos. Perfectly proportioned and sheathed in marble, it's an early Renaissance gem. Notice how the architect, Pietro Lombardo, squeezed the structure into the space, and then made it look bigger with various optical illusions: varying the color of the marble exterior to create the effect of distance; using extra pilasters to make the building's canal side look longer; and slightly offsetting the arcade windows to make the arches look deeper. The structure is best appreciated from the Ponte dei Miracoli, where you can catch a glimpse of how the side of the church actually hangs out over a rio. With the exception of those on the coffered ceilings, there are no paintings in the interior, but if you happen to be here when the afternoon sunlight filters through the large round window, the exquisite marble decorations come alive with soft pink shades. The immaculate, elegant flight of steps that leads up to the main altar with the holy icon of the Virgin has made "I Miracoli" a favored Venetian wedding stage. On the parapet are four small, delightful sculptures by Tullio Lombardo (1455–1532), among them *San Francesco* and *Santa Chiara,* both saints known for their devotion to the Madonna. ⊠ *Campo Santa Maria Nova, Castello,* ☎ *041/5235293; 041/2750462 Chorus.* 🎫 *€1.55, €7.75 Chorus ticket.* ☉ *Mon.–Sat. 10–5, Sun. 1–5.*

㊵ Santa Maria Formosa. This graceful white marble church was inspired by a vision of *una Madonna formosa* that appeared to San Magno in the 7th century. The "curvaceous" Madonna told him to follow a white cloud and to found a church wherever it settled. The present building, designed by Codussi in 1492, was grafted onto the foundations of an earlier 12th-century church that replaced San Magno's original. The interior is a unique architectural blend that merges Renaissance decoration with Codussi's collection of Byzantine cupolas, barrel vaults, and narrow-columned screens. Of interest are two fine paintings: Bartolomeo 's *Madonna of the Mercy,* sheltering a group of petitioners under her cloak, and Palma Il Vecchio's *Santa Barbara,* the patron saint of gunpowder. Outside, the square bustles with a few sidewalk cafés and a produce market on weekday mornings. ⊠ *Campo Santa Maria Formosa, Castello,* ☎ *041/5234645; 041/2750462 Chorus.* 🎫 *€1.55, €7.75 Chorus ticket.* ☉ *Mon.–Sat. 10–5, Sun. 1–5.*

★ **㊾ Santi Giovanni e Paolo.** A better proportioned, more luminous version of San Polo sestiere's Santa Maria Gloriosa dei Frari, San Zanipolo (as it's commonly called) is the only church in Venice to have benefited from the work of the glass masters of Murano. The stained glass in the great window near the side entrance is breathtaking for its brilliant colors and beautiful figures, which were made in the 15th century from drawings by Bartolomeo Vivarini and Gerolamo Mocetto (their signatures appear near St. Theodore). The five orders of images, culminating in the *Blessing Eternal Father,* are easy to read despite their great distance. From top to bottom and left to right they include *Annunciation and Two Prophets*; *St. Paul, the Virgin, the Baptist, St. Peter*; the *Four Evangelists*; the *Four Doctors of the Church*; and the *Four Dominican Saints with St. George, Sts. John and Paul, and St. Theodore.* The second official church of the Republic after San Marco, this is Venice's equivalent of London's Westminster Abbey, with a great number of important people, including 25 doges, buried here. Artistic highlights include an outstanding polyptych by Giovanni Bellini (right nave, second altar); Alvise Vivarini's *Christ Carrying the Cross* (right transept); Lorenzo Lotto's *Charity of St. Antonino* (right transept); and the Cappella del Rosario (Rosary Chapel), off the left transept. The chapel was built in the 16th century to commemorate the victory of Lepanto in 1571, when Venice and a combined European fleet finally succeeded in destroying the Turkish navy; it was devastated by a fire in 1867. Restored in the early years of the 20th century, it was entirely redecorated with works from other churches—among them the sumptuous Veronese ceiling paintings.

However quick your visit, two of the tombs should not be missed: the monument to Pietro Mocenigo by the ubiquitous Pietro Lombardo and his sons (on the wall to the right of main entrance); and, in the choir, the sepulchre of Doge Michele Morosini, according to Ruskin "the richest monument of the Gothic period in Venice." Oddities include a foot of St. Catherine of Siena and an urn containing the skin of commander Marcantonio Bragadin, tortured and flayed alive by the Turks during the siege of Cyprus in 1571. ⊠ *Campo Santi Giovanni e Paolo, Castello,* ☎ *041/5235913.* 🎫 *Free.* ☉ *Mon.–Sat. 7:30–12:30 and 3:30–6, Sun. 3:30–6.*

★ ⑤ **San Zaccaria.** This church was in large part the result of the foreign policy successes of the 12th doge, Giustiniano Partecipazio, who had gone to Constantinople to pay a gesture of submission to the emperor. Leo V was so pleased with the doge's visit that he presented Venice with the remains of St. Zachary, father of St. John the Baptist, and even sent along a group of masons, decorators, *scalpellini* (stonecutters), and mosaic artists to build the church dedicated to the saint. The adjacent Benedictine convent quickly became the richest—and least chaste—in the city. This was the convent in town where the girls whose families couldn't afford the marriage dowry ended up, by misfortune rather than choice or devotion. San Zaccaria always enjoyed the protection of the doge, who attended Easter Mass here every year. The tilted square bell tower dates from the 13th century.

The striking Renaissance facade, with central and upper portions representing some of Codussi's best work, is only the last chapter in the long story of the building, which features a coronet of four chapels instead of the apse—a Gothic layout typical of the great northern European cathedrals but unusual for Italy. Eight of the earliest doges are buried in the crypt (visitable but frequently flooded), which corresponds to the apse of the primitive church. Giovanni Bellini's celebrated altarpiece is easily recognizable in the left nave. It portrays one of the artist's best Madonnas, this time in the company of an angel playing the viola and four very silent saints. Ask the custodian to show you to the **Cappella di Sant'Atanasio,** also called Cappella del Coro, to see the rough copy of the magnificent choir stalls that once belonged to the church of Sant'Elena in Castello Basso. The five gilded chairs on display were used by the doge and his entourage during his annual visit. The **Cappella di San Tarasio** displays frescoes by Tuscan Renaissance artists Andrea del Castagno (1423–57) and Francesco da Faenza (1400 or 1410–1451); the three outstanding Gothic polyptychs attributed to Antonio Vivarini and Giovanni d'Alemagna (unknown–1450) earned it the nickname "Golden Chapel." From here, you might want to step down to the spooky crypt. ⊠ *Campo San Zaccaria, 4693 Castello,* ☎ *041/5221257.* 🎫 *Church free, chapels and crypt €1.00.* ☉ *Mon.–Sat. 10–noon and 4–6, Sun. 4–6.*

★ ㊻ **Scuola di San Giorgio degli Schiavoni.** This scuola was founded in 1451 by the local Dalmatian community, which still owns it. Many of the private chapels and meeting halls in Venice's scuole were decorated lavishly by the most fashionable artists of the day, but here one single master did it all, creating an unpretentious, harmonious ambience and one of the most beautiful rooms in all of Italy. Not well known outside Venice, where he spent all of his life, Vittore Carpaccio painted devotional *teleri* (large narrative canvases of legendary and religious scenes) against a background of Venetian architecture, combining a keen sense of observation, a spirit of fantasy, and a warm sense of color. For this scuola, Carpaccio concentrated on scenes from the lives of three saints especially venerated in Dalmatia: George, Tryphone, and Jerome. The two paintings to the left and the one opposite the entrance tell the story of St. George, who was passing through the town of Selene (in Libya) and found the beautiful virgin daughter of the king, who had been offered as a sacrifice to a dragon. To read the episodes in chronological order, start with the exuberant *St. George Charging the Dragon*; then turn your attention to the scene in which St. George baptizes the king and queen, who had to become Christian before the saint agreed to slay the dragon. The central painting shows the happy ending, with St. George standing triumphant over the monster, and the royal family, with the freed princess, in all its official splendor. The fourth painting shows the holy child St. Tryphone, miraculously freeing the emperor's daughter from the devil. Paintings five and six are called, respectively, the *Agony in the Garden* and the *Calling of St. Matthew.* The remaining three teleri are dedicated to St. Jerome, who in the seventh painting is about to take a thorn out of the lion's paw while the other monks flee in terror. The *Funeral of St. Jerome* and the *Vision of St. Augustine* follow. This last work—especially vivid in detail—is the faithful representation of the "office" of a 15th-century humanist. Augustine is writing a letter to his dear friend Jerome, when the latter appears and delivers the news that he'd died and gone to heaven.

The adjoining little room has a display of old garments and other objects used by the brotherhood. The first floor features many portraits of brothers and sisters. Try to visit in the morning, as the fraternal order sometimes closes the church in the afternoon for its own private ceremonies. ✉ *Calle dei Furlani, 3259/a Castello,* ☎ *041/5228828.* ✉ €2.60. ✆ *Apr.–Oct., Tues.–Sat. 10–12:30 and 3:30–6:30, Sun. 9:30–12:30; Nov.–Mar., Tues.–Sat. 10–12:30 and 3–6, Sun. 10–12:30.*

CASTELLO BASSO

Until about 100 years ago, the neighborhood of Castello Basso was made up of fishermen, lace artisans, pearl stringers, and shipbuilders who worked at the Arsenale. Here there are no noble palaces, and the fancy shops that line the streets of the center of town have not replaced the small workshops, bakeries, butchers, and bars. Castello Basso is one of the few places where you are likely to catch the aroma of stewed squid and see laundry hung from lines stretched across the narrow streets. Only on Sunday do throngs of people hurry through the streets; Venice's soccer team rejoined the first division of the Italian League in 2000, and their stadium is in Sant'Elena, near the church. Plans are under way to build a new one in the mainland near Mestre.

A good portion of the area is taken up by the Sant'Elena quarter, made up of two large islands and some marshes, which the Austrians reclaimed in the 19th century in order to have a large area in which to stage military exercises. (Today a portion of it is occupied by a military high school run by the Italian Naval Academy.) The absence of bridges and canals in view makes a visit to Sant'Elena seem almost like a walk on the mainland. During the Austrian occupation, its open spaces became a favorite Sunday retreat for the many Venetians without a villa in the country. In the 1920s the Fascist government made it into a working-class residential quarter (note the relatively modern look of some of the buildings and the streets, here called "*viali*" as in any other Italian town) and reopened the parish church of Sant'Elena, which, like many other Venetian churches, had been sacked and closed by Napoléon. The breezy little pine grove is slowly recovering after a freak disaster struck on a warm September afternoon in 1971, when a part of the sky suddenly blackened and a small but violent storm pulled roofs off and trees up by their roots and tossed a vaporetto up in the air, killing 89 Venetians.

Numbers in the text correspond to numbers in the margin and on the Castello Basso map.

A Good Walk

Starting from Piazzetta San Marco, cross Ponte della Paglia and continue along the Riva degli Schiavoni, a wide promenade built to accommodate the *passeggiata,* the ritualistic evening stroll, as well as several rows of vendors. Vendors selling candy and running the bumper cars and Ferris wheel (in wintertime) are the modern descendants of those who sold dried meat and fish here during Republican times. They came from Dalmatia, modern-day Croatia, which in Venetian dialect was called "Schiavonia." If it's open, pop into the **Chiesa della Pietà** ⑤⑤, where, in an adjoining room, there is also a tiny collection of Baroque musical instruments that includes a violin that once belonged to Antonio Vivaldi. The large, 15th-century buildings with the crenellated facades between Calle dei Forni and Ponte dell'Arsenale once housed Venice's military bakeries and bread storehouses. Down the Ponte dell' Arsenale, built in 1936 to replace a retractable iron bridge, is the **Museo Storico Navale** ⑤⑥, which doesn't quite do justice to the rich, noteworthy maritime history of the Venetian Republic but displays a worthwhile collection of modern and ancient naval models. Proceed straight down the promenade. Up ahead is the pine grove of Sant'Elena, marked on maps with its official (but never used) name of Parco delle Rimembranze. Walk along Via Quattro Novembre and turn left onto Viale Piave; then take the first bridge to the right to the church of **Sant' Elena** ⑤⑦. Retrace your steps and bear right toward the dock for a look at the tiny harbor at the end of Fondamenta di Sant'Elena. Cross the rio to reach **San Pietro di Castello** ⑤⑧, Via Calle del Pasubio, Paludo Sant' Antonio, San Giuseppe (Sant'Isepo in Venetian), and Fondamenta Sant'Anna. After visiting the church, go over the wooden bridge and find your way to Via Garibaldi, where you can mingle with the locals and rest at one of several unpretentious bars with tables outside offering a selection of hot and cold snacks. Up on your feet again, take any of the right turns that lead to Fondamenta della Tana, cross the rio of the same name, follow the long and narrow Campo della Tana, and make a right in the direction of the **Arsenale** ⑤⑨, with its mighty gateway guarded by lions. From here, head to Campo Bandiera e Moro, walking past the church of San Martino, and visit the late-Gothic **San Giovanni in Bragora** ⑥⓪, with a wonderful painting by Cima da Conegliano.

TIMING

On a fine day this walk makes a very scenic wander that's not too heavy on sights. Allow a full morning if you want to include the Museo Storico Navale (which adds an hour). After lunch at a nearby restaurant or a quick snack from one of the several bars in Via Garibaldi, you can have a sit-down coffee or gelato along the Riva, and then spend the rest of the afternoon taking a trip to the Giudecca and the Isola di San Giorgio, where from atop the bell tower you have a panoramic view of the buildings and domes you walked past in the morning.

Sights to See

★ ⑤⑨ **Arsenale.** The immense Arsenal dockyard was founded, according to tradition, by Doge Falier in 1104 and was built up considerably throughout the 16th century. For a republic founded on sea power, having a huge, state-of-the-art shipyard was of paramount importance, and this one was legendary for its size and efficiency. Galleys 200 ft long were built here, capable of carrying 300 tons of ginger, pepper, silk, and silver. Until the middle of the 16th century, when slaves began to be used in the galleys, the crew was made up of men who volunteered in exchange for an opportunity to amass pounds of precious merchandise from ports all around the Eastern Mediterranean, to be resold if they survived the perils of the trip. With 16,000 "Arsenalotti" on the payroll, a perfectly armed warship could be built in just 12 hours; 100 ships were built in 60 days in 1597 for the battle against the Turks at Cyprus. After that war, the old Venetian word *arzanà* (from the Arabic *darsina'a,* meaning workshop) was adopted by another 14 languages. Dante visited the shipyards several times, and the half-naked bodies of the workers, armed with pitches and boiling tar, inspired his vision of the seventh plane of Hell for his *Inferno.*

The impressive Renaissance **gateway** (1460) is guarded by four lions, war booty of Francesco Morosini, who took the Peloponnese from the Turks in 1687. The 10-ft-tall lion to the left started its career as a sentinel more than 2,000 years ago in a harbor not far from Athens. A mysterious inscription in Viking runes engraved on its back has been interpreted as "graffiti" left by a Viking mercenary soldier who fought in the revolts against Pyrrus in the 11th century. When in 1995 the Greek government unsuccessfully tried to have the lion returned, some Venetians made a human wall around it to protect it from a surprise raid. Note that the Gospel between the paws of the winged lion above the doorway is closed and without the familiar motto wishing Pax: peace cannot be invoked by a factory of war machines.

Modernized under the Austrians and the Kingdom of Italy, the Arsenale made several of the battleships used in the first World War, but they marked its swan song. Dismantled and completely closed to the public except during the Biennale, the Arsenale today belongs to the Italian Navy, which at the very least protects it from further decay until the city decides among various restoration projects. To catch a glimpse of the interior, take vaporetto Line 23, which, in the summer only, connects San Zaccaria to Murano by cutting through Rio delle Galeazze, where a portion of the shipbuilding once took place. ⊠ *Campo dell' Arsenale, Castello.*

⑤⑤ **Chiesa della Pietà.** Unwanted babies were left on the steps of this religious institute, founded by a Franciscan friar in 1346. The girls were immediately taken in at the adjoining orphanage, which provided the children with a musical education. The church flourished during the years of the Venetian Republic, when it was traditionally visited by the doge on Palm Sunday, protected by the pope, and supported by generous benefactors. The quality of the performances here reached continental fame—the in-house conductor was none other than Antonio Vivaldi (1675–1745), who wrote some of his best compositions here for the hospice. The original church was rebuilt in the 15th century, and again after the death of the great musician. Today, with its ceiling frescoes by Tiepolo, it is an elegant example of a Venetian sacred site, and more like a small theater than a church. In an adjoining room to the left of the entrance is a tiny collection of Baroque instruments, including the violin played by Vivaldi. Often closed during the day, the Pietà hosts Baroque concerts, usually with Venetian composers such as Vivaldi,

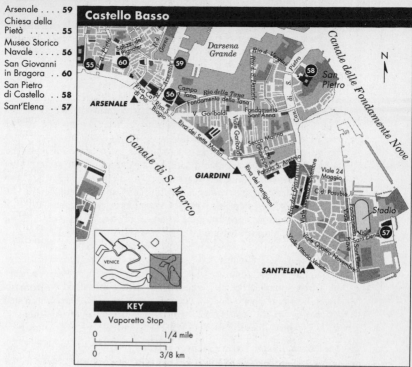

Castello Basso

Galuppi, and Marcello on the program. Some are performed in 17th-century costume. ⊠ *Riva degli Schiavoni, Castello.*

🖑 **56** **Museo Storico Navale** (Museum of Naval History). Peggy Guggenheim's private gondola, a gondola with a romantic cabin like those used during the time of Casanova, and a good-size replica of the doge's ceremonial boat, the *Bucintoro,* are among the highlights of this museum. Models, parts from galleys, old and modern naval weapons, fishermen's ex-votos, and even a few real boats round out the interesting collection. Maps and scale models of the Arsenal will help you appreciate this "town within the town." The museum also houses a large seashell collection, donated to the city by Venetian-born fashion designer Roberta da Camerino. ⊠ *Campo San Biagio, Castello, near the Arsenale,* ☎ *041/5200276.* 💷 *€1.55.* ☉ *Weekdays 8:45–1:30, Sat. 8:45–1.*

★ **60** **San Giovanni in Bragora.** This rather humble redbrick church is so old that there's no record of the significance of its name. At the beginning of the 8th century, San Magno, the same bishop who dreamed of the beautiful Virgin prior to the construction of Santa Maria Formosa, wanted to build a church dedicated to St. John the Baptist. It is thought that St. John's remains were brought to Venice just 200 years later, but the relics in the second chapel to the right belong to St. John the Almsgiver, not the Baptist. After undergoing two restorations, the church was completely redone in a light Gothic style in 1475. Inside are two works by Alvise Vivarini (1445–1503), son of Antonio and leader of the Veneto school of painting in the late decades of the 15th century: *Madonna with Child* (left nave) and *Risen Christ* (above the altar of the Sacrament), in which the figure of Christ is, for the first time in Venice, rendered with freedom from linear constraints. But the real highlight is in the sanctuary: the *Baptism of Christ* by Cima da Conegliano (circa 1459–1517), a luminous painting in which a realistic, gaunt St. John calmly administers the sacrament to an absorbed Jesus praying against a background of the Veneto countryside. ✉ *Campo Bandiera e Moro, Castello,* ☎ *041/5205906.* ✉ *Free.* ☉ *Weekdays 8:30–11 and 3:30–6, Sat. 8:30–11, Sun. 9:30–11.*

★ ⑤⑧ **San Pietro di Castello.** A 7th-century church had been dedicated on this site to Sergio and Bacchus, two Byzantine saints of less-than-grand importance judging from the fact that just two centuries later the Venetians built a new church there in honor of St. Peter the Apostle. At the end of the 16th century the facade was redone based on a design by Palladio. The imposing campanile, the first in Venice built from the marblelike Istrian stone rather than in brick, stands out against the peaceful Renaissance cloister, for years a sort of squatters' colony, and the rather picturesque, workaday slips along the Canale di San Pietro. The Veneti had settled here long before Venice ever existed, but now the "island" is a particularly tranquil, almost forgotten place, with nothing to suggest that for more than 1,000 years this church served as Venice's cathedral until the Basilica di San Marco superseded it in 1807. The church features some minor 17th-century art and an archaic Cattedra (Chair) di San Pietro in the right nave. According to legend, this marble throne, made from an Arab funerary tomb inscribed with verses from the Koran, was used by Peter at Antioch. ✉ *Campo San Pietro Apostolo, Castello,* ☎ *041/5238950; 041/2750462 Chorus.* ✉ *€1.55, €7.75 Chorus ticket.* ☉ *Mon.–Sat. 10–5, Sun. 1–5.*

⑤⑦ **Sant'Elena.** Built to receive pilgrims en route to and from the Holy Land and aptly dedicated to Emperor Constantine's mother, this church once stood alone, surrounded by the lagoon. A make-do soccer stadium to the left and a long brick wall to the right (covered with unlikely graffiti by local hooligans) flank a surreal path that leads to the ex-Olivetan complex, rebuilt in 1435. The focal point of the late-Gothic facade is a beautiful Renaissance doorway surmounted by a sculptural group by Antonio Rizzo portraying Commander Vittore Cappello kneeling before St. Helen. The interior is strangely touching in its simplicity. Three medallions on the cross vault represent the lion of San Marco, San Benedetto, and San Nicola da Bari, patron saint of navigators. Frescoes with floral and angelic motifs hang tenuously, awaiting restoration, around the wall of the single nave. Completed in 1505, a monastic choir with 60 wooden stalls finely inlaid in Olivetan style used to be in front of the presbyter, separated from the faithful by two altars and a gate to the cloister. Dismantled and sent to France by Napoléon, the choir had won such admiration that the nuns of San Zaccaria had a "rough" copy made for their own church, which today suggests how the original might have been. To the right of the entrance a chapel holds the relics of St. Helen, recovered in the 1930s from the bottom of the lagoon; the friars had tossed the holy urn in the water to hide it from Napoléon. It is said that the beauty of the church rested not only in the choir stalls but also in the tombs of the various Venetian patricians, some of which were relocated, some buried beneath two layers of floor added later. The modern bell tower in reinforced cement is obviously a poor match for the church. The story goes that the tower had originally been commissioned in the 1950s for a church in Milan. When the local Milanese friars came up short on funds, they sent the campanile (and the bill) to their better-off Venetian brothers. Although the monstrous tower is so heavy it is sinking the foundation of the church, it is unlikely that it will be removed. Italian law prohibits architectural changes to structures that are more than 40 years old. ✉ *Sant'Elena, Castello,* ☎ *041/5205144.* ✉ *Free.* ☉ *Tues.–Sun. 6:30–12:30 and 4–7, Mon. 5–7.*

SAN GIORGIO MAGGIORE AND THE GIUDECCA

Beckoning all travelers across St. Mark's Basin, sparkling white through the mist, is the island of San Giorgio Maggiore, separated by a small channel from the Giudecca. A tall brick campanile on that distant bank perfectly complements the Campanile of San Marco. Behind it looms the stately dome of one of Venice's greatest churches, San Giorgio Maggiore. The island of Giudecca, a crescent cupped around the southern shore of Venice, is one of the most mysterious neighborhoods in the city, with an obscure history and a somber feel.

Numbers in the text correspond to numbers in the margin and on the San Giorgio Maggiore and the Giudecca map.

A Good Boat Trip

Take vaporetto Line 82 from San Zaccaria near San Marco across the lagoon to the island of San Giorgio Maggiore. Palladio's **San Giorgio Maggiore** ⑥ and its adjacent Monastero di San Giorgio Maggiore occupy the entire island. After visiting the church and campanile, proceed by vaporetto (Line 82) to the nearby island of **Giudecca** ⑥. Explore the neighborhood and visit the **Chiesa del Redentore** ⑥, another work of Palladio. From here the vaporetto crosses the Giudecca Canal to the Zattere, with one of the best promenades in Venice.

TIMING

A half day should give you plenty of time to enjoy the sights. Allow at least an hour to visit the Chiesa di San Giorgio and its campanile, including the time to get there from San Zaccaria, and another two hours to visit the Giudecca neighborhood and the Redentore, plus whatever time you want to spend on the Zattere promenade.

Sights to See

⑥ **Chiesa del Redentore.** Palladio's church has a tranquil, stately facade, actually a series of superimposed temple fronts topped by a dome and a pair of slim, almost minaret-like bell towers. The interior, like San Giorgio Maggiore's, is perfectly proportioned and airy, in contrast to the dusky Byzantine mystery of the Basilica di San Marco. ✉ *Fondamenta San Giacomo, Giudecca,* ☎ *041/5231415; 041/2750462 Chorus.* ✆ €1.55, €7.75 *Chorus ticket.* ☉ *Mon.–Sat. 10–5, Sun. 1–5.*

⑥ **Giudecca.** Seeing Venice from the Giudecca is a bit like seeing the earth from the moon. Only from here is it possible to take in a comprehensive view of the city, stretching from the Giardini della Biennale to the right as far as the fuming factories of Marghera industrial complex in the distance to the left, with San Marco's square right in the middle. The best time to come is from April to September, or on a clear winter day; rainy or foggy weather turn an otherwise perfect walk into cold misery. Few tourists explore the streets beyond the Redentore, and even Venetians rarely go the Giudecca unless it is for a swim in the beautiful pool at Sacca Fisola, or for a change of scene on a breezy Sunday morning. The island's name is something of a mystery. According to some, it derives from the possible settlement of Jews here in the 14th century. Others believe it was so called because in the 9th century nobles condemned to exile were sent here (*giudicato* means judged or sentenced). It became a pleasure garden for wealthy Venetians during the long and luxurious decline of the Republic. In one regard it is still the province of the wealthy: the exclusive Cipriani hotel lies secluded on its eastern tip. But aside from the Cipriani and a couple of stately buildings, here you'll find only homely neighborhoods dotted here and

San Giorgio Maggiore and the Giudecca

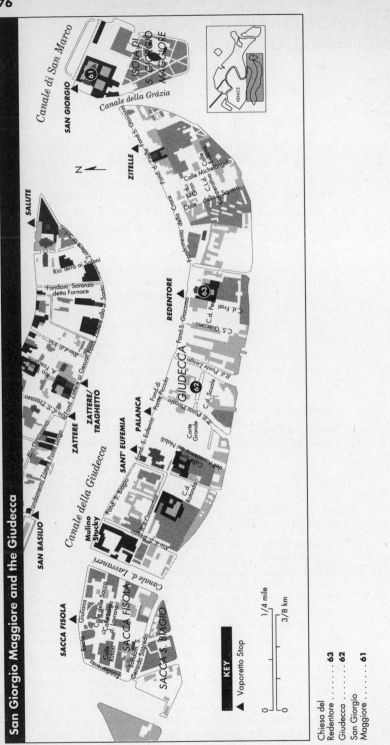

Canale di San Marco

ISOLA DI S. GIORGIO MAGGIORE

▲ SAN GIORGIO

Canale della Grázia

VENICE

▲ ZITELLE

Calle Michelangelo
Calle del Gran
C. d.
Calle della Croce
C. d. Scuola
Fond. delle Zitelle Fond. S. Giovanni
Fondamenta delle Croce

▲ SALUTE

Rio Terra ai Saloni
Fondam. Soranzo detta Fornace

▲ REDENTORE

Fond. S. Giacomo
C.S. Giacomo
C. d. Froli C. d. Pesaro

Rio di S. Vio
Rio di S. Tommaso
A. Foscarini

ZATTERE
ZATTERE / TRAGHETTO

Fond. Zattere ai Gesuati Fond. Zattere allo Santo

R. d. Ponte Lungo

▲ PALANCA

Fond. di Ponte Piccolo
C. d. Scuole

Fondamenta Zattere Ponte Lungo

Rio di S. Biagio

Canale della Giudecca

GIUDECCA

▲ SANT' EUFEMIA

Fond. S. Eufemia
Calle dell'Accademia dei Nobili

Corte Grande

▲ SAN BASILIO

Rio di S. Biagio

Mulino Stucky

C. d. Rotonda

Canale d. Lavraneri

SACCA FISOLA

Basio
Giuliana
Calle delle Sacca
Calle Lunga d. Lavraneri
Calle Rimini
Fondam. S.
Campo Scarpa
Fondamenta

SACCA FISOLA

SACCA S. BIAGIO

KEY

■ Vaporetto Stop

▲ Vaporetto Stop

0 — 1/4 mile
0 — 3/8 km

there by the ruins of a brief industrial past: an intriguing string of empty mills and factories, all dating from the 19th century, strikes a different note in the by-now familiar Venetian landscape. Towering over Fondamenta San Biagio is the brick Mulino Stucky, a neo-Gothic flour mill built in 1895, abandoned for years and closed to the public while the city contemplates various restoration projects.

OFF THE
BEATEN PATH **LIDO –** Separating the lagoon from the sea, the Lido is a long and narrow island that served for centuries as Venice's most fertile garden. Only its southern end, Malamocco—which in the 8th century was the administrative center of the Republic—was inhabited, the rest being all cultivated land. But from the 1850s through World War II, the Lido became a fashionable sea resort, and its name was subsequently borrowed by many seaside resorts throughout the world. This was where the Austrian Archduke Maximilian built his summer residence (since destroyed), Thomas Mann wrote and staged *Death in Venice,* and Emperor Reza Pahlavi came to water-ski. The Lido's popularity peaked in the late 1930s, following the launching of the Biennale film festival, the building of one of Italy's first airports (now used only for private traffic), and the opening of the casino (now closed). Some of the glamour and architecture of those days remains in the Moorish-looking Grand Hotel Excelsior and on the quiet streets branching from Viale Santa Maria Elisabetta, adorned with many Art Deco villas. Today, the Lido is a satellite neighborhood of Venice, where locals keep holiday houses and crowds of commuters from Venice and the mainland spend a good portion of their summers. The water looks murky because of the fine sand celebrated by Byron and Shelley, but it's actually quite clean and, due to the lack of big waves, relatively safe for swimming. The best way to explore the Lido is by renting a bicycle, alternating sightseeing with sunbathing. ✉ *By vaporetto: from San Zaccaria stop, Line 1, 4 (June–Sept.), 6, 14, 51 (52 back), or 82; from Rialto stop, Line 1, 4 (June–Sept.), or 82. From Piazzale Roma stop: direct Line 61 (62 back); or Grand Canal Lines 1, 4 (June–Sept.), and 82.*

61 **San Giorgio Maggiore.** A church has been on this island since the late 8th century, with a Benedictine monastery added in the 10th century. The present church was begun in 1566 by Palladio. Two of Palladio's hallmarks are mathematical harmony and architectural elements borrowed from classical antiquity, both demonstrated in this superbly proportioned neoclassical church of red brick and white marble. Inside, it's refreshingly airy and simply decorated. Two important late Tintoretto paintings hang on either side of the chancel: the *Last Supper* and the *Gathering of Manna.* Over the first altar on the right-hand side of the nave is an *Adoration of the Shepherds* by Jacopo Bassano (1517–92), a painter from Bassano del Grappa who possessed considerable originality and was especially adept at portraying nature and country life. The campanile is so high that it was struck by a lightning bolt in 1993. Take the elevator to the top; the views from here are some of the finest in town. ✉ *Isola di San Giorgio,* ☎ *041/5227827.* ✆ *Free, elevator €2.60.* ☉ *June–Sept., daily 9–12:30 and 2:30–6:30; Oct.–May, daily 9–12:30 and 3–5:30.*

OFF THE
BEATEN PATH **SAN LAZZARO DEGLI ARMENI –** When a leprosy epidemic hit Venice in 1185, those infected were confined to a hospital on a far-flung island in the lagoon, which was subsequently dedicated to San Lazzaro (St. Lazarus), the leper mentioned in the Vangel. San Lazzaro later served as a shelter for beggars. In 1717 Doge Giovanni Corner II gave the island to Peter of Manug, better known as Father Mekhitar ("the Consoler"), an Armenian priest who had founded an order of Catholic-Armenian monks

in Morea (today's Peloponnese). Armenia had been the first country in the world to adopt Christianity as its state religion but did not recognize the pope's authority. Following the Turkish invasion of Greece, Mekhitar fled to Venice, where a small but wealthy Armenian community had thrived since the 13th century. On San Lazzaro he built the monastery that still stands today, more than tripled the size of the island with landfill, and established what was then the world's largest center of Armenian culture outside of Armenia.

Only 15 minutes from the San Zaccaria vaporetto stop, San Lazzaro feels a world apart from the touristy hubbub of San Marco. Its 322,920 sq ft are covered with trees, orchards, and gardens impeccably kept by a community of some 20 Mekhitarist priests and seminarians. Apart from the monastery, San Lazzaro houses a flock of sheep, a church, a picture gallery, a museum, two libraries, and a collection of precious manuscripts.

The guided visit begins at the 14th-century church, partially rebuilt by Mekhitar, which features rococo decorations and stained glass made in Innsbruck in 1901. Under a turquoise ceiling you'll be given a brief lesson on Armenian history. In the refectory is an 18th-century *Last Supper* inspired by Leonardo da Vinci's masterpiece. Mekhitar's staircase leads to the picture gallery, with about 100 paintings by Armenian artists from the 18th to 19th century, and to Mekhitar's room, adorned with his personal objects. With about 150,000 volumes, the main library holds the world's richest collection of Armenian books; some 40,000 antique books belonged to Mekhitar himself. Napoléon destroyed all the monasteries in Venice except this one, which he believed to be more of an academy and a center of learning than a religious institution. A fresco by Tiepolo, *Peace and Justice,* adorns the ceiling of the entrance to an eclectic museum collection, which reflects the Mekhitarist encyclopedic passion for culture: Armenian pottery, swords, and silver artwork share space with an Egyptian mummy, an Indian throne made of ivory and wood, a Sanskrit Buddhist manuscript, Chinese ivory carvings, and fragments of Roman urns. A few steps lead down to Byron's room, displaying his portrait. The poet spent some months here between 1816 and 1817 recovering from his separation from Anne Isabelle Milbanke and England. To soothe his soul and pass the time, Byron dedicated himself to the difficult task of learning the Armenian language—he even helped write an Armenian-English grammar book (still printed by the convent's press), which is on sale in the gift shop next to the more famous homemade *marmellata di rose* (rose jam). Finally, the round library contains nearly 5,000 Armenian manuscripts dating from the 9th to the 17th century; some of these, embellished by precious golden illuminations, are on display. ⊠ *Vaporetto Lines 10 and 20 from San Zaccaria stop,* ☏ *041/5260104.* 🕮 *€5.15.* 🕙 *Guided tours only, leaving daily 3:25 sharp (until 5); no reservation required.*

ISLANDS OF THE LAGOON

The perfect vacation from your Venetian vacation is an escape to the magical islands of the city's lagoon—Murano, Burano, and Torcello—which can provide a welcome relief after the brooding, enclosed charms of Venice itself. Far from the madding crowd, Torcello is the actual birthplace of Venice, today visited for its haunting melancholy, its great Byzantine-era church, and that famous outpost of elegance, the Locanda Cipriani. The island is also perfect for picnics, but bring food from Venice. Burano is a toy town of little houses all painted in a riot of colors—blue, yellow, pink, ocher, and dark red. Here visitors love to shop for

"Venetian" lace, despite the fact that these days most of it is machine made and comes from Taiwan. Murano is known the world over for its glass, but guided tours usually involve high-pressure attempts to make you buy, with little time left for anything else. It's worth the extra effort to make your own way around the islands, using the good vaporetto connections. There are several options in getting to these islands: Lines 12 and 14 to Murano, Burano, and Torcello from the landing stage at Fondamente Nuove, almost due north of San Marco; and Line 41, which you can pick up at the San Zaccaria stop, off Piazza San Marco, and which runs to Fondamente Nuove, San Michele, and Murano, where you change to Line 14 to continue to Torcello and Santa Maria Elisabetta on the Lido.

Numbers in the text correspond to numbers in the margin and on the Islands of the Lagoon map.

A Good Boat Trip

Take Line 41 from the San Zaccaria stop near Piazza San Marco to the Fondamente Nuove stop (or if you are already near the Campo Santi Giovanni e Paolo, begin at Fondamente Nuove). From there it's only a five-minute ride to **San Michele** ⑥④, the cemetery island home to the church of San Michele in Isola. Another five minutes on Line 41 takes you to **Murano** ⑥⑤—get off at the Navagero or Museo stop. From the Museo stop, turn right and it's only a few steps along Fondamenta Giustinian to the Museo Vetrario, with a fascinating display of glass objects from the oldest Roman period (AD 1st–3rd centuries) to the 19th century. Find your way to the Faro landing stage, at the south end of the Canal Grande di Murano, and take Line 12 to **Burano** ⑥⑥, about 30 minutes farther, where you can see traditional lace making at the Scuola di Merletti di Burano. Line 12 continues from the Burano landing stage to the sleepy green island of **Torcello** ⑥⑦, only five minutes away. A brick-paved lane leads up from the landing stage and follows the curve of the canal toward the center of the island. You pass the Locanda Cipriani, one of Hemingway's haunts. Just beyond is the grassy square that holds the island's only surviving monuments. Next to it is the 11th-century cathedral of Santa Maria Assunta.

TIMING

Line 41 boats leave every 20 minutes from San Zaccaria or the Fondamente Nuove, and the trip to Murano from San Zaccaria takes about 50 minutes each way. Stopping on every island and visiting the various sights will take a full day. If, however, you limit yourself to Murano, a full morning or a full afternoon will suffice.

Sights to See

★ ⑥⑥ **Burano.** Dotting this fishing village are houses painted in cheerful colors and a raffishly raked bell tower on the main square, about 100 yards from the landing stage. Lace is to Burano what glass is to Murano, but be prepared to pay a lot—$1,000 to $2,000 for a 10-inch doily—for the real thing. Stalls line the way from the landing stage to Piazza Galuppi, the main square. The vendors, many of them fishermen's wives, are generally good-natured and blessedly unfamiliar with the techniques of the hard sell.

Museo del Merletto (Lace Museum) is the best place to learn the intricacies of the lace-making traditions of Burano, plus the nature of the skills needed to make the more expensive lace. ⊠ *Piazza Galuppi,* ☎ *041/730034.* ▨ *€4.15; €15.50 combined ticket also allows entry to Biblioteca Marciana, Ca' Rezzonico, Palazzo Mocenigo, Museo Archeologico, Museo Correr, Museo Vetrario, and Palazzo Ducale.* ◷ *Apr.–Oct., Wed.–Mon. 9–5; Nov.–Mar., Wed.–Mon. 10–4.*

Islands of the Lagoon

 ★ ⑥⑤ **Murano.** Like Venice, Murano is made up of a number of smaller islands linked by bridges. It is known for its **glassworks**, which were moved
here from Venice in the 13th century because of fire hazard. You can
visit them daily to see how glass is made. Many of these line the **Fondamenta dei Vetrai**, the canal-side walkway leading away from the
Colonna landing stage. It's likely you'll be offered a tour of the glassworks by one of the many "tourist-catchers" cruising Piazza San
Marco, and a complimentary boat ride to Murano is indeed hard to
resist. But unless you are ready to vanish upon landing, you'll pay dearly
for the free lift, having to endure the hard sell that's always a part of
such group tours, even when organized by the best hotels. However,
you're welcome to come on your own and look around, and you won't
usually be pushed to buy anything you don't want.

The houses of Murano are simpler than many of their Venetian counterparts; traditionally they were workmen's cottages. Just before the
junction with Murano's Grand Canal—250 yards up from the landing stage—is the church of **San Pietro Martire**. This 16th-century reconstruction of an earlier Gothic church has several works by Venetian
masters, notably, the *Madonna and Child* by Giovanni Bellini and *St.
Jerome* by Veronese.

The Venetian glass at the **Museo Vetrario** (Glass Museum) ranges from
priceless antique to only slightly less-expensive modern. The museum
details authentic Venetian styles and patterns and the history of Murano's glassworks. ⊠ *Murano,* ☎ *041/739586.* 🎟 *€4.15; €9.30 combined ticket with Biblioteca Marciana, Palazzo Mocenigo, Museo del
Merletto, Museo Archeologico, Museo Fortuny, Palazzo Ducale, Palazzo
Mocenigo, and Museo Correr.* ☉ *Apr.–Oct., Thurs.–Tues. 10–5; Nov.–
Mar., Thurs.–Tues. 10–4.*

OFF THE
BEATEN PATH

SAN FRANCESCO DEL DESERTO – A clump of 4,000 cypress trees floating south of Burano, St. Francis of the Desert is too green and surrounded by too much water to feel like a desert. But with its peaceful medieval monastery and cloistered spaces, it's certainly as far as you can get from the bustle of central Venice. The story goes that St. Francis of Assisi came here in 1220 with his follower Illuminato on the way back from his preaching tour of Palestine. The pair had planned to settle on Torcello but found that island too rich for their tastes. They rowed to the tiny island then known as Due Vigne ("Two Vineyards"), and when St. Francis planted his pilgrim's stick into the ground, it miraculously grew into a pine tree and birds came to sing for him. When he reached Assisi, he sent some friars to the island, who in 1228 built the first church that was dedicated to the saint. You will be told more about Franciscan lore while being shepherded around by one of the 10 resident friars. ⊠ *Vaporetto Line 12 from Fondamente Nuove stop to Burano, from Burano to San Francesco del Deserto,* ☎ *041/5286863.* 🖼 *Donation; fishermen's boats €12.00 round-trip, private water taxi €26.00 round-trip.* ☉ *Tues.–Sun. 9–11 and 3–5.*

⁶⁴ **San Michele.** Venice's cypress-lined cemetery island is home to the pretty Renaissance church of **San Michele in Isola,** designed by Codussi in 1478, and Venice's cemetery. It is a unique experience to walk among the gravestones with the sound of lapping water on all sides. The American poet Ezra Pound (1885–1972), the great Russian impresario and art critic Sergey Diaghilev (1872–1929), and the composer Igor Stravinsky (1882–1971) are buried here. For most Venetians, however, the stay here is short lived, as the cemetery has a policy of transferring those interred more than 10 years to another, less grandiose cemetery, making room for more recent burials. ☎ *041/2730111.* 🖼 *Free.* ☉ *Nov.–Mar., daily 7:30–4; Apr.–Oct., daily 7:30–6.*

★ ⁶⁷ **Torcello.** This is where the first Venetians landed in their flight from the barbarians 1,500 years ago. Even after many settlers left to found the city of Venice on the island of Rivo Alto (Rialto), Torcello continued to grow and prosper until its main source of income, wool manufacturing, was priced out of the marketplace. It's hard to believe, looking at this almost deserted island, that in the 16th century it had 20,000 inhabitants and 10 churches.

The island's cathedral, **Santa Maria Assunta,** dates from the 11th century. The ornate Byzantine mosaics are testimony to the importance and wealth of an island that could attract the best artists and craftsmen of its day. The vast mosaic on the inside of the facade depicts the *Last Judgment* as artists of the 11th and 12th centuries imagined it: figures writhe in vividly depicted contortions of pain. Facing it, as if in mitigation, is the calm mosaic figure of the Madonna, alone in a field of gold above the staunch array of Apostles. ⊠ *Torcello,* ☎ *041/730084.* 🖼 *€2.60.* ☉ *June–Sept., daily 10:30–6; Oct.–May, daily 10–4 (last entry ½ hr before closing).*

NEED A
BREAK?

Locanda Cipriani (⊠ Torcello, ☎ 041/730150), closed Tuesday and early January–early February, is an inn famous for its good food and the patronage of Ernest Hemingway, who often came to Torcello for the solitude. These days Locanda Cipriani—not to be confused with the Cipriani hotel on Giudecca—is about the busiest spot on the island, as well-heeled customers arrive on high-speed powerboats for lunch.

2 DINING

At both fancy restaurants and popular holes in the wall, the catchword in Venice is fish, often at its tastiest when it looks like nothing you've seen before. How do you learn first-hand about the catch of the day? An early morning visit to the Rialto's *pescheria* (fish market) is more instructive than any book. Making a bacaro crawl in search of *cicheti* (savory snacks) may be Venice's most engaging eating experience.

By Carla
Lionello

Additional
reviews by
Robert
Andrews

N VENICE, YOU SHOULD TAKE CARE in selecting where you sit down for a meal—the city has more than its share of overpriced, mediocre eateries that prey on tourists. Avoid places with cajoling waiters standing outside, and beware of restaurants that don't display their prices. At the other end of the spectrum, showy *menu turistico* (tourist menu) boards make offerings clear in a dozen languages, but for the same 13–16 euros you'd spend at such places you could eat much better in a *bacaro,* the local version of a wine bar with delicious snacks.

Bacari (the name harkens back to Bacchus, the Greek god of wine) provide the most quintessentially Venetian dining experience, and they aren't to be missed. They're the pillars of the city's social life: here fishermen and bankers alike line up for a glass of the house *vino da ombra*—"wine of the shadow," so named because in the past wine merchants kept their demijohns cool in the shadow of the Campanile. In a bacaro, *ombre* are enjoyed with *cicheti,* the Venetian word for the small, savory snacks served at the counter, usually made of fish, inexpensive cuts of meat, grilled vegetables, boiled eggs, and onions. Most typical are *baccalà mantecato* (a delicious, fluffy dried-cod spread), served on bread or polenta squares, and *folpetti* (baby octopus), which is boiled and tossed with olive oil, lemon, and parsley. In recent years, a good number of Venice's bacari have become rather refined, adding some of northern Italy's best wines to their more typical local offerings.

An upsurge of *bacari con cucina,* sort of family-run trattorias with limited menus that cater mostly to Venetians, has made it possible to eat a full, well-prepared meal without spending a fortune. Tablecloths are often considered a luxury in these places, but the atmosphere is friendly, allowing you to catch a glimpse of the local way of life. Service is fast without being brisk, and there's no need to dress up.

Although pizzerias are not hard to find, Venice is not much of a pizza town—standards aren't what they are elsewhere in Italy, and local laws impede the use of wood-burning ovens. Beware of the gooey, soggy pizza at bar-pizzerias, which is commonly precooked and reheated. *Tramezzini,* the triangular white-bread sandwiches served in bars all over Italy, however, are particularly good in Venice. Many bars here still make their own mayonnaise, and few skimp on the fillings.

Be sure to keep some cash on hand, because *osterie,* bacari, and pizzerias usually do not take credit cards. Meals start earlier in the north of Italy than in Rome and the South, and Venice is no exception. Plan on lunch being served between 12:30 and 2, dinner between 7:30 and 10. You might notice that many bacari open as early as 8 AM, but they do not serve typical breakfast items or coffee; some Venetians partake of cicheti and tramezzini for their morning meal.

Sparkling prosecco, a wine from the Veneto, is often taken as an aperitif or stirred into fresh fruit juice to make some of the most famous mixed drinks in the lagoon, including the peachy Bellini cocktail. Prosecco di Valdobbiadene is one of the region's favorites. The better restaurants offer good selections of Italian and French wines. Osterie more often have a limited choice of wines from the region. Popular reds include merlot, valpolicella, Raboso, Bardolino, the more-refined Cabernet Pramaggiore, and Amarone. Good table whites are Recioto, Tocai Lison, Soave, and the sauternes-like Torcolato.

Tiramisu lovers will have ample opportunity to sample this creamy concoction made from ladyfingers that are soaked in espresso and covered with sweetened mascarpone cheese. It was invented here in the

Veneto. In addition to sorbets and *semifreddi* (frozen ice cream and cake desserts), other sweets that frequently appear on Venetian menus are almond cakes and strudels, as well as dry cookies served with sweet white wine. Ice cream is sold at every corner but, with a few notable exceptions, rarely rises above mediocrity.

CATEGORY	COST*
$$$$	over €23
$$$	€18–€23
$$	€13–€18
$	under €13

Prices are for a main course (secondo piatto)

Burano

$$ ✕ **Al Gatto Nero da Ruggero.** Even cats know that this restaurant dedicated to one of their own offers the best fish on the island. The "Black Cat" has a vivid blue facade that stands out among the low, brightly colored buildings that animate the picturesque Fondamenta della Giudecca, where in warm weather amateur painters set up their easels. Anything you order will taste fresh and genuine, from sweet *gamberetti* (shrimp) to tender folpetti. The spaghetti *alla scogliera* comes in a seafood sauce with cherry tomatoes; the *fritto misto* (fish fry) is outstanding for its lightness and variety of fish. ✉ *Fondamenta della Giudecca 88, Burano (vaporetto Line 12, Burano stop),* ☎ *041/730120. AE, DC, MC, V. Closed Mon. and 3 wks in Nov.*

Cannaregio

$$$–$$$$ ✕ **Il Sole sulla Vecia Cavana.** This restaurant opened in 2001 and im-
★   mediately became a star of the Venice dining scene. Owner Stefano Monti and his young, talented kitchen team create winning Italian and Venetian dishes such as *filetti di pesce a cottura differenziata* (fish fillet, cooked at the bottom and rare on top), tender baby cuttlefish, and, among desserts, *gelato al basilico* (basil ice cream). The 18th-century *cavana* (boathouse) maintains its original low columns, arches, and brick walls, but has been decorated with contemporary flair. A large marble slab by the entrance serves as a communal table for those who want to sample chic cicheti. ✉ *Rio Terà SS. Apostoli, 4624 Cannaregio,* ☎ *041/5287106. AE, DC, MC, V. Closed Mon. and 2 wks in Jan.*

$$$ ✕ **Antica Mola.** You'll find a warm welcome at this family-run trattoria. Whether you choose the terrace overlooking the canal or the shaded garden in back, owners Giorgio, Antonietta, and Franco, will entertain you with their lively presence. The cooking is reliably good, homey fare with the accent on seafood—spaghetti *coi caparozzoli* (with clams) is a favorite. ✉ *Fondamenta dei Ormesini, 2800 Cannaregio,* ☎ *041/717492. AE, DC, MC, V. Closed Wed. and Aug.*

$$$ ✕ **Fiaschetteria Toscana.** This cordial restaurant in a former Tuscan wine and oil storehouse merits a trip to Cannaregio for its cheerful and courteous service, fine *cucina* (cooking), and noteworthy cellar. The owners, Albino and Mariuccia Busatto, make their presence felt as they walk among the well-appointed tables, opening special bottles of wine and discussing the menu. Gastronomic highlights include a light *tagliolini* (thin fettuccine), perhaps prepared *alla buranella* (with shrimp), and *zabaione* (zabaglione). In warm weather, the best tables are under the arbor on the square. ✉ *Campo San Giovanni Crisostomo, 5719 Cannaregio,* ☎ *041/5285281. AE, DC, MC, V. Closed Tues. and 4 wks July–Aug. No lunch Mon.*

$–$$ ✕ **Al Bacco.** Located not far from the Ghetto, this ancient osteria caters to young locals and those tourists who make the effort to seek it out. Among the classic Venetian dishes, sample the *sarde sotto sale* (salted sardines) or the old favorite, *bigoli in salsa* (rough-shaped spaghetti in an anchovy sauce). For alfresco dining, the charming garden has a few tables. ✉ *Fondamenta Capuzine 3054 Cannaregio,* ☎ *041/717493. AE, DC, MC, V. Closed Mon. and 1–2 wks July–Aug.*

$–$$ ✕ **Anice Stellato.** Hidden away on one of the most romantic fondamente of Cannaregio, this family-run bacaro-trattoria is the place to stop for fairly priced, great-tasting food in a part of town that doesn't teem with restaurants. The space has plenty of character: narrow columns rise from the colorful mosaic-like floor, dividing the room into cozy booths. The traditional Venetian fare is enriched with such offerings as *carpacci di pesce* (thin slices of raw tuna, swordfish, or salmon dressed with olive oil and fragrant herbs), tagliatelle with king prawns and zucchini flowers, and several tasty fish stews. ✉ *Fondamenta de la Sensa, 3272 Cannaregio,* ☎ *041/720744. AE, DC, MC, V. Closed Mon. and 3 wks in Aug.*

$–$$ ✕ **Bentigodi da Andrea.** *Bentigodi* is Venetian for "you'll enjoy yourself," and such a jaunty name is well suited to this trendy osteria, decorated with fishing-boat lamps and old-fashioned prints on whitewashed walls. The menu includes tartare of tuna and swordfish, steamed orata with green apple and lemon, *masorini con alici e capperi* (local duck with anchovies and capers), and game in winter. Good homemade desserts include cakes made with pumpkin and almond or chocolate and walnut, a rich bread pudding, and simple *panna cotta* served with fresh fruit. ✉ *Calesele, 1423 Cannaregio,* ☎ *041/716269. No credit cards. Closed Sun. and 3 wks in Jan.*
★

$–$$ ✕ **Da Bepi.** This neighborhood hangout is run by an energetic mamma who, judging from the allegiance shown by local regulars, must know the way to diners' hearts. At peak times you might have to wait a few minutes before receiving any attention, but you'll be consoled by the inviting odors wafting through the busy dining room. All dishes are fresh and well prepared: try the *tortelli con spinaci, patate, e ricotta* (ravioli filled with spinach, potato, and ricotta cheese) or, for a break from the usual Venetian fare, the *spiedini di pollo* (chicken on skewers). ✉ *Salizzada del Pistor, off Campo Santi Apostoli, 4550 Cannaregio,* ☎ *041/5285031. No credit cards. Closed Thurs.*

$–$$ ✕ **Vini da Gigio.** A quaint, friendly, family-run trattoria on the quay side of a canal just off the Strada Nuova, da Gigio is very popular with Venetians and other visiting Italians, who appreciate the affable service; the well-prepared homemade pasta, fish, and meat dishes; the imaginative and varied cellar; and the high-quality draft wine. It's good for a cheap, simple lunch at tables in the barroom. ✉ *Fondamenta de la Chiesa, 3628/a Cannaregio,* ☎ *041/5285140. AE, DC, MC, V. Closed Mon., 3 wks Jan.–Feb., 1 wk in June, and 3 wks Aug.–Sept.*
★

$ ✕ **Da Alberto.** An amicable trattoria that doubles as a bacaro, Alberto is always packed with locals. The faux-antique decor makes the place look old, but missing is the characteristic bacaro odor that comes from years of serving wine. However, what you cannot smell, you see: heaping barrels and demijohns full of vino da ombra. Vegetarians will appreciate the range of nonmeat dishes on the menu. Pasta is made to order, and fish can be better here than in most of the city center's pricier restaurants. ✉ *Calle Giacinto Gallina, 5401 Cannaregio,* ☎ *041/ 5238153. MC, V. Closed Sun. and 3 wks July–Aug.*

$ ✕ **Gam-Gam.** At the edge of the Jewish Ghetto near Ponte delle Guglie is one of the very few kosher restaurants in Italy, with a name that in Hebrew means "more-more" and recalls the Italian word *gnam-gnam* ("yum-yum"). The informal dining room is narrow and pink. The Or-

Venice Dining

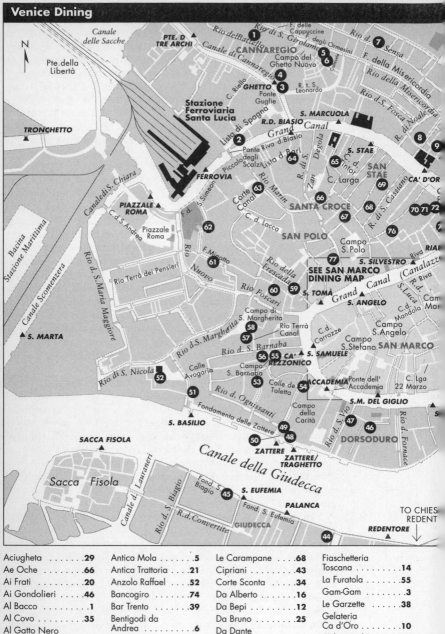

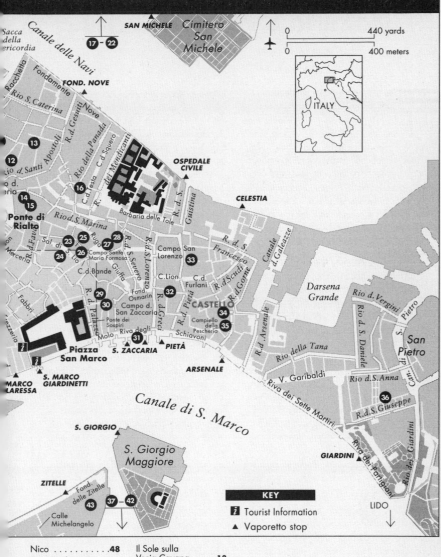

NAVIGATING A VENETIAN MENU

THE SEAFOOD PILED HIGH at the Rialto *pescheria* (fish market) comes from local waters and carries names peculiar to Venice. Inevitably, much of it finds its way to Venetian tables: *moeche* (soft-shell crabs) are caught at molting time (spring and fall) and fried in an egg-and-Parmesan batter. *Seppie in tecia* (tender baby cuttlefish) turn deep black after being stewed in their ink and a dash of tomato sauce and are customarily served with golden yellow polenta.

A vast array of tasty shellfish, including *caparozzoli* (carpet-shell clams), *garusoli* (snail-like mollusks), and *peoci* (mussels), are tossed with pasta, stirred into risotto or soups, or simply boiled and dressed with olive oil, lemon juice, and parsley. *Capesante* (sea scallops) are usually baked, either plain or with bread crumbs, Parmesan, and parsley. Crustaceans include *gamberetti* (shrimp), *scampi* (king prawns), *schie* (tiny gray shrimp), *granseola* (spider crab), and *canocie* (mantis shrimp). One very traditional preparation for fish, found on just about every bacaro, osteria, and restaurant, is *sarde in saor*, or just saor (boned sardines fried in olive oil, then marinated in a sauce of sautéed onion, vinegar, raisins, and pine nuts).

Less strictly Venetian but nevertheless often found on menus throughout the city are dishes featuring fish from the Mediterranean such as *branzino* (sea bass, also called *spigola*), *orata* (gilthead), *sogliola* (sole), *rombo* (turbot), and *dentice* (sea bream). Common preparations include *ai ferri* (grilled), *al forno* (baked, usually with potatoes), *al sale* (baked under a seasalt crust), and *a filetti* (as fillets).

A Venetian specialty savored all over Italy is *fegato alla veneziana* (thin slices of calf's liver quickly sautéed and dressed with onion, then briefly stewed in olive oil and butter, and generously sprinkled with parsley). Adventurous diners should try *bisatto all'ara*, a local variety of fleshy eel with a very thin skin cooked on a bed of bay leaves. Bisatto can also be deep-fried or stewed.

Although pasta with seafood sauce is generally well prepared, other pasta dishes are better in central and southern Italy. The Veneto region is Italy's risotto homeland, and Venice has its own special risotto made in springtime with local peas called *risi e bisi*. The fertile, salty soil of the larger islands of the lagoon was legendary for the quality of its produce (now just a few stalls at the Rialto market sell locally grown vegetables), and home gardening is still very strong throughout the region.

Spring treats are the fat white asparagus from Bassano and artichokes, either called *castraure* (baby artichokes sautéed with olive oil, parsley, and garlic) or *fondi* (hearts of globe artichokes, simmered in olive oil, parsley, and garlic). In winter, roughly from mid-December to early March, red radicchio *di Treviso* (from Treviso) comes to market and is best grilled or used as a base for risotto. Fall brings small, brown wild mushrooms called *chiodini* and *zucca barucca*, a warty squash often baked, used in soups, or stuffed into ravioli. In the cooler months, keep an eye out for *pasta e fasioi*, a thick bean soup enriched with fresh pasta, known elsewhere in the region as *pasta e fagioli*.

Without doubt, tiramisu is the most popular dessert in town, but no matter how many times you try it, it will always taste a bit different, as each restaurant follows its own tiramisu creed. Just to mention a few of the possible variations, sweet liqueur can be added to the coffee, whipped cream or crème anglaise stirred in the basic mascarpone and egg-yolk filling, or bits of bitter chocolate scattered on top instead of cocoa. A close second is *panna cotta*, literally "cooked cream," a sort of flourless and eggless cream pudding, at its best when served with a sauce made from fresh berries.

Buon appetito!

— Carla Lionello

thodox staff is helpful in explaining the blend of Israeli and Eastern European dishes, which include falafel with tahini sauce, a meat stew called *cholent,* and gefilte fish. Vegetarians might create their own salad from the salad bar or try the *piatto di melanzane,* with eggplant done many ways. ⊠ *Sottoportico del Ghetto Vecchio, 1122 Cannaregio,* ☎ *041/715284. AE, DC, MC, V. Closed Sat. No dinner Fri.*

$ ✕ **Osteria Ca' d'Oro.** Known commonly as La Vedova (the Widow), this warm osteria not far from the Ca' d'Oro was opened as a low-key bacaro by the owner's great-grandparents. The high quality of the food is due to the energetic Widow—the owner's mother—whose presence is still felt even though she's long gone. A rough Venetian floor, old marble counter, and long tables invite conviviality. Cicheti include tender *seppie roste* (grilled cuttlefish), *polpette* (meatballs), and baccalà mantecato. The house winter pasta is the *pastisso de radicio rosso* (lasagna with sausage, radicchio, and béchamel sauce). In the spring, the chef switches to *pastisso de asparagi* (with asparagus). ⊠ *Calle del Pistor, 3912 Cannaregio,* ☎ *041/5285324. No credit cards. Closed Thurs., Aug., 1st wk in Sept., and 2 wks after Carnevale.*

$ ✕ **Tiziano.** A handy place for a quick detour and snack, this *tavola calda* (snack bar) sells pizza by the meter, which you eat standing up at the counter or perched on a stool. At lunchtime you can also order from the variety of pasta dishes, and sandwiches are always on offer if you are in need of refueling in between meals. ⊠ *Salizzada San Giovanni Crisostomo, 5747 Cannaregio,* ☎ *041/5235544. No credit cards.*

Castello

$$$$ ✕ **Al Covo.** This small, charming osteria changes its menu according
★ to the day's bounty—mostly local seafood caught just hours before and specialties from other European waters. Cesare Benelli and his American wife, Diane, insist on only the freshest ingredients and claim not to use butter or animal fat. Try the *zuppa di pesce* (fish soup) followed by the fish of the day, either grilled, baked, or steamed. Diane will guide you through some of her homemade desserts and the extensive wine selection. At lunch, only a fixed-price menu (€30.00, with several options) is served; dinner is à la carte. ⊠ *Campiello della Pescaria, 3968 Castello,* ☎ *041/5223812. No credit cards. Closed Wed.–Thurs., 1 wk in Aug., and 4 wks Dec.–Jan.*

$$$–$$$$ ✕ **Do Leoni.** The "Two Lions," located in the Londra Palace hotel, is a sumptuous setting (with wood paneling, soft light, mirrored walls, and burgundy leather chairs) in which to sample Venetian cuisine. The menu features traditional fish risotto and sarde in saor as well as lobster and oysters, and the desserts are suitably decadent—chocolate cake, mascarpone ice cream with *mostarda* (sweet-and-sour fruit chutney), and *spuma di zabaione* (zabaglione stirred into whipped cream) are among the offerings. World travelers will appreciate the professional service, with waiters fluent in English and French. The summer terrace occupies a good portion of the Riva. ⊠ *Riva degli Schiavoni, 4171 Castello,* ☎ *041/5200533. Reservations essential. AE, DC, MC, V.*

$$$ ✕ **Alle Testiere.** A strong local following can make it tough to get one
★ of the five tables at this tiny trattoria near Campo Santa Maria Formosa. Chef Bruno Gavagnin's dishes stand out for lightness and balance: try the *gnocchetti con moscardini* (little gnocchi with tender baby octopus), linguine with *coda di rospo* (angelfish tail), or the baked *rombo* (turbot) with radicchio di Treviso. The Testiere also offers a refined selection of cicheti, which can be taken as appetizers before a full meal. A short but well-assembled wine list allows for interesting combinations. Save room for a slice of homemade pear tart. ⊠ *Calle del*

Mondo Novo, 5081 Castello, ☎ *041/5227220. Reservations essential. MC, V. Closed Sun., 3 wks in Aug., and 3 wks Dec.–Jan.*

$$–$$$ ✕ **Da Bruno.** A country *taverna* (tavern) in the center of Venice, this popular restaurant grills its meat over an open fire. First, though, don't overlook the cicheti, such as the paper-thin prosciutto wrapped around *grissini* (thin bread sticks), at the counter. As for main courses, you can take your pick from such Italian specialties as fillet of beef with pepper sauce or veal with wild mushrooms. Fish fans might gravitate toward the squid with polenta, scampi, or calamari. ✉ *Calle del Paradiso, 5731 Castello,* ☎ *041/5221480. AE, DC, MC, V.*

$$ ✕ **Corte Sconta.** What happens when a hotel porter and a trade union
★ leader open up a bacaro near the Arsenal? They choose an old tavern, where the poor once brought food from their unheated homes in order to drink a glass of wine and share the warmth of a roaring stove, and leave the decor as is. The menu, written in Venetian dialect, is strictly focused on fish, and only the freshest ingredients are used. Cicheti, served as starters, come by the dozen, but save room for primi like spaghetti *neri alle capesante e zucchine* (cuttlefish-ink pasta with scallops and zucchini) and secondi such as squid stuffed with radicchio di Treviso. The house dessert is a warm zabaglione with cookies. ✉ *Calle del Pestrin, 3886 Castello,* ☎ *041/5227024. Reservations essential. AE, DC, MC, V. Closed Sun.–Mon., 4 wks Jan.–Feb., 4 wks July–Aug.*

$$ ✕ **Da Remigio.** This popular family-run trattoria near San Giorgio dei Greci turns out reliably tasty fish and meat dishes. You're likely to eat dishes Venetians have been enjoying for centuries, including the *gnocchetti alla pescatora* (tiny potato dumplings with a fish sauce) and *seppie in tecia* (cuttlefish stew). This is the place to enjoy an informal meal in the company of hungry, chatty locals. ✉ *Salizzada dei Greci, 3416 Castello,* ☎ *041/5230089. Reservations essential. AE, DC, MC, V. Closed Tues., 2 wks July–Aug., and 4 wks Dec.–Jan. No dinner Mon.*

$–$$ ✕ **Al Mascaron.** The convivial, crowded Al Mascaron, with its paper tablecloths and informal atmosphere, is always filled with Venetians who drop in to gossip, drink, play cards, and eat cicheti at the bar. You can bet on delicious seafood, pastas, risottos, and seafood salads. Mascaron has become so popular that the owners, Gigi and Momi, have opened an offshoot called La Mascareta, a few doors down the calle (at No. 5183), where you can enjoy a glass of wine and snacks. ✉ *Calle Lunga Santa Maria Formosa, 5225 Castello,* ☎ *041/5225995. No credit cards. Closed Sun. and mid-Dec.–mid-Jan.*

$ ✕ **Dai Tosi.** Finding a restaurant in Castello Basso can be difficult; this neighborhood trattoria is the only fairly priced place near San Pietro di Castello. The red, hand-painted sign above the window reflects the homey interior and also the cheerfulness of service: *tosi* refers to the "young lads" on the waitstaff, as opposed to the grumpy, aging career waiters you might encounter elsewhere. Step inside to sample a dish of pasta with seafood, or tossed with fresh veggies, and to taste some well-prepared cicheti. In the evening and on Thursday at lunch you can also opt for pizza; on Monday, Tuesday, and Thursday evenings there's only pizza. ✉ *Seco Marina, 738 Castello,* ☎ *041/5237102. No credit cards. Closed Wed. and 2–3 wks in Aug.*

$ ✕ **Osteria al Portego.** At this bacaro, located on a calle where bacari have thrived for centuries, the emphasis is more on food than on wine. Regulars swear by the gelatinous *nervetti* (veal knee cartilage) served with beans and *spienza* (beef spleen), but you might take their word for it and turn your attention to the deep-fried crab claws, folpetti, or hard-boiled eggs with pickles and anchovies. A big pot of risotto is made once or twice a day and served on the spot. ✉ *Calle della Malvasia, 6015 Castello,* ☎ *041/5229038. No credit cards. June–Sept., closed* *weekends; Oct.–May, closed Sun., no dinner Sat.; closed over Christ-mas, 2 wks in June, and 2 wks in Aug.*

$ ✗ **Rivetta.** A reasonably priced trattoria among sandwich shops and tourist traps, Rivetta is a safe bet for a bite to eat near Piazza San Marco. Crowded and not particularly charming, it is redeemed by fast service and a solid selection at the counter: try *insalata di mare* (seafood salad) and *un bianco* (a glass of house white wine). If you take a seat, con-sider the *pasticcio* (fish lasagna) pasta special. If you have recently taken a gondola ride, there's a fair chance you will run into your gondolier: those who park at the nearby Ponte della Canonica, San Zaccaria, and Bacino di San Marco are regulars here. ✉ *Ponte San Provolo, 4625 Castello,* ☎ *041/5287302. No credit cards. Closed Mon.*

Dorsoduro

$$$ ✗ **Ai Gondolieri.** This is the place for those who appreciate meat and
★ the food of the mainland, and despite the tourist-trap name, it's a fa-vorite with Venetians. Feast on *filetto di maiale con castraure* (pork fillet with baby artichokes), duck breast with apple and sweet onion, or on more traditional dishes from the Veneto hills such as horse meat and game, gnocchi and polenta. The wine list is above average in qual-ity and variety. ✉ *Fondamenta Zorzi Bragadin, 366 Dorsoduro,* ☎ *041/5286396. AE, DC, MC, V. Closed Tues.*

$$–$$$ ✗ **L'Incontro.** This trattoria between San Barnaba and Campo Santa
★ Margherita has a faithful clientele of Venetians and visitors, attracted by flavorful Sardinian cucina, sociable service, and reasonable prices. Starters include Sardinian sausages, but you might sample the delicious traditional primi like *culingiones* (large ravioli filled with pecorino, saf-fron, and orange peel). The selection of secondi is heavy on herb-crusted meat dishes such as *coniglio al mirto* (rabbit baked on a bed of myrtle sprigs) and the *costine d'agnello con rosmarino e mentuccia* (unweaned lamb's ribs with rosemary and wild mint). ✉ *Rio Terrà Canal, 3062/a Dorsoduro,* ☎ *041/5222404. AE, DC, MC, V. Closed Mon., Jan., and 2 wks in Aug. No lunch Tues.*

$$–$$$ ✗ **Locanda Montin.** Peggy Guggenheim used to take leading artists of her day—including Jackson Pollock and Mark Rothko—to this archety-pal Venetian inn not far from her Palazzo Venier dei Leoni. The walls are still covered with modern art, but it's far from the haute bohemian hangout it used to be, except for when the Biennale crowd takes over. Outside, you can dine under an elongated arbor and enjoy such spe-cialties as rigatoni *ai quattro formaggi* (with four cheeses), spaghetti Adriatica (with fish sauce), and antipasto Montin (seafood antipasto). ✉ *Fondamenta di Borgo, 1147 Dorsoduro,* ☎ *041/5227151. AE, DC, MC, V. Closed Wed., Jan. 7–26, and 2–3 wks in Aug. No dinner Tues.*

$$ ✗ **Cantinone Storico.** On a quiet, romantic canal near the Accademia, this comfortable trattoria with alfresco tables serves well-prepared specialties such as risotto *terra mare* (with seafood, vegetables, and porcini mushrooms) and tagliolini *alla granseola* (with spider-crab sauce). It's heavily advertised and draws mostly tourists, but it's hard to beat for location and reasonable prices. The house stocks a good selection of wines. ✉ *Fondamenta di Ca' Bragadin, 660/1 Dorsoduro,* ☎ *041/5239577. AE, MC, V. Closed Sun. and 2 wks in Nov.*

$$ ✗ **La Furatola.** The name means simply "The Restaurant" in Old Venetian dialect, reflecting the plain style of the decor, but it hardly does justice to the fine fish offerings available within. There's a selec-tion of seafood cicheti on display as you enter, and for the main course, the fish are presented for your approval before being cooked. When it's available, the John Dory is truly remarkable. It's a small place—

just one room—so you should book ahead to avoid waiting in line. ⊠ *Calle Lunga San Barnaba, 2870 Dorsoduro,* ☎ *041/5208594. Reservations essential. AE, DC, MC, V. Closed Thurs., last 3 wks in Jan., and Aug. No lunch Mon.*

$–$$ ✕ **Anzolo Raffael.** A long way from the madding crowd, this trattoria has a clientele evenly divided between locals and visitors, all eager to eat something simple and authentic at a fraction of the price of comparable Venetian restaurants. Take a seat at a wooden table in the nononsense back room and listen to the kind signora (her husband is a few steps away in the kitchen) recite the short menu. Choose from two pastas or a fish soup, two vegetable side dishes, and a main course of fish, either grilled or fried. Plan on dessert elsewhere—the signore doesn't make sweets. ⊠ *Campo Anzolo Rafael, 1722 Dorsoduro,* ☎ *041/5237456. No credit cards. Closed Mon.–Tues.*

$ ✕ **Alla Dona Onesta.** The virtue of the "Honest Woman" is still maintained by the owners of this small, neat trattoria perched along the rio. Through the glass door you'll see a well-kept old structure with no frills—the style is dark-brown wooden chairs and white tablecloths. The menu posted outside offers a reasonable choice of staple Italian pasta dishes, fish, and meat. Few tourists stop here, and the little English you'll hear is likely to be a conversation among professors of the nearby Università Ca' Foscari, who are lunchtime regulars. ⊠ *Ponte de la Dona Onesta, 3922 Dorsoduro,* ☎ *041/710586. AE, DC, MC, V.*

$ ✕ **Randon Enoteca.** If you only visit one enoteca in Venice, make it Enoteca Randon, arguably the best wine bar in town, with tables outside in summer and a good, informal restaurant open for dinner. The decor is modern but warm and comfortable, and behind the counter you can see the cooks at work in the kitchen. They might be preparing old Venetian favorites such as baked sardines or saor, but also lasagna, *gnocchi ai cinque formaggi* (in a rich cheese sauce), lamb on skewers, and home-smoked fish. ⊠ *Campo San Barnaba, 2852 Dorsoduro (not far from the Accademia Gallery),* ☎ *041/5224410. AE, DC, MC, V. Closed Sun. No lunch Mon.*

$ ✕ **Ristorante alle Zattere.** This is a perfect spot on a summer evening to watch the *passeggiata* of gondolas, rowboats, and vaporetti, as it's one of the few restaurants with a terrace that overlooks the Canale della Giudecca. The fare is rather predictable—spaghetti *alle vongole* (with clams), seppie in tecia, or fegato alla veneziana—but you might be happy with a plain but appetizing pizza (served also at lunch) in view of the marvelous backdrop. ⊠ *Zattere, 795 Dorsoduro,* ☎ *041/5204224. MC, V. Closed Tues. and 4–6 wks Nov.–Dec.*

$ ✕ **San Trovaso.** A wide choice of Venetian dishes served in robust portions, economical fixed-price menus, pizzas, and house wine by the glass or pitcher keep this two-floor, no-nonsense tavern abuzz with young Venetians and budget-conscious visitors in the know. It's always packed, and table turnover is fast. Not far from the Gallerie dell'Accademia, this is a good place to slip into while sightseeing in Dorsoduro. ⊠ *Fondamenta Priuli, 1016 Dorsoduro,* ☎ *041/5203703. AE, MC, V. Closed Mon. and 1 wk Dec.–Jan.*

Giudecca

$$$$ ✕ **Cipriani.** A cut above most Italian restaurants in ambience, service,
★   and view, the Cipriani is an expensive, world-class experience worth having once. In white-peach season (July to early September), start with the famous blossom-scented Bellini. The cuisine is rooted in Venetian tradition, prepared with a star chef's hand, and matched with a superb wine list. Sole fillets instead of whole sardines are used for the saor; deep-fried prawns, coated in semolina flour, stay wonderfully crisp.

Desserts are spectacular: a decadent tiramisu is served in a bitter-chocolate shell topped by a gondola. ⊠ *Fondamenta San Giovanni 10, Giudecca (vaporetto Line 82, Zitelle stop),* ☎ *041/5207744. Reservations essential. AE, DC, MC, V. Closed mid-Nov.–mid-Mar.*

$ ✕ **Altanella.** This Giudecca institution facing a large canal is the right
★ place to taste some of the strange-looking fish sold at the stalls in the Rialto's *pescheria* (fish market). The Altanella is a favorite among locals, although a trilingual menu makes it clear that visitors find their way here as well. Start with a salad of folpetti, followed by a creamy risotto or gnocchi with a seppie (cuttlefish) sauce. Secondi include grilled or deep-fried fish, or seppie *in umido* (in a stew with its black ink and a dash of tomato sauce), served with polenta. Wine is not this rustic place's strong suit. ⊠ *Calle delle Erbe 270, Giudecca (vaporetto Line 82, Redentore or Palanca stops),* ☎ *041/5227780. No credit cards. Closed Mon.–Tues., 2 wks in Aug., and 3 last wks in Jan.*

Lido

$$–$$$ ✕ **Trattoria Favorita.** This neighborhood eatery has been in the same family's hands since the 1920s and offers you the choice between a wood-beamed dining room and a vine-covered garden. Seafood is the specialty, always fresh and lovingly prepared; you won't go wrong ordering the tagliolini with shrimp and zucchini or the divine gnocchi con granseola. ⊠ *Via Francesco Duodo 33, Lido,* ☎ *041/5261626. Reservations essential. AE, DC, MC, V. Closed Mon. and mid-Jan.–mid-Feb. No lunch Tues.*

$$ ✕ **Al Vecio Cantier.** The wild scenery, with intersecting canals and reeds, contributes to the appeal of one of the trendiest places on the Lido, always filled to the gills during the film festival. There's efficient cicheti service, but the restaurant deserves a longer visit for a relaxing meal in the best Venetian tradition: whipped baccalà with polenta and tagliolini *con gamberetti e carciofi* (with shrimp and artichokes) in spring. Homemade desserts include lemon and almond tarts, or you can dip cookies in a glass of *vino passito,* a dessert wine. Outside dining is in a pretty garden. ⊠ *Via della Droma 76, Lido (vaporetto Lines 1, 6, 14, 51/52, or 82, Lido stop; then bus Line B to the Alberoni),* ☎ *041/ 5268130. AE, DC, MC, V. Closed Mon. No lunch Tues., Nov., or Jan.*

$$ ✕ **Le Garzette.** A small, family-run trattoria inside the agriturismo of the same name, Le Garzette cooks very fresh fish, homegrown vegetables, and home-raised poultry, including duck. Meals are served to non-boarders on Friday evenings and weekends. You won't find anything new here, but everything tastes genuine and the staff won't look down on you if you are wearing shorts. ⊠ *Lungomare Alberoni 32, Lido (vaporetto Lines 1, 6, 14, 51/52, or 82, Lido stop),* ☎ *041/731078. Reservations essential. No credit cards. Closed Dec.–Feb. No lunch weekdays.*

$ ✕ **Bar Trento.** This neat, old-style osteria 10 minutes from Piazzale Santa Maria Elisabetta has a soft spot for meat and innards (one of the owners was a *bechèr,* or butcher). Lunch is the only meal served, but it stays open from 8 to 8 for ombre and cicheti. Descriptions of tasty snacks from century-old recipes are left out, as they might put off nonnatives. More recognizable options include be baccalà *alla vicentina* (stewed with onion, milk, and Parmesan); pasta with seafood; and several seasonal risottos. As a secondo, fish can be cooked any way you want. Don't be suspicious of the surprisingly low prices: you are far enough away from San Marco's bells. ⊠ *Via Sandro Gallo 82, Lido (vaporetto Line 1, 6, 14, 51/52, or 82, Lido stop),* ☎ *041/5265960. No credit cards. Closed Sun. No dinner except during Biennale.*

Murano

$$–$$$ ✕ **Valmarana.** This is the most upscale restaurant on the island, housed in a palace on the *fondamenta* (street) across from the Museo Vetrario. Stuccoed walls and glass chandeliers complement well-appointed tables, and although the menu contains no surprises, the cuisine is more refined than at other places on Murano. Try the baked sea scallops or crab with fresh herbs, or the rich risotto *alla pescatora,* containing all kinds of fish. In warm weather, reserve a table in the back garden or on the terrace overlooking the canal; inside, there's a no-smoking room. ⊠ *Fondamenta Navagero 31, Murano (vaporetto Line 12, 13, 23, 41/42, or 61/62, Navagero stop),* ☎ *041/739313. AE, DC, MC, V. Closed 3 wks in Jan. No dinner.*

$$ ✕ **Ai Frati.** A walk along the Fondamenta dei Vetrai brings you to the large iron bridge spanning Murano's Grand Canal; down to the left, hanging over the Canale degli Angeli, is the attractive terrace of Ai Frati. As elsewhere in Venice, the key word here is fish, prepared any way you want. The risottos are nicely done, and if you want to taste a famous dish from Murano, ask ahead for the *bisatto sull'ara,* a local variety of fleshy eel traditionally cooked on a bed of bay leaves. ⊠ *Fondamenta Sebastiano Venier 4, Murano (vaporetto Line 12, 13, 23, 41/42, or 61/62, Venier stop),* ☎ *041/736694. V. Closed Thurs. and Feb. No dinner.*

$–$$ ✕ **Antica Trattoria.** This lunch-only trattoria can be easily spotted by the bright red walls close to the Grand Canal on the island of Murano. For company you'll probably find local glass workers with a *caffè corretto con grappa* (espresso with grappa) in front of them. If it's more solid nourishment you're after, go for the freshly grilled fish or the seppie in tecia, served in the rear garden. ⊠ *Riva Longa 20, Murano,* ☎ *041/739610. AE, DC, MC, V. Closed Sat. and Feb. No dinner.*

$–$$ ✕ **Busa alla Torre da Lele.** A pretty square with olive trees and a well sets the stage for Da Lele, a favorite of the Muranese. On the ground floor of a dark-red building with a loggia, the restaurant stretches out on the campo, where you eat in the shade of large umbrellas. Check the blackboard for such daily specials as antipasto Busa, with granseola and garusoli; *bavette alla busara* (flat spaghetti with a hot prawn and tomato sauce); and baked rombo or branzino with potato. Homemade cookies are served with *fragolino,* a sweet, sparkling wine redolent of strawberries. ⊠ *Campo Santo Stefano 3, Murano (vaporetto Line 12, 13, 23, 41/42, or 61/62, Faro stop),* ☎ *041/739662. AE, DC, MC, V. No dinner.*

San Marco

$$$$ ✕ **Al Graspo de Ua.** Opened in the 19th century as a small osteria, the "Bunch of Grapes" became the meeting place of artists and movie stars back in the 1960s. Today, it serves a faithful clientele of wealthy Italians. The decor is a miscellanea of plants, sculpture, candlelight, and paintings set against brick and white-stucco walls. The owner, Lucio Zanon, speaks fluent English and will introduce you to a wide-ranging menu of fresh pasta, seasonal risotto, and meat and seafood. A treat in late spring is the fat, white asparagus from Bassano, which, with a couple of fried eggs, is eaten as a main course. Desserts are all homemade. ⊠ *Calle dei Bombaseri, 5094 San Marco,* ☎ *041/5223647. AE, DC, MC, V. Closed Mon. and 1 wk in Jan.*

$$$$ ✕ **Antico Pignolo.** Hidden in the maze of alleys north of Piazza San Marco, the "Old Pine Nut" occupies a former spice shop, but its name is the most modest thing about it: a row of impeccably set tables and a smart bar create a sophisticated air, with high prices to match. Although the cuisine focuses on fish, the style is less Venetian than else-

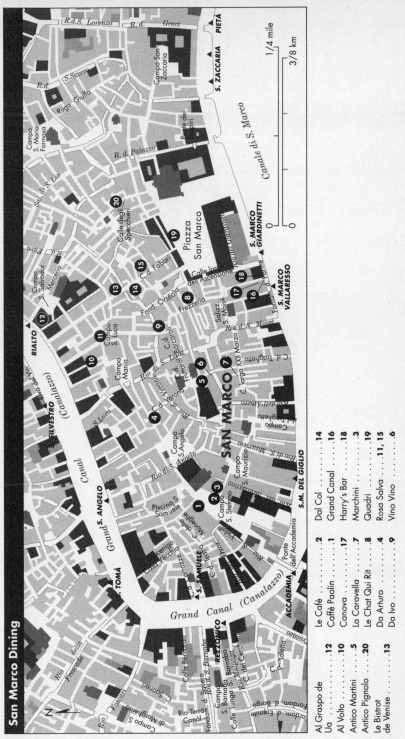

San Marco Dining

Al Graspo de Ua **12**
Al Volto **10**
Antico Martini **5**
Antico Pignolo **20**
Le Bistrot de Venise **13**

Le Café **2**
Caffè Paolin **1**
Canova **17**
La Caravella **7**
Le Chat Qui Rit **8**
Da Arturo **4**
Da Ivo **9**

Dal Col **14**
Grand Canal **16**
Harry's Bar **18**
Marchini **3**
Quadri **19**
Rosa Salva **11, 15**
Vino Vino **6**

where, with organic dishes and oysters available (the latter on a day's notice). In the fall there's also a menu based on white truffles from Alba. The *fritti* (deep-fried dishes) deserve special mention, and the wine list, with nearly 1,000 labels, is impressive. ⊠ *Calle degli Specchieri, 451 San Marco,* ☎ *041/5228123. AE, DC, MC, V.*

$$$$ ✕ **Da Ivo.** An enclave of Tuscan cuisine two minutes from Piazza San Marco, Da Ivo is a cozy, relaxing trattoria, with paintings and copper pots hanging on white walls and candlelight at dinner. Start with a vegetable soup, or the less-Tuscan tagliolini *alla bottarga* (with roe). The reputation of the restaurant has been built on its famous *fiorentine* (2-pound Chianina beef steaks grilled over olive-wood charcoal), but game and fish are also reliable standards. Top it off with a warm zabaglione with ricotta. The wine list focuses on reds from Piedmont, the Veneto, and Tuscany. ⊠ *Ramo dei Fuseri, 1809 San Marco,* ☎ *041/5285004. AE, DC, MC, V. Closed Sun. and Jan.*

$$$$ ✕ **Grand Canal.** The restaurant of the Hotel Monaco & Grand Canal is a favorite with Venetians, who enjoy eating on the lovely canal-side terrace in summer and in the cozy dining room in winter. All the pasta is made fresh daily on the premises, and the smoked and marinated salmon are also prepared here. The chef's traditional Venetian cuisine is top-flight; you'll marvel over savory dishes such as *scampi alla Buséra* (shrimp in a cognac sauce). Jackets are required for men at dinner. ⊠ *Hotel Monaco & Grand Canal, Calle Vallaresso, 1325 San Marco,* ☎ *041/5200211. AE, DC, MC, V.*

$$$$ ✕ **Harry's Bar.** The humble door of this less-than-humble watering hole leads to the legendary Venetian hangout of such notables as Hemingway, Maugham, and Onassis. Such company doesn't come cheap, but Harry's is still known for the driest martinis and the most heavenly Bellinis in town, as well as fine, though overpriced, *cucina veneta.* The decor is boring beige-on-beige, but the view upstairs—looking out on spectacular Chiesa di Santa Maria della Salute—competes with the finest Canaletto *vedute* (scenic paintings). ⊠ *Calle Vallaresso, 1323 San Marco,* ☎ *041/5285777. Reservations essential. AE, DC, MC, V.*

$$$$ ✕ **Quadri.** In the 19th century, princes, dukes, and countesses dined here, and you'll feel like one when you walk into the gilded salons of Venice's most beautiful restaurant. The decor is stunning—Quadri's second-floor aerie gives you a pigeon's-eye view of Piazza San Marco—and the cuisine is classic Venetian, with lots of fish. (Truffles are a major draw in the fall.) Come September, when the Biennale is in session, the sequins-and-sunglasses set takes over. ⊠ *Piazza San Marco, 120–124 San Marco,* ☎ *041/5289299. Reservations essential. AE, DC, MC, V. Closed Mon. Nov.–Apr. except during Christmas and Carnevale.*

$$$–$$$$ ✕ **Antico Martini.** This place was born as a caffè in 1720, and its original quarters are impeccably maintained by the current owner, Signor Emilio Baldi. Intimate tables, candlelight, antique oil paintings, and a patrician air are paired with traditional yet inventive dishes. Salmon rolls filled with caviar and sour cream might be followed by homemade tagliatelle with prawn and arugula or angelfish with black peppercorns. Finish up with a slice of apple and raspberry tart, or consider booking a soufflé. There's no need to rush out, as the Antico Martini has a piano bar open until 3 AM. ⊠ *Calle del Cafetier, off Campo San Fantin, 1983 San Marco,* ☎ *041/5224121. Reservations essential. Jacket required. AE, DC, MC, V. Closed Tues. No lunch Wed.*

$$$–$$$$ ✕ **Canova.** The restaurant of the Hotel Luna Baglioni is on the pricey side, but the excellent service, tasteful surroundings, and inventive dishes all make for one of the most reliably good dining experiences close to Piazza San Marco. Fresh, nicely presented dishes might include a warm salad of scallops and cannellini beans in a lemon rosemary sauce,

and veal medallions with champagne vinegar, capers, and herbs. ✉ *Luna Baglioni, 1243 San Marco,* ☎ *041/5289840. AE, DC, MC, V.*

$$$–$$$$ ✕ **Da Arturo.** The tiny eatery on the Calle degli Assassini has the distinction in Venice of *not* serving seafood. Instead you'll choose from salads and fresh vegetable dishes; tasty, tender, meat courses in generous portions, including the subtly pungent *braciola alla veneziana* (pork chop schnitzel with vinegar); and an authentic creamy homemade tiramisu to finish. The good food and intimate atmosphere can make for a very pleasant evening. ✉ *Calle degli Assassini, 3656 San Marco,* ☎ *041/5286974. Reservations essential. No credit cards. Closed Sun., 10 days after Carnevale, and 4 wks in Aug.*

$$$–$$$$ ✕ **La Caravella.** Affixing your gaze on the chateaubriand, bouillabaisse, and fegato alla veneziana, you might think you had wandered into a temple of French haute cuisine. Continue reading the extensive menu to discover some of the best Venetian specialties in town, such as creamy *taglierini* (narrow fettuccine-shape pasta) alla granseola and fillets of local branzino and sole. The front room of this old favorite—long admired for its fine wine list and cordial, gracious service—is like the dining saloon of an old Venetian sailing ship. The pretty garden courtyard is open from May to September. ✉ *Saturnia Internazionale, Calle Larga XXII Marzo, 2397 San Marco,* ☎ *041/5208901. Reservations essential. AE, DC, MC, V.*

$–$$ ✕ **Le Bistrot de Venise.** Live music, poetry readings, and art exhibits attract a young crowd to this café-brasserie. Centrally located, it's open until 1 AM and serves 16th-century Venetian cuisine such as *l'ambroyno* (spiced chicken with nuts and raisins) and *capirotta* (meat soup). ✉ *Calle dei Fabbri, 4685 San Marco,* ☎ *041/5236651. MC, V.*

$–$$ ✕ **Le Chat Qui Rit.** This self-service cafeteria-pizzería, right on the main tourist stamping ground, is popular for its homemade dishes at reasonable prices and also for its family-friendly atmosphere. A dozen fish dishes and as many meat platters are always available, including cuttlefish with polenta and steaks served either plain or with herbs. ✉ *Calle Frezzeria, 1131 San Marco,* ☎ *041/5229086. No credit cards. Closed Sat. and about 4 wks in winter.*

$ ✕ **Vino Vino.** The annex of the extremely expensive Antico Martini restaurant is an informal wine bar where you can sample Italian wines and snack on a limited selection of (microwaved) dishes from the kitchens of its upscale big sister next door. ✉ *Calle delle Veste, near Campo San Fantin, 2007/a San Marco,* ☎ *041/5237027. Reservations not accepted. AE, DC, MC, V. Closed Tues.*

San Polo

$$$$ ✕ **Osteria Da Fiore.** Tucked away in a little calle off the top of Campo
★ San Polo, Da Fiore is a favorite among high-end diners for its superbly prepared Venetian cuisine and refined yet relaxed atmosphere. The long dining room, softly lit and warmly decorated with wooden wainscoting, is run by sure-handed waiters in white coats. Delicate antipasti of moeche, capesante, and folpetti might be followed by a succulent risotto or tagliolini *con scampi e zucchini* (with shrimp and zucchini) and a perfectly cooked main course of rombo or branzino. ✉ *Calle del Scaleter, 2202/a San Polo,* ☎ *041/721308. Reservations essential. AE, DC, MC, V. Closed Sun.–Mon., Aug., and Dec. 25–Jan. 20.*

$$–$$$ ✕ **Poste Vecie.** A tiny wooden bridge connects this historic osteria with the Rialto pescheria. In the 16th century, Poste Vecie (Old Post Office) served as a base for Venetian couriers, who stopped here to sort the mail between a glass of wine and a bowl of risotto. The place went upscale, but the large fireplaces are still here, along with the wooden ceiling, hand-painted plates, and some bizarre frescoes depicting alle-

gories of vices (Gluttony has been left out). The menu is based on what's available at the fish market. Besides the usual Venetian specialties, you'll find the more rare bisatto *in umido* (stewed with polenta) and moeche in springtime. An inner garden opens up in warm weather. ⊠ *Pescheria, 1608 San Polo,* ☎ *041/721822. AE, DC, MC, V. Closed Tues.*

$$ ✕ **Le Carampane.** Classics like saor and spaghetti with mussels are rarely missing here, and you might come across *caperossoli alla Savonarola* (seafood sautéed in olive oil and Parmesan) and John Dory fillets with radicchio di Treviso. Homemade cookies and *crostatine* (individual jam tarts) make up for the lack of more dessertlike treats. ⊠ *Rio Terrà delle Carampane, 1911 San Polo,* ☎ *041/5240165. No credit cards. Closed Sun.–Mon., 4 wks July–Aug., and 1 wk in Jan.*

$–$$ ✕ **Alla Madonna.** In a town with no fewer than 20 churches dedicated to the Virgin, why not a restaurant where you can get fish after mass on any day but Wednesday? Don't judge the place from the outside—the rooms are actually well kept and, by Venetian standards, rather elegant, with some decent artwork. Boiled granseola and seafood salads can be followed by a hearty fish soup with croutons, or deep-fried eel for the more adventurous. Grilled vegetables, meat ravioli, and a simple grilled beef fillet *al sangue* (rare) are all welcome alternatives to fish. ⊠ *Calle della Madonna, 594 San Polo,* ☎ *041/522384. AE, DC, MC, V. Closed Wed. and part of Aug.*

$–$$ ✕ **Da Ignazio.** Conveniently located on the route from Campo San Polo to the Frari, this pleasant family restaurant serves good, honest Venetian cuisine. The house specialty is a generous portion of creamy white polenta topped by shelled scampi, in the fall served with porcini. Poorly prepared elsewhere in town, the *capesante gratinate* (scallop gratin) here is made with just enough bread crumbs to make it nice and crusty on top. Desserts—standards such as crème caramel—are homemade and light. The garden is a charming spot to dine in fair weather. ⊠ *Calle dei Saoneri, 2749 San Polo,* ☎ *041/5234852. AE, DC, MC, V. Closed Sat., 2 wks over Christmas, and 2 wks in July.*

Santa Croce

$$–$$$ ✕ **Do Spade.** A rough Venetian floor and the motto *Vinum bonum fortificat cor hominis* (good wine fortifies the man's heart) are tip-offs to the character of this classic bacaro that was once the haunt of Casanova. The plump host, Giorgio Lanza, is the town's unofficial authority on little sandwiches. He coined the term *paperini* for his own creations, and after tasting one you'll happily add the word to your Venetian vocabulary. At mealtimes, the bacaro doubles as a trattoria; stick to more authentic dishes like *salsicce* (sausage) di secole, bean soup, baccalà, and cuttlefish. ⊠ *Calle Do Spade, 860 San Polo,* ☎ *041/5210574. No credit cards. Closed Sun., 2 wks in Aug., and 10 days in Jan.*

$$ ✕ **Antica Besseta.** Tucked away in a quiet corner of Santa Croce, with a few tables under an ivy shelter, the Antica Besseta dates from the 18th century, and it retains some of its old feel. The menu focuses on vegetables and fish, according to what's at the market: spaghetti with caparozzoli or cuttlefish ink, *schie* (tiny gray shrimp with polenta), and plenty of grilled fish. ⊠ *Salizzada de Ca' Zusto, 1395 Santa Croce,* ☎ *041/5240428. AE, V. Closed Mon.–Tues. No lunch Wed.*

$$ ✕ **Ribò.** Signor Martini loves Thoroughbreds, so when he took over
★   the restaurant Brodo di Giuggiole in 2001, he renamed it after the champion European horse Ribot. His kitchen puts out purebred Venetian cuisine—food that's is fanciful but not fancy. Several homemade pasta dishes are always on the menu, and the fish rolls with eggplant, when available, are worth a medal. The pleasant interior garden is a rarity for Venetian restaurants. ⊠ *Fondamenta Minotto, 158 Santa Croce,*

☎ 041/5242486. AE, DC, MC, V. Closed Mon., 10 days in Jan., and 2 wks in Aug. No dinner Sun.

$$ ✕ **Vecio Fritolin.** Until not so long ago, fish was fried and sold "to go" throughout Venice just as in London, except that it was paired with polenta rather than chips. An old sign advertising fried fish to go still hangs outside the "Old Fry Shop," but nowadays you can only dine in. A second sign, announcing cicheti available to go, still holds true. At this neat bacaro con cucina you can have a traditional meal featuring such dishes as bigoli in salsa, *totanetti* (squid) in tecia, baked fish with herbs, and non-Venetian lamb chops. ⊠ *Calle della Regina, 2262 Santa Croce,* ☎ *041/5222881. No credit cards. Closed Mon., 2 wks in Jan., and 2 wks in Aug. No lunch Tues.*

$–$$ ✕ **Bancogiro.** Set in the heart of the Rialto market, in a 15th-century
★ loggia that was home to one of the world's first banks, this gem of a bacaro doubles as informal restaurant at mealtimes. Tables are upstairs, in a carefully restored no-smoking room with a view of the Grand Canal. The market location assures access to the freshest possible ingredients, and the resulting combinations of fish, herbs, and vegetables taste just perfect: simple but intriguing, light but full of flavor. Try such treats as Sicilian-style *sarde incinte* (stuffed, or "pregnant," sardines) and *rombo con castraure* (turbot fillet with baby artichokes). ⊠ *Campo San Giacometto 122 (under the porch), Santa Croce,* ☎ *041/5232061. No credit cards. Closed Mon. No dinner Sun.*

$ ✕ **Ae Oche.** There's nothing Venetian about this saloonlike pizzeria with
★ shelves of imported stouts and a no-smoking room. Seventy-nine pizza combinations include the Campagnola, lavishly topped with a mix of tomato, mozzarella, mushroom, Brie, and *speck* (smoked prosciutto). Purists can stick to the *margherita,* with tomato, mozzarella, and basil. A selection of 16 salads plus a few pasta dishes make the Oche an ideal stop for a light meal between sights. ⊠ *Calle delle Oche, 1552/a–b Santa Croce,* ☎ *041/5241161. AE, DC, MC, V.*

$ ✕ **La Zucca.** Young couples crowd the closely spaced tables of cheerful Zucca, where dishes are adapted from the travels of the owners: there are flavors from Mexico (lemon chicken with guacamole), North Africa (beef with chickpeas and couscous), and Greece (grilled chicken breast with cucumber-yogurt sauce). Delicious starters include Sicilian pasta and, from the Veneto, a salad with *sfilacci di cavallo* (smoked horse meat). Fresh vegetables such as squash and artichokes are paramount in seasonal flans, soups, and stews. ⊠ *Calle del Tintor, 1762 Santa Croce,* ☎ *041/5241570. AE, DC, MC, V. Closed Sun., 1 wk in Aug., and over Christmas.*

Torcello

$$$–$$$$ ✕ **Locanda Cipriani.** Owned by the nephew of Arrigo Ciprianió–the founder of Harry's Bar—this inn profits from its idyllic location on the island of Torcello. Hemingway, who loved the silence of the lagoon, came here often to eat, drink, and brood under the green veranda. The food is not exceptional, especially considering the price, but dining here is more about getting lost in Venetian magic. The menu features pastas, *vitello tonnato* (shredded veal in a tuna and caper sauce), baked orata with potatoes, and lots of seafood. There's vaporetto service all night long, though only once an hour after 11 PM. The alternative is an expensive water taxi. ⊠ *Piazza Santa Fosca 29, Torcello,* ☎ *041/730150. AE, DC, MC, V. Closed Tues. and early Jan.–early Feb.*

Bacari: Andar per Ombre

Not all bacari double as bacari con cucina. Some do not even have tables for eating your cicheti. But even when they are little more than hole-in-the-walls with blackened beams and rustic trappings, they qualify as the redeeming counterpart to all those tourist-oriented fast-food joints and bars that line the city's main streets. More often than not, bacari are hard to find. Tucked away in narrow calli, few have signs on the doors or storefront windows. Although in some cases plastic chairs and veneered tables have replaced generations-old furnishings, the spirit of bacari is still rooted in diehard traditions. A real bacaro would never dream of selling soft drinks, beer, or mineral water, and hosts would find it inconceivable to offer green salads and "lite" preparations.

All bacari serve wine by the glass and have at least a dozen cicheti available, from *folpetti* (baby octopus) to *polpette* (meat patties), from *melanzane alla griglia* (grilled eggplant) to *cipolline* (sweet-and-sour baby onions). Table service is the exception rather than the rule, and you should go to the counter and pick what you want. Keep track of what you eat and drink, and pay for everything (in cash only) at the end. Plan on spending €12.00–€15.00 on a hearty helping of cicheti. Hours of operation vary. Some bacari are open nonstop from 8 in the morning to 8 or 9 in the evening; others take a lunch break, closing around 1 or 1:30 and reopening at 5. Most are closed on Sunday. The list below is by no means exhaustive: Venetians themselves don't know how many bacari thrive in their hometown.

Al Volto. Dark and with a ceiling lined with wine-bottle labels, the Volto has the atmosphere of a grotto or cellar, despite its location a stone's throw from the Rialto bridge. Ombre and appetizing cicheti are to be sampled until 10 PM, and at lunchtime the small kitchen prepares pasta and risotti made to order, vegetables done many ways, and more. ✉ *Calle Cavalli, 4081 San Marco,* ☎ *041/5228945. Closed Sun.*

Aciugheta. A mediocre pizzeria-trattoria, Aciugheta (Tiny Anchovy) leads a secret life as an enoteca, with some of the best bottles in town. Show up in the late afternoon and let wine expert Gianni Bonaccorsi guide you. Cicheti and a variety of other tasty bites—including tiny pizzas, stuffed red peppers, and a fine selection of cheeses—will keep you from going hungry between sips. ✉ *Campo SS. Filippo e Giacomo, 4357 Castello,* ☎ *041/5224292.*

Candela del Bomba. This neighborhood bacaro with a tiny inner garden and a long communal table is frequented by the gondolieri operating the nearby traghetto. Choose from a selection of "green" cicheti, made with seasonal produce, plus the usual Venetian fish snacks and *soppressa* (fresh sausage). ✉ *Calle dell'Oca, off the Strada Nova, 4297 Cannaregio,* ☎ *041/2411146. Closed Mon. and Aug.*

Cantina Do Mori. This bacaro par excellence—cramped but warm and cozy under hanging antique copper pots—has been catering to the workers of the Rialto market since the 15th century. In addition to young, local whites and reds, the well-stocked cellar offers about 600 more refined labels, many available by the glass. Between sips you can munch on crunchy grissini draped with prosciutto or a few well-stuffed, tiny tramezzini, appropriately called *francobolli* (stamps). Don't leave without tasting the delicious baccalà mantecato. ✉ *Calle dei Do Mori, 429 San Polo,* ☎ *041/5225401. No credit cards. Closed Sun., 3 wks in Aug., and 1 wk in Jan.*

Cantinone. A beautiful 19th-century osteria opposite the *squero* (gondola repair shop) of San Trovaso, this bacaro has original furnishings and one of the best wine cellars in town. No cicheti are offered here, but you won't regret trying one of the huge *panini* (sandwiches) filled with first-rate cheeses and cured pork. It also serves warm *crostini* (toasted bread) topped with tasty spreads like tuna and onion or egg and mushrooms. ✉ *Fondamenta Nani, 992 Dorsoduro,* ☏ *041/5230034. Closed Sun. after 2 PM and 2 in wks Aug.*

Da Dante Alle Alpi. A little oasis thriving in the deserted lands of Castello, this bacaro has the usual fish cicheti, including folpetti *consi* (with olive oil, parsley, and boiled potatoes). ✉ *Corte Nova, near the Scuola di San Giorgio degli Schiavoni, 2877 Castello,* ☏ *041/5285163. Closed Sun.*

Da Pinto. At the heart of the Rialto market and with tables outside, Da Pinto has its cicheti all ready by 8 in the morning. A necessary stop for curious visitors and a second home of stall vendors and clerks of the nearby Tribunale (Court of Justice), this ever-packed bacaro is worth elbowing your way into. ✉ *Campo delle Becarie, 367 San Polo,* ☏ *041/5224599. Closed Mon. and 2 wks in Nov.*

La Mascareta. An offspring of the extremely popular Al Mascaron, the Mascareta offers refined cicheti and a selection of cured pork and cheeses, washed down with quality ombre like Chardonnay Friuliano. This is one of the prettiest bacari in town, and one of the very few that stay open after midnight. ✉ *Calle Lunga Santa Maria Formosa, 5183 Castello,* ☏ *041/5230744. Closed Sun. and over Christmas.*

Minibar da Lele. A three-minute stroll from Piazzale Roma, Lele's 6-by-10-ft place is a real blessing for hungry commuters on their way to work. Not strictly a bacaro, it offers equally good food and wine. Try the freshly made, enormous tramezzini and tiny panini filled with vegetables and cured pork. ✉ *Campo dei Tolentini, 183 Santa Croce,* ☏ *no phone. Closed weekends.*

Osteria da Toni. This unpretentious bar-bacaro sits on the western edge of the Zattere promenade, near a pretty and breezy side canal. It caters mainly to workers from the harbor over the bridge, and you might luck into a dish of homemade lasagna if you show up during lunch hours. ✉ *Fondamenta San Basilio, 1642 Dorsoduro,* ☏ *041/5286899. Closed Mon. and 3 wks Aug.–Sept.*

Rivetta. Except for the loss of the bower in back, nothing seems to have changed at the Rivetta over the course of its long history. Aging customers cluster around the counter, topped by a traditional wine-proof marble slab, while owner-host Franco distributes panini and cicheti. This is perhaps the only bacaro in Venice with opera playing on the hi-fi. ✉ *Calle Sechera, 637/a Santa Croce,* ☏ *no phone. Closed Sun.*

Pasticcerie

Venetians have always loved pastry, not so much in the way of desserts at the end of a meal but rather as something that could go well with a glass of sweet wine or a cup of hot milk. Traditional cookies are sold in *pasticcerie* (pastry shops) throughout town, both by weight and by the piece, and often come in attractive gift packages. Search for *zaeleti* (cookies made with yellow corn flour and raisins), *buranelli* (S-shape cookies from Burano, which also come in heavy, fat rings), or *baicoli* (crunchy cookies made with yeast). Many bakeries also sell pastry by the portion: from apple strudel to *crostate* (jam tarts) and *torta di mandorle* (almond cake)—just point out what you want. After Christmas and through Carnevale, a great deal of frying takes place behind the counter to prepare the tons of pastries annually devoured by Venetians and tourists alike in the weeks preceding Lent: *frittole* (doughnuts with pine nuts, raisins, and candied orange peel, rolled in sugar), best eaten warm; the ribbonlike *galani* (crunchy, fried pastries sprinkled with confectioners' sugar); and walnut-shape *castagnole* (fried pastry dumplings rolled in sugar).

Dal Col. This is a good spot near Piazza San Marco for coffee and pastry on the run, with bar (coffee and beverage) service at the counter. ☒ *Calle dei Fabbri, 1035 San Marco,* ☎ *041/5205529. Closed Sun.*

Dal Mas. Crisp croissants, pastries such as *kranz* (a braided pastry filled with almond paste and raisins) and strudel from the Friuli region, and bar service make this a great place for breakfast. ☒ *Lista di Spagna, 150/a Cannaregio,* ☎ *041/715101. Closed Tues.*

Giovanni Volpe. This is the only place in town that all year round still bakes traditional Venetian-Jewish pastry and delicious *pane azimo* (matzo bread), although the days of operation give it away that the shop is not kosher. ☒ *Calle del Ghetto Vecchio, 1143 Cannaregio,* ☎ *041/715178. Closed Sun. and Wed. afternoon.*

Harry's Dolci. With tables outside in warm weather and an elegant room inside, Harry's makes for a perfect break while exploring the Giudecca, or fill your bag to go. ☒ *Fondamenta San Biagio 773, Giudecca,* ☎ *041/5208337. Closed Tues. and Nov.–Mar.*

Maggion. Make the trip to the Lido even in bad weather for celebrated, custom-made fruit tarts (to be ordered one day ahead; no bar service). ☒ *Via Dardanelli 48, Lido,* ☎ *041/5260836. Closed Mon.–Tues.*

Marchini. The best-known and most expensive pasticceria in town has a fantastic display of tarts and gifts (no bar service). ☒ *Ponte San Maurizio, 2769 San Marco,* ☎ *041/5229109. Closed Tues.*

Rizzardini. This is the tiniest and prettiest pastry shop in Venice, with a counter dating from the late 18th century. Frittole and *pastine di riso* (pastry with a creamy rice filling) are especially good. ☒ *Campiello dei Meloni, 1415 San Polo,* ☎ *041/5223835. Closed Tues.*

Rosa Salva. Headquarters of one of the oldest pasticcerie in town, this small shop has a wide selection of pastry and savory snacks as well as bar service at the counter. ☒ *Calle Fiubera, 951 San Marco; Campo San Luca, 4589 San Marco;* ☎ *041/5210544; 041/5225385. Closed Sun.*

Tonolo. Students from the nearby Università di Ca' Foscari crowd the counter at Tonolo, which makes for a nice break while visiting the Frari district. ☒ *Calle San Pantalon, 3764 Dorsoduro,* ☎ *041/5237209. Closed Sun. 1 PM–Mon. Oct.–May, and Sun.–Mon. June–Sept.*

Vio. Besides the usual selection of small pastry and drinks, here you can get a piece of *crostata di marroni* (chestnut tart) or a bag of spicy cookies made with chili. ☒ *Fondamenta Rio Marin, 890 Santa Croce,* ☎ *041/718523. Closed Wed.*

Gelaterie

So the story goes that Marco Polo "imported" a dessert called *panna in ghiaccio* (literally, "cream on ice"), a brick of frozen cream between wafers, from China. Although there is no historical evidence to prove this, several local *gelaterie* (gelato shops) make this supposed "ancestor" of gelato, but you'll have to ask around for it, because it's almost never kept on display. Gelato, like pizza, tends to be better prepared in central and southern Italy, but you can enjoy some fairly good gelato in Venice, although you shouldn't expect to discover anything out of this world. On a hot summer day, nothing is better than a cup of fruit-flavor gelato to restore your energy: light and refreshing, it will help you go that extra mile before you call it a day. Most gelaterie are open nonstop from mid-morning to late evening, and some keep longer business hours in the summer.

Boutique del Gelato. Good value and a large choice of flavors have won this gelateria a dedicated following. ✉ *Salizzada San Lio, 5727 Castello,* ☎ *041/5223283. Closed Jan.*

Caffè Paolin. The morning sun draws crowds of all ages and nationalities to take a seat on busy Campo Santo Stefano and enjoy a little cup at this favorite bar-gelateria. Ask for an extra topping of whipped cream and *amarene* (sour cherries). ✉ *Campo Santo Stefano, 3464 San Marco,* ☎ *041/5220710. Closed Sat.*

Da Titta. On the Lido, strategically located on the main drag between the vaporetto stop and the most central beaches, Titta is one of the oldest gelaterie in Venice. Get your receipt at the *cassa* (register) for a cone to go, or enjoy one of the special combinations while swinging in a chair under the trees that line the Gran Viale. It also has bar service. ✉ *Gran Viale Santa Maria Elisabetta 61, Lido,* ☎ *041/5260359. Closed Nov.–early Mar.*

Gelateria Ca' d'Oro. Here you'll find the usual array of flavors, plus panna in ghiaccio and some chocolate-covered specials in the freezer on the side of the counter. ✉ *Strada Nova, near Campo Santi Apostoli, 4273/b Cannaregio,* ☎ *041/5228982.*

Gelateria Il Doge. This popular take-out gelateria, just off Campo Santa Margherita, offers a good selection of flavors, from a few low-calorie options to the extrarich *strabon* (Venetian for "more than good," made with cocoa, espresso, and chocolate-covered almonds), as well as granitas in summer. It's open late most of the year. ✉ *Campo Santa Margherita, 3058/a Dorsoduro,* ☎ *041/5234607. Closed Nov.–Feb.*

Le Café. On Campo Santo Stefano across from Paolin, with see-and-be-seen tables outside year-round, Le Café is the Häagen Dazs outpost in Venice and something of a nightspot. It also has bar service and afternoon tea and offers a variety of hot chocolate drinks and desserts. ✉ *Campo Santo Stefano, 2797 San Marco,* ☎ *041/5237201.*

Nico. With an enviable terrace on the Zattere, Nico is the city's gelateria with a view. The house specialty is the *gianduiotto,* a brick of dark chocolate ice cream flung into a tall glass filled with freshly whipped cream. It also has bar service. ✉ *Zattere, 922 Dorsoduro,* ☎ *041/5225293. Closed Thurs. mid-Oct.–Apr.*

3 LODGING

Whether you are staying in a grand hotel
or budget find, Venetian magic still lingers
when you retire for the night. Many Venetian
hotel rooms are swathed in brocades and
glitter with Murano chandeliers. Even in the
less grand *pensioni* you stand a chance of
finding antiques, Persian carpets, and a
lovely canal view. No music or satellite TV
to keep you company? Just open the
window and listen to the gondoliers'
serenades or watch the ebb and flow
of city life in the campo below.

E VERYONE LOVES VENICE, and hotels here cater to all tastes and price ranges. Deluxe and upscale hotels are often filled with antiques and art collections and retain much of the feel of the past, with coffered ceilings, frescoes, stucco, and fireplaces in the best rooms. Renovations are usually made as discreetly as possible, wisely paying respect to Gothic and Renaissance structures. With a few exceptions, there's a widespread dislike for modern design among Venetian hoteliers, and even the moderately priced establishments usually opt for copies made in the 18th-century Venetian style. This means curvaceous, carved furnishings lacquered in soft colors—pale yellow and green are big favorites—with gilded or flowery decorations.

By Carla Lionello

Additional reviews by Robert Andrews

Before choosing a hotel, decide in advance what's important to you and don't be afraid to ask detailed questions. The staff at most Venetian hotels speaks English. Most hotels are housed in old buildings, and preservation laws prohibit elevators in some, so ask ahead if an elevator is vital to you. Space is at a premium, and even exclusive hotels have some small, dowdy Cinderella-type rooms. Rooms tend to be different even on the same floor: windows with canal views and windows looking onto bleak alleyways are both common. In the $–$$ price categories, hotels may not have lounge areas, and some rooms may be cramped. Bathrooms are also on the small side (tubs are considered a luxury) but are usually well equipped with courtesy sets, hair dryers, and towel warmers.

Carpeted floors are very rare, so pack a pair of slippers if you dislike wood and marble under your bare feet. Air-conditioning can be essential if you suffer in summer heat; note that some hotels charge a supplement for it. Although the city has no cars, it does have boats plying the canals and pedestrians chattering in the streets, even late at night, so ask for a quiet room if noise bothers you. During the summer months, don't leave your room lights on *and* your window wide open at night: mosquitoes can descend en masse.

The busiest times for hotels are spring and autumn, December 20 to January 2, and the two weeks during Carnevale. You can save off-season—November to March, excluding Christmas and Carnevale—but prices remain generally high relative to those in other Italian towns, while quality and service often are not. Double-booking is not uncommon, so always ask for a written confirmation of your reservation with a description of your special requirements, if any (tub or shower, first or top floor, and so on). Planning your trip four to five months ahead will grant you freedom of room choice, and although in Venice you cannot go terribly wrong in terms of "good" areas to stay (as long as it's not on the mainland), each neighborhood offers different advantages. You must always book well in advance.

If you don't have reservations, try your luck at **AVA** (Venetian Hoteliers Association; ☎ 041/5228004 for administration), which will make same-day reservations for those who come in person to its booths at Piazzale Roma (☎ 041/5231397), open daily 9 AM–10 PM, €4.00 commission; inside the Santa Lucia train station (☎ 041/715288 and 041/715016), open daily 8 AM–9 PM, €0.50 commission; and at the Marco Polo Airport (☎ 041/5415133), open daily 9 AM–10 PM, €2.00 commission. A deposit, which will be deducted from your hotel bill, is required to hold the room (€11.00–€47.00 per person; V and MC accepted). Alternatively, Venezia Sì offers a free reservation service over the phone: ☎ 800/843006 toll-free in Italy Mon.–Sat. 9 AM–7 PM; ☎ 0039/0415222264 or FAX 0039/0415221242 from abroad). Many hotels accept reservations on-line; the handy Web site (WEB www.veniceinfo. it) offers free information (with pictures) about most hotels in town.

It is *essential* to know how to get to your hotel when you arrive, as transport can range from arriving in a water taxi or gondola direct to the front door to wandering down anonymous alleys and side streets—luggage in hand—with relapses of déjà vu.

CATEGORY	COST*
$$$$	over €260
$$$	€180–€260
$$	€100–€180
$	under €100

All prices are for two people in a standard double room, including tax and service.

For further information about lodging in Venice and the Veneto, *see* Lodging *in* Smart Travel Tips A to Z.

Cannaregio

$$$$ 🏨 **Grand Hotel Palazzo dei Dogi.** Don't read too much into the name: this hotel doesn't look like Palazzo Ducale, nor is it anywhere near Piazza San Marco and the city's other grand hotels. Instead the Palazzo dei Dogi, housed in an old Venetian palace that once served as the French embassy, is a rare "budget five-star." It offers easy access to the northern lagoon, a private garden, lounges with tall Renaissance-style windows, and majestic Murano chandeliers. Well-appointed rooms featuring red Venetian floors, Oriental carpets, and antique-looking furnishings are all here at two-thirds the price of comparable hotels in Venice. The quiet and romantic beauty of the surroundings makes the (relative) splurge worth the stay. ⊠ *Fondamenta Madonna dell'Orto, 3500 Cannaregio, 30121,* ☎ *041/2208111,* FAX *041/722278,* WEB *www.boscolo.com. 70 rooms, 6 suites. Restaurant, bar, breakfast room, air-conditioning, meeting room. AE, DC, MC, V.*

$$$ 🏨 **Giorgione.** Tucked away in a little-visited part of town not far from Rialto Bridge, the Giorgione is a dignified cross between old and new. A 15th-century palace and a modern building with many common areas are set around a private garden with a lily pond. Guest rooms feature golden brocades on the walls, carpeted floors, and unusual furnishings in a Venetian-Chinese style: red lacquered headboards decorated with Oriental motifs, rounded chests of drawers, and nightstands. Some split-level rooms come with the lovely bonus of a small, private balcony. ⊠ *Calle dei Proverbi, near Campo Santi Apostoli, 4587 Cannaregio, 30121,* ☎ *041/5225810,* FAX *041/5239092,* WEB *www.hotelgiorgione. com. 56 rooms. Bar, breakfast room, air-conditioning, billiards. AE, DC, MC, V.*

$$ 🏨 **Abbazia.** The only Venetian abbey turned into a hotel, the Abbazia is not recognizable as such from the outside. The guest rooms are in the former convent—a low, white stucco structure with no exposed brick or Gothic windows. Numerous details survive from the building's religious past: tiny wooden pulpits hang on the walls, and holy-water bowls await around many corners. Brass chandeliers befit the austerity of the place, as does the cream-white and beige decor of the rooms (considerably larger than monks' cells), although some touches of gaudy colors have been added on the tapestries and couches. Breakfast is served in the spacious, relaxing inner garden. There is no elevator. ⊠ *Calle Priuli, 68 Cannaregio, 30121,* ☎ *041/717333,* FAX *041/ 717949,* WEB *www.venezialberghi.com. 40 rooms. Bar, air-conditioning. AE, DC, MC, V.*

$$ ⊞ **Hesperia.** A quiet, friendly hotel housed in a two-floor building (no elevator) just across from the Jewish Ghetto, the Hesperia is within walking distance to the train station but also safely removed from the noise and commercial clutter. Half the rooms offer a beautiful view of the wide (and clean) Cannaregio Canal. The decor doesn't lend much atmosphere, with basic furniture, spare tapestry in pastel shades, and humble, black-and-white versions of Venetian floors, but the space is less cramped than in comparable hotels. Its not-so-central location makes it a possibility when the rest of town is booked solid. ⊠ *Calle Riello, 459 Cannaregio, 30121,* ☎ *041/715251,* ℻ *041/715112. 15 rooms, 13 with bath. Restaurant. AE, DC, MC, V.*

$ ⊞ **Bernardi Semenzato.** This is a particularly inviting little place just
★ off Strada Nova and near the gondola ferry to the Rialto market. Rooms are well maintained, with exposed ceiling beams, matching headboard-bedspread sets, and tiled bathrooms. The nearby *dipendenza* (annex) has more the feeling of a private apartment, with large rooms featuring inlaid wooden floors, Murano chandeliers, and several 19th-century antiques. ⊠ *Calle dell'Oca, 4366 Cannaregio, 30121,* ☎ *041/5211052,* ℻ *041/5222424. 24 rooms, 14 with bath. Air-conditioning. AE, MC, V. Closed 2 wks Nov.–Dec. and 2 wks before Carnevale.*

$ ⊞ **Minerva e Nettuno.** This friendly, family-run place located near the train station is popular with backpackers and Italian families. It offers spotless rooms with solid wood furniture. The "vippina" treatment for €20 extra entitles you to a soft bath robe, and your own copy of a booklet with literary extracts about Venice, and lunch or dinner at I Quattro Rusteghi, located in the heart of the Jewish Ghetto. ⊠ *Lista di Spagna, 230 Cannaregio, 30121,* ☎ *041/715968,* ℻ *041/5242139. 27 rooms, 11 with bath. AE, DC, MC, V.*

$ ⊞ **Rossi.** The rather cantankerous owner stands guard at the reception desk against large groups and has not made this hotel popular with travel agents or group tours. Most of the clientele is made up of guests who appreciate the reasonable price and the convenient, if not central, location not far from the train station. Rooms are comfortable and clean, with tile floors and dark, solid wood furniture. Some face an adjacent private garden that houses a colony of songbirds, others the dead-end street below. Skip the house breakfast and instead take advantage of the hotel's vicinity to Cannaregio's best pastry shop, Dal Mas. ⊠ *Off Lista di Spagna, 262 Cannaregio, 30121,* ☎ *041/715164,* ℻ *041/717784. 14 rooms. MC, V.*

$ ⊞ **Santa Lucia.** Set in a narrow alleyway just off the Lista di Spagna—steps from the train station and a stone's throw from a vaporetto stop—this small and plain hotel makes a quiet oasis in the midst of the hustle and bustle. The best feature is the surprisingly spacious garden, where you can picnic (there's a fountain for washing fruit) or take breakfast. Rooms (some without private bathroom) are simply furnished but benefit from facing the garden. ⊠ *Calle della Misericordia, 358 Cannaregio, 30121,* ☎ *041/715180,* ℻ *041/710610. 15 rooms, 9 with bath. AE, DC, MC, V. Closed Jan. 10–Feb. 10.*

Castello

$$$$ ⊞ **Colombina.** True romantics will opt to arrive at this hotel by gondola or water taxi. Newly opened in 1999, the hotel—just steps from Piazza San Marco—has exquisite rooftop views over the Ponte dei Sospiri. Rooms are spacious and elegant, and the predominant tone is old Venetian, though modern comforts are not sacrificed. ⊠ *Calle del Rimedio, 4416 Castello, 30122,* ☎ *041/2770525,* ℻ *041/2776044,* ▦ *www.hotelcolombina.com. 32 rooms. Bar, breakfast room, meeting room. AE, DC, MC, V.*

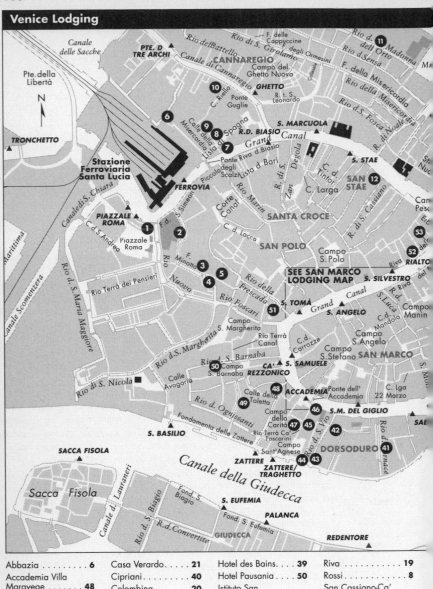

SAN MICHELE ▲ Cimitero San Michele

0 ———————— 440 yards
0 ———————— 400 meters

ITALY

Sacca della Misericordia

Canale delle Navi

Canale delle Navi

FOND. NOVE ▲

Racchetta
Fondamente
Rio S. Caterina
R. d. Gesuiti Nove
R. d. Testa C. d. Squero
R. dei Mendicanti
Rio della Panada

OSPEDALE CIVILE ▲

CELESTIA

14
13
Rio d. Santi
od.
eria

Apostoli
R. d. S. Marina

Barbaria delle Tole
Giustina

R. d. S. Francesco

Canale d. Galeazze

Ponte di Rialto

22

Campo Santa Maria Formosa

Ruga Giuffa

Campo San Lorenzo

C. Lion

Campo San Zaccaria

CASTELLO

Darsena Grande

Rio d. Vergini

15 16 17
18 19 20 21

R. d. S. Severo
R. S. Lorenzo

C. d. Bande

C. d. Furlani

R. d. Scudi d. Gorne

Rio d. S. Daniele

S. Pietro

San Pietro

Fabbri
Mercerie R. d. Fava
Merzerie

See Inset

Ponte dei Sospiri

Riva degli

33 34 30
31

R. d. Pietà
R. d. Greci

R. d. Arsenale

Rio della Tana

Rio d. S. Anna

i

Piazza San Marco

S. ZACCARIA ▲

Molo

PIETÀ ▲

ARSENALE ▲

32

V. Garibaldi

R. d. S. Giuseppe

S. MARCO GIARDINETTI ▲

MARCO RARESSO

S. MARCO GIARDINETTI

C. d. Vin 23
Rio del Vin 24 28
29 27
25 26

Rio dei Greci

Riva dei Sette Martiri

Riva dei Partigiani

Rio dei Giardini

S. GIORGIO ▲

Riva degli Schiavoni

Canale di S. Marco

Detail

Canale di S. Marco

GIARDINI ▲

ZITELLE ▲

S. Giorgio Maggiore

Fond. delle Zitelle

40 35 — 39

Calle Michelangelo

LIDO ▲

KEY

ℹ️ Tourist Information

▲ Vaporetto stop

$$$$ 🔝 **Danieli.** You'll feel like a doge in Venice's largest luxury hotel, a series of newer buildings set around a 15th-century palazzo built for the Doge Dandolo, all with sumptuous Venetian decor. Rooms with a view of the lagoon are the most prized. The four-story-high lobby is supreme, its chic salons and bar offering relaxation and celebrity sightings. The rooftop terrace restaurant has a heavenly view, but the food is unexceptional. May through October, guests have access to the pool, tennis courts, and private beach of the Hotel Excelsior on the Lido. ☒ *Riva degli Schiavoni, 4196 Castello, 30122,* ☎ *041/5226480,* 🄵🄰🄷 *041/5200208,* WEB *www.luxurycollection.com. 219 rooms, 11 suites. Restaurant, bar, air-conditioning. AE, DC, MC, V.*

$$$$ 🔝 **Londra Palace.** Fine views of the lagoon and the church of San Giorgio floating in the background offer a soothing counterpoint to the plush carpets and costly tapestries in a thousand and one patterns that fill the over-the-top Londra Palace, one of the long-established grand hotels of Venice. Handsome Biedermeier tables, couches, and writing desks in the common areas stand out against the numerous marble columns (apparently needed to support so much weighty luxury). Rooms overlooking the Riva cost 10% more than the smaller, top-floor rooms with mansard ceilings. The hotel's ground-floor restaurant, Do Leoni, offers pricey but solid Venetian cuisine. Extras include a complimentary Mercedes for a one-day excursion to the mainland. ☒ *Riva degli Schiavoni, 4171 Castello, 30122,* ☎ *041/5200533,* 🄵🄰🄷 *041/5225032,* WEB *www.hotelondra.it. 36 rooms, 17 suites. Restaurant, piano bar, air-conditioning. AE, DC, MC, V.*

$$$$ 🔝 **Metropole.** Only a few minutes' stroll from Piazza San Marco, the
★ Metropole is the most intimate and affordable of the top-notch hotels that stretch along the Riva degli Schiavoni. The ample, bright hall is cluttered with oil paintings and enough antiques to fill a dealer's shop, and an impressive collection of old crucifixes, clocks, fans, corkscrews, nutcrackers, and locks is displayed all around. An original *felze* (gondola cabin) is perched on top of some old marble steps. The spacious, carpeted rooms upstairs feature original period furniture, Murano chandeliers, and occasional oddities like intricately carved headboards. ☒ *Riva degli Schiavoni, 4149 Castello, 30122,* ☎ *041/5205044,* 🄵🄰🄷 *041/5223679,* WEB *www.hotelmetropole.com. 67 rooms, 7 suites. Restaurant, bar, air-conditioning. AE, DC, MC, V.*

$$$–$$$$ 🔝 **Bisanzio.** Managed by the Busetti family since 1969, this fine hotel is in a restored 16th-century building, right by the church of La Pietà, where Vivaldi was choirmaster and violin master. The peaceful rooms are decorated in Venetian antique style. Generous buffet breakfasts are served in a bright and airy salon, and a lounge opens onto an old courtyard, close to a private mooring for gondolas and other boats. Better rooms have private balconies. ☒ *Calle della Pietà, 3651 Castello, 30122,* ☎ *041/5203100,* 🄵🄰🄷 *041/5204114,* WEB *www.bisanzio.com. 40 rooms. Restaurant, bar. DC, MC, V.*

$$$–$$$$ 🔝 **Gabrielli-Sandwirth.** Beyond the soft orange stucco-and-stone facade of this 13th-century Gothic palace are rambling marbled halls, an inner dining courtyard, a flower-filled garden, and a large rooftop sun terrace. But ask careful questions before you book: the mazelike parquet passageways lead to some of the most glamorous rooms in town but also to overpriced rooms that are nothing special. In summer avoid those with windows facing the restaurant. The better rooms have a view of the lagoon, inlaid wood floors, antiques, impeccable old-style tapestry, and sparkling Murano chandeliers. ☒ *Riva degli Schiavoni, 4110 Castello, 30122,* ☎ *041/5231580,* 🄵🄰🄷 *041/5209455. 100 rooms. Restaurant, bar, air-conditioning. AE, DC, MC, V.*

$$$-$$$$ ⊞ **Savoia e Jolanda.** The location and views are the best features of this hotel, facing San Giorgio Maggiore on one side, the church of San Zaccaria on the other. All guest rooms are decorated with sumptuous tapestry and Murano glass chandeliers. Some rooms are designated no-smoking, and most have balconies; the less expensive rooms are in the new annex close by. ⊠ *Riva degli Schiavoni, 4187 Castello, 30122,* ☎ *041/5206644,* FAX *041/5207494,* WEB *www.hotelsavoiajolanda.com. 83 rooms. Restaurant, bar, no-smoking rooms. AE, DC, MC, V. Closed Jan.*

$$$ ⊞ **Da Bruno.** A fairly priced hotel in a very central location, Da Bruno is just a five-minute walk from Piazza San Marco and the Rialto. Rooms are simple and well maintained, done up in Venetian style with chairs and bed stands in carved wood, mirrors set in glass frames, and glass chandeliers. You can sip hot and cold drinks on the *terrazzino* (terrace) upstairs in perfect quiet—it's so tiny it holds just one table (first come, first served). There are two floors but no elevator, and if you find it picturesque to watch the flow of pedestrians from your window, ask for a room with a view of the Salizzada. ⊠ *Salizzada San Lio, 5726/a Castello, 30122,* ☎ *041/5230452,* FAX *041/5221157,* WEB *www.hoteldabruno.it. 32 rooms. Bar. AE, DC, MC, V.*

$$$ ⊞ **Santa Marina.** In the small neighborhood campo that's home to this hotel, five minutes from the Rialto Bridge, you will probably see more Venetians than tourists passing by. Immaculate rooms are outfitted with pastel colors and lacquered Venetian-style furniture. There are no sitting areas, but in summer a cheerful veranda is set up on the square and breakfast is served behind rows of pink geraniums by the kind and helpful staff. ⊠ *Campo Santa Marina, 6068 Castello, 30122,* ☎ *041/5239202,* FAX *041/5200907,* WEB *www.hotelsantamarina.it. 20 rooms. Breakfast room, air-conditioning. AE, DC, MC, V.*

$$$ ⊞ **Scandinavia.** Central but off the main tourist arteries, the Scandinavia is housed in a building dating from the 11th century. Despite the name, the rooms are done in Venetian style, with brocade tapestry and Murano chandeliers. The top suite has a beautiful, private, covered veranda with a view of the nearby church. Ask for air-conditioning, as it's only available in some rooms. ⊠ *Campo Santa Maria Formosa, 5240 Castello, 30122,* ☎ *041/5223507,* FAX *041/5235232,* WEB *www.scandinaviahotel.com. 33 rooms, 1 suite. Breakfast room, air-conditioning (some). AE, MC, V.*

$$ ⊞ **Al Piave.** This is a stylish little hotel with modest rates, set on a busy street but not too noisy inside. Rooms are a bit cramped but tastefully furnished, though with no views to speak of. Breakfast is included in the price. ⊠ *Ruga Giuffa, Campo Santa Maria Formosa, 4838–40 Castello, 30132,* ☎ *041/5285174,* FAX *041/5238512,* WEB *www.elmoro.com/alpiave. 8 rooms. AE, DC, MC, V.*

$$ ⊞ **Bucintoro.** A glorious name for a glorious view, the Bucintoro stands halfway down the promenade from Piazza San Marco to the Isola di Sant'Elena and a few steps away from the Museo Storico Navale (where the original Bucintoro, the doge's ceremonial boat, is on display). Many Venetian hotel brochures show striking panoramas that are visible from only a few choice rooms, but here nearly every room has an expansive view of the lagoon, the Isola di San Giorgio, and the Bacino di San Marco. The decor, however, does not live up to the view: modern wood furniture, plain white walls and bedcovers, fake lace curtains, and linoleum floors. Plus, there is no elevator. Beds, however, are comfortable, and the price is attractive by Venetian standards. ⊠ *Riva San Biagio, 2135 Castello, 30122,* ☎ *041/5223240,* FAX *041/5235224. 28 rooms. No credit cards.*

$$ ⊞ **Campiello.** The good location, old-fashioned appointments, and modest prices are the best reasons to come to this hotel. Marble floors and gracious furnishings add a certain luster to the public rooms, and guest rooms are functional if unexceptional. There is a bar but no restaurant, though plenty of dining choices exist in the neighborhood. ⊠ *Campiello del Vin, 4647 Castello, 30122,* ☎ *041/5205764,* FAX *041/5205798,* WEB *www.hcampiello.it. 15 rooms. Bar. AE, MC, V. Closed Jan.*

$$ 🏨 **Casa Verardo.** Close to the Campo Santa Maria Formosa and just a few minutes from San Marco, this hotel is one of the best bargains in the district. Rooms, three of which have canal views (two others look onto a small courtyard), are spotless and have a predominantly antique tone. There is no restaurant, but you don't need to venture far to find a good selection. ⊠ *Calle della Chiesa, 4765 Castello, 30122,* ☎ *041/5286127,* FAX *041/5232765,* WEB *www.chipsandcolors.com/casaverardo. 9 rooms. MC, V.*

$$ 🏨 **La Residenza.** The word *residenza* in Italian connotes a good deal
★ of aristocratic elegance, and this hotel, with more the feeling of a private noble house than a hotel, does not disappoint. The hall occupies the whole *portego* (entryway) of the patrician apartment of Palazzo dei Badoari-Partecipazi già Gritti and looks almost disproportionately opulent for this quiet hotel. Well-preserved 18th-century stuccowork adorns the ceilings and walls, along with precious oil paintings. Oriental carpets partially hide the beautiful Venetian floor. Breakfast is served on the many coffee tables placed by the couches and armchairs in the hall. Rooms are done up in faux-antique style, and the choice ones overlook the pretty campo below. ⊠ *Campo San Giovanni in Bragora, 3608 Castello, 30122,* ☎ *041/5285315,* FAX *041/5238859. 14 rooms. AE, DC, MC, V.*

$$ 🏨 **Paganelli.** The lagoon views here so impressed Henry James that he wrote the Paganelli up in the preface to his *Portrait of a Lady.* This enchanting small hotel on the waterfront near Piazza San Marco is tastefully decorated in the Venetian style. The quieter annex in Campo San Zaccaria is a former convent, and some rooms preserve the original coffered ceilings. ⊠ *Riva degli Schiavoni, 4687 Castello, 30122,* ☎ *041/5224324,* FAX *041/5239267,* WEB *www.hotelpagnelli.com. 22 rooms, 19 with bath. Bar, breakfast room, air-conditioning. AE, MC, V.*

$$ 🏨 **Wildner.** Right between the superdeluxe Danieli and Londra Palace hotels, this pleasant, unpretentious, family-run pensione enjoys the same views. The rooms are spread over four floors (no elevator), half with a view of San Giorgio and half looking out onto the quiet Campo San Zaccaria. The simple, no-nonsense decor features parquet floors and solid, dark furniture matched by brown leather headboards. Light, white curtains and creamy bedspreads further enhance the Wildner's subtle and sober atmosphere. ⊠ *Riva degli Schiavoni, 4161 Castello, 30122,* ☎ *041/5227463,* FAX *041/5265615,* WEB *www.veneziahotels.com. 16 rooms. Breakfast room, air-conditioning. AE, DC, MC, V.*

$ 🏨 **Doni.** This former palace occupies a prime position on a canal a couple of stone's throws from Piazza San Marco. The rooms at the front look out onto gondolas through ogee windows. It's a family-run place with wooden floors, solid if uninspiring furniture, and old-fashioned wallpaper to match, although some rooms have frescoed ceilings and chandeliers. ⊠ *Fondamenta del Vin, 4656 Castello, 30122,* ☎ FAX *041/5224267; 041/5206682 in Jan. 13 rooms, 3 with bath. AE, DC, MC, V. Closed Jan.*

$ 🏨 **Istituto San Giuseppe.** This religious institution, in an excellent location north of Piazza San Marco, is one of several lodgings in Venice run by nuns. Rooms are spartan in decor but spotless and very quiet, overlooking the inner cloister. Book well ahead, as the unbeatable prices draw crowds, mostly Italians in the know. Curfew is at 11 PM (10:30 in the winter), and no breakfast is served. ⊠ *5402 Castello, 30122,* ☎ *041/5225352,* FAX *041/5224891. 16 rooms. No credit cards.*

$ ⊞ **Riva.** This small hotel, close to San Marco, is at the junction of three canals much used by all manner of Venetian watercraft. Although they are endlessly fascinating to watch, here you take the good with the bad—the passing gondolier at sunset travels the same waters as the buzzing water taxi at dawn. Rooms differ in size, and climbing up to the fourth floor (no elevator) wins you a better view. The decor is typical of Venetian hotels—a mix of Murano chandeliers, 18th-century-style furniture, exposed ceiling beams, and beds lacquered in pastel shades. ⊠ *Ponte dell'Angelo, 5310 Castello, 30122,* ☎ *041/5227034,* FAX *041/5285551. 12 rooms, 10 with bath. No credit cards. Closed mid-Nov.–Carnevale (except 2 wks at Christmas).*

Dorsoduro

$$$ ⊞ **American.** At first sight, it's hard to pick out this quiet, family-run
★ hotel from the houses along the fondamenta: there are no lights, flags, or big signs on the hotel's yellow stucco facade. A hall decorated with antique-style furniture, Oriental carpets, and contemporary images of Venice on the walls leads to a breakfast room reminiscent of a theater foyer, with red velvet chairs and gilded wall lamps. Rooms vary in size and shape, but sage green and delicate pink fabrics and lacquered Venetian-style furniture are found throughout. Several rooms on the top floor have wooden ceilings, and those facing Rio di San Vio have as many as four windows. ⊠ *Fondamenta Bragadin, 628 Dorsoduro, 30123,* ☎ *041/5204733,* FAX *041/5204048,* WEB *www.hotelamerican. com. 28 rooms. Bar, breakfast room, air-conditioning. AE, DC, MC, V.*

$$$ ⊞ **Hotel Pausania.** From the moment you ascend the grand staircase rising above the fountain of this 14th-century palazzo, you sense the combination of good taste and modern comforts that characterizes Hotel Pausania. Light-shaded rooms are spacious, with comfortable furniture and carpets with rugs thrown over them. Some rooms face the small canal (which can become a bit noisy early in the morning) in front of the hotel, while others look out over the large garden courtyard. The hotel has a convenient car service (€40.00) to and from the airport. ⊠ *Fondamenta Gherardini, 2824 Dorsoduro, 30123,* ☎ *041/5222083,* FAX *041/5222989. 26 rooms. Bar, breakfast room, air-conditioning, airport shuttle. AE, DC, MC, V.*

$$$ ⊞ **Pensione Seguso.** This venerable establishment, run by the third gen-
★ eration of the Seguso family and housed in a modern building with good views of the Giudecca Canal, is the last true pensione in Venice. The required half-board adds character to your stay, with meals served in the impeccable dining room adorned with heirloom silver plate and old wall lamps. Rooms are spare—no TV, minibars, or phones, and some don't have their own bathrooms—but they're decorated with attractive wooden furniture that will charm the flea-market lover in you. Persian rugs, leather couches, and dark-wood paneling set the tone for the intimate reading salon. ⊠ *Zattere, 779 Dorsoduro, 30123,* ☎ *041/5286858; 041/5222472 when closed,* FAX *041/5222340, 36 rooms, 16 with bath. Restaurant, bar. AE, DC, MC, V. MAP. Closed Dec.–Carnevale.*

$$–$$$ ⊞ **Accademia Villa Maravege.** A secret garden awaits just beyond an
★ iron gate, complete with a mini Palladian-style villa, flower beds, stone cupids, and verdant trees—all rarities in Venice. Aptly nicknamed "Villa of the Wonders," this patrician retreat once served as the Russian embassy and was the residence of Katharine Hepburn in the movie *Summertime.* Conservative rooms are outfitted with Victorian-era antiques and fine tapestry. The location is on a promontory where two side canals converge with the Grand Canal, which can be seen from the garden. Book well in advance. ⊠ *Fondamenta Bollani, 1058 Dorsoduro, 30123,*

☎ *041/5210188,* FAX *041/5239152,* WEB *www.pensioneaccademia.it. 27 rooms. Bar, breakfast room, air-conditioning. AE, DC, MC, V.*

$$ ⊞ **Agli Alboretti.** Slightly overpriced, the Alboretti is one of the many hotels clustered at the foot of the Ponte dell'Accademia. Its unpretentious, rather small rooms are blessed with plenty of light. Their nautical decor, with original pieces taken from old ships' cabins, goes well with the cries of seagulls living along the nearby Giudecca Canal. Some steep climbing might be part of your stay, as there are four floors and no elevator. In warm weather, breakfast is served in an inner courtyard under a rose bower. ⊠ *Rio Terrà Foscarini, 884 Dorsoduro, 30123,* ☎ *041/5230058,* FAX *041/5210158,* WEB *www.aglialboretti.com. 20 rooms. Restaurant, bar, air-conditioning. AE, DC, MC, V.*

$$ ⊞ **Antica Locanda Montin.** Only a street lamp hanging above the entrance marks this waterway inn, which, in spite of its low-key looks, won the hearts of Ruskin, Guggenheim, and Italian poet Gabriele d'Annunzio. Without a doubt, part of its charm lay in the trattoria on the ground floor, which once served delicious Venetian food. Rooms are a collection of Venetian floors, worn decor, cheap furniture, and good contemporary paintings left by the many artists who have stayed here in years past. A romantic view of the canal or the pretty internal garden and a durable reputation as a den for artists and literati keep the Locanda full all year long. ⊠ *Fondamenta delle Eremite, 1147 Dorsoduro, 30123,* ☎ *041/5227151,* FAX *041/5200255. 11 rooms, 5 with bath. Restaurant. AE, DC, MC, V.*

$$ ⊞ **La Calcina.** The Calcina sits in an enviable position along the sunny
★ Zattere, with views across the wide Giudecca Canal. You can sunbathe on the *altana* (wooden terrace) or enjoy an afternoon tea in one of the reading corners of the shadowy, intimate hall with flickering candlelight and barely perceptible classical music. A stone staircase (no elevator) leads to the rooms upstairs, with shiny wooden floors, original Art Deco furniture and lamps, and firm beds. Some rooms suffer from a lack of storage space. A courteous staff helps make this one of Venice's most comfortable places to lay your head. The annex nearby offers lower-priced rooms without a view. ⊠ *Zattere 780 Dorsoduro, 30123,* ☎ *041/5206466,* FAX *041/5227045. 42 rooms. Breakfast room, air-conditioning. AE, DC, MC, V.*

$$ ⊞ **Messner.** Located in a modest, two-story palace on a luminous fon-
★ damenta, this is a budget hotel that fulfills all your best expectations. Several rooms, the best featuring Gothic-style balconies, face the clean and sunny *rio* (canal) below. All rooms have sturdy wooden furniture, white curtains, and blue carpeting, plus private bathrooms, hair dryers, satellite TV, and air-conditioning. You can opt for the half-board formula by paying just €13.00 more per day. The annex has 23 lessexpensive rooms without a view. ⊠ *Fondamenta Ca' Balà, 216 Dorsoduro, 30123,* ☎ *041/5227443,* FAX *041/5227266. 33 rooms. Bar, air-conditioning. AE, DC, MC, V. MAP.*

$–$$ ⊞ **Galleria.** For atmosphere and location, this hotel is the gem of its
★ price range, but the secret is out, and you will probably need to book months ahead for the sensational view of the Grand Canal and the Accademia Bridge. Rooms differ in size and shape but are all classically Venetian, with a few whimsical touches, such as huge cane armchairs, faux liberty-style lamps, and sumptuous brocades on the walls. Although there is no breakfast room, a small Italian-style *colazione* (breakfast) of croissants and hot drinks is served in the rooms. The Galleria is a few steps away from the convenient Accademia vaporetto landing. ⊠ *Accademia Bridge, 878/a Dorsoduro, 30123,* ☎ *041/5232489,* FAX *041/5204172,* WEB *www.hotelgalleria.it. 9 rooms, 7 with bath. AE, DC, MC, V.*

$ ⊞ **Locanda Ca' Foscari.** Although an unprepossessing choice, this is a homey and relaxed pensione between Dorsoduro and San Polo where the English-speaking owner will proudly show you to your modest-size but surprisingly well-decorated and comfortable room. Booking ahead may ensure you get one of the few rooms with a pleasant view, and breakfast is included in the tab. ⊠ *Calle della Frescada, 3887/b Dorsoduro, 30123,* ☎ *041/710401; 041/521–1365 when closed,* ℻ *041/710817. 11 rooms, 5 with bath. MC, V. Closed 10 days July–Aug. and Nov. 21–Jan. 21.*

Giudecca

$$$$ ⊞ **Cipriani.** It's impossible to feel stressed in this oasis of stunning rooms and suites, some with garden patios. The hotel launch whisks you to Giudecca from San Marco and back at any hour; those dining at the exceptional Ristorante Harry Cipriani can use it as well. The restored 17th-century-style Palazzo Vendramin is preferable to the main hotel and the Palazzetto, a modern annex facing the Canale della Giudecca. Prices are high even by Venetian standards, but this is the only place in town with such extensive facilities and services, from an Olympic-size pool and tennis courts to cooking courses and fitness programs. ⊠ *Giudecca 10, 30133,* ☎ *041/5207744,* ℻ *041/5207745,* ⒲ *www. hotelcipriani.it. 54 rooms, 50 suites. 2 restaurants, bar, air-conditioning, no-smoking rooms, saltwater pool, massage, sauna, spa, tennis court, health club, solarium, meeting room. AE, DC, MC, V. Closed Dec.– Apr.; Palazzo Vendramin closed 2nd wk Nov.–early Mar.*

Lido

$$$$ ⊞ **Hotel des Bains.** This is a perfect spot to soak up some of the atmosphere in Venice's Lido district. Thomas Mann wrote his haunting novella *Death in Venice* here, and it appeared in the book's film adaptation. The Art Deco tone has survived pretty much intact, making this a favorite stopover for the beautiful people during the Biennale. Rooms are sumptuously furnished, overlooking either the garden or the sea, and the facilities, including the beach, are superb. A minibus links the hotel with the nearby Excelsior, from which water taxis cross to San Marco every 30 minutes. ⊠ *Lungomare Marconi 17, Lido, 30126,* ☎ *041/5265921,* ℻ *041/5260113,* ⒲ *www.sheraton.com. 291 rooms, 1 suite. Restaurant, bar, sauna, tennis court, gym. AE, DC, MC, V. Closed mid-Nov.–mid-Mar.*

$$$$ ⊞ **Quattro Fontane.** This fine hotel in a well-maintained mansion run
★ by a Danish couple offers the serenity of the Lido, although you will be a 15-minute walk and a 20-minute boat ride from Piazza San Marco. Well-decorated rooms, with period furniture and tasteful tapestry, overlook the surrounding garden. Common areas contain an odd collection of mason's aprons, pipes, ex-votos, masks from Jakarta, Roman seals, and seashells. A huge fireplace adds warmth and character in the colder months. After a full day you can relax in the library, stocked with books in many languages. ⊠ *Via delle Quattro Fontane 16, Lido, 30126,* ☎ *041/5260227,* ℻ *041/5260726,* ⒲ *www.quattrofontane. com. 59 rooms. Restaurant, bar, air-conditioning, library, meeting room. AE, DC, MC, V.*

$$$$ ⊞ **Villa Mabapa.** Built as a private house in the 1930s and subsequently converted into a hotel, this lodging is still run by the original owners and conserves its air of a family home. A charming rustic atmosphere prevails, and the shady garden is an excellent spot for an alfresco dinner of classic Venetian dishes. If you're wondering about the name, it's a combination of *mamma, bambini,* and *papa.* ⊠ *Riviera San Nicolò 16, Lido,*

30126, ☎ *041/5260590,* FAX *041/5269441,* WEB *www.villamabapa.it. 69 rooms. Restaurant, bar, meeting room. AE, DC, MC, V.*

$$$$ 🔲 **The Westin Excelsior.** The Excelsior's imposing, Oriental-style building dominates the Lido's beaches for a couple of miles. The green cupolas and Moorish inner courtyard, complete with potted lemon trees and fountains, suggest the southern Mediterranean. No longer a haunt of the noble and famous of the dolce vita days (except during the Biennale), the hotel nonetheless offers the same panache, luxury, and space as ever. Rooms are tastefully modern, done in bright colors, and face either the inner garden or the beach below. Facilities include tennis courts, a pool, and cabanas. A shuttle boat between the hotel and San Zaccaria is at guests' disposal. ⊠ *Lungomare Marconi 41, Lido, 30126,* ☎ *041/5260201,* FAX *041/5267276,* WEB *www.westin.com. 196 rooms, 18 suites. Restaurant, bar, air-conditioning, pool, 6 tennis courts, beach, parking (fee). AE, DC, MC, V. Closed mid-Nov.–mid-Mar.*

$ 🔲 **Le Garzette.** As the only *agriturismo* (working farm with guest accommodations) available in Venice, this place is a bit of an oddity, situated at the greener end of the island about a half hour from San Marco. The quiet guest rooms, some of which have balconies facing the sea, are furnished with 19th century antiques. The restaurant—which is open to nonguests on weekends—takes its ingredients directly from the surrounding orchards and gardens. Bicycles are available free, and the beach is literally steps away. With so few rooms available, you'd do well to book early. ⊠ *Lungomare Alberoni 32, Lido, 30011,* ☎ *041/731078,* FAX *041/2428798,* WEB *www.welcome.to/legarzette. 5 rooms. Restaurant, bicycles. No credit cards. Closed mid-Dec.–mid-Jan.*

San Marco

$$$$ 🔲 **Bauer.** Divided into two wings, the 18th-century Palazzo at the Bauer and the modern Bauer Hotel, this hotel is the last word in luxury, with individually furnished rooms, many with balconies or terraces that afford breathtaking city views. Suites are decorated with designer fabrics, silks, and glassware. The lounge Settimo Cielo (Seventh Heaven), which opens out onto Venice's highest terrace, must be the ultimate breakfast venue. ⊠ *Campo San Moisè, 1459 San Marco, 30124,* ☎ *041/5207022,* FAX *041/5207557,* WEB *www.bauervenezia.it. 196 rooms, 60 suites. Restaurant, hot tub, massage, sauna, spa, health club, dock. AE, DC, MC, V.*

$$$$ 🔲 **Bonvecchiati.** The owner here is a passionate collector of contemporary paintings, and the works adorning the walls contribute to the hotel's character. Adorned in cool shades of blue, green, or salmon, rooms have wooden floors, Oriental rugs, and either smart modern furniture or antique-looking pieces with elaborate carvings. A few small but choice rooms on the fifth floor overlook the domes of the Basilica di San Marco. From sunset to midnight there is intense gondola traffic outside, with noisy singers entertaining tourists. Avoid rooms on lower floors facing the mezzanine terrace restaurant. Prices are in the lower range of the category. ⊠ *Calle Goldoni, 4488 San Marco, 30124,* ☎ *041/5285017,* FAX *041/5285230,* WEB *www.hotelinvenice.it. 87 rooms. Restaurant, bar, air-conditioning. AE, DC, MC, V.*

$$$$ 🔲 **Cavalletto & Doge Orseolo.** The curved, yellow stucco facade was clearly remade in recent times, but this choice spot next to Piazza San Marco has been familiar to travelers and visitors since 1308, when the earliest version of the Cavalletto was founded here under the Latin name Taberna ad Cavaletum. The French windows of the bright hall and breakfast room open onto the largest gondola parking lot in town. The same view is enjoyed from all the "superior" rooms (well worth the supplement), which feature king-size beds and spacious marble bath-

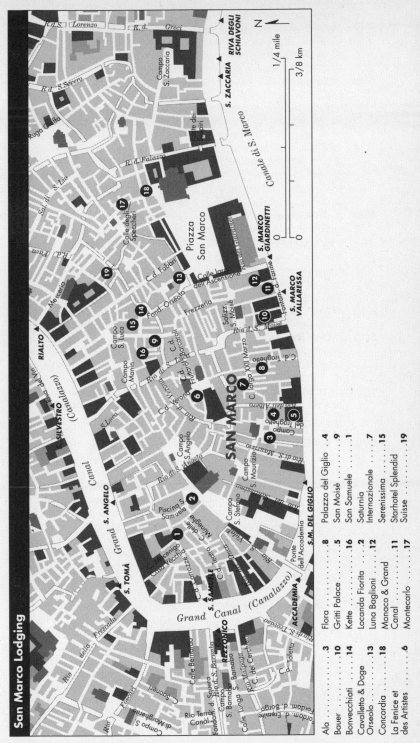

San Marco Lodging

rooms, some with bathtubs. The decor varies from room to room: expect soft colors, warm parquet floors, and lacquered furniture. ⊠ *Calle del Cavalletto, 1107 San Marco, 30124,* ☎ *041/5200955,* FAX *041/ 5238184,* WEB *www.sanmarcohotels.com. 88 rooms, 7 junior suites. Restaurant, bar. AE, DC, MC, V.*

$$$$ ⊡ **Concordia.** Half of the rooms in this attractive, well-run hotel catch a side view of the Basilica di San Marco, as does the spacious breakfast room–bar, where light meals and snacks are served all day. Rooms are decorated with brocade tapestry and have cream, aqua, or peach color schemes. The romantic *mansarda* (rooftop room) has a panoramic view over the Piazza San Marco. The management offers good deals at off-peak times, so check when booking. ⊠ *Calle Larga San Marco, 367 San Marco, 30124,* ☎ *041/5206866,* FAX *041/5206775,* WEB *www. hotelconcordia.com. 54 rooms, 3 suites. Bar, breakfast room, air-conditioning. AE, DC, MC, V.*

$$$$ ⊡ **Gritti Palace.** Queen Elizabeth, Greta Garbo, and Winston Churchill
★ made this their Venetian address. The feeling of being in an aristocratic private home pervades this legendary hotel, replete with fresh flowers, fine antiques, sumptuous appointments, and old-fashioned service. The dining terrace on the Grand Canal is best enjoyed in the evening when the boat traffic dies down. Guests have access to pool and tennis courts. ⊠ *Campo Santa Maria del Giglio, 2467 San Marco, 30124,* ☎ *041/ 794611,* FAX *041/5200942,* WEB *www.luxurycollection.com. 87 rooms, 6 suites. Restaurant, bar, café, air-conditioning. AE, DC, MC, V.*

$$$$ ⊡ **Luna Baglioni.** Two minutes from San Marco, this handsome hotel has elegant rooms, several with a view of the Grand Canal. Breakfast is served in a salon fit for a king, adorned with frescoes by the school of Tiepolo, 18th-century furniture, and Venetian floors. Most suites are lavish affairs, with fireplaces, jetted tubs, and terraces. Restaurant Canova offers modern Venetian cuisine. ⊠ *1243 San Marco, 30124,* ☎ *041/5289840,* FAX *041/5287160,* WEB *www.baglionihotels.com. 111 rooms, 7 suites. Restaurant, air-conditioning. AE, DC, MC, V.*

$$$$ ⊡ **Monaco & Grand Canal.** Between the view onto the Bacino di San
★ Marco and the touches of elegance and comfort found at this luxurious hotel, you may find little motivation to leave. The common rooms on the ground floor are flooded with the shimmering light coming off the lagoon, and the piano bar, with velvety light-sage couches, comes alive every night. Rooms are spacious but warm and intimate, with carpeted floors, satin-lined walls, handsome, antique-style furniture, and ample terra-cotta bathrooms. The half-board option, with meals à la carte in the worthwhile Grand Canal restaurant, is a good choice. ⊠ *Calle Vallaresso, 1325 San Marco, 30124,* ☎ *041/5200211,* FAX *041/ 5200501. 64 rooms, 7 suites. Restaurant, bar, piano bar. AE, DC, MC, V. MAP.*

$$$$ ⊡ **Saturnia Internazionale.** You'll find lots of old-fashioned charm and tranquillity in this historic palace near Piazza San Marco. Beamed ceilings, damask-hung walls, and authentic Venetian decor impart real character to the comfortable rooms and salons. Many rooms are endowed with glamorous, large bathrooms. La Caravella restaurant, which serves traditional Venetian dishes and haute French cuisine, is of special note. ⊠ *Calle Larga XXII Marzo, 2398 San Marco, 30124,* ☎ *041/5208377,* FAX *041/5207131,* WEB *www.hotelsaturnia.it. 95 rooms. Restaurant, bar, air-conditioning. AE, MC, V.*

$$$$ ⊡ **Starhotel Splendid Suisse.** This hotel in the heart of the Mercerie is made up of two buildings connected by a suspended bridge. The upper floors are high enough to offer panoramic views of town. Well equipped to accommodate business travelers, small conferences, and groups, the Suisse stands out for tasteful decor, a blend of voluptuous quilted black leather couches, angular cherrywood furniture, and low-pile carpets in

neutral colors. In some rooms the light ocher walls are contrasted by exposed wooden beams. A computer in the entrance hall is available for you to check e-mail. ✉ *Merceria San Zulian, 760 San Marco, 30124,* ☎ *041/5200775,* FAX *041/5286498,* WEB *www.starhotels.it. 158 rooms, 8 suites. Restaurant, bar, air-conditioning, meeting room. AE, DC, MC, V.*

$$$ ⊡ **Ala.** The Ala is in the "aristocratic" part of town, between Piazza San Marco and Campo Santo Stefano a few steps from the Santa Maria del Giglio vaporetto and traghetto stop. The owner's collection of armor is displayed in the hall and sitting rooms, where daily English-language newspapers are at your disposal. Some rooms are large, with coffered ceilings and old-style furnishings; others are smaller with more modern decor. Most come with a view of either the campo below or of the side canal. ✉ *2494 San Marco, 30124,* ☎ *041/5208333,* FAX *041/5206390,* WEB *www.hotelala.it. 85 rooms. Breakfast room, air-conditioning. AE, DC, MC, V.*

$$$ ⊡ **Flora.** This hotel has what many in this category lack: plenty of sitting rooms and a pretty courtyard. It's in a quiet but central spot near San Moisè and Piazza San Marco. Rooms have Venetian period decor and are a bit dark; a handful are small, with tiny bathrooms. Ask for a room with a view of the courtyard or the garden. ✉ *Calle Bergamaschi, off Calle Larga XXII Marzo, 2283 San Marco, 30124,* ☎ *041/5205844,* FAX *041/5228217,* WEB *www.hotelflora.it. 44 rooms. Bar, air-conditioning. AE, DC, MC, V.*

$$$ ⊡ **Kette.** Positioned next to a canal, this hotel has a busy feel on account of the tour groups passing through. It's clean and efficiently run, even if the meager facilities lend a somewhat functional feel. Guest rooms are on the small side, but the swank marble bathrooms, brocade tapestry, and Murano glass chandeliers help to compensate for the shortage of space. You might prefer to take your morning cappuccino and pastry from one of the numerous bars in the neighborhood, though the hotel bill includes breakfast. ✉ *Piscina San Moisè, 2053 San Marco, 30124,* ☎ *041/5207766,* FAX *041/5228964,* WEB *www.hotelkette. com. 70 rooms. Bar. AE, DC, MC, V.*

$$$ ⊡ **La Fenice et des Artistes.** The timeworn facade of this hotel on Campo San Fantin hides a rather unusual internal layout. The building was once divided into a fashionable atelier, a warehouse, and private apartments. Rambling corridors and common areas lead to the rooms, some of which overlook the two inner gardens, where breakfast is served in fair weather. Try to reserve an antique-style room (several have balconies), as a few bedrooms have modern, rather disappointing furniture. Ask in advance for air-conditioning, which isn't available in all rooms. ✉ *Campo San Fantin, 1936 San Marco, 30124,* ☎ *041/5232333,* FAX *041/5203721. 65 rooms. Bar, meeting room. AE, DC, MC, V.*

$$$ ⊡ **Montecarlo.** There's plenty of atmosphere in this hotel housed in a 17th-century palazzo behind Piazza San Marco and only a short stroll from the Rialto Bridge. Typical Venetian-style rooms are well equipped with modern comforts, including air-conditioning and satellite TV. Chandeliers and paintings by old Venetian masters add to the refined ambience. The well-regarded Antico Pignolo restaurant serves traditional Venetian fare. ✉ *Calle degli Specchieri, 463 San Marco, 30124,* ☎ *041/5207144,* FAX *041/5207789. 48 rooms. Restaurant, bar, air-conditioning. AE, DC, MC, V.*

$$$ ⊡ **Palazzo del Giglio.** A whole block of orange stucco houses overlooks Campo Santa Maria del Giglio at this hotel and short-term residence with modern, if not too charming, decor. Guest rooms lack views and are rather overpriced in high season. The real appeal lies in the apartments, which have hotel service, house two to six people, and offer

views of the Campo below. The larger units are outfitted with two bed-rooms, two bathrooms, a spacious common area, and a fully equipped kitchen. One features an altana from which you can converse with the trumpet-playing angel perched on the church's facade across the street. It's essential to reserve months ahead. ⊠ *Campo Santa Maria del Giglio, 2462 San Marco, 30124,* ☎ *041/2719111,* ℻ *041/5205158,* WEB *www.hotelgiglio.com. 12 rooms, 12 apartments. Air-conditioning. AE, DC, MC, V.*

$$$ ⚏ **San Moisè.** The closest you can get to staying in an 18th-century
★ Venetian house, the San Moisè deserves special mention for its warm decor, which in this part of town usually comes at a much higher price. Rooms share the same motifs as the cozy portego: Oriental rugs, glass chandeliers, rich tapestries, handsome furniture, and in some cases pleasantly irregular dimensions. Some rooms have a view of the rio, and others face a small inner courtyard, home to a lush wisteria tree. There is no elevator, but you won't have to climb any higher than to the second floor. ⊠ *Piscina San Moisè, 2058 San Marco, 30124,* ☎ *041/5203755,* ℻ *041/5210670,* WEB *www.sanmoise.it. 16 rooms. Bar, air-conditioning. AE, DC, MC, V.*

$$ ⚏ **Serenissima.** Run with pride by the Dal Borgo family since 1960, the Serenissima offers quiet rooms in the heart of town at very fair prices. An effort to create some warmth has been made in the common areas, but the waxed wooden floors, Oriental rugs, and dark-burgundy leather couches are too new to create any real atmosphere. A similar style characterizes the guest rooms, which, within their category, stand out for good maintenance and comfort. As busy Calle Goldoni below does not count as a view, your best bets are the quieter rooms at the back, all facing an inner courtyard. ⊠ *Calle Goldoni, 4486 San Marco, 30124,* ☎ *041/5200011,* ℻ *041/5223292,* WEB *www.hotelserenissima. it. 38 rooms. AE, DC, MC, V. Closed mid-Nov.–Carnevale.*

$ ⚏ **Locanda Fiorita.** This welcoming, small hotel is tucked away in a sunny little square near the Ponte dell'Accademia. The entrance is through a vine-covered porch, a section of which belongs to the best guest room. Beamed ceilings give some character to otherwise bland but practical furnishings. Eight of the rooms are in an annex on Campo Santo Stefano. Air-conditioning is available in some rooms. ⊠ *Campiello Novo o dei Morti, 3457/a San Marco, 30124,* ☎ *041/5234754,* ℻ *041/ 5228043,* WEB *www.locandafiorita.com. 18 rooms, 14 with bath. AE, MC, V.*

$ ⚏ **San Samuele.** Near the Grand Canal and Palazzo Grassi, this friendly hotel has clean, sunny rooms in surprisingly good shape for the price. Five of the bathrooms, with white and gray-blue tiles, are relatively new, and the walls are painted in crisp, pleasant shades of pale pink or blue. Curtains and bedspreads are made from antique-looking fabrics, and although the furniture is of the boxy modern kind, the owners are gradually adding more interesting-looking pieces. ⊠ *Salizzada San Samuele, 3358 San Marco, 30124,* ☎ ℻ *041/5228045. 10 rooms, 7 with bath. No credit cards.*

San Polo

$$$ ⚏ **Marconi.** With its location next to the Rialto Bridge in the Riva del Vin area—once renowned for its taverns—it is no surprise to learn that the Marconi was itself an *osteria* until its conversion in the 1930s into one of the most elegant hotels in town. Rooms are furnished in an-tique style but equipped with up-to-date facilities. Two of the guest rooms enjoy outstanding views overlooking the Grand Canal, though they are on the small side. The bustling produce market is steps away. ⊠ *Ri-alto, Riva del Vin, 729 San Polo, 30125,* ☎ *041/5222068,* ℻ *041/*

5229700, WEB *www.hotelmarconi.it. 26 rooms. Restaurant, bar, air-conditioning, minibars. AE, DC, MC, V.*

$$ ⊞ **Sturion.** You might recognize the facade of the hotel in a painting by Carpaccio that hangs at the Gallerie dell'Accademia. Once frequented by merchants who traded at the nearby Rialto market, this small, family-run hotel has rooms done in red-and-gold brocade (two overlooking the Grand Canal) and a small but pretty breakfast room. Some rooms are reserved for nonsmokers. ⊠ *Calle del Sturion, 679 San Polo, 30125,* ☎ *041/5236243,* FAX *041/5228378,* WEB *www. locandasturion.com. 11 rooms. Breakfast room, air-conditioning, no-smoking room. AE, DC, MC, V.*

Santa Croce

$$$$ ⊞ **Sofitel.** Housed inside a new, well-maintained pink palazzo just 300 yards from Piazzale Roma and with access to all main vaporetto lines, the Sofitel is the luxury hotel of choice for travelers with children, as kids under 12 stay free in their parents' bedroom. You'll find an efficient staff and modern comforts, including soft carpets, noise insulation, and spacious bathrooms with tubs and windows. The tasteful decor mixes wooden furniture, large mirrors, glass chandeliers, and pastel-shade walls. The hotel organizes "secret itineraries" through the lesser-known parts of town, boat excursions in the lagoon, and day trips to the Palladian villas (for a fee). ⊠ *Giardini Papadopoli, 245 Santa Croce, 30135,* ☎ *041/710400,* FAX *041/710394,* WEB *www.sofitel.com. 95 rooms, 5 suites. Restaurant, bar, air-conditioning. AE, DC, MC, V.*

$$$ ⊞ **Al Sole.** "The Sun" overlooks the sunny Rio dei Tolentini, where one of the last fruit-selling boats in Venice sets up shop, and is housed in the striking Gothic Ca' Marcello, dating from the 15th century. Plants and fresh flowers, along with a superb life-size model of a galley, decorate the hotel's lovely Venetian portego. Compact rooms have simple Venetian chandeliers, nightstands painted with mock doge designs, and views of either the rio or inner garden; some have old wooden ceilings. This is a particular bargain in winter, but the restaurant is open from June through September only. ⊠ *Fondamenta Minotto, 136 Santa Croce, 30135,* ☎ *041/710844,* FAX *041/714398,* WEB *www. alsolepalace.com. 62 rooms. Restaurant, bar, air-conditioning. AE, DC, MC, V.*

$$$ ⊞ **San Cassiano-Ca' Favretto.** This 16th-century red-stucco and stone
★ building was home to the families of several doges before being purchased by the Venetian painter Giacomo Favretto (1849–87). The spacious portego preserves the original 20-ft beamed ceiling, from which hang two huge Murano chandeliers fit for a royal ballroom; old tapestries arranged high on the walls add glamour and a medieval feel. All rooms are furnished with either real antiques or well-made replicas. Nearly every window frames a great view; those facing the Grand Canal open on the lacy facade of the Ca' d'Oro, which at sunset picks up magic shades of pink. ⊠ *Calle della Rosa, 2232 Santa Croce, 30135,* ☎ *041/5241768,* FAX *041/721033,* WEB *www.sancassiano.it. 35 rooms. Bar, breakfast room, air-conditioning. AE, DC, MC, V.*

$$$ ⊞ **Santa Chiara.** You can drive your car to the entrance of the Santa Chiara and yet still find yourself staying in a room overlooking the Grand Canal. The hotel was built where the convent and church of Santa Croce once stood; a surviving wall is incorporated into the present-day structure. Wood-beam ceilings and red-and-white check floors give character to the common areas. Rooms are bright and well appointed and generally larger than average within this price category. Some windows open on the Piazzale Roma, while others have a view of the Grand Canal. The most coveted room is the attic, with a private terrace and panoramic

view. ✉ *Piazzale Roma, 548 Santa Croce, 30135,* ☎ *041/5206955,* FAX *041/5228799,* WEB *www.hotelsantachiara.it. 28 rooms. Bar, air-conditioning, free parking. AE, DC, MC, V.*

$$ ⊡ **Falier.** The name Falier (recalling a former doge) is a bit misleading for this simple, decidedly undogelike hotel. In fact, if it weren't for the red-and-white floor of the portego, the decor wouldn't be at all Venetian. Terra-cotta floors and basic wood furniture recall a budget mountain chalet; in most rooms the feeling is enhanced by rustic wooden ceilings and short curtains. Bathrooms are on the small side and have showers only. Views are not great, and the first floor is rather dark. The exception is room 41, with a lovely little terrace set amid the neighboring roofs. ✉ *Salizzada San Pantalon, 130 Santa Croce, 30135,* ☎ *041/710882,* FAX *041/5206554,* WEB *www.hotelfalier.com. 19 rooms. Bar, air-conditioning. AE, DC, MC, V.*

$ ⊡ **Dalla Mora.** On a quiet calle beyond the main flow of traffic, this
★ hotel occupies two simple, well-maintained houses, both with a view. The cheerful, tiny entry hall leads upstairs to a terrace lined with potted geraniums, the perfect place to catch the breeze on summer evenings. Rooms are all quite spacious, with basic wooden furniture and tile floors. The annex across the calle has rooms without private bathrooms and others with only showers and sinks. The excellent price and good views make this an especially attractive place to stay if you're on a budget. ✉ *Off Salizzada San Pantalon, 42 Santa Croce, 30123,* ☎ *041/ 710703,* FAX *041/723006. 14 rooms, 6 with bath. AE, DC, MC, V.*

4 NIGHTLIFE AND THE ARTS

Why descend into a cramped Venetian nightspot when the setting sun turns the city itself into an immensely romantic open-air stage? Because *ombre*, *cicheti*, and live music until 2 AM might just be as Venetian as all those canals. For an unforgettable night, try a concert of Baroque music performed in 18th-century costume, a late meal at an *osteria musicale*, and a toast to the rising sun from Isola di San Giorgio after a quiet, intimate ride along the Grand Canal.

By Carla
Lionello

Y OUR FIRST IMPRESSION WILL PROBABLY BE that Venice doesn't live much at night. As the last bit of daylight slips away, so, too, does the noise of an active if not busy town. Boat traffic drops to the occasional passing vaporetto, shutters roll down, and signs go dark. Even most *bacari* (wine bars), which seem like natural spots for after-hours gathering, turn out the lights around 9 PM. But there is a night scene in Venice, subtly spread among many neighborhood *locali* (nightspots) that stay open until 1 or 2 AM, many with live music. Still, things never get too wild, except perhaps during Carnevale. There are no venues suited to loud concerts and few options for dancing on weeknights. Aside from the piano bars, nightlife tends to be student oriented.

Venice is a stop for major traveling exhibits, from Maya art to contemporary art retrospectives. In odd years, usually from mid- or late June to early November, the Biennale dell'Arte draws the work of several hundreds of contemporary international artists. Classical music buffs can rely on a rich season of concerts, opera, chamber music, and some ballet performed at the Palafenice theater. Minor venues and churches offer less-expensive shows, often focusing on Venetian Baroque music. There is no English-language theater or cinema in Venice, but during Carnevale foreign companies act in their mother tongue, and all movies participating in the Biennale del Cinema are shown in the original language, which most often happens to be English.

For a detailed listing of what's going on, pick up the monthly *Venezia News* from a newsstand. It has plenty of information in English about concerts, opera, ballet, theater, exhibitions, movies, sports, sightseeing, and a useful "Servizi" section with late-night pharmacies, operating hours for the busiest vaporetto and bus lines, and a listing of the main trains and flights from Venice. The tourist office puts out *Venezia da Vivere* (www.veneziadavivere.it), a seasonal brochure in Italian with weekly listings of what's going on in most of the nightspots. More entertainment and lifestyle information can be found in *Meeting Venice* (www.meetingvenice.it), *Leo Bussola,* and *Un Ospite di Venezia* (www.aguestinvenice.com), all in Italian with English translations. They are free and available at the tourist office.

THE ARTS

The arts in Venice are commonly marked by celebration. The Biennale is a whirlwind of fine arts, film, and music festivals, and Carnevale, with its mix of concerts, traditional masks, and elaborate parties, is equal parts history and revelry. Musical performances are frequent; they often involve period costume and can take place in churches, palaces, or even gondolas afloat on the Grand Canal.

Art Exhibitions

Venice's major site for temporary exhibits is **Palazzo Grassi** (✉ Campo San Samuele, 3231 San Marco, ☎ 041/5231680, WEB www.palazzograssi.it), a stately 18th-century palace on the Grand Canal that since the early 1980s has been hosting art and cultural shows of international importance, ranging from contemporary painting to Etruscan finds. The **Fondazione Bevilacqua La Masa** (✉ Fondamenta Gherardini, off Campo San Barnaba, 2826 Dorsoduro, ☎ 041/5207797), houses contemporary fine arts events.

THE BIENNALE: AN INTERNATIONAL ART FEAST

A VENETIAN CULTURAL institution for over 100 years, the **Biennale** (as the name suggests) started as an art exposition held every two years. It now refers to a film festival and a music festival as well, and falls at slightly irregular intervals: the Esposizione Internazionale d'Arte (Biennale dell'Arte) has been held in odd-numbered years since 1993, from mid-June to early November. The Mostra Internazionale del Cinema (Biennale del Cinema) is held every year for 10 days in early September. The Festival Internazionale di Musica Contemporanea (Biennale Musica) was launched in 1930 by Conte Volpi. From 1937 onward it was intended to occur annually, but due to poor management and a lack of funds it failed to occur regularly and became the most unpredictable of all Biennale events. In an encouraging trend, it did take place consistently in the first years of the 21st century. The Biennale Danza (Ballet) and Biennale Teatro (Theater) saw their inaugural performances in 1999. For information on all events, contact La Biennale di Venezia (✉ 1364/a San Marco, Ca' Giustinian, ☎ 041/5218711, ⒻⒶⓍ 041/5227539).

The **Biennale dell'Arte** is traditionally displayed at the Giardini della Biennale, located in Castello between the Arsenal and the neighborhood of Sant'Elena. Exhibits are organized into national pavilions, some of them just temporary shelters, others permanent exhibition spaces and interesting works of art in their own right. The Corderie dell'Arsenale (where ships' ropes were made inside the Arsenal) has also been used recently as a setting for satellite displays, allowing you a rare glimpse of the interior of the glorious Arsenal. What doesn't find space here is arranged by the artists along the Riva dei Sette Martiri. Expect to see anything from huge sculptures and avant-garde paintings to colored pebbles set in mystical patterns and "landscapes" made of smelly straw cones.

The **Biennale del Cinema**, while not quite as prestigious as Cannes, is nonetheless one of the film world's most noteworthy festivals. Films are shown in several theaters at the Palazzo del Cinema on the Lido (✉ Lungomare Guglielmo Marconi 90, Lido, 30126 Venice, ☎ 041/2726511; vaporetto stop Lido Casinò), a low, boxy affair that looks more like a train station than a movie house from the outside. Closed 355 days a year, it comes to life in early September with a fresh coat of paint, scores of bright lights, potted plants, and flags. Screenings run from about 9 AM to 2 AM. In addition to the films that vie for the various awards (including the prestigious grand prize, the Leone d'Oro, or Golden Lion), there are retrospectives and "debuts" of mainstream commercial releases. Non-Italian films are shown in their original language with Italian subtitles. It is a good idea to buy tickets in advance for the most eagerly awaited films (contact the tourist office for details). There is also an open-air cinema on Campo San Polo, where the bigger films are shown.

The **Biennale Musica** has attracted many world-famous composers and performers in years past. Igor Stravinsky premiered his *Rake's Progress* during the 1951 festival, and three years later George Gershwin did the same with *Porgy and Bess*. In 1984, the deconsecrated church of San Lorenzo housed Luigi Nono's opera *Prometeo*: a gigantic wooden structure designed by the composer filled the interior of the church, serving as a stage, seating area, and resonance chamber. After decades of stunted growth, the successful 1999, 2000, and 2001 editions made the Biennale Musica take off as never before. Plans are to once more make it an official annual event, taking place from mid-May to October, with a special section for street instruments like cymbalon and accordion, rarely employed in "serious" composition.

The latest additions, **Biennale Danza**—directed by world-famous dancer and choreographer Carolyne Carlson—and **Biennale Teatro** focus on contemporary ballet and theater from all over the world. Both sections are expected to occur annually, with dozens of shows occurring from May to October.

— Carla Lionello

From time to time, museums and picture galleries such as Palazzo Ducale, Ca' Rezzonico, Museo Correr, Pinacoteca Querini-Stampalia, Galleria di Palazzo Cini, and the Peggy Guggenheim Collection host temporary exhibits having some relevance to their permanent collections. Normally, there's no extra charge to visit such shows. All exhibits are well advertised on the city walls and on banners as well as in the entrance hall of each museum; publications such as *Leo, Meeting Venice, A Guest in Venice* (available from APT) and *Venezia News* (on sale at news kiosks) fully cover what's on in the city.

Carnevale

The first historical evidence of Carnevale (Carnival) in Venice dates from 1097, and for centuries the city marked the days preceding *quaresima* (Lent, the 40 days of abstinence leading up to Palm Sunday) with abundant feasting and wild celebrations. The word *carnival* is derived from the words for meat (*carne*) and to remove (*levare*), as eating meat was prohibited during Lent. It was in the 18th century that Venice acquired an international reputation as the "city of Carnevale," largely due to the masquerades and theatrical shows that characterized Carnevale celebrations during that century. But with the fall of the Republic in 1797, the city lost a great deal of its vitality, and the tradition of Carnevale celebrations was abandoned.

Fast-forward to 1979, when the city government decided to revive Carnevale in Venice with an eye toward stimulating business and tourism at a normally slow time of the year. The rejuvenation has been an unqualified success: between the visitors that stay in the city and those who come in for the day, more than half a million people experience Venetian Carnevale every year. The festivities last 10 to 12 days and consist of concerts, street performances, masquerade balls, historical processions, fashion shows, contests for the best mask, and special theater performances. The tourist office (☎ 041/5298711, WEB www.venezia.provincia/apt.it) has detailed information about daily events well in advance, or contact the **Consorzio Carnevale di Venezia** (✉ 468/b Santa Croce, ☎ 041/2510811, FAX 041/5200410).

The most coveted Carnevale parties fill up quickly—book well ahead. The **Ballo del Doge** is held at Palazzo Pisani-Moretta on the last Saturday of Carnevale. Tickets cost roughly $425 per person, dinner included; for reservations, contact Antonia Sautter (☎ 041/5224426, FAX 041/5287543, WEB www.ballodeldoge.com) at least three months in advance). The **Belle Epoque Ball** is usually held at Palazzo Albrizzi. Contact Oltrex Viaggi (✉ Riva degli Schiavoni, 4192 Castello, ☎ 041/5242840, FAX 041/5221986, WEB www.venicesystem.com), which also organizes a gondola procession following the Grand Canal pageant during the last weekend of Carnevale. **Count Emile Targhetta d'Audiffret** (✉ 6293 Cannaregio, 30121 Venezia, ☎ 041/5230242) opens his palazzo on the Fondamente Nuove for evenings of masquerade, dancing parties, and follies; write to the count for information. For general information about Carnevale events, contact **Consorzio Comitato per il Carnevale di Venezia** (✉ 1714 Santa Croce, 30135 Venezia, ☎ 041/717065, FAX 041/5200410, WEB www.meetingeurope.com).

Many find Carnevale the perfect time not to visit Venice. Enormous crowds clog the streets as at no other time of the year. One-way street traffic regulations are enforced, the bridges become "no-stopping" zones to avoid collapse, and hotel prices skyrocket.

Concerts

The lack of large rock venue hasn't stopped some major groups from playing here—many Venetians still recall the time in 1989 when the Rolling Stones played a free concert on a pontoon floating in the lagoon—but for the most part Venice remains isolated from the European tour circuit. Contemporary music gets highlighted during the Biennale Musica and in various clubs around town, but the vast majority of music played in Venice is classical.

For up-to-date information, consult local publications or pay a visit to the tourist information office inside the **Venice Pavillon** (⊠ next to the Giardinetti Reali, ☎ no phone). The **Vela** office (⊠ Calle dei Fuseri, 1810 San Marco, ☎ 041/2418029), open Monday–Saturday 7:30–7, handles tickets for some musical events.

If you hear something you like, there is a good chance it's on sale at **Nalesso** (⊠ Calle dello Spezier, off Campo Santo Stefano, 2765 San Marco, ☎ 041/5203329), a shop that specializes in Venetian classical music of all kinds and handles tickets for some concerts. The English-speaking staff is a good source of information about the musical events in town. It's open Monday–Saturday and most Sundays 10–1 and 3–7.

Classical

The churches of Santo Stefano, San Stae, San Lio, San Giacometo, Santa Maria Formosa, Sant'Agnese, and the Frari host concerts throughout the year, although performance quality tends to be uneven. The city occasionally sponsors free concerts by visiting choirs and musicians.

Chiesa della Pietà has long been associated with Vivaldi, and frequent concerts here often feature his music. Over Christmas and during Carnevale, concerts are held every evening. Shows by such groups as I Virtuosi dell'Ensemble di Venezia, Le Venexiane, and Le Putte Veneziane di Vivaldi are performed in 18th-century costume. The Pietà is also a regular venue for the performances of the Virtuosi dell'Ensemble di Venezia. Tickets, sold at the church and at various agencies, often include admission to a tiny museum of Baroque instruments. ⊠ *Riva degli Schiavoni, Calle delle Pietà, Castello,* ☎ *041/5231096 information and reservations,* 𝔽𝔸𝕏 *041/917257,* 𝕎𝔼𝔹 *www.vivaldi.it.* 🎫 *€20.00.*

Chiesa di San Bartolomeo, at the foot of the Rialto Bridge, is the official seat of the string group Interpreti Veneziani, which plays Vivaldi, Paganini, Rossini, and lesser-known composers such as Tartini and Corelli. Attending a concert is the best way to visit this church, which is not normally open. ⊠ *Campo San Bartolomeo, 5096 San Marco,* ☎ *041/2770561,* 𝕎𝔼𝔹 *www.interpretiveneziani.com.* 🎫 *€18.00.*

From April to September, the association Musica & Musica puts on historical alfresco **gondola concerts** along the Grand Canal. A party of 11 gondolas (10 for the audience and 1 for the performers in 18th-century costume) leaves from the gondola ferry stop at San Tomà, heading in the direction of the Accademia bridge; at the end of the performance, viewers and musicians disembark at Rialto. Concerts are held Monday and Thursday–Saturday at 8:30 PM. ☎ *041/5210294,* 𝕎𝔼𝔹 *www.musicaemusicasrl.com.* 🎫 *€44.00.*

Gruppo Accademia di San Rocco plays a varied repertoire. Its summer season takes place at the **Scuola Grande di San Rocco** (⊠ Campo San Rocco, 3054 San Polo, ☎ 041/5234864), and in the winter it moves to the more central **Ateneo Veneto** (⊠ Campo San Fantin, 1897 San Marco, ☎ 041/5224459). ⊠ *Booking and information: Via Ca' Ve-*

nier 8, 31132 Mestre, ☎ *041/962999,* WEB *www.musicinvenice.com.* ⌨ *€18.00–€26.00.*

Perhaps the best classical concerts in Venice are those put on by **L'Offerta Musicale,** *the city's main chamber orchestra. Performances take place in churches and other music venues around town.* ⊠ Calle dei Botteri, 1541 San Polo, ☎ 041/5241143.

On certain days (at press time every Friday and Saturday), **Museo Querini-Stampalia** hosts concerts of *musica antica,* music dating from before the 15th century. Entrance is included in the admission price of the museum. ⊠ *Campiello Querini-Stampalia, near Campo Santa Maria Formosa, 4778 Castello,* ☎ *041/2711411.* ⌨ *€6.20.*

From April to mid-January, the musicians of **Musici Veneziani** play in 18th-century costume at the Scuola Grande di San Teodoro in Campo San Salvador, near the Rialto bridge. The rest of the year they move to the Ateneo San Basso in Piazzetta dei Leoncini (close to the Basilica di San Marco). Aside from the ever-present Vivaldi, you might also hear Albinoni, Bach, Handel, and Mozart—but the ticket prices reflects the tailoring bills. ⊠ *Booking and information:* ☎ *041/5210294,* WEB *www.musicaemusicasrl.com.* ⌨ *€21.00–€31.00.*

The Orchestra di Venezia performs concerts in costume at the **Scuola Grande di San Giovanni Evangelista,** with two added bonuses: a baroque ballet and a soprano singing along to the notes of Vivaldi, Albinoni, Boccherini, and Cesti. ⊠ *Booking and information: Campiello della Scuola, 2454 San Polo,* ☎ 041/5235807 or 041/786764. ⌨ *€21.00–€31.00.*

Contemporary

The **Aula Magna Tolentini** (⊠ 191 Santa Croce, near Chiesa dei Tolentini, ☎ 041/2571806) hosts occasional contemporary and ethnic concerts. Contemporary music and dance are often staged at **Teatro Fondamente Nuove** (⊠ 5013 Cannaregio, near Chiesa dei Gesuiti, ☎ 041/5224498).

Festivals

Festa della Madonna della Salute

This popular festival gives thanks every November 21 to the Virgin Mary for having liberated Venice from the terrible plague of 1629–30, which in less than two years killed nearly a third of the city's 145,000 inhabitants. In gratitude, the Republic built a votive temple to the Madonna della Salute. To make the pilgrimage easier for the aged and the infirm, between Campo Santa Maria del Giglio and the sestiere of Dorsoduro, a bridge made up of boats is traditionally set up across the Grand Canal. The weather is usually cold and foggy, and the Venetians inaugurate the winter season with a stew, made according to an age-old recipe, called *castradina. Frittelle* (fritters), *palloncini* (balloons on strings), and votive candles are sold along the main streets that lead to the church.

Festa della Sensa

The oldest Venetian festival, the Festival of the Ascension, was initiated by Doge Pietro Orseolo II in the year 1000, after he led the Venetian fleet to victory over the Slavic pirates (who had invaded the Istrian-Dalamatian coast) on Ascension Day. Originally the Ascension was a very simple ceremony in which the doge led a procession of boats to the entrance of the port of San Nicolò di Lido to meet the religious leader of the period, the bishop of San Pietro di Castello, who blessed the waters as a sign of peace and gratitude.

In 1177, with the famous "Peace of Venice" between Emperor Frederick Barbarossa and Pope Alexander III, the festival was transformed into the so-called "wedding with the sea." The story goes that following the occupation of Rome by Barbarossa's troops, Alexander III escaped to Venice disguised as a pilgrim, and after having passed the first night in the open air on the Sottoportego della Madonna near the Church of Sant'Aponal (now marked by a wooden plaque), he found work in the kitchens of the Convento della Carità (today home of the Gallerie dell'Accademia). Some time later, Alexander III was recognized by a Roman high prelate who was visiting the monastery. When the doge Sebastiano Ziani heard of this, he immediately began peace talks with the emperor. But Barbarossa did not want to make peace, so the doge armed a strong fleet and with the blessing of Alexander III set off from Piazzetta di San Marco to attack the imperial ships in the Istrian waters. The Venetians won and captured Barbarossa's son, thereby forcing the emperor to negotiate. In gratitude the pope gave a gold ring to the doge, with which he could remarry Venice with the sea every year.

In Republican times, the Ascension began with a series of performances and celebrations that went on for 15 days and culminated with a large fair in Piazza San Marco. Today the Ascension is held on the Sunday following Ascension Day, the Thursday that falls 40 days after Easter, and begins at about 9 AM with a procession of ships led by the mayor, who tosses a ring into the water and pronounces the ritual phrase: "In segno di eterno dominio, noi, Doge di Venezia, ti sposiamo o mare!" (As a symbol of our eternal dominion, we wed you, o sea!). Masses in the Chiesa di San Nicolò and boat races follow later in the afternoon. In the Sala del Maggior Consiglio in Palazzo Ducale, you can see several objects that are part of the ceremony, such as the thick candle, the umbrella, the gilded throne, and the eight white, red, blue, and yellow banners. The Museo Storico Navale has an 18-ft-long scale model of the gilded boat used by the doge.

Festa del Redentore

On the third Sunday of July, crowds of pilgrims cross the Canale della Giudecca by means of a pontoon bridge, which is traditionally built every year to commemorate the doge's annual visit to Palladio's Chiesa del Redentore to offer thanks to the Redeemer for the end of a 16th-century plague. The festival starts the previous night with *foghi* (fireworks) exploding over the lagoon. This sensational fireworks show starts around 11 o'clock and lasts with uninterrupted "compositions" for nearly an hour. Early in the evening, most Venetians take to the water in boats decorated with vines and leaves and colored lanterns to secure a good place from which to enjoy the show, their portable coolers stuffed with watermelon, white wine, fruit salads, and cold snacks. (The "proper" dish to serve used to be stuffed duck, but these days few go to the trouble.) Many hotels with terraces overlooking the Bacino di San Marco organize special dinners and parties (reserve well ahead), and you can buy a seat in one of the several *motonavetti da turismo,* the big tourist boats that for the occasion turn into musical boats. If you prefer to see the fireworks from Piazza San Marco, any free spot between the monument to Vittorio Emanuele in the Riva degli Schiavoni and the Giardinetti Reali will do; you can also watch from the Zattere. The closer to the water, the better, but most of the fireworks are shot high in the sky and are visible from the middle of the crowds. The show is not held in the rain, but no one can recall the last time it rained during the Festa del Redentore.

Festa di San Marco

The festival in honor of the great Evangelist who for 1,000 years protected his city is today in part eclipsed by the fact that April 25 is also a national holiday (Liberation Day). The only unusual tradition observed is the sale of the buds of *boccoli* (red roses), which every Venetian man buys for all the ladies in his life (wife, mother, sisters, cousins, friends)—the longer the stem the deeper the token of love. According to the legend, a soldier enamored of the daughter of the doge was mortally wounded during a battle in a far-off land. His blood, as it spilled, bore red roses, which he entrusted to his companion to bring to the girl. The story doesn't say if the flowers arrived on St. Mark's Day, but by tradition Venetians celebrate the pagan miracle on this date.

Opera and Ballet

Teatro La Fenice, located between Piazza San Marco and Campo San Stefano, is one of Italy's oldest opera houses. It's a shrine and pilgrimage site for all opera lovers and the scene of many memorable operatic premieres, including, in 1853, the dismal first-night flop of Verdi's *La Traviata*. The theater was badly damaged by fire in January 1996; delays and scandal jeopardized its reconstruction until 2001. Careful "philological" restoration work is expected to begin in January 2002. It will take 630 days and nearly €53,000,000 to complete the job—helped in large part by donations from opera-lovers around the world. Until the Fenice reopens in September 2003, opera, symphony, and ballet performances are held year-round at the **Palafenice** (✉ Cassa di Risparmio bank, Campo San Luca, ☎ 041/5210161; 041/5204010 ticket information) near the Tronchetto parking area.

For avant-garde ballet, check the schedule of **Teatro Fondamente Nuove** (✉ 5013 Cannaregio, near Chiesa dei Gesuiti, ☎ 041/5224498).

The **Teatro Malibran** (✉ Calle del Teatro at Corte del Milion, Cannaregio), built by the powerful Grimani family in 1677, was one of Europe's most famous opera theaters before it was converted into a movie theater in 1927. It was reopened in 2001 after lengthy restoration, and it now hosts opera and symphony performances.

On the mainland, **Teatro Toniolo** hosts an interesting mix of events, including contemporary music concerts, operas with renowned international singers, fringe theater pieces (in Italian or dialect), and classic plays (in Italian). ✉ *Piazzetta Battisti, off central Piazza Ferretto, Mestre,* ☎ *041/971666.*

NIGHTLIFE

Most nightspots fit into three categories. The so-called *osterie musicali* offer full meals, *cicheti* (little savory snacks), beer, inexpensive wine, and live music several nights a week. Many of them also serve as galleries for local artists, whose paintings decorate the walls and are for sale. Then there are the English- and Irish-style pubs, with beer on tap and occasional live music, which are especially popular with the younger crowd. Finally, there are the late-night cafés and piano bars that offer more nocturnal diversion.

Bars

For a delicious late dinner of *panini* (sandwiches) or breakfast and a nap in the sun after a late night, consider **Al Chioschetto.** Live funk, reggae, jazz, or soul is on tap once a week, usually on Wednesday, and there's a romantic view of the Giudecca at night. ⊠ *Zattere Ponte Lungo, 1406/a Dorsoduro,* ☎ *338/1174077. Closed Sun. Oct.–Apr.*

Caffè Blue is a music bar and *birreria* (Italian-style pub) rolled into one. It has live music on Friday, frequent art openings, a no-smoking room (until 8 PM), and an array of tiny sandwiches filled with smoked or cured pork or game. Whisky drinkers, take note: Caffè Blu has one of the widest selections in Venice. Happy hour runs from 8:30 to 9:30. ⊠ *Calle dei Preti (also known as Calle Lunga San Pantalon), 3778 Dorsoduro,* ☎ *041/710227. Closed Sun.*

Codroma, is one of the few bacari that might stay open late into the night, though the hours are utterly unpredictable. Sometimes there's live jazz, but the biggest attraction is the after-hours cappuccino. This is a Venetian institution, founded at the beginning of the 20th century by the bearded cook shown in the picture near the window. ⊠ *Ponte del Soccorso, off Campo dei Carmini, 2540 Dorsoduro,* ☎ *041/ 5246789. Closed Sun. Sept.–June and weekends July–Aug.*

Il Caffè, known as "Bar Rosso" (red bar) because of its bright-red exterior, hosts occasional jazz concerts in summer and has tables outside. It's a favorite with students and has a reputation for strong *spritz* (pronounced "spriss"), the Venetian aperitif of choice, invented at the time the Austrians ruled Venice. The drink is made with white wine, Campari or Aperol, soda water, and a twist of lemon. ⊠ *Campo Santa Margherita, 2963 Dorsoduro,* ☎ *041/5286255. Closed Tues.*

In addition to a unique menu of Renaissance Venetian dishes and a variety of crepes, **Le Bistrot de Venise** has poetry reading and cabaret sessions (in Italian) once or twice a week. ⊠ *Calle dei Fabbri, 4685 San Marco,* ☎ *041/5236651.*

Paradiso Perduto (Paradise Lost) has been catering to night owls since the late 1970s. It's always been a hybrid nightspot with food (mostly inexpensive fish dishes), drinks, interesting wines (try the sparkling white Il Grigio Collavini), and music—live jazz and ethnic music on Sunday and Monday, harsh metal the rest of the week. Set up in a huge room with closely placed tables, this is a captivating place for togetherness and conviviality. ⊠ *Fondamenta della Misericordia, 2540 Cannaregio,* ☎ *041/720581. Closed Wed.*

With live music every Friday and a hundred tables outside in a breezy campo at the west end of the Zattere promenade, **Suzie** is cheerful bar and popular summer nightspot. It has a decidedly friendly atmosphere and welcomes gay clientele. The food choices include a good selection of panini and a limited pasta menu. ⊠ *Campo San Basilio, 1527 Dorsoduro,* ☎ *041/5227502. Closed weekends Oct.–Apr.*

At **Torino@notte,** acoustic jam sessions once a week, usually on Wednesday, are the draw. Cocktails are available (rum and Coke, here called a *cubino,* is popular), and there's a short menu of snacks. ⊠ *Campo San Luca, 459 San Marco,* ☎ *041/5223914.*

Zanzibar, a bar-gelateria in the style of a beach kiosk with tables outside, has live jazz or Irish music every Friday in the summer. Located along a canal in front of the Chiesa di Santa Maria Formosa, it serves homemade gelato and lots of natural, freshly prepared fruit treats (salads, smoothies, and juices), as well as hamburgers and beer. ⊠ *Campo Santa Maria Formosa, 5840 Castello,* ☎ *347/1460107 or 339/2006831.*

Casino

The city-run gambling **Casino** at the splendid Palazzo Vendramin-Calergi has lost some of its clientele to the charmless Ca' Noghera, set up in a boxy building near the airport in 1999. While Palazzo Vendramin-Calergi has only slots and traditional French games, Ca' Noghera has a large selection of Las Vegas–style games. There's a minimum age of 18. ⊠ *Ca' Nogari: Via Triestina 222, Tessera,* ☎ *041/5416237; Palazzo Vendramin-Calergi:* ⊠ *San Marcuola vaporetto stop,* ☎ *041/5297111.* 🎫 *€7.75.* ⊙ *Daily 11* AM–*2:30* AM.

Dance Clubs

With only two discos in the historic center, Venice's club scene is rather skimpy. Local dedicated dancers are often ready to face long and dangerous nocturnal drives to reach the celebrated clubs in Rimini and Riccione to the south of Venice in the Emilia-Romagna region. On the strip of terra firma closer to Venice, clubs come and go frequently, and their opening hours are often unpredictable. Below is a list of dependable discos; however, it's always a good idea to call ahead. If you go to Mestre or Jesolo, you can plan your night so that you return to Venice in time to see the sun rise over the lagoon, but make sure you check public transportation details before you leave town.

Disco and live performances are the lure at **Acropolis,** a trendy spot on the Lido with a large marble dance floor, a pedestal for *cubiste* (provocative dancing girls), and a view of the sea. In summer you can dance on the spacious terrace jutting out over the beach. The bar serves gelato, little sandwiches, *pizzette* (little pizzas), and other savories to fuel you until breakfast. ⊠ *Lungomare Marconi 22, Lido,* ☎ *041/5260466.* 🎫 *€10.00 includes 1 drink. Closed Mon.–Tues., Thurs., and Sun. May–mid-Oct.; closed Sun.–Fri. mid-Oct.–Apr.*

Metallic walls, red leather couches, big projection screens, and theme nights are in store at **Casanova,** a medium-size restaurant-cabaret-disco. ⊠ *Lista di Spagna, 158/a Cannaregio,* ☎ *041/2750199.* 🎫 *€10.00 includes 1 drink. Closed Mon., Wed. in Aug., and 1st wk of Sept.*

Disco Club Piccolo Mondo, a tiny venue with few lights and a bunch of small tables arranged around the dancing area, welcomes visitors as well as students looking for a late-night drink and a dance floor. The place is gay friendly, and the music (mostly commercial house) is not so loud as to make conversation impossible. ⊠ *Calle Contarini, close to the Gallerie dell'Accademia, 1056/a Dorsoduro,* ☎ *041/5200371.* 🎫 *€6.00–€10.00 includes 1 drink.*

Set up in an old refrigerator warehouse on the mainland in Mestre, **Magazzino Frigorifero** is a hybrid disco-pizzeria decorated with industrial relics. Greatest-hits sound tracks, plus live music, salsa, and merengue during the week, get things pumping. Conversation requires strong vocal chords. Take buses 4 and 4/ from Piazzale Roma to Corso del Popolo. ⊠ *Via Altobello 107, Mestre,* ☎ *041/5319293.* 🎫 *Free. Closed Sun.–Tues. and Aug.*

Sound Garden Rock Café features music by period rock cult artists such as Jimi Hendrix and the Cure, but on Friday and Saturday it also has live performances by cutting-edge local bands. For a break from dancing, there are also three pool tables and an Internet café. It takes about 70 minutes to reach Jesolo, where the club is located, from Piazzale Roma by ATVO buses (☎ *041/5205530;* last departure mid-June–Aug. 12:40 AM; Sept.–mid-June 9:40 PM). ⊠ *Piazza Mazzini, Jesolo,* ☎ *338/8752823.* 🎫 *€5.50 includes 1 drink.*

Late-Night

Campo Santa Margherita, where you'll find Il Caffè, Gelateria Il Doge, and Margaret Duchamp, is one of the livelier gathering places in town after dark.

Midnight Snacks

Venice may be a sleepy city, but there are a number of places where you can answer the call of late-night hunger.

Arca, something between a bacaro and a trattoria, is a well-established part of the Venetian after-hours scene, particularly with the local university crowd. There's live music on Tuesday from October through May, and an enticing array of snacks is available. ⊠ *Calle Lunga San Pantalon, 3757 Dorsoduro,* ☎ *041/5242236. Closed Sun.*

Gelateria Il Doge has about 50 flavors of gelato—including Venice's only "dietetic" version, made lighter in taste and a bit lower in calories (no sugar and no milk). Popular non-dietetic flavors include *sacher* (cocoa, sponge cake, and apricot jam), *bounty* (coconut and chocolate), and *strabon* (Venetian for "more than good," made with cocoa, espresso, and chocolate-covered almonds). In the summer you'll also find refreshing lemon, peach, sour cherry, and Coca-Cola granitas. It's open until 1 or 2 AM in the summer, with slightly earlier closing in the spring and October. ⊠ *Campo Santa Margherita, 3058 Dorsoduro,* ☎ *041/5234607. Closed Nov.–Feb.*

With tables outside along a canal and a no-smoking room (a rarity in Italian nightspots), **Gibo Bar,** a health-conscious bar-gelateria that also serves cicheti, is a dependable address all year round. Board games and an Internet corner don't make for a fast turnover, but you can sit down in Venetian style on the canal wall. ⊠ *Ponte della Donna Onesta, Fondamenta della Misericordia, 2925 San Polo,* ☎ *041/5229969. Closed 1 wk mid-Aug.*

Wooden chairs and tables line **Iguana,** a lively nightspot festooned with colored sombreros and paper chains. A wide selection of Mexican beers and tequilas, Mexican snacks, and rather forgettable burritos is served until 2 AM. Once or twice a week, usually on Tuesday, there's live Brazilian music. ⊠ *Fondamenta della Misericordia, 2515 Cannaregio,* ☎ *041/ 713561. Closed Mon.*

The French-sounding name **Margaret Duchamp** befits this café-brasserie (no crepes) with an artfully minimalist decor that's light-years away from that of any bacari around town. Warm sandwiches and light salads take the place of cicheti, but you won't pay more for the "designer's touch." It's open till 2 AM. ⊠ *Campo Santa Margherita, 3019 Dorsoduro,* ☎ *041/5286255.*

Moscacieka is a wine bar with *bruschette* (slabs of toasted bread with toppings), grilled sandwiches, and vegetables. The walls and ceiling of the bizarre "Blind Fly," which also means "Blindman's Bluff" in Italian, feature huge, blue Styrofoam flies; there's a matching blue Murano-glass counter and a dozen dark wooden tables. There's no live music, but the location is handy, and it remains open until 1 AM. ⊠ *Calle dei Fabbri, 4717 San Marco,* ☎ *041/5208085. Closed Sun. Oct.– May; closed weekends June–Sept.*

The hole-in-the-wall pizza-to-go place **Pizza al Volo** sells pizzas with classic toppings such as *margherita* (tomato and mozzarella), *ai funghi* (margherita with mushrooms), and *al prosciutto* (margherita with

ham). You can get it either whole or by the slice until 1 or 1:30 AM.
⊠ *Campo Santa Margherita, 2944/a Dorsoduro,* ☎ *041/5225430.*

Nightcaps

During Carnevale, many ordinary bars, which close around dinnertime the rest of the year, stay open around the clock.

Far less famous than the café around the corner on the Piazza San Marco proper, **Bar Al Todaro** is a worthy alternative, especially on a clear day when the view out toward San Giorgio and the Giudecca rivals that of the grand Piazza and Basilica. On most summer nights there's live music much like what's heard on the Piazza. ⊠ *Piazzetta San Marco, 3 San Marco,* ☎ *041/5285165.*

Caffè Florian opened up in 1720 as Venezia Trionfante (Triumphant Venice) but was soon renamed after its founder, Floriano Francesconi. The café started as a fashionable spot for a hot chocolate, but during the Austrian domination of Venice it became the favorite meeting place of Italian patriots and intellectuals who boycotted the rival Caffè Quadri across the piazza because of its Austrian military clientele. Stuccoes, mirrors, wooden carvings, and intimate booths date back to 1859, but the historical atmosphere comes at a price: an espresso here costs €5.00, and afternoon tea can end up costing as much as a meal when the waiter counts out the pieces of pastry missing from the platter and charges accordingly. No wonder it's one of the few cafés in all of Italy to accept credit cards. ⊠ *Under the Procuratie Nuove, 56 Piazza San Marco,* ☎ *041/5205641. Closed Nov.–Mar. and Wed.*

Opened in the late 18th century, **Caffè Quadri** was the first place in Venice to serve Turkish coffee—back before the espresso had been invented. Less glamorous and less intimate than the Florian across the piazza, this equally historic (and pricey) café has had its fair share of famous regulars, including Stendhal, Balzac, and the hard-to-please Proust. It stays open late during summer, with music outside. ⊠ *Under the Procuratie Vecchie, 120 Piazza San Marco,* ☎ *041/5289299. Closed Mon. Nov.–Mar.*

Venice has its share of famous places for a nightcap or an aperitif, none more so than **Harry's Bar,** once a favorite haunt of Hemingway's. If you want to follow in such illustrious footsteps, though, you'll pay for the privilege. The place was an old rope works when the father of the current owner, Arrigo Cipriani, bought it with the help of a loan from an American named Harry Pickering. Step inside the cozy, wood-paneled cocktail bar to join the crowds sipping Bellinis, a treat not to be missed if you happen to visit during peach season (June to early September). The trademark drink is made with fresh white peach juice stirred into sparkling prosecco. (Little green "shake-and-pour" Bellinis sold in town compare to the real thing like concentrated orange juice does to succulent oranges.) ⊠ *Calle Vallaresso, 1323 San Marco,* ☎ *041/5285777.*

Randon Enoteca is an attractive, well-stocked wine bar with tables outside in warm weather. There are always a dozen wines available by the glass and a small but a tasty selection of food, including desserts, at mealtimes. ⊠ *Campo San Barnaba, 2852 Dorsoduro,* ☎ *041/5224410. Closed Sun.*

Piano Bars

On the ground floor of the prestigious Hotel Baglioni, **Caffè Baglioni** is perfect for an intimate chat in the cold winter months. There's live piano music on Wednesday, Friday, and Saturday. ⊠ *Hotel Baglioni, 1243 San Marco,* ☎ *041/5289840. Closed June–Sept.*

The piano bar in the luxe **Hotel Monaco & Grand Canal** is especially pleasant in the winter, when the fireplace adds extra warmth to the refined, romantic ambience. ⊠ *Calle Vallaresso, 1325 San Marco,* ☎ *041/ 5200211. Closed July–Sept.*

The **Martini Scala Club** is an elegant piano bar with a restaurant. Music starts at 10 and goes until the wee hours. ⊠ *Calle del Cafetier, 1007 San Marco,* ☎ *041/5224121. Closed July–Aug.*

Pubs

Night sailors in need of a moorage can stop at **Capo Horn Pub,** a roomy watering hole on two floors, decorated to resemble the interior of an old ship, with wooden benches, ropes, brass lamps, and the like. Wine, 50 kinds of beer, and a good selection of aged whisky are available, and from the galley you can get salads and made-to-order sandwiches. ⊠ *Fondamenta degli Ormesini, 2754 Cannaregio,* ☎ *041/ 5242177.*

Devil's Forest Pub, one of the more popular Irish pubs in town, has lots of board games and Irish beer on tap. There's pasta, too. ⊠ *Calle dei Stagneri 5185, off Campo San Bartolomio,* ☎ *041/5200623.*

Fiddler's Elbow is a typical Irish pub (of the Italian variety), with plenty of grub, gab, and creamy Guinness. ⊠ *Corte dei Pali, off the Strada Nova, 3847 Cannaregio,* ☎ *041/5239930.*

Olandese Volante (The Flying Dutchman) is decorated to resemble the interior of an old ship, but with more attractive tables in the pretty campo outside. The central location makes this a convenient stop for a simple late-night bite and glass of beer. ⊠ *Campo San Lio, 5658 Castello,* ☎ *041/5289349.*

Ignore the fake country-pub decor and join in the midnight *spaghettata* (communal spaghetti bowl—you don't get to choose the sauce) at **Pier Dickens Inn.** Italian comedians and bands perform once a week, usually on Tuesday. ⊠ *Campo Santa Margherita, 3410 Dorsoduro,* ☎ *0339/4430617.*

Senso Unico, a popular neighborhood hangout, is a sparsely decorated pub with Guinness on tap and a substantial display of panini. Inside, the best table has a view of the canal. ⊠ *Calle della Chiesa, off Campo San Vio, 684 Dorsoduro,* ☎ *no phone. Closed Mon.*

5 OUTDOOR ACTIVITIES AND SPORTS

Venice a sports town? It may not be the soccer capital of Italy, but the local squad is respectable, and though recreational sports facilities are at a minimum, the very nature of a city where you have to walk down alleys and across bridges just about anywhere you go ensures that local (and tourist) legs always get a workout.

WITH ALL THE BRIDGES TO CROSS and streets to walk, simply getting from place to place is the principal exercise for many Venetians. You will find recreational facilities here, but as is the case with so many aspects of life in Venice, you have to put conventional expectations aside and accept the city on its own terms. A jog in La Serenissima may not be obstacle-free, but it will be memorable. There are uniquely Venetian spectator sports as well: the various boat races, often incorporating centuries-old traditions, could only happen here.

By Carla
Lionello

BEACHES

The Lido's 12 km (8 mi) of beaches have very fine sand (unlike many other Italian beaches), which makes for wonderful barefoot walks but which also turns the water murky—a shame, since this part of the Adriatic is much less polluted than other Italian waters. The lack of big waves and the shallowness of the sea—you have to walk 200 to 250 ft before losing the ground under your feet—make these beaches an ideal place for toddlers and young children, who can safely play in the water or hunt for the few surviving crabs.

The best-kept beaches are all privately run. Located all less than a 2-km (1-mi) walk from the vaporetto landing (there is also a bus), they have first-rate facilities, with hot showers, shady porches, *capanne* (cabanas), mini-bungalows with eating areas, and bars serving ice cream, hot and cold drinks, fruit, salads, and sandwiches. With a reputation for catering to the working class, **Zona A** (⊠ on Lungomare G. D'Annunzio, ☎ 041/5260236; 041/5261249 in winter) has *camerini* (tiny dressing rooms with locks where you can leave your valuables) for the day ranging between €11.00 and €19.00, as well as *ombrelloni* (umbrellas, €9.00 per day), and *sdraii* (chaise lounges, €3.00 per day). The tiny **Sorriso** (⊠ on Lungomare Marconi after the Excelsior, ☎ 041/5261066; 041/5260729 in winter) tends to be less crowded that larger beaches, and it makes a good base for exploring the Murazzi area, sandless coastline with less murky water than elsewhere. The exclusive **Bagni Des Bains** (⊠ at the beginning of Lungomare Marconi, ☎ 041/2716836) is only a 15-minute walk from the vaporetto landing; to the left of the main entrance stand a few of the straw-roofed bungalows that used to be the main attraction here before most were destroyed in a flood in the early 1980s. The Oriental-looking dome of the Hotel Excelsior towers over the Lido's most famous beach, the **Bagni Excelsior** (⊠ Lungomare Marconi, ☎ 041/2716836). In the 1950s and '60s it became a favorite of movie stars and their wealthy companions; the stylish huts, made from white cotton fabric and dark wood, served as scenery in Lichino Visconti's haunting film *Death in Venice*. Middle-class **Consorzio** (also known as Capli, ⊠ Lungomare Marconi, ☎ 041/5260356) rents camerini and huts by the day, ranging between €16.00 and €72.00. The higher price gets you an ample dressing room, a table, four chairs, a *lettino* (camp bed), a chaise lounge, and a shady veranda. At most private beaches you can rent a *pedalò* (paddleboat) or *moscone* (wooden pontoon) by the hour: these are the best ways to get a good tan under the breeze or go for a swim away from the crowds.

You have to go a ways to find the *spiagge libere* (free beaches) of San Nicolò and Alberoni, on either side of the Lido. These beaches do not offer shelter or drinking water, so it is a good idea to bring along food, water, and sunscreen. The term *spiagge libere* still applies, though it hasn't made any sense since the 1970s, when the privately run beaches described above were compelled to let in nonguests, in accordance with a law that prevented private ownership of the sea and the first 6½ ft of sand. Of course, this sudden freedom of access came at a price: Swiss standards of quiet and cleanliness dropped to regular Italian levels, and although the Des Bains and Excelsior beaches still stand out for comforts and potted flowers, they are no longer what they once were.

Although nobody can stop you from entering the "private beaches," nonguests are forbidden to use the facilities, including the bathrooms and the areas protected by windbreaks. In practice many locals discreetly use them anyway. In general, the best times to visit the Lido beaches are in June and September, when you can take long walks or play *racchettoni* (a paddle game) and swim without human obstacles. April–May and October are great for walks, but it's too cold to swim. July and August are, predictably, the busiest months of the year.

PARTICIPANT SPORTS

Venice doesn't have the large recreational spaces found in most other cities. Walk a bit off the beaten path and you're sure to come across some hopeful young soccer players practicing their footwork along the stones of their home *campo* (square). If your idea of exercise is more than a good walk, you may have to be equally resourceful, but there are facilities available.

Biking

The best way to move from coast to coast on the Lido island is by bike or tandem, both of which can be rented by the hour or day. Quadricycles with canopy roofs are especially popular with families (perhaps because *Papà* is typically left to do all the work). Prices are the same everywhere and start at €3.00 per bike per hour, €8.00 for the day. Central **Bruno Lazzari** (✉ Gran Viale 21/b, ☎ 041/526–8019) is only two minutes from the vaporetto landing; it's open June–September, daily 8–8, and October–May, Monday–Saturday 8:30–1 and 2:30–7. **Giorgio Barbieri** (✉ Via Zara 5, ☎ 041/526–1490), open March–October, daily 8:30–8, also has repair service.

The Lido is a flat, long, and narrow island, so easy to explore that a map isn't necessary. Make a point to ride down pretty Via Lepanto, which runs along a canal at the heart of the Lido, and its neighboring tiny streets lined with shady trees and Art Deco villas. For a full, adventurous day you can also take the ferry to Pellestrina and Chioggia. Helmets are not mandatory in Venice, nor are they available for rent.

Boating

Expert sailors with a passion for historic boats should contact the **Associazione Vela al Terzo,** a private association that organizes regattas and social activities on board traditional lagoon sailing boats, some 200 years old, with their characteristic yellow and orange sails. Contact Signor Gino Luppi, reachable at his hardware store, Trevissoi s.a.s. (✉ 555 San Marco, ☎ 041/5224250), near the Mercerie, and be prepared to speak Italian. If you have sailed into Venice and want to rent a slip, contact **Diporto Velico** (✉ Porticciolo Zottis, Sant'Elena, ☎ 041/5231927). Although officially there are no reservations, it's a good idea to call a few hours ahead to secure a *parcheggio* (mooring spot); daily parking fees range from €13.00 to €54.00, depending on the length of the boat—those longer than 45 ft are not accepted.

If you have fallen in love with the lagoon, you might consider hiring a motorboat to explore it thoroughly. See what's available by the hour (€21.00) or by the day (€130.00) at **Brussa** (⊠ near Ponte delle Guglie, 331 Cannaregio, ☎ 041/715787), open daily 7–5:30. **Signor Davide** (☎ 0335/259435; 041/739767 home phone) rents boats starting at €78.00 for half a day. The place where pick up your boat is named "Oscar" (⊠ near the Scuola di San Giorgio degli Schiavoni, 3255 Castello).

Fitness Centers

The few tiny gyms that appeared in damp cellars around town when judo, karate, yoga, and bodybuilding became popular with young Venetians in the 1970s have been replaced by modern fitness centers, and a few are open to short-term visitors. Most of the classes are conducted in Italian.

Fitness Point (⊠ Calle del Pestrin, near Campo Santa Maria Formosa, 6141 Castello, ☎ 041/5209246), open weekdays 9 AM–10 PM and Saturday 9–5, has daily aerobics and step-dance classes. A onetime visit costs €15.50, five visits €39.00.

Palestra Club Delfino (⊠ Zattere, 788/a Dorsoduro, ☎ 041/5232763, WEB www.palestraclubdelfino.com) offers custom training sessions available in English by appointment, intensive wellness weeks, cardio machines, and stretching. A day pass costs €12.50. It's open September–June, weekdays 9 AM–10 PM and Saturday 9–noon; July–August, Monday–Wednesday and Friday 9 AM–9:30 PM.

Wellness Center (⊠ Calle della Pietà, off Riva degli Schiavoni near the Chiesa della Pietà, 3697 Castello, ☎ 041/5231944) has custom training sessions in English by appointment, sauna, and a tanning center in a 2,000-square-ft space on two floors. One entry costs €15.50, a three-day pass €36.00. It's open September–June, weekdays 8 AM–9 PM, Saturday, 9–1; July–August, Monday, Wednesday, and Friday 8 AM–9 PM, Tuesday and Thursday 3–9, Saturday 9–1.

Golf

The decent 18-hole **Golf Club Lido di Venezia** (⊠ Via del Forte, Alberoni, Lido, ☎ 041/731333), closed Monday, is on Lido island. You can rent clubs for €18.00 a day, and greens fees are €46.50 per person Tuesday–Saturday, €52.00 Sunday.

Horseback Riding

Although the iron rings that were once used to tie horses have remained on the walls of old buildings around town, horses can only be found on the Lido—but they are no longer allowed to trot on the beaches.

Circolo Ippico Veneziano (⊠ Ca' Bianca, Lido, ☎ 041/5265162), closed Sunday afternoon and Monday, rents horses for riding trails on the premises, and it can refer you to terra firma clubs around the Veneto.

Rowing

Venice's most traditional participant sport is *canottaggio,* or rowing. Several *società di canottieri* (rowing clubs) operate in the lagoon. The **Società Canottieri Bucintoro** (⊠ Zattere, 15 Dorsoduro, ☎ 041/5205630), founded in 1882, is the oldest and best-known club and has produced several national champions. Unfortunately, it does not rent out its boats or offer courses to nonmembers. You must join the club to take part in its activities, ranging from lagoon exploring to serious training, but should your vacation grow into a longer stay, you might want to consider this quintessentially Venetian sport.

Running

Your best bet is to combine exploration and fitness by running through town, but beware of dog droppings and the slippery steps on bridges. Here are a few routes: the **Fondamente Nuove,** near Campo Santi Giovanni e Paolo in the Cannaregio and Castello sestieri, offer good uninterrupted stretches away from the crowds, and the northern exposure makes the area one of the cooler places to be in midsummer. You can return to the center on Calle Racchetta and Strada Nova or take Via Barbaria delle Tole and Campo Santa Maria Formosa in the opposite direction. The **Zattere** promenade is definitely scenic, but there are likely to be many passersby to dodge. A pleasant, central route starts from the **Riva degli Schiavoni** (✉ past the busy San Zaccaria landing area, from the Chiesa della Pietà onward) and goes to the pine grove at Sant' Elena; you can return by way of the island of San Pietro di Castello and Via Garibaldi. For long-distance training, the best places to go are the **Lido beaches,** unpaved but with compact sand near the water (the bathing season goes from June to September, and in these months the best time is either before 9 AM or after 7 PM). From the San Zaccaria vaporetto stop, it will take you 40 to 50 minutes on Lines 6, 14, 32, or 51 (52 back) to reach the beaches.

The **Venice Marathon** is usually held the last Sunday of October. The course is the standard 42 km (26 mi), but it begins on terra firma in the town of Strà near Padua and follows the Brenta River to Mestre and Marghera before crossing to Venice, where it goes through Giudecca island, which for the occasion is connected to Piazza San Marco by a floating bridge, and finishes at Sant'Elena. In recent years, annual participation has reached nearly 6,000. Fees are lower with early registration. For information in Italy contact **Venicemarathon** (✉ Via Felisati 34, 30171 Mestre, ☎ 041/940644, FAX 041/940349); and from the States try **Marathon Tours & Travel** (✉ 261 Main St., Boston, MA 02129, ☎ 800/444–4097, FAX 617/242–7686).

Su e Zo per i Ponti (Down and Up the Bridges), an informal race through Venice traditionally held on a Sunday in March or April, is a fun event, more popular with local joggers-for-a-day and children than with international athletes. It starts around 9 AM in Piazza San Marco, where you can register right before the start. There are several itineraries of varying lengths to choose from, between 3 km (2 mi) and 14 km (9 mi). All participants receive a souvenir medal. You can get further information from the tourist office (☎ 041/5298711).

Swimming

With all the water around, you might well assume that Venetians learn to swim at a young age. But the first public swimming pool in Venice opened only in 1986. It was not too long ago that most children learned to swim with their waist securely tied to a rope held by a teacher standing on top of a bridge. Until boat traffic got too heavy after World War II, daily swimming races from Piazzetta di San Marco to the Lido were part of Venetian summers.

Venice's best public indoor pool, eight lanes wide and 26 meters long, is the **Piscina Comunale** (✉ Sacca Fisola island, far western end of Giudecca, ☎ 041/5285430), with a glass wall overlooking the lagoon. It's open daily September–mid-June (call ahead for hours); fees are €4.15

per hour, €36.15 for a 10-visit pass, and €45.00 for a monthly pass allowing three visits a week. To get there, take Line 82 to Sacca Fisola. A four-lane, 25-meter public pool is located near the **Sant'Alvise** church and bears the church's name (⊠ 3161 Cannaregio, ☎ 041/713567). It's open daily September–mid-July, with fees of €4.15 per hour, €36.15 for a 10-visit pass, and €45.00 for a monthly pass allowing three visits a week. It's housed in a well-preserved building that once served as the community laundry. Both pools have good shower facilities and spacious changing rooms but no lockers (you can leave your valuables with the attendants for free). The deluxe **Hotel des Bains** (⊠ Lungomare Marconi 17, Lido, ☎ 041/5260201) opens its small, kidney-shape outdoor pool with diving board (no lanes) to nonguests for an exorbitant fee (€52.00 per day). On the Lido, **Club Ca' del Moro** (⊠ Via F. Parri 6, ☎ 041/770965) has an outdoor pool (no lanes) open in summer (€15.50 per day).

Tennis

The **Hotel des Bains** (⊠ Lungomare Marconi 17, Lido, ☎ 041/5260201) rents tennis courts to nonguests. The exclusive **Sea Gull Club** of the Cipriani hotel (⊠ Giudecca 10, ☎ 041/5207744) will let nonguests play for a fee. Several tennis clubs are run on the Lido, including **Lido Tennis Club** (⊠ Via Sandro Gallo 163, ☎ 041/5260954); fees are €7.00 per person per hour. The Lido's **Club Ca' del Moro** (⊠ Via F. Parri 6, ☎ 041/770965) has tennis for €8.50 per court per hour.

SPECTATOR SPORTS

Unless your Venetian holiday corresponds with one of the few annual sports-related festivals, seeing a Sunday soccer match in the dated but cozy stadium at Sant'Elena is about all there is, apart from grade-school pickup games on *campi* (squares) throughout town.

Boat Races

La Vogalonga

Teams hold their oars high in the air until a cannon shot signals the start of the race, along with the ancient cry "Viva San Marco!" The oars drop to the water and the boats begin their *vogata lunga* (long row), a 30-km (19-mi) race in the lagoon. The event is held on the first, second, or third Sunday of May and is open to any oar-powered boat. It was begun by locals in 1974 as a symbol of protest against the devastating waves created by motorboats around the lagoon, which have done more damage to the old foundations of the city than the centuries of high water. It also was intended to relaunch old Venice rowing traditions. The number of boats participating has steadily risen over the years from 500 to 1,700, with more than 5,000 people from all over the world taking part. The rediscovery of *voga alla veneta* (standing rowing) has kept in business a good number of the city's boat workshops, where skiffs and oars are still made of wood. The race begins at 9 AM and wraps up at around 2 PM; the start and finish can be seen from Piazzetta San Marco and the Molo di San Marco, but there is competition for good standing places, so arrive a couple of hours early. To participate in La Vogalonga, you need to be over 16, pay a €9.50 registration fee, and come with your own boat. For information and registration, contact **Comitato Organizzatore Vogalonga** (⊠ c/o Rosa Slava, 951 San Marco, 30124 Venice, ☎ 041/5210544, FAX 041/5200771, WEB www.vogalonga.it).

Regata delle Befane

Since 1977, every January 6 the rowing club Società Canottieri Bucintoro has organized the Regata delle Befane. The majority of the club's
historic boats take part in the elimination rounds leading up to the final
race on the Grand Canal, in which five boats compete. The event co-
incides with the holiday of the Epiphany, the celebration of the day
when the three Wise Men came to see and worship the baby Jesus. On
this day the Santa Claus–like Befana (a mythical old woman with a
hooked nose, warts, secondhand clothes, and a scarf over her gray hair)
brings candy to good children and charcoal (black sugar lumps) to bad
ones. At midnight between January 5 and 6 she rides a broomstick
(though technically she's not a witch) and makes deliveries via chimneys. In the final race of the Regata, the rowers all dress as the Befana,
and the winning team gets an enormous flag strung on a the Befana's
broomstick.

Regata Storica

The first Sunday of every September since 1315 has been dedicated to
the Regata Storica, a series of four races on the Grand Canal, culminating with the season championship of the *gondolini* (two-oared,
gondola-like boats). The fame of the regatta derives in large part from
the procession of historic boats, with crews and passengers in Renaissance
costume, that kicks off the festivities. The procession honors Caterina
Cornaro (1454–1510), whose visit to Venice marked the beginning of
Venetian dominance over the island of Cyprus.

Other races during the Regata Storica include one for young children,
one for women in *mascarete* (small, oval-shape boats), and one for men
in *caorline* (heavy transport boats with six oars). The top four com-
petitors in each race receive a cash prize and a coveted flag: red for
first place, white for second, green for third, and blue for fourth. The
regatta starts and finishes at Ca' Foscari on the Grand Canal, and a
window overlooking the Grand Canal is the best place for viewing the
proceedings. Alternatively, secure a spot along the Riva del Vin or the
Riva del Carbon near the Rialto Bridge, in Campiello San Vio, or in
Campo San Samuele.

Soccer

After more than 30 years in the minor leagues, Venice's soccer team,
Venezia, was promoted in 1998 to Serie A (First Division). It was rel-
egated to Serie B (Second Division) in 2000, then promoted again to
Serie A in 2001. This means that every two weeks the Campo Sportivo
on the island of Sant'Elena hosts some of the best Italian teams.
Decades of neglect, due to lack of interest in what was once a hope-
less team, have turned this old stadium into one of the worst in Italy.
At press time, plans for a brand-new stadium to be built in the sub-
urbs of Mestre were well under way. The construction was expected
to start by the the beginning of 2002 and to last for two or three years.
The plan is then to convert the present structure, which dates back to
1913 and holds only 13,000 spectators, into a large public sports center, with a track, tennis courts, and the like. Tickets for the games are
sold at the Vela office (⊠ Calle dei Fuseri, San Marco 1810, ☎ 041/
2418029), open Monday–Saturday 7:30–7. If you want to sit among
the local green-and-black-clad fans, reserve ahead through your hotel.
For information about professional soccer in Venice, contact the tourist
office or **Venezia Calcio** (⊠ Via Alfredo Ceccherini 19, Mestre 30175,
☎ 041/2380711, WEB www.veneziacalcio.it). Matches are usually played
in the early afternoon on Sunday.

6 SHOPPING

Bring an extra suitcase to export your booty, because Venice is paradise found for shoppers of all varieties. There's no better place for gifts and souvenirs, from kitschy to one-of-a-kind. The hunting ground is vast, and if the city center is devoted to high fashion, glass artworks, and antiques, quieter parts of town are home to a number of artisans' shops, where paper is glued, pressed, and shaped into masks, and gilded cherubs are born from the hands of wood-carvers.

ALLURING SHOPS ABOUND IN VENICE. You'll find countless vendors of trademark Venetian wares such as glass and lace; the authenticity of some goods can be suspect, but they're often pleasing to the eye regardless of their heritage. For more sophisticated tastes (and deeper pockets), there are jewelers, antiques dealers, and high-fashion boutiques, on a par with those in Italy's larger cities but often maintaining a uniquely Venetian flair.

By Carla
Lionello

It's always a good idea to mark the location of a shop that interests you on your map; otherwise you may not be able to find it again in the maze of tiny streets. Regular store hours are usually 9–12:30 and 3:30 or 4–7:30 PM; some stores are closed on Saturday afternoon or Monday morning. Food shops are open 8–1 and 5–7:30, and are closed all day Sunday and on Wednesday afternoon. However, many tourist-oriented shops are open all day, every day. Some shops close for both a summer and a winter vacation. If you plan on a major purchase, take advantage of tax-free shopping with the value-added tax (VAT, or IVA in Italian) refund, whereby non-EU residents are entitled to a tax refund (roughly 13% of the purchase price) on purchases greater than €155.00 (pretax) of clothing and luxury goods made in one store.

Department Stores

You wouldn't expect to find a big department store sandwiched between Venice's canals and narrow alleys, but two of Italy's three department-store chains have managed to settle into some of Venice's largest storefronts. Middle-market **Standa** (⊠ Ponte San Felice, on the Strada Nova, 3659 Cannaregio, ☎ 041/5238046) has clothing, perfume, housewares, and a supermarket; the larger outlet on the Lido (⊠ Via Corfù 1/a, ☎ 041/5265720) is conveniently located on the way to the beaches. Decidedly more upmarket, **Coin** (⊠ Salizzada San Crisostomo, near Campo San Bartolomio, ☎ 041/5203581, WEB www.coin.it) sells clothing, leather goods, and housewares; in 2001, Coin opened a second outlet inside the former Standa store off Campo San Luca (⊠ 4546 San Marco, ☎ 041/5238444), but there you'll find only perfume and lingerie.

Markets

The itinerant flea markets that operate on the mainland never include Venice in their tours, and the only markets left in town trade in food. The morning open-air **fruit and vegetable market** at the Rialto district (open Monday–Saturday, roughly 8–1), in business since the 11th century, offers animated local color and commerce. With the decline of the Republic the market slowly lost its fame as a world trade center. The adjacent **Rialto Fish Market,** or *pescheria*, offers an impressive lesson in ichthyology, with species you've certainly never seen before (open Monday–Saturday, roughly 8–1). Smaller, lively food markets are located on Via Garibaldi, near the Giardini della Biennale, and on Strada Nova, not far from the train station (both open Monday–Saturday, roughly 8–1).

Shopping Districts

Piazza San Marco

The rule here is simple: the closer you are to Piazza San Marco, the higher the prices, especially for low-end market stuff. The serious jewelry and glasswork in the windows of the shops of the Procuratie Vecchie and Nuove make for a pleasant browse, and during the summer your stroll will be accompanied by the music from the bands that set up in front of Caffè Quadri and Florian. Under the arcades you'll also find an art gallery, a few old-fashioned shops selling kitschy souvenirs, and an assortment of lace, linen blouses, and silk ties and scarves. Masks haven't landed here, yet.

Mercerie
The network of streets between the tower clock in Piazza San Marco and Campo San Salvador near Rialto is called the Mercerie. For centuries this was where Venetians came to shop—the word *merceria* comes from *merce* (goods). Only a few refined shops survive—the rest are spread out along other streets in the center of town—and a run of anonymous clothing shops and cheap souvenir boutiques has taken their place. On Campo San Zulian is Cartier, worth a look for its rather dour facade, and around the corner in Merceria San Zulian is a long-established jewelry shop (with no name) selling exquisite antique pieces.

Gucci is on Merceria dell'Orologio, but it has little of the flair and selection you'll find at its sister shops in Rome and Milan. Venice's top lace retailer, Jesurum, opened a second showroom on Merceria del Capitello, and from there it's a short walk (in the direction of Campo San Salvador) to Rosa Salva, one of the best pastry shops in town. Up ahead on the campo is the lingerie boutique La Perla, with lingerie so elegant you could wear it to a party, and Marforio, Venice's standby for high-quality leather.

Campo San Bartolomio and Rialto
Other good shopping areas surround Campi San Salvador and San Bartolomio. The department store Coin is just past the central post office and down Ponte dell'Olio. The Rialto district is the mecca for buyers of traditional, inexpensive souvenirs: *furlane,* or *pantofole del gondoliere,* velvety slippers with rubber soles that resemble the traditional gondoliers' shoes; 18th-century-style wooden trays and coasters that will look better after a little wear; and glass "candies," which make a nice, inexpensive (if inedible) gift. Clothing and shoe shops are concentrated between the Rialto Bridge and San Polo, along Ruga Vecchia San Giovanni and Ruga Ravano, and around Campo Sant'Aponal.

West of Piazza San Marco
The San Marco sestiere has its fair share of boutiques, jewelry shops, antiques dealers, and the most important art galleries in the city, including Bugno.

Specialty Shops
Antiques and Art Dealers
You may not ship home an 19th-century bed from Venice, and even a relatively common item like an Art Deco chest of drawers is more easily found in Rome, Florence, or Naples. But if you have a taste for odd accessories from another age, Victorian silver plate, prints, or portable antiques with a *je ne sais quoi* to fill an empty corner, you might just find what you weren't even looking for. In recent years, art galleries have sprouted up here and there, and, after centuries of commercial slumber, Venice seems on its way to finally catching up with the world's contemporary art scene.

Do the huge windows of **Antichità Pietro Scarpa** (✉ Campo della Carità, 1023 Dorsoduro, ☎ 041/5239700) show off well-made replicas of the originals inside the Gallerie dell'Accademia next door? Not a chance—these are all originals, so you'll have to confess to Signor Scarpa that it's really hard having to choose between a Titian and a Canaletto. Maybe you'll take both?

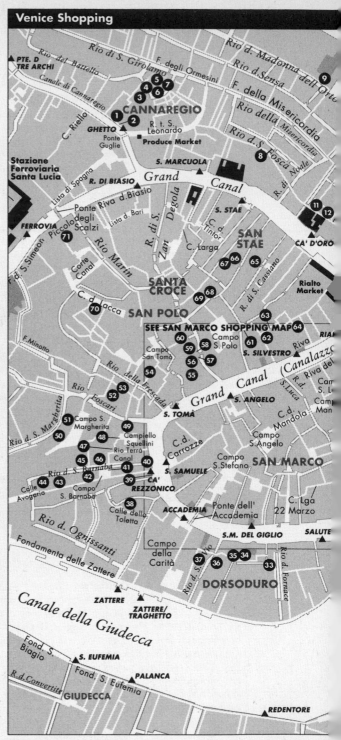

Venice Shopping

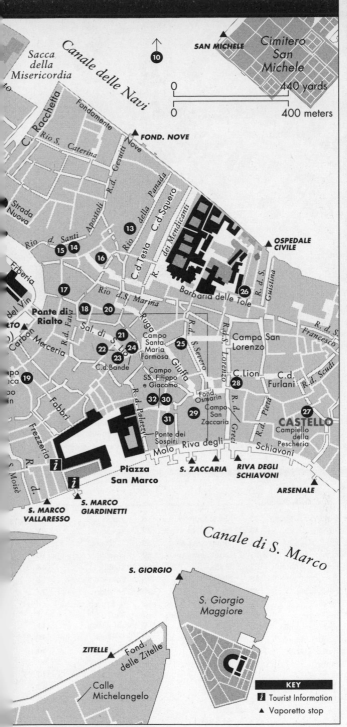

Sacca della Misericordia

Canale delle Navi

SAN MICHELE

Cimitero San Michele

440 yards

400 meters

FOND. NOVE

Canale delle Navi

Fondamente Nove

Rio S. Caterina

C. Racchetta

Rio d. Santi

Strada Nuova

R. d. Gesuiti

R. d. della Panada

C. d. Sauero

dei Mendicanti

OSPEDALE CIVILE

Barbaria delle Tole

R. d. S. Giustina

Erberia

del Vin

Ponte di Rialto

Carbon

Merceria

Rio d. S. Marina

Ruga Giuffa

Sal. di

C. d. Bande

Campo Santa Maria Formosa

Campo SS. Filippo e Giacomo

R. d. Fava

R. S. Severo

R. d. Lorenzo

Campo San Lorenzo

Campo San Lorenzo

C. Lion

C. d. Furlani

R. d. S. Francesco

R. d. Scudi

Fabbri

Frezzeria

R. d. Palazzi

Fond. Osmarin

Campo San Zaccaria

R. d. Greci

R. d. Pietà

CASTELLO

Campiello della Pescheria

Ponte dei Sospiri

Molo

Riva degli

Riva degli Schiavoni

Piazza San Marco

S. ZACCARIA

RIVA DEGLI SCHIAVONI

ARSENALE

S. MARCO VALLARESSO

S. MARCO GIARDINETTI

S. R. d. Moisè

Canale di S. Marco

S. GIORGIO

S. Giorgio Maggiore

ZITELLE

Fond. delle Zitelle

Calle Michelangelo

KEY

ℹ️ Tourist Information

▲ Vaporetto stop

148

San Marco Shopping

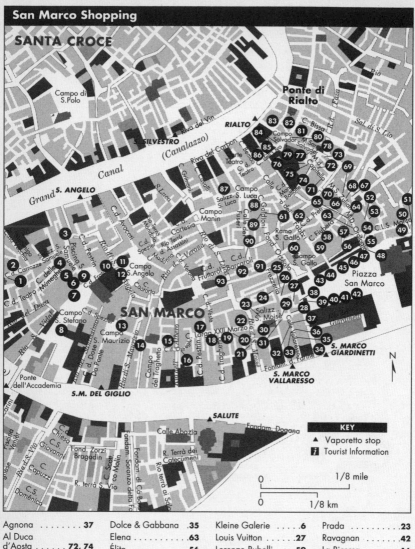

SANTA CROCE

Antiquus (✉ Calle delle Botteghe, 3131 San Marco, ☎ 041/5206395), a cozy shop from another era, sells a bit of everything, from old-master paintings to jewelry. Among the hottest items are the lovely earrings and brooches in the shape of Venetian Moors' heads.

Claudia Canestrelli (✉ Campiello Barbaro, near the Peggy Guggenheim Collection, 364/a Dorsoduro, ☎ 041/5227072 or 347/4812388) is a tasteful shop with a limited choice of antiques, small paintings, and plenty of interesting-looking bric-a-brac, including silver ex-votos and period souvenirs such as brass ashtrays in the shape of lions' heads.

Kleine Galerie (✉ Calle delle Botteghe, 2972 San Marco, ☎ 041/5222177) is a good address for antique books and prints, majolica, and ceramics.

La Luna nel Pozzo (✉ Calle Lunga San Barnaba, 2860 Dorsoduro, ☎ 041/5237072), or the "Moon in the Well," smells of flea markets and old attics. Old table silver plate with ivory handles, antique glass, lamps, beautiful pewter plates, bowls, and pitchers fill the place. The knowledgeable lady who runs the shop gives a special discount to shoppers on Thursday morning.

Luisa Semenzato (✉ Merceria San Zulian, 732 San Marco, ☎ 041/5231412) offers a good selection of furniture, a few paintings by minor masters, and European ceramics, as well as a miscellanea of more affordable objets d'art.

Art Galleries

Bac Art Studio (✉ Fondamenta Venier, near the Gallerie dell'Accademia, 862 Dorsoduro, ☎ 041/5228171, WEB www.bacart.com) was founded in 1977 by Paolo Baruffaldi and Cadore, two etchers with a soft spot for angels, views of Venice and the lagoon, flowers, cats, and insects. The gallery also hosts exhibits of other local artists. Prices start around €10.00 for a 2-inch x 1-inch etching.

Bugno (✉ Campo San Fantin, 1996/a San Marco, ☎ 041/5231305), a retailer of contemporary art, puts together windows representative of the whole gallery—most notably, Missagia's fruit and apples on "textured" backgrounds made of pasted newspaper and cardboard and Demarchi's sexy wooden sculptures.

Contini (✉ Campo Santo Stefano, 2765 San Marco, ☎ 041/5207525) shows only figurative artists of the 20th century, including big names like Picasso, Chagall, Magritte, and Giacometti. It's also Italy's only dealer for Botero, Navarro Vires, Zoran Music, and the marble and bronze sculptures by Mitorag.

Gallery Holly Snapp (✉ Calle delle Botteghe, 3133 San Marco, ☎ 041/5210030) focuses on the works by the eclectic English-born artist Geoffrey Humphries, including paintings, drawings, and etchings of a great variety of subjects, from landscapes to portraits; among them are watercolors of Venice.

Melori & Rosenberg (✉ Campo del Ghetto Nuovo, 2919 Cannaregio, ☎ 041/2750039, WEB www.melori-rosenberg.com) shows young Italian artists on their way up, including Luigi Rocca (hyper-realist scenes of modern life), Francesco Mancini (views of Venice and nudes in the impressionist style), Michele Giorgio Riva (still lifes), and expressionist Henry Vigino.

Ravagnan (✉ under Procuratie Nuove, Piazza San Marco 50/a, San Marco, ☎ 041/5203021, WEB www.ravagnangallery.com) has since 1967 been the exclusive dealer of some of the most noted living artists on the Italian scene, including Venetian surrealist Ludovico de Luigi and metaphysical painter Andrea Vizzini. You'll also find here glass sculptures by Primo Formenti and collages by Piero Principi.

Ceramics

With all the glass around town, it's not surprising that Venice has never been known for its pottery. You can find replicas of 19th-century chocolate cups, usually cream-white and delicately gilded (not for daily use); pottery from Bassano, typically decorated with reliefs of fruit and vegetables; and some modern, handmade plates and mugs.

Angela Greco (✉ Campo Santa Maria del Giglio, 2433 San Marco, ☎ 041/5234573), a must for collectors and lovers of antique ceramics, has affordable items such as replicas of 19th-century Venetian chocolate cups.

Atelier (✉ Calle del Pestrin, near Campo dell'Arsenale, 3876 Castello, ☎ 041/5225895 or 348/7249249) stocks black-and-white ceramics with subjects inspired by famous erotic Italian cartoons. There are also more chaste pieces, some reminiscent of pop art. It's closed Wednesday and mornings.

Bottega del Vasaio (✉ Campo Santa Margherita, 2904 Dorsoduro, ☎ 347/5387318) has vases turned on a wheel, plates, cups, and tiles, all handmade and painted in bright colors. The house specialty is the *tazza da colazione* (breakfast cup), a large cup attached to a kidney-shape saucer and meant for morning cappuccino.

Margherita Rossetto (✉ Sotoportego della Siora Bettina, off Campo San Cassiano, San Cancian in Venetian, 2345 Santa Croce, ☎ 041/723120) creates faience-style majolica on a white background, with figures of animals, flowers, and fruit designed in oxidized copper.

Rigattieri (✉ Calle dei Frati, between Campo Santo Stefano and Campo Sant'Angelo, 3532 San Marco, ☎ 041/5231081) sells pottery from Bassano, ranging from white plates with a lace border to serving bowls in the shape of hens and geese to platters with asparagus in relief. They also sell lanterns in blown glass that will give a Venetian touch to your garden or porch.

Clothing

Venetian streets lined with so many designers' boutiques and tiny pricey stores may leave you wondering where Venetians buy their everyday clothes. The truth is that fancy garments are not worn much here. Venice is a town without office buildings, banks, or government offices, and the casual dress code favored here agrees with the mileage to be covered on foot everyday. You will undoubtedly see a few impeccably dressed *signore* (ladies) who manage the bridges in high heels without a misstep, but most Venetians prefer a more relaxed and creative style than that of the fashion-conscious Milanese and Romans. Bargain-hunters should know that the best clothing sales typically occur from January 7 until mid–February and from mid- to late July to early September.

Agnona (✉ Calle Vallaresso, 1307 San Marco, ☎ 041/5205733) has incredibly warm cashmere and wool knitwear and winter coats—all in soft natural colors (creamy white and various shades of beige) and clean cuts. In the summer, the designers switch to linen. Angora slippers make a great gift.

Al Pupo (✉ Campo Santa Fosca, 2215 Cannaregio, ☎ 041/721748) is one of the few surviving Venetian shops selling clothes for infants and children. It's a cut above the rest, with good prices and assortments. They even make Carnevale costumes for toddlers.

Armani (⊠ Calle Goldoni, 4412 San Marco, ☎ 041/5234758), in a rather grand space, delivers its superlative signature style and service—women's silk shirts are especially striking for quality, design, and price. Those waiting for the dressing rooms can rest on comfortable couches.

Camiceria San Marco (⊠ Calle Vallaresso, 1340 San Marco, ☎ 041/5221432) is the town's top custom shirtmaker, with a good assortment of blouses and shirts. Only the finest fabrics are used (they can also be bought by the meter). Elegant pajamas, gowns, and ladies' dresses complete the scene.

Elysée (⊠ Calle Goldoni, 4485 San Marco, ☎ 041/5223020; ⊠ Frezzeria, 1693 San Marco, ☎ 041/5223020) stocks mostly Armani or Armani-style clothing.

Emporio Armani (⊠ Calle dei Fabbri, 989 San Marco, ☎ 041/5237808) flaunts the famous stylist's casual line, with his eagle symbol fastened onto just about everything.

Fiorella Mancini (⊠ Campo Santo Stefano, 2806 San Marco, ☎ 041/5209228) is your best bet for original creations and the craziest look in town.

La Coupole (⊠ Calle Larga XXII Marzo, 2366 San Marco, ☎ 041/5224243; ⊠ Calle Larga XXII Marzo, 2031 San Marco, ☎ 041/5232754; ⊠ Calle Larga XXII Marzo, 2254 San Marco, ☎ 041/5231273), with three shops a stone's throw from one another, offers an excellent selection of name-brand *alta moda* (high fashion).

La Tour (⊠ Calle Larga San Marco, 287 San Marco, ☎ 041/5225147) carries labels such as Versace, Ferré, and the unparalleled Malo cashmere-wear.

Venice's **Prada** (⊠ Campo San Moisè, 1479 San Marco, ☎ 041/5283966) is one of the largest Prada stores in Italy. Suit up in clean-cut, modern-looking articles made out of high-tech materials, leather, or not-so-delicate natural fibers.

Trussardi (⊠ Spadaria, 695 San Marco, ☎ 041/5285757) houses the clothing, shoes, and bags of its famous namesake Italian designer.

MEN'S FASHIONS

Al Duca d'Aosta (⊠ Merceria del Capitello, 4946 San Marco, ☎ 041/5220733) stocks such classics as Burberry and Ralph Lauren.

Ceriello (⊠ Campo SS. Filippo e Giacomo, 4275 San Marco, ☎ 041/5222062) is the only shop in Venice with Brioni suits.

Élite (⊠ Calle Larga San Marco, 284 San Marco, ☎ 041/5230145) is the source for not-so-casual Italian outdoor wear and the quintessentially English Aquascutum coats and suits that are ubiquitous in Italy. There are also silk ties and cashmere scarves.

La Bottega (⊠ Merceria dell'Orologio, 223 San Marco, ☎ 041/5225608) is the place to go if you like the comfort and style of leading Italian classic designers Cerruti and Ermenegildo Zegna.

Otello (⊠ Calle dell'Acqua, 4989 San Marco, ☎ 041/5223142) has a great selection of brightly colored waistcoats and bow ties—not for the conservative dresser.

WOMEN'S FASHIONS

Al Duca d'Aosta (⊠ Merceria del Capitello, 4922 San Marco, ☎ 041/5204079), no longer the Venetian bulwark of classy Italian fashion, now offers a selection of international pret-a-porter on its two floors: Jil Sander, Rebecca Moses, Donna Karan, and Ralph Lauren.

Arabesque (✉ Ponte dei Greci, 3403 Castello, ☎ 041/5228177) sells the serviceable foulards that designer Barbieri started creating in 1945. These days, new, "technologic" fibers are woven in with silk or linen to give classic scarves a dramatic sparkling effect.

Arras (✉ Campiello Squellini, 3234 Dorsoduro, ☎ 041/5226460) sells exclusive scarves as well as a few blouses and jackets, all hand-woven in wool or silk. It also occasionally organizes weaving workshops.

Caberlotto (✉ Calle Mazzini, 5114 San Marco, ☎ 041/5229242) has cornered the market on fabulous fur coats and hats and interesting wool blazers for those cold walks about town. There are also pashmina shawls by Rosenda Arcioni Meer.

Dolce & Gabbana (✉ Calle Vallaresso, 1314 San Marco, ☎ 041/5205733) design most of their collections—usually characterized by a mild transgressive flair—for the slim, fit, and highly fashion-conscious.

Gucci (✉ Merceria dell'Orologio, 258 San Marco, ☎ 041/5229119) sells shoes, bags, accessories, and some clothes as well in two side-by-side shops.

Hermès (✉ Procuratie Vecchie, 127 San Marco, ☎ 041/5210117) offers the famous French foulards and accessories.

Hibiscus (✉ Calle dell'Olio, near the Rialto Market, 1060 San Polo, ☎ 041/5208989) is a hip boutique selling loose-fitting women's clothing (which look better on you than they do drooping from hangers) and matching accessories. The style is very youthful, the prices very adult.

Kenzo (✉ Ramo dei Fuseri, 1814 San Marco, ☎ 041/5205733) stocks trendy clothes for young people with big wallets. Neat, slim cuts are daringly matched to brightly colored, often floral patterns, which at their best recall sumptuous tapestry. Wear a Kenzo jacket and you need-n't worry about being missed in a crowd.

La Fenice (✉ Calle Larga XXII Marzo, 2255 San Marco, ☎ 041/5231273) has an assortment of the major Italian and foreign stylists, including evening dresses and shoes to match.

La Perla (✉ Campo San Salvador, 4828 San Marco, ☎ 041/5226459) specializes in extremely elegant lingerie that's comfortable, too.

Le Ragazze di Cima (✉ Strada Nova, near Ponte San Felice, 3683 Cannaregio, ☎ 041/5234988) carries the best Italian brands of lingerie, from glossy silk to cotton lace.

Malo (✉ Calle de le Ostreghe, 2359 San Marco, ☎ 041/5232162) is recognized as one of Italy's highest-quality producers of cashmere garments. Its styles are tasteful and refined, designed and made to be worn for many years.

Mario Borsato (✉ Calle Vallaresso, 1318 San Marco, ☎ 041/5210313) is a local designer who creates sober outfits for real ladies only. If you like the look, inquire about his large shop in Treviso.

Missoni (✉ Calle Vallaresso, 1312 San Marco, ☎ 041/5205733) sells scarves and clothing made of wool, linen, or cotton, but all rigorously knitted and dramatically colorful.

The **Shirt Shop** (✉ Campo Sant'Angelo, 3820 San Marco, ☎ no phone) specializes in good-quality cotton shirts and blouses and well-made stockings.

Valentino (✉ Salizzada San Moisè, 1473 San Marco, ☎ 041/5205733) only sells clothing signed by the famous stylist of the same name.

Valeria Bellinaso (✉ Campo Sant'Aponal, 1226 San Polo, ☎ 041/5223351) designs attractive (and expensive) straw hats, perfect for a romantic date in the park. The store also features shawls full of character and foldable silk bags that are light as a feather yet large enough to pack for the weekend.

Costumes and Accessories

Atelier Pietro Longhi (✉ Rio Terrà dei Frari, 2604/b San Polo, ☎ 041/714478) rents out and sells costumes inspired by authentic 18th- and 19th-century models, with masks (for sale only) to match, available also in large sizes for both sexes.

Flavia (✉ near Campo San Lio, 6010 Castello, ☎ 041/2413200) is a good address for historical costumes, either made-to-order or for rent; you can also rent tuxedos all year round.

Laboratorio Arte & Costume (✉ Calle del Scaleter, near Campo San Polo, 2235 San Polo, ☎ 041/5246242) is the place if you are making your own costume and need some professional help with scissors and needles. Monica Daniele will fix your problem as quickly as her sewing machine will go. In the meantime you can take a look at the assorted hats, bags, and vintage clothing.

At **Laboratorio Parrucche Carlotta** (✉ Campo Widman, 5415 Cannaregio, ☎ 041/5207571) wigmaker Carlotta Carisi believes that at Carnevale details count, and her sensational creations are the ideal way to top off an elegant costume. Note that the quality comes at a price (€230.00–€500.00), and credit cards are not accepted.

Nicolao Atelier (✉ Calle del Magazin, near Campo SS. Apostoli, 5590/a Cannaregio, ☎ 041/5209749) is the largest costume-rental shop in town, with nearly 7,000 ranging from the historical to the fantastic, including thematic costumes ideal for group masquerades. At the **tailor's workshop** (✉ Calle del Bagatin, near Campo SS. Apostoli, 5565 Cannaregio) you can see the costumes being made (by appointment only).

At **Venetia** (✉ Frezzeria, 1286 San Marco, ☎ 041/5224426) the colorful, fanciful display window of 18th-century Venetian outfits often makes passersby stop to admire the mannequins. Less-glamorous medieval-style garments, masks, and accessories are kept behind the curtains inside.

English-Language Books

Although there aren't any strictly English bookshops in Venice, some places carry small selections of books in English. For newspapers and magazines in English, the best-stocked newsstand is on Bocca di Piazza near the Museum Correr.

Ca' Foscarina (✉ Campiello Squellini, 3259 Dorsoduro, ☎ 041/5229602) is the bookstore of nearby Università di Venezia Ca' Foscari, with the town's largest selection of books in English. Shelves are heavy with literature and history, but there's also a corner devoted to travel books and a handful of best-sellers.

Demetra (✉ Campo Sant'Aponal, 1128 San Polo, ☎ 041/5208760), part of a bookstore chain, has a small number of books in English (best-sellers and guide books) plus an interesting selection of Italian titles (with plenty of self-explanatory color pictures) dedicated to handicrafts.

Fantoni (✉ off Campo San Luca, 4119 San Marco, ☎ 041/5220700) specializes in coffee-table books on art, architecture, photography, and design, mostly in Italian, but the beautiful illustrations speak for themselves. You'll find books in English on Venice and Italian food.

Filippi (✉ Calle del Paradiso, 5763 Castello, ☎ 041/5236916) might not have any books in English, but if you read Italian you're likely to be impressed by the selection of books about Venetian history and folklore.

Libreria San Pantalon (✉ Crosera, also known as Calle Lunga San Pantalon, 3950 Dorsoduro, ☎ 041/5224436) specializes in children's books (some in English), minor arts and crafts, and books on music and opera (in Italian).

Studium (✉ Calle della Canonica, 337/C San Marco, ☎ 041/5222382) is a good stop for books in English, especially guidebooks and books on Venetian culture and food.

Gifts

At **Angelo Dalla Venezia** (✉ Calle del Scaleter, off Campo San Polo, 2204 San Polo, ☎ 041/721659), Signor Angelo makes wooden "eggs" for mending socks and knitwear and hard-to-find wooden bobbins for lace making.

Antichità Santomanco della Toffola (✉ Frezzeria, 1504 San Marco, ☎ 041/5236643) sells Russian and English silver work, paintings, period glass and jewelry, and bric-a-brac.

Fusetti Diego Baruch (✉ Ghetto Vecchio, 1218 Cannaregio, ☎ 041/720092) has all manner of handmade Jewish handicrafts, including replicas of antique menorahs, in glass, bronze, gold, silver, and mosaic. It's closed Saturday.

Giro Vago (✉ Ponte dei Miracoli, near the Chiesa dei Miracoli, 6019 Cannaregio, ☎ 348/2924991) is a creative workshop that produces groovy handmade copper jewelry and leather bags. It's almost always open, but sometimes the owner is out of town at markets and fairs, so it's a good idea to call ahead.

Giuliana Longo (✉ Calle del Ovo, 4813 San Marco, ☎ 041/5226454) is a hat shop with a very special corner dedicated to accessories for antique cars; the leather goggles and helmets are also great for skiing.

Il Baule Blu (✉ Calle Prima, off Campo San Tomà, 2916/a San Polo, ☎ 041/719448, ⬜ www.ilbauleblu.com) specializes in *orsi artistici,* teddy bears to collect and treat with great care. All fastidiously handmade and different from one another, these old-fashioned toys have articulated paws and glass eyes and when squeezed on their tummy can either grumble or play a carillon tune. Some are stark naked; others are dressed in old baby garments trimmed with lace and ribbons. They come in all sizes, ages, and colors.

La Stamperia del Ghetto (✉ Calle del Ghetto Vecchio, 1185/a Cannaregio, ☎ 041/2750200) sells black-and-white prints of the old Ghetto. It's closed Saturday.

La Venexiana (✉ Frezzeria, 1135 San Marco, ☎ 041/5286888), an Aladdin's cave full of last-minute gift treasures, sells mostly Carnevale-oriented keepsakes.

Le Sculture di Livio de Marchi (✉ Calle delle Carrozze, near Palazzo Grassi, 3157/a San Marco, ☎ 041/5285694, ⬜ www.liviodemarchi.

com) received national news coverage during the 1999 Carnevale season when Signor De Marchi created a costume for boats: a car body made of wood. His swift hands turn wood into gold, or rather into outstanding full-scale sculptures that perfectly reproduce everyday objects such as hats, laundry hung out to dry, telephones, jackets, books, fruit, lace—even underwear. Prices start at about €80.00 but can easily reach four figures. It's closed weekends.

Perle Veneziane (✉ Ponte della Canonica, 4308 San Marco, ☎ 041/5289059; ✉ inside the airport at Tessera, ☎ 041/5415871), two minutes from Piazza San Marco, fits the bill when you've got gifts to buy and you're short on time. There's an assortment of necklaces, faux-period Venetian glass jewelry and loose modern beads, but also *murrine,* pour tops for olive oil bottles, and an assortment of glass curios.

Signor Blum (✉ Fondamenta Gherardini, off Campo San Barnaba, 2840 Dorsoduro, ☎ 041/5226367, 𝖂𝖤𝖡 www.signorblum.com) makes solid large-piece puzzles (painted or in natural wood colors) depicting animals, views of Venice, and trompe l'oeil scenes. Ideal toys for toddlers, the puzzles also make a nice pictures to hang.

Strafanti & Cavalieri (✉ Campo del Ghetto Nuovo, 2920 Cannaregio, ☎ 041/2440176) is operated by Luigina Checchini, a Venetian who returned home in 1999 after 10 years spent in Kenya. In her small shop she sells African pottery, hand-printed clothing, and necklaces made of painted beads and brass. The "Venetian corner" features soap made according to a medieval recipe and a selection of collectible handmade books about the region. Like jewelry made with *vetro murrina*? Luigina will tell you in fluent English how she is the only one in town to have the real McCoy. The shop is closed Monday.

Tabaccheria Grandesso (✉ Campo Santa Margherita, 2979 Dorsoduro, ☎ 041/5238626) stocks old-fashioned school pads and notebooks, as well as period postcards.

Glassware

Glass, most of it made in Murano, is Venice's number one product, and you'll be confronted by mind-boggling, often kitschy displays of traditional and contemporary glassware. Take your time and be selective. If you want to make an investment, the important producers to remember are Barovier, Pauly, Poli, Seguso, Toso, and Venini. Freelance designers create pieces for more than just a single glasshouse: look for signatures and certificates of authentication. Bear in mind that the value of any piece—signature and shape apart—is also based on the number of colors, the presence of gold, and, in the case of goblets, the thinness of the glass. Prices are about the same all over, but be warned that some shops sell glass made in Taiwan. All shops will arrange for shipping.

Al Campanil (✉ Calle Lunga Santa Maria Formosa, 5184 Castello, ☎ 041/5235734) specializes in replicas of antique Murano pieces and jewelry made with tiny glass Venetian beads.

Antichità (✉ Calle della Toletta, 1195 Dorsoduro, ☎ 041/5223159) has an attractive display of period objects made with the tiniest Murano glass beads "woven" on linen threads, as well as new creations, such as stunning flowers and necklaces in the shape of snakes. The old and new are hard to tell apart, as they are crafted with the same antique beads. Here you can also purchase small quantities of antique beads for making your own jewelry.

Domus (✉ Fondamenta dei Vetrai 82, Murano, ☎ 041/739215) has a selection of smaller objects and jewelry from the best glassworks.

Ferro & Cimegotto (⊠ Ramo dei Saoneri, 2672/a San Polo, ☎ 041/5227794) uses glass, enamel, and gold to make traditional Venetian plaques, coats-of-arms, and crucifixes, all for wall display. They take custom orders.

Galleria San Nicolò (⊠ Calle del Traghetto, near the Ca' Rezzonico vaporetto stop, 2793 Dorsoduro, ☎ 041/5221535) is owned by the American glass expert Louise Berndt. It shows the best of contemporary glass, including superb work by Yoichi Ohira, a Japanese designer who has lived in Venice for many years. It's closed Sunday and Monday.

Genninger Studio's (⊠ Calle dei Barcaroli, 1845 San Marco, ☎ 041/5225565; ⊠ Calle del Traghetto, off Campo San Barnaba, 2793/a Dorsoduro, ☎ no phone) is the retail outlet for Leslie Ann Genninger, an American from Ohio who was the first woman to enter the male-dominated world of Murano master bead makers. She established her own line of jewelry, called Murano Class Act, in 1994 using period glass beads, and when she could no longer find antique beads, she started designing her own. Here you'll also find glasswork signed by Venetian Lucio Bubacco.

Gianfranco Penzo (⊠ Campo del Ghetto Nuovo, 2895 Cannaregio, ☎ no phone) decorates Jewish ritual vessels in glass and makes commemorative plates. He takes special orders.

L'Isola (⊠ Campo San Moisè, 1468 San Marco, ☎ 041/5231973) has chic, contemporary glassware signed by Carlo Moretti.

Marina Barovier's Gallery (⊠ Calle delle Botteghe, off Campo Santo Stefano, 3216 San Marco, ☎ 041/5236748) has an excellent selection of collectible contemporary glass. It's closed Sunday and Monday.

Paropàmiso (⊠ Frezzeria, 1701 San Marco, ☎ 041/5227120) sells stunning Venetian glass beads and jewelry from all over the world.

Pauly (⊠ Ala Napoleonica, 73–77 San Marco, ☎ 041/5209899) has a large showroom in Piazza San Marco, with a wide array of glassware and chandeliers.

Tre Erre (⊠ Piazza San Marco 79/b, ☎ 041/5201715) is a reliable and respected firm for both traditional and contemporary glass designs.

Venini (⊠ Piazzetta dei Leoncini, 314 San Marco, ☎ 041/5224045, WEB www.venini.it) has been an institution since the 1930s, attracting some of the foremost names in glass design.

Vetri d'Arte (⊠ Piazza San Marco 140, ☎ 041/5200205) offers moderately priced glass jewelry.

Gold, Wood, and Metalwork

Venice's passion for glittering golden objects, which began with the decoration in the Basilica di San Marco and later spread into the finest noble homes, kept specialized gold artisans (called *doradori*) in business for several centuries. They still produce lovely cabinets, shelves, wall lamps, lanterns, candleholders, banisters, headboards, frames, and the like by applying gold leaf to wrought iron and carved wood. A bunch of skilled silversmiths still cater to the faithful, and in their workshops you'll find silver devotional icons of the Madonna della Salute and of the Madonna Nicopeia, traditionally hung in Venetian bedrooms. Most foundries have long since closed their doors, but you can still find top-quality brass pieces at Valese Fonditore.

Cornici Trevisanello (⊠ Fondamenta Bragadin, off Campo San Vio, ☎ 041/5207779) is special for wonderful handcrafted frames, made of gold-leafed wood and inset with antique glass beads, mosaic tesserae, and small ceramic tiles. Either Byzantine or rich Renaissance in appearance, the more elaborate pieces are at their best when used to frame an old mirror.

Dorador (✉ Campo San Barnaba, 2808 Dorsoduro, ☎ no phone) trades in gilded carved wood, including flying cherubs playing trumpets.

E. Pandian e Figli (✉ Campo Santa Maria Mater Domini, 2171 Santa Croce, ☎ 041/5241398) creates artisanal silver work, most notably icons of venerated Venetian Madonnas.

Gilberto Penzo (✉ Calle Seconda dei Saoneri, 2681 San Polo, ☎ 041/719372) is the gondola expert in Venice. He creates scale models of gondolas and lagoon boats and real gondola *forcole* (crotches where gondoliers balance their oars) in his *laboratorio* (workshop) nearby. (If the shop is closed, a sign posted on the door will explain how to get ahold of Mr. Penzo.) When he's not busy sawing and sanding, Mr. Penzo writes historical and technical books about gondola building. Here you'll also find gondola model kits, a great gift for the boatbuilder in your life.

Jonathan Ceolin (✉ Ponte Marcello off Campo Santa Marina, 6106 Castello, ☎ 041/5200609), in his tiny workshop near Campo Santa Maria Formosa, makes traditional wrought-iron chandeliers, wall lamps, and Venetian lanterns, either plain black or gilded (like in the old days).

Maurizio Sumiti (✉ Calle delle Bande, 5274 Castello, ☎ 041/5205621) is a good place for traditional wrought-iron chandeliers and lamps: they come plain, gilded, or tastefully enameled in bright colors. Here you'll also find conspicuous, 5-ft-tall wooden sculptures of *mori veneziani* (Venetian Moors).

Valese Fonditore (✉ Calle Fiubera, 793 San Marco, ☎ 041/5227282; workshop: ✉ 3535 Cannaregio, near Madonna dell'Orto, ☎ 041/720234), the Valese foundry, here since 1913, works in brass, bronze, copper, and pewter. The various metals are then cast into artistic handles, menorahs, Carnevale masks, and real gondola decorations (which make great paperweights, bookends, or unusual shelf pieces). The coups de grâce are the brass chandeliers, exactly like those that hang in the Oval Office in the White House. The foundry is open only by appointment on Friday mornings.

Jewelry

Venetians have always liked gold, and the city is packed with first-class jewelry shops, as well as more modest shops found outside the San Marco area, most notably around the Rialto district. One of the most typical pieces of inexpensive jewelry that you can buy is a murrina, a thin, round slice of colored glass (imagine a bunch of colored spaghetti firmly held together and sliced) encircled with gold and sold as pendants or earrings. Their manufacture is well explained in the Museo del Vetro at Murano.

Bastianello (✉ Via Due Aprile, off Campo San Bartolomio, 5042 San Marco, ☎ 041/5226751) has classic jewelry as well as pieces made with semiprecious stones.

Bulgari (✉ Calle Larga XXII Marzo, 2282 San Marco, ☎ 041/2410553, WEB www.bulgari.com) is one of the best-known Italian jewelry designers.

Cartier (✉ Campo San Zulian, 606 San Marco, ☎ 041/5222071) has watches and jewelry by the famous designer.

Elena (✉ Merceria dell'Orologio, 214 San Marco, ☎ 041/5226540) carries pieces signed by world-famous jewelers Fabergé, Buccellati, Chanel, Piguet, and Damiani.

Gianmaria Buccellati (✉ Merceria dell'Orologio, 214 San Marco, ☎ 041/5226540) is an Italian big name for watches and jewelry.

Gualti (✉ Rio Terà Canal, near Campo Santa Margherita, 3111 Dorsoduro, ☎ 041/5201731, WEB www.gualti.com) makes creative jewelry in colored resin that looks as fragile as glass but is as strong and soft as rubber. Earrings take the shape of mysterious sea creatures—sea anemones or jellyfish—broaches look like fall leaves, and necklaces are reminiscent of Queen Elizabeth's ruffled collars. Silk shoes can be custom "garnished" with jewelry.

La Bauta (✉ Merceria del Capitello, 705 San Marco, ☎ 041/5200324) is devoted to Tiffany creations.

At **Laboratorio Orafo Guido Carbonich** (✉ Ponte delle Guglie, 1297 Cannaregio, ☎ 041/720461) Guido Carbonich's interest in Byzantine and Oriental art comes out in his unique jewels, made from silver, coral, and precious and semiprecious stones. Huge rings (meant for men more than for women), sensual bracelets in the shape of snakes, and earrings in the shape of Moors' heads are his strong points. For precious yet affordable bracelets and rings out of the ordinary, this is *the* place.

Missiaglia (✉ Procuratie Vecchie, 125 San Marco, ☎ 041/5224464) is one of the Piazza San Marco's shopping landmarks, selling fabulous jewelry and a few silver accessories.

Nardi (✉ under Procuratie Nuove, 69 San Marco, ☎ 041/5225733) sells exquisite *moretti*—earrings and brooches in the shape of Moors' heads—studded with diamonds, rubies, or emeralds.

Pomellato (✉ Salizzada San Moisè, 1298 San Marco, ☎ 041/5201048) is a leading Italian designer, with shops also in Rome and Milan.

Rizzo (✉ Merceria San Zulian, 706 San Marco, ☎ 041/5229380) has no sign posted but is the place to come for antique brooches, earrings, pendants, and ceramic display pieces. With discretion and good manners, prices can be bargained down a bit.

Salvadori (✉ Merceria San Salvador, 5022 San Marco, ☎ 041/5230609) specializes in precious watches, but it also has sparkling diamonds and the like.

Leather Goods

In Venice you'll find a good assortment of leather goods, especially shoes and ladies' bags. All shoe shops listed below are for both men and women. Unless stated otherwise, these shops tend to carry rather upmarket designer articles. For less fancy items, you should explore the areas of Rialto and Campo San Polo.

Bata (✉ Merceria San Salvador, 4979/a, ☎ 041/5229766) is part of an enormous chain of shoe stores catering to a younger crowd. It offers a rich assortment of trendy models at low prices.

Casella (✉ Via Due Aprile, 5048 San Marco, off Campo San Bartolomio, ☎ 041/5228848) has a good selection of everyday shoes—no glamour but rather low prices.

Emporium (✉ Spadaria, 670 San Marco, ☎ 041/5235911) has traveling bags and suitcases by Alviero Martini, typically decorated with maps in light colors, and Trussardi accessories.

Fanny (✉ Calle dei Saoneri, 2723 San Polo, ☎ 041/5228266), run by a family of market stall sellers, combines good value, friendly service, and cheerful design. Leather and suede bags come in many different colors and sizes and can be embroidered; soft leather gloves are warm but not bulky.

Fendi (✉ Salizzada San Moisè, 1474 San Marco, ☎ 041/5205733) carries bags, shoes, and leather and fur winter clothing designed by the Fendi sisters.

Fratelli Rossetti (✉ Campo San Salvador, 4800 San Marco, ☎ 041/ 5230571) has bags, boots, leather jackets, and shoes of the Rossetti brothers—for once, the selection here is better than in the Roman shop.

Glamour (✉ Ponte delle Guglie, 1298 Cannaregio, ☎ 041/716246) is a tiny neighborhood shop with a sign proudly stating CHAUSSURE DE TENDENCE (trendy shoes). Vic Matiè and Shilla are designers on the rise, who make cute, reasonably priced low-heeled sandals; you'll also find cork platform shoes and boots.

Kalimala (✉ Salizzada San Lio, near Campo Santa Maria Formosa, 5387 Castello, ☎ 041/5283596, WEB www.kalimala.it) should not be missed if you are looking for soft leather bags, a perfect match for almost any outfit, or very pretty, inexpensive copper jewelry.

La Bottega Veneta (✉ Calle Vallaresso, 1337 San Marco, ☎ 041/ 5228489) is a prestigious Italian chain selling bags typically made with intertwined strips of leather, plus smooth bags and elegant low-heeled shoes (for ladies only).

La Parigina (✉ Merceria San Zulian, 727 San Marco, ☎ 041/5226743; ✉ Merceria San Zulian, 733 San Marco, ☎ 041/5231555) is a Venetian institution, with five large windows spread in two neighboring shops. You'll find the house collection here, plus a dozen other famous names such as Piero Guidi and Alexander Nicolette.

Louis Vuitton (✉ Calle Larga dell'Ascensione, 1255 San Marco, ☎ 041/ 5224500), the famous French maker of travel bags and boxes, reopened here in 2001 after a prolonged absence from the Venetian shopping scene.

At **Macri** (✉ Calle dell'Ascensione, 1296 San Marco, ☎ 041/5231221), René Caovilla's terrific shoes are meant for showing off, not walking around town (especially in Venice). These high-heeled works of art are studded with sparkling bits of multicolored leather and crystal and decorated with feathers, flowers, and butterflies. Prices start at €300.00.

Marforio (✉ Campo San Salvador, 5033 San Marco, ☎ 041/5225734) is a quality shop with good prices, well stocked with bags, suitcases, belts, wallets, and leather accessories like cases for glasses and shoe-polish boxes. Among the designer items, you'll find Valentino, Armani, and the famous natural leather Florentine line called the Bridge.

Mariani (✉ Calle del Teatro, off Campo San Luca, 4775 San Marco, ☎ 041/5222967) is one of Venice's best shoe shops, with very affordable prices.

Rolando Segalin (✉ Calle dei Fuseri, 4365 San Marco, ☎ 041/5222115) founded the custom shoe workshop bearing his name in 1932. The team of artisans here can give life to your wildest shoe fantasy (see the gondola and cat-paw creations in the window) as well as make the most classic designs.

Vogini (✉ Salizzada San Moisè, 1292 San Marco, ☎ 041/5222573) is well stocked with designer bags by Armani, Moschino, Fendissime

(Fendi's less expensive line), and Versace and also has its own line of classic bags in real crocodile, lizard, and ostrich leather.

Masks

Not everyone knows that the boom of mask shops started only in the early '80s, due to the resurrection of the Carnevale tradition, which the municipality dreamed up in 1979 as a way to draw tourists to Venice during what used to be the city's dead season. The mask business has grown so quickly over the last 20 years that if in the past it was enough to say that visitors rarely left Venice without a piece of glass, today it must be added "or a mask of some sort."

Scores of mask shops cluster around famous sights. You'll encounter in them thousands of different sizes, colors, designs, and materials. Prices go up dramatically for leather and gilded masks, and you might come across expensive *pezzi da collezione* (pieces for collectors)—single pieces whose cast is destroyed. In general, you'll get better deals from direct producers, so make a point to visit several of the largest workshops.

Ca' Macana (✉ Calle delle Botteghe, off Campo San Barnaba, 3172 Dorsoduro, ☎ 041/2776142, WEB www.maskvenice.com), a large workshop offering lots of gilded creations, both traditional and new, is a must-see.

Il Canovaccio (✉ Calle delle Bande, 5369 Castello, ☎ 041/5210393) is a treasure trove of papier-mâché objects, panels, and masks designed for the theater stage. Mask-making classes are offered by appointment.

Laboratorio Artigiano Maschere (✉ Barbaria delle Tole, near Campo dei Santi Giovanni e Paolo, 6657 Castello, ☎ 041/5223110) is home to Giorgio Clanetti, credited with starting the current revival in mask making; here you'll find the town's best masks of the Commedia dell'Arte.

Mondo Novo (✉ Rio Terrà Canal, off Campo Santa Margherita, 3063 Dorsoduro, ☎ 041/5287344) is a cut above most other mask stores and a real pleasure to browse through.

Tragicomica (✉ Calle dei Nomboli, off Campo San Tomà, 2800 San Polo, ☎ 041/721102, WEB www.tragicomica.it) has a good selection, and it's a useful resource for information about Carnevale parties. It also turns out a limited production of Carnevale costumes and hats made in hand-printed cotton fabric.

Paper Goods

Twenty years ago there was only one *legatoria* (bookbindery) in town. Nowadays you find dozens of them, usually next door to a mask shop. Hand-printed paper and fancy diary books bound in leather marked with St. Mark's lion are hot souvenirs, and the young folks who run these shops come out with new ideas all the time, the latest invention being a glass pen to dip into colored ink (a matching ink bottle is, of course, provided)—a necessary accessory to complete your desk, after you have already bought handmade writing paper, wax, and seals. How's that for a break from e-mail?

Antica Legatoria Piazzesi (✉ Campo della Feltrina, near Campo Santa Maria del Giglio, 2511 San Marco, ☎ 041/5221202), the oldest bookbindery in Venice, used to make wonderful hand-printed paper using carved wood *stampi* (plates for a press), which the artisans carefully filled with colored inks. The stampi are on exhibit in the shop, and the last of this gorgeous paper is slowly being sold off. Due to the high

VENETIAN MASKS UNVEILED

VENETIAN MASK MAKING has experienced a rebirth: in the time of the Republic, the mask trade was vibrant (Venetians used masks all year long to go about town incognito), but it died out under Napoléon, who suppressed the practice along with many religious and traditional holidays, including Carnevale. When Carnevale was revived in the late 1970s, mask making returned as well. Though many of the current workshops stick to centuries-old techniques, none have been in business for more than 30 years.

A landmark date in the history of Venetian masks is 1436, when the *mascareri* (mask makers) founded their own guild. By then the techniques that are replicated today had been well established: a mask is first modeled in clay, and then a chalk cast is made from it and lined with layers of papier-mâché, glue, gauze, and wax. (You can buy a molded mask at this stage of production and paint it yourself.)

But masks were popular well before the mascareri's guild was established. Local laws regulating their use appeared as early as 1268, often intended to prevent people from carrying weapons when masked or to prohibit the then-common practice of masked men disguised as women entering convents to seduce nuns. Even on religious holidays—when masks were theoretically prohibited—they were commonly used by Venetians going to the theater or attempting to avoid identification at the city's numerous brothels and gaming tables.

In the 18th century masks started being used by actors playing the traditional roles of the commedia dell'arte. Arlecchino, Pantalone, Pulcinella, and company would wear leather masks designed to amplify or change their voices. Inexpensive papier-mâché versions of these traditional, all-black masks can be found everywhere. Arlecchino has the round face and surprised expression, Pantalone is the one with the curved nose and long moustache, and Pulcinella has the protruding nose.

The least expensive mask is the white Bauta, smooth and plain with a short, pointed nose. It's also reproduced in ceramic and brass. Invented in the 18th century as a disguise, a properly made Bauta will also alter the tone of the wearer's voice. It was particularly popular for women going to the theater, and whether worn by a man or woman, it was always accompanied by a black three-cornered hat and an ample black cloak. The pretty Gnaga, which resembles a cat's face, was used by gay men to "meow" compliments and proposals to good-looking boys. The basic Moretta is just a black oval with eyeholes. The most interesting-looking of the traditional masks is perhaps the Medico della Peste (Plague Doctor), with an enormous nose shaped like a bird's beak and surmounted by a pair of glasses. During the terrible plague of 1630 and 1631, doctors took some protective measures against infection: as well as wearing masks, they examined patients with a rod to avoid touching contagious bodies and wore waxed coats that didn't "absorb" the disease. Inside the nose of the mask they put medical herbs and fragrances thought to filter and clean the infected air, while the glasses protected the eyes.

FOLLOWING THE BOOM of mask shops, numerous costume rental stores opened in the 1990s. Here you'll find an assortment of masks and simplified versions of 18th-century costumes (for men both civil and military) that are warm enough to be worn outdoors and at the same time suitable for dances and parties. They can be rented for one or more days (with reduced rates for longer periods), and most models are also for sale. If you plan to rent a costume during Carnevale, it's a good idea to make a reservation several months in advance.

— Carla Lionello

production costs, this kind of paper is now only made to order. Although Piazzesi is a charming little place of great historical value, you'll probably find a more attractive selection in the new, more up-market places.

Cartavenezia (✉ off Campo Santa Maria Mater Domini, 2125 Santa Croce, ☎ 041/5241283) stands out in the showy panorama of Venetian bookbindery shops. From handmade writing paper to cards and paper objects, everything is white here, so you'll be kindly asked to wear gloves while browsing.

Il Pavone (✉ Fondamenta Venier, 721 Dorsoduro, ☎ 041/5234517; ✉ Calle delle Carrozze, off Palazzo Grassi, 3287 San Marco, ☎ 041/5238216), aptly called "The Peacock," offers a great selection of *coda di pavone*, a kind of paper with colors and patterns resembling peacock feathers. Little prints with grapes, cherubs, and more peacocks make inexpensive gifts.

La Ricerca (✉ Ponte delle Ostreghe, near Campo Santa Maria del Giglio, 2431 San Marco, ☎ 041/5212606), together with the affiliated **Arcobaleno** ✉ Calle delle Rasse, near Campo SS. Filippo e Giacomo, 4615 Castello, ☎ 041/5237282), is the biggest bookbindery in town, where you'll find marbled paper, writing paper, bookmarks, leather-bound diaries, notepads, photo albums, colored prints of Venice to send as postcards, and even a medieval writing kit, complete with personalized wax seal.

Precious Fabrics, Lace, and Linen

Not everybody knows that in Venice the tradition of weaving brocades, damasks, and velvets is still very much alive, with top manufacturers catering to royal courts, theaters, and the movie industry. With the tourist boom in the 1980s, the descendants of underpaid embroiderers opened up fine lace and handicraft boutiques. Prices range from €120.00 per meter for old-style fabrics woven on power looms to €1,500.00 a meter for handmade silk velvets of unparalleled softness and beauty. On the lower end of the price range are striking lampases, brocades, and damasks, which come in different floral and striped patterns as well as in solid colors. Sometimes the fabrics are hand-dyed after they've been woven to obtain mellow watercolor effects. It's always worth inquiring about sales for designs that are being discontinued—you might want to give a Venetian look to your favorite reading chair.

Although most of the lace sold in town is machine-made in China or Taiwan, you can still find something that more closely resembles the real thing in the best shops. Paradoxically, period lace (made between 1900 and 1940) is easier to find and less expensive than contemporary lace, even though the former is a finer product, made *ad ago* (with the needle), while the latter is made with thicker threads or *a fusello* (with the bobbin). A visit to the Museo del Merletto (Lace-Making Museum) in Burano will give you an idea of how lace once looked. Despite the recent reopening of the Scuola del Merletto (Lace-Making School), students and teachers no longer sell their creations in shops, but older lace makers might accept jobs on commission. The best way to contact them is to ask around in Burano (as they object to having their names put down in print), but consider that a 10-inch doily takes about 400 hours to make, and the price will show it. So go ahead and buy what you like, but do not believe any "handmade in Burano" signs.

Annelie (✉ Calle Lunga San Barnaba, 2748 Dorsoduro, ☎ 041/5203277) has some lace baby clothing and a small selection of nightgowns and towels.

Bevilacqua (shop: ✉ Fondamenta della Canonica, 337/b San Marco, ☎ 041/5287581; factory (visits by appointment only): ✉ Campiello della Comare, 1320 Santa Croce, ☎ 041/721576) has kept the weaving tradition alive in Venice since 1875, using 18th-century hand looms for its most precious creations. Its repertoire of 3,500 different patterns and designs yields a ready-to-sell selection of several hundreds of brocades, Gobelins, damasks, velvets, taffetas, and satins. In the little shop near Piazza San Marco you'll also find tapestry, cushions, and braiding. Fabrics made by this prestigious firm have been used to decorate the Vatican, the Royal Palace of Stockholm, and the White House.

Capricci e Vanità (✉ Calle San Pantalon, 3744 Dorsoduro, ☎ 041/5231504), a small shop near the Church of San Pantalon, is where lace-lover Signora Giovanna Gamba sells her wonderful authentic Burano lace. She specializes in tablecloths and lingerie made on the bobbin as well as more rare and precious pieces made with a needle in the extralight Burano stitch.

Frette (✉ Calle Larga XXII Marzo, 2070/a San Marco, ☎ 041/5224914) sells high-quality sheets and bath towels—lace and embroidery are machine made, but the general effect is nonetheless luxurious and elegant.

G. Scarpa (✉ Campo San Zaccaria, 4683 San Marco, ☎ 041/5287883) is an old-fashioned shop with no dressing room: you'll have to make do in a tiny corner behind a foldable screen. Its top-of-the-line silk lace shirts, at only €40.00, are well worth the trouble, as are the lace cooking aprons.

You need to ring the bell to be admitted inside **Gaggio** (✉ Piscina San Samuele, near Campo Santo Stefano, 3451 San Marco, ☎ 041/5228574), one of Venice's most prestigious fabric shops. Bedcovers, cushions, tapestry, and the like are available, plus a line of delightful small bags made in silk velvet with dark wooden frames. The colors of the fabric are never garish—they tend toward mellow autumn tones. It's closed weekends.

Il Merletto (✉ Sotoportego del Cavalletto, under the Procuratie Vecchie, 95–96 Piazza San Marco, ☎ 041/5208406), removed from Piazza San Marco by way of a private bridge, seems to make a point of putting on display just the low end of what's sold upstairs. To see the difference, ask for the authentic, handmade lace kept in the drawers behind the counter. This is the only place in Venice connected with the students of the Scuola del Merletto in Burano, who, officially, do not sell to the public.

Jesurum (✉ Procuratie Nuove, 60–61 San Marco, ☎ 041/5229864; ✉ Merceria del Capitello, 4857 San Marco, ☎ 041/5206177; WEB www.jesurum.it) is Venice's top name for lace and embroidered linen. Here you'll find an assortment of dreamy gowns and nightshirts, sheets, bedcovers, and towels ready to buy, or you can order yours custom-made.

La Bottega di Cenerentola (✉ Calle dei Saoneri, 2718/a San Polo, ☎ 041/5232006, WEB www.cenerentola.net), or "Cinderella's Workshop," creates unique handmade lamp shades out of silk, old lace, and real parchment, embroidered and decorated with gold braids and cotton or silk trim. The pieces on display are a perfect match for country- and antique-style furniture. The owner, Lidiana Vallongo, will be happy to discuss special orders.

La Fenice Atelier (✉ Calle dei Frati, down the bridge on Campo Sant' Angelo, 3537 San Marco, ☎ 041/5230578) sells attractive lace nightdresses and handwoven bath towels at affordable prices.

Lorenzo Rubelli (✉ Campo San Gallo, 1089 San Marco, ☎ 041/ 5216411) offers the same sumptuous brocades, damasks, and cut velvets used by the world's most prestigious decorators.

Norelene (✉ Calle della Chiesa, near the Peggy Guggenheim Collection, 727 Dorsoduro, ☎ 041/5237605) sells hand-printed scarves and clothing, either in solid colors or in geometrical patterns inspired from the mosaic floors in the Basilica di San Marco. Tapestries and cushion covers are available and can also be made to order. Prices start at €130.00, but you can treasure a velvety souvenir for free: just step inside and ask for a business card. It's closed Sunday and Tuesday.

Pina Bonzio (✉ Merceria dell'Orologio, 298 San Marco, ☎ 041/ 5226791) offers the usual array of inexpensive lace souvenirs, from handkerchiefs and baggy blouses to lovely bookmarks; the news is that, despite the proximity to pricy Piazza San Marco, the prices can't be beat.

Trois (✉ Campo San Maurizio, 2666 San Marco, ☎ 041/5222905) is one of those humble little shops often overlooked by passersby. But the Trois family has the exclusive rights to the "Tessuti Artistici Fortuny," the handwoven and hand-dyed fabrics "invented" by Mariano Fortuny, which are great for curtains, bedspreads, cushions, and more. The stunningly vibrant colors of these fabrics are all obtained from natural pigments. You can browse through a catalog of roughly 400 patterns. All fabrics are sold for the same price, currently at €220.00 for 100 x 150 centimeters, a bargain if you consider that it takes each worker a whole day to make 40 centimeters.

Venetia Studium (✉ Calle Larga XXII Marzo, 2403 San Marco, ☎ 041/ 5229281; ✉ Merceria San Zulian, 723 San Marco, ☎ 041/5229859; ✉ Calle della Madonnetta, off Campo San Polo, 3006 San Polo, ☎ 041/ 52713393; WEB venetiastudium.com) has antique-looking velvety fabric, beautiful Fortuny-inspired lamps, pleated silk scarves in solid colors, and little drawstring purses that make perfect evening bags.

Venetian Floors

Another traditional Venetian craft is the installation of pavement made from cement and marble dust. One of the last surviving places where this centuries-old art is kept alive is worth seeking out for the dozens of different samples on display—you won't actually see workers laying out floors, but you can get a general idea of how the job gets done.

Benito Turco (✉ Calle della Lacca, 2458 San Polo, ☎ 041/5240999) started making *terrazzi alla veneziana* (Venetian floors) when still in primary school, and he may very well be Venice's last artisan capable of laying down these gorgeous floors without the help of any modern machinery. One wall of his tiny showroom is covered with samples of many different colors, but the technique is basically the same: multicolored pebbles or marble particles are scattered (either at random or following a design for "carpetlike" effects) onto a bed of cement dyed with colored marble dust; the floor is pressed flat and left to dry, then polished to a high shine and waxed. The whole operation takes several months, but prices are not as high as you'd expect, due to the low cost of the materials involved. The logistics of getting a floor shipped are difficult, but not impossible. For most visitors, though, this is primarily a place to observe a uniquely Venetian craft.

7 SOUTHERN VENETO

PADUA, VERONA,
VICENZA, LAKE GARDA

The art and architecture of every city in the
Venetian Arc—Verona, Vicenza, Padua—
echo in some way the graces and
refinements of Venice. Here you'll find
Padua, a city of university students and
ancient archways ennobled by Giotto's
frescoes; Verona's romantic *piazze* and
riverside promenade; the medieval walled
towns of Monselice and Montagnana; and
the villas of Andrea Palladio, where 16th-
century aristocrats once led the privileged
life.

By Robert
Andrews

Updated
by Robin
Goldstein

AS ROME PRESIDES OVER LAZIO, the arc that stretches west from Venice to Verona and south as far as Rovigo falls under the historical and spiritual influence of its great seafaring namesake city. The region's architecture, paintings, and way of life all bask in the reflected splendor of La Serenissima, and much of the pleasure of exploring this area comes from discovering the individual variations on the Venetian theme, conferring special charm on the towns you'll visit.

Whether in the cities or the small towns, the winged lion of St. Mark, the emblem of Venice (irreverently referred to as "the cat"), is very much in evidence, either emblazoned on palazzi or atop a lofty column. Long before its arrival, however, Ezzelino III da Romano (1194–1259), the larger-than-life scourge who was excommunicated by Pope Innocent IV and even had a crusade launched against him, laid claim to as much land as he could, seizing the cities of Verona, Padua, Este, Montagnana, and Monselice and their surrounding territory. After he was finally ousted, powerful families such as the Carrara in Padua and the della Scala (Scaligeri) from Verona vied with each other during the 14th century to annex these towns.

When not destroying each other, the noble families of the region bestowed on their progeny a rich legacy of architectural and artistic jewels, infusing an opulence into the area that is today the hallmark of Padua, Vicenza, and Verona. This trio of cities, though sharing the Venetian patrimony, has a diverse and multifaceted appeal, their individual characters well defined long before Venice arrived on the scene. Padua had established itself as a city-state during the 12th century, its university, founded in 1222, counting Galileo among its teachers and drawing the poets Dante and Petrarch into its orbit. In the 14th century, the cultural flowering found its most sublime expression in the frescoes of Giotto, a landmark in the history of art, and later in the painters and sculptors of the Renaissance, most notably Donatello and Mantegna.

Vicenza lays claim to a scion who was to have a predominant influence on the course of western architecture, Andrea di Pietro della Gondola—better known as Palladio, whose mark can be seen in practically every capitol in the United States. Not only did Palladio create new buildings, he grafted his classically inspired designs on the existing Gothic palazzi, and his spirit prevails, too, in the numerous villas in the surrounding countryside. In Verona, on the other hand, there's no escaping a much earlier epoch, for this was once a Roman city, its awe-inspiring arena the third largest in Italy. Here, "circuses" still astound audiences, though the spectacles have moved on from the gladiatorial to the operatic, in the shape of large-scale productions complete with animals. Among the performances, the Roman theater currently hosts an annual Shakespeare Festival, as who can forget that this is the home of that most fabled of love stories, *Romeo and Juliet*?

In the hinterland, redbrick castles and fortifications with fishtail or square crenellations bear testimony to the struggles of the medieval warring families. A better example would be hard to find than walled Montagnana, a town that changed hands no less than 13 times in the course of its history, or Monselice with its beautifully restored castle. Once Venice had established its presence in the region, a time of relative peace ensued, exquisitely marked by the blooming of Venetian palazzi and the works of masters. The three Ts—Titian, Tintoretto, and Tiepolo—have all contributed to the impressive heritage of the zone. These sophisticated traces contrast with the simpler delights of the Euganean Hills, south of Padua, where the unspoiled medieval village of Arquà Petrarca seems to exist in a separate dimension, unruffled by time's encroachments. A similar sense of peace reigns in and around Lake Garda, of which the German poet Goethe wrote, "I could have reached Verona by nightfall, but only a few steps away was this spectacular exhibition of nature, this stupendous panorama known as Lake Garda, and I simply could not tear myself away." Similar sentiments have been echoed by throngs of newcomers, who have added the joys of windsurfing and other lake sports to the delights of walking and taking in grand mountain scenery.

When Venetians took vacations, they made sure they did it in style, their retreats designed by the best architects and decorated by the best painters of the day. Needless to say, Palladio was first choice for the job, and his work is nobly illustrated by the superlative Villa La Rotonda near Vicenza, and Villa Foscari near Venice. For two centuries, Palladian villas sprouted up in prime locations such as along the Brenta Canal, many of them in private hands, but some open to the public. For requirements of the flesh, Abano Terme and Montegrotto Terme provided an excuse for pampering the body and rolling in mud, while the bustling fishing port of Chioggia is *the* place to savor fish.

Pleasures and Pastimes

Concerts and Opera

The love of Italian culture need not stop at Venice. Verona and Vicenza offer some of the most spectacular opportunities for indulging in the passions of open-air operas and concerts. Sit in the ancient Roman amphitheater and watch the grand spectacle of *Aida* or a Shakespearean tragedy or comedy unfold before you, or just enjoy a free jazz or folk concert on a warm summer evening. Alternatively, sit back like a true-born aristocrat and listen to a concert in the grand setting of a Vicentine villa. You can also treat yourself to an unforgettable performance in Palladio's Teatro Olimpico. You'll find that the smaller towns run concert seasons, too.

Dining

In the main cities of the Veneto region, restaurants are generally moderately priced, but in smaller towns and in the countryside you can find some real bargains. Seafood is the specialty along the coast, of course, where there's almost an embarrassment of choices, from struggling with the saltwater-vs-freshwater fish dilemma to weighing the virtues of sea bass, gilthead, sardines, or eels against carp, trout, and tench, all vying to find their way onto your plate. And then there are the crustacea to ponder over. Inland, the cuisine varies from delicate and creamy risotto, radicchio di Treviso, and asparagus to hearty grills, game, snails, and frogs. Don't be surprised if you come across horse meat on the menu or see whole shops devoted to its sale. Jewish influence has left its mark in such dishes as *risi e bisi* (rice and peas), *sarde in saor* (fried sardines marinated in vinegar, onions, pine nuts, and raisins), and *bigoli in salsa* (thick, rough spaghetti in anchovy sauce). Montagnana is famous for its deliciously sweet prosciutto and *schizoto,* a sort of unleavened bread. Polenta, a creamy cornmeal concoction, is a staple throughout the area, served with thick, rich sauces or grilled as an accompaniment to meat.

The Veneto produces more D.O.C. (Denominazione di Origine Controllata) wines than any other region in Italy. The country's main trade wine fair, Vinitaly, takes place in Verona in April. The southern shores of Lake Garda and the gentle Euganean Hills provide optimum conditions for growing the grapes that will eventually enhance your meals.

By far the region's crowning achievement, Amarone is a robust and powerful red wine with an alcohol content as high as 16%. Valpolicella and Bardolino are other notable varietals. *Ripasso* is made from adding unpressed or partially dried grape skins to Amarone wines after spring fermentation and strikes a balance between the powerful Amarone and the more mild Valpolicella. The best of the whites are Soave; sweet, sparkling *prosecco*; *pinot bianco* (pinot blanc); and Tocai (though the best of the last come from Friuli).

CATEGORY	COST*
$$$$	over €18
$$$	€13–€18
$$	€8–€13
$	under €8

Prices are for a main course (secondo piatto)

Lodging

The area around Venice has been playing host to visitors for centuries, and the result is a range of comfortable accommodations at every price. As with dining, common sense should tell you that the slightly out-of-the-way small hotel will cost you less than its counterpart in a the bigger town, especially at trade-fair time. Expect to pay more as you approach Venice, since many of the mainland towns absorb the overflow during the times when Venice becomes most crowded, such as Carnevale (Carnival, the two weeks preceding Lent) and throughout the summer. However, at no time do prices approach those in Venice proper. Padua, in fact, can be used in dire circumstances as a base for Venice-exploring day trips. Be aware that prices in the Lake Garda area as much as double during high season.

CATEGORY	COST*
$$$$	over €155
$$$	€105–€155
$$	€50–€105
$	under €50

All prices are for two people in a standard double room, including tax and service.

Villas and Palazzi

Countless villas and palaces are sprinkled throughout the Venetian hinterland. These gracious country homes give insight into the way wealthy Venetians used to—and still do—spend leisure time. Many of the villas are privately owned but are open to the public at certain times or by special request. Local tourist offices can be helpful in providing information on visiting these jewels.

Exploring Southern Veneto

Lake Garda and the trio of towns, Padua, Verona, Vicenza, are easily and quickly reached from Venice by the A4 autostrada and the parallel S11 running west as far as Milan. Public transport is frequent and fast, with regular services from Verona, the jumping-off point for buses and trains to Peschiera and buses to Sirmione, both on the southern shore. The S249 hugs the lake's eastern shore and leads to Garda and Malcesine.

Numbers in the text correspond to numbers in the margin and on the Southern Veneto; Padua; Vicenza; and Verona maps.

Great Itineraries

Hard as it may seem to leave the unique beauty of Venice behind, the Venetian Arc is the perfect complement to a stay in La Serenissima. The towns are often beautiful, flawlessly mixing grand architecture and medieval ambience. One of these towns, Verona, also unknowingly produced the most tragic of all *storie d'amore* (love stories)—*Romeo and Juliet*—which it has never allowed visitors to forget.

You could visit most of the towns and cities in this chapter on a day trip from Venice. A three-day itinerary would limit you to the principal cities. A five-day exploration would give you time to take in the cities, and either the mountain scenery of Lake Garda or the group of smaller walled towns south of Padua, which you could combine with a visit to Chioggia, by the sea. A seven-day trip would allow a fuller exploration of the area embracing all of these possibilities.

IF YOU HAVE 3 DAYS

If you only have a short time, Padua, Vicenza, and Verona are the three cities that beckon, steeped as they are in art and architecture and all easily connected by the A4 autostrada. **Padua** ①–⑮ holds the wondrous Giotto frescoes in the Cappella degli Scrovegni and the Venetian masters, Titian, Tiepolo, and Tintoretto in the nearby Musei Civici degli Eremitani. As you head west, **Vicenza** ⑯–㉖, the Palladian city, is home to the Teatro Olimpico, the oldest theater in Europe, with an alarmingly tilted backdrop. Try to find time for the Palladian villa par excellence, La Rotonda, close by. Continuing west along the A4, visit **Verona** ㉗–㊸, whose awesome Arena offers a night at the opera, leaving time in the afternoon to browse among the fabulous shops along Via Mazzini. And you can't leave Verona without viewing that most famous of balconies, at the Casa di Giulietta.

IF YOU HAVE 5 DAYS

Having visited the essential sights at **Padua** ①–⑮, **Vicenza** ⑯–㉖, and **Verona** ㉗–㊸, it's only a short hop to Lake Garda, where the resort of **Sirmione** ㊾ has inspiring views across the azure water to the mountains from the Grotte di Catullo. Then head north up the lake's eastern shore to **Malcesine** ㊼, where you can take a cable car up Monte Baldo for alpine views and fine walks. Spend your last night in one of the southern walled towns of **Montagnana** (58) and **Monselice** (55), their restored castles and encircling walls oozing medieval atmosphere; or, if you long for the beach, in the **Chioggia-Sottomarina** ㊺ area, where beach fans may not be able to resist the temptation to take a dip and fish-eaters can get their fill of the bounty of the lagoon.

IF YOU HAVE 7 DAYS

Take in the towns of **Padua** ①–⑮, **Vicenza** ⑯–㉖, and **Verona** ㉗–㊸ on your first three days, spending your fourth night in **Sirmione** ㊾. Next, head to **Monselice** (55), within striking distance of the equally atmospheric **Montagnana** (58) and **Este** (57). From here, you could either drive south to spend the night in the quiet inland town of **Rovigo** ㊻, whose 16th-century church of La Rotonda is unmissable, or spend some time exploring the Euganean Hills and the charming medieval village of **Arqua Petrarca** (56) and pampering yourself at the baths at **Abano Terme** (53) or **Montegrotto Terme** (53). Spend your last night in **Chioggia-Sottomarina** ㊺, with a celebratory evening meal at one of the fish restaurants of Chioggia.

When to Tour

To get the most out of your stay, consider coming during late spring or early summer (May, June, or July) or September, when the weather conditions are most comfortable and when opera and theater buffs can enjoy outdoor performances to their hearts' content. Spring, the season of blossom, is always enchanting, and Lake Garda is especially enticing during the summer months, when there's always a cooling breeze blowing from the mountains and the water is comfortably warm. Sum-

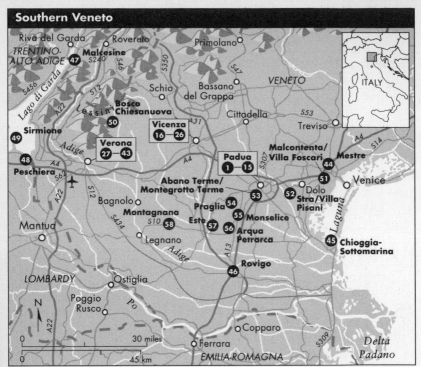

Southern Veneto

mer also sees crowds, however, and neither will you be alone in such places as Verona and Sirmione during this period. You'll have more elbowroom during winter, but the sights will have shorter opening hours and hotels are often closed in November and February (so check first). This is also the season when fogs can descend, and you'll certainly find snow on the higher ground. Visitors in February or March, however, will encounter Carnevale shenanigans—Carnevale is not only the preserve of Venice—and you could find yourself sitting next to bearded nuns on the train, being served cappuccino by a long-tailed cat in the local bar, or smiling at a clown dining with a mouse at the next table.

PADUA

Bustling with bicycles and lined with frescoes, Padua has long been one of the major cultural centers in northern Italy. It's home to the peninsula's—and the world's—second-oldest university, founded in 1222, which attracted the likes of Dante (1265–1321), Petrarch (1304–74), and Galileo Galilei (1564–1642), thus earning the city the sobriquet *La Dotta* (The Learned). Padua's Basilica di Sant'Antonio, begun not long after the university in 1234, is dedicated to St. Anthony, the patron saint of lost and found objects, and attracts grateful pilgrims in droves, especially on his feast day, June 13. Three great artists—Giotto (1266–1337), Donatello (circa 1386–1466), and Mantegna (1431–1506)—left great works here, with Giotto's Scrovegni chapel one of the best-known, and most meticulously preserved, works of art in the country. Today, cycle-happy students still rule the roost, flavoring every aspect of local culture. Don't be surprised if you spot a *laurea* (graduation) ceremony marked by laurel leaves, mocking lullabys, and X-rated caricatures. If you plan to visit many of the local sites, consider a cumulative ticket, *Padova Arte*; at €7.75 it's a good deal, allowing entry to the Cappella degli Scrovegni, Musei Civici degli

Eremitani, Palazzo della Ragione, Battistero, Scoletta del Santo, Musei Antoniani, and the Orto Botanico. It is available from the tourist office or any of the sites it covers.

Exploring Padua

The train station lies a few minutes' walk north of the main Corso del Pòpolo, the bus station a few minutes east. The *corso* leads south through the walls into the heart of the city and the oval square, Prato della Valle, changing its name as it goes to Corso Garibaldi and Via VIII Febbraio, where it meets the university. The core of the city spreads north and west from here and includes the central squares of Piazza delle Frutte and Piazza delle Erbe. To the south, the Basilica di Sant' Antonio (Il Santo) and the Prato della Valle are within easy walking distance.

If you arrive by car, leave your vehicle in one of the garages on the outskirts or at your hotel, as much of the center is given over to pedestrians. Coming to Padua by autostrada, exit at Padova Est and there's a parking area in Via Tommaseo. Coming from Padova Ovest or Sud, park in Prato della Valle. Buses 3, 8, 10, and 12 go to the center. If you're staying in a central hotel, expect to pay to park.

A Good Walk

Start your tour at the **Cappella degli Scrovegni** ① for the Giotto frescoes. The **Musei Civici degli Eremitani** ② and the **Chiesa degli Eremitani** ③ are close by. Following Corso del Popolo will bring you to the university and its main building, the **Palazzo del Bo'** ④. Stop at the Piazza delle Frutte or Piazza delle Erbe for a quick bite from the market, or else nip into one of the many bars or caffès around here before visiting the famed equestrian statue in the **Palazzo della Ragione** ⑤, which straddles the two piazzas. Head west to the **Piazza dei Signori** ⑥ for the **Duomo** ⑦ and the **Battistero del Duomo** ⑧ to see Giusto de'-Menabuoi's frescoes. Next to the Duomo are the **Oratorio di San Giorgio and Scuola del Santo** ⑨. Retrace your steps to the Via VIII Febbraio and stop for a coffee at **Caffè Pedrocchi** ⑩; then head southward along Via Roma and Via Umberto I to the spacious **Prato della Valle** ⑪, site of the **Chiesa di Santa Giustina** ⑫. From here, Via Belludi leads north to the monumental **Basilica di Sant'Antonio** ⑬, where you can mingle with the pilgrims and explore the **Musei Antoniani** ⑭. Finally, take a well-deserved rest in the shady **Orto Botanico** ⑮.

TIMING
You could easily spend a day following this walk, but if you don't want to stop at every sight, half a day will be enough.

Sights to See

★ ⑬ **Basilica di Sant'Antonio.** Thousands of worshipers throng to Il Santo, a cluster of Byzantine domes and slender, minaret-like towers that gives it an Asian-inspired style, reminiscent of San Marco in Venice. The interior is sumptuous, too, with marble reliefs by Tullio Lombardo (1455–1532), the greatest in a talented family of marble carvers who decorated many churches in the area, among them Santa Maria dei Miracoli in Venice. The artistic highlights here, however, all bear Donatello's name; the 15th-century Florentine master did the remarkable series of bronze reliefs illustrating the life of St. Anthony—whose feast day, June 13, draws pilgrims from all over Europe—as well as the bronze statues of the Madonna, the saints on the high altar, and the life-size bronze crucifix. The **Cappella del Santo** was built to house the green marble tomb of the saint and is now the object of votive offerings. Reconstructed in the 16th century, it shows Italian High Renaissance at

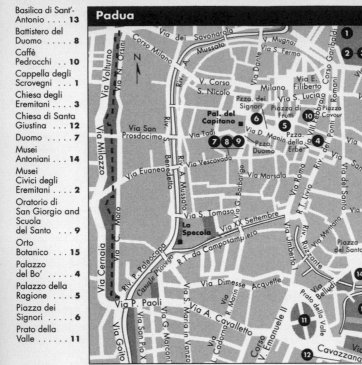

Padua

its best. Note the nine panels of sculptured reliefs that commemorate the saint's miraculous healing powers. The **Cappella del Tesoro** (☉ daily 8–noon and 2:30–7) holds the not-so-pristine tongue of the saint in a 15th-century reliquary. Standing in front of the church is Donatello's powerful statue of the *condottiere* (mercenary general) *Gattamelata*, which was cast in bronze—a monumental technical achievement—in 1453 and was to have an enormous influence on the development of Italian Renaissance sculpture. ⊠ *Piazza del Santo,* ☎ *049/8242811.* ☉ *Mon.–Sat. 6:30 AM–7 PM, Sun. 6:30 AM–7:45 PM.*

⑧ Battistero del Duomo. The Baptistery next to the Duomo is more interesting than the cathedral itself. A prime example of Romanesque Lombardic art, the 1378 interior is covered with the finest example of frescoes by the Florentine painter Giusto de'Menabuoi (died 1397). The vibrant cycle starts in the cupola with a depiction of Paradise and the *108 Saints,* a compendium of Paduan saints commissioned by the Carrara family to watch over their tomb. ⊠ *Piazza del Duomo,* ☎ *049/ 662814.* ⊡ *€1.55.* ☉ *Apr.–Oct., daily 9:30–1:30 and 3–7; Nov.–Mar., daily 9:30–1 and 3–6.*

⑩ Caffè Pedrocchi. This neoclassical building was designed by Giuseppe Jappelli (1753–1852) in 1831 for Antonio Pedrocchi, called by Stendhal "the best caterer in Italy." Take the outside staircase up one flight to the *piano nobile* (first floor) for a delightful series of rooms decorated in a melee of antique styles—Etruscan, Roman, Egyptian, Renaissance—not to mention the Rossini Room or the Herculaneum Room. ⊠ *Piazzetta Pedrocchi,* ☎ *049/8205007.* ⊡ *€2.60.* ☉ *Daily 9:30–12:30 and 3:30–6.*

★ ① Cappella degli Scrovegni (Scrovegni Chapel). Perhaps the most famous chapel in Italy after Michelangelo's magnum opus in the Vatican, this one was erected in the 13th century by a wealthy Paduan, Enrico

Scrovegno, to atone for the usury of his deceased father, Reginaldo, as chronicled in Dante's *Inferno* (the fresco above the door, which depicts the dedication of the chapel, shows Enrico dressed in violet, the color of penitence). Scrovegno called on Giotto to decorate its interior, a task that occupied the great artist and his helpers from 1303 to 1305. They created a magnificent fresco cycle, arranged in typical medieval comic-strip fashion, illustrating the lives of Mary and Christ, allegorical forms of the seven deadly sins and the seven virtues, and the Last Judgment. The realism in these frescoes—which include the first blue skies in Western painting—was revolutionary. Today, in glorious restoration, Giotto's starry firmament glows in splashes of brilliant color. ⊠ *Piazza Eremitani 8,* ☎ *049/8204550.* ⊡ *€5.15, €7.75 combined ticket with Musei Civici.* ☼ *Feb.–Oct., daily 9–7; Nov.–Jan., daily 9–6. Reservations required.*

❸ **Chiesa degli Eremitani.** The 13th-century church contains some fragments of frescoes—most, however, were destroyed by the Allied bombing of 1944—by Andrea Mantegna, the brilliant locally born artist. In the vestibule is a bronze copy of a *Pietà* by Antonio Canova (1757–1822). ⊠ *Piazza Eremitani 10,* ☎ *049/8204550.* ⊡ *Free.* ☼ *Daily 8:30–5:30.*

⑫ **Chiesa di Santa Giustina.** Two red marble griffins flank the steps of the unclad brick facade of this church, whose eight cupolas are reminiscent of Sant'Antonio's basilica. Inside are finely carved and inlaid 15th-century choir stalls and a colossal altarpiece, *The Martyrdom of St. Justina,* by Veronese (1528–88). Among the monuments are the sarcophagus that once contained the body of St. Luke, and in the Chapel of St. Luke, the resting place of Elena Piscopia, the first woman to ever receive a university degree. ⊠ *Prato della Valle,* ☎ *049/8751628.* ☼ *Apr.–Oct., daily 7–1 and 3–8; Nov.–Mar., daily 8:30–noon and 3–7.*

❼ **Duomo.** Padua's cathedral was designed by a pupil of Michelangelo. The 17th- to 18th-century interior contains many paintings dating from the same era, as well as some 14th-century pieces in the sacristy such as *Virgin and Child* and *Life of St. Sebastian,* both by Nicolò Semitecolo (1353–70). ⊠ *Piazza del Duomo,* ☎ *049/662814.* ☼ *Mon.–Sat. 7:30–noon and 3:45–7:30, Sun. 7:45–1 and 3:45–8:30.*

OFF THE
BEATEN PATH

LA SPECOLA – See the astronomical instruments used by Galileo himself, and use the more up-to-date versions for observing the Italian sky at night. ⊠ *Vicolo dell'Osservatorio 5,* ☎ *049/8754949; tickets: Agenzia Next Tour,* ⊠ *Via Bonporti 16,* ☎ *049/8754949.* ⊡ *€3.60.* ☼ *Guided visits Sept.–May, Sun. at 10, 11 AM, and 4 PM; Tues., Wed., and Fri. at 9 PM and 10 PM.*

⑭ **Musei Antoniani.** To mark the 800th anniversary of the birth of St. Anthony in 1195, these new galleries were opened in 1995 on the first floor of the church cloister building, with 300 exhibits relating to the image of the saint and of the basilica. ⊠ *Piazza del Santo,* ☎ *049/ 8225656.* ⊡ *€2.60.* ☼ *Easter–Oct., daily 9–1 and 2–6:30; Nov.– Easter, Tues.–Sun. 10–1 and 2–5.*

★ ❷ **Musei Civici degli Eremitani** (Civic Museums of the Hermit). The museum is housed in what used to be the monastery of the church and divided into three parts. The ground floor houses the **archaeological** section containing Etruscan, Roman, Egyptian, Greek, and early Christian objects. The **Pinacoteca** (Art Gallery) upstairs displays an array of Veneto masters from the 14th to 19th century and some Flemish and Dutch works. Notable are the Giotto Crucifix that was once in the Scrovegni chapel, the *Heavenly Host in Battle* by Guariento (1338–1368 or 1379), and the *Portrait of a Young Senator* by Bellini (1432–

1516). The corridors are hung with 19th- and 20th-century prints and paintings, and the **Museo Bottacin** holds an important collection of more than 50,000 coins and medals. ⊠ *Piazza Eremitani 10,* ☎ *049/8204550.* ☞ *€5.15, €7.75 combined ticket with Cappella degli Scrovegni.* ⊙ *Feb.–Oct., Tues.–Sun. 9–7; Nov.–Jan., Tues.–Sun. 9–6.*

⑨ Oratorio di San Giorgio and Scuola del Santo. The San Giorgio Oratory and adjoining gallery are next to the basilica. The Romanesque oratory served as a prison in Napoleonic times. It displays frescoes dating from 1384 by two pupils of Giotto, Altichiero di Zevio (1320 or 1330–95) and Jacopo Avanzo (1378–84), that illustrate the lives of St. George, Catherine of Alexandria, and St. Lucy. The **Scuola,** up a pretty stairway on the first floor, came into being after the canonization of St. Anthony in 1231; the present building was completed in 1504. The walls of the upper part are lined with frescoes, four of which are attributed to Titian. They depict the life and work of St. Anthony, including the saint's reattaching the foot of a young man, and bringing back to life a child who had fallen into a cauldron of boiling water. ⊠ *Piazza del Santo,* ☎ *049/8755235.* ☞ *€1.55.* ⊙ *Apr.–Sept., daily 9–12:30 and 2:30–5; Oct.–Mar., daily 9–12:30 and 2:30–5.*

⑮ Orto Botanico. The Botanic Garden was founded in 1545 by order of the Venetian Republic to supply the university with medicinal plants and is one of the few Renaissance gardens to have kept its original layout. The so-called Palm of St. Peter, planted in 1585, still stands, protected in its private little greenhouse. It was admired by Goethe (1749–1832) on his travels through Italy in 1786. Take time to wander through interesting hothouses, beds of plants that were first introduced to Italy in this garden, and the arboretum. ⊠ *Via Orto Botanico 15, in front of the Basilica di Sant'Antonio,* ☎ *049/8272119.* ☞ *€2.60, combined ticket €7.75.* ⊙ *Apr.–Oct., daily 9–1 and 3–6; Nov.–Mar., weekdays 9–1.*

④ Palazzo del Bo'. The 16th-century palace houses the **Università di Padova,** founded in 1222. The building, which now features an 18th-century facade, is named after the Osteria del Bo' ("Ox"), an inn that once stood on the site. The exquisite and perfectly proportioned anatomy theater was built in 1594. William Harvey (1578–1657), famous for his theory of the circulation of the blood, took a degree here in 1602, at the same time as Galileo was teaching. Galileo's *cattedra* (desk) is still on display. In the courtyard there's a statue of Elena Lucrezia Cornaro Piscopia (1646–84), who, in 1678, was the first woman in the world to be confirmed with a university degree. If you're superstitious, don't jump over the chain in this courtyard, as, according to students, it will bring you bad luck. ⊠ *Via VIII Febbraio,* ☎ *049/8209711 or 049/8209773.* ☞ *€2.60.* ⊙ *Guided visits Tues., Thurs., and Sat. at 9, 10, and 11; Mon., Wed., and Fri. at 3, 4, and 5.*

⑤ Palazzo della Ragione. Also known as Il Salone, this impressive palace was built in the Middle Ages as the seat of Padua's parliament. Today its street-level arcades shelter shops and caffès. The **Salone** (Salon) on the upper level is, at 85 ft high, one of the largest and most architecturally pleasing halls in Italy, covered by a wooden roof and frescoed with religious and astrological subjects. Inside pride of place is taken by an enormous wooden horse, a replica of the bronze steed in Donatello's equestrian statue of Gattamelata and originally built for a tournament held in the Piazza dei Signori in 1446. In the northeast corner is the Railing Stone where debtors had to sit three times repeating "Cedo bonis" (I give up all worldly goods) before leaving the city. ⊠ *Piazza della Ragione, enter from Via VIII Febbraio,* ☎ *049/8205006.* ☞ *€3.60.* ⊙ *Tues.–Sun. 9–6.*

⑥ **Piazza dei Signori.** The large, sequestered square exhibits examples of 15th- and 16th-century buildings. On the west side the **Palazzo del Capitanio** sports an impressive **Torre dell'Orologio,** which has a fine astronomical clock dating from 1344.

⑪ **Prato della Valle.** Laid out in 1775, this immense space with a central oval park is surrounded by a canal along which stand 78 statues of local worthies. It hosts a general market on Saturday and an antiques market on the third Sunday of the month.

Dining and Lodging

$$$ ✕ **Antico Brolo.** Housed in a 16th-century building not far from central Piazza dei Signori, charming Antico Brolo is one of the best restaurants in town. Seasonal specialties are prepared with a flair and might include starters like tiny flans with wild mushrooms and herbs or fresh pasta dressed with zucchini flowers. The wine list won't disappoint you. ⊠ *Corso Milano 22,* ☎ *049/664555. AE, DC, MC, V. Closed Mon.*

$$–$$$ ✕ **La Vecchia Enoteca.** The ceiling is mirrored, the shelves are filled with books and wine, the silverware on which the meals are served once belonged to a shipping line, and the flower displays are extravagant. In this luxurious ambience enjoy *branzino in crosta di patate* (sea bass with a potato crust) or beef with rosemary and balsamic vinegar, followed by a homemade dessert such as *crema catalana* (cream caramel). Reservations are advised. ⊠ *Via Santi Martino e Solferino 32,* ☎ *049/ 8752856. MC, V. Closed Sun. No lunch Mon.*

$$ ✕ **Angelo Rasi.** Perfect for a light dinner on a breezy summer evening, this wine bar with tables along the river offers delicious fish salads but also a few pasta dishes and simple meat courses. ⊠ *Riviera Paleocapa 7,* ☎ *049/8719797. V. Closed Mon. No lunch Tues.*

$$ ✕ **Bastioni del Moro.** The genial owner devises his own recipes according to season, with vegetarians and calorie watchers in mind, although meat eaters are well cared for, too. Gnocchi, eggplant, artichokes, and pumpkin all appear on the menu in different guises. For starters, you could try *tagliolini gratinati con prosciutto* (thin ribbons of egg noodles with prosciutto) or *gnocchi con capesante e porcini* (gnocchi with local fish and field mushrooms). The garden is put to good used in summer. Reservations are recommended. ⊠ *Via Pilade Bronzetti 18,* ☎ *049/8710006. AE, DC, MC, V. Closed Sun.*

$$ ✕ **Cavalca.** A family-run establishment with a long tradition, Cavalca is just off Piazza dei Signori in the heart of Padua. The place is crammed with rugby trophies, though the decor is otherwise classic and service is simple but courteous. The specialties are *pasta e fagioli* (pasta and bean soup), *capretto arrosto* (roast kid), or a platter of *arrosti misti* (assorted roast meats). ⊠ *Via Manin 8,* ☎ *049/8760061. Reservations essential. AE, DC, MC, V. Closed Wed., 2 wks mid-Jan., and 3 wks late July. No dinner Tues.*

$ ✕ **Vecchia Padova.** The low-beamed and vaulted ceilings are hung with copper cauldrons, and a medley of antiques covers the walls. Very popular with locals, this eatery relies on self-service at lunch, while the evening brings waiter service. The tempting *crespelle* (pancakes filled with cheeses, fresh herbs, tomatoes, or pancetta) change daily; the *panzerotti alla zucca* (pasta with pumpkin) and the *risotto al prosecco* get the taste buds going. ⊠ *Via Zabarella 41,* ☎ *049/8759680. Reservations essential. AE, DC, MC, V. Closed Mon.*

$$–$$$$ 🏨 **Villa Ducale.** Set in its own stately gardens, one of the country residences built along the Brenta River by Venetian noblemen has been turned into a stylish hotel with stuccoed walls and ceilings, Murano glass chandeliers and mirrors, and Venetian-style marble floors. This is not in Padua but in Dolo, halfway between Venice and Padua (20

km [12 mi] east of Padua), and is connected to both by a regular local train service. The restaurant, which serves excellent seafood, closes Tuesday. ⊠ *Riviera Martiri della Libertà 75, 30031 Dolo*, ☎ *041/5608020*, FAX *041/5608004. 11 rooms. AE, DC, MC, V.*

$$$ 🏨 **Milano.** This is a modern hotel just outside the historic center on a main road. The rooms are soundproofed, with built-in remote controls on the bedside table. The clean lines induce a '30s feel, and the gleaming marble lets you know you are in Italy. ⊠ *Via Pilade Bronzetti 62, 35138*, ☎ *049/8712555*, FAX *049/8713923*, WEB *www.hotelmilano-padova.it. 83 rooms. Restaurant, bar, free parking. AE, DC, MC, V.*

$$$ 🏨 **Plaza.** Guest rooms are luxurious and spacious, with flowery fabrics and full appointments, but they don't have antique furnishings. The hotel caters mainly to businesspeople and includes a buffet breakfast in the price. ⊠ *Corso Milano 40, 35139*, ☎ *049/656822*, FAX *049/661117. 135 rooms, 8 suites. Restaurant, parking (fee). AE, DC, MC, V.*

$$–$$$ 🏨 **Donatello.** Directly opposite the Basilica di Sant'Antonio, Donatello has rooms with a view of the square and church, but it can get noisy. The entrance hall is all chandeliers and marble, the rooms contemporary. ⊠ *Via del Santo 102/104, 35123*, ☎ *049/8750634*, FAX *049/8750829*, WEB *www.hoteldonatello.net. 49 rooms. Restaurant, bar, parking (fee). AE, DC, MC, V. Closed Dec. 15–Jan. 15.*

$$–$$$ 🏨 **Majestic Toscanelli.** The elegant entrance, with potted evergreens flank-
★   ing the steps, sets the tone in this stylish, central hotel close to the Piazza delle Frutte. Plants feature strongly in the breakfast room as well, and the charming bedrooms are furnished in different styles from 19th-century mahogany and brass to French Empire. ⊠ *Via dell'Arco 2, 35122*, ☎ *049/663244*, FAX *049/8760025*, WEB *www.toscanelli.com. 32 rooms. Restaurant, bar, parking (fee). AE, DC, MC, V.*

$$ 🏨 **Leon Bianco.** The quiet colors, intimate lounge, and screens make this a relaxed place to stay. It's very central, with the Caffè Pedrocchi a few steps away, viewable from the roof terrace. ⊠ *Piazzetta Pedrocchi 12, 35122*, ☎ *049/8750814*, FAX *049/8756184. 23 rooms. Parking (fee). AE, DC, MC, V.*

$ 🏨 **Al Fagiano.** Close to the Basilica di Sant'Antonio and the river, this modest hostelry has basic facilities (some with shower only), an amiable staff, and a calm atmosphere. The rooms are functional if uninspiring, and some have views of the basilica's spires and cupolas. ⊠ *Via Locatelli 45, 35100*, ☎ FAX *049/8753396. 16 rooms. Restaurant, bar. AE, DC, MC, V.*

Nightlife and the Arts

The Arts

The **Auditorium Pollini** (⊠ Via Carlo Cassan 15, ☎ 049/8759880) puts on recitals and concerts. Ticket prices start at €10.30 for concerts and €18.10 for the opera. The **Teatro Verdi** (⊠ Via dei Livello 32, ☎ 049/8760339) holds a regular program of opera, concerts, and ballet.

Nightlife

BARS

An over-25 crowd fills the small **Le Petit Palais** (⊠ Via Vecellio 1, ☎ 049/600134), with a dance floor and commercial house music downstairs and a lounge upstairs. It's closed Monday and mid-July to mid-August. **Limbo** (⊠ Via San Fermo 44, ☎ 049/656882) has a pool table and game room upstairs and live music downstairs. **Victoria** (⊠ Via Savonarola 149, ☎ 049/8721530) is a *birreria* (Italian-style pub) with live jazz concerts on Thursday.

When you pack your MCI Calling Card, it's like packing your loved ones along too.

Your MCI Calling Card is the easy way to stay in touch when you travel. Use it to call to and from over 125 countries. Plus, every time you call, you can earn frequent flier miles. So wherever your travels take you, call home with your MCI Calling Card. It's even easy to get one. Just visit **www.mci.com/worldphone.**

EASY TO CALL WORLDWIDE

1. Just enter the WorldPhone® access number of the country you're calling from.
2. Enter or give the operator your MCI Calling Card number.
3. Enter or give the number you're calling.

Country	Access Number
Austria ◆	0800-200-235
Belgium ◆	0800-10012
Czech Republic ◆	00-42-000112
Denmark ◆	8001-0022
Estonia ★	0800-800-1122
Finland ◆	08001-102-80
France ◆	0-800-99-0019
Germany	0800-888-8000
Greece ◆	00-800-1211
Hungary ◆	06 ▼-800-01411
Ireland	1-800-55-1001
Italy ◆	172-1022
Luxembourg	8002-0112
Netherlands ◆	0800-022-91-22
Norway ◆	800-19912
Poland ✛	00-800-111-21-22
Portugal ✛	800-800-123
Romania ✛	01-800-1800
Russia ◆ ✛	747-3322
Spain	900-99-0014
Sweden ◆	020-795-922
Switzerland ◆	0800-89-0222
Ukraine ✛	8 ▼ 10-013
United Kingdom	0800-89-0222
Vatican City	172-1022

◆ Public phones may require deposit of coin or phone card for dial tone. ★ Not available from public pay phones.
▼ Wait for second dial tone. ✛ Limited availability.

EARN FREQUENT FLIER MILES

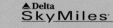

SEE THE WORLD
IN FULL COLOR

Fodor's Exploring Guides bring all the great sights vividly to life with hundreds of photographs, fascinating historical background, and colorful anecdotes. Detailed maps and practical information keep you headed in the right direction.

Pair a **Fodor's** Exploring Guide with your trusted Gold Guide for a complete planning package.

Fodor's EXPLORING GUIDES

At bookstores everywhere.

Caffè Margherita (⊠ Piazza delle Frutte 44, ☎ 049/8760107) is the perfect place to watch the busy world of the piazza unfold and admire the nearby Palazzo della Ragione. It's closed on Sunday.

The ever-popular **Caffè Pedrocchi** (⊠ Piazzetta Pedrocchi, ☎ 049/8752020), in a monumental 19th-century neoclassical coffeehouse, looks like a cross between a museum and a stage set, with rooms ranging in color from red to white to green. You can indulge in a full-scale lunch or just sip a cappuccino here. Previously a haunt for the city's intellectuals and open 24 hours a day, it now observes regular hours and is closed on Monday.

NIGHTCLUB

Big Club (⊠ Via Armistizio 68, ☎ 049/680934) has pizza and live music on Thursday and Sunday; on Friday and Saturday it becomes a disco. It's closed Monday and Tuesday.

Outdoor Activities and Sports

Golf

The 18-hole **Golf Club Padova** (⊠ Via Noiera 57, Valsanzibio di Galzignano Terme, ☎ 049/9130078) is 23 km (15 mi) south of Padua.

Tennis

Green Tennis (⊠ Via Pilade Bronzetti 33, ☎ 049/8719774) has public courts. Book in advance.

Shopping

Markets

Padua's Saturday market in **Prato della Valle** has a wide range of goods. An antiques market is held the third Sunday of every month with some 220 stalls—you're sure to find a bargain, but it's more likely to be '50s or '60s bric-a-brac than a genuine antique. A regular fruit and vegetable market is held weekday mornings and all day Saturday in the **Piazza delle Erbe.** In the nearby **Piazza delle Frutte,** a general market is held Monday, Tuesday, and Wednesday mornings and all day Thursday through Saturday. **Padova Fiere** (Padua Trade Fair, ⊠ Via Tommaseo 59, ☎ 049/840111) is the venue for conventions and exhibitions, including regular antiques and art fairs.

Specialty Stores

CLOTHING

There's no lack of fashion boutiques in Padua's center. You'll find many in the **Galleria Ezzelino** just off the Piazza delle Erbe. Close to the same piazza is **Paolo Prata** (⊠ Via Santi Martino e Solferino 42, ☎ 049/665508), specializing in women's clothes.

CRYSTAL

Swarovski (⊠ Via Cesare Battisti 15, ☎ 049/8753721), a shop that has been established for more than 100 years, specializes in crystal miniatures with prices ranging from €26.00 to €103.00.

FOODSTUFFS AND WINE

R. Vignato (⊠ Via Roma 64, ☎ 049/8751320) is well known for its cheese, salami, olive oil, honey, and wine. It sells potato chips by the scoop, too.

JEWELRY

Alberto Cesarotto (⊠ Corso Milano 7, ☎ 049/8761550) specializes in designer silverware with names such as Christian Dior and Gucci. **Vittorio Burgo** (⊠ Via Umberto I 40–44, ☎ 049/8760436) has a wonderful array of silver, watches, coral work, and gemstones.

VICENZA

Vicenza bears the distinctive signature of the 16th-century architect Andrea Palladio and was designated by UNESCO in 1994 as a preeminent site of world cultural heritage. The architect, whose name is the root of the style referred to as "Palladian," gracefully incorporated elements of classical architecture—columns, porticoes, and domes—into a style that reflected the Renaissance celebration of order and harmony. His elegant villas and palaces were influential in propagating classical architecture in Europe, especially Britain, and later in America—most notably, at Thomas Jefferson's Monticello.

In the mid-16th century, Palladio (1508–80) was given the opportunity to rebuild much of Vicenza, which had suffered great damage during the bloody wars waged against Venice by the League of Cambrai, an alliance of the Papacy, France, the Holy Roman Empire, and several neighboring city-states. He imposed upon the city a number of his grand Roman-style buildings—rather an overstatement, considering the town's status. With the basilica, begun in 1549 in the very heart of Vicenza, he ensured his reputation and embarked on a series of lordly buildings, all of which proclaim the same rigorous classicism. Much as it was at the end of the 18th century, today Vicenza is a center of Italy's publishing and computer industries and is ranked among the richest of Italian cities. This is readily apparent in the mod style of dress, the elegance of the shops, and the array of BMWs and Mercedes.

Exploring Vicenza

Vicenza can easily be covered in a day or less. The broad main street, Corso Palladio, cuts through the historical center, leading east from Piazza del Castello to Piazza Matteotti. Palladio's buildings line this street as well as banks, offices, and elegant boutiques. The main Piazza dei Signori lies to the south of the corso, from where it's an easy walk to the Teatro Olimpico. Make sure you save some time to visit the Villa La Rotonda, just south of the city.

A Good Walk

The creeper-covered courtyard of the **Palazzo Chiericati** ⑯ and the **Teatro Olimpico** ⑰ make a good starting place for a tour of the city. From here, it's a short walk along Corso Palladio to the church of **Santa Corona** ⑱, with works by Veronese and Bellini. Cross Contrà Santa Corona and go down Contrà Santo Stefano, site of the church of **Santo Stefano** ⑲ and its fine *Madonna and Child*. Head down Contrà Riale to **Contrà Porti** ⑳, where the Palazzo Porta Festa is one of Palladio's works. Turning back toward the main corso takes you to the Palazzo Barbaran da Porto and Palazzo Thiene—one of the many unfinished projects of Palladio—which face one another across the Contrà Porti. If you cross the Corso Palladio and head for the Piazza dei Signori, you'll come to Palladio's earliest work, the **Basilica** ㉑, with the landmark adjacent **Torre di Piazza** ㉒. Take a break for a drink at the Pasticceria Sorarù, some shopping, or for a bite to eat. The **Loggia del Capitaniato** ㉓, also in the piazza, is an unfinished work by Palladio. Then passing through Piazza delle Erbe on the south side of the Basilica, find the narrow Contrà Pigafetta for the **Casa Pigafetta** ㉔, from where it's not far to the **Duomo** ㉕. Retracing your steps, Contrà Fogazzaro is home to the Palazzo Valmarana Braga, with its armored statues in place of columns. If you haven't had your fill of Palladio by now, the majestic Palazzo Bonin Longhare, at the end of the **Corso Palladio** ㉖ at No. 13, awaits you at the opposite end of the Piazza del Castello.

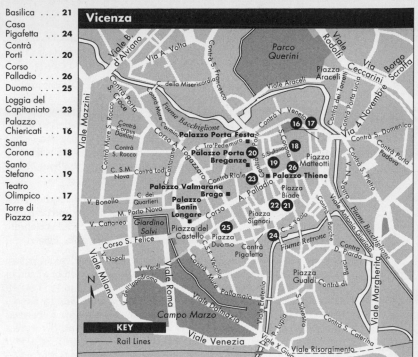

Sights to See

㉑ Basilica. At the heart of Vicenza, Palladio's **Palazzo della Ragione** is more commonly known as La Basilica, a confusing way to refer to it, as it is not a church but rather a courthouse and public meeting hall. An early Palladian masterpiece, the Palazzo was actually a medieval building that the architect modernized. The skill with which he wedded the graceful two-story exterior *loggias* (Tuscan Doric above and Ionic below) to the existing Gothic structure is remarkable. The beautiful, huge Gothic hall was rebuilt in 1460 after a fire in 1444 and is now used for exhibitions. ✉ *Piazza dei Signori*, ☎ *0444/323681.* ⌨ *Fee varies according to exhibition.* ☉ *Tues.–Sat. 9:30–noon and 2:30–5, Sun. 9:30–noon (Apr.–Sept., also Sun. 2–7); hrs vary with exhibitions.*

㉔ Casa Pigafetta. This ornate, red marble house was built shortly before the birth of the sailor after whom it is named. Antonio Pigafetta (1491–1534) was a member of Magellan's crew in his circumnavigation of the globe in 1519. ✉ *Contrà Pigafetta.*

㉒⓪ Contrà Porti. A fine cluster of Palladio's buildings centers on this short street. He contributed a wing to **Palazzo Thiene,** at No. 47, which was started in 1484 and incorporates another Renaissance palace by Lorenzo da Bologna (1489). At Contrà Porti 21, the **Palazzo Porta Festa** (1552) was begun but not finished by Palladio. With its mullioned windows, the strikingly Gothic **Palazzo Porta Breganze,** on the corner with Contrà Riale, is not Palladio's work, but his **Palazzo Barbaran da Porto** (1570), beyond, is now the home of the International Center of Palladian Architectural Studies (CISA). On Via Fogazzaro, **Palazzo Valmarana Braga** (1566) is a perfect example of Palladio's ability to integrate his buildings with the surroundings. All these buildings can be admired from the outside.

㉖ Corso Palladio. The main avenue in town is lined with a succession of imposing palaces and churches that run the gamut from Venetian Gothic to Baroque. At the start of the Corso, near the Piazza del Castello, **Palazzo Bonin Longhare** was probably built by Palladio's follower, Vincenzo Scamozzi (1552–1616), and has a good courtyard.

㉕ Duomo. Vicenza's Gothic cathedral is notable for a gleaming altarpiece by the 14th-century Venetian painter Lorenzo Veneziano (1356–72). The marble high altar could be an early work of Palladio as it comes from the workshop of Pedemuro, where he was employed as a novice. The cathedral itself was partly destroyed in World War II, but nearly all the damaged areas have been restored. The Romanesque bell tower stands apart from it. ⊠ *Piazza del Duomo.* ☉ *Daily 10:30–noon and 3:30–7.*

㉓ Loggia del Capitaniato. Opposite the Basilica in Piazza dei Signori, this building was commissioned for the commander of the city and designed, but never completed, by Palladio. The reliefs on the facade celebrate the defeat of the Turks at Lepanto in 1571. ⊠ *Piazza dei Signori.*

★ **⑯ Palazzo Chiericati.** The exquisite and unmistakably Palladian palace houses the **Museo Civico**, with a representative collection of Venetian paintings including Tiepolo (1696–1770) and Tintoretto (1519–94). Also noteworthy are the stucco relief *Madonna and Child* by Sansovino (1486–1570) and, in the Flemish room, another *Madonna and Child* attributed to Brueghel the Elder (circa 1520–69) and *Three Ages of Man* by Van Dyck (1599–1641). ⊠ *Piazza Matteotti,* ☎ *0444/ 321348.* 🎫 *€6.20 includes Teatro Olimpico.* ☉ *Apr.–May and Sept.– Mar., Tues.–Sun. 9–5; June–Aug., Tues.–Sun. 10–7.*

⑱ Santa Corona. Begun in 1261 to hold a thorn from Christ's crown, a gift from Louis IX of France, this church is said to possess the oldest Gothic interior in the Veneto. In addition to the Holy Thorn, which is kept in a gold reliquary and displayed only on Good Friday, it also holds an exceptionally fine *Baptism of Christ* (1500) by Giovanni Bellini (1430–1516) over the altar on the left, just in front of the transept, and an equally fine *Adoration of the Magi* by Paolo Veronese (1528–88). The high altar is a splendid example of 18th-century craftsmanship in inlaid marble and mother-of-pearl. The church was the original burial place of Palladio until his remains were transferred in the 19th century to the cemetery of Santa Lucia. The cloisters are now home to the **Museo Naturalistico-Archeologico,** containing remains of a Roman theater excavated in the 19th century and a natural history and geology section upstairs. ⊠ *Contrà Santa Corona,* ☎ *0444/320440.* 🎫 *Museum €6.20 includes Teatro Olimpico and Palazzo Chiericati.* ☉ *Church daily 8:30–noon and 2:30–6. Museum Apr.–May and Sept.– Mar., Tues.–Sun. 9–5; June–Aug., Tues.–Sun. 10–7.*

⑲ Santo Stefano. This small church is worth tracking down for the fine painting contained within, the *Madonna and Child with Sts. George and Lucy* by Palma Vecchio (1480–1528), who was to influence Veronese's paintings. ⊠ *Contrà Santo Stefano.* ☉ *Daily 8:30–noon and 2:30–6.*

★ **⑰ Teatro Olimpico.** This is Palladio's last, and perhaps most exciting, work. It was completed in 1584 by Vincenzo Scamozzi (1552–1616), who was also responsible for the permanent set. Based closely on the model of the ancient Roman theater, it represents an important development in theater and stage design and is noteworthy for its acoustics and the cunningly devised false perspective of a classical street in the permanent backdrop. The anterooms are all frescoed with important figures in Venetian history. ⊠ *Piazza Matteotti,* ☎ *0444/323781.* 🎫 *€6.20* *includes Palazzo Chiericati.* ⊙ *Apr.–May and Sept.–Mar., Tues.–Sat. 9–5, Sun. 9–12:30; June–Aug., Tues.–Sun. 10–7.*

㉒ **Torre di Piazza.** This slender tower at the corner of the basilica was built in the 12th century and is all that remains of the original structure to which Palladio made his additions. ⊠ *Piazza dei Signori.*

OFF THE
BEATEN PATH

VILLA LA ROTONDA – This is the most famous Palladian villa of all. In truth, it can hardly be called a villa, since Palladio was inspired by ancient Roman temples. For this villa, his inspiration was the Pantheon in Rome. Serene and symmetrical, Villa La Rotonda was the model for Jefferson's Monticello. Take the time to admire it from all sides and you'll see that it was the inspiration not just for Monticello but also for nearly every state capitol in the United States. The interior is typical of Palladio's grand style, with a unique juxtaposition of solids and voids. You can walk 3 km (2 mi) south along the Riviera Berica from Vicenza, or take Bus 8 from Viale Roma and ask the driver to let you off at the villa. Note that the interior is open Wednesday only during limited months. ⊠ *Via della Rotonda 29,* ☎ *0444/321793.* ⊠ *Grounds €2.60, villa €5.15.* ⊙ *Grounds mid-Mar.–early Nov., daily 10–noon and 3–6; interior mid-Mar.–early Nov., Wed. 10–noon and 3–6.*

VILLA VALMARANA AI NANI – A short walk from Villa La Rotonda, this 18th-century country house is decorated with a series of marvelous frescoes by Giambattista Tiepolo. These are fantastic visions of a mythological world, including one of his most stunning works, the *Sacrifice of Iphegenia*. The neighboring Foresteria, or guest house, holds more frescoes depicting vignettes of 18th-century Veneto life at its most charming, executed by Tiepolo's son, Giandomenico (1727–1804). In case you're wondering, *nani* means "dwarves": story has it that the villa is protected by the dwarf servants of a girl who used to live here. The dwarves were subsequently turned to stone, and you can see their statues all along the garden wall. ⊠ *Via dei Nani 2/8,* ☎ *0444/321803.* ⊠ *€4.13.* ⊙ *Mid-Mar.–mid-Nov., Wed., Thurs., and weekends 10–noon and 2–6; Tues. and Fri. 10–noon.*

Dining and Lodging

$$–$$$ ✕ **Da Remo.** About 1 km (½ mi) or so outside town, Da Remo is worth the taxi ride simply because it is one of Vicenza's best restaurants. In an attractive country house setting, with light, airy dining rooms and a garden terrace, you can enjoy a relaxing meal of Venetian specialties, among them *faraona* (guinea hen) with radicchio, and risotto with seasonal vegetables. ⊠ *Via Ca' Impenta 14,* ☎ *0444/911007. AE, DC, MC, V. Closed Mon., Aug., and Dec. 23–Jan. 6. No dinner Sun.*

$$ ✕ **Agli Schioppi.** You'll find traditional cooking employing seasonal ingredients at this rustic and intimate trattoria. Specialties include *tartufo nero dei Colli Berici* (tagliolini with local black truffles) and *coniglio con rosmarino* (rabbit with rosemary). ⊠ *Contrà Castello 26,* ☎ *0444/543701. Reservations essential. AE, DC, MC, V. Closed Sun. and July 16–Aug. 11. No dinner Sat.*

$$ ✕ **Conte Negroni.** People come for the stupendous location (in front ★ of the Basilica Palladiana), but you can eat reasonably well here. The small menu offers such appealing Italian classics as tagliolini *con tartufo* (sprinkled with truffle slivers) and linguine *alle vongole* (with clams and parsley), as well as the city's specialty, *baccalà alla vicentina* (dried cod stewed with onions, anchovies, milk, and Parmesan). In warm weather you can reserve a table outside. ⊠ *Piazza dei Signori 5,* ☎ *0444/542455. DC, V. Closed Wed.*

$-$$ ✕ **Al Paradiso.** This pizzeria-trattoria just off the Piazza dei Signori is one of a pair right next door to each other, owned by two brothers; the other is Vecchia Guardia (✉ Via Vecchia Guardia 15, ☎ 0444/321231; closed Mon.). This place is particularly attractive in summer, when you can sit at tables outside. The pizzas and other dishes are tasty and very reasonably priced. ✉ *Via Pescherie Vecchie 5, ☎ 0444/322320. AE, DC, MC, V. Closed Mon.*

$$$-$$$$ 🏨 **Campo Marzio.** This elegant and luxurious hotel sits right in the center of the city. The rooms are furnished in different styles—Chinese, modern, or floral—and the bathrooms have nice ceramic washstands. The price increases at trade fair times, but you'll always get a good buffet breakfast. ✉ *Via le Roma 21, 36100,* ☎ *0444/545700,* FAX *0444/320495,* WEB *www.hotelcampomarzio.com. 35 rooms. Restaurant, bar, air-conditioning, bicycles, free parking. AE, DC, MC, V.*

$$-$$$ 🏨 **Castello.** Predominantly charming pink with spacious rooms, this hotel has a cordial atmosphere and offers a discount if you dine in the restaurant Agli Schioppi next door. Cheaper rooms have shared bathrooms in the hallway. ✉ *Contrà Castello 24, 36100,* ☎ *0444/323585,* FAX *0444/323583. 18 rooms, 16 with bath. Breakfast room, parking. AE, DC, MC, V.*

$$ 🏨 **Alfa.** As it's close to the autostrada Vicenza Ovest exit and the Fiera (Exhibition Center), this modern hotel will have its fair share of business clientele. However, the whirlpool and Turkish baths may be just what you need after a hard day's sightseeing. ✉ *Via dell'Oreficeria 52, 36100,* ☎ *0444/565455,* FAX *0444/566027. 90 rooms, 3 suites. Restaurant, bar, gym. AE, DC, MC, V.*

$ 🏨 **Due Mori.** In the heart of Vicenza just off Piazza dei Signori, this small hotel is a favorite with regular visitors and a very good value. It's light and airy, yet cozy at the same time. The rooms are individually furnished with nice antique furniture and wooden fittings in the bathrooms. ✉ *Contrà Do Rode 26, 36100,* ☎ *0444/321886,* FAX *0444/326127. 26 rooms, 23 with bath. Breakfast room, free parking. AE, MC, V. Closed last 2 wks in July.*

Nightlife and the Arts

The Arts

MUSIC AND THEATER

The monthly *Informa Città*, available from the tourist office, will give you details of all events, including walking trips. Contact the tourist office for details of **Concerti in Ville,** a series of concerts held in nearby villas during June and July. Vicenza's **Teatro Olimpico** has a concert season in May and June, as well as a classical drama season in September. Even if your Italian is dismal, it's particularly thrilling to see a performance in Palladio's magnificent theater. For details, contact (☎ 0444/323781).

A **Jazz Festival** (☎ 0444/222101, FAX 0444/222155) takes place in May in various sites over the city. The **Teatro Zuccato** (✉ Strada Communale di Polegge 84, ☎ 0444/595533) offers a varied program of concerts, operetta, and folklore; tickets start at €6.20.

Nightlife

BARS

Bar Borsa (✉ Piazza dei Signori 26, ☎ 0444/546636) puts on live jazz on Wednesday. **Enocibus** (✉ Vicolo Pomodoro 3, ☎ 045/594010), one block off Piazza Bra, serves great wine and great food—and no smoking, a rarity in Italy. **Rebar** (✉ Via Zugliano 43, ☎ 0444/500151) has live rock, jazz, and funk on Friday.

Outdoor Activities and Sports

BIKING

Bikes can be rented from the luggage lost and found at the **train station** (☎ 0444/392528) for a very reasonable €0.50 per hour or €5.15 per day.

Shopping

Markets

A daily fruit and vegetable market is held in **Piazza delle Erbe,** behind the basilica. A general market is held Thursday in Piazza dei Signori.

Shopping Districts

Shops center on the main Corso Palladio, Contrà Cavour, and Piazza Signori.

Specialty Shops

CERAMICS AND GLASS

A good place to pick up a gift is **L'Idea** (✉ Piazza dei Signori 56, ☎ 0444/542052), which sells contemporary ceramics and glass.

CLOTHING

For a nice selection of classic and stylish shirts and skirts, visit **Zanolini** (✉ Piazza dei Signori 5, ☎ 0444/540768).

JEWELRY

Vicenza is one of Italy's leading centers for the production and sale of jewelry. For gold, silver, jewelry, and watches at factory prices, visit **Cash & Gold** (✉ Viale della Scienza 14, ☎ 0444/965947), a complex of more than 100 traders. Buses 12 and 15 from the train station will get you there. **Fiera di Vicenza** (✉ Via dell'Oreficeria, ☎ 0444/969111) holds a series of trade fairs, most of which are open to the general public. These include jewelry, pictures, ceramics, and coins.

PASTICCERIE

If you see a procession of people carrying beribboned packages across the Piazza dei Signori, you can be sure they're coming from **Pasticceria Sorarù** (✉ Piazzetta Palladio 17, ☎ 0444/320915), a heavenly place to buy cakes and pastries. You'll find it hard to leave without stopping to taste the *paste* (pastries) and savoring the old-fashioned atmosphere.

VERONA

On the banks of the fast-flowing Adige River, enchanting Verona lays claim to classical and medieval monuments, a picturesque town center where bright geraniums bloom in window boxes, and a romantic reputation, thanks to its immortalization as the setting of Shakespeare's *Romeo and Juliet*. It is one of Italy's most alluring cities, despite extensive industrialization and urban development in its newer sections. There's an opulence in the air and in the shops that line the red Verona marble pavements with their enticing and elegant wares. Inevitably, with its lively Venetian feel, proximity to Lake Garda, and renowned summer opera season, it attracts hordes of tourists, especially vacationing Germans and Austrians, who drive over the Brenner Pass.

Verona grew to power and prosperity within the Roman Empire as a result of its key commercial and military position in northern Italy. After the fall of the Empire, the city continued to flourish under the guidance of Barbarian kings such as Theodoric, Alboin, Pepin, and Berenger I, reaching its cultural and artistic peak in the 13th and 14th centuries under the della Scala (Scaligeri) dynasty. You'll see the *scala,* or ladder, emblem all over town. In 1404, however, Verona traded its independence for security and placed itself under the control of Venice. The other recurring architectural motif is the winged lion of St. Mark, symbol of Venetian rule. Verona remained under Venetian protection until 1797, when Napoléon invaded. In 1814 the entire Veneto region was won by the Austrians, and it was finally united with the rest of Italy in 1866.

Exploring Verona

With its small streets, secret courtyards, elegant boutiques, and comely air, Verona is an extremely walkable city. Please note that the Duomo and churches in Verona enforce a strict dress code: no tank tops, sleeveless shirts, shorts, or short skirts. You might want to consider buying the €4.15 combined ticket that allows admittance to most churches in town, including the Duomo, San Zeno, and Sant'Anastasia. Drivers should be aware that cars are not allowed in the historic center from 7:30 to 10 and 1:30 to 4:30. Numerous parking areas are found beyond the center, and one-hour disk parking is permitted in the nearby streets.

A Good Walk

Start at the **Arena di Verona** ㉗ in Piazza Brà, the vast and airy square at the center of the city. Built by the Romans in the 1st century AD, the arena is one of the largest and best-preserved Roman amphitheaters anywhere. Take Via Mazzini, the main shopping street in town, to **Piazza delle Erbe** ㉘, a busy square with an open-air market. The **Casa di Giulietta** ㉙, with the most famous balcony in Italy, is a block down Via del Cappello. Return and take a few moments to stroll around **Piazza dei Signori** ㉚, and admire the **Palazzo della Ragione** ㉛, **Loggia del Consiglio** ㉜, and **Palazzo degli Scaligeri** ㉝. Don't miss the **Arche Scaligere** ㉞, and, if you've time, take a trip to the top of the **Torre dei Lamberti** ㉟ for the view. From here it's a short walk to Ponte Nuova and across the river toward the **Santa Maria in Organo** ㊱ and the **Giardino Giusti** ㊲. Then follow Via Santa Maria in Organo up to the Teatro Romano, site of the **Museo Archeologico** ㊳. The Romanesque **Duomo** ㊴ is just over Ponte Pietra. From there either walk down Via Duomo and Corso Sant' Anastasia to **Sant'Anastasia** ㊵ and Via Forti and the **Galleria d'Arte Moderna** ㊶. Or, turn toward the riverbank and stroll (or alternately take Bus 76) down to the 14th-century **Castelvecchio** ㊷, looking like a fairy-tale castle guarding the bridge over the Adige River. The stunning Romanesque **San Zeno Maggiore** ㊸ is another few minutes' walk downriver.

TIMING

It takes about an hour or two to walk the route, and three hours or more to see the sights.

Sights to See

㉞ **Arche Scaligere.** The impressive marbled Gothic monuments of the Scaligeri family tombs are set in the grounds of the church of Santa Maria Antica. Cangrande I ("Big Dog") looks down from atop his pinnacled tomb—this statue is a copy of the original that stands in the Castelvecchio. Mastino II ("Mastiff") is buried to the left of the church close to Cansignorio ("Top Dog"). Look for the ladder motif on the wrought-iron grille surrounding the tombs. ⊠ *Via Arche Scaligere.* ☉ *Visible at all times.*

㉗ **Arena di Verona.** Only the Colosseum and the arena in Capua can outdo this amphitheater in size. Just four arches remain of the outer arcade of the arena, but the main structure is so complete that it takes little imagination to picture it as the site of the cruel deaths of countless gladiators, wild beasts, and Christians. Today it hosts, among other events,

Verona

Verona's summer opera, famous for spectacular productions and audiences of as many as 16,000. The best operas to see here are the big splashy ones that demand huge choruses, enormous sets, lots of color and movement, and, if possible, camels, horses, and/or elephants. The music can be excellent, and the acoustics are fine, too. If you go, be sure to take or rent a cushion—four hours on 2,000-year-old marble can be an ordeal. ✉ *Arena di Verona, Piazza Brà 5,* ☎ *045/8003204.* 🎫 *€3.10, €1.05 1st Sun. of month.* ◷ *Sept.–June, Tues.–Sun. 9–6:30; July–Aug., Tues.–Sun. 8–3:30.*

㉙ **Casa di Giulietta** (Juliet's House). The balcony in the small courtyard will help to bring Shakespeare's play to life, even if it was built in the 20th century. Historians now believe that the couple had no real-life counterparts, but this hasn't discouraged anyone from imagining that they did. After all, historians are not as renowned for their storytelling as Shakespeare is. You can see the balcony without paying to enter. ✉ *Via Cappello 23,* ☎ *045/8034303.* 🎫 *€3.10.* ◷ *Tues.–Sun. 9–6:30.*

Casa di Romeo. Folklore has it that Romeo's house was in Via Arche Scaligere, where at No. 4 a plaque marks the spot.

㊷ **Castelvecchio** (Old Castle). This crenellated, russet brick building with massive walls, towers, turrets, and a vast courtyard was built for Cangrande II della Scala in 1354. It presides over a street lined with attractive old buildings and palaces of the nobility. Inside, the **Museo di Castelvecchio** gives you a good look at the castle's vaulted halls and some treasures of 15th- to 18th-century Veronese painting and sculpture. Look out for the Via Trezza precious 14th-century jewels, Cangrande's belt and sword in Room VIII, and the original painted walls of Room XI. In the courtyard Cangrande I stands imposingly on a pedestal. ✉ *Corso Castelvecchio 2,* ☎ *045/594734.* 🎫 *€3.10, free 1st Sun. of month.* ◷ *Tues.–Sun. 9–6:30; hrs vary according to exhibition.*

OFF THE
BEATEN PATH

TOMBA DI GIULIETTA – Romantic souls may want to see the pretty spot claimed to be Juliet's tomb. Authentic or not, it is still popular with lovesick Italian teenagers, who leave notes for the tragic lover. A museum of frescoes is inside. ✉ *Via del Pontiere 5,* ☎ *045/8000361.* 🎫 *€2.60, free 1st Sun. of month.* ◷ *Tues.–Sun. 9–6:30.*

GIARDINI DI VILLA ARVEDI – Formal gardens surround a 17th-century villa 8 km (5 mi) northeast of town. ✉ *Statale per Grezzana,* ☎ *045/907045.* 🎫 *€5.20.* ◷ *By appointment; minimum 10 people.*

㊴ **Duomo.** The ornate red-and-white striped Romanesque Duomo, dating back to the 12th century, has a grand organ and a wealth of decorative architectural detail especially around each chapel. The first chapel on the left holds an *Assumption* (1535) by Titian. Fine reliefs on the 12th-century south porch depict *Jonah and the Whale,* and on the west porch are statues of *Roland* and *Oliver,* paladins of Charlemagne. ✉ *Via Duomo,* ☎ *045/592813.* 🎫 *€2.05.* ◷ *Nov.–Feb., Tues.–Sat. 10–4, Sun. 1:30–5; Mar.–Oct., Tues.–Sat. 10–5:30, Sun. 1:30–5:30.*

㊶ **Galleria d'Arte Moderna** (Gallery of Modern Art). The handsome Palazzo Forti was the 13th-century home of Ezzelino III and once provided lodgings for Napoléon. The gallery hosts contemporary painting exhibitions of well-known artists such as Marcel Duchamp (1887–1968) and Andy Warhol (1928–87). ✉ *Via Forti 1, entrance on Corso S. Anastasia,* ☎ *045/8001903.* 🎫 *Fee varies according to exhibition.* ◷ *Sept.–June, Tues.–Sun. 9 AM–10 PM; July–Aug., Tues.–Sun. 9–7.*

㊲ **Giardino Giusti.** The formal gardens, laid out on several levels around a 16th-century villa, is a symbol of things long gone. There's a fine view of the city from the terrace, from which the German poet and drama-tist Johann von Goethe recorded his inspiration. Formal box hedges, cypresses, statues, fountains, and a maze will provide a diversion from city sightseeing. ⊠ *Via Giardino Giusti 2*, ☎ *045/8034029*. ☞ *€4.15.* ☉ *July–Aug., daily 9–8; Sept.–June, daily 9–sunset.*

㉜ **Loggia del Consiglio.** The graceful structure was built in the 12th cen-tury to house city council meetings and still serves as the seat of the provincial government. Over the door is the inscription bearing testi-mony to Verona's loyalty to Venice and Venice's love for Verona, *Pro summa fide summa amor MDXCII* ("Greatest love for the greatest loy-alty 1592"). ⊠ *Piazza dei Signori.*

㊳ **Museo Archeologico.** An old monastery above the **Teatro Romano** houses fine Greek, Roman, and Etruscan artifacts. The theater, built in the same era as the Arena di Verona and now restored, is still used for dramatic productions and a jazz festival. ⊠ *Regaste del Redentore 2*, ☎ *045/8000360.* ☞ *€2.58, free 1st Sun. of month.* ☉ *Apr.–Oct., Tues.–Sun. 9–6:30; Nov.–Mar., Tues.–Sun. 9–3.*

㉝ **Palazzo degli Scaligeri.** This was the medieval stronghold from which the della Scalas ruled Verona with an iron fist. ⊠ *Piazza dei Signori.*

㉛ **Palazzo della Ragione.** The 12th-century palace has a somber court-yard, a Gothic staircase, and a medieval tower overlooking the piazza. ⊠ *Piazza dei Signori.*

㉚ **Piazza dei Signori.** Verona's great piazza has been at the center of things for more than 1,000 years, but the impressive facades and arched en-trances surrounding it date from the early Renaissance.

㉘ **Piazza delle Erbe** (Vegetable Market Square). A Roman forum once bustled on this site, and today a colorful morning market (daily ex-cept Monday) with huge rectangular umbrellas raised to shade the neat ranks of fruits and vegetables gets under way daily.

★ ㊸ **San Zeno Maggiore.** What is possibly the finest example of a Ro-manesque church in Italy, with a 13th-century rose window representing the Wheel of Fortune and 12th-century portal, is set between two me-dieval bell towers. Of special note are the 11th- and 12th-century bronze doors depicting biblical scenes and episodes from the life of San Zeno, Verona's patron saint, and Mantegna's triptych the *Madonna and Saints* over the main altar. San Zeno is buried in the crypt, and a peaceful cloister lies off the left nave. ⊠ *Piazza San Zeno*, ☎ *045/ 8006120.* ☞ *€2.05.* ☉ *Nov.–Feb., Tues.–Sat. 10–4, Sun. 1–5; Mar.–Oct., Tues.–Sat. 8:30–5:30, Sun. 1–6.*

㊱ **Santa Maria in Organo.** The choir and sacristy of this medieval church are decorated with inlaid-wood masterpieces by the 15th-century monk Fra Giovanni. A series of panels depicts varied scenes—local buildings, an idealized Renaissance town, wildlife, and fruit—that radiate a love of life and reveal the artist's eye for detail. ⊠ *Via Interrato dell'Acqua Morta*, ☎ *045/591440.* ☞ *€1.55.* ☉ *Apr.–Oct., daily 7:30–noon and 3–6; Nov.–Mar., daily 7:30–noon.*

㊵ **Sant'Anastasia.** Verona's largest church, completed in 1481, is a fine example of Gothic brickwork. The Gothic interior contains numerous frescoes, of which the most outstanding are the richly decorative and glowing *St. George and the Princess* by Pisanello (1377–1455) in the sacristy and one by Altichiero (1320–95) in the Cavalli chapel. As you come in, look for the *gobbi* (hunchbacks) supporting the holy water stoup, with holes in their pants. ⊠ *Piazza Sant'Anastasia*, ☎ *045/*

592813. ✆ *€1.55.* ☉ *Nov.–Feb., Tues.–Sat. 10–4, Sun. 1–5; Mar.–Oct., Tues.–Sat. 9–5:30, Sun. 1–6.*

③⑤ Torre dei Lamberti. Standing 285 ft above Piazza dei Signori, this tower was begun in the 12th century and finished in the 15th. Taking the elevator will only cost you €0.50 more than walking up the 368 steps for the panoramic view. ⊠ *Piazza dei Signori,* ☎ *045/8032726.* ✆ *Elevator €2.05, stairs €1.55.* ☉ *Apr.–Oct., Tues.–Sun. 9–6; Nov.–Mar., Tues.–Sun. 10–1 and 1:30–4.*

Dining and Lodging

$$$$ ✕ **Le Arche.** True to its name, this elegant restaurant is in a medieval
★   building a step away from the della Scala tombs. The art-nouveau dining room features candlelight and flowers, imparting a turn-of-the-20th-century air. Only seafood is served, absolutely fresh and superlatively prepared. Try the *raviolone al branzino e spinaci in salsa di foie gras e tartufo* (pasta squares stuffed with sea bass and spinach with foie gras and truffle sauce) and the unusual *salsiccia di pesce* (fish sausage made with sea scorpion, sea bass, and salmon). ⊠ *Via Arche Scaligere 6,* ☎ *045/8007415. AE, DC, MC, V. Closed Sun., last 2 wks in Jan., and first 2 wks in Feb. No lunch Mon.*

$$$–$$$$ ✕ **Dodici Apostoli.** Vaulted ceilings, frescoed walls, and a medieval ambience make this an exceptional place to enjoy classic local and regional dishes. Near Piazza delle Erbe, it stands on the foundations of a Roman temple. Specialties include *zuppa scaligera* (soup of meat stock with vegetables and bread) and *vitello Lessinia* (veal with mushrooms, cheese, and truffles). ⊠ *Vicolo Corticella San Marco 3,* ☎ *045/596999,* WEB *www.12apostoli.com. AE, DC, MC, V. Closed Mon. and June 15–July 7. No dinner Sun.*

$$$–$$$$ ✕ **Maffei.** The mirrored old-world elegance of the interior of this restaurant, right on the end of Piazza delle Erbe, betrays the remarkable creativity of the dishes that await. Unlikely bedfellows take on unprecedented form in the *risotto ai bruscandoli e ragout di rane con fiori di luppolo fritti* (risotto with hop sprouts, frog ragout, and fried hop flowers). Even more shockingly, at least for Italy, Siennese fried pig is topped with soy sauce—wonderful sacrilege. ⊠ *Piazza Erbe 38,* ☎ *045/ 8010015,* WEB *www.ristorantemaffei.it. AE, DC, MC, V.*

$$$–$$$$ ✕ **Osteria All'Oste Scuro.** Two local gourmets turned this ex-family trat-
★   toria into a first-class fish restaurant. Specialties might include *spaghettini ai gamberetti e cannellini* (little spaghetti with shrimp and Tuscan beans), and more traditional dishes like grilled crab and prawn or baked fish with potatoes are always on the menu. ⊠ *Vicolo San Silvestro 10,* ☎ *045/592650. Reservations required. V. Closed Sun. and Aug. 8–25. No lunch Mon.*

$$–$$$ ✕ **Al Calmiere.** This congenial trattoria on the lovely piazza in front of San Zeno Maggiore is the ideal place to enjoy Veronese specialties of tagliatelle *con fegatini di pollo* (with chicken-liver sauce), various types of pasta in *brodo* (broth), meats, and local wines (there are some 20 different Valpolicellas alone available) at reasonable prices. The interior, with an enormous open fireplace used for cooking, is especially cozy in winter. ⊠ *Piazza San Zeno 10,* ☎ *045/8030765. AE, DC, MC, V. Closed Thurs., 1st wk in Jan., and 1st 3 wks in July. No dinner Wed.*

$$–$$$ ✕ **La Greppia.** The classic decor with vaulted ceilings sets the tone in this bustling restaurant off Via Mazzini between the Arena and Piazza delle Erbe. The kitchen produces fine versions of local and regional dishes, especially *tortelli di zucca* (pasta filled with squash) and *bolliti* (assorted boiled meats served with a choice of sauces). Service is courteous and efficient. ⊠ *Vicolo Samaritana 3,* ☎ *045/8004577. AE, DC, MC, V. Closed Mon., last 3 wks in Jan., and last 2 wks in June.*

$$ ✕ **La Stueta.** Perhaps the best bargain in town, La Stueta is a friendly trattoria not far from the Giardino Giusti across the river. Try the gnocchi *con la pastisada* (with a horse-meat sauce), baccalà, or *maiale all'amarone* (pork shin in a red wine sauce served with polenta). ⊠ *Via del Redentore 4/b,* ☎ *045/8032462. AE, DC, MC, V. Closed Mon. and July. No lunch Tues.*

$ ✕ **Pizzeria Vesuvio.** Between Castelvecchio and San Zeno Maggiore, this authentic Neapolitan pizzeria has tables on the riverbank in summer, with a lovely breezy view of the Adige. ⊠ *Via Rigaste 41,* ☎ *045/ 595634. No credit cards. Closed Mon.*

$$$–$$$$ ▥ **Gabbia d'Oro.** Set in a historic building off Piazza delle Erbe in the
★   ancient heart of Verona, this hotel is a tasteful fantasia of romantic ornamentation, exquisite fabrics, and gorgeous period pieces. Individually decorated rooms have frescoes, beamed ceilings, pretty wallpaper, antique prints and furnishings, and canopy beds, and some are festooned with flying cupids and peaceful cherubs. You can relax outdoors in the medieval courtyard, in the comfortable orangerie, or on the roof terrace. The breakfast buffet is a celestial affair. ⊠ *Corso Porta Borsari 4/a, 37121,* ☎ *045/8003060,* 𝐅𝐀𝐗 *045/590293,* 𝐖𝐄𝐁 *www.hotelgabbiadoro. it. 19 rooms, 8 suites. Restaurant. AE, DC, MC, V.*

$$$–$$$$ ▥ **Villa del Quar.** This tranquil 16th-century villa is surrounded by gar-
★   dens and vineyards in the Valpolicella country, 10 minutes by taxi from the city. Architect Leopoldo Montresor and his wife, Evelina, who live here with their children, converted part of the villa into a stylish and sophisticated hotel. No expense has been spared: all rooms have marble bathrooms (some with whirlpool baths) and European antiques. ⊠ *Via del Quar 12, 37020 Loc. Pedemonte, S. Pietro Incariano, 5 km (3 mi) north of Verona,* ☎ *045/6800681,* 𝐅𝐀𝐗 *045/6800604. 19 rooms, 4 suites. Restaurant, pool. AE, DC, MC, V.*

$$–$$$ ▥ **Colomba d'Oro.** This attractive four-star hotel right by the Arena occupies a building that dates from the 14th century. It has retained its clubby atmosphere and European charm while providing up-to-date comfort. ⊠ *Via Cattaneo 10, 37121,* ☎ *045/595300,* 𝐅𝐀𝐗 *045/594974. 45 rooms, 10 suites. Parking (fee). AE, DC, MC, V.*

$–$$ ▥ **Torcolo.** The warm welcome extended by the owners, Signoras
★   Diana and Silvia, the pleasant rooms decorated unfussily, and the central location on a peaceful street close to Piazza Brà and the Arena make the Torcolo an outstanding value in its class. Breakfast is served outside on the terrace in front of the hotel in summer. ⊠ *Vicolo Listone 3, 37121,* ☎ *045/8007512 or 045/8003871,* 𝐅𝐀𝐗 *045/8004058. 19 rooms. Closed Jan. 7–Feb. 8. AE, MC, V.*

Nightlife and the Arts

The Arts

MUSIC AND CONCERTS

The Teatro Romano is the setting for the annual summer **Shakespeare Festival** (⊠ Via Rigaste del Redentore 2, ☎ 045/8077219). In the first week of June, an **International Jazz Festival** (⊠ Via Rigaste del Redentore 2, ☎ 045/8077111) is held at the Teatro Romano with added venues in the Arena and Teatro Nuovo.

The city is awash in cultural events in July and August—the Arena doesn't have a monopoly on all the entertainment. From Thursday to Saturday in both the afternoon and evening, free concerts called **I Concerti Scaligeri** take place in Piazza dei Signori. There's a wide range of national and international offerings, from Mozart to Gershwin, country to Indian ragas. ☎ *045/8077532 or 8077497 for information.*

LOVE AND DEATH IN VERONA

> While Verona by that name is known,
> There shall no figure at such rate be set
> As that of true and faithful Juliet.
> (*Romeo and Juliet*, Act V, Scene 3)

So promised Lord Montague to Lord Capulet, as they ended the ancient family feud that doomed Romeo and Juliet to their tragic end. By the looks of things, he's kept his vow. Romeo and Juliet are said to have made their ill-fated match in the 13th century, and Shakespeare's play dates to the 16th, but no matter—English literature's best-known lovesick teenagers are even today the first couple of Verona, and they've turned this somewhat staid northern town into a mecca for romantic pilgrims with a literary bent.

Italy was a favorite dramatis loca for Shakespeare, and he set plays all along the peninsula, from Messina (*Much Ado About Nothing*) to Venice (*The Merchant of Venice*). No other city, however, wears its Shakespearean legacy as much on its sleeve as "fair Verona." In fact, the timeless story of doomed love was originally Verona's, not Shakespeare's—the tale of young lovers torn apart by feuding between the Montecchi (Montagues) and Cappellelli (Capulets) was first published in the 16th century by Veronese Luigi Da Porto, then popularized by retellings in French and English, one of which, *Brooke's Romeus and Juliet: Being the Original of Shakespeare's Romeo and Juliet,* by Arthur Brooke, is thought to have inspired Shakespeare's play.

Shakespeare's play, in turn, seems to have inspired Verona—or at least the tourists that flock there. Romeo and Juliet live on in the names of restaurants and hotels, and star-crossed-lover postcards and T-shirts are sold at every turn. The city hosts a Shakespeare festival every summer, with guess what play taking center stage? (Hint: it's not *Two Gentlemen of Verona*.) Some Veronese romantics have formed a Juliet Club, dedicated to answering letters for Juliet they say arrive from all over the world. Each year, they sponsor a love-letter writing contest on Juliet's birthday, September 16. The City of Romeo and Juliet basks in its reputation for romance, attracting flocks of lovebirds every year.

Starry-eyed visitors can stroll hand-in-hand down not one but two Lovers' Lanes (Via Amanti and Vicolo Amanti), gaze wistfully up at the balcony of Juliet's house (Via Cappello 23), and dab moist eyes at Juliet's red marble tomb next to the Museo degli Affreschi on Via del Pontiere. The more literal- or cynically minded will note that historians doubt Romeo and Juliet ever lived, much less loved, and that "Juliet's Balcony," built in 20th century, is attached to a house that was not the Cappellellis' (although the Casa di Romeo, at Via Arche Scaligere, was indeed the Montecchi home). But what's in a name? What are authentic are the remains of the more than 700 defense towers and fortresses dating from the 13th century, testament to the real family feuding that took many more lives than Romeo's poison and Juliet's dagger.

— Valerie Hamilton

Of all the venues for enjoying opera in the region, the best is probably the **Arena di Verona.** The season runs from July through August, and the 16,000 in the audience sit on the original stone terraces that date from the time when gladiators fought to the death. The opera stage is huge and best suited to grand operas such as *Aïda,* but the experience is memorable no matter what is being performed. Sometimes, while sipping a drink in a caffè at **Piazza Brà,** you can overhear the opera. A 15% advance-sale fee is added to the price of a ticket for bookings made more than 24 hours before a performance. *Contact: Fondazione Arena di Verona,* ✉ *Piazza Brà 28, 37121 Verona,* ☎ *045/8051811. Box office:* ✉ *Via Dietro Anfiteatro 6B,* ☎ *045/8005151.* ☼ *Weekdays 9–noon and 3:15–5:45, Sat. 9–noon.*

From the end of August through September, strolling players perform Shakespeare's *Romeo and Juliet* in the very place where the story is said to have unfolded. In addition, many churches put on concerts throughout the year. Contact the tourist office (☎ 045/8000861) for details. The beautiful **Teatro Filarmonico** (✉ Via dei Mutilati 4/k, ☎ 045/8002880) puts on an international program of traditional and experimental concerts, opera, and ballet attracting such renowned artistes as José Carreras. Prices start from €10.35.

Nightlife

Alter Ego (✉ Via Torricelle 9, ☎ 045/915130) packs a twentysomething crowd with a vague alternative edge. **Berfi's** (✉ Via Lussemborgo 1, ☎ 045/508024) is a popular and expensive spot. **Excalibur** (✉ Via Provolo 24, ☎ 045/594295) attracts a young crowd.

Outdoor Activities and Sports

Biking

Bikes are available for rent from **Noleggio Bici** (☎ 045/582389 in summer; 0338/9550056 in winter) on Piazza Brà.

Golf

The 18-hole **Golf Club Verona** (✉ Ca' del Sale 15, Sommacampagna, ☎ 045/510060), closed Tuesday, is 16 km (10 mi) west of Verona and 2 km (1 mi) from the Sommacampagna exit on the A4 autoroute.

Shopping

Markets

Verona's **Piazza delle Erbe** daily market, open Monday through Saturday 8 to 1 and 3:30 to sundown, has a selection of food, wine, clothing, antiques, and even pets. On the third Saturday of every month an antiques and arts-and-crafts market is held in **Piazza San Zeno.**

Specialty Stores

The area around the Gothic church of Sant'Anastasia is full of antiques shops, most of them catering to serious collectors. Picnic on the Piazza dei Signori in the cool breeze after a strenuous day of antiques hunting. The perfect place for a pricey modern gift or imaginative decorative piece is **Fornasetti** (✉ Via Rosa 8/d, ☎ 045/8000064), displaying the geometric black-and-white designs of the namesake artist imparted onto everything from ties and umbrellas to pillowcases, lacquer furniture, and plates. Everything for the kitchen can be found in **Cose di Casa** (✉ Via Oberdan 8, ☎ 045/8013861), including colorful glass bottle stoppers, designer corkscrews, and modern crystal. **Cesare Soprana**

(✉ Via Rosa 4/b, ☎ 045/8032224) sells Versace silver and exquisite (and expensive) miniature knights in armor.

CLOTHING AND ACCESSORIES

Via Mazzini is full of the well-known names—Maxmara, Versace, Marina Rinaldi to name but a few. At **Carcereri** (✉ Via Roma 4/a, ☎ 045/8030238) you can pick up romantic dresses trimmed with fur and feathers, along with hats and scarves. **Furla** (✉ Via Mazzini 60, ☎ 045/8004760) displays its distinctive bags, watches, umbrellas, and key rings. **Pollini** (✉ Via Mazzini 64, ☎ 045/8032247) is nirvana for shoe collectors. **Prada** (✉ Corso Porta Borsari, ☎ 045/8013861) features Miuccia's postmodern designs.

ENGLISH-LANGUAGE BOOKS

The **Bookshop** (✉ Via Interrato dell'Acqua Morta 3/a, ☎ 045/8007614) has a good range of English books and an English-speaking staff.

THE LAGOON AND THE ADRIATIC

Crossing the lagoon from Venice over the Ponte della Libertà to the mainland, you'll be confronted with the sight of oil tankers and red-and-white striped cranes. Nevertheless, it can make a less-hectic and less-expensive base for exploring the Veneto and Venice itself, which is a mere 10 minutes away by bus or train, and some attractive hotels and restaurants are worth seeking out. What's more, you'll have no parking problems here. Crossing the flat expanse of the lagoon from Venice in the other (southerly) direction brings you to Chioggia, scene of a decisive naval battle between the rival sea powers Venice and Genoa in 1379. Now a bustling fishing port, it's based on a grid alleyway system and has excellent fish restaurants. The long strip of beach at nearby Sottomarina makes it a popular vacationing spot for Italians. Rovigo, an inland town due south of Padua on A16, is a working city that's not geared up for tourists, but it does have a good art gallery and its own fine Rotonda. The area between Rovigo and the sea, the Po delta, with its slow-moving rivers, fields, and marshes, offers opportunities for quiet walks, bird-watching, and contemplation.

Mestre

🐸 *9 km (5½ mi) northwest of Venice.*

The Italian playwright Carlo Goldini (1707–93) likened Mestre to a "little Versailles"—but that was in the days when the Venetians were building numerous villas in the areas for their country retreats and rural enjoyment. Since then, and particularly with the development of the port at Marghera in 1919, Mestre has become the focus for industrial development and the destination for an exodus of Venetians forced out by high rents and sinking houses. Although in many ways it is the town where the "real Venetians" now live, Mestre hardly fits the tourist idea of Italy. Most of it is more '70s-style suburb than culture-infused outskirt. However, the small historic center still reveals a few remnants of the medieval defense system: the tower in the main square, Piazza Ferretto; the 14th-century **Scuola dei Battui,** now a retirement home; and the **Torre dell'Orologio** in Piazzetta Mattei. This brick tower with typical dovetail battlements dates from 1100, but the clock was added in the 16th century. Via Palazzo, the main street, makes for a pleasant stroll, lined as it is with arcaded buildings from the 16th to the 20th century. Note that the train station is marked "Venezia Mestre."

Dining and Lodging

$$ ✕ **Pizzeria Columbus.** The cool colors and unrushed service make this a relaxing place to dine. Pizzas are not the only attraction: try as an

antipasto *chele di granchio fritte* (fried crab claws), followed by a choice of three different kinds of fettuccine *alla pescatora* (with fish) and, for a *secondo*, *scaloppa alla boscaiola* (veal with wild mushrooms). ⊠ *Via Piave 68,* ☎ *041/950068. AE, DC, MC, V. Closed Mon.*

$$ 🏨 **Garibaldi.** Established 20 years ago in the center of town, this hotel has a quiet family atmosphere. The impressive foyer is flanked by modern columns offset by a pink marble floor. The bedrooms are contemporary and stylish. ⊠ *Viale Garibaldi 24, 30173,* ☎ *041/5350455,* FAX *041/5347565. 28 rooms. Bar, parking (fee). AE, DC, MC, V.*

$ 🏨 **Cris.** You'll spot this charming small hotel, not far from the train station, by its attractive terra-cotta and green exterior. The antiques-filled reception area makes you feel at home, and the rooms, though not luxurious, are adequate and comfortable. ⊠ *Via Montenero 3, 30171,* ☎ FAX *041/926773. 14 rooms, 11 with bath. Bar. MC, V.*

Chioggia-Sottomarina

45 *44 km (27 mi) south of Mestre, 35 km (22 mi) south of Venice.*

Only a thin strip of the lagoon separates Chioggia from Sottomarina, but they're as different as chalk from cheese. If you skip the outskirts of Chioggia (after Venice it's the largest settlement on the lagoon), you'll find a gridded series of *calli* (alleyways) and a busy fishing port. Cross the Ponte Translagunare and you'll come to 9 km (5 ½ mi) of beach stretching to the river Brenta, and all the glitz of a popular resort. Direct boat service on Carimero runs from Venice once a day in summer; contact the Chioggia tourist office (⊠ Lungomare Adriatico 101, 30019 Chioggia, ☎ 041/401068) for details. Practically all the hotels are situated in Sottomarina; you'll find the good restaurants in Chioggia.

Chioggia suffered terrible destruction from 1379 to 1380, when the Republics of Genoa and Venice clashed in the bid for supremacy of the Adriatic Sea, from which Venice emerged triumphant. The city then enjoyed a long period of calm under the sway of Venice until Napoléon arrived on the scene in 1797. Topped by the ubiquitous symbol of Venice, St. Mark's lion (locally known as "the cat"), the **Vigo Column** marks the eastern end of wide Corso del Popolo that runs the length of the town and along which you'll find the main monuments. It's impossible to get lost in this grid plan. Parallel to the Corso, the Canale Vena is spanned by eight bridges, the most picturesque of which is the **Ponte Vigo** at the eastern end, Chioggia's version of the Rialto. Take an hour or so to stroll along the main drag, or poke around the fish market (held Tuesday through Saturday) and the narrow alleys with gently flapping washing strung across their balconies.

Walking down the corso from the Vigo column, you'll pass the 18th-century church of **Sant'Andrea.** After going by Sant'Andrea, you'll soon arrive at the **Palazzo del Granaio** (1322), formerly the town granary and one of the few buildings to have survived the sea battle. A niche on the facade has a *Madonna and Child* by the sculptor Jacopo Sansovino (1486–1570). The **Chiesa della Santa Trinità** contains paintings by the schools of Tintoretto and Veronese. ⊠ *Piazzetta XX Settembre.* ⊙ *Open for Mass.*

The Romanesque bell tower predates the **Duomo** designed by Baldassare Longhena (1604–82). The interior holds some fine 18th-century paintings including work by Piazzetta (1683–1754) and Tiepolo (1696–1770). ⊠ *Piazza del Duomo 77,* ☎ *041/400496.* ⊙ *Daily 7–noon and 4–6.*

San Domenico has stood on a little island of the same name since 1745. The high altar is dominated by a 12-ft-high wooden Crucifix said to have been carved by fishermen. Found within are the last work of Vittore Carpaccio (1455–1526), *San Paolo,* along with the *Apparition of Jesus to St. Thomas Aquinas* by Tintoretto (1518–94). ⊠ *Via Canale 6, San Domenico,* ☎ *041/403526.* ☉ *Call to check opening hrs.*

The **Museo Civico** is housed in the former monastery of San Francesco Fuori le Mura, and the collection illustrates the history of lagoon life, with a number of traditional boats on display. ⊠ *Campo Marconi,* ☎ *041/5500911.* 🖼 *€2.05.* ☉ *Tues.–Wed. 9–1, Fri.–Sun. 9–1 and 3:30–7:30.*

At the Sottomarina end of the bridge, the Venetian-Gothic church of **San Martino** was built by the townspeople after the battle of 1379. It holds two polyptychs by Veronese. ⊠ *Piazza Ballarin,* ☎ *041/40054.* ☉ *Daily 7–noon and 4–7:30.*

It's not churches but hotels that are the dominant feature in this part of town. They stretch out along the **Lungomare Adriatico,** scene of a permanent *passeggiata* (stroll), even in winter. The beach is visible from the upstairs windows of hotels but not from the road, so encumbered is it with a barrier of buildings. You'll have to pay to get on the beach unless you walk to the far western end, though many hotels will have their own strip for guests. You'll find the usual crop of discos, swimming pools, bars, entertainment, opportunities for horseback riding, sailing, boat trips, and a teeming nightlife with karaoke on the beach and outdoor films. In summer, classical concerts are held in the town's churches and in the museum garden.

Dining and Lodging

$$ ✕ **Ai Vaporetti.** This restaurant overlooks the lagoon and Ponte La-
★ gunale: a perfect spot for a summer evening. Downstairs, the whole of the ceiling is covered by a canvas fishing boat's sail, and above the intimate alcoves is a mezzanine level with a wrought-iron balcony. The menu is restricted to fish cooked over a wood fire. You could go for the eels, or maybe the clams in tomato sauce. There's a good local wine list. ⊠ *Campo Traghetto 1256,* ☎ *041/400841. Reservations essential in summer. AE, DC, MC, V. Closed Tues. and 3 wks in Nov.*

$$ ✕ **Antico Toro.** In bygone days, great fun was had at Carnevale time by letting 12 ferocious dogs chase a bull that was customarily housed in this restaurant before its release. Don't worry, though, if you see *al toro* on the menu; you won't be getting bull, just a special fish sauce. It comes with *gnocchetti* (little potato dumplings). The spaghetti with vongole or *granseola* (spider crabs) is worth fighting for. ⊠ *Corso del Popolo 1306,* ☎ *041/400560. Reservations essential. AE, DC, MC, V. Closed Wed. and Nov.*

$$ ✕ **Bella Venezia.** In summer you can eat in the courtyard amid the glory of the plants. The chef recommends *branzino al carpaccio* (marinated slices of raw sea bass) and *bianco nero alla scoglio* (a mix of cuttle-fish-ink pasta with shrimp, clams, and squid), a specialty to this area. Try chilled port or grappa with it. ⊠ *Calle Corona 51,* ☎ *041/400500,* 🌐 *www.bellavenezia.com. Reservations essential in summer. AE, DC, MC, V. Closed Thurs. and Jan. No dinner Wed. and Oct.–Feb.*

$$ ✕ **El Gato.** Signor Silvano cooks the vegetables grown in his own garden and Signora Alba is an old hand at the *dolci* (desserts). It's a winning combination. Try a creamy risotto with shrimp or fish, *cappellacci* ("little hat" pasta) with a fish sauce, and the linguine *con molluschi* (with shellfish with a smoky flavor). The brick arches and wooden ceiling give a rustic air to the proceedings. ⊠ *Campo Sant'Andrea 653,* ☎ *041/401806,* 🌐 *www.elgato.it. Reservations essential. AE, DC, MC, V. Closed Mon. and late Jan.–mid-Feb. No lunch Tues.*

$$$ 🏨 **Grande Italia.** This hotel, established in Chioggia since 1914, is solid
★ and reliable and in a perfect position overlooking the lagoon and ma-

rina. Rooms are well appointed in a restful green color, and the suites are spacious. The very elegant (and expensive) restaurant closes on Tuesday. ⊠ *Rione Sant'Andrea 597, 30015,* ☎ *041/400515,* FAX *041/ 400185,* WEB *www.hotelgrandeitalia.com. 49 rooms, 8 suites. Restaurant, bar, sauna, health club, parking (fee).* AE, DC, MC, V.

$$ ⊞ **Airone.** If you like bright, plain, and primary colors, then this is the hotel for you. The reception area has a large mural of flamingos flying over the blue sea and intriguing modern sculptures. It's no nursery, though, preserving elegance and class. There's a lively bar downstairs. ⊠ *Via Lungomare Adriatico 50, 30019,* ☎ *041/492266,* FAX *041/ 5541325. 97 rooms. Restaurant, bar, pool, beach, free parking.* AE, MC, V.

$$ ⊞ **Bristol.** Of the many hotels along the Lungomare, this is one of the most tasteful and spacious, with service that does not take itself too seriously. All rooms have a terrace. There's an opulent restaurant and piano accompaniment in the evenings. ⊠ *Lungomare Adriatico 46, 30019,* ☎ *041/5540389,* FAX *041/5541813,* WEB *www.hotelbristol.net. 70 rooms. Restaurant, bar, air-conditioning, pool.* AE, DC, MC, V.

$–$$ ⊞ **Stella d'Italia.** Set back a little from the Lungomare and full of clutter and greenery, this is one of the smaller hotels to stay open all year, so it's always busy and most likely full of children. ⊠ *Viale Veneto 37, 30019,* ☎ *041/400600,* FAX *041/400322,* WEB *www.hotelstelladitalia.net. 40 rooms. Restaurant, bar, free parking.* AE, DC, MC, V.

Nightlife and the Arts

FESTIVALS

The Palio **La Maciliana** takes place in the third week of June with medieval fun and games. The **Sagra del Pesce** (Fish Festival) celebrates the lagoon's bounty the third week in July, with fish-tasting, music, poetry, and theater. Contact the tourist office (⊠ Lungomare Adriatico 101, 30019 Chioggia, ☎ 041/401068) for information.

Outdoor Activities and Sports

BOATING

Rendez-vous Fantasia (⊠ Via San Marco 1720, ☎ FAX 041/5540016) rents houseboats by the week. For sailing boats with or without a skipper, contact **Morgan Yachting** (⊠ Viale Trieste 31/a, ☎ 041/5506094 or 0336/491401). It also runs short cruises in July and August.

GUIDED TOURS

You can have a free tour of **Chioggia by Night** on Monday and Thursday from June to September. Get details from the tourist office (⊠ Lungomare Adriatico 101, 30019 Chioggia, ☎ 041/401068).

HORSEBACK RIDING

Contact **Villaggio Turistico Isomar** (⊠ Via Isomar 9, Sant'Anna di Chioggia, ☎ 041/498100) for lessons and rides in the surrounding countryside.

Rovigo

46 *70 km (44 mi) southwest of Venice, 53 km (33 mi) southwest of Chioggia-Sottomarina.*

Between Chioggia and Rovigo the land is flat, given over to market gardening and agriculture. Rovigo itself is largely a prosperous business and university city and the capital of the province. In the main squares you'll be very aware of business talk in action. Brave the **Caffè Borsa** (⊠ Piazza Garibaldi 2, ☎ 0425/21999) for a power espresso or snack. It's closed Thursday. If you're in the center of the city, the first thing to catch your eye will most likely be the **Torre Dona,** one of the tallest towers in Italy, and the **Torre Mozza,** the one remaining tower of the castle built in 920 by the Bishop of Adria. Both appear to be rather alarmingly out of kilter. Like other towns and cities in the area, Rovigo submitted to the yoke of Venice, which controlled the town from 1482 until the end of the Republic.

The main **Piazza Vittorio Emanuele II** holds some fine palazzi, including the **Palazzo Roncale** designed in 1555 by Sanmichele (1484–1559). Also in the main piazza is the **Accademia dei Concordi,** which was founded in 1580 and now houses the Pinacoteca (Art Gallery), with a fine, intimate collection of Veneto masters. Stop and admire Bellini's *Madonna,* the portraits of Alessandro Longhi (1733–1813), and the paintings of the late-17th-century artist Elizabeth Marchioni, a native of Rovigo. A small Roman, Greek, and Egyptian collection includes a touching mummy with child and in a room downstairs some Flemish tapestries by pupils of Rubens (1577–1640). ⊠ *Piazza Vittorio Emanuele II 14,* ☎ *0425/21645.* ⊡ *€2.60.* ☉ *Sept.–June, weekdays 9:30–noon and 3:30–6:30, Sat. 9:30–noon; July–Aug., Mon.–Sat. 10–1.*

★ An impressive dual row of pine trees leads up to the church of Santa Maria del Soccorso di Rovigo, better known as **La Rotonda.** Contrasting against the trees stands the white, Palladian-influenced octagon, surrounded by a portico of Tuscan columns. It was designed by Francesco Zamberlan (1529–1606) in 1594, and the brick campanile was added in 1673 by Baldassare Longhena. The interior, both walls and dome, is entirely and sumptuously covered by 17th-century Veneto paintings. ⊠ *Piazza XX Settembre 37,* ☎ *0425/24914.* ⊡ *Free.* ☉ *Easter–Oct., daily 8:30–noon and 3–6; Nov.–Easter, daily 8:30–noon and 4:30–7.*

Dining and Lodging

$$$ ✕ **Tavernetta Dante.** You can be sure of good quality in this long-established restaurant, where you can choose between two rooms, one with warm pink, plaster, and brick, the other in cool shades of green and filled with plants. The menu changes frequently and there's always a vegetarian option. Meat dishes include tagliolini *con verdura conigliano* (with rabbit and greens). The restaurant is popular with businesspeople. ⊠ *Corso del Popolo 212,* ☎ *0425/26386. MC, V. Closed Sun. and Aug. 10–31.*

$–$$ ✕ **Antico Canevone.** Tucked away in a little alley, this modern, stylish restaurant and *birreria* puts on live music every Thursday and attracts a younger set. Taste the beer in *braciole alla birra rossa* (beef stewed in beer). ⊠ *Vicolo Canevone 4,* ☎ *0425/27787. No credit cards. Closed Sun. and 1 wk in mid-Aug.*

$–$$ ✕ **Taverna.** This no-nonsense restaurant with its cheerful plaid table-
★ cloths is a real find and very popular. At lunchtime, the city's workers stream in and out. Especially good are the salads, complete meals in themselves: a big bowl of *radicchio, rucola, pere, grana, a scaglie e mandorla* (radicchio, arugula, pear, Grana Padano, and almonds) or *verdure crude, uove, tonno, mozzarella, mais e olive* (tuna-and-egg salad) will sustain you for the rest of the day. ⊠ *Piazza Merlin 20,* ☎ *0425/ 21653. DC, MC, V. Closed Fri. and last 2 wks in Aug. No lunch Sat.*

$$ 🏨 **Corona Ferrea.** Right in the center of the city, this hotel offers polite, friendly service. The decor bears the same hallmark of discretion— modern and elegant, the colors understated and quiet. You'll probably be rubbing shoulders with businesspeople. ⊠ *Via Umberto I 21, 45100,* ☎ *0425/422433,* 🖷 *0425/422292. 30 rooms. Bar, parking (fee). AE, DC, MC, V.*

$$ 🏨 **Villa Regina Margherita.** The most attractive of Rovigo's hotels, this
★ early 20th-century villa glows a welcoming pink and reflects a Liberty style. Large comfortable armchairs, velvet upholstery, and potted palms

give an air of luxury, and there's a good restaurant. Book ahead, as rooms fill quickly. ⊠ *Viale Regina Margherita 6, 45100,* ☎ *0425/ 361540,* FAX *0425/31301. 18 rooms, 2 suites. Restaurant, bar, parking (fee). AE, DC, MC, V.*

Nightlife and the Arts

The **Teatro Sociale** (⊠ Piazza Garibaldi 14, ☎ 0425/25614) puts on musicals and symphony concerts as well as plays.

Shopping

For food shopping, wander through the arcaded **Piazza Annonaria** and marvel at the variety of vegetables—red and green, veined and smooth. You'll probably want to try the salami, but most likely you'll be giving the horse-butcher a miss.

LAKE GARDA

Lake Garda is the most popular of the Italian lakes as well as the largest, spanning the borders of three regions—the Veneto, Trentino, and Lombardy. The size of the lake actually has an impact upon the climate, making the summers cooler and the winters warmer. Vacationers on packages love it, especially the German and the French, who invade the large number of hotels. If you plan to spend any time during the summer in the busiest resorts, such as Sirmione, book well ahead. Of course, if you're a windsurfer or a sailor, then this is your heaven, with breezes tailor-made for you. The funicular ride up the slopes of Monte Baldo is spectacular. You can even arrange for a mountain bike to meet you at the top or take a paragliding trip. Glorious walking can be enjoyed in the mountains that enclose the narrow northern part of the lake, tapering off to the south to give way to flatter country. On the gentle slopes are lush olive and lemon groves, oleanders and palm trees, and the vines that provide the grapes for the local wines such as Valpolicella and Bardolino. Enchanting castles and little medieval towns complete the picture.

Malcesine

47 *179 km (111 mi) northwest of Venice, 67 km (42 mi) northwest of Verona.*

One of the loveliest areas along the upper eastern shore of Lake Garda, Malcesine is principally known as a summer resort with sailing and windsurfing schools. The 13 campsites and tourist villages do tend to make the town a little crowded in summer. There are, however, some nice walks from the town toward the mountains behind. The town hall was the seat of the Captains of the Lake during the 16th and 17th centuries. Dominating the town is the 13th- to 14th-century **Castello Scaligero,** built by the della Scalas. Inside are several small museums, one of which is devoted to Goethe, who in 1786 spent a short spell in prison here—while sketching the lake he was thought to be an Austrian spy and promptly arrested. Another shows pictures of the ships being hauled to Torbole. There's a fine view from the tower. ⊠ *Via Castello,* ☎ *045/7400837.* ☜ *€3.10.* ☉ *May–Sept., daily 9–6; Oct.– Apr., weekends 9–6.*

OFF THE
BEATEN PATH
    MONTE BALDO – If you are fond of cable cars take the 15-minute *funivia* (funicular) ride to the top of Monte Baldo (5,791 ft) for a great view of the whole lake in summer, or possibly a short ski run in winter (expect a wait). The mountain is also a great place for mountain biking, and you can even arrange for bikes to meet you at the top. Because of the variety of vegetation found here, from olive and lemon groves to beech

woods, not to mention the profuse Alpine flowers, the mountain was once known as the *hortus europae* (garden of Europe).

Outdoor Activities and Sports

MOUNTAIN BIKING

Furioli (⊠ Piazza Matteotti 11, ☎ 045/7400089) rents bikes for €16.55 per day. Contact **Funivia Malcesine-Montebaldo** (☎ 045/7400044) for mountain-bike rentals and paragliding.

SKIING

Malcesine (☎ 045/7400555) is a well-equipped resort with six lifts and more than 11 km (7 mi) of runs of varying degrees of difficulty.

WINDSURFING

In Malcesine **Wind Square** (⊠ Località Sottodossi, ☎ 045/7400413) offers windsurfing courses and rents out equipment. **Marco Segnana** (⊠ Foci del Sacra, Torbole, ☎ 0464/505963) in Torbole, just north of Malcesine, can arrange windsurfing weekends, including lessons and equipment rental, and also arranges mountain-bike rentals and hotel accommodation.

Peschiera

48 *46 km (29 mi) southwest of Malcesine, 140 km (90 mi) west of Venice.*

At the southern end of the Lake Garda, Peschiera is a pleasant place to wander around for a half day or so. It's less touristy than other lake towns and makes an alternative to staying in Sirmione if that resort is full or if you fancy a lower-key scene. Sports enthusiasts will find all the usual water sports on hand. The town is surrounded by hefty bastion walls that were begun by the Venetians in 1553 and subsequently strengthened by Napoléon and later the Austrians. Crossing the bridge from the harbor brings you through the defenses to the historic center and the *lungolago* (lake promenade) lined with villas now defended by dogs. The Roman writer Pliny (AD 23–79) noted that Peschiera was the place for eels, and indeed the eel is featured on the town's coat of arms. So don't be surprised if you see them on the menu.

Vittorio Emanuele III held a meeting at the **Museo della Palazzina Storica** on November 8, 1917, to debate the course of the war. The museum commemorates this fact and also displays local artifacts. ⊠ *Via Parco Catullo 1,* ☎ *045/7550938.* ⊡ *Free.* ☉ *Tues.–Sun. 10–11 and 4–6.*

OFF THE BEATEN PATH | **PARCO GIARDINO SIGURTÀ** – Over a period of 40 years, Count Doctor Carlo Sigurtà transformed the hillside into a sumptuous garden, introducing walkways through lawn carpets, woods, canals with water lilies, surrealist sculptures in boxwood, rosebushes, grottoes, and cypresses. It makes a magical place to spend an afternoon. ⊠ *Valeggio sul Mincio, 8 km (5 mi) south of Peschiera,* ☎ *045/6371033.* ⊡ *€15.50 per vehicle.* ☉ *Mar.–Nov., daily 9–6.*

Dining and Lodging

$$ ✕ **Il Cantinone.** This quiet courtyard in the historic center is an ideal place to sample tagliolini *al ragu di trota* (with trout) or *pappardelle con lepre* (broad ribbons of pasta with hare). Follow it with fish from the lake, or eels. If it's not warm enough to eat out, the inside is cozy with lots of reproduction paintings on the walls. ⊠ *Via Galileo Galilei 14,* ☎ *045/7551162. Reservations essential. AE, DC, MC, V. Closed Tues., 1 wk in Nov., and 10 days in Jan.*

$ ✕ **Bellavista.** Right on the lake and with a garden, this is a pleasantly old-fashioned restaurant and pizzeria with brisk service. Inside, the gold tablecloths and gilt mirrors give it a glitzy air. Of the 30 different types of pizza to choose from, the ones with the local porcini mushrooms are recommended. ✉ *Lungolago Mazzini 1,* ☎ *045/7553252. MC, V. Closed Thurs. and mid-Nov.–mid-Dec.*

$–$$ 🏠 **Bell'Arrivo.** This pink-washed, family-run hotel on the banks of the Mincio River makes for an attractive place to stay in the center of town. There's a tempting, rather grand marbled *pasticceria* (pastry shop) underneath. The management rents out canoes and bicycles. ✉ *Piazza Benacense 29, 37019,* ☎ *045/6401322,* FAX *045/6401311,* WEB *www. hotelbellarivo.it. 27 rooms. Bar, boating, bicycles. AE, DC, MC, V. Closed Jan. 11–Feb. 7. FAP, MAP.*

$–$$ 🏠 **San Marco.** As the address implies, the hotel sits right on the lake with a large covered terrace for dining in summer. The reception rooms hit you with vibrant reds, turquoises, and purples, toned-down versions of which prevail in the bedrooms. Bathrooms are stylish with pink marble fittings. ✉ *Lungolago Mazzini, 37019,* ☎ *045/7550077. 33 rooms. Restaurant, bar, parking (fee). AE, DC, MC, V. FAP, MAP.*

Outdoor Activities and Sports

BOAT TRIP

Gestione Governativa (✉ Piazza Matteotti 2, Desenzano, ☎ 030/ 9149511 or 167/551801) runs a daily ferry to Riva del Garda from April through October, leaving Peschiera at 9:45 AM and returning at 7:15 PM.

Sirmione

★ ㊾ *14 km (9 mi) northwest of Peschiera, 150 km (94 mi) west of Venice.*

The ruins at this enchanting town on an isthmus at the southwestern shore of Lake Garda, complete with narrow, cobbled streets that wind their way through medieval arches, are a reminder that Garda has been a holiday resort for the leisurely well-to-do since the height of the Roman era. Most of the historic town, which stretches the length of the spit, is inaccessible to cars, so you must park at the bottom of the historic center and walk the rest of the way. The locals will almost certainly tell you that the so-called **Grotte di Catullo** (Grottoes of Catullus) were once the site of the villa of Catullus, one of the greatest pleasure-seeking poets of all time. Present archaeological wisdom, however, does not concur, and there is some consensus that this was the site of two villas of slightly different periods, dating from about the 1st century AD. But never mind—the view through the cypresses and olive trees is lovely, and even if Catullus didn't have a villa here, he is closely associated with the area and undoubtedly did once plop down somewhere nearby. The ruins are at the top of the isthmus and are badly signposted: walk through the historic center and past the various villas to the top of the spit; the grottoes are on the right. ✉ *Grotte di Catullo, Sirmione,* ☎ *030/916157.* 🎫 *€4.15.* ☉ *Mar.–Sept., Tues.–Sun. 8:30–6; Oct.– Feb., Tues.–Sat. 8:30–4:30, Sun. 9–4:30.*

The **Castello Scaligero** was built, along with almost all the other castles on the lake, by the della Scala family. As hereditary rulers of Verona for more than a century before control of the city was seized by the Visconti in 1402, they counted Garda among their possessions. The inside of the castle offers a nice view of the lake from the tower. Entry to the old part of town is gained through the castle's gates, over what was originally a drawbridge. ✉ *Piazza Castello, Sirmione,* ☎ *030/ 916468.* 🎫 *€4.15.* ☉ *June–Sept., Tues.–Sat. 9–6, Sun. 9–1; Oct.–Apr., Mon.–Sat. 9–1.*

OFF THE
BEATEN PATH

GARDALAND AMUSEMENT PARK – This park has more than 40 different rides and water slides and is one of Italy's biggest amusement parks at which to thrill your children. It is 16 km (10 mi) east of Sirmione. There is a free transfer service from Peschiera train station, less than 5 km (3 mi) up the road. ⊠ *Castelnuovo del Garda*, ☎ *045/6449777*. ☎ €*13.95*. ⊘ *July–mid-Sept., daily 9 AM–midnight; Apr.–June, daily 9–6 (some days until 7 or 8); mid- to late Mar. and Oct., weekends 9–6.*

Dining and Lodging

$$$-$$$$ ✗ **La Rucola.** This restaurant prides itself on attention to detail, in the courteous service, elegance of the surroundings, and, of course, the food. Recommended dishes include *timballo di luccio* (timbale of pike) and risotto with local mushrooms. The spiced and iced zabaglione is also worth dipping into. ⊠ *Vicolo Strentelle 7*, ☎ *030/916326. Reservations essential. AE, DC, MC, V. Closed Thurs. and Jan.*

$$$ ✗ **Vecchia Lugana.** At the base of the peninsula and outside the town,
★ this restaurant is considered one of Italy's best. Adventurous diners will reap the most rewards, including such wonders as wood mushroom soup with river prawns or venison fillet with artichoke puree. The menu changes seasonally. There's also an elegant garden. ⊠ *Piazzale Vecchia Lugana 1, Lugana di Sirmione*, ☎ *030/919012. AE, DC, MC, V. Closed Tues. and Jan.–mid-Feb. No dinner Mon.*

$$ ✗ **Ristorante Al Pescatore.** The specialty of this simple, rustic, and very popular restaurant is lake fish. Try grilled trout with a bottle of local white wine and finish your meal with a walk in the nearby public park. ⊠ *Via Piana 20*, ☎ *030/916216. DC, MC, V. Closed Jan.–Feb. and Wed. Oct.–May.*

$$$$ ▦ **Villa Cortine Palace.** A formidably decorative early 19th-century villa
★ in a secluded park, Villa Cortine is in danger of being just plain ostentatious, but only just: it is saved by the sheer luxury of its setting and the extraordinary professionalism of its staff, which, although a little too formal and cold, will leave you wanting for virtually nothing—except your wallet. It dominates a low hill, and the grounds—a colorful mixture of lawns, trees, statues, and fountains—go down to the lake. Rooms in the original villa have easy old-world charm, and those in the newer wing have better lake views. ⊠ *Via Grotte 12, 25019,* ☎ *030/9905890,* ☎ *030/916390,* ⅦⅢ *www.hotelvillacortine.com. 51 rooms, 6 suites. Restaurant, bar, pool, tennis court, beach. AE, DC, MC, V. Closed Oct. 22–Apr. 5. FAP, MAP.*

$$$-$$$$ ▦ **Hotel Sirmione.** Just inside the city walls, near the Castello, this hotel
★ and spa sits amid lakeside gardens and terraces. Some rooms display superb execution, with comfortable Scandinavian slat beds, matching floral draperies and wall coverings, and built-in white furniture. Many guests have been returning for years, largely due to the homespun feel and the attentiveness of the staff. ⊠ *Piazza Castello 19, 25019,* ☎ *030/916331,* ☎ *030/916558. 76 rooms. Restaurant, bar, pool, spa, meeting room. AE, DC, MC, V. Closed Dec.–Apr. 9. FAP, MAP.*

$$-$$$ ▦ **Continental.** Overhanging the lakefront, right next to a spa, the Continental is a bright yellowish structure in that ubiquitous '70s style. The hotel operates on a half-pension basis only during the summer. This works to keep the cost in check, and the hotel has the amenities and feel of a much more expensive establishment. Most rooms have balconies, but ask specifically for a lake view. ⊠ *Via Punta Staffalo 7, 25019,* ☎ *030/9905711,* ☎ *030/916278. 51 rooms. Pool, beach. AE, DC, MC, V. Closed Dec.–Mar. MAP.*

Bosco Chiesanuova

50 *68 km (42 mi) northeast of Sirmione, 125 km (78 mi) northwest of Venice.*

It's a treacherous road that takes you to Bosco Chiesanuova, the stopping-off point for exploration of **Parco Regionale della Lessinia** (Lessinia Regional Park). Best reached from Verona (31 km [19 mi] south), the park lies between the Adige Valley to the west and the Piccoli Dolomiti to the north. The park features a gentle but rugged landscape, ideal for exploring either on foot, by mountain bike, or on horseback and, in winter, by cross-country ski. Among the cherry trees, beech groves, and meadows edged with dry-stone walls are houses made from the local *pietra di Prun,* a type of stone that, in the not-so-distant past, was used in the construction of underground ice houses where ice was stored to be sold for summer use. This is a karst limestone area, so the pastures are riven with deep gorges and sprinkled with small lakes and waterfalls. At **Ponte di Veja,** the natural attraction is the stone bridge that has been created purely by water erosion. The area is renowned for its fish fossils. The small **Museo Civico** has a nice display of artifacts and photographs of the traditions, art, and costumes of the area. ⊠ *Bosco Chiesanuova,* ☎ *045/7050022.* ☜ *€0.52.* ⊘ *Apr.–Sept., Tues., Thurs., and weekends 9–7; Oct.–Mar., Sun. 9–6:30.*

Lodging

$ ⊞ **Lessinia.** This hotel is small, modern, and functional, furnished in Tyrolean style. The rooms are plain and cheerful, with pine furniture. The restaurant (closed Wednesday) offers local specialties such as dishes prepared with Monte Veronese cheese, and a gelateria is just below. ⊠ *Piazzetta Alpini 2, 37021,* ☎ *045/6780151,* ℻ *045/6780098. 20 rooms. Restaurant, bar, parking (fee). MC, V. FAP, MAP.*

Outdoor Activities and Sports

MOUNTAIN BIKING

From June 6 until September 13 you can take your mountain bike on the special bus that leaves Verona for Bosco Chiesanuova at 9 AM, returning at 6:30 PM (€9.30 round-trip). You can get tickets from the **Verona bus station** (☎ 045/8004129) and information on biking trails from the tourist office in Verona (☎ 045/8068680).

SKIING

For skiing information, contact **Lessinia Turistsport** (⊠ Piazza della Chiesa 3, ☎ 045/6780224).

WALKING AND HIKING

Bosco's **tourist office** (⊠ Piazza Chiesa 34, 37021 Bosco Chiesanuova, ☎ ℻ 045/7050088) has information on walks.

THE BRENTA

Once upon a time, the Brenta River was a constant source of trouble to the settlers of the area, as it was prone to flooding and caused the lagoon to silt up. Steps had been taken to regulate matters since the 11th century, but it was not until Venice took control of the area in 1405 that matters were really taken in hand, diversions were created, banks strengthened, and the deposit of silt controlled. By the 16th century the land was safe enough for extensive farming and for wealthy Venetians to enjoy *villeggiatura,* a vacation from harried city life, by building princely residences on their country estates. The best architects, sculptors, and artists were summoned, and elegant symmetry and Baroque sumptuousness remain the characteristic style. Some of the 100 or so villas built served as farmhouses, while others were just used for pleasure. A handful of these are now open to the public, often for only a couple of days a week, so check before arranging your itinerary. Two of the best villas, each reflecting the different basic designs of Palladio, are the Villa Pisani and the Villa Foscari.

Malcontenta/Villa Foscari

51 *8 km (5 mi) west of Venice.*

Malcontenta is the first village along the Brenta River from Venice. Legend has it that the name "Malcontenta" (unhappy) was derived from the wife of one of the Foscari brothers, who was banished here for "inappropriate behavior," but the real explanation is likely to be more prosaic, as the name was already in use before the arrival of the Foscari. Built in 1560 by—who else—Palladio, **Villa Foscari** is not one of his long, low designs but one of his large cubes with portico and dome, its lawn running down to the river. Giovanni Batista Zelotti (1526–78) lent his hand in decorating the walls inside, covering them with allegorical and mythological figures in mock architectural effects. ⊠ *Malcontenta,* ☎ *041/5470012.* 🎟 *€5.15.* ☉ *May–Oct., Tues. and Sat. 9–noon.*

Stra/Villa Pisani

☕ ★ **52** *37 km (23 mi) west of Malcontenta, 34 km (21 mi) west of Venice.*

This extraordinary house (also called Villa Nazionale) in Stra is the most spectacular of all the villas in the region. Villa Pisani may remind you more of Versailles. It's an imposing 18th-century edifice designed by Francesco Maria Preti (1701–74) that once belonged to Napoléon, who appreciated its similarities to Versailles. In 1934 it was the scene of the first meeting between Hitler and Mussolini. See the grandiose frescoes by Giambattista Tiepolo on the ceiling of the ballroom and Napoléon's elaborate bed and bathroom. If you have youngsters surfeited with the old masters in tow, explore the gorgeous **park** and the **maze.** ⊠ *Stra,* ☎ *049/502074.* 🎟 *Villa, maze, and grounds €5.15; maze and grounds only, €2.60.* ☉ *Apr.–Sept., daily 9–7; Oct.–Mar., daily 9–4. Maze open only Apr.–Sept.*

Euganean Hills: Abano Terme/Montegrotto Terme

53 *12 km (7 mi) south of Padua, 49 km (30 mi) west of Venice.*

Rising abruptly out of the plain, the volcanic Euganean Hills are a pleasure to explore in any season, the gentle slopes strewn with chestnut trees, olive groves, and vineyards that encroach right upon the road. The hills themselves enfold unspoiled villages, and at their feet you'll find abbeys and villas. Take time to wander along the paths marked for walkers, look for wild mushrooms, and enjoy the microclimates that produce Mediterranean and Alpine flowers, myrtle, and even prickly pears. In spring the blossom of almond and cherry trees turns the hills a frothy pink and white. For information about the regional park contact the **Parco Regionale dei Colli Euganei** (⊠ Via Fontana 2, Arqua Pertarca, ☎ 0429/777144).

Fango (mud) is the one thing that draws people in droves to these two conjoined resorts, considered among the foremost in Europe. There is no escaping the steam that rises from streets and gardens at every turn and is channelled into the collection of hotels and thermal clinics that make up Abano Terme and Montegrotto Terme. Water emanates from the Dolomites after a journey deep underground and resurfaces at a temperature of 87°F, full of salt, bromine, and iodine. Each hotel will have its series of slimy mud basins and clients in dressing gowns submitting to mud massage, inhalations, or irrigations. If it's not mud you're after, or indulge in one of the nine five-star hotels, you'll get more out of your trip by staying in one of the small towns in the area.

Abano Terme shows its Roman origin in its name, Abano deriving from the Roman god of healing, Aponeus. Although some buildings were a result of the design by Giuseppe Jappelli in the early 19th century, most hotels and parks have appeared in 20th century.

The small **Museo D'Arte** contains 16th- and 17th-century Venetian and Flemish masters. ⊠ *Via Pietro d'Abano 20,* ☎ *049/8245375.* ☐ *Free.* ☉ *Tues.–Sat. 10–noon and 4–7.*

The name **Montegrotto Terme** derives from "Mons Aegrotorum" (Mount of the Sick). It became a Roman colony in 184 BC, was the birthplace of the historian Livy (59 BC–AD 17), and was much praised for the properties of its algae by a succession of Roman worthies— Pliny, Suetonius, and Plutarch to name but three. The **archaeological zone** consists of the remains of Roman Baths (Terme Romane), and a theater dating from the era of Augustus (63 BC–AD 14) can be seen from the outside at all times. If you spot a statue of a medieval dame rotating, it'll be the one commemorating the story of Berta che Filava (Bertha Spinning), to whom the wife of Henry IV of Germany gave as much land as could be surrounded by the thread on her spinning wheel. Tickets for guided visits must be booked from the library by calling ahead. ⊠ *Via Scavi,* ☎ *049/793700.* ☉ *Guided visits June–July and Sept.–Oct., Sat. at 9, 10, and 11.*

Dining and Lodging

$$–$$$ ✕ **Casa Vecia.** Most hotel guests will be taking dinner as part of their
★   package, but if you're eating out, this is probably the best in town. Try *funghi e baccalà con aceto di lamponi* (mushrooms and dried cod with raspberry vinegar) or *spuma di pomodoro fresco e burrata in salsa di basilico* (fresh tomato foam with butter in basil sauce). Finish with a mouthwatering dessert. There's a wide and well-chosen wine list and excellent service. ⊠ *Via Ghislandhi 5,* ☎ *049/8669910. AE, D, MC, V. Closed Wed. and last 2 wks in Mar.*

$$ ✕ **Al Bosco.** A 3-km (2-mi) drive out of Montegrotto in the Torreglia
★   direction (signposted left) brings you to this rustic setting in the woods. Inside you'll find large copper pans and cowbells. Cooking is done *alla brace* (barbecued) in summer and the accent is on meat. There's a choice of 20 different *secondi* (seconds), which can be eased down with one of the local red wines. The tagliatelle with *vitello* (veal) or *selvaggina* (game) is good. ⊠ *Via Cogolo 8, Parco dei Colli Euganei,* ☎ *049/ 794317. AE, MC, V. Closed Wed. and Jan. 10–31.*

$$ ✕ **Aubergine.** This restaurant is tasteful, contemporary, and spacious, but if it's an intimate dinner you're after, opt for one of the alcoves. If it's miniature golf you want, though, there's a course handy. The menu changes every month, but you'll always find a good selection of chocolate desserts. Before dipping into these, try the polenta with truffles, chicken breasts with ham and sage, or the spinach and cheese gnocchi. A range of pizzas includes one, of course, with eggplant. ⊠ *Via Ghislandhi 5,* ☎ *049/8669910. AE, MC, V. Closed Wed. and last 2 wks in Mar.*

$$$ ⊞ **Esplanade Tergesteo.** The brochure shows nothing but red Ferraris parked outside, but these are not compulsory accessories for a stay at this large and modern five-star hotel. Service is friendly and natural, with all the requisite mud treatments on hand. You can opt for a game of tennis, or bike or horseback ride. Or maybe just laze around the pool, or be entertained by an evening concert. ⊠ *Via Roma 54, 35036*

Montegrotto Terme, ☏ *049/8911777,* FAX *049/8910488. 139 rooms, 14 suites. Restaurant, bar, pool, spa, golf privileges, tennis court, horseback riding. AE, DC, MC, V. Closed Dec. 1–19 and Jan. 11– Feb. 20.*

$$–$$$ 🖭 **Bristol Buja Spa.** One of the modern hotels in Abano Terme's western zone offers all the usual mud treatments, a diet regime, and exercise classes in the outdoor pool. The indoor pool has a colorful stained-glass roof, and rooms are prettily decorated. You'll be well looked after here. ⊠ *Via Monteortone 2, 35031 Abano Terme,* ☏ *049/ 8669390,* FAX *049/667910. 116 rooms, 25 suites. Restaurant, bar, 2 pools, spa, golf privileges. AE, DC, MC, V. Closed Nov. 21–Dec. 19.*

$ 🖭 **Ai Buoni Amici.** Situated on the outskirts of Montegrotto, this unpretentious but well-furnished and quiet little hotel has no mud. But, unlike some of the other establishments around here, you can feel the proximity of the Euganean Hills. Ignore the kitsch pictures and enjoy the friendly family management. ⊠ *Via Neroiane 11, 35036 Montegrotto Terme,* ☏ FAX *049/8910730. 22 rooms. Restaurant, bar, free parking. AE, MC, V.*

Outdoor Activities and Sports

BIKING

Brombin (⊠ Via Roma 10, Montegrotto, ☏ 049/793491) rents mountain bikes for €6.20 per day, €15.50 for 6 days, and €20.66 for 10 days.

GOLF

For information on courses in the area contact **Golf Point** (⊠ Largo Marconi 16, Abano Terme, ☏ 049/667143). There's miniature golf at **Via Caposeda** (☏ 049/793406).

HORSEBACK RIDING

Courses and excursions can be arranged through **Centro Equestre Montagnon** (⊠ Via Mezzavia 49, ☏ 049/793289).

Praglia

★ ⑤④ *8 km (5 mi) west of Abano Terme, 12 km (7 mi) southwest of Padua.*

You can tour the evocative 15th-century halls and cloisters of this Benedictine monastery set at the foot of the Euganean Hills. The monastery was founded in the 11th century, but the present buildings date from the 15th and 16th centuries and consist of four cloisters, two refectories—one with a fine *Crucifixion* by Montagna—and the church with its Romanesque campanile containing paintings by Veneto masters. The monastery is known for its book restoration, with its library containing more than 100,000 books on its 16th-century shelves. As well as books and meditation, the monks produce wine and honey that are for sale. ☏ *049/9900010.* 🖾 *Free; donations appreciated.* 🕐 *Tours Apr.–Oct., Tues.–Sun. every ½ hr 3:30–5:30; Nov.–Mar., Tues.–Sun. every ½ hr 2:30–4:30.*

Monselice

⑤⑤ *7 km (4½ mi) south of Montegrotto Terme, 61 km (38 mi) southwest of Venice.*

Rising out of the Paduan plain, Monselice's defensive walls skirt the base of the volcanic hill around which the town is ranged, making its lofty position unique in this part of the country. The foremost build-

★ ing of the town is the **Castello di Monselice**, or Ca' Marcello—a must to visit. Passing through the hands of Ezzelino III da Romano, who extended the original 12th-century building, and then to the Carrara and Marcello families, this castle has been lovingly and meticulously restored by Count Vittorio Cini, into whose care it came after World War I. As you enter the Salone d'Onore, you will immediately notice the wonderful chimney with its tiered arches on columns of majolica set against the red-and-white checkerboard walls. It's everything a medieval castle should be, both inside and out. ⊠ *Via del Santuario 24,* ☎ *0429/72931.* ☞ *€4.15.* ☉ *Guided tours Apr.–Nov., Tues.–Sun. at 9, 10, and 11* AM *and 3, 4, and 5* PM.

The Via Santuario leads to the **Via Sette Chiese,** a private road that climbs up the hill to the **Villa Duodo,** summer residence of the Duodo family built in 1593 by Scamozzi. At the lower end stands the Romanesque Gothic **Duomo Vecchio** (☎ 0429/72130) and six little pilgrimage churches, where those in need of forgiveness could stop and pray on their way to the seventh, **San Giorgio,** which houses relics of some of the first Christian martyrs. These were transferred from the catacombs of Rome at the behest of the Duodo family and are displayed in glass cases. Among the relics are those of St. Valentine, and surely it's no surprise to hear that there's an annual pilgrimage here on February 14. San Giorgio is open on Sunday; contact the tourist office (⊠ Via Roma 1, 35043 Monselice, ☎ FAX 0429/783026) for opening hours at other times.

Dining and Lodging

$$$ ✕ **Alla Posta.** As the name implies, this modern restaurant was once a coach house. The interior, green with plants, looks out onto a walled courtyard where you can dine in summer beneath the shade of the pomegranate tree. Fish is the specialty here, and the risotto *alla marinara* (with fish) is particularly good. Grilled meats also hold their own. From the extensive wine list, consider choosing something local from the Euganean Hills. ⊠ *Via XXVIII Aprile,* ☎ *0429/782816,* WEB *www.ristoranteallaposta.com. AE, DC, MC, V. Closed Tues.*

$$$ ✕ **Savellon Molini.** A 2-km (1-mi) drive from Monselice toward Padua will bring you to this converted barn, with its wooden beams and benches, set among log stacks and vineyards. Signor Bruno and his family run a jolly, rustic establishment. Opt for the *carni alla brace* (game and grills)—there's a huge barbecue grill in summer—and local vegetables. Reservations are advised. ⊠ *Via Savellon Molini 52,* ☎ *0429/ 73135. AE, DC, MC, V. Closed Tues. No dinner Mon.*

$$ ✕ **La Torre.** You can't dine in the castle, but the next best thing is a meal in the medieval walls. The accent here is on seasonal ingredients, especially vegetables. If you're here in April you can sample the local white asparagus, but just as delightful are the *fior di zucca* (zucchini blossoms), which in summer, along with wild porcini, are picked as fillings for the homemade ravioli. You'll find truffles as well, but you'll be digging deep in your pocket for the tubers. ⊠ *Piazza Mazzini 14,* ☎ *0429/73752. Reservations essential. AE, DC, MC, V. Closed Mon. and Aug. No dinner Sun.*

$–$$ 🛏 **Hotel Ceffri.** Though the service can be a mite condescending, and the antiques don't quite marry with the general decor, rooms are spacious and quiet, each one with its own balcony. There's a pleasant garden next to the pool, a perfect place for sipping a long drink or a *thè freddo* (iced tea) in summer. The adjacent restaurant associated with the hotel, the Villa Corner provides local and international dishes and a tourist menu at €18.10. To be recommended is the dessert *strudel con crema e pinoli* (strudel with cream and pine nuts). ⊠ *Via Orti 7/ b, 35043,* ☎ *0429/783111,* FAX *0429/783100,* WEB *www.ceffri.it. 42 rooms, 2 suites. Restaurant, piano bar, pool. AE, DC, MC, V. FAP, MAP.*

Nightlife and the Arts

FESTIVALS

On the third Sunday of September, Monselice relives medieval feasting and games with the **Giostra della Rocca.** Feats of strength are performed with millstones, archers strive for glory, and horses gallop around the town in the *quintana* (medieval competition). To add to it all, there's a market with stall workers in medieval costume. Contact the tourist office (✉ Via Roma 1, 35043 Monselice, ☎ FAX 0429/ 783026) for details.

MUSIC

Every Sunday in April and May, a music performance is given at the castle. For information contact the **local library** (☎ 0429/72628) or the Monselice tourist office.

Shopping

MARKETS

From May to September a flea market is held the last Saturday of the month. A general market is held all year on Monday and Friday in Piazza Mazzini.

Arqua Petrarca

56 *9 km (5½ mi) northeast of Este, 22 km (14 mi) south of Padua.*

It would be a shame to miss this little jewel of a village tucked away in the Euganean Hills. The narrow cobbled streets wind their way between unspoiled medieval houses and pretty gardens surrounded by the mellow green of the hills and vineyards. It's a good spot for lunch. The poet Francesco Petrarca (1304–74) spent the last four years of his life in this little haven: his house, **Casa Petrarca,** is visitable and his life traceable through the medieval frescoes on its walls (they were retouched in the 17th century). You can see his chair and desk here and later visit his sarcophagus by the church in the center of the village. ✉ *Via Valesella 4,* ☎ *0429/718294.* ✇ €3.10. ☉ *Feb.–Sept., Tues.–Sun. 9–12:30 and 3–7; Oct.–Jan., Tues.–Sun. 9–noon and 2:30–5:30.*

Dining

$$ ✕ **La Montanella.** The oil used in this restaurant is cold pressed from
★ the century-old olive trees in the garden, and you can admire them, the rest of this lovely garden, and the view from the veranda of the restaurant. You'll be hard put to choose between the pheasant, venison, and boar, the orange blossom or quail risotto, or even the *papero alla frutta* (duck with pear, grapes, or cherries), made to an original 17th-century recipe. Homemade bread and Cabernet from the Euganean hills top it off. ✉ *Via Costa 33,* ☎ *0429/718200,* WEB *www.montanella. it. AE, DC, MC, V. Closed Wed., Jan. 1–Feb. 13, and Aug. 7–21. No dinner Tues.*

Nightlife and the Arts

The **Festa della Sacra Trinità** (Feast of the Holy Trinity) in early June involves local food and wine tastings, theater performances, and music. Call the **Comune di Arqua Petrarca** (☎ 0429/777100) for information.

Este

57 *9 km (5½ mi) southwest of Monselice, 80 km (50 mi) southwest of Venice.*

Este was an important center of the Veneto before becoming Roman Ateste, retaining its prominent role under the rule of the Este family, later to become dukes of Ferrara. Power was then transferred to Venice. Dominating the town is the **Castello dei Carraresi,** now in ruins, although the gardens are open to the public. Abutting the walls, housed in a 16th-century palazzo, is the **Museo Nazionale Atestino,** where you can see the Veneto's best collection of pre-Roman and Roman artifacts, including some fine bronzes such as the 7th-century *Situla Benvenuti* and the *Dea di Caldevigo* dating from the 5th century. ⊠ *Via Guido Negri 2,* ☎ *0429/2085.* 🎫 *€2.05.* ☉ *Tues.–Sun. 9–7.*

The Baroque **Duomo** is dedicated to Santa Thecla, who is represented in a large painting by Tiepolo. ⊠ *Piazza Santa Thecla 6,* ☎ *0429/2009.* ☉ *10–noon and 4–6.*

Dining and Lodging

$$ ✗ **Sapio.** Tucked up a little alley, in the center of town, this is the place for wine lovers, for it's an *enoteca* (wine shop/bar) as well as a restaurant. With more than 250 different wines to choose from, the management will be happy to help you with your selection. There's no set menu—the chef is inventive and likes to use local ingredients such as lamb, goose, and seasonal vegetables. Homemade desserts such as *torta della nonna* ("grandma's tart," made with pine nuts), *torta al cioccolato* (chocolate cake), and seasonal fruit tarts are a specialty. The decor is plain with terra-cotta accents, and there's a quiet garden for alfresco eating in warm weather. ⊠ *Via Madonetta 2/c,* ☎ *0429/602565. Reservations essential. AE, DC, MC, V. Closed Mon.*

$–$$ ✗ **Antica Torre.** Live music, a piano bar, and sing-alongs are what you can expect from this lively restaurant just 3 km (2 mi) out of Este on the Montagnana road. In summer, the barbecue sizzles and pizzas are cooked in a wood-burning oven. The menu changes daily and you'll find local dishes such as *petta da oca fresca con crostini* (breast of goose and croutons) or *macheroncini con oca e piselli* (little macaroni with goose and peas). ⊠ *Località Ponte della Torre,* ☎ *0429/3484. DC, MC, V. Closed Tues. No lunch Sat.*

$ 🏠 **Beatrice d'Este.** The statues set among the trees leading up to the entrance to this hotel against the backdrop of the castle walls make you think it's going to be rather grand. It is, but it's also family run and a very good value. Sink down into one of the comfy armchairs and you may not want to get up again. The hotel is named after one of the most renowned women of her day (1475–97), an intelligent and cultured beauty married at the age of 16 to the seventh Duke of Milan (who commissioned Leonardi da Vinci to paint *The Last Supper*). ⊠ *Viale delle Rimembranze 1, 35042,* ☎ *0429/600533,* 🄵🅰🅇 *0429/601957. 30 rooms. Restaurant, bar. AE, DC, MC, V.*

$ 🏠 **Castello.** Though the stairs and passages of this modest hotel are rather cramped, guest rooms are serviceable, and the bathrooms are well equipped. Underneath is a busy caffè full of gossiping locals. The price only just enters this category. ⊠ *Via San Girolamo 7/a, 35042,* ☎ *0429/602223,* 🄵🅰🅇 *0429/602418. 12 rooms. AE, DC, MC, V.*

Nightlife and the Arts

FESTIVALS

The **Settembre Euganeo** in September heralds theater performances, an antiques market, an exhibition of local handicrafts, and a pumpkin feast. Contact the tourist office (⊠ Piazza Maggiore 9, 35042 Este, ☎ 🄵🅰🅇 0429/3635) for information.

Montagnana

❺❽ *42 km (26 mi) west of Este, 85 km (53 mi) southwest of Venice.*

You could almost be forgiven for thinking that you have been transported back to the 1300s as you approach the medieval walls and tall, crenellated towers that surround Montagnana, glowing pink against the green of the moat. Might you even hear the noise of the hooves of horses galloping past? If you're here in September, then your ears may not be deceiving you, as this is when the 10 bareback jockeys compete for the *pallium* (a red cloth), from which the name *palio* is derived. In this the whole town celebrates the end of the rule of the tyrant Ezzelino III, who in 1242 practically destroyed the town by fire. It was thanks to the Carrara family that the defensive walls, with their 24 towers and four gates, were subsequently put in place; these now rank among the best preserved in Europe, even boasting two castles. One of them, the **Rocca degli Alberi,** was built in 1362 to defend the western approaches but now is only subject to invasions by backpackers, functioning as a youth hostel.

Montagnana's eastern gate (Porta Padova) is defended by the town's oldest fortification, the **Castello di San Zeno,** a survivor from Ezzelino's time. It presently houses the **Museo Civico,** consisting of memorabilia of two famous tenors born in the town in 1885, Giovannni Martinelli and Aureliano Pertile. For a panoramic view over the red roofs and a different perspective on the walls, take a trip up the tower. ⊠ *Piazza Tieste 15,* ☎ *0429/804128.* 🎫 *Castle €1.55, tower €0.50.* ☉ *Museum guided tours Apr.–Oct., Wed.–Fri. at 11 and weekends at 11, noon, 3, 4, 5, and 6; Nov.–Mar., Wed.–Fri. at 11 and weekends at 11, noon, 3, 4, and 5. Tower Apr.–Oct., Wed.–Mon. 9:30–12:30 and 4–7; Nov.– Mar., Wed.–Mon. 9:30–12:30 and 3–6.*

The brick **Duomo** reflects both Gothic and Renaissance styles. In its spacious nave, your eye might be caught by the altarpieces by Veronese and Buonconsiglio (died circa 1536) but will probably dwell longer on the lively painting of the decisive *Battle of Lepanto* (1571) by Vassilacchi (known as Aliense), fought against the Turkish invaders. ⊠ *Piazza Vittorio Emanuele,* ☎ *0429/81009.* 🎫 *Free.* ☉ *Apr.–Oct., daily 8–noon and 3–7; Nov.–Mar., daily 3–6.*

NEED A BREAK?	Whatever the time of year, it's worth a stop for a delicious ice cream at the **Bottega del Gelato** (☎ 0429/800855), across the square from the cathedral. Also, don't leave town without strolling through the cobbled streets and buying some prosciutto *di Montagnana,* as sweet and tasty as any you'll find in Italy.

The Duomo is the dominant feature of the main square, **Piazza Vittorio Emanuele.** Of the Quattrocento buildings gracing the rest of the square, perhaps the finest is the Venetian Gothic **Palazzo Lombardesco,** with its balconies and five-paned windows. Notice the ornamental chimneys sprouting like flowers from the roofs.

Dining and Lodging

$$ ✗ **Marco Polo.** This is a serious fish restaurant, full of locals concentrating on their food. It's a little ways out from the town center, small and elegant with stained-glass windows. At this no frills place, make your way past the stacked-up piles of plates and try out the risotto with prawns, scampi, or *polipo* (octopus). ⊠ *Via San Zeno 37,* ☎ *0429/ 81509. Reservations essential. AE, MC, V. Closed Wed.*

$–$$ ✗ **Pizzeria Palio.** The shields and crossbows on the walls remind you that you're sitting right up against the medieval walls. This place is bright and busy, and the pizzas cooked in the wood-burning oven are bustled to your table. Try the Brie and *speck* (Tyrolean bacon) pie. Pasta dishes are available as well, and the light grilled salmon with peppers is tasty. ⊠ *Piazza Trieste,* ☎ *0429/804188. MC, V. Closed Tues.*

$$ 🏨 **Aldo Moro.** Pink marble, parquet floors, and polished furniture
★ imbue this little hotel with ineffable charm. Formerly an inn, the building is steeped in style and warmth, enhanced by beamed ceilings and

creaking floors. Bathrooms are pink marble, too. If you dine in the restaurant (closed Monday), make sure you taste the prosciutto di Montagnana, then perhaps some *oca* (goose) or, as an extravagant novelty, tagliolini *al cacao con funghi porcini e tartufo* (with cocoa, mushrooms, and truffles). For secondi, try *lumache con nocciole* (snails with hazelnuts). ⊠ *Via Guglielmo Marconi 27, 35044,* ☎ *0429/81351,* 𝖥𝖠𝖷 *0429/ 81842. Closed Jan. 3–10 and July 25–Aug. 10*

$ ▣ **Concordia.** Whether you come to eat or stay here, you'll be sure of a warm welcome in this family-run establishment. You're not in the historic center, but you're surrounded by a modest, homey atmosphere with folksy furnishings to match. There are only a small number of rooms, so book ahead. A full meal here of traditional home cooking chosen from the simple menu will cost you around €15.50 and might include prosciutto, grilled *selvaggina* (game), or *pollo alla griglia* (grilled chicken). An inexpensive house wine from the Colli Euganei will set it all off nicely. ⊠ *Via San Zeno 148, 35044,* ☎ 𝖥𝖠𝖷 *0429/81673. 8 rooms. Restaurant, bar. AE, MC, V.*

Nightlife and the Arts

The **Palio** takes place on the first Sunday in September. Ten districts compete in a horse race. You can get information from the **Comitato Palio dei 10 Communi** (☎ 0429/80448) or the tourist office (⊠ Piazza Trieste 3, 35044 Montagnana, ☎ 𝖥𝖠𝖷 0429/81320).

SOUTHERN VENETO A TO Z

To research prices, get advice from other travelers, and book travel arrangements, visit www.fodors.com.

AIRPORTS AND TRANSFERS

The main airport serving the Venetian Arc is Aeroporto Marco Polo, 10 km (6 mi) north of Venice, which handles international and domestic flights. A few European airlines schedule flights to Aeroporto Catullo di Villafranca, also served by a number of charter flights.

➤ AIRPORT INFORMATION: **Aeroporto Catullo di Villafranca** (⊠ 10 km [6 mi] southwest of Verona, ☎ 045/8095666). **Aeroporto Marco Polo** (☎ 041/2609260).

TRANSFERS

From Padua, Landomas Service provides a minibus service to Venice airport. A regular bus service connects Villafranca with Verona's Porta Nuova railway station.

➤ TAXIS AND SHUTTLES: **Landomas Service** (☎ 049/8601426 or 049/ 8600819).

BOAT AND FERRY TRAVEL

ACTV operates a once-daily direct boat service in the summer connecting Venice (San Zaccaria) with Chioggia and Sottomarina departing Sottomarina at 9:15 and Venice at 5 PM.

➤ BOAT AND FERRY INFORMATION: **ACTV** (☎ 041/5287886).

BUS TRAVEL TO AND FROM VENICE AND THE VENETO

Frequent buses from Venice to the region's major cities are operated by ATVO and ACTV, both operating from the bus station at Piazzale Roma in Venice. There are interurban and interregional connections throughout the Veneto. Local tourist offices may be able to provide details of timetables and routes; otherwise contact the local bus station, or in some cases the individual bus companies operating from the station. Lake Garda is more easily explored by bus; frequent services run between the towns.

➤ BUS INFORMATION: **ACTV** (✉ Piazzale Roma, Venice, ☎ 041/5287886). **ATVO** (✉ Piazzale Roma, Venice, ☎ 041/5205530).

BUS TRAVEL WITHIN THE VENETO

Contact ACTV for buses from Venice to Brenta Riviera, Padua, and Chioggia; ATVO covers the Conegliano–Vittorio and Veneto–Cortina routes. Contact APT for Lake Garda, Montagnana, and Bosco Chiesanuova. In Verona, AMT gets you around. In Vicenza, FTV serves the region, and ACI takes you around the city; minibuses run every few minutes from the parking lots to the town center Monday through Saturday. Take Line A from Via Bassano, Line B from Via Farini and Via Cairoli, and Line C from Viale Cricoli.

➤ BUS INFORMATION: **ACI** (✉ Viale della Pace 260, Vicenza, ☎ 0444/510501). **ACTV** (✉ Piazzale Roma, Venice, ☎ 041/5287886). **AMT** (✉ Via Torbido, 1, Verona, ☎ 045/8871111). **APT** (✉ Piazza XXV Aprile, Verona, ☎ 045/8004129). **ATVO** (✉ Piazzale Roma, Venice, ☎ 041/5205530). **FTV** (✉ Viale Milano 138, Vicenza, ☎ 0444/223115).

CAR RENTAL

➤ LOCAL AGENCIES: **Avis** (✉ Piazza Stazione 1, Padua, ☎ 049/664198; ✉ Via Monte Baldo 3, Peschiera, ☎ 045/6401164; ✉ Corso del Popolo 329, Rovigo, ☎ 0425/23028; ✉ Stazione FS, Verona, ☎ 045/26636; ✉ Viale Milano 88, Vicenza, ☎ 0444/321622). **Hertz** (✉ Piazza Stazione 5, Padua, ☎ 049/657877; ✉ Stazione FS, Verona, ☎ 045/25832; ✉ Viale Europa 50, Vicenza, ☎ 0444/321313).

CAR TRAVEL

The main access roads to the region are both linked to the A1 (Autostrada del Sole), which connects Bologna, Florence, and Rome. They are the A13, which culminates in Padua, and the A22, which passes through Verona in a north–south direction. The road linking the region from east to west is the A4, the primary route from Milan as far as Trieste.

The main highway in the region is A4, which connects Verona, Padua, and Venice with Trieste. The A13 connects Padua with Monselice and Rovigo. The A4 and SS11 pass the southern edge of the Lago di Garda, and the A22, which connects Verona with Trento, runs along the lake's eastern shore.

EMERGENCIES

For first aid, ask for *pronto soccorso,* and be prepared to give your address. All pharmacies post signs on the door with addresses of *farmacie di turno* (pharmacies taking shifts), which stay open at night, on Saturday afternoon, and on Sunday.

➤ EMERGENCY SERVICES: **Police, Ambulance, Fire** (☎ 113).

➤ HOSPITALS: **Ospedale Civile** (✉ Via Rodolfi 37, Vicenza, ☎ 0444/993111). **Ospedale Civile e Policlinico dell'Università** (✉ Via Giustiniani 1, Padua, ☎ 049/8211111). **Ospedale Civile Maggiore** (✉ Piazza Stefani, Verona, ☎ 045/8071111).

LODGING

The Landmark Trust offers accommodation in the Villa Saraceno, a Palladian villa in Finale di Agugliaro, south of Vicenza. In summer it takes parties of 16 but from November to February parties of 5.

Local agencies that rent out villas around Malcesine include Paola Farina, La Costa Blu, and Little Villa. In the Vicenza area, you can contact individual villas direct: Villa Franceschini-Canera di Salasco, 8 km (5 mi) south of Vicenza; the Palladio-designed Villa Godi Malinverni, 22 km (14 mi) north of Vicenza; and Ville Da Schio, 10 km (6 mi) south of Vicenza, after La Rotonda on SS247.

➤ LOCAL AGENTS: **La Costa Blu** (✉ Via Gardesana 62, 37018 Malcesine, ☎ 045/7400699). **Little Villa** (✉ Via Gardesana 32, 37018 Malcesine, ☎ 045/7401547). **Paola Farina** (✉ Via Butura 8, 37018 Malcesine, ☎ 045/7400532). **Ville Da Schio** (✉ Piazza Giovanni da Schio 4, Località Longare, 36023 Costozza, ☎ 0444/555896 or 0444/ 555073). **Villa Franceschini-Canera di Salasco** (✉ Via Roma 5, 36057 Arcugnano, ☎ 0444/270113). **Villa Godi Malinverni** (✉ Via Palladio 44, 36030 Lonedo di Lugo, ☎ 0445/860561 or 0330/6221287).

➤ RENTAL LISTINGS: **The Landmark Trust** (✉ Shottesbrooke, Maidenhead, Berkshire SL6 3SW, England, ☎ 01628/825925, FAX 01628/ 825417).

TOURS

You'll find that many of the best tours begin and end in Venice because so much of the region is accessible from there. Local tourist offices will be able to provide you with a list of authorized guides, for whom there is an official tariff rate.

BOAT TOURS

Between March and November, the Burchiello excursion boat makes an all-day villa tour along the Brenta Canal, departing from Padua on Wednesday, Friday, and Sunday; you can admire more than 50 villas en route, but only stop and visit three, the Villas Pisani, Valmarana, and Foscari, and there's a lunchtime break at the Burchiello restaurant at Oriago. Contact American Express for details. For those who prefer to go it alone, the most practical way is to hire a car for the day or to take a bus from Padua.

➤ FEES AND SCHEDULES: **American Express** (✉ Salizzada San Moisè, 1471 San Marco, Venice, ☎ 041/5200844, FAX 041/5229937).

SPECIAL-INTEREST TOURS

You can have a free tour of "Chioggia by Night" on Monday and Thursday, June through September. Get details from the tourist office. During July you can take guided tours by night for "music and culture under the stars" in the towns of the Euganean Hills (Monselice, Montagnana, Este, Arqua Petrarca). Call Centro Guide Padova for information.

➤ FEES AND SCHEDULES: **Centro Guide Padova** ☎ 049/8209711). **Chioggia Tourist Office** (☎ 041/401068).

PRIVATE GUIDES

For an individual guide in Padua, call the Sindacato Guide Turistiche. Ippogrifo in Verona can provide escorted trips on foot, by car, or bus.

➤ CONTACTS: **Ippogrifo** (✉ Via Roncisvalle 76, ☎ 045/8278959). **Sindacato Guide Turistiche** (☎ 049/8209711).

WALKING TOURS

The Comune di Padova organizes nocturnal tours of Padua.

➤ FEES AND SCHEDULES: **Comune di Padova** (☎ 049/8204562, 049/ 8204547, or 049/8204573).

TRAIN TRAVEL

The most important train routes arriving from the south will stop almost every hour in either Verona, Padua, or Venice. From northern Italy and the rest of Europe, trains usually enter via Milan to the west or through Porta Nuova station in Verona. Call Ferrovia dello Stato toll-free for fare and schedule information.

From Venice, the main line running across the north of Italy connects Padua (20 mins), Vicenza (1 hr), and Verona (1½ hrs) with most routes continuing west to Milan (3 hrs). From Padua, there are regular connections for Monselice, Este, Montegrotto Terme, and Rovigo, which in turn connect with Chioggia. The nearest train stations for Lake Garda are Peschiera, in the south, and Rovereto (in Trentino), from which there are frequent bus connections for Riva del Garda. Again, call Ferrovia dello Stato for toll-free train information.

➤ TRAIN INFORMATION: **Ferrovia dello Stato** (☎ 147/888088).

TRAVEL AGENCIES

➤ LOCAL AGENTS: **A. Palladio Viaggi** (✉ Contrà Cavour 16, Vicenza, ☎ 0444/546738). **Caldieri** (✉ Via Negrelli 1, Monselice, ☎ 0429/783396). **Eniana** (✉ Via Guglielmo Marconi 25, Montagnana, ☎ 0429/82188). **Fabretto Viaggi/American Express** (✉ Corso Porta Nuova 11/f, Verona, ☎ 045/8009040). **Felicity** (✉ Riviera Magellano 4, Mestre, ☎ 041/980899). **Piacare Viaggi** (✉ Viale Veneto 8/a, Chioggia, ☎ 041/5500470). **Revox Viaggi** (✉ Corso del Popolo 290/c, Rovigo, ☎ 0425/28283). **Tiarè Viaggi/American Express** (✉ Via Risorgimento 20, Padua, ☎ 049/666133).

VISITOR INFORMATION

Vicenza offers special weekend package deals ("Vicenza Weekend") that include discounts in hotels and restaurants, free or reduced-price entrance to a selection of the city's main tourist attractions, and guided tours. Contact the Vicenza tourist offices (✉ Piazza Matteotti 12, 36100 Vicenza, ☎ 0444/320854). Verona has a free hotel booking service through Cooperativa Albergatori Veronesi. Vicenza's Consorzio di Promozione Turistica can provide info about hotel and restaurant discounts.

➤ TOURIST INFORMATION: **Consorzio di Promozione Turistica** Vicenza è (✉ Via Enrico Fermi, 36100 Vicenza, ☎ 0444/994770). **Cooperativa Albergatori Veronesi** (✉ Via Patuzzi 5, 37100 Verona, ☎ 045/8009844, FAX 045/8009372). **Tourist Offices** (✉ Via Pietro d'Abano 18, 35031 Abano Terme, ☎ 049/8669055; ✉ Via Castello 6, 35032 Arqua Petrarca, ☎ 0429/777145; ✉ Piazza Chiesa 34, 37021 Bosco Chiesanuova, ☎ FAX 045/7050088; ✉ Lungomare Adriatico 101, 30019 Chioggia, ☎ 041/401068; ✉ Piazza Maggiore 9, 35042 Este, ☎ FAX 0429/3635; ✉ Via Capitanato del Porto 6, 37018 Malcesine, ☎ 045/7400555; ✉ Corso del Populo 65, 30174 Mestre, ☎ 041/975357; ✉ Via Roma 1, 35043 Monselice, ☎ FAX 0429/783026; ✉ Piazza Trieste 3, 35044 Montagnana, ☎ FAX 0429/81320; ✉ Viale Stazione 60, 35036 Montegrotto Terme, ☎ 049/793384; ✉ Stazione Ferroviaria, 35100 Padua, ☎ 049/8752077; ✉ Piazza del Santo, 37019 Padua, ☎ 049/8753087; ✉ Piazzale Betteloni 15, 37019 Peschiera, ☎ 045/7551673; ✉ Via Dunant 10, 45100 Rovigo, ☎ 0425/361481; ✉ Stazione Ferroviaria, Porta Nuova, 37100 Verona, ☎ 045/8000861; ✉ Piazza delle Erbe 38, 37121 Verona, ☎ 045/8068680, WEB www.tourism.verona.it; ✉ Piazza Matteotti 12, 36100 Vicenza, ☎ 0444/320854).

8 NORTHERN VENETO

TREVISO, THE DOLOMITES

The works of man and nature have never met in such felicitous union as in this northern region of Alps and Art. The marriage has resulted in Canova's silky sculptures, Titian's noble portraits, and frescoes unlimited, all within a short ride of sparkling rivers, air crisp enough to bottle, craggy-peaked ski slopes, and the choicest food and drink from the mountain pastures. You'll never want to go home.

By Robert
Andrews

Updated
by Robin
Goldstein

T**HE REGION AROUND TREVISO** called Marca Trevigiana was known by its early admirers as *gioiosa et amorosa* ("joyful and lovely"), which remains a good encapsulation of its attractions today. The area's historic towns have spawned some of Italy's supreme painters and sculptors, whose magnificent works of art and architecture are very much in evidence. The region to the north provides a natural complement to these works of men in the form of the mighty Dolomites.

The arcaded town of Treviso, dubbed "the painted city" for its prolific frescoes, yields abundant artwork by Giotto's heir, Tomaso da Modena. The walled town of Castelfranco boasts a much-admired altarpiece by the Renaissance painter Giorgione. Great art and architecture can be discovered in the same building at the Villa Barbaro at Maser, the only point where the two geniuses of the 16th century, Palladio and Veronese, coincided. Conegliano—wine capital of the Veneto—is the birthplace of the 15th-century painter Cima. The unassuming village of Possagno displays one of the largest collections of Canova's sculptures and plaster casts anywhere. Last but not least, the mountain village of Pieve di Cadore has produced yet another master, Titian, whose modest house still remains.

The Dolomites are masterpieces in their own right, particularly when the last rays of the setting sun shed their pink spell on the sheer and jagged heights. Here, follow your whim, either to hobnob in Cortina d'Ampezzo's bars and restaurants during the ski season or to experience the thrill of the mountains while walking, fishing, or horseback riding—best done on the gentler slopes of the southerly Pieve di Cadore districts. Higher up are some of the most dramatic driving routes in Italy. You'll find some excellent restaurants in these parts, many tucked away in the woods, as well as a wide range of upmarket or cozy hotels.

The shadow of Venice, of course, is still ever present, its influence stretching to Belluno, strategically placed as its northernmost ally. La Serenissima was responsible for rebuilding the town of Feltre after it was sacked by Emperor Maximilian in 1509, thus making Feltre one of the best places to absorb the feel of small-scale 16th-century Italy. The lion of St. Mark sits proudly atop a column in the piazza at Bassano del Grappa, a town made even more picturesque by the wooden bridge designed by Palladio. Marostica, famous for its human chess match held each September, was ruled by Venice for nearly 400 years and vaunts two castles with walls that tier down the hillside. Imposing defense works also gird the small centers of Castelfranco and Cittadella.

With its red walls rising above and sheltering the town within, Cittadella is perhaps the supreme example of a small fortified Italian town. It was one of the strongholds of Ezzelino III da Romano (1194–1259), a name that comes up in any account of this area. A much-hated man who terrorized the region during the 13th century, he was known as the "Son of Satan"—so monstrous and tyrannical were his deeds that he was condemned to boil in a river of blood in Dante's *Inferno*. When Ezzelino died, the remainder of his family was massacred by the citizens of Asolo to prevent his like from ever being seen again.

Pleasures and Pastimes

Dining

The cuisine of the Treviso area combines robust country cooking and more refined urban-inspired dishes. Great use is made of the food that grows in the wild, especially in the hills. Chestnuts, berries, mushrooms, herbs, and *verdure* (greens) all have their place on the menu. You can't make a journey through this zone without encountering radicchio. The other Treviso specialty is delicate, white asparagus. Game figures on the menu in the mountain zones, and in winter, steaming bowls of *pasta e fagioli* (pasta and bean soup), creamy risotto, and polenta are staples. Treviso is reputedly the birthplace of tiramisu (literally "pick me up"), that delight composed of espresso, mascarpone cheese, sugar, ladyfingers, liqueur, and cocoa powder.

The cattle that graze on the mountain pastures and the fertile lowlands produce excellent cheese that comes with a D.O.C. (Denominazione di Origine Controllata) mark, a guarantee of quality. Look out for Montasio and Asiago, both in mild, medium, and strong varieties. Grana Padano and Provolone Val Padana are piquant and flavorful. In summer try for Morlacco, a soft, salty cheese that comes from the mountains, and Casatella, a creamy cheese made by local farmers.

CATEGORY	COST*
$$$$	over €18
$$$	€13–€18
$$	€8–€13
$	under €8

Prices are for a main course (secondo piatto)

Grappa

You can't fail to be intrigued by the elegant bottles full of clear liquid on display in any area *alimentari* (food shop), *enoteca* (wine shop), or restaurant. This is grappa, a spirit distilled from grape pomace (the skins, seeds, and stems left over from the wine-making process). The process has been refined over the years, leading eventually to the commercial production in distilleries, especially in the Bassano del Grappa area. Of these, perhaps the most famous is the Nardini distillery, which, if you're visiting the Ponte degli Alpini here, will no doubt lure you in.

Lodging

Hotels in the small towns of the region offer excellent value. Treviso caters largely to the business sector, with hotels sited away from the historic center. If you're planning a stay in Cortina in the peak skiing season, be sure to book well ahead. The quieter resorts will have more low-key hotels, but still check on availability. Bear in mind that many hotels in the mountains close between Easter and June.

CATEGORY	COST*
$$$$	over €155
$$$	€105–€155
$$	€50–€105
$	under €50

All prices are for two people in a standard double room, including tax and service.

Wine Roads

An ideal way to explore the southern stretch of this region is by following the wine roads, tours that blend the picturesque with the culture and delights of the grape. Authorized wine shops where you can stop and sample are marked with a sign showing a triangular arrangement of red and yellow grapes. You can choose between three routes, or do them all.

MONTELLO AND ASOLO HILLS WINE ROAD

This route winds its way from Nervesa della Battaglia, a couple of miles south of Conegliano, through two key sights of the area, the lovely village of Asolo and the Villa Barbaro at Maser. Asolo produces good prosecco, whereas Montello favors merlot and cabernet. Both areas also yield pinot and chardonnay.

The circular route starts and ends in Conegliano. It follows the river Piave and runs through orchards, woods, and hills. Of the red and white wines here, the Raboso del Piave ages well and is the perfect complement for local dishes such as beans and pasta or goose stuffed with chestnut. The other reds are cabernet, merlot, and cabernet sauvignon. As an accompaniment to fish, choose a Verduzzo del Piave or, for an aperitif, the lovely warm-yellow Pinot Grigio del Piave. The gems of the area are the D.O.C. Torchiato di Fregona and Refrontolo Passito, both made according to traditional methods.

PROSECCO WINE ROAD

This route runs for 47 km (29 mi) from Valdobbiadene to Conegliano, where vines grow either in straight rows or on pergolas. Prosecco, a white wine enjoyed since Roman times, ranges in color from green-tinged to a straw-yellow hue. Prosecco *tranquillo* (still) is served chilled and goes well with starters; *spumante* (sparkling) is recommended as an aperitif wine served at an optimum of about 45°F, and *frizzante* (lightly sparkling, the most common), from the hilly area around Cartizze, is served at a slightly higher temperature—the best is Superiore di Cartizze.

Exploring Northern Veneto

Half an hour's drive due north of Mestre on the A27 brings you to Treviso, the chief town of the region. Set among gentle hills, the area's numerous walled and medieval towns lie to the north and west of this town, though the region becomes more mountainous at Bassano del Grappa in the west and at Vittorio Veneto, farther north of Treviso. From Belluno, dramatically placed on the Piave River on the edge of the Dolomites, the S51 continues north to Pieve di Cadore and Cortina d'Ampezzo in the heart of Dolomites. If you're without a car, this range is most easily explored by bus, and it's easy to connect with any of the other smaller towns in this region by public transportation.

Numbers in the text correspond to numbers in the margin and on the Northern Veneto map.

Great Itineraries

IF YOU HAVE 3 DAYS

Even with three days at your disposal, you can experience both the mountains and the small towns covered in this area. Starting off in "the painted city" of ▦ **Treviso** ①, spend some time taking in the town's artworks and diverse shops in the morning before heading west to make a brief circuit of the medieval walls of ▦ **Cittadella** ④. After a bite of lunch, head off to the lovely Palladian bridge in ▦ **Bassano del Grappa** ⑤, the place to indulge in a grappa, and a possible hotel stop; alternatively, spend the night in ▦ **Asolo** ②, a town famed for its "hundred vistas." From either of these places, head north toward the Dolomites, perhaps stopping in ▦ **Belluno** ⑩ for lunch. The grandeur of the mountains becomes a constant presence as you progress up the Piave River valley to ▦ **Cortina d'Ampezzo** ⑬ or to the quieter ▦ **Pieve di Cadore** ⑫ for your second night, dining well in one of the local restaurants. Your third day could be spent walking and admiring the stunning mountain views before returning south, on the way passing through ▦ **Vittorio Veneto** ⑨ and ▦ **Conegliano** ⑦, both of them with fine artistic and architectural treasures on view, before returning to Treviso.

IF YOU HAVE 5 DAYS

Five days would allow you to tour the area at a more leisurely pace. Following the same basic route from ▦ **Treviso** ① as before, you could take in ▦ **Castelfranco Veneto** ③ for the Giorgione connection en

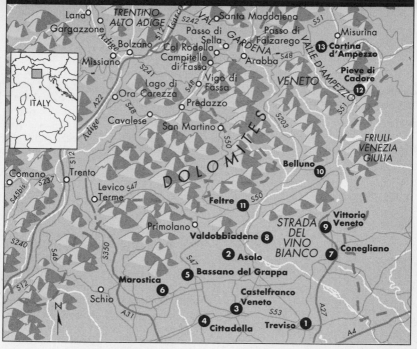

Northern Veneto

Lana
Gargazzone
TRENTINO ALTO ADIGE
Santa Maddalena
Passo di Sella
Passo di Falzarego
Misurina
Bolzano
Missiano
Col Rodella
Campitello di Fassa
Arabba
Cortina d'Ampezzo **13**
ITALY
Lago di Fassa
Vigo di Fassa
VENETO
Pieve di Cadore **12**
Ora Carezza
Predazzo
Cavalese
San Martino
FRIULI-VENEZIA GIULIA
Comano
Trento
DOLOMITES
Belluno **10**
Levico Terme
Feltre **11**
Primolano
Valdobbiadene **8**
STRADA DEL VINO BIANCO
Vittorio Veneto **9**
Asolo **2**
Conegliano **7**
Marostica **6**
Bassano del Grappa **5**
Schio
Castelfranco Veneto **3**
Cittadella **4**
Treviso **1**

route to ⊞ **Cittadella** ④, spending the night in ⊞ **Bassano del Grappa** ⑤. From here, it's a short hop west to ⊞ **Marostica** ⑥ to see the famous checkered square. Doubling back through Bassano, head northeast to Possagno to admire Canova's graceful sculptures; then spend your second night at ⊞ **Asolo** ②, where you'll have time for the famous vistas and the Palladian villa at Maser. Taking the road north, you should stop next in the walled Venetian town of ⊞ **Feltre** ⑪, and then visit ⊞ **Belluno** ⑩, beautifully sited against the backdrop of the mountains, before spending your third night in either ⊞ **Cortina d'Ampezzo** ⑬ or **Pieve di Cadore** ⑫. If you're a fan of mountain scenery, spend a second night here; otherwise drive south to **Vittorio Veneto** ⑨, still within the shadow of the mountains, and then continue on for your fourth night at ⊞ **Conegliano** ⑦. Here you can pick up the wine route almost all the way back to Treviso.

When to Tour Northern Veneto

Touring the Treviso region or the Dolomites in late spring or early summer is a visual feast, when the vines are in full leaf and the meadows lush with flowers (the cherry blossom is a sight to behold in April and May). Many of the smaller towns hold festivals in the fall, when there is much feasting and gaiety. In winter, the crucial question is: snow or no snow? Snowfalls can make driving treacherous, though main roads are kept clear and tourist offices always have up-to-the-minute reports on conditions. Skiing varies wildly year by year but is almost always best in late February and March, after a full season of snow. Whatever time you plan your trip, you'll always be here at the right time for the mountains, which are stunning in all seasons.

TREVISO AND ENVIRONS

The prosperous center of Treviso provides easy access to a handful of towns in the region, including the beautiful walled towns of Castelfranco, home to one of the most famous of Giorgione's paintings, and Cittadella, resonant with reminders of its long history. Bassano del Grappa, with its lovely Palladian bridge and ceramics, is only a hop away, as are Marostica, renowned for its checkerboard square, and Asolo, antique retreat of the Venetian aristocracy. North of Treviso, the Renaissance can be savored in the streets of Vittorio Veneto and the thriving wine center of Conegliano. If you're interested in white wine, the abundant wine trails in the area invite exploration, while if sculpture's your bag, you can refresh your spirit by gazing on Canova's masterpieces in his museum at Possagno. And if you really can't leave the region without shopping, you'll find all the well-known names in Treviso, as well as a plethora of crafts and ceramics shops here and in the smaller centers, not to mention the gourmet delicatessens bulging with local specialties.

Treviso

❶ *30 km (19 mi) north of Venice.*

"Little Venice" is probably a somewhat inflated claim for Treviso, though the town does have canals and a Venetian air; "the painted city" is a less extravagant title, and an apt one: you'll come across frescoes practically everywhere you look. Treviso is a busy commercial center, with fashionable shops and boutiques at every turn. Treviso was already well established long before it came within the sphere of Venetian influence in the late 14th century, minting its own coins as early as the 8th century and becoming a center for literary and artistic excellence by the 13th. Much of the city was embellished by Tomaso da Modena (1325–79), the foremost northern Italian painter following the death of Giotto, responsible for decorating many of the Gothic churches with his frescoes in the 14th century.

Most of the frescoes you see on the outside of Treviso's buildings were put there by happy accident—the lack of any alternative stone with which to finish the facades in the 13th century. Together with the arcaded streets and mossy banked canals, where weeping willows trail their fronds in the water, these help to create an appealing town center, unmarred by the postwar constructions erected after a bombing raid on Good Friday 1944, when about half the city was destroyed. Other buildings, some dating from the 15th century, have been expertly restored.

The early 15th-century walls are best preserved around the Porta dei Santa Quaranta, the main gate west of the center. Borgo Cavour leads past the Museo Civico to Via Calmaggiore and the main **Piazza dei Signori,** in the heart of the medieval city. Some impressive public buildings line the piazza. Behind one of them, the early 13th-century **Palazzo dei Trecento,** restored after the bombing raid of 1944, follow a small alley for about 200 yards to the *pescheria* (fish market) on an island in one of the canals flowing through town. The nearby church of **Santa Lucia** holds frescoes by Tomaso da Modena.

NEED A BREAK?	Nearby, **Nascimben** (✉ Via Calmaggiore 32, ☎ 0422/540871), closed Monday, is the best *pasticceria* (pastry shop) in town, a good place for the requisite sampling of the local tiramisu before more exploring.

Treviso's seven-domed **Duomo** was founded in the 12th century. Within, the Malchiostro Chapel contains fine paintings and frescoes: an *Annunciation* by Titian (circa 1488–1576) and frescoes by Pordenone (1484–1539), including the *Adoration of the Magi.* The crypt is worth a visit for its array of 12th-century columns. ⊠ *Piazza del Duomo,* ☎ *0422/545720.* ☉ *Daily 8:30–noon and 3–7.*

Housed in the Canoniche Vecchie near the Duomo, the **Museo Diocesano d'Arte Sacra** contains archaeological material, a frescoed lunette by Tomaso da Modena, church silver, and vestments. ⊠ *Canoniche Vecchie, Via Canoniche 3,* ☎ *0422/416707.* ☜ *Free.* ☉ *Mon.–Thurs. 9–noon, Sat. 9–noon and 3–6.*

★ The most important church in Treviso is **San Nicolò,** an imposing Gothic building with an ornate vaulted ceiling. San Nicolò has more frescoes of the saints by Tomaso da Modena on the columns. Particularly charming is the depiction of *St. Agnes* on the north side, but the artist's best work here is the remarkable series of 40 portraits of Dominican friars in the seminary next door. These are astoundingly realistic considering that some were painted as early as 1352 and include one of the earliest-known portraits of a subject wearing glasses. ⊠ *Capitolo dei Domenicani, Seminario Vescovile, Via San Nicolò,* ☎ *0422/ 3247.* ☉ *Mon.–Sat. 9–noon and 3–6:30, Sun. 3–6:30. To enter, ring at custodian's desk at seminary entrance.*

The **Museo Civico** holds an archaeological section on the ground floor, including a collection of bronze sword blades dating from the 7th and 6th centuries BC and Roman remains. Upstairs is the picture gallery, the **Galleria Communale d'Arte Moderna.** Room 11 holds the best: portraits by Titian and Lorenzo Lotto (circa 1480–1556) and a *Crucifixion* by Jacopo Bassano (circa 1510–92). In contrast to these are the 19th- and 20th-century sculptures, bronzes, ceramics, and charcoal drawings by the Trevisan artist Arturo Martini (1889–1947) and the painter Gino Rossi (1884–1947). ⊠ *Borgo Cavour 24,* ☎ *0422/591337.* ☜ *€1.55.* ☉ *Tues.–Sat. 9–12:30 and 2:30–5, Sun. 9–noon.*

The **Chiesa di Santa Caterina,** on the east side of the city, holds more frescoes by da Modena, his *Ursula Cycle.* Other frescoes attributed to his school are found in the **Cappella degli Innocenti.** This deconsecrated church is in the process of being restored and is currently closed. Contact the Museo Civico or the tourist office (⊠ Piazzetta del Monte di Pietà, 31100 Treviso, ☎ 0422/547632) for information. ⊠ *Piazzetta Mario Botter.*

Dining and Lodging

$$$ ★ ✗ **Da Alfredo.** This restaurant belongs to the El Toulà group, a small chain of high-class restaurants in Italy and abroad. This is your chance to enjoy the art nouveau decor and classic international cuisine for which it became famous. Among regional dishes are risotto *con funghi* (with mushrooms) and asparagus in season. For cooking, ambience, and service, it's one of the region's best. ⊠ *Via Collalto 26,* ☎ *0422/540275. AE, DC, MC, V. Closed Mon. and Aug. No dinner Sun.*

$$-$$$ ★ ✗ **Beccherie.** In a town known for good eating, this rustic inn is a favorite. It's in the heart of old Treviso, behind the main square, and there are tables outside for fair-weather dining under the portico. In winter, look for *crespelle al radicchio* (crepes with radicchio) and *faraona in salsa peverata* (guinea hen with a peppery sauce). Spring brings risotto enriched with greens, *stinco di vitello* (veal shin), and *pasticcio di melanzane* (eggplant casserole). ⊠ *Piazza Ancillotto 11,* ☎ *0422/ 540871. AE, DC, MC, V. Closed Mon. and July 15–31. No dinner Sun.*

$-$$ ★ ✗ **Toni del Spin.** Wood-paneled with '30s decor, this place oozes delightful, old-fashioned character. Locals love the friendly and bustling feel as well as the wholesome food. The menu changes twice a week and is chalked on a hanging wooden board: try the filling *zuppa d'orzo e fagioli* (barley and bean soup) or the pasta e fagioli, delivered with panache and care. You shouldn't leave without quaffing a glass or two of prosecco. ⊠ *Via Inferiore 7,* ☎ *0422/543829. Reservations essential summer. AE, MC, V. Closed Sun. and Aug. No lunch Mon.*

$–$$ ✕ **La Colonna.** Everything in this small hotel set in a creeper-covered,
★ 15th-century courtyard is crisp and white. Flower-frescoed ceilings and old-fashioned washstands in the bathrooms add to the quaint charm. It's essential to book one of the only six rooms well ahead. You can feel the history seeping through the walls in the associated restaurant of the same name, where you can dine among the pillars, beamed ceiling, and low arches of the main room or on the mezzanine floor. The chef favors fish, and beef with rosemary is a perfumey delight. ⊠ *Via Campana 27, 31100,* ☎ *0422/544804,* FAX *0422/419177. 6 rooms. AE, DC, MC, V. Closed Mon. No dinner Sun.*

$$$ **Continental.** You'll find this hotel within the old city walls, between the train station and the sights. Rich fabrics and Oriental rugs lend an air of opulence to this traditional four-star hotel offering solid comfort. ⊠ *Via Roma 16, 31100,* ☎ *0422/411216,* FAX *0422/55054. 81 rooms. AE, DC, MC, V.*

$$ **Campeol.** This hotel is associated with the Beccherie restaurant, just across the way. Frescoes adorn the stairways leading to adequate rooms that can get a little noisy in summer. You can park in the evening in the *piazzetta* without charge. ⊠ *Piazza Ancillotto 108, 31100,* ☎ *0422/56601,* FAX *0422/540871. 14 rooms. AE, DC, MC, V.*

Nightlife and the Arts

CONCERTS

Estate Trevigiano, a series of open-air events consisting of music, concerts, theater, and dance, takes place in the summer. Contact the tourist office (☎ 0422/547632) for information.

PIANO BAR

The piano bar **Nilo Blu** (⊠ Via della Repubblica 7/c, ☎ 0422/420469), 3 km (2 mi) north of the center on the road to Vittorio Veneto and Conegliano, features live jazz and rock bands most evenings but is primarily a place to lounge and talk. **Soda Pop** (⊠ Via Fonderia 46, ☎ 0422/424487) has live music and a young crowd.

Outdoor Activities and Sports

HORSEBACK RIDING

You can get horse carriage rides at **Cervara Cavalli** (⊠ Azienda Agricola, Via Padovana 20, Cervara, ☎ 0422/477100), 11 km (7 mi) from Treviso toward Padua. River trips can also be arranged.

Shopping

A general market is held Tuesday and Saturday mornings just behind the main Piazza Signori. The wrought iron and copper for which Treviso is known might be a little difficult to transport home, but there are plenty of small shops to explore in addition to the usual well-known names.

CERAMICS

For ceramics, visit **Ceramiche Bregantin** (⊠ Borgo Cavour 39, ☎ 0422/541820). **Ceramiche Artistiche di Visentin** (⊠ Piazza Garibaldi 16, ☎ 0422/590990) also sells beautiful painted ceramics.

GIFTS

Craighero (⊠ Via Calmaggiore 13, ☎ 0422/549225) is good gift-shopping territory, with perfumes, jewelry, shaving supplies, and hair accessories. At **Mangiafuoco-Vecchi Giochi** (⊠ Via Roggia 54, ☎ 0422/541738) you can find models of characters from fairy tales and handmade boxes made of paper, wood, and fabric. **Polo Pelleterie** (⊠ Via Inferiore 19, ☎ 0422/540896) sells handmade leather bags, briefcases, and belts.

Asolo

★ ❷ *35 km (22 mi) northwest of Treviso, 65 km (41 mi) northwest of Venice.*

The romantic, charming hillside hamlet of Asolo was the consolation prize of an exiled queen. At the end of the 15th century, Venetian-born Caterina Cornaro was sent here by Venice's doges to keep her from interfering with their administration of her former kingdom of Cyprus, which she had inherited. To soothe the pain of exile, she established a lively and brilliant court in Asolo. In this court Cardinal Pietro Bembo (1470–1547), one of the foremost literary figures of the time, wrote the love letters: *Gli Asolani,* coining the word *asolare,* meaning to while away the time in idle pleasures. Over the centuries, Venetian aristocrats continued to build gracious villas on the hillside, and in the 19th century Asolo once again became the idyllic haunt of musicians, poets, and painters. The man of letters and ideologue Gabriele d'Annunzio (1863–1938) was smitten with the beauty of the place, as was the English poet Robert Browning (1812–89). From the outside, you can explore villas once inhabited by Browning and also the actress Eleonora Duse (1850–1924), called *"La Divina del teatro italiano."* Famous as much for her stormy love life as for her roles in Ibsen and Shakespeare. Her tomb can be found in the cemetery of the church of Sant'Anna, along with that of the English explorer and writer Freya Stark (1893–1993), who lived here for most of her life.

Asolo has not always been a scene of tranquillity. In the early 13th century it fell, like many other towns of the area, under the sway of the tyrant Ezzelino III da Romano. Upon his death in 1259 the people of Asolo made sure that his ilk was never seen again by massacring all remaining members of his family. The peaceful old-world atmosphere vaporizes, too, on holiday weekends when the crowds pour in. Book your accommodation well ahead if you can.

In Asolo's town center, **Piazza Maggiore** is the site of Renaissance palaces and antique cafés. The Piazza Maggiore is also home to the frescoed 15th-century **Loggia del Capitano,** which contains the **Museo Civico,** displaying memorabilia of Asolo's dead coterie—Eleonora Duse's correspondence, Browning's spinet, manuscripts, and portraits of Caterina Cornaro. ✉ *Piazza Maggiore.* 🎟 *€3.10.* ⊙ *Weekends 10–12:30 and 3–7.*

NEED A BREAK?	While away some idle moments at the famous **Caffè Centrale** (✉ Via Roma 72, ☎ 0423/952141, WEB www.caffecentrale.com), which has overlooked the fountain in Piazza Maggiore and the Duomo since about 1700.

The **Duomo** was rebuilt in 1747 on the site of Roman baths. Caterina Cornaro donated the baptismal font, and Jacopo Bassano (circa 1510–92) and Lorenzo Lotto (1480–1556) both painted *Assumption* altarpieces. ✉ *Piazzetta S. Pio X 192,* ☎ *0423/952376.* ⊙ *Daily 9–noon and 4–7.*

Walking along Via Browning takes you past smart shops, Browning's house at No. 153, and the enoteca **Alle Ore** (✉ Via Browning 183, ☎ 0423/952070), where you can sample the local wine and grappa. It's closed Monday. Uphill from the piazza, you'll go past Caterina's ruined **Castello** (✉ Piazzetta E. Duse, ☎ 0423/952361), whose theater was transported to Florida in 1930. It is closed for renovation. Then as you go farther past some Gothic-style houses, you'll find the medieval fortress **La Rocca,** standing on the summit. It's only open on weekends, and hours vary according to the month—it's best to check with the tourist office first. It's worth the stiff climb for the views. ✉ *Monte Ricco,* ☎ *0423/529046 tourist office or 049/710977.* ⌦ *€1.55.* ☉ *Weekends only; hrs vary (check with tourist office).*

Dining and Lodging

$$$ ✗ **Hosteria Ca' Derton.** Right on the main square, Ca' Derton has a pleasant, old-fashioned ambience, adorned with early photos of Asolo and bouquets of dried flowers. The friendly proprietor takes pride in the homemade pasta, which might include *lasagnette* (flat, square noodles) with partridge sauce and radicchio, and game-themed *secondi* like loin of deer with pomegranate sauce. ✉ *Piazza D'Annunzio 11,* ☎ *0423/ 952730,* WEB *www.caderton.com. AE, DC, MC, V. Closed Mon., Feb. 1–15, and July 25–Aug. 8. No dinner Sun.*

$$ ✗ **Due Mori.** What could be better than sitting on the terrace in summer and enjoying the view over the valley in this "town of a hundred horizons"? Add to your pleasure by trying *bigoli all'anatra* (pasta with duck), the chicken, and the *ai ferri* (*barbecued*) dishes, but leave room for the homemade desserts. ✉ *Piazza d'Annunzio 5,* ☎ *0423/ 952256,* WEB *www.hotelduse.com. Reservations essential in summer. AE, DC, MC, V. Closed Wed. and Feb.*

$$$$ 🏨 **Villa Cipriani.** A romantic garden surrounded by gracious country ★ homes on a hillside on the outskirts of Asolo is the setting for this historic villa, now part of the Sheraton chain. Tastefully furnished with 19th-century antiques, it offers an oldfangled atmosphere, every creature comfort, and discreet service. Past guests have included Prince Philip, Aristotle Onassis, and Queen Juliana. The superb restaurant (closed Monday) has a terrace overlooking the garden, a perfect place to sip an aperitif. ✉ *Via Canova 298, 31011,* ☎ *0423/523411,* FAX *0423/ 952095,* WEB *www.sheraton.com/villacipriani. 31 rooms. Restaurant, bar. AE, DC, MC, V.*

$$$ 🏨 **Al Sole.** The smell of the polished wooden floor greets you as you enter this 1920s pink-washed hotel overlooking the main square. The rooms are large and furnished in antique style, cheerful with patterned rugs. The decoratively tiled bathrooms come equipped with hydro-massage showers. ✉ *Via Collegio 3, 31011,* ☎ *0423/528111,* FAX *0423/ 528399. 22 rooms, 1 suite. Bar, breakfast room, golf privileges, horseback riding. AE, DC, MC, V.*

$$ 🏨 **Duse.** Quality is the hallmark of this small hotel set on the arcaded Via Browning. Rooms are prettily decorated, and those higher up have beamed ceilings and views across to the Duomo. Best of all is the attic suite up a winding staircase, with different levels. ✉ *Via Robert Browning 190, 31011,* ☎ *0423/55241,* FAX *0423/950404,* WEB *www.hotelduse. com. 13 rooms, 1 suite. Bar, breakfast room. AE, MC, V.*

Outdoor Activities and Sports

GOLF

Asolo Golf Club (☎ 0423/543226), an 18-hole golf course at Cavaso, is 10 km (6 mi) north of Asolo on SP16.

Nightlife and the Arts

FESTIVALS

During the third weekend of September a **Palio** is held, commemorating the history of Asolo from Roman times until the arrival of Caterina Cornaro. It takes the form of a Roman chariot race through the streets and is attended by much feasting.

Shopping

An **antiques market** sets up in Asolo's center on the second Sunday of the month (except July and August).

FOODSTUFFS

For a shop that is pure theater, make sure you visit the century-old **Ennio** (✉ Via Robert Browning 159, ☎ 0423/529109). Once you've ogled longingly in front of the many windows, where food is displayed in all its glory—the biggest bowls of preserves and olives you've ever seen, graceful bottles of grappa, jars of truffle, enticing pastries, formidable cheeses—a visit inside is obligatory, as all these delights will be lovingly extolled by the expansive owner.

GIFTS

You can see the ceramic artist at work at **La Guizza Ceramiche** (✉ Via Robert Browning 166, ☎ 0423/55430). For jewelry **Rosso** (✉ Via Regina Cornaro 221, ☎ 0423/55544) has tasteful pieces.

OFF THE
BEATEN PATH

POSSAGNO – Just 8 km (5 mi) northwest of Asolo, this small town nestling at the foot of Monte Grappa merits a visit for its **Gipsoteca Museo Canoviano,** birthplace of the sculptor and architect Antonio Canova (1757–1822). Set in a typical Venetian garden, with vistas over the mellow countryside, the *gipsoteca* (collection of plaster casts) was built in 1836 and contains about 300 plaster, wax, and terra-cotta models that illustrate his way of working. Little nails (*rèpere*) were first studded all over the plaster cast; then by means of a pantograph (measuring device) the proportions were transferred to the final marble version. This is documented in his studio, part of his native house, alongside his charming and elegant paintings, mainly of disporting Greek nymphs. In the airy halls, marvel at the force of *Hercules and the Lion* and the beauty of *The Three Graces.* ✉ Piazza Canova, ☎ 0423/544323. ☑ €2.60. ۞ May–Sept., Tues.–Sat. 9–noon and 3–6, Sun. 9–noon and 3–7; Oct.–Apr., Tues.–Sun. 9–noon and 2–5.

On the other side of the road an imposing drive leads to the **Tempio,** a church designed by Canova as the resting place for his mortal remains that is reminiscent of the Pantheon. ✉ Stradone del Tempio. ۞ May–Sept., Tues.–Sat. 9–noon and 3–6, Sun. 9–noon and 3–7; Oct.–Apr., Tues.–Sun. 9–noon and 2–5.

Maser/Villa Barbaro

★ *4 km (2½ mi) east of Asolo, 60 km (38 mi) northwest of Venice.*

Just outside the town of Maser, Villa Barbaro is one of Palladio's most gracious Renaissance creations. The fully furnished villa is still inhabited by its owners, who make you wear heavy felt slippers over your shoes to protect the highly polished floors. The elaborate stuccos and opulent frescoes by Paolo Veronese bring the 16th century to life. After La Rotonda in Vicenza, this is Palladio's greatest villa and is definitely worth going out of your way for (before making the trip, note restricted hours). On the grounds, the **Tempietto** (little church) is one of Palladio's last projects, the only church designed by him lying outside Venice. At press time, the Tempietto was closed for restoration. A **cantina** also on the grounds offers wine tastings. ✉ Via Cornuda 2, ☎ 0423/923004. ☑ €4.65. ۞ Mar.–Oct., Tues. and weekends 3–6; Nov.–Feb., weekends 2:30–5. Closed Dec. 24–Jan. 6.

Dining

$$
★

✗ **Agnoletti.** In the town of Giavera del Montello near Maser, Agnoletti is an 18th-century inn of a bygone era with a lovely summer garden. The kitchen can produce an all-mushroom menu; but if you order something else, at least try the mushroom *zuppa* or *crostata di funghi* (mushroom tart). ✉ Via della Vittoria 190, Giavera del Montello, ☎ 0422/776009. No credit cards. Closed Mon.–Tues. and 3 wks in Jan.

$–$$ ✕ **Da Bastian.** A good place to stop for lunch before visiting the Villa Barbaro, this contemporary place has a pleasant garden for outdoor dining. Varied antipasto of pâtés, homemade vegetarian ravioli, and broiled meat with tasty sauces top the menu. ⊠ *Via Cornuda (follow sign), Loc. Muliparte, Maser,* ☎ *0423/565400. No credit cards. Closed Thurs. and Aug. No dinner Wed.*

Castelfranco Veneto

❸ *27 km (17 mi) west of Treviso, 45 km (28 mi) northwest of Venice.*

The stocky, battlemented walls with green banks and trees running down to the moat are not quite in the league of Cittadella's but nevertheless lend character to this small town. Erected in the 12th century by the Trevisans as protection against Padua, they encircle the old center or Castello. The most famous name associated with this town is that of Giorgione (1478–1510), the least known of all the figures of the High Renaissance. Dying young, possibly of the plague, graced with physical beauty and musical talents, he possessed all the attributes of poetic remembrance. The **Casa Giorgione** contains a small museum about the artist and, on the first floor, a chiaroscuro frieze attributed to him. ⊠ *Piazzetta San Liberale,* ☎ *0423/491240.* ☜ *€1.30.* ☺ *Apr.–Oct., Tues.–Sun. 9:30–12:30 and 3–6:30; Nov.–Mar., Tues.–Sun. 9–noon and 3–6.*

The neoclassical **Duomo,** modeled on Palladio's Chiesa del Redentore in Venice, holds frescoes by Paolo Veronese (1528–88) and Zelotti (1526–78). Castelfranco's greatest treasure, however, is Giorgione's altarpiece *Madonna and Child with SS. Francis and Liberale,* known as *La Pala.* The poetic and enigmatic mood his paintings evoke is ably demonstrated here. Commissioned in 1504 to commemorate the death of a young man of 18, Matteo Costanza, it shows three figures gazing dolefully out of the picture. Mary is set apart, at one with the landscape and isolated from the two saints in the foreground. ⊠ *Via Francesco Maria Preti,* ☎ *0423/495202.* ☺ *Daily 9–noon and 3–6.*

The restored **Teatro Accademico** was built to a design of F. M. Petri, also responsible for the cathedral. It's an elegant example of 18th-century work, in which concerts and performances can still be enjoyed in season. ⊠ *Via Garibaldi,* ☎ *0423/494500.* ☜ *Free.* ☺ *By appointment.*

Outside the walls are some fine palaces, notably the stuccoed 18th-century **Palazzo Soranzo Novello** (⊠ Corso XXIX Aprile), now a bank.

The broad Borgo Treviso leads to the **Parco Revedin Bolasco,** a tranquil garden with lakes, canals, little bridges, and hillocks. It complements the villa built in the 19th century by Giovan Battista Meduna. Here you'll find a Moorish greenhouse on an island and a circle of statues surrounding an amphitheater that was originally used as an exercise ground for horses. ☎ *0423/472114.* ☜ *Free.* ☺ *Mar. 21–Nov. 2, Thurs. and Sat. 10–12:30 and 3:30–7.*

Dining and Lodging

$$$$ ✕ **Alle Mura.** Castelfranco is not the sort of town where you would
★   expect to find this tropical-style restaurant, where the exotic festoons of fruit and flowers, chirping birds, and leopard-skin chairs are a veritable assault on the eye. If that is not enough, the pictures on the wall might suggest you've been transported to the South Seas, as do the Pacific island recipes, which include fish and shellfish specialties. ⊠ *Via Francesco Maria Preti 69,* ☎ *0423/498098. Reservations essential. AE, DC, MC, V. Closed Thurs., Jan. 10–31, and Aug.*

$$ ✕ **Ai Do Mori.** Typical dishes from the Veneto are served in this small restaurant up a little street just within the walls. If you've never got around to tasting *trippa* (tripe), now is your chance, but if you're not tempted by the trippa *alla parmigiana* (with Parmesan), maybe you'll feel safer with the *polenta e oca* (goose with polenta and herbs). ✉ *Vicolo Montebelluna 24,* ☎ *0423/495725. AE, DC, MC, V. Closed Thurs. No dinner Wed.*

$$ 🏨 **Al Moretto.** In the hands of the same family for generations, this refined but understated hotel offers welcoming service. The public rooms are intimate and at the same time light, soothing, and summery, with wicker furniture and chintz armchairs. In summer breakfast is served in the beautiful garden with a lily pond. Among the range of services offered here are bicycle tours and rafting, and a guide service can also be arranged. ✉ *Via San Pio X 10, 31033,* ☎ *0423/721313,* 🖷 *0423/ 721066. 34 rooms. Bar, breakfast room. AE, DC, MC, V.*

$$ 🏨 **Alla Torre.** The clock tower of Castelfranco's medieval castle overlooks this hotel, and the original brick wall is even incorporated into some of the suites. Rooms are modern and spacious, and the plaid carpets add a touch of hominess. A terrace gives onto the square. ✉ *Piazzetta Trento Trieste 7, 31033,* ☎ *0423/498707,* 🖷 *0423/498737. 46 rooms, 9 suites. Bar, breakfast room, air-conditioning, free parking. AE, DC, MC, V.*

Outdoor Activities and Sports

The nine-hole **Golf Club Castelfranco** (✉ Via Loreggia Postioma 44, ☎ 0423/493428) is open to the public and requires no handicap.

Cittadella

★ ❹ *13 km (8 mi) southeast of Marostica, 61 km (38 mi) northwest of Venice.*

Of all the walled cities in the Brenta Valley, Cittadella conveys most fully the sense of enclosure and protection. The lofty and battlemented walls rise up on either side as you enter through the brick arches of the Porta Padua, painted with the red *carra* (wagon) emblem of the Carrara family. Imagine, as you pass the **Torre di Malta,** the plight of the prisoners abandoned here to die of starvation by the tyrant Ezzelino III da Romano. The town was built on a Roman site by the Paduans as a counter to Castelfranco, a Trevisan stronghold, and then passed to a succession of powerful families including, of course, Ezzelino's. The lines of the streets follow the original Roman plan, with gates at the four cardinal points.

Via Garibaldi leads to the main **Piazza Pierobon** and the early 19th-century square **Duomo** with its massive columns and, inside, paintings by Jacopo Bassano, including *La Cena in Emmaus* in the sacristy. ✉ *Via Marconi 5,* ☎ *049/5970237.* ☉ *Daily 8–noon and 3–7.*

For the best view over the red-tiled roofs, pale ocher houses, and soaring walls, climb the bell tower of the Duomo, the **Torre Campanaria,** which doubles as a museum. As you go up, you'll see the walls festooned with vestments, candelabra, and other ecclesiastical exhibits. ✉ *Duomo, Via Marconi 5,* ☎ *049/5970237.* 🎟 *€1.05.* ☉ *Tues.–Fri. 9–11:30, Sat. 4–6, Sun. 9–11:30 and 4–6.*

On Via Indipendenza, the neoclassical **Teatro** has a facade by Japelli (1783–1852). The **Palazzo Pretorio** on Via Marconi, with a fine 16th-century marble portal and frescoes, was headquarters of whoever was in control of the city. You can visit upon request; contact the tourist office (✉ Via Marconi 5, 31033 Cittadella, ☎ 🖷 049/5970627).

A pleasant end to your visit can be a walk around the exterior of the walls through the **Giardini Pubblici,** open daily 8:30–5:30.

Dining and Lodging

$$ ✕ Al Teatro. Colorful tablecloths, ceramic dishes, and big pumpkins scattered about the dining area contribute to the farmhouse atmosphere. Before tucking into *porchetta Trevigiana* (whole pigs roasted on the spit and served cold with radicchio), try the *bigoli al Teatro* (pasta with tomato, basil, and mozzarella) or the gnocchi with a tomato cream sauce. ⊠ *Via Mura Rotta 11,* ☎ *049/9402317. AE, DC, MC, V. Closed Wed.*

$ ✕ Ai Giardini. This is a simple, honest haunt of locals, whom you'll probably encounter playing cards. The dish of the day varies: it might be *baccalà alla vicentina* (dried cod with milk and polenta) or *bigoli con sugo al anitra* (pasta with sweet duck sauce). You'll always find pasta with seasonal vegetables in a creamy sauce. ⊠ *Via Tezzon 22,* ☎ *049/5970740. Reservations essential weekends. AE, DC, MC, V. Closed Wed.*

$$ ▥ La Cittadella. This hotel is beautifully decorated and possesses every comfort. The accent is emphatically floral, from the dried flower arrangements to the frescoes and wallpaper, and there are even tasseled canopies over the beds. The management can arrange visits to local towns, though there are plenty of opportunities to relax on the premises. It's in a quiet location just outside the walls and represents very good value for the money. ⊠ *Via Monte Pertica 3, 35013,* ☎ *049/9402434,* ℻ *049/5975544. 26 rooms, 9 suites. Bar, breakfast room, indoor pool, sauna, gym, baby-sitting, parking (fee). AE, DC, MC, V.*

$$ ▥ La Filanda. A 19th-century spinning factory has been restored and adapted to house one of Cittadella's most stylish hotels, patronized by mostly businesspeople. You can still see the tall brick chimney and old machinery, but the interior is now bright, spacious, and furnished to a high standard. The restaurant (closed August) serves local and national dishes, in summer under a garden gazebo. ⊠ *Via Palladio 34, 35013,* ☎ *049/940000,* ℻ *049/9402111. 71 rooms. Restaurant, bar, hot tub, sauna, gym, squash. AE, DC, MC, V.*

Bassano del Grappa

❺ *13 km (8 mi) north of Cittadella, 76 km (47 mi) northwest of Venice.*

Beautifully positioned directly above the swift-flowing waters of the Brenta River at the foot of the Monte Grappa massif (5,880 ft), Bassano has old streets lined with low-slung buildings flanked by wooden balconies and pretty flowerpots. Bright ceramic wares produced here and in nearby Nove are displayed in shops along byways that curve uphill toward a centuries-old square, and, even higher, to a belvedere with a good view of Monte Grappa and part of the Val Sugana.

Bassano's most famous landmark is the **Ponte degli Alpini** (also called Ponte Vecchio), which has spanned the Brenta since the 13th century. Rebuilt countless times (floods are frequent), the present-day bridge is a postwar reconstruction using Andrea Palladio's 16th-century design. The great architect astutely chose to use wood as his medium, knowing that it could be replaced quickly and cheaply. For the best view, cross to the far side; then take Via Marcello and follow the *Veduta Panoramica* (panoramic view) sign. The bridge itself is named after the Alpini regiment who fought in the World War I campaigns on Monte Grappa and above Asiago and who were responsible for the present-day reconstruction. The small **Museo degli Alpini** documents this in the Taverna al Ponte. ⊠ *Via Angarono 2,* ☎ *0424/503662.* ▦ *Free.* ☾ *Tues.–Sun. 8–8.*

Almost as famous as the bridge is the liquor shop **Nardini** (✉ Ponte Vecchio 2, ☎ 0424/527741), right by the bridge, where grappa has been distilled for more than two centuries. Stop in for a sniff or a snifter. It's closed Monday October–May.

The center of town focuses on two adjacent squares, the Piazza Libertà and the Piazza Garibaldi. Most of the buildings date from the 16th century, a period of stability under Venetian rule. Looking down on the bustle of Piazza Garibaldi is the **Torre Civica,** once part of the earlier 13th-century defense system. Also dominating the piazza is the campanile of the Gothic church of **San Francesco,** which houses an interesting 13th-century wooden crucifix, on the arms of which are carved the sun and moon. The cloister of this church is home to the **Museo Civico,** whose downstairs section is devoted to archaeological finds, notably the Chini collection of 1st-century BC vases from Apulia, a good collection of 18th-century engravings, and theatrical memorabilia and costumes of the baritone Tito Gobbi (1913–84), who was a native of the town. Upstairs, the museum features paintings from three generations of the da Ponte family, predominantly Jacopo Bassano (1510–92). Note the dirty feet and wrinkled skin of the peasants in *The Adoration of the Shepherds,* a prosaic touch that heralded a new realism in Venetian painting. One room is devoted to the works of Canova; the library owns 2,000 of his drawings and 7,000 letters. ✉ *Piazza Garibaldi,* ☎ *0424/522235; 0424/523464 campanile.* ▨ *€6.20 includes Palazzo Sturm.* ☉ *Tues.–Sat. 9–noon and 3:30–6:30, Sun. 3:30–6:30; campanile daily 7–noon and 3–7.*

NEED A BREAK? A table set outside the **Bar Daniele** (✉ Piazza Garibaldi 39, ☎ 0424/529322) is a great place from which to watch life unfold on the piazza. It's closed Tuesday afternoon and Wednesday.

The museum's ceramics collection is to be found in the 18th-century **Palazzo Sturm,** on the river's east bank. Walk through the attractive courtyard, past frescoes by Giorgio Anselmi (1723–97), to view the town's famed majolica pieces including 17th-century Manardi ware and later ware from Nove and Faenza. ✉ *Via Ferracina 16,* ☎ *0424/524933.* ▨ *€3.60 includes Museo Civico.* ☉ *Apr.–Oct., Tues.–Sun. 9–12:30 and 3:30–6:30; Nov.–Mar., Fri. 9–12:30, weekends 3:30–6:30.*

Dining and Lodging

$$ ✕ **Al Sole.** You'll see whistling men astride animals in this restaurant. These hefty ceramic whistles, characteristic of the locality, were used by locals in bygone days to warn of the approach of enemies. In the two large dining areas, you can taste such dishes as *anitra al melograna* (duck with pomegranate, Torcolato wine, and rosemary), seasonal game, and white asparagus in season. ✉ *Via Jacopo Vittorelli 41/43,* ☎ *0424/523206. AE, DC, MC, V. Closed Mon. and July 15–Aug. 15.*

$$ ✕ **Trevisani.** A lovely 14th-century tower in the old walls of Bassano houses this restaurant, whose 17th-century interior is filled with a rich panoply of period decorations, all warmed by an open fireplace. Traditional local fare—radicchio, asparagus, mushrooms, and strawberries in summer—is incorporated in the classic cuisine, which features game, smoked meats, and a wide range of antipasti. The wine cellar has more than 120 varieties, and there's a busy *osteria* (tavern) attached, which also serves as the ticket office for the bus. Reservations are advised. ✉ *Piazzale Trento 13,* ☎ *0424/522201. AE, DC, MC, V. Closed Sun. and 2 wks in mid-Aug.*

$$–$$$ ⊞ **Belvedere.** This historic hotel has richly decorated public rooms with
★ period furnishings and Oriental rugs. A fireplace and piano music in
the lounge and an excellent restaurant with a garden make for a very
pleasant stay. The rooms are decorated in traditional Venetian or chic
contemporary style. ⊠ *Piazzale Giardino 14, 36061,* ☎ *0424/529845,*
FAX *0424/529849,* WEB *www.bonotto.it. 83 rooms, 4 suites. Restaurant.
AE, DC, MC, V.*

$–$$ ⊞ **Al Bassanello.** Established for more than 50 years this neat, white
hotel offers rooms furnished in a modern style with comfy candlewick
bedspreads and contemporary rugs on the tiled floor so your feet
won't get cold. ⊠ *Via Trozzetti 2, 36061,* ☎ *0424/35347,* FAX *0424/
35347. 12 rooms. Restaurant, bar. AE, DC, MC, V.*

Nightlife and the Arts

ROMAN FEASTS

Throughout the year, the dining group **Ristoratori Bassanesi** arranges
special dinners featuring either a traditional ingredient such as the white
asparagus or the whole works in a gala dinner. Contact the tourist office (☎ 0424/524351) or Promo Bassanopiù (☎ 0424/228651) for dates
and participating restaurants.

FESTIVALS

During July and August, Bassano stages the **Opera Estate Festival,** a
season of classical and jazz music, dance, opera, cinema, and theater.
Contact the tourist office or call ☎ 0424/524214 for information and
reservations. Ticket prices range from €4.15 for the cinema to €28.40
for the opera.

Shopping

There's a general market on Thursday and Saturday in Piazza Garibaldi
and surrounds.

CERAMICS

Bassano del Grappa and nearby Nove are the best bets for ceramic items.
A large number of shops in town feature wrought-iron and copper utensils, many made on the premises. **Luigi Parise** (⊠ Salita Ferracina 4,
☎ 0424/228359) sells hand-painted ceramics.

CLOTHING

Battista Cenere (⊠ 18–20 Via Giacomo da Ponte, ☎ 0424/523322)
sells a range of elegant contemporary clothing.

Marostica

❻ *18 km (11 mi) west of Asolo, 82 km (51 mi) northwest of Venice.*

Ruled by Venice between 1404 and 1797, Marostica exudes a powerful sense of history, immediately apparent at the first glimpse of its
formidable fortifications. From the **Castello Superiore,** perched on a
hill overlooking the surrounding countryside, the ramparts tier down
to enclose the main square and a second castle. The enclosed castle,
the **Castello Inferiore,** affords marvelous views from whichever direction. The castle was built by the Scaligeri family in the 13th century,
ousting the despotic Ezzelino III da Romano, who had taken over from
Ezzelino the Stutterer and Ezzelino the Monk. If you take a guided tour
of the castle, you'll see the oldest and largest ivy in Europe, which is
more than 420 years old, as well as a reconstructed catapult, the frescoed Sala del Consiglio, where the town council still meets, and the
costumes used for the historic chess game on which the fame of the
town rests. ⊠ *Piazza Castello,* ☎ *0424/72127.* ⛁ *€1.05.* ⊙ *Mon.–
Sat. 10–noon and 3:30–6, Sun. 3:30–6.*

The harmonious Piazza Castello is marked out in red and white stone checkerboard fashion and on the second weekend in September in even-numbered years is the venue for a human chess game, the **partita a scacchi.** In 1454, rival suitors for the hand of a fair maiden decided to fight it out, not by means of the sword but with chess pieces. Nowadays a set game is enacted to the accompaniment of solemn proclamations, fanfares, processions, and flag waving, with a total of 500 participants dressed in medieval garb and 20 horses in attendance, the whole thing culminating in a dramatized wedding ceremony. If you want to see it, have your tickets bought by June.

After you've admired the square, drop into the nearby hostelry, the **Osteria alla Madonetta** (⊠ Viale Vajenti 21), to see a model of Marostica, handmade in wood by the proprietor. It looks like a bed but is in fact a seating arrangement in which to play chess, using the miniature piazza as the board. Take a seat at the long, polished wood tables by the fireplace for a glass of Moscato wine, while absorbing the quaint charm of the clutter here. There's a ceramics shop next door at No. 23, **Alla Vecia Bottega** (☎ 0424/73674), where you can see the ceramicist in action and buy some of his wares. The 15th-century church **Sant' Antonio** contains a fine 16th-century altarpiece by the painter Jacopo Bassano. ⊠ *Via Sant'Antonio,* ☎ *0424/72007.* ☉ *Daily 8–11.*

Marostica's soil and climate conspire to produce Italy's most luscious cherries. During May and June, the square is covered with stalls selling Morello, Sandre, Roane, and Marostegane varieties.

Dining and Lodging

$$ ✕ **Al Castello Superiore.** This place is right in the hillside castle: wind up the corkscrew road and through the gate to be greeted by the stupendous view onto the square. There's a terrace for summer eating, and a fireplace and suits of armor for the winter. Try the *tagliatelle ai torresani* (pasta with pigeon sauce, sage, and onions) or the veal with asparagus. If you haven't tasted tiramisu, now's your chance. ⊠ *Via Consignorio della Scala,* ☎ *0424/73315. AE, DC, MC, V. Closed Wed., 3 wks in Jan., 1st wk in Feb., and 1 wk in mid-Aug. No lunch Thurs.*

$–$$ 🏨 **Europa.** In the heart of Marostica, this modern hotel is comfortably filled with reproduction antique furniture. The restaurant offers Spanish cuisine as well as cooking from the Veneto. ⊠ *Via Pizzamano 19, 36063,* ☎ *0424/77842,* 🅵🅰🆇 *0424/72480. 23 rooms. Restaurant, bar. AE, DC, MC, V.*

$ 🏨 **La Rosina.** With fabulous views, this quiet spot a couple of miles north of Marostica. The hotel is spic and span, with wooden furniture and polished parquet floors. The restaurant prides itself on the freshness of seasonal ingredients. ⊠ *Contrà Marchetti 4, 36063 Valle San Floriano,* ☎ *0424/470360,* 🅵🅰🆇 *0424/470290. 12 rooms. Restaurant, bar. AE, DC, MC, V. Closed Tues., Aug. 3–28, and Jan. 20–Feb. 4. No dinner Mon.*

Nightlife and the Arts

FESTIVALS

Marostica's game of **partita a scacchi** (human-scale chess) takes place on the second weekend in September in even-numbered years (tickets go on sale in April). For information, call Associazone Pro Marostica (☎ 0424/72127, 🅵🅰🆇 0424/72800). The **Sagra delle Ciliege** (Cherry Festival) is held on the last Sunday in May in the castle yard. Growers from the surrounding regions attend, and plenty of eating and drinking accompanies the revelry.

Shopping

Soffieria Parise (✉ Corso della Ceramica 18, ☎ 0424/470262), out of the center toward Nove, specializes in handblown glass.

Conegliano

❼ *28 km (17 mi) north of Treviso, 60 km (37 mi) northwest of Venice.*

Conegliano lies in the heart of wine-producing country, an attractive town with Venetian-style villas, frescoed houses, arcades, and cobbled streets. The walls that once girded the city did not succeed in repelling the series of assaults between the 12th and 14th centuries, when after being subjected to Padua, Treviso, Feltre, Belluno, the Carraresi, and Scaligeri families, the city finally declared its allegiance to Venice. It turned out to be a good move: Conegliano enjoyed nearly 300 years of peace and stability after the pact.

Shops, bars, and restaurants now line Conegliano's main street, the Via XX Settembre, housed in former palaces that bear witness to the Venetian influence. As well as being known as a thriving center of wine, prosecco in particular, Conegliano is also the birthplace of the painter Giambattista Cima (1460–1518), a follower of Giorgione who enjoyed great popularity in Venice.

The **Casa del Pittore Giambattista Cima,** the modest house where Cima died in 1517, contains reproductions of his paintings and some archaeological finds discovered when the house was restored. ✉ *Via Cima 24,* ☎ *0438/21660.* ⌑ *€1.55.* ☉ *Apr.–Sept., weekends 3:30–7; Oct.–Mar., weekends 3–6:30. At other times call 0438/34387 for an appointment.*

The 14th-century **Duomo** has an arcaded facade frescoed in the 16th century by Ludovico Pozzoserrato (1550–1603/05). Inside, Cima's 1493 masterpiece, *La Madonna in Trono e Santi,* graces the altar, as well as paintings by Palma the Younger (1548–1628) and frescoes by Pordenone (1484–1539). ✉ *Via XX Settembre,* ☎ *0438/22606.* ☉ *Daily 9–noon and 3–6.*

It's a steep walk up the cobbled Calle Madonna della Neve to the Castello, where you'll find the **Museo Civico** in the tower. It's full of local artifacts and memorabilia, some frescoes by Pordenone, and a good bronze by Giambologna (1529–1608). Make your way to the roof and you'll be rewarded with a fine view over the city to the gentle hills and their vines. ✉ *Piazzale San Leonardo,* ☎ *0438/22871.* ⌑ *€1.55.* ☉ *Apr.–Sept., Tues.–Sat. 10–12:30 and 3:30–7; Oct–Mar., Tues.–Sat. 10–12:30 and 3–6:30.*

The Duomo gives onto **Sala dei Battuti,** which was previously the meeting place for the Confraternità dei Flagellanti. It is covered with frescoes by Girolamo da Treviso (circa 1455–97) and Jacopo da Montagnana (15th century) among others. ✉ *Via XX Settembre,* ☎ *0438/ 22606.* ☉ *Sun. 10–12:30 and 3:30–7, or weekday mornings by appointment (find a parishioner).*

Dining and Lodging

$$–$$$ ✕ **Al Salisà.** Taking its name from the Venetian dialect word for a cobbled street, this restaurant is cool and fresh, with white walls and wrought-iron work. Fish ranks high on the menu and there's a good range of soups including minestrone and *minestra a base di riso e singole verdure* (clear broth with rice and vegetables). Reservations are advised in summer. ✉ *Via XX Settembre 2,* ☎ *0438/24288. AE, DC, MC, V. Closed Wed. and Aug. No dinner Tues.*

$$ ✕ **Città di Venezia.** It's no surprise to see the striped poles and lions in this restaurant, for it was here that the doges came on vacation. It is the oldest eating place in the town, with a 14th-century room with heavy beams across the ceiling and a terrace on the street. Try the sauce that is particular to this area—*saor* (onions marinated in vinegar and fried with sultanas and pine nuts). Reservations are advised. ⊠ *Via XX Settembre 77/79,* ☎ *0438/23186. AE, DC, MC, V. Closed Mon. and Aug. 10–31. No dinner Sun.*

$ ✕ **Al Bacareto.** You sit in little wooden compartments in this little osteria, where the jovial owner will recite the menu (in English) that includes hearty soups, fish choices, and local beer. ⊠ *Via Cavour 6,* ☎ *0438/411666. No credit cards. Closed Mon.*

$$ ⊞ **Canon d'Oro.** The town's oldest inn, the Canon d'Oro is in an arcaded and frescoed 16th-century building in a central location near the train station. The antique furniture, lovely bed linen, and terraced garden all add to its charm. The restaurant's decor provides a soothing ambience in which to appreciate the good food, mainly regional specialties such as risotto, *Canon d'Oro gnocchi* (gnocchi with a rich meat sauce), baccalà alla vicentina, and *fegato alla veneziana* (liver with onions). ⊠ *Via XX Settembre 129, 31015,* ☎ *0438/34246,* FAX *0438/ 34246. 35 rooms. Restaurant, bar. AE, MC, V.*

$ ⊞ **Sporting Hotel Ragno d'Oro.** Just out of the center amid the greenery of the Parco Rocca, this modern hotel offers generous facilities for relaxing or exercising. There's an 8-km (5-mi) running course nearby, if all that good Italian food and wine has gone to your waistline. Guest rooms are plain and wood-paneled. ⊠ *Via Diaz 37, 31015,* ☎ *0438/ 412300,* FAX *0438/412310. 17 rooms. Bar, pool, sauna, 2 tennis courts. AE, DC, MC, V.*

Nightlife and the Arts

Musical and literary events take place each weekend in September, leading up to the **Dama Castellana** on the first weekend in October—a human chess match in celebration of victory over Treviso in 1241. Processions, flag-waving, and fireworks accompany the proceedings.

Shopping

For gifts, **Follies** (⊠ Via Beato Ongaro 5, ☎ 0438/21201) has a wide selection of antiques and craftwork. **Ornamenta** (⊠ Via Beato Ongaro 7, ☎ 0438/35527) carries local crafts and antiques.

Valdobbiadene

❽ *36 km (22 mi) north of Treviso, 66 km (41 mi) northwest of Venice.*

If you're following the Prosecco Wine Road, Valdobbiadene will be your end destination. As you wind your way through the hills, the vines practically creep up onto the road.

The pasticceria **Emilio Carnia** (⊠ Viale Vittoria 1, ☎ 0423/972209), established as a family-run business since 1935, also doubles as a wine shop. Signor Carnia, the versatile pastry maker, not only makes excellent biscuits and pastries but chooses the grapes for the prestigious Cartizze prosecco wine. The terrace will tempt you to indulge in a breakfast croissant, a Mozart *plait* (a kind of biscuit), or an evening aperitif before continuing on your way. It's closed Wednesday.

Dining and Lodging

$$ ✕ **Alla Vecia Hostaria.** In this simple and homey trattoria you might be given a tour of the kitchen to see Mamma cooking the day's specialty. It could be *strozzapretti* (gnocchi with spinach), duck with brandy and onion, or venison with rosemary. Start your meal with very fresh salami to the accompaniment of nonna's homemade pickles, and finish with a swig or two of the white grappa. ⊠ *Via Piva 60,* ☎ *0423/ 973867. No credit cards. Closed Sun.*

$ ☷ **Diana.** The warm hues of the exposed stone walls and tiled floor of this modern hotel set off the discreet lighting and colorful rugs. The large, airy restaurant has an impressive trussed wooden roof under which to dine. Service is courteous. ⊠ *Via Roma 49, 31049,* ☎ *0423/976222,* ℻ *0423/972237. 47 rooms. Restaurant, bar, parking. AE, MC, V.*

Vittorio Veneto

⑨   *14 km (7 mi) north of Conegliano, 70 km (43 mi) northwest of Venice.*

Vittorio Veneto owes its name to the unification of Italy in 1866 and its first king, Vittorio Emanuele II. The two towns of Ceneda and Serravalle were joined to form Vittorio Veneto, with a new town hall and train station built between them. The town extends along the main road, with Ceneda, the commercial center, in the south. To the north, Serravalle is the historic quarter enclosed within a gorge that sports a more Alpine feel. After Serravalle's annexation to Venice in 1337 it became an important economic center and money market, with one of the largest Jewish communities in the north of Italy.

Although Serravalle is by far the more attractive of the two parts, Ceneda does have two sights, the first of which is the church of **Santa Maria del Meschio,** which holds a heavenly *Annunciation* by Andre Previtali (circa 1470–1528). ⊠ *Piazza Meschio,* ☎ *0438/53581.* ⊙ *Daily 8– noon and 3–7.*

The second is the **Museo della Battaglia,** dedicated to the Battle of Vittorio, which in 1918 marked the final engagement of the Italian army in World War I. It is housed in the graceful **Loggia del Cenedese,** which is attributed to Jacopo Sansovino (1486–1570). ⊠ *Piazza Giovanni Paolo I,* ☎ *0438/57695.* ▨ *€2.55 includes Museo del Cenedese and San Lorenzo dei Battuti.* ⊙ *May–Sept., Tues.–Sun. 10–noon and 4–6:30; Oct.–Apr., Tues.–Sun. 10–noon and 2–5.*

Franco Zeffirelli was so taken by Serravalle that he used it as a location for his 1970s film *Romeo and Juliet,* and indeed its charm rests on the fact that nothing much has changed since the 16th century. Via Martiri della Libertà leads up to the main square in Serravalle, lined with 15th- and 16th-century buildings and ending at the Loggia Serravalle, a fine building emblazoned with shields. It's now the home of the **Museo del Cenedese.** This collection contains local archaeological bits and pieces, minor paintings, and frescoes. ⊠ *Piazza Flaminio,* ☎ *0438/57103.* ▨ *€2.55 includes Museo della Battaglia and San Lorenzo dei Battuti.* ⊙ *May–Sept., Tues.–Sun. 10–noon and 4–6:30; Oct.– Apr., Tues.–Sun. 10–noon and 3–7.*

The church of **San Lorenzo dei Battuti** houses an excellent fresco cycle painted in the mid-15th century. The damage suffered when Napoléon's men used the church as a kitchen has since been rectified. ⊠ *Piazza Vecellio,* ☎ *0438/57103.* ▨ *€2.55 includes Museo della Battaglia and Museo del Cenedese.* ⊙ *May–Oct., Wed.–Mon. 10–noon and 4:30– 6:30; Nov.–Apr., Wed.–Mon. 10–noon and 3–7.*

Crossing the river Meschio from Piazza Flaminio, you come to the **Duomo,** notable for its Titian altarpiece *The Virgin with S. Peter and S. Andrew.* ⊠ *Piazza Giovanni Paolo I,* ☎ *0438/53401.* ⊙ *May– Sept., daily 6:30–noon and 2:30–7:30; Oct.–Apr., daily 6:30–noon and 2:30–6:30.*

Dining and Lodging

$$ ✕ **Taverna da Peo.** You'll get a good meal served at plain wooden tables in this bustling osteria-cum-trattoria. Typical Veneto cooking is seasonal and comes in the form of fegato alla veneziana or *salsiccetta con polenta* (sausage and polenta). Service is friendly. ⊠ *Via Martiri della Libertà 25,* ☎ *0438/554930. DC, MC, V. Closed Tues., 2nd and 3rd wks Jan., last wk in June, and 1st wk in July. No dinner Mon.*

$–$$ ✕ **Locanda al Postiglione.** A post office in the time of Emperor Franz Josef, this hotel preserves its 18th-century atmosphere with beamed ceilings and wooden paneling. The menu changes daily. Regional dishes prevail, but the choice extends wider to encompass international dishes, too. Noteworthy are the *lumache* (snails) and smoked meats. Fish is served on Thursday and Friday. ⊠ *Via Cavour 39,* ☎ *0438/556924. AE, DC, MC, V. Closed Tues. and July 20–Aug. 10.*

$$ ☷ **Terme.** Service is courteous in this modern hotel that looks out over a garden at the back. The restaurant places an emphasis on seasonal greenery, wild mushrooms, and berries. ⊠ *Via delle Terme 4, 31029,* ☎ *0438/554345,* ℻ *0438/554347. 39 rooms. Restaurant, bar. AE, MC, V.*

$ ☷ **Hotel Flora.** This small and functional hotel built at the beginning of the 20th century is situated by the public garden in town center. It has a good fish restaurant with a terrace for summer eating and an open fire in winter. ⊠ *Viale Trento Trieste 28, 31029,* ☎ *0438/53625,* ℻ *0438/941440. 21 rooms. Restaurant, bar. AE, DC, MC, V.*

Outdoor Activities and Sports

Tennis Club (⊠ Via Cadore 13, Località Anzano, ☎ 0438/53422) has three uncovered courts and one covered, open 10 to midnight in summer and noon to midnight in winter.

Shopping

Distilleria de Negri (⊠ Via Martiri della Libertà 43, ☎ no phone), closed Wednesday, has a large stock of grappa. **Tochetti** (⊠ Via Martiri dei Libertà, ☎ 0438/450025) is good for a range of fresh mountain cheeses.

THE DOLOMITES

Turn northward to enter one of Italy's grandest mountain landscapes, an exhilarating land of lush, flower-laden meadows cut through by lakes and river valleys. The towns of Belluno and Feltre lie on the mighty Piave River, the first of these a relatively neglected holiday destination dramatically sited against the jagged mountain backdrop. Feltre, a walled city perched high on a ridge with stunning views, reveals some unexpected examples of Renaissance architecture. For a more glamorous aspect of the Alps, repair to the ritzy Cortina d'Ampezzo ski resort. The scenery around Cortina is as good as anything you'll find in these mountains and can be just as scintillating in summer as in the winter months, and certainly more accessible for rambling through. The rich and creamy food here, including fondues, polentas, and barley soups, reflects the Alpine climate and Austrian and Swiss influence; there are a number of dishes unique to the zone, such as *schiz*—fresh cheese that is sliced and fried in butter, sometimes with cream added, great for your cholesterol level.

Belluno

❿ *78 km (49 mi) north of Treviso, 108 km (67 mi) north of Venice.*

The Dolomites set the mood in Belluno, spread out over a plateau above the junction of the Piave and Ardo rivers. It's the northernmost town of the Veneto and, given its strategic position, prospered as an ally of Venice. Now a provincial capital and busy commercial center, the city attracts a few tourists, though most prefer to stay higher up within the mountain range, so Belluno's hotels are fairly quiet. You could spend a rewarding half day wandering around the old town, and there are some good spots for lunch. It's best to park on the lower side near the river and take the escalator up, enjoying the panorama as you go.

Take a stroll along the impressively broad main square, **Piazza dei Martiri,** complete with a grove of evergreens and bordered on one side by a unified row of arcaded palazzi. To the south lies the Piazza del Duomo, where the pale-ocher **Duomo,** first built in the 16th century to a design of Tullio Lombardo (1455–1532), had to be rebuilt after two earthquakes, once in 1873 and again in 1936. Inside there are 16th-century paintings by Jacopo Bassano. Next to it, topped by a green onion-shape cupola, stands the tall campanile, Belluno's most prominent monument, built in the 18th century by the Sicilian architect and stage designer Filippo Juvara (1678–1736). ✉ *Piazza del Duomo,* ☎ *0437/941908.* ⊘ *Daily 7–noon and 3–7.*

The **Palazzo dei Rettori,** an ornate 15th-century building with Baroque touches, seat of the Venetian governors and now an administrative building, fills one side of the square. The best view from the town can be had if you head for the **Porta Ruga** at the end of the main street, Via Mezzaterra.

NEED A BREAK?

For interesting contemporary art in situ it's worth a visit to the **café** under the Albergo Centrale (✉ Via Loreto 2/a, ☎ 0437/943349). The artist-owner has molded each chair and table into a sculpture, either in an abstract or concrete form in primary colors, as bright as the candies in the jars on the shelves.

The **Museo Civico,** housed in a 17th-century palazzo, has a good collection of work by the locally born painters Sebastiano Ricci (1659–1734) and Marco Ricci (1679–1729), and the sculptor Andrea Brustolon (1662–1732). ✉ *Piazza del Duomo 16,* ☎ *0437/944836.* 🖾 *€2.05.* ⊘ *Apr.–Oct., Tues.–Sun. 10–noon and 3–6.*

Dining and Lodging

$$ ✕ **Al Borgo.** Cross the river to find this lovely rustic restaurant, an 18th-century villa in a park colored in shades of terra-cotta, green, and cream. The chef uses wild herbs and greenery from the mountains, whatever's in season. Spring might produce risotto *selvatico e lupolo* (with hops and herbs), while in summer you can find gnocchi with *zucca* (pumpkin) and lamb with rosemary. On rare occasions you might be offered *pinza da noze,* a traditional wedding cake made with ricotta cheese. ✉ *Via Anconetta 8,* ☎ *0437/926755. Reservations essential. AE, DC, MC, V. Closed Tues. and last 2 wks in Jan. No dinner Mon.*

$$ ✕ **Terracotta.** This plain but elegant little restaurant likes to provide both traditional and inventive Bellunese dishes such as *formai schiz e rösti di patate* (cheese and roasted potatoes) as well as more exotic fare such as Indonesian and Malayan, with music to match the type of cuisine. You're likely to find a youngish clientele, and there are memorable vistas across to the mountains from the candlelit terrace, open on summer evenings. ✉ *Via Garibaldi 61,* ☎ *0437/942644. MC, V. Closed Sat. lunch and Sun..*

$ 🏨 **Alle Dolomiti.** This is an adequate if unexceptional hotel, with simple rooms. Don't let the numerous photographs of famous Italian actors and personalities raise your expectations, whatever the grande dame of the establishment would have you believe. ✉ *Via Carrera 46, 32100,* ☎ *0437/941660,* ℻ *0437/941436. 32 rooms. Bar. AE, DC, MC, V.*

Feltre

⑪ *31 km (19 mi) east of Belluno, 88 km (55 mi) northwest of Venice.*

Approaching along one of the river valleys below the town, you'll soon see the mellow tones of Feltre's historic center rearing above you on its narrow fortified ridge. To reach the old quarter, either wend your way up the main cobbled street from the modern zone, or opt for the steeper but more rewarding toil up one of the various flights of stone steps that thread up through the old town. Either way, you'll be stepping back into the 16th century, when Venice had Feltre almost completely rebuilt after it was sacked in 1509 by the League of Cambrai, as punishment for the town's allegiance to La Serenissima.

Via Mezzaterra, marked by gates at either end, is lined with harmonious houses, many of which are adorned with frescoes by Lorenzo Luzzo (died 1526), the town's best-known painter, who bore the unfortunate nickname of "Il Morto da Feltre" (the Dead Man of Feltre) due to his pallid complexion. Midway along, the road pans out into the **Piazza Maggiore,** the main square that holds the medieval **Castello** and the **Palazzo della Ragione,** with its Palladian portico. Here you can see the frescoed Sala Consiglio and the little wooden theater, La Scena, rebuilt in 1802 by Gian Antonio Selva, the designer of La Fenice in Venice. Call the Museo Civico for visiting hours.

Via Mezzaterra continues into Via Luzzo to the **Museo Civico,** containing a collection of paintings by Luzzo including his *Madonna with S. Vitus and S. Modestus,* as well as a portrait by Gentile Bellini (1429–1546) and a triptych by Cima da Conegliano (1460–1518). Luzzo's masterpiece, a *Transfiguration,* is housed in the sacristy of the **Chiesa di Ognissanti.** ✉ *Via Lorenzo Luzzo 23,* ☎ *0439/885242.* 🎟 *€4.15.* ☉ *Tues.–Sat. 10–1 and 3–6.*

In the street parallel to Via Mezzaterra, the **Galleria d'Arte Moderna Carlo Rizzarda** has wrought-iron work on display, mostly by Carlo Rizzarda (1883–1931), whose decorative pieces reveal Liberty, art nouveau, and Art Deco influences. In 1929 Rizzarda presented the town with his collection and his house. ✉ *Via Paradiso 8,* ☎ *0439/885234.* 🎟 *€1.55.* ☉ *June–Sept., Tues.–Sun. 10–1 and 4–7.*

At the bottom of the 16th-century stairway that leads down from Piazza Maggiore you'll reach the Porta Pusterla and the **Duomo** with its baptistery. Look for the 6th-century carved Byzantine cross inside the much-altered 15th-century cathedral. ✉ *Piazza del Duomo,* ☎ *0439/2312.* ☉ *Daily 8–noon and 3–7.*

Dining and Lodging

$$ ✗ **Hostaria Novecento.** In the heart of the old town, Signor Cuman places the emphasis on seafood. Try the marinated fish as a starter and follow it with *sgoda con funduta e porcini* (soft polenta with cheese fondue and mushrooms) or *salmone con pepe verde* (salmon with green pepper). The surroundings are intimate and elegant, with copper decorations decking out a 15th-century building and a summer garden. ✉ *Via Mezzaterra 24,* ☎ *0439/80193. MC, V. Closed Mon.*

$–$$ 🏨 **Doriguzzi.** This is a functional hotel on the main road into town with light wooden furniture and big comfy armchairs. Service is friendly and obliging. ✉ *Viale Piave 2, 32032,* ☎ *0439/2003,* ℻ *0439/83660. 23 suites. Restaurant, bar. AE, DC, MC, V.*

$ ⊞ **Nuovo.** This is a small, modern hotel near the river in town center. An open fireplace crackles in winter; in summer relax in the garden or on the terrace. The rooms are light and airy and full of plants, though some of the bedroom furniture has seen better days. The management is cheerful and hospitable. ✉ *Via Fornere Pazze 5, 32032,* ☎ *0439/ 2110,* ⅢX *0439/89241. 23 rooms. Bar. AE, DC, MC, V.*

Pieve di Cadore

⑫ *43 km (27 mi) north of Belluno, 130 km (81 mi) northwest of Venice.*

The Cadore region of the Dolomites extends as far as the Austrian frontier. Pope John Paul II has vacationed in the area for years, as do many other overheated city folk, though it does not have the feel of a tourist zone. The region's most important artistic center, Pieve di Cadore, is small, scenic, set on a hill, and quickly explored. A bronze statue of Pieve's most illustrious son, the painter Titian (circa 1480–1576) guards the **Casa di Tiziano,** where he was born. It's furnished as in Titian's time but contains nothing of his. ✉ *Via Arsenale,* ☎ *0435/32262.* 🎫 *€2.55 includes admission to the Museo dell'Occhiale.* ☉ *Mid-June– mid-Sept., Tues.–Sun. 9:30–12:30 and 4–7; other times by appointment.*

The **Museo dell'Occhiale** claims to be the only one of its kind in the world. It exhibits more than 2,000 glasses (spectacles) from medieval times to the present day, including the earliest French, English, and Chinese models and the first pair of sunglasses, used by the 18th-century Venetian dramatist Carlo Goldoni. ✉ *Via degli Alpini 39,* ☎ *0435/ 500213.* 🎫 *€2.55.* ☉ *Sept.–June, Mon.–Sat. 8:30–12:30; July–Aug., Mon.–Sat. 8:30–12:30 and 4:30–7:30.*

The pretty church of **Parrochiale di Santa Maria Nascente** was completed in the early 19th century and the mosaicked facade dates from 1876. Inside, the Titian altarpiece in the Cappella di San Tiziano is said to bear likenesses of the painter's family, his daughter Lavinia representing the Virgin Mary and his son Pomponio Bishop Tiziano. ✉ *Piazza Tiziano 41,* ☎ *0435/32261.* ☉ *Daily 8–noon and 3–6.*

If you're here before Christmas, drop a note at the **Casa di Babbo Natale** (House of Father Christmas) on the nearby hill of Montericco and maybe Father Christmas will bring you what you've asked for.

Dining and Lodging

$$$ ✕ **La Chiusa.** It may be the secluded position in a hillside copse that
★   entices you here, or the smell of the wood smoke in winter. Within, the ceiling beams are tree trunks and the wood paneling is imported from Turkey and Pakistan. But the star attraction is the fare itself. The genial Benito Perismascietti subscribes to the slow-food philosophy and positively encourages you to linger over your victuals (he has a poem in the menu to this effect). Indeed this is not difficult: here you can enjoy pasta stuffed with potatoes, walnuts, and sage, or carrot dumplings with a cream and arugula sauce. This gourmet heaven is 20 km (12 mi) southeast of Cortina and 10 km (6 mi) west from Pieve di Cadore on the SS51. ✉ *Località La Chiusa, Ruvignan, Vodo di Cadore,* ☎ *0435/489288. Reservations essential. AE, DC, MC, V. Closed Mon., 2 wks in late May–early June, 1st 2 wks in Oct.*

$ ⊞ **Villa Marinotti.** This lovely wooden chalet set on a gentle slope was once a private home, now converted into suites, and there are a pair of bungalows on the grounds. All the accommodations are beautifully furnished with a luxuriously light and spacious feel. In winter there's a *fogher* (open fireplace). It makes an ideal center for walking, horseback riding, and fishing. The gracious and hospitable owner speaks excellent English. ✉ *Via Manzago 21, Tai di Cadore, 32040,* ☎ *0435/*

32231, FAX *0435/33335. 4 suites, 2 bungalows. Restaurant, sauna, tennis court. AE, DC, MC, V.*

Outdoor Activities and Sports

BIKING

From June to September, mountain bikes can be rented from **Dynamic Line** (⊠ Via XX Settembre 63, Valle di Cadore, ☎ 0435/519260).

FISHING

Permits can be bought from **Cadore Sport Camping** (⊠ Via Cortina 63/65, Pieve di Cadore, ☎ 0435/30251).

HORSEBACK RIDING

Contact **Agriturismo di Masi Alessandro** (⊠ Via Campo Sportivo, Vallsella di Domegge, ☎ 0435/7284).

TENNIS

Courts (⊠ Via Arsenale, ☎ 0435/31363) can be booked.

WALKING

For walking trips, contact **Gruppo CAI di Pieve di Cadore** (⊠ Località Valcalda, ☎ 0435/31515).

Cortina d'Ampezzo

★ ⑬ *30 km (19 mi) northwest of Pieve de Cadore, 155 km (97 mi) northwest of Venice.*

"The Pearl of the Dolomites" is set in a lush meadow 4,000 ft above sea level. Dense forests adjoin the town, and mountains encircle the whole valley. The town sprawls on the slopes along a fast-moving stream; a public park extends along one bank. Luxury hotels and the villas of the rich are conspicuously scattered over the slopes above the town—identifiable by their attempts to hide behind stands of firs and spruces.

The bustling center of Cortina d'Ampezzo has little nostalgia for old-time atmosphere, despite its Alpine appearance. The tone is set by elegant shops and stylish cafés, as opulent as their well-dressed patrons, whose corduroy pants may well have been tailored by Armani. Don't look for authentic Tyrolean gemütlichkeit here: Cortina is the place for a whiff of the heady aromas of wealth and sophistication and retains a more Italian feel than some of its German-speaking Alto Adige neighbors.

Dining and Lodging

$$$–$$$$ ✕ **De la Poste.** There are two lively restaurants in the exclusive De la Poste hotel on Cortina's main square. There's a refined, high-ceilinged main dining room with three big chandeliers where you can dine on soufflés and nouvelle-cuisine dishes (every Friday fresh fish is served). There's also a more informal grill room with wood paneling and the family pewter collection. ⊠ *Piazza Roma 14,* ☎ *0436/4271,* WEB *www. hotels.cortina.it/delaposte. Reservations essential. Jacket and tie in dining room. AE, DC, MC, V.*

$$$ ✕ **Leone e Anna.** Decorated in Sardinian style in dusky pink, with leather sofas, this warm and welcoming restaurant specializes in Sard cuisine. To be recommended are spaghetti *alla bottarga* (pasta with tuna eggs seasoned with oil and lemon), *porceddu alla sarda* (roast piglet with raw seasoned vegetables), and the homemade Sard desserts. ⊠ *Via Alverà 112,* ☎ *0436/2768. Reservations essential. AE, DC, MC, V. Closed Tues., May–June, and Nov.*

$$ ✕ **Tavernetta.** Near the Olympic ice-skating rink, this popular restaurant has an authentic Tyrolean ambience, with wood-paneled dining rooms and a local clientele. Here you can try Cortina specialties such as *zuppa di porcini* (wild mushroom soup), ravioli *di cervo* (stuffed with

venison), and game. ⊠ *Via dello Stadio 27/a,* ☎ *0436/867494. AE, DC, MC, V. Closed mid-June–mid-July, Nov., and Wed. No lunch Thurs. in May and Sept.*

$$$$ 🏨 **Miramonti Majestic.** This imposing and luxurious hotel, more than a century old, has a magnificent mountain valley location about 1 km (½ mi) south of town. A touch of old-world formality accompanies the imperial Austrian design. There's always a roaring fire in the cozy bar, and the hotel's recreation rooms are framed by plate-glass windows overlooking mountain vistas. The history of Cortina is intricately tied into the Miramonti, and you'll feel a part of it all here. ⊠ *Località Peziè 103, 32043,* ☎ *0436/4201,* 𝔽𝔸𝕏 *0436/867019,* 𝖶𝖤𝖡 *http://cortina.dolomiti. org/hmiramonti. 105 rooms. Restaurant, pool, sauna, golf course, tennis court, gym. AE, DC, MC, V. Closed Easter–June and Sept. 15– Dec. 20.*

$$$ 🏨 **De la Poste.** Skiers who want to see and be seen return year after year to this lively hotel, one of Cortina's social centers. The hotel has been under the same family management since 1826, and the furnishings feature antiques in characteristic Dolomite style. Almost all rooms have wooden balconies. In winter, the hotel offers pricier half-board plans only. ⊠ *Piazza Roma 62, 32043,* ☎ *0436/4271,* 𝔽𝔸𝕏 *0436/ 868435,* 𝖶𝖤𝖡 *www.hotels.cortina.it/delaposte. 83 rooms. Restaurant, bar. AE, DC, MC, V. Closed mid-Apr.–mid-June and mid-Oct.– mid-Dec.*

Nightlife and the Arts

At **Europa** hotel (⊠ Corso Italia 207, ☎ 0436/3221) you can expect to mingle with the couture set at the VIP disco; nonguests are welcome, but don't expect to spend less than €25.85.

Outdoor Activities and Sports

The tourist office (⊠ Piazzetta San Francesco 8, 32043 Cortina d'Ampezzo, ☎ 0436/3231, 𝔽𝔸𝕏 0436/3235) will supply information about hiking paths and a good trail map.

Cortina d'Ampezzo has downhill slopes to challenge all levels of skiers. The most impressive views (and steepest slopes) in town are on **Monte Cristallo,** based at **Misurina.** The **Faloria** gondola runs from the center of town. From its top, you can get up to most of the other central mountains. Farther out of town, don't miss the **Cinque Torri** and **Passo Falzarego** runs either. All runs are covered by the **Dolomiti Superski** pass (☎ 0471/795397, 𝖶𝖤𝖡 www.dolomitisuperski.com), good for the entire region.

NORTHERN VENETO A TO Z

To research prices, get advice from other travelers, and book travel arrangements, visit www.fodors.com.

AIRPORTS AND TRANSFERS

Treviso's Aeroporto San Giuseppe is also served by charter flights. Flights to Treviso usually include transportation from the airport to Venice or other destinations; otherwise there is an ATVO local bus service to Treviso every 30 minutes during the day, or a taxi will come from Treviso, only 6 km (4 mi) away, to pick you up. However, most people still fly into Venice's Aeroporto Marco Polo.

➤ AIRPORT INFORMATION: **Aeroporto San Giuseppe** (⊠ 5 km [3 mi] southeast of Treviso, 32 km [19 mi] north of Venice, ☎ 0422/315131).
➤ TAXIS AND SHUTTLES: **Taxi** (☎ 0422/431515).

BUS TRAVEL TO AND FROM TREVISO

Taking one of the frequent ACTV buses from Venice will bring you to Treviso in a half hour. An equally frequent service runs from Padua with La Marca.

FARES AND SCHEDULES

➤ BUS INFORMATION: **ACTV** (✉ Piazzale Roma, Venice, ☎ 041/5287886). **La Marca** (✉ Lungosile Mattei 29, Treviso, ☎ 0422/412222).

BUS TRAVEL WITHIN TREVISO AND THE DOLOMITES

More so than elsewhere in the boot, bus is a reasonable choice in the Dolomites. La Marca has connections throughout the province including the Conegliano bus station. From Bassano del Grappa FTV runs hourly buses to Marostica and Vicenza. ACTM serves Asolo, Maser, and Possagno. The Dolomites are served by Dolomiti Bus. Buses run frequently between Conegliano and Valdobbiadene along the Prosecco Wine Road.

FARES AND SCHEDULES

➤ BUS INFORMATION: **ACTM** (☎ 0424/522201). **Conegliano Bus Station** (✉ Piazza Fili Zoppas, ☎ 0438/21011). **Dolomiti Bus** (✉ Piazzale Stazione, Belluno, ☎ 0437/941237). **FTV** (✉ Piazzale Trento, ☎ 0424/30850). **La Marca** (✉ Lungosile Mattei 29, Treviso, ☎ 0422/412222).

CAR RENTAL

CUTTING COSTS

➤ LOCAL AGENCIES: **Avis** (✉ c/o Garage Cima, Conegliano, ☎ 0438/34687). **Europcar Italia** (✉ Via Noalese, Treviso, ☎ 0422/23396). **Hertz** (✉ Via di Salce 5/a, Belluno, ☎ 0437/915140; ✉ c/o ACI, Largo delle Poste 53, Cortina d'Ampezzo, ☎ 0436/86092; ✉ Via Trevigiana 1, Feltre, ☎ 0439/80373; ✉ Piazza S. Pio X, Treviso, ☎ 0422/411311).

CAR TRAVEL

If you're heading from Venice, the SS11 connects with Mestre, from where the SS13 leads due north to Treviso. The autostrada A4 runs north of Mestre and continues north of Belluno. From Padua, the SS47 goes north to Bassano del Grappa.

Westward from Treviso, it's a straight run on the SS53 to Castelfranco and Cittadella. The SS47 connects Cittadella with Bassano del Grappa. Joining the autostrada A27 at Treviso Nord takes you as far as Belluno. The SS51 heads up to Pieve di Cadore following the River Piave, and then northwest to Cortina d'Ampezzo. The SS13 and SS51 connect Treviso with Conegliano and Vittorio Veneto.

ROAD CONDITIONS

Beware: wind and snow conditions in the region can be treacherous at times in the winter.

EMERGENCIES

For first aid, ask for *pronto soccorso,* and be prepared to give your address. All pharmacies post signs on the door with addresses of *farmacie di turno* (pharmacies taking shifts), which stay open at night, on Saturday afternoon, and on Sunday.

➤ EMERGENCY SERVICES: **Ambulance, Police, and Fire** (☎ 113). **First aid** (☎ 118).

➤ HOSPITALS: **Bassano del Grappa** (Ospedale Civile, ✉ Via dei Lotti 40, ☎ 0424/888111). **Belluno** (Ospedale Civile, ✉ Viale Europa, ☎ 0437/216111). **Treviso** (Ospedale Generale, ✉ Viale Vittorio Veneto

18, ☎ 0422/4281). **Vittorio Veneto** (Ospedale Civile, ⊠ Via Forlanini, ☎ 0438/5671).

TOURS

Contact the tourist office at Castelfranco for tours of the town. Free guided tours of Feltre are offered on weekends in summer from 10 to 1 and 4 to 7 and at other times by appointment. Call the number listed below Tuesday through Friday between 9:30 and 10:30 AM for information. Vichival Tour will arrange a gastronomic or cultural tour of the Treviso area.

➤ FEES AND SCHEDULES: **Feltre Tours** (☎ 0439/83879). **Vichival Tour** (⊠ Via Piva 76, 31049 Valdobbiadene, ☎ 0423/976322).

TRAIN TRAVEL

The Treviso train station lies on the FS line from Venice to Udine. Trains run several times an hour, and the journey takes half an hour. The FS line connects Treviso with Castelfranco, Cittadella, and Conegliano. On the Padua–Belluno line you pass through Castelfranco and Feltre. Bassano del Grappa has frequent trains to Cittadella, Venice, and Padua. Belluno connects with Conegliano and Padua. The nearest station to Cortina d'Ampezzo is at Calalzo, 32 km (19 mi) southeast, from where there are frequent connecting buses.

FARES AND SCHEDULES
➤ TRAIN INFORMATION: **FS** (☎ 147/888088). **Treviso Train Station** (⊠ Piazzale Duca d'Aosta, ☎ 0422/542976).

TRAVEL AGENCIES

➤ LOCAL AGENTS: **Agenzia Esprit Tour** (⊠ Viale d'Alviano 52, 31100 Treviso, ☎ 0422/410999). **ASVI** (⊠ Piazza Martiri 27/e, 32100 Belluno, ☎ 0437/941746). **Cadore** (⊠ Via XX Settembre 18, 32044 Pieve di Cadore, ☎ 0435/31644). **Dynamic Tour** (⊠ Corso Italia 185, 32043 Cortina d'Ampezzo, ☎ 0436/867130). **Giorgione** (⊠ Piazza Giorgione 46, 31033 Castelfranco, ☎ 0423/493601). **Grizzly Viaggi** (⊠ Piazzale Parmeggiani 23, 32032 Feltre, ☎ 0437/942726, WEB www. grizzlyviaggi.it). **Viaggi Montegrappa** (⊠ Via Giuseppe Barbieri 40, 36061 Bassano del Grappa, ☎ 0424/523007).

VISITOR INFORMATION

➤ TOURIST INFORMATION: **Tourist Offices** (⊠ Piazza Gabriele D'Annunzio 2, 31011 Asolo, ☎ 0423/529046, FAX 0423/524137; ⊠ Largo Corona d'Italia, 36061 Bassano del Grappa, ☎ 0424/524351, FAX 0424/525301; ⊠ Piazza dei Martiri 7, 32100 Belluno, ☎ 0437/940083, FAX 0437/940073; ⊠ Via Francesco Maria Preti 39, 31033 Castelfranco, ☎ 0423/495000, FAX 0423/720760; ⊠ Via Marconi 5, 31033 Cittadella, ☎ FAX 049/5970627; ⊠ Via Colombo 45, 31015 Conegliano, ☎ 0438/21230, FAX 0438/428777; ⊠ Piazzetta San Francesco 8, 32043 Cortina d'Ampezzo, ☎ 0436/3231, FAX 0436/3235; ⊠ Piazzetta Trento e Trieste 9, 32032 Feltre, ☎ 0439/2540, FAX 0439/2839; ⊠ Piazza Castello, 32032 Marostica, ☎ 0424/72127, FAX 0424/72800; ⊠ Piazza Venetia 20, 32040 Tai di Cadore, ☎ 0435/31644, FAX 0435/31645; ⊠ Piazzetta del Monte di Pietà, 31100 Treviso, ☎ 0422/547632, FAX 0422/419092; ⊠ Piazza del Popolo 18, 31029 Vittorio Veneto, ☎ 0438/ 57243, FAX 0438/53629).

9 FRIULI-VENEZIA GIULIA

Tucked away in Italy's northeastern corner, Friuli-Venezia Giulia is off most tourist tracks and gains as a result. It's a packed wedge of extremes, from the green, mountainous region of Carnia to the ragged coast of the Golfo di Trieste, a hodgepodge of cultures and climates, marched through, fought over, hymned by patriots and poets, and scene of war atrocities. The capital is the old Hungarian port of Trieste, a longtime symbol of Italian nationalist aspirations that, together with the medieval city of Udine, makes a perfect excursion base.

By Robert
Andrews

Update
by Robin
Goldstein

IN THE 19TH CENTURY, the great Italian novelist Ippolito Nievo described this region as "a small abridged version of the universe." Bounded by the Adriatic to the south, the Slovenian and Austrian borders to the north and east, and a ring of mountains to the north, this part of Italy is also as diverse in its culture, architecture, and cuisine as it is in its landscape.

The region has in turn suffered invasions from Romans, Lombards, Cossacks, and Nazis. The rule of Venice was felt at Udine, and the Habsburgs dominated Trieste. During the 19th century, Trieste was the focus for Irredentism, a movement that sought liberation from Austrian rule and ended with the arrival of Italian troops in 1918. Some of the fiercest fighting of World War I took place on the Carso hinterland behind Trieste, now remembered in war memorials and cemeteries containing thousands of fallen soldiers, at Oslavia, Udine, and, with as many as 100,000 interred, Redipuglia. During World War II, Italian fascism found a stronghold in Trieste, the city holding one of Italy's two concentration camps, still visitable. In 1991 border posts witnessed confrontations between Yugoslav and Slovene troops in the battle for Slovenian independence. Trieste's culture and architecture remain distinctly Eastern compared with the rest of the country.

The landscape of Fruili-Venezia Giulia shows an extraordinary diversity, from the mountainous north, essentially Alpine in character, and the limestone karst of the plateau around the Slovenian border, to the flat lagoons and dramatic coastline of the Adriatic. The varied topography is reflected in the patchwork past of this border zone. Whereas the palazzi of Udine reveal Venetian influence, Grado and Aquileia are strongly redolent of their Roman and early Christian past. Trieste, the capital of the region, only became Italian soil after World War II. Its peculiar frontier ambience proved a breeding ground for literary talent in the early years of the 20th century, providing refuge for James Joyce, Richard Burton, Rainer Maria Rilke, and the native Ettore Schmitz, all living here. Joyce (1882–1941) lived in Trieste with his wife for spells before and after World War I and wrote *Portrait of the Artist as a Young Man* and part of *Ulysses* here. Sir Richard Burton (1821–90), explorer and writer, was British consul from 1872 until his death and completed his translation of *A Thousand and One Nights* in Trieste. Rilke (1875–1926) composed the *Duino Elegies* near here, and Schmitz, better known as Italo Svevo, wrote his masterpiece, *Confessions of Zeno.*

Pleasures and Pastimes

Dining

In 1784 a decree was passed allowing peasants around Trieste to sell their own produce for eight days a year. This led to the setting up of *osmizze,* eateries where local food and wine were offered, a tradition that still continues today. Osmizze provide probably the best, and certainly the cheapest, way to experience authentic home cooking in the region—fresh cheeses, bread, prosciutto, soups, and wine in a rustic setting. Look for the *frasco,* a bunch of leaves on a post.

Trieste itself is famous for its self-service buffets, from which the aromas of *cren* (horseradish), paprika, *capuzi garbi* (sweetkraut), and *jota* (sauerkraut and bean soup) waft invitingly through the streets. Don't be surprised to hear these Slavic syllables issuing forth from mouths or to find a strange dialect on menus. These dishes are what give a distinctive flavor to the cuisine of this corner of the Italian peninsula. Seafood abounds here, in some restaurants to the exclusion of everything else. Look out for the soups made from a diverse range of seafood—mackerel, sardines, clams, squid, and octopus to name but a few. When sated on seafood, try the well-known San Daniele ham, either cooked or cured. In the Carnia district you're sure to come across *cjalsòns*—ravioli stuffed with ricotta and spinach. Here and in other rural areas, you should make a point of savoring the *verdure* (herbs and greens picked from the mountains) or the wild fruits and berries. Sweet specialties include gnocchi stuffed with prunes and coated in cinnamon and sugar.

CATEGORY	COST*
$$$$	over €18
$$$	€13–€18
$$	€8–€13
$	under €8

Prices are for a main course (secondo piatto)

Lodging

As this area is not very well known to tourists, apart from Austrians, it shouldn't be too hard to find accommodations. In the rural districts you'll certainly find good value for your money. The smaller country hotels often have a restaurant with an open *fogher* (hearth), which gives an intimate and cozy air and is more than welcome in chilly winter months. Your options on the seaside vary from the plethora of hotels in Grado to tranquil spots in Duino. Trieste is busy and caters mainly to the business crowd. You'll find excellent hotels along the water here.

CATEGORY	COST*
$$$$	over €155
$$$	€105–€155
$$	€50–€105
$	under €50

All prices are for two people in a standard double room, including tax and service.

Wine

Friuli produces some of the best wines in northeast Italy. The local wine par excellence, a denomination that has now attained international stature, is Tocai Friulano, a dry, lively white made from Tocai grapes. The red of choice is Terrano, a deep, dry, ruby wine produced from Refosco vines. Among the region's other esteemed reds are those from Isonzo, Carso, and Grave del Friuli. The D.O.C. (Denominazione di Origine Controllata e Garantita) wines, which meet production and quality standards, include Malvasia Carso and Carso Terrano. Cheaper cabernet sauvignon and merlot are made in Aquileia. The Collio designation indicates wines from vineyards in the eastern part of Friuli, up against the Slovenian border. The Collio Pinot Bianco from here, a fragrant white, is cool and refreshing. One of the best known and rarest wines produced is the sauternes-like Picolit, made in very limited quantities.

Exploring Friuli-Venezia Giulia

The region is easily accessed from Venice by the A4 autostrada, which terminates at Trieste. Palmanova (90 km [56 mi] from Venice) marks a crossing point for the region. From here the A23 heads north to Udine and border country with Slovenia to the east, or farther north to connect with the S52, which bisects the mountainous Western Carnia region, following the line of the River Tagliamento, the longest river of the region. Heading farther west will entail taking a tortuous mountain pass—not so easy in winter. South from Palmanova, the historic towns of Aquileia and Grado can easily be reached by the straight Roman road. All towns are well served by public transportation.

Numbers in the text correspond to numbers in the margin and on the Friuli-Venezia Giulia and Trieste maps.

Great Itineraries

IF YOU HAVE 3 DAYS

Spend your first day and night in ⊞ **Trieste** ①–⑫, where your first port of call should be the panoramic **Castello di San Giusto** ⑧ and the nearby cathedral. Break from your perambulations in a buffet-restaurant for lunch; then take in the dramatically positioned **Castello di Miramare** ⑬ in all its opulence, perhaps leaving time for a walk along the coastline at ⊞ **Duino** ⑭. The next day, make the short journey west to ⊞ **Aquileia** ⑮ to explore the unmissable early Christian treasures and mosaics in the basilica, as well as the remains and museum exhibits from the Roman era. For your last day, head north via the city of ⊞ **Udine** ⑱, home to some stunning work by Tiepolo, en route to the mountains of Carnia, the place to sample game or wild produce and do some hill walking, spending a quiet night at the village of ⊞ **Forni di Sopra** ⑳. Alternatively, spend a day at the picturesque town of ⊞ **Cividale del Friuli** ⑲, with its early Christian and Roman treasures and delightful setting by the river. Carry on from here to venture farther into the Dolomites, or else retrace your steps to Trieste.

IF YOU HAVE 5 DAYS

Spend your first two days as above in ⊞ **Trieste** ①–⑫ and ⊞ **Aquileia** ⑮, making excursions to the **Castello di Miramare** ⑬, the coast around ⊞ **Duino** ⑭, and the island town of ⊞ **Grado** ⑯. On your third day, head north to ⊞ **Gorizia** ⑰, right on the Slovenian border, then northwest to stay the night at ⊞ **Udine** ⑱. Spend the next day here exploring the town's Venetian art and architectural heritage; then move on east to ⊞ **Cividale del Friuli** ⑲ for your fourth night in this charming town in sight of the mountains. For your last day, head northward again into the idyllic Alpine scenery of the Carnia region, perfect for sampling the bracing mountain air, ideally on a hike. Just set off in your car, and pick your spot. A good base here would be the village of ⊞ **Forni di Sopra** ⑳, where there is a choice of hotels for your fifth night, and plenty of opportunity to sample rural specialties in the local restaurants. From Forni, you can retrace your steps south to Udine, alternatively continue west, either to further penetrate the Alps or to catch the SS51 south toward Belluno, the Lakes, Treviso, and Venice.

When to Tour Friuli-Venezia Giulia

The beauty of being in the shadow of tourist-hungry Venice is that there is never an overwhelming presence of other visitors. Any season is a pleasure here, though winter snows may make the roads difficult in Carnia, which sees a fair number of ski enthusiasts between December and March. Spring and autumn will bring walkers to this mountain zone, but never enough to spoil your enjoyment. Friuli would also be a cool haven from the heat of summer, when the coastal regions can be sultry. Tourist offices can update you about the weather and offer advice on walking conditions.

TRIESTE

Surrounded by rugged countryside and beautiful coastline, Trieste is a lovely architectural melange built on a hillside above what was once the chief port of the Austro-Hungarian Habsburg Empire. The spacious streets hold a lively mix of monumental, neoclassical, and Liberty

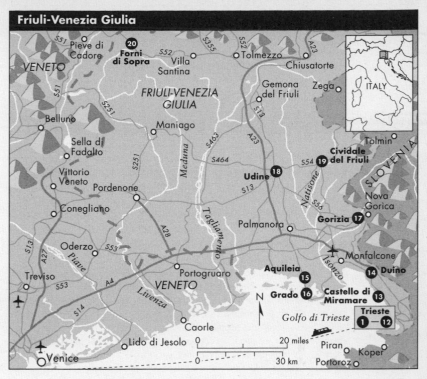

Friuli-Venezia Giulia

styles, granting an air of stateliness to the city. On the downside, Trieste is also brash and clogged with traffic and can be a little overwhelming until you settle in.

Trieste was the Roman city of Tergeste. Having chafed under a brief Venetian dominion, the city placed itself in 1382 under the protection of Leopold III of Habsburg, whose overlordship gradually developed into Austrian possession. In 1719, the city was proclaimed an imperial free port, its economy taking an upturn at the instigation of Maria Teresa, Empress of Austria (1717–80), under whom a program of building started around the Grand Canal. From this anchorage for sailing ships, a regular pattern of spacious streets developed to the west of Piazza Unità d'Italia, called the Borgo Teresiano, an area still lined with grand neoclassical buildings and embellished with statues and bas-reliefs. Much of the city's pre-19th-century identity, in fact, has been submerged under this Austrian layer. The feeling of a Mittel-European city is compounded by the many cafés that grew up at the end of the 19th century. Like Vienna's coffeehouses, these are the social and cultural centers of the city, and much-beloved refuges from the city's prevailing northeast wind, the *bora*.

On becoming Italian in 1918, the port lost much of its business and Trieste suffered a period of decline. The quays are now used as parking lots, and the container port has moved to the south side of Trieste. In recent years, however, the city has undergone a degree of rejuvenation and has become something of a center for science and the computer industry. Having absorbed new waves of Slavic and eastern European immigrants, Trieste still has an international air, a tattered romance, and the offbeat ambience of a remote frontier town.

Exploring Trieste

If you're bringing a car into Trieste, find a space to park along the quay, as negotiating the city's new system of one-way streets can be a nightmare. From the Stazione Centrale the Corso Cavour leads westward to the Riva, the broad quay that changes its name four times—Rivas Tre Novembre, del Mandracchio, Nazario Sauro, Tommaso Gulli, Grumula—as it skirts the seafront. The Borgo Teresiano extends behind the Corso and the Riva's first section (Riva Tre Novembre); adjoining this area, the main Piazza Unità d'Italia opens out onto the sea. Behind the piazza, you can wind your way up through the historical center, pausing along the way at places of interest before reaching the Castello and a rewarding view of the city. On the seafront beyond the piazza, the long white building on the pier, formerly the Stazione Marittima, is now a conference center. From Piazza Oberdan a *tranvia* (cable tramway) runs every 20 minutes to Opicina and the Carso plateau.

A Good Walk

Start at **Piazza Unità d'Italia** ① and walk eastward along Riva Mandracchio and Riva Nazario Sauro past the fish market. Turn left into Piazza Venezia for the **Museo Revoltella e Galleria d'Arte Moderna** ② and the **Museo Sartorio** ③. From the square, take Via Torino and turn left into Via di Cavana to return to Piazza Unità d'Italia. Head south to the Scala Medaglie steps, which lead to the churches of **San Silvestro** ④, dating from the 11th century, and the Baroque **Santa Maria Maggiore** ⑤. From here it's only a few paces to Piazza Barbacan. At the far end of the piazza, stop at the Roman **Arco di Riccardo** ⑥ before winding your way uphill along Via della Cattedrale to the **Cattedrale di San Giusto** ⑦ for its exquisite mosaics and the **Castello di San Giusto** ⑧ for the view and the museum within. The **Museo Civico di Storia ed Arte** ⑨ lies across Via della Cattedrale from here. If you're set to visit the **Museo Morpurgo** ⑩, follow Via Spellico down, turning left onto Corso Italia and right onto Via Imbriani. Alternatively, head down Via Rota from the cathedral to the **Teatro Romano** ⑪ and the **Piazza della Borsa** ⑫, where you can stop for an espresso, or else wait until you return to Piazza Unità d'Italia, just the other side of Teatro Verdi.

TIMING

The route would take a couple of hours to walk, half a day to tour the sites on the Capitoline Hill, and longer still if you're going to stop in the museums.

Sights to See

⑥ **Arco di Riccardo.** The Roman arch was built in AD 33 in honor of the Emperor Augustus (63 BC–AD14) and served as a city gate. Its name recalls the belief that Richard I of England, "the Lionheart," (1157–99) was imprisoned here after a spell in the Holy Land. ⊠ *Piazza Barbacan.*

⑧ **Castello di San Giusto.** The Venetians, who always had an eye for the best vantage point in the cities they controlled, built the castle in the 14th century during one of their brief sojourns in Trieste. The Habsburgs enlarged it to its present size in 1470. Inside, some of the best exhibits in the **Museo Civico del Castello di San Giusto** are the weaponry and armor, but you can also admire an array of Flemish tapestries, a painted ceiling by Andrea Celesti (1637–1712), and period furnishings. From the ramparts, you can have a view of the area as far as the Dolomites. ⊠ *Piazza Cattedrale,* ☎ *040/309362.* ☞ *€1.55.* ☉ *Castle Tues.–Sun. 9–1; museum Oct.–Mar., daily 9–5; Apr.–Sept., daily 9–7.*

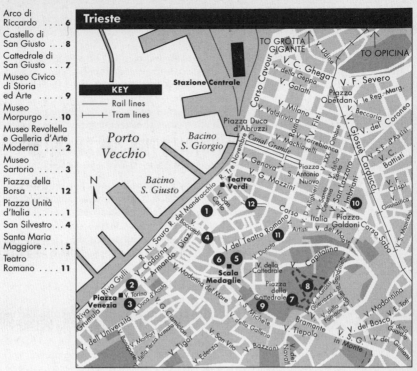

⑦ Cattedrale di San Giusto. Fragments of Roman tombs and temples can be seen among the jumble of styles on the exterior of this 14th-century cathedral; you can see these most clearly on the pillars of the main doorway. The structure incorporates two much older churches, one dating from the 5th century. The facade has a fine and lovely Gothic rose window. The highlights of the interior are the 13th-century mosaics and frescoes, green and golden and beautifully decorated. Look up and you'll see the wooden ceiling studded with stars. ⊠ *Piazza Cattedrale,* ☎ *040/309666.* ☉ *Apr.–Sept., Mon.–Sat. 8–noon and 3:30–7:30, Sun. 8–1 and 3:30–8; Oct.–Mar., Mon.–Sat. 8–noon and 2:30–6:30, Sun. 8–1 and 3:30–8.*

⑨ Museo Civico di Storia ed Arte. Statues from the Roman theater and artifacts from Egypt as well as Greece and Rome are on show at the eclectic Civic Museum of History and Art, including sculptures, glass, and manuscripts. From here you can gain access to the **Orto Lapidario** (Lapidary Garden), where you'll find classical statuary and pottery and a small Corinthian temple that houses the remains of the archaeologist and proponent of neoclassicism, J. J. Winckelmann (1717–68). He was murdered here in Trieste by a thief who coveted his collection of gold coins. ⊠ *Via Cattedrale 15,* ☎ *040/310500.* ⊞ *€1.55.* ☉ *Tues. and Thurs.–Sun. 9–1, Wed. 9–7.*

⑩ Museo Morpurgo. The building and its contents were left to the city in 1943 by Mario Morpurgo, a wealthy banker. It's still very much as it was in the last decades of the 19th century, and you can wander through the rooms with their glass, ceramics and porcelain, 19th-century paintings, and Japanese prints. ⊠ *Via Imbriani 5,* ☎ *040/636969.* ⊞ *Free.* ☉ *Tues. and Thurs.–Sun. 9–1, Wed. 9–7.*

NEED A
BREAK?

For the best ice cream in town, head for **Zampolli** (⊠ Via Ghega Carlo 10, ☎ 040/364868).

② **Museo Revoltella e Galleria d'Arte Moderna.** In 1872 the Venetian Baron Revoltella left the city his palazzo, library, and art collection. Original furniture, inlaid floors, and enameled stoves set the tone in the older part of the museum. A modern annex designed by Carlo Scarpa (1906– 78), holds one of the most important collections of 19th- and 20th-century art in Italy, including work by the metaphysical painter Giorgio De Chirico (1878–1978). In July and August the museum is open until midnight with a bar on the terrace featuring splendid views. ⊠ *Via Diaz 27,* ☎ *040/311360.* ☞ *€6.20.* ☉ *Wed.–Mon. 10–7.*

③ **Museo Sartorio.** The 19th-century rooms of this museum, once the private home of a well-to-do family, display decorative arts including ceramics from the 16th century, local majolica, and Venetian paintings. The highlight of the collection is the Santa Chiara triptych, which is attributed to Paolo Veneziano (1335–60) and depicts the Life of Christ in 36 miniature scenes. ⊠ *Largo Papa Giovanni XXIII,* ☎ *040/ 301479.* ☞ *€2.60.* ☉ *Tues.–Sun. 9–1.*

⑫ **Piazza della Borsa.** This square contains Trieste's original stock exchange, the **Borsa Vecchia,** a neoclassical building with a four-columned portico, now serving as the Chamber of Commerce. The statues on the top represent Asia, Europe, Africa, and the Americas, along with Mercury and Vulcan. Presiding over the square from a column is a **Statue of Leopold I** (died 994), Emperor of Austria. In the same square, you can sample Liberty style à la Trieste in the lightly decorated facade of the **Casa Bartoli,** designed in 1905 by Max Fabiani.

① **Piazza Unità d'Italia.** This spacious square inevitably recalls Piazza San Marco in Venice. Both are focal points of architectural interest abutting the water. Inhabitants of Trieste, however, argue that their piazza is superior to that of San Marco, as it opens out directly onto the seafront. Imposing late-18th- and 19th-century buildings flank the square, most prominently the **Palazzo Comunale** (Town Hall) taking up the entire southern end of the piazza, designed in grand imperial style in 1877. The sidewalk caffès here have always been popular meeting places for literary and political figures and still make grand watering holes.

OFF THE
BEATEN PATH

RISIERA DI SAN SABBA – Originally used for the preparation of rice, this building was turned into a prison and subsequently became, in 1943, one of the only two concentration camps used by the Germans in Italy. A railway line ran to the crematorium, where it is estimated that 5,000 inmates were burned before liberation by the Yugoslavs on May 1, 1945. Now a museum, it serves as a reminder of the Fascist past. Bus 10 will get you here, or drive southeast out of town on Via Gabriele D'Annunzio. ⊠ *Ratto della Pileria 43,* ☎ *040/826202.* ☞ *Free.* ☉ *Tues.–Sun. 9–1.*

④ **San Silvestro.** Now used by Evangelicals, this solid little church is the oldest place of worship in Trieste. It's of plain-fronted Romanesque construction, dating from the 11th century, and said to have been erected on the site where two local martyrs, Sts. Tecla and Eufemia, once lived. ⊠ *Piazza di San Silvestro,* ☎ *040/632770.* ☉ *Mon.–Sat. 10–noon.*

⑤ **Santa Maria Maggiore.** In contrast to San Silvestro next door, this church, begun in 1627, has a square Baroque facade with slender columns giving height and lightness. The interior has an altarpiece by Francesco

Maffei (circa 1625–60). ⊠ *Via del Collegio 6,* ☎ *040/632920.* ◐ *Daily 7–noon and 3–7.*

⑪ **Teatro Romano.** Quintus Petronius Modestus, procurator of the Emperor Trajan, endowed Tergeste, as it was known in Roman times, with this amphitheater in the late 1st century AD. The 6,000 spectators it once held have been replaced with grass and flowers. The statues that once adorned the proscenium arch are now in the Museo Civico di Storia ed Arte. The theater only resurfaced in 1938 after demolition work in the area. ⊠ *Via del Teatro Romano.*

OFF THE BEATEN PATH — **GROTTA GIGANTE –** This is the largest cave in the world open to tourists. It is more than 300 ft high, 900 ft long, and 200 ft wide, with spectacular stalactites and stalagmites. Reserve 45 minutes for the tour. It is not far from Trieste, about 10 km (6 mi) north of the city (take Bus 42 from Piazza Oberdan). ☎ *040/327312.* ▣ *€6.70 includes guided tour.* ◐ *Tours every ½ hr Nov.–Feb., Tues.–Sun. 10–noon and 2–4; Apr.–Sept., Tues.–Sun. 10–6; Mar. and Oct., Tues.–Sun. 10–4.*

Dining and Lodging

$$$–$$$$ ★ ✕ **Harry's Grill.** One of the city's most elegant restaurants, you'll be impressed with the sophisticated surroundings of either the inner sanctum (polished parquet floor, brass, plants, chandeliers) or the glass-doored conservatory that overlooks the Piazza Unità. The caring owner and chef, Dario Basso, devises a new menu nearly every month, and complements it with an extensive selection of 800 wines. Choose from foie gras, truffle, or lobster, or even dare to try *bocconcini di rana pescatrice con olive, capperi, e pinoli* (tidbits of frog with olives, capers, and pine nuts). There's a set dinner menu, and from Thursday through Saturday you'll have piano accompaniment. ⊠ *Piazza dell'Unità d'Italia 2, 34121,* ☎ *040/365646. Reservations essential. AE, DC, MC, V. Closed Sun.*

$$–$$$ ✕ **Città di Cherso.** Light and white and restful in atmosphere, this restaurant right in the heart of downtown specializes in fish. Try the gnocchi *con seppie* (with cuttlefish, brandy, tomatoes, and cream) or the *zuppa di pesce spinate* (spiny fish soup). Desserts are a must, wonderful concoctions of chocolate and cream. ⊠ *Via Cadorna 6,* ☎ *040/366044. Reservations essential. AE, DC, MC, V. Closed Tues. and Aug.*

$$–$$$ ✕ **Delfini.** This restaurant in Riviera and Maximilian's hotel is the perfect place for a tête-à-tête dinner or tryst with its curtained-off little areas—like eating in a four-poster bed. Of the regional and international fish menu, the shrimp risotto and *tagliolini in busara* (pasta with shrimp, onions, anchovies, tomatoes, and brandy) are standouts. The homemade cakes are not to be missed. ⊠ *Strada Costiera 22,* ☎ *040/224551. AE, DC, MC, V. Closed Nov.–Apr. No lunch Sun.*

$$–$$$ ✕ **Hostaria alle Bandierette.** Try to keep from bumping into the tank of crayfish; then squeeze past the beds of flatfish and shellfish on crushed ice—yes, you're in seafood territory. In fact, this restaurant serves nothing else but. It's small, hectic, and full of serious eaters admiring the cooks in full view. Fish risottos, squid spaghetti, and lobsters with capers will all hit the spot. Dine on the outdoor patio in summer. ⊠ *Riva Nazario Sauro 2,* ☎ *040/300686. Reservations essential. AE, DC, MC, V. Closed Mon. and Jan. 1–15.*

$$ ★ ✕ **Suban.** Though in the hills on the edge of town, this historic trattoria is worth the taxi ride. The rustic decor is rich in dark wood, stone, and wrought iron, and you'll find typical regional fare with imaginative variations. Among the specialties are *jota carsolina* (typical local minestrone made of cabbage, potatoes, and beans) and duck breast in

CAFFÈ CULTURE

TRIESTE BEING ONE OF THE MOST famous coffee towns in the world, perhaps it's no coincidence that its mayor is Riccardo Illy, patriarch of the eponymous über-roaster, Illycaffè, which can be credited with supplying caffeine fixes to most Italians and much of the free world. The elegant civility of Trieste plays out beautifully in a *caffè* culture that rivals Vienna. In Trieste, as in all of Italy, ask for a *caffè* and you'll get a thimbleful of high-octane, but no less delicious, espresso. Know that in Trieste your cappuccino will come in said espresso cup, with only half as much frothy milk and a dollop of whipped cream. Many cafés are part of a *torrefazione* (roasting shop), so you can sample the beans before you buy. You can taste the local brews at both the Cremecaffè and Caffè La Colombiana.

Few cafés in Trieste, Italy, and the world can rival **Antico Caffè San Marco** (✉ Via Cesare Battisti 18, ☎ 040/363538) for its glimmering Art Deco style and old-world patina. It was completely destroyed in World War I, and when it was rebuilt in the 1920s, it became the meeting place for local intellectuals. On Friday and Saturday it hosts live music; it's closed Monday. **Caffè Tommaseo** (✉ Riva Tre Novembre 5, ☎ 040/362666) has been the haunt of politicians and businessmen since 1830. Sober and elegant, it has mirrors that were imported from Belgium more than 100 years ago. It's closed Monday.

Caffè Pasticceria Pirona (✉ Largo Barriera Vecchia 12, ☎ 040/636046) was patronized by the likes of James Joyce. Imagine him garnering inspiration for his *Ulysses* as he sipped his *macchiato* (literally "spotted," espresso with a touch of steamed milk). Founded in 1900 by Alberto Pirona and still in the family, the place has maintained an old-fashioned look with its cherrywood fittings but has no place to sit down: it's a spot for coffee and its famously scrumptious cakes on the go. It's closed on Monday. **Cremecaffè** (✉ Piazza Goldoni 10, ☎ 040/636555), closed Sunday, may not be the place to sit down and read the paper, lest you get jostled by the caffeine-craving crowd, but it's nonetheless one of the most-frequented cafés in town, with 20 different blends to choose from.

ONE OF THE CITY'S FINEST roasting shops, **Caffè La Colombiana** (✉ Via Carducci 12, ☎ 040/370855), closed Sunday, has stood here since the 1940s—still without tables or eats, but the coffee hasn't changed since those days. There is no better location in town than **Caffè Piazza Grande** (✉ Piazza Unità d'Italia 5, ☎ 040/369878), with a great view of this grand piazza. It's closed Sunday. **Il Gran Bar Malabar** (✉ Piazza San Giovanni 6, ☎ 040/636226) is yet another wonderful stop for a coffee or an aperitif, with an excellent wine list as well and tastings every Friday.

Tocai sauce. ✉ *Via Emilio Comici 2,* ☎ *040/54368. AE, DC, MC, V. Closed Tues., 3 wks in Aug., and 1 wk in Jan. No lunch Mon.*

$–$$ ✕ **Buffet da Pepi.** Established here for more than a century and reportedly the crème de la crème of Trieste's restaurants, this place represents excellent value for the money and always has a good crowd. If you're on a tour of the city, stop here for lunch and sample the sausages and hams with your slice of bread and glass of the local Terrano red or a draft beer. ✉ *Via Cassa di Risparmio 3,* ☎ *040/366858. No credit cards. Closed Sun. and mid-July–mid-Aug.*

$$$$ **Duchi d'Aosta.** On the spacious Piazza dell'Unità d'Italia, this hotel is beautifully furnished in lavish Venetian Renaissance style. Who would think it began life as a dockers' café, its beautiful facade added in 1873? Rooms have dark-wood antiques, rich carpets, and drapes. The restaurant Harry's Grill is situated in the hotel, but independent of it. ⊠ *Piazza Unità d'Italia 2/1, 34121,* ☎ *040/7600011,* FAX *040/366092,* WEB *www.grandhotelduchidaosta.com. 50 rooms, 2 suites. Bar. AE, DC, MC, V.*

$$–$$$ 🏨 **Colombia.** Unpretentious but adequate, this small hotel caters mainly to a business clientele. There is no restaurant, but there's a typical beer cellar–restaurant close by. ⊠ *Via della Geppa 18, 34121,* ☎ *040/369333,* FAX *040/369644. 40 rooms. AE, DC, MC, V.*

$$–$$$ 🏨 **Savoia Excelsior.** Right on the waterfront, this imposing hotel retains its Habsburg heritage with its ornate public rooms adorned with molded friezes, gilded ceilings, and voluptuous chandeliers. Bedrooms each have a small balcony, are individually furnished in contemporary style, and have tea-making facilities. The excellent restaurant provides both international and local dishes. ⊠ *Riva del Mandracchio 4, 34124,* ☎ *040/77941,* FAX *040/638260. 116 rooms, 39 suites. Restaurant, bar, baby-sitting, parking (fee). AE, DC, MC, V.*

$$ 🏨 **Riviera and Maximilian's.** Seven kilometers (4 miles) north of Tri-
★ este, this lovely hotel with private access to the beach below commands stunning views across the Golfo di Trieste to Castello di Miramare. Rooms are beautifully furnished in modern style, some with balconies. Delfini is the hotel's restaurant of choice and highly recommended. Full- and half-board arrangements are available. ⊠ *Strada Costiera 22, 34010,* ☎ *040/224551,* FAX *040/224300. 45 rooms, 4 suites. Bar, golf privileges, beach. AE, DC, MC, V.*

$–$$ 🏨 **Al Teatro.** This hotel overlooking the main piazza served as head-quarters for the British army after World War II. Now it's a favorite with theatrical people and business types as well as travelers. The rooms have parquet floors and are plain but comfortably furnished, with distinctive blue drapes that fall to one side of the window. ⊠ *Capo di Piazza Bartoli 1, 31131,* ☎ *040/366220,* FAX *040/366560. 45 rooms. Parking (fee). AE, DC, MC, V.*

$–$$ 🏨 **San Giusto.** Oriental rugs on the marble floor, potted palms, and chandeliers complement the elegant Art Deco style of this hotel, positioned away from the sea. The hotel caters mainly to businesspeople. ⊠ *Via dell'Istria 7, 34137,* ☎ *040/764824,* FAX *040/763826. 62 rooms. Restaurant, bar, parking (fee). AE, DC, MC, V.*

Nightlife and the Arts

The Arts

CONCERTS, OPERA, AND BALLET

The concert, opera, and ballet season in Trieste runs from October through May, with events taking place in the **Teatro Verdi** (⊠ Piazza Giuseppe Verdi). Various music and dance events are held at the **Sala Tripcovich** (⊠ Piazza Libertà). The **Festival Internazionale dell'Operetta** is held in July and August. Prices start at €7.75. For information on all these events call the **Teatro Verdi** (☎ 040/6722500) or contact the tourist information office (⊠ Via San Nicolò 20, 34121 Trieste, ☎ 040/67961, FAX 040/416806).

FESTIVALS

Details of events and festivals are published in the daily paper, *Il Piccolo.*

Films from central and eastern Europe are shown during the **Alpe-Adria Film Festival,** held in December and January. Contact the **Teatro Miela** (⊠ Piazza Duca degli Abruzzi 3, ☎ 040/365119).

The **Barcolana Autumn Cup Regatta** gets under way on the second Sunday in October, attracting more than 1,000 sailing boats.

Four kilometers (2½ miles) south of Trieste, Muggia is famous for its **Carnevale** in February, which goes back as far as 1420, but it also has a crowd-pulling "summer edition" in July and August with music, dancing, and theater. Call the Commune di Muggia (☏ 040/3360340) for further information.

MUSEUMS

In August and September, the **Museo Civico di Storia ed Arte** arranges Musei Sera, an opportunity to make an evening visit to a local museum with an expert guide. Call ☏ 040/310500 for more information; tickets cost around €5.15.

Nightlife

DISCOS

Machiavelli (✉ Viale Miramare 285, ☏ 040/44104) attracts a lively crowd. **Tor Cucherna** (✉ Via Chiauchiara 7, ☏ 040/368874), just as hopping, has an American bar.

Outdoor Activities and Sports

Golf

The nine-hole **Golf Club Trieste** (✉ Padriciano 80, ☏ 040/226159), closed Tuesday, is 6 km (4 mi) from town center.

Horseback Riding

Ippodromo di Montebello (✉ Piazzale de Gasperi 4, ☏ 040/393176) is a stable with rides available throughout the year.

Scuba Diving

For scuba diving in the Riserva Naturale Marina di Miramare, contact **Riserva Naturale** (☏ 040/224147), which also provides scuba diving equipment.

Shopping

Trieste's busy shopping street, **Corso Italia,** is reached from Piazza della Borsa. Trieste has some 60 antiques dealers, jewelers, and secondhand shops. For small items of glass and porcelain the nameless antiques shop at Piazza Vecchia 2/c is excellent. You'll find similar shops along the Via del Ponte.

Markets

At the beginning of November, Trieste plays host to the region's biggest antiques fair—a good opportunity to find those art nouveau pieces. Contact **Promotrieste** (Centro Congressi, ✉ Stazione Marittima, ☏ 040/304888). Antiques markets crowd the streets of the city's old center on the third Sunday of each month. Markets are held Tuesday through Saturday. You'll find general markets in Piazza della Libertà and Via Carducci and fish, fruit, and flowers in Piazza di Ponterosso and at Riva Nazario Sauro 1.

Specialty Shops

CLOTHING

Alexandra (✉ Via XXX Ottobre 14, ☏ 040/634401) has fine Italian selections. For clothes, try **Cesana** (✉ Via Mazzini 40, ☏ 040/632020). **Fendi** (✉ Capo di Piazza 1, ☏ 040/366464) stocks its trademark leather goods. For elegant, stylish shoes, try **Malvestiti** (✉ Via Santo Spiridione 12, ☏ 040/638803).

JEWELRY

For nice stocks of silverware and gemstones, there are several options: **Cavallar** (✉ Via S. Lazzaro 15, ☏ 040/630335), **Cella** (✉ Via Battisti 5, ☏ 040/370640), and **G. Bin** (✉ Via Giulia 10/c, ☏ 040/569450).

For small leather gifts, try **Isolachenonc'è** (✉ Via Punta del Forno, ☎ no phone).

FROM THE COAST TO SLOVENIA

From Trieste, the road eastward follows the coast under the shadow of the huge geological formation called the Carso, a barren expanse of limestone that forms a giant ledge, most of which is across the border in Slovenia. Italian territory extends only a couple of miles inland on this narrow strip, and Italy's small Slovene minority ekes out an agricultural existence in the region, which has changed hands countless times since the final days of Imperial Rome. Forty or so kilometers (25 miles) west of Trieste, Aquileia was the principal Roman center in the region. In 313, Theodore became its first Christian patriarch (bishop), founding a basilica whose richly allegorical early Christian mosaics are among the finest to be seen in Italy today.

The Roman population of Aquileia found safe refuge from the ravaging Huns and Lombards in the island town of Grado, whose small historic center lies adjacent to some of the region's best beaches. There is more than a passing resemblance to Venice in the layout of this port and resort, and no lack of hotels just a short walk from the sands, not to mention fish restaurants galore. Between Trieste and Grado, Miramare and Duino offer more coastal pleasures but without the bustling beach culture of other resorts along this stretch. The shore here is picturesquely cliffy, the tramping ground and inspiration for both Dante and Rilke. To the north, Gorizia lies right on the Slovenian border, literally bisected by it. The hilltop castle here holds a World War I museum, recalling the conflict that devastated this region. The Slavic element is strong here; make sure you sample the local goulash.

Castello di Miramare

★ **⓭** *8 km (5 mi) northwest of Trieste, 138 km (86 mi) east of Venice.*

This waterfront castle in Miramare is a 19th-century extravaganza in white stone, built for the Archduke Maximilian of Habsburg (1832–67, brother of Emperor Franz Josef). Maximilian spent a brief, happy time here until Napoléon III of France took Trieste from the Habsburgs and sent the poor archduke packing. He was given the title of emperor of Mexico in 1864 as a compensation but met his death before a Mexican firing squad in 1867. The interiors preserve much of the original fittings and ornaments: bohemian glass chandeliers, inlaid furniture, and ornately molded ceilings, including the elaborate Gothic ceiling in the vast throne room. Lush grounds surround the castle, affording stupendous views over the Adriatic. In summer, son-et-lumière shows are staged here, including a version in English. ✉ *Miramare,* ☎ *040/224143,* WEB *www.castello-miramare.it.* 🎟 *Castle €4.15; guided visit €1.55; grounds free.* ⊙ *Castle daily 9–7 (ticket office closes ½ hr before closing). Grounds Nov.–Feb., daily 8–5; Mar. and Oct., daily 8–6; Apr.–Sept., daily 8–7.*

Duino

⓮ *20 km (12 mi) northwest of Trieste, 12 km (8 mi) northwest of Castello di Miramare.*

The small fishing village of Duino is a picture of tranquillity, largely unspoiled, consisting of a few houses, hotels, and a police station. The contrast with the neighboring bay of Sistiana, which is chock-full of yachts and pleasure boats, couldn't be greater. You can walk the 2-km (1-mi) path from Sistiana, passing through woodland along the panoramic rocky coast, where you might even glimpse a peregrine falcon. Two castles are at Duino—one, the **Castello Vecchio,** is in ruins; the other **Castello** once hosted the German poet Rilke and is still inhabited by descendants of the original owners, the Della Torre e Tasso family (part of it now belongs to an international school). Rilke used the path for his musings and composed the *Duino Elegies,* among his last and most famous works, while staying here. This castle is not open to the public, but you can reach the Castello Vecchio easily enough, crowning an impressive headland jutting out to sea. The site is famed for the Dama Bianca (White Lady), a white rock named after a legendary episode in which the lord Duino hurled a woman for whom he had no further use out of the castle. Before hitting the water, she turned to stone, the white rock. The locality is also said to have been a favorite haunt of Dante (1265–1321); the cliff on which he meditated bears his name.

Dining and Lodging

$ X▥ **La Dama Bianca.** Right on the shore, with glorious sunset views,
★   the balconied rooms here are blue, cool, light, and airy. The lush foliage in the restaurant will make you feel as if you're in a greenhouse—albeit a tremendously romantic one. With the twinkling of the lights on the tables at night and on the boats out to sea, it's the perfect setting for the delights that the affable Branca Miladinovic concocts from the catch of her fisherman husband. Try the crab served in its shell and the crescent-shape ravioli with shrimp, basil, and poppy seeds. The desserts, devised from Signora Branca's own recipes, are to die for, and there's an excellent local wine list. ✉ *Duino Porto 61/c, 34013,* ☎ *040/ 208137,* ℻ *040/208258. 7 rooms. Restaurant, bar. AE, DC, MC, V. Restaurant closed Wed. and Thurs. in Jan.*

$$ ▥ **Duino Park Hotel.** This is a nice, quiet lodging a little way up the hill from the sea and run by genial management. Rooms are individually furnished with balconies overlooking the bay. The wicker furniture in the public area set off by big terra-cotta floor tiles adds to the charm. Breakfast is taken on the terrace in warm weather. ✉ *Via Duino 60/c, 34013,* ☎ *040/208184,* ℻ *040/208526. 21 rooms. Bar, breakfast room, pool, sauna. AE, DC, MC, V.*

Aquileia

⓯   *77 km (48 mi) west of Trieste, 18 km (11 mi) west of Monfalcone.*

Nowadays, it is difficult to believe that this sleepy little town was, in the time of Emperor Augustus, Italy's fourth most important city (after Rome, Milan, and Capua). The patriarchate (bishopric) of Aquileia was founded here around 314, the basilica commissioned shortly afterward, and, after several centuries of decline and frequent pillaging, the town regained its prominence from the 11th to the end of the 14th century. Prominent past visitors include Herod the Great, who was received by Augustus in 10 BC; Sts. Jerome and Ambrose, who attended a council of bishops in AD 381; and Attila the Hun, who sacked the town in 452. Aquileia's magnificent Roman and Byzantine remains are strongly evocative of this patchwork past, beautifully preserved right in the middle of the serene village and refreshingly free of the mass tourism that you might expect to find given the cultural riches.

Aquileia's **Basilica** was founded by Theodore, its first patriarch, and later extended. It owes its present form to the patriarch Poppo (or Popone) who rebuilt it between 1021 and 1031, though it has accumulated different elements including the Romanesque portico and the Gothic bell tower. But the highlight of this monument is the staggering 4th-century mosaic covering the entire floor, one of the finest relics of the early Christian period in Italy and the biggest of its kind. From the vibrancy of the colors, the floor appears as if it has just been laid, and with good reason, as it was only uncovered at the beginning of the 20th century. It survived a major earthquake in 1328—just: it now ripples in corrugated waves as a consequence. Christian images combine with the pagan in this marine extravaganza of dolphins, squid, and lobsters, among which Jonah is swallowed and spewed out of an extraordinary sea monster, and cherubs fish from a boat.

Before the Edict of Constantine (the proclamation in 313 that established religious toleration for Christianity under the Romans), Christians adopted images of pagan symbolism to express their faith, some of which can be seen here. The winged figure of Victory with her laurel wreath and palm frond equates with triumph over death; the tortoise with its carapace symbolizes darkness, and the cockerel, which crows at dawn, is light. Fish, of course, represent Christ, from Ichthos—Greek for fish and an acronym for Jesus Christ, Son of God, Savior—and birds such as peacocks represent immortality. Down a flight of steps, the **Cripta degli Affreschi** contains soft-hued frescoes, among them St. Peter sending St. Mark to Aquileia and the beheading of Saints Hermagoras and Fortunatus, to whom the basilica is dedicated. The **Cripta degli Scavi** contains more mosaics and was closed at press time. ⊠ *Piazza Capitolo,* ☎ *0431/91067.* ⊡ *Basilica free; crypt €0.50; campanile €0.50.* ☉ *Apr.–Oct., daily 8:30–7; Nov.–Mar., daily 8:30–12:30 and 2:30–5:30.*

Beyond the basilica and across the road from it, the **archaeological site** among the cypresses reveals Roman remains of the forum, houses, cemetery, and port. The little stream was once a navigable and important waterway extending to Grado. The area is well signposted. WEB *www. museoarcheo-aquileia.it.* ⊡ *Free.* ☉ *Daily 8:15–one hr before sunset.*

Of the two museums the **Museo Archeologico** is the most rewarding, containing a wealth of material from the Roman era. Notable are the portrait busts from Republican times, semiprecious gems, amber- and gold-work—including preserved flies—a fine glass collection in iridescent hues, and miniature priapic bronzes. ⊠ *Via Roma 1,* ☎ *0431/91096,* WEB *www.museoarcheo-aquileia.it.* ⊡ *€4.15.* ☉ *Oct.–May, Mon. 8:30–2, Tues.–Sun. 8:30–7:30; June–Sept., Mon. 8:30–2, Tues.–Fri. 8:30–7:30, Sat. 8:30–10:45 PM, Sun. 8:30–7:30.*

The **Museo Paleocristiano** houses more mosaics and traces the development of art from Roman to Christian times. ⊠ *Località Monastero,* ☎ *0431/91131,* WEB *www.museoarcheo-aquileia.it.* ⊡ *Free.* ☉ *Oct.–May, Mon. 8:30–1:45, Tues.–Sun. 8:30–7:30; June–Sept., Mon. 8:30–1:45, Tues.–Fri. 8:30–7:30, Sat. 8:30–10:45 PM, Sun. 8:30–7:30.*

Dining and Lodging

$$–$$$ ✕ **La Colombara.** The fogolar in this friendly, family-run restaurant is used for cooking, and the fare is mainly fish. Everything is homemade—pasta, bread, and cakes. In August and September the restaurant organizes Roman evenings (come in a toga) when the tables are cleared for the triclinia (reclining couches). When not eating Roman style, try the stuffed calamari with artichokes or the ravioli with mixed fish. ⊠ *Via San Zilli 42,* ☎ *0431/91513,* WEB *www.lacolombara.it. AE, DC, MC, V. Closed Mon. and Jan. 7–17.*

$ ✕⚏ Patriarchi. You can open your shutters onto a view of the basilica from this hotel. It's well run and very friendly and offers good service in modern rooms with colorful rugs on the floor and plenty of space. Book ahead for stays in July and August, when an umbrella on Grado's beach is included in the price. The simple restaurant serves its own salami or baby octopus in *salsa piccante* (spicy sauce) as antipasti on unusual glass plates. Follow it with gnocchi with salmon and cognac or *scarpena alla siciliana* (scorpion fish with black olives, tomato, and oregano). Everything is deliciously light. The restaurant closes Wednesday. ⊠ *Via Giulia Augusta 12, 33051,* ☎ *0431/919595,* ℻ *0431/919596. 22 rooms. Restaurant, bar. AE, DC, MC, V. Closed Nov. 10–25.*

Grado

⓰ *11 km (7 mi) south of Aquileia, 52 km (32 mi) west of Trieste.*

Grado is an island town set among lagoons and approached by causeway from Aquileia or Monfalcone. The town has a compact and attractive historic center, but most people flock here for its 20 km (12 mi) of sandy beaches, as clean and safe as you'll find anywhere in Italy. All the usual sunning and swimming facilities are on hand, as well as thermal baths, but it's worth leaving the serried ranks of umbrellas to take a stroll round the harbor and the alleys and piazzas of the old town. This small quarter has an engaging, slightly decaying air to it and holds the best restaurants. With Grado still an active fishing port, seafood is high on the menu.

The old town's Venetian architecture sets the tone, a legacy of the period when Grado came under the Republic's sway in the 15th century. Its history, however, extends back further, for this was an outpost of Roman Aquileia, the place to which the inhabitants of that inland town fled in the 5th century to escape the invasions of Huns. In the 6th century, Grado became the principal patriarchal seat and grew in importance. Three absorbing buildings remain from that time, in each of which you can see mosaic pavements from the 6th century.

The 6th-century **Basilica di Sant'Eufemia** has some 20 different columns with Byzantine capitals, a patterned geometrical mosaic floor, and an embossed, silver Venetian altar frontal dating from the 14th century. Remarkable, too, is the lovely 13th-century hexagonal *ambo* (pulpit) decorated with bold symbols of the Evangelists and covered by an Oriental cupola. ⊠ *Campo Patriarca Elia,* ☎ *0439/80146.* ☉ *Daily 8–8.*

Close to the Basilica in Campo dei Patriarchi, the 6th-century **Battistero** (Baptistery) also has a mosaic pavement. In the same square, the church of **Santa Maria delle Grazie** displays more Byzantine columns and mosaics.

Dining and Lodging

$$–$$$ ✕ De Toni. Right in the old town, this pretty restaurant exposes its floor so that you can see the foundations of the old Roman walls. Dining outside in summer is almost de rigueur. The chef has his own special recipe for fish soup. *Zuppa di vongole* (clam soup) is good, too, as is *triglia* (red mullet) in bread crumbs with vinaigrette. Reservations are advised in summer. ⊠ *Piazza Duca d'Aosta 37,* ☎ *0431/80104. AE, DC, MC, V. Closed Wed. in Sept.–June, and Jan.*

$ ✕ Al Balaor. As you might expect in this fishing port, seafood is the specialty. Pull up a button-backed chair in this elegant and plush restaurant with blue-green furnishings, and tuck into the fresh fish antipasti, coquilles St. Jacques with polenta, *frogolezzi* (small gnocchi) with shrimp, or swordfish. As the restaurant has its own pasticceria, the cakes are superb. Reservations are advised in summer. ⌧ *Calle Zanini 3,* ☎ *0431/80150. AE, DC, MC, V. Closed Thurs. and 10 days in Nov.*

$$$ ⊞ **Hannover.** The best thing about this small four-star hotel is its position overlooking the fishing port. Rooms are spacious and modern in a standard way, offset by the pink and green marble of the public rooms. The beach is also nearby, and access to this and the changing rooms is included in the price. ⌧ *Piazza XXVI Maggio, 34073,* ☎ *0431/ 82264,* FAX *0431/82141. 23 rooms, 3 suites. Restaurant, bar, hot tub, sauna, health club, parking. AE, DC, MC, V. Closed 2 wks in Jan.*

$$ ⊞ **Antares.** A pleasant, small, plant-filled hotel, it's right on the waterfront and has a quiet location. All rooms have a balcony, and there's a terrace for sunbathing. ⌧ *Via delle Scuole 4, 34073,* ☎ *0431/84961,* FAX *0431/82385. 19 rooms. Bar, parking (fee). AE, DC, MC, V. Closed Nov. 20–Feb. 10.*

$$ ⊞ **Savoy.** Light and spacious, this is the only Grado hotel to offer both indoor and outdoor swimming pools. Guest rooms are elegantly minimalist. The stately striped sofas in the lobby combine with the modernistic pink and white columns to lend an almost 18th-century flavor. ⌧ *Via Carducci 33, 34073,* ☎ *0431/897111,* FAX *0431/83305,* WEB *www. hotelsavoy-grado.it. 83 rooms. Restaurant, bar, 1 indoor and 1 outdoor pool, hair salon. AE, DC, MC, V. Closed Nov.–Mar.*

Outdoor Activities and Sports

BEACH

Before or after sightseeing in the old town, take a dip in the sea: the beach umbrellas are backed by cabins on lidos where you pay a small daily fee, and there's a free beach at the western end. The water is shallow and clean, making it ideal for kids.

BOAT TRIPS

The **Motonave Cristina** (☎ 0337/898055) sails twice a day from Grado to Portobuso, with a stop for lunch on the isle of Anfora.

GOLF

The **Golf Club Grado** (⌧ Rotta Primero, ☎ 0431/896896), a nine-hole course, is open year-round.

Gorizia

🄱 *51 km (39 mi) northwest of Trieste, 43 km (27 mi) north of Grado.*

Like Trieste, Gorizia bears the hallmark of the Habsburgs, having remained under the control of the Austrian dynasty until 1916. After World War II, the Treaty of Paris split the town, Italy keeping the western half and Yugoslavia the eastern, which is now Nova Goricia. A quiet place, Gorizia is still imbued with a mixture of Italian and Slavic cultures, and a stroll around town reveals grand streets, arcades, parks, and gardens.

A pleasant garden surrounds the Borgo Castello, a hilltop area fortified by the Venetians. Climb up the steps on the hill's steep western side, or take the Viale D'Annunzio on the gentler southern side to reach the red-roofed and battlemented **Castello.** The walls were reinforced in 1508 by the Venetians, who left their ubiquitous mark in the form of a winged lion in bas-relief over the castle entrance. In the inner court, it's possible to see the original 11th- and 12th-century foundations of the keep. ⌧ *Borgo Castello 36,* ☎ *0481/535146.* 🎟 €*3.10.* ⊗ *Tues.– Sun. 9:30–1 and 2–7:30.*

Within the castle complex is the church of **Santo Spirito,** built in 1398. It's notable for the hanging porch and 16th-century large wooden crucifix on the facade—actually a copy, the original squirreled away for safekeeping. ⊠ *Borgo Castello,* ☎ *0481/530193. Church rarely open; check at Museo di Storia e Arte for entry.*

Also in the Borgo Castello, the **Museo di Storia e Arte** contains a folklore and local handicraft collection, though it has been closed for years for restoration work. The **Palazzo Attems** in Piazza de Amicis is a fine neoclassical building, designed in 1745 by Nicolò Pacassi (1711–90), which houses the town's art gallery and historical archives. Local painters are represented from the 18th to the 20th century, including portraits by the painter Giuseppe Tominz (1790–1865) and the Impressionist Italico Brass.

The area around Gorizia saw some of the bloodiest battles of World War I, as documented by the town's **Museo della Grande Guerra,** one of Italy's most important museums relating to the Great War, particularly the Carso campaign fought by Italian and Austrian troops. Fourteen kilometers (8½ miles) south of Gorizia, the war cemetery at Redipuglia contains 100,000 graves of the fallen. ⊠ *Borgo Castello 15,* ☎ *0481/533926.* ⌨ €3.10. ☉ *Tues.–Sun. 9:30–1 and 2–7:30.*

Dining and Lodging

$$ ✕ **Ai Tre Soldi Goriziani.** This long dining room with plain white walls and a refined atmosphere is popular with locals on their night out. Try dishes with Eastern European flair such as the *gnocchi di pane al sugo di goulasch* (bread gnocchi with goulash) or the Weiner schnitzel. ⊠ *Corso Italia 38,* ☎ *0481/531956. Reservations essential. AE, DC, MC, V. Closed Mon. and Aug.*

$$ ✕ **Rosenbar.** There's a predominantly dark-red tone at this restaurant with wooden paneling and a copper bar. One part is more formal, the other around the bar less so. It's a popular spot, usually fairly lively, and with hospitable service. The small menu is handwritten and changes regularly. Try the pumpkin soup and the strudel of potato and radicchio, both delicious. Homemade puddings are a delight. ⊠ *Via Duca d'Aosta 96,* ☎ *0481/522700. AE, DC, MC, V. Closed Sun.–Mon. and 2 weeks in Feb.*

$–$$ ✕ **Alla Luna.** A simple, family-run establishment, Alla Luna manages to be both rustic and elegant. Dishes include gnocchi, and goulash with polenta and *zuppa di fagioli* (bean soup). ⊠ *Via Oberdan 13,* ☎ *0481/ 530374. No credit cards. Closed Mon. and last 2 wks in Aug. No dinner Sun.*

$ ⊞ **Palace.** Fancy trimmings at this modern hotel right in the center of town are confined to the impressive glass chandelier in the lobby. The place is a bit tattered around the edges, but it's conveniently priced, offers standard comfort, and is a decent place to stay if you're considering day-tripping to Slovenia. ⊠ *Corso Italia 63, 34170,* ☎ *0481/82166,* FAX *0481/31658. 70 rooms. Restaurant, bar, parking. AE, DC, MC, V.*

UDINE AND POINTS NORTH

Infused with the spirit of Venice, the inland town of Udine holds a cluster of absorbing attractions and is also the starting point for some fine sights in the vicinity, including a couple of the region's best museums, both enclosed within the old castle. Although there are good lodgings to be found at Udine, you might prefer the quieter milieu of Cividale del Friuli, almost within spitting distance of the Julian Alps and washed through by the lovely Natisone River. Some excellent museum collections are here, particularly the Museo Cristiano annexed to the Duomo.

You don't have to venture far from Cividale to feel the Alpine earth under your feet. Carry on northward, past Tolmezzo, to enter the charmed environment of Carnia, a mountain region lacking the epic grandeur of the Dolomites but containing enough natural beauty to satisfy the most jaded urban sensibility. Aside from a few larger hotels catering to skiers and hikers, the lodgings here are generally small and inexpensive, where hospitality is the watchword and the meals are designed to cure the deepest hunger induced by the clean air and healthy exertions.

Udine

18 *64 km (40 mi) north of Trieste, 100 km (62 mi) east of Venice.*

The second city of the region of Friuli-Venezia Giulia, Udine has a very different atmosphere than Trieste. The city of Udine, almost sleepy in its provincialism, commands a view of the surrounding plain and the Alpine foothills. According to legend, it stands on a mound erected by Attila the Hun so he could watch the burning of the important Roman center of Aquileia to the south. Udine flourished in the Middle Ages, thanks to its good location for trade and the rights it gained from the local patriarch to hold regular markets. There is a distinct Venetian feel to the city, noticeable in the architecture of Piazza della Libertà, which lies under the stern gaze of the lion of St. Mark. Like Venice, the city can boast a rich artistic patrimony, including a good selection of works by Tiepolo.

Udine's **Duomo,** consecrated in 1335, completed in the 15th century but much altered in the Baroque period, is an essential stop for its altarpieces and frescoes by the great Venetian artist, Giambattista Tiepolo (1696–1770). ☒ *Piazza Duomo,* ☎ *0432/505302.* ☒ *Free.* ☉ *Daily 7–noon and 4–7.*

Opposite the cathedral, the **Oratorio della Purità** is well worth a visit for more Tiepolo frescoes and, by his son, Giandomenico, grisaille (graytoned) biblical friezes. Ask the sacristan at the cathedral to let you in; late afternoon is probably the best time. ☒ *Piazza Duomo,* ☎ *0432/505032.*

The Palazzo Arcivescovile houses the **Galleria del Tiepolo,** which contains superlative examples of Tiepolo's frescoes from the Old Testament, depicting the stories of Abraham, Isaac, and Jacob and the *Judgment of Solomon* in beautiful pastel colors. In the same building, the **Museo Diocesano** features a collection of sculptures from Friuli churches from the 13th to the 18th century. ☒ *Piazza Patriarcato 1,* ☎ *0432/25003.* ☒ *€3.60 includes Museo Diocesano.* ☉ *Wed.–Sun. 10–noon and 3:30–6:30.*

Udine's large main square, **Piazza Libertà,** features the Palazzo del Comune, a typical 15th-century Venetian palazzo, built in imitation of the Palazzo Ducale in Venice. Opposite is the Renaissance Porticato di San Giovanni and the Torre dell'Orologio, a clock tower complete with *mori* (the name for naked Moors who strike the hours) on the top—another reference to Venice and the Torre d'Orologio in Piazza San Marco.

Pass through the **Arco Bollani,** a triumphal arch by Palladio, and climb the steps to the castle hill. In the castle area itself, the 13th-century church of **Santa Maria di Castello** contains frescoes contemporary with the building and can be opened on request; inquire at the Galleria d'Arte Antica.

From Udine's **Castello,** rebuilt after earthquakes in 1511 and 1976, the stunning panoramic views extend as far as Monte Nero in Slovenia (7,360 ft). In summer, concerts are held in the gardens here. The castle now holds the city's two main museums. The **Galleria d'Arte Antica** is a wide-ranging collection of local and Italian art including

canvases by the prolific Neapolitan Luca Giordano (1632–1705), the
Venetians Vittore Carpaccio (circa 1460–1525) and Tiepolo, and a paint-
ing of St. Francis receiving the stigmata, attributed to Michelangelo
Merisi Caravaggio (circa 1571–1610). ⊠ *Piazzale del Castello,* ☎
0432/502872. ▧ *€5.15, free Sun.* ☉ *Tues.–Sat. 9:30–12:30 and 3–6,*
Sun. 9:30–12:30.

The **Museo Archeologico** is the best place to trace the history of the
area and the importance of Udine and nearby Cividale del Friuli in the
formative period following the collapse of the Roman Empire. A large
collection of Lombard artifacts includes weapons, jewelry, and domestic
wares from this warrior race, which swept into what is now Italy in
the 6th century. ⊠ *Piazzale del Castello,* ☎ *0432/502872.* ▧ *€5.15,*
free Sun. ☉ *Tues.–Sat. 9:30–12:30 and 3–6, Sun. 9:30–12:30.*

West of Piazza Libertà, **Piazza Matteotti,** surrounded on three sides by
arcades and on the fourth by the church of San Giacomo, is the central piazza of Udine. The balcony of San Giacomo holds an outside
altar, allowing mass to be said while business could carry on uninterrupted in the market below.

Dining and Lodging

$$ ✕ **Antica Maddalena.** Just a few steps from Udine's pretty Piazza del-
★   l'Unità is where you'll find this elegant eating place, defined by its owner
as a deluxe trattoria. Lots of warm wood tones, fresh flowers, and stained
glass complement a menu of regional and Italian specialties, among
them *zuppa di funghi porcini* (porcini mushroom soup) and gnocchi
con zucca e ricotta (with squash and ricotta cheese). ⊠ *Via Pellicerie*
4, ☎ *0432/25111. AE, DC, MC, V. Closed Sun. and 2 wks in Aug.*
No lunch Mon.

$-$$ ✕ **Alla Buona Vite.** This traditional restaurant in the town center specializes in seafood. *Tagliolini dello chef* (long, thin noodles with a creamy
shrimp sauce) and *rombo al limone e capperi* (turbot with lemon and
capers) are among the many choices here. ⊠ *Via Treppo 10,* ☎ *0432/*
21053. AE, DC, MC, V. Closed Mon. and Aug. No dinner Sun.

$-$$ ✕ **Trattoria al Lepre.** A characteristic fogolar in one of the dining
rooms is a symbol of traditional local cooking, and that's what you'll
enjoy in this simple establishment. The specialties include tagliatelle
con funghi (with mushrooms) and *stinco di maiale* (shin of pork). ⊠
Via Poscolle 27, ☎ *0432/295798. AE, DC, MC, V. Closed Tues. and*
2 wks in Aug.

$$-$$$ 🛏 **Astoria Hotel Italia.** Centrally located, the Italia offers soundproofed
rooms furnished in traditional style. Public rooms have Venetian glass
chandeliers and comfortable armchairs. ⊠ *Piazza XX Settembre 24,*
33100, ☎ *0432/505091,* FAX *0432/509070. 75 rooms. Restaurant,*
minibars. AE, DC, MC, V.

$ 🛏 **Quo Vadis.** A 10-minute walk from the train station, this modest,
plant-filled hotel has an older part and modern annex with its own small
terrace. Facilities are basic and there's no restaurant, but Udine has a
good choice of eating places and the Don can recommend a couple of
clean tablecloths nearby. Rooms are small but comfortable. Choose one
facing away from the main road to cut down on traffic noise. ⊠ *Pi-*
azzale Cella 28, 33100, ☎ *0432/21091,* FAX *0432/21092. 14 rooms.*
Bar, free parking. AE, DC.

Cividale del Friuli

⑲ *17 km (11 mi) east of Udine, 52 km (29 mi) north of Trieste.*

For space, serenity, and beautiful scenery, venture east of Udine to the
foothills of the Julian Alps and the town of Cividale del Friuli, which

ranks as one of the most pleasant and picturesque towns of the region. The Natisone River tumbles down from the Alps to cut a limestone swath through the town, where it is crossed by the Ponte del Diavolo (Devil's Bridge)—legend has it that the devil himself threw into the river the large stone on which the central pier of the bridge rests. The town dates from the time of Julius Caesar, who was commander of Roman legions in the area and who had it named the Forum Julii—from which the Friuli region is named. In AD 568 it became the first Lombard duchy formed in Italy and after the demise of the Lombards was dominated by Franks, when the name was changed to Civitas Austriae—hence the name Cividale. Until 1238 it was the seat of the patriarchs of Aquileia, becoming a university town in 1353, though it declined from 1420 onward when it fell to Venice with the rest of Friuli and lost much of its influence to Udine. As a result, it has maintained a small, manageable size and is brimming with the impressive relics of various periods, all coverable in the less than a day. The **Duomo,** with its Gothic-Renaissance facade, contains a magnificent 12th-century silver altarpiece, a gift of the patriarch Pellegrino II (in office 1195–1204). It depicts a multitude of saints who surround the archangels Michael and Gabriel, who in turn flank the Virgin Mary. ⊠ *Piazza del Duomo,* ☎ *0432/731144.* ⊙ *Daily 9–noon and 3:30–6.*

Two masterpieces of Lombard sculptures are preserved in the **Museo Cristiano,** right next door to the Duomo and accessible from there. First of these is the octagonal baptistery, which incorporates 5th-century columns and capitals. This was named after Callisto, the first patriarch of Aquileia to live in Cividale (between 730 and 756). It was he who commissioned this baptistery, which is beautifully decorated with bas-reliefs, to stand originally beside the cathedral. The second piece is the altar that was carved for Ratchis, the Duke of Cividale and King of the Lombards from 744 to 749. The sides of the altar hold more bas-reliefs, depicting *Christ in Triumph,* the *Visitation,* and the *Adoration of the Magi.* Look out, too for the sculpted rhinoceros elsewhere in the museum. ⊠ *Piazza del Duomo,* ☎ *0432/731144.* ⊠ *Free.* ⊙ *Apr.–Sept., Mon.–Sat. 9:30–noon and 3–7, Sun. 3–7; Oct.–Mar., Mon.–Sat. 9:30–6, Sun. 3–6.*

Also in Piazza Duomo is the **Museo Archeologico,** installed in a building dating from the late 16th century and ascribed to Palladio. It houses an important and well-displayed collection of artifacts, including Roman mosaics and bronzes, Romanesque reliefs, and the Psalter of St. Elizabeth of Hungary. Cividale was a flourishing artistic center during Lombardic times, particularly in the goldsmith's field, to which the many finely crafted and delicate pieces here attest. ⊠ *Piazza Duomo,* ☎ *0432/700700.* ⊠ *€2.05.* ⊙ *Apr.–Oct., Mon. 9–1:30, Tues.–Sun. 9–6:30; Nov.–Mar., daily 8:30–1:30.*

Heading toward the river, you'll soon come to the **Ipogeo Celtico,** reached by a flight of steep steps at the bottom of which are underground chambers thought to be either a Celtic place of burial or a Roman prison. On the walls are crudely carved heads possibly dating from the 3rd century BC. ⊠ *Via Monastero Maggiore 2,* ☎ *0432/701211.* ⊠ *Free.* ⊙ *Daily 8 AM–10 PM (get key from adjacent Bar Ipogeo).*

Farther down Via Aquileia lies the river and the **Ponte del Diavolo,** the double-arched bridge crossing the Natisone. On the other side, you can browse among the stalls selling basketwork. The pretty, cobbled Via Monastero Maggiore leads along the river to what must count as one ★ of the most evocative early medieval buildings in Italy. The **Tempietto Longobardo,** a little gem of Lombard church-building, stands in a perfect and peaceful location above the meandering river. Though damaged by earthquakes, there remains a remarkable 8th-century stucco procession of female figures on either side of an arch, and lovely friezes with a vine motif. The carved and canopied wooden stalls date from the 14th century as do the frescoes. The epiphany scene is unique in that instead of the usual three kings it depicts two kings and a queen, the last in the procession, possibly in recognition of Giseltrude, a Lombard queen at the time of the chapel's construction. ✉ *Via Monastero Maggiore,* ☎ *0432/700867.* 🎫 *€2.05.* ⊘ *Apr.–Oct., Mon.–Sat. 9:30–1 and 3–6:30, Sun. 9:30–12:30 and 2:30–6; Nov.–Mar., Mon.–Sat. 9:30–12:30 and 3–5, Sun. 9:30–12:30 and 2:30–6.*

NEED A BREAK?	The **Caffè Longobardo** (✉ Via Carlo Alberto 6) is a pleasant place to sit and sample a traditional *gubana,* a sort of brioche with pine nuts and raisins, or a grappa and watch the passersby on the piazza. It's closed Monday.

Dining and Lodging

$–$$ ✕ **Al Monastero.** You can dine here either under the wooden roof or in an arcade whose walls were frescoed in the 1930s by an itinerant painter. There's a fogolar, and if you happen to be here in January you might catch a medieval banquet. If not, don't fret: the modern food, such as the local prosciutto San Daniele with pears, *maltagliati all'anitra* (duck with tomatoes and cream), or the tournedos of beef *del Monastero* (with speck and smoked ricotta baked in red wine), will still go down very nicely. The restaurant produces its own wine. ✉ *Via Ristori 11,* ☎ *0432/700808,* 🕸 *www.almonastero.com. Reservations essential. AE, DC, MC, V. Closed Mon. No dinner Sun.*

$ ✕ **Taverna Longobarda.** This place is pink and elegant, has an open fireplace, and is popular with locals. Cooking is traditional with the accent on meat, game in particular. Try the hare with polenta or the *cinghiale* (wild boar). In summer you can eat in the garden. ✉ *Via Monastero Maggiore 5,* ☎ *0432/731655. AE, MC, V. Closed Wed.*

$ 🏨 **Al Castello.** At the beginning of the 19th century, this creeper-covered, crenellated hotel, set on a peaceful hillside, was a monastery. Rooms are spacious and furnished in different styles, some antique, some modern, and with nice, big bathrooms. The redbrick restaurant, popular for Sunday lunch (and closed Wednesday and the first two weeks of February), has a Friulian fogolar and serves national as well as local dishes, both fish and meat. In spring, find something that includes asparagus and you won't be disappointed. ✉ *Via del Castello 20, 33043,* ☎ *0432/733242,* 📠 *0432/700901,* 🕸 *www.infotech.it/castello. 17 rooms. Restaurant, bar, tennis court. AE, DC, MC, V.*

$ 🏨 **Al Pomo d'Oro.** Pink seems to be a predominant color for little hotels in Italy and this one is no exception, presenting a charming facade with its shutters and geraniums. It was an inn in the 12th century but has since undergone considerable renovation; rooms are furnished in a plain, modern style. The location is excellent, a few steps away from the cathedral. The restaurant is closed Wednesday. ✉ *Piazza San Giovanni 20, 33043,* ☎ 📠 *0432/731489,* 🕸 *www.alpomodoro.com. 13 rooms. Restaurant, bar. AE, DC, MC, V.*

$ 🏨 **Roma.** Situated right in the center of Cividale, this is a modern family-run hotel. Public and private rooms are attractively furnished in cherrywood, and the pale green decor gives a cool and mellow ambience. ✉ *Piazza Picco 14/a, 33043,* ☎ *0432/731871,* 📠 *0432/701033. 50 rooms. Restaurant, bar. AE, DC, MC, V.*

Shopping

A general market is held every Saturday morning in Piazza Garibaldi; by the bridge you'll find good stalls selling wicker baskets of every description. The goldsmith at **Bottega Longobarda** (⊠ Stretta Santa Maria di Corte 20, ☎ 0432/730932), on the ground floor of the 13th-century Casa Medioevale, makes and sells distinctive jewelry in a Lombard style.

Forni di Sopra

⑳ *100 km (62 mi) northwest of Cividale, 153 km (95 mi) northwest of Trieste.*

Forni di Sopra sits on the edge of the Parco Regionale delle Dolomiti Friulane and at the foot of the Passo di Mauria, the mountain pass connecting Carnia with the eastern Dolomites. In summer, the area is a walker's nirvana, although you'll find plenty of space to yourself, as the area is not on any major tourist routes. The lush meadows are filled with flowers, and there are trails for mountain biking and horseback riding. The tourist office (☎ 0433/886767) can furnish you with information on these activities as well as hikes. Excellent food can be found in small trattorias, many with an open fireplace, that make good use of wild plants and herbs in their cooking. Winter, of course, brings streams of skiers to the district, and there are places to rent equipment if you want to join them.

Dining and Lodging

$ ✕ **Osteria di Nonta.** Relax at this lovely, hospitable old restaurant in the village of Nonta di Socchieve, 26 km (16 mi) east of Forni di Sopra and 15 km (9 mi) west of Tolmezzo. It has long, polished wooden tables; a fogolar with a cauldron; a frilly curtain; a wind-up telephone (that almost works); and lace lamp shades. The obliging lady of the house devises a different menu each day of extremely traditional food; taste the local specialty, *cjalsòns* (ravioli) if you haven't already; here it's cjalsòns *di Rualp* (ravioli with ricotta, nutmeg, and onion). The *brovada* (turkey stuffed with spinach, rolled and sliced) also deserves mention. ⊠ *Nonta di Socchieve,* ☎ *0433/80596. Reservations essential. No credit cards. Closed Mon.*

$$–$$$ 🏨 **I Larici.** This is a long, low hotel with clean, elegant lines and good facilities. It's a favorite hostelry for skiers (bus to the ski lift is included in the price) and hikers, offering a range of evening entertainment and generous meals in its restaurant. ⊠ *Via Chianeit 5, 33024,* ☎ *0433/886701,* ℻ *0433/886710. 68 rooms, 3 suites. Restaurant, bar, sauna, gym, dance club. MC, V. Closed Sept. 16–June 8.*

$$ 🏨 **Davost.** This hearty, no-nonsense hotel is next to good sporting facilities, including an ice rink and tennis courts. The terrace has fine views of the mountains. In the basement there's a large pizzeria with a wood-burning oven and a reasonably priced tourist menu. Try the local specialty *frico* (cheese) with gnocchi, onion, speck, and mushrooms. ⊠ *Via Tagliamento 12, 33024,* ☎ *0433/88103,* ℻ *0433/88550. 34 rooms, 2 suites. Restaurant, bar. MC, V.*

$ 🏨 **Nuoitas.** In a quiet location 4 km (2½ mi) north of Forni di Sopra, circled by evergreens, this is a traditional chalet hotel with wooden furniture in an Alpine style. The bathrooms are attractive, and rooms have good views from their wooden balconies. It represents very good value for the money. The restaurant is closed Tuesday. ⊠ *Località Nuoitas Nord-Ovest, 33024,* ☎ *0433/88387,* ℻ *0433/886956. 18 rooms. Restaurant, bar. AE, DC, MC, V. Closed May 7–18.*

FRIULI-VENEZIA GIULIA A TO Z

To research prices, get advice from other travelers, and book travel arrangements, visit www.fodors.com.

AIRPORTS AND TRANSFERS

There are domestic flights to Aeroporto Ronchi dei Legionari, 35 km (22 mi) northwest of Trieste, linked by regular SAITA bus service to Via Flavio Gioia, near Trieste's train station. There is also a SAITA connection to Udine from the airport.

➤ AIRPORT INFORMATION: **Aeroporto Ronchi dei Legionari** (✉ Redipuglia, ☎ 0481/773224, WEB www.aeroporto.fvg.it). **SAITA** (☎ 040/425001 for connection to Trieste; 0432/503004 for Udine connection).

BOAT AND FERRY TRAVEL

Boats from Greece, Albania, Slovenia, and Croatia dock in Trieste. Contact Adriatica di Navigazione, through the agent Agemar.

➤ BOAT AND FERRY INFORMATION: **Adriatica di Navigazione** (✉ Piazza Duca degli Abruzzi 1/a, ☎ 040/363737, FAX 040/365015).

BUS TRAVEL

Interurban and interregional bus connections serve the Veneto and Friuli-Venezia Giulia. Regular buses run from Piazzale Roma in Venice to Trieste, and there are frequent connections from Padua and Treviso. Local tourist offices may be able to provide details of timetables and routes; otherwise contact the local bus station.

The bus station in Trieste is at Piazza della Libertà; ACT operates services in and around Trieste. SAITA operates services within the province and to Slovenia and Croatia. Gradese buses travel among Trieste, Aquileia, Cividale, and Udine.

➤ BUS INFORMATION: **ACT** (☎ 167/016675 toll-free). **Gradese** (☎ 0432/503004). **SAITA** (☎ 0481/425001). **Trieste Bus Station** (✉ Piazza della Libertà 11).

CAR RENTAL

➤ LOCAL AGENCIES: **Avis** (✉ Molo Bersaglieri 3, Stazione Marittima, Trieste, ☎ 040/300820; ✉ Aeroporto Ronchi dei Legionari, Trieste, ☎ 0481/777085; ✉ Viale Leopardi 5/a, Udine, ☎ 0432/501149). **Hertz** (✉ Molo Bersaglieri 3, Stazione Marittima, Trieste, ☎ 040/3220098; ✉ Aeroporto Ronchi dei Legionari, Trieste, ☎ 0481/777025; ✉ Via Crispi 19, Udine, ☎ 0432/609160).

CAR TRAVEL

The good A4 autostrada runs eastward past or through Verona, Vicenza, and Venice to Trieste, off of which the A23 highway branches north to Udine; both are toll routes. The A27 links the A4 with Treviso and continues northward until it ends north of Belluno, from where you can pick up the SS51, then turn eastward on the SS52 to reach Carnia.

From Trieste the SS14 runs northwest along the coast to Monfalcone, and the SS202 takes the more inland route. The A4 runs from Sistiana to Udine and north almost to Tolmezzo from where the SS52 leads eastward to Carnia and Forni di Sopra. Aquileia is easily reached from the SS14, from where the straight SS352 traverses the causeway to Grado. Gorizia is easily reached from Monfalcone and Cividale from Udine along the SS54.

EMERGENCIES

All pharmacies post signs on the door with addresses of *farmacie di turno* (pharmacies taking shifts), which stay open at night, on Saturday afternoon, and on Sunday.

➤ EMERGENCY SERVICES: **Police** (☎ 112 or 113). **Ambulance** (☎ 118).

➤ HOSPITALS: **Ospedale Civile** (✉ Via Chiusaforte 41, Udine, ☎ 0432/ 480062). **Ospedale Maggiore** (✉ Via Stuparich 1, Trieste, ☎ 040/ 3991111).

TOURS
Trieste offers a variety of tours throughout the year; "Trieste Romantica" (a Habsburg tour); "Il Liberty a Trieste," and "Winckelmann e il Neoclassico." Tours cost €5.15 and details can be obtained from the tourist office, or call the number below.

➤ FEES AND SCHEDULES: **Trieste Tours** (☎ 040/6796111 or 040/420182).

TRAIN TRAVEL
There are 14 daily services linking Venice with Trieste and hourly services between Treviso and Udine. Trieste also connects easily with Budapest, Ljubljana, and Vienna. All towns within this region are connected by train with the exception of Grado and Aquileia and Forni di Sopra, which are reachable by bus. Contact FS for train information.

FARES AND SCHEDULES
➤ TRAIN INFORMATION: **FS** (☎ 888088). **Stazione Gorizia** (✉ Piazzale Martiri Libertà d'Italia, ☎ 147/888088). **Stazione Trieste Centrale** (✉ Piazza della Libertà 8, ☎ 147/888088). **Stazione Udine** (✉ Piazzale d'Annunzio, ☎ 147/888088).

TRAVEL AGENCIES
➤ LOCAL AGENTS: **Gotour** (✉ Via Nazario Sauro 12, Gorizia, ☎ 0481/ 531213). **Non Stop Viaggi** (✉ Via Nazario Sauro 12, Monfalcone, ☎ 0481/791096). **Paterniti Viaggi/American Express** (✉ Corso Cavour 7, Trieste, ☎ 040/366161). **Ribi** (✉ Viale Europa Unita 5, Grado, ☎ 0431/80166). **Viaggi Uno** (✉ Viale Europa Unita 36, Udine, ☎ 0432/ 25123).

VISITOR INFORMATION
Trieste offers a special weekend package deal ("T for you") that includes discounts in hotels and restaurants, free or reduced-price entrance to a selection of the cities' main tourist attractions, and some guided tours. Contact the Trieste tourist office (☎ 040/67961). Promhotels offers a booking service for the Grado hotels and can arrange excursions.

➤ TOURIST INFORMATION: **Promhotels** (✉ Riva Zaccaria Gregori 9, 34073, ☎ 0431/82347, FAX 0431/84980). **Tourist Offices** (✉ Piazza Capitolo, 33043 Aquileia, ☎ FAX 0432/731398; ✉ Piazza Capitolo, 33051 Cividale del Friuli, ☎ 0431/919491, FAX 0431/91086; ✉ Via Cadore 1, 33024 Forni di Sopra, ☎ 0433/886767, FAX 0433/886686; ✉ Via Roma, 34170 Gorizia, ☎ 0481/386225, FAX 0481/386277; ✉ Viale Dante 72, 34073 Grado, ☎ 0431/98991, FAX 0431/899278; ✉ Via San Nicolò 20, 34121 Trieste, ☎ 040/67961, FAX 040/416806; ✉ Piazza I Maggio 7, 33100 Udine, ☎ 0432/295972, FAX 0432/504743).

10 BASICS AND BACKGROUND

Smart Travel Tips A to Z

Italian Vocabulary

ESSENTIAL INFORMATION

ADDRESSES

In Venice addresses are made up of
the name of one the city's six neighborhoods and a number. The hitch is
that the numbers don't go in any
sequential order, so San Marco 3672
and 3673 might well be several narrow winding streets away from one
another. Accordingly, the Venetian
addresses in this book include the
nearest campo, bridge, or calle when
helpful.

Italian addresses outside of Venice
are fairly straightforward: the street
is followed by the street number.
However, you might see an address
with a number plus "bis" or "A"
(e.g., Via Verdi 3/bis or Via Mazzini
8/A). This indicates that 3/bis or 8/A
is the next entrance or door down
from Via Verdi 3 and Via Mazzini 8,
respectively.

In rural areas, some addresses give
only the route name or the distance in
kilometers along a major road (e.g.
Via Fabbri, km 4.3), or sometimes
only the name of the small village in
which the site is located.

AIR TRAVEL

BOOKING

When you book **look for nonstop
flights** and **remember that "direct"
flights stop at least once.** Try to avoid
connecting flights, which require a
change of plane. For more booking
tips and to check prices and make on-
line flight reservations, log on to
www.fodors.com.

CARRIERS

When flying internationally, you must
usually choose between a domestic
carrier, the national flag carrier of the
country you are visiting, and a foreign carrier from a third country. You
may, for example, choose to fly
Alitalia to Italy. National flag carriers
have the greatest number of nonstops.

Domestic carriers may have better
connections to your home town and
serve a greater number of gateway
cities. Third-party carriers may have a
price advantage.

Alitalia—in addition to other major
European airlines and smaller, privately run companies such as Meridiana and Air One—has an extensive
network of internal flights in Italy.
Ask your domestic or Italian travel
agent about discounts, which include
a 50% family reduction and up to
30% off certain night flights.

Direct service from Heathrow to
Venice is provided daily by Alitalia
and British Airways. From Manches-
ter there are three direct BA flights
daily to Milan, and daily flights to
Rome.

➤ To & FROM ITALY: **Alitalia** (☎
800/223–5730 in the U.S.; 020/7602–
7111 in the U.K.; 06/65641 in Rome;
848/865641 elsewhere in Italy, WEB
www.alitalia.it) to Rome, Milan, and
Venice. **American Airlines** (☎ 800/
433–7300 in the U.S.; 02/679141 in
Milan, WEB www.aa.com) to Milan
and Rome. **British Airways** (☎ 800/
247–9297 in the U.S.; 0345/222–111
in the U.K.; 06/65011575 in Rome;
848/812266 elsewhere in Italy, WEB
www.britishairways.com) to Rome,
Milan, and Venice. **Continental
Airlines** (☎ 800/231–0856 in the
U.S.; 06/47675205 in Rome; 800/
296230 elsewhere in Italy, WEB www.
flycontinental.com) to Rome and
Milan. **Delta Air Lines** (☎ 800/241–
4141 in the U.S.; 800/864114 in
Italy, WEB www.deltaairlines.com) to
Rome, Milan, and Venice. **Meridiana**
(☎ 020/7839–2222 in the U.K.; 06/
478041 in Italy, WEB www.meridiana.
it) from London to Florence, Bologna,
Turin, and Catania. **Northwest Airlines** (☎ 800/225–2525 in the U.S.;
02/218981 in Italy, WEB www.nwa.
com) to Rome and Milan. **United
Airlines** (☎ 800/538–2929 in the

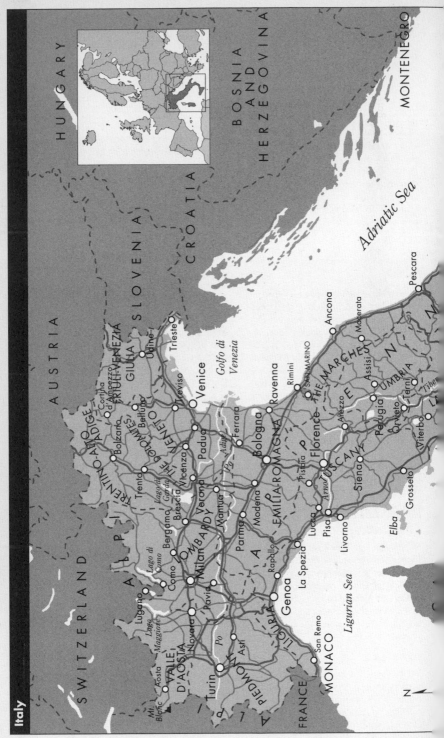

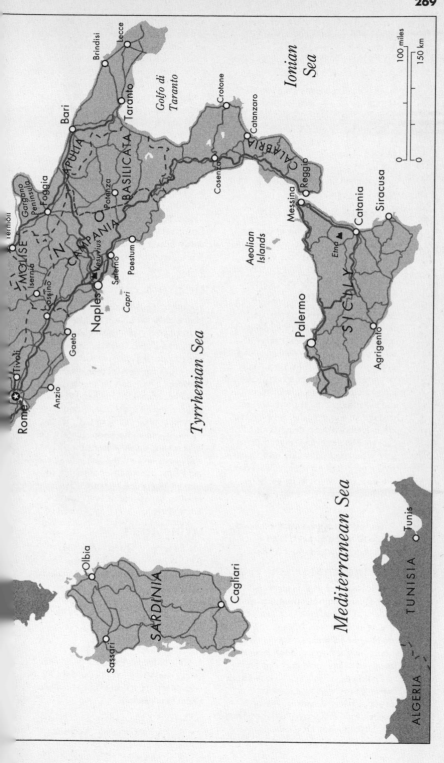

U.S.; 02/667481 in Italy, WEB www. unitedairlines.com) to Milan. US Airways (☎ 800/428–4322 in the U.S.; 848/813177 in Italy, WEB www. usairways.com) to Rome.

➤ AROUND ITALY: **Air One** (☎ 06/ 488800 in Rome; 848/848880 elsewhere in Italy). **Alitalia** (☎ 800/223– 5730 in the U.S.; 020/7602–7111 in the U.K.; 06/65641 in Rome; 848/ 865641 elsewhere in Italy, WEB www. alitalia.it). **Meridiana** (☎ 020/7839– 2222 in the U.K.; 06/478041 in Italy, WEB www.meridiana.it).

CHECK-IN & BOARDING

Always **ask your carrier about its check-in policy.** Plan to arrive at the airport about 2 hours before your scheduled departure time for domestic flights and 2½ to 3 hours before international flights.

Assuming that not everyone with a ticket will show up, airlines routinely overbook planes. When everyone does, airlines ask for volunteers to give up their seats. In return, these volunteers usually get a certificate for a free flight and are rebooked on the next flight out. If there are not enough volunteers, the airline must choose who will be denied boarding. The first to get bumped are passengers who checked in late and those flying on discounted tickets, so **get to the gate and check in as early as possible,** especially during peak periods.

Always **bring a government-issued photo ID to the airport;** even when it's not required, a passport is best.

CUTTING COSTS

The least expensive airfares to Venice and other Italian destinations must usually be purchased in advance and are nonrefundable. It's smart to **call a number of airlines,** and when you are quoted a good price, **book it on the spot**—the same fare may not be available the next day. Always **check different routings** and look into using different airports. Travel agents, especially low-fare specialists (☞ Discounts & Deals, *below*), are helpful.

Consolidators are another good source. They buy tickets for scheduled international flights at reduced rates from the airlines, then sell them at prices that beat the best fare available directly from the airlines, usually without restrictions. Sometimes you can even get your money back if you need to return the ticket. Carefully read the fine print detailing penalties for changes and cancellations, and **confirm your consolidator reservation with the airline.**

➤ CONSOLIDATORS: **Cheap Tickets** (☎ 800/377–1000). **Discount Airline Ticket Service** (☎ 800/576–1600). **Unitravel** (☎ 800/325–2222). **Up & Away Travel** (☎ 212/889–2345). **World Travel Network** (☎ 800/409– 6753).

ENJOYING THE FLIGHT

For more legroom, **request an emergency-aisle seat.** Don't sit in the row in front of the emergency aisle or in front of a bulkhead, where seats may not recline. If you have dietary concerns, **ask for special meals when booking.** These can be vegetarian, low-cholesterol, or kosher, for example. On long flights, try to maintain a normal routine, to help fight jet lag. At night, **get some sleep.** By day, **eat light meals, drink water** (not alcohol), and **move around the cabin** to stretch your legs. For additional jet-lag tips consult *Fodor's FYI: Travel Fit & Healthy* (available at bookstores everywhere).

FLYING TIMES

Flying time to Milan is 8½ hours from New York, 10–11 hours from Chicago, 11½ hours from Dallas (via New York), 11½ hours from Los Angeles. It's 2½ hours from London to Venice, 23½ hours from Sydney to Rome.

HOW TO COMPLAIN

If your baggage goes astray or your flight goes awry, complain right away. Most carriers require that you **file a claim immediately.**

➤ AIRLINE COMPLAINTS: U.S. Department of Transportation **Aviation Consumer Protection Division** (✉ C-75, Room 4107, Washington, DC 20590, ☎ 202/366–2220, WEB www.

dot.gov/airconsumer). **Federal Aviation Administration Consumer Hotline** (☎ 800/322–7873).

AIRPORTS

Venice's Aeroporto Marco Polo is served by domestic and international flights, including connections from London, Amsterdam, Brussels, Frankfurt, Munich, Paris, Vienna, and Zurich.

The major gateways to Italy are Rome's Aeroporto Leonardo da Vinci, better known as Fiumicino, and Milan's Aeroporto Malpensa 2000, which handle domestic, intercontinental, and European traffic. If you land in Rome or Milan and plan to take a train to Venice, you will first need to get to the main train stations in either town. In Rome you will need to take a train or a taxi to Stazione Termini; in Milan, take the convenient buses to Stazione Centrale. Trains for Venice are frequent during the day. The trip takes four to five hours from Rome, three hours or less from Milan, on the fastest trains being the Eurostar. Smaller, minor gateways are served by domestic and some international flights.

➤ AIRPORT INFORMATION: **Aeroporto Malpensa 2000** (✉ 45 km [28 mi] north of Milan, ☎ 02/74852200, WEB www.sea-aeroportimilano.it). **Aeroporto Marco Polo** (✉ 10 km [6 mi] north of Venice, Tessera, ☎ 041/2609260; 041/2609222 lost baggage, WEB www.veniceairport.it). Aeroporto Leonardo da Vinci, also known as **Fiumicino** (✉ 35 km [20 mi] southeast of Rome, ☎ 06/65953640, WEB www.adr.com).

AIRPORT TRANSFERS

By Boat: This is the most convenient (and scenic) way to get to Venice from Aeroporto Marco Polo. The most direct boat trip is from the Alilaguna launch, with regular scheduled service from 6.15 AM until midnight; it takes about an hour to get to the landing (just off Piazza San Marco), stopping at the Lido on the way, and the fare is €9.00 per person, including luggage. A water taxi, a sleek, modern motorboat known as a *motoscafo,* from the airport costs about €75.00 for two people (more

for larger groups), but it is always essential to **agree on a water-taxi fare before boarding.** The trip takes 40 minutes to San Marco.

By Bus: Blue ATVO buses make the 25-minute nonstop trip from the airport to Piazzale Roma; from here you can get a vaporetto to the landing nearest your hotel. The ATVO fare is €2.60 (with added fees for luggage), and tickets are available on the bus when the airport ticket booth is closed. The local ACTV bus (Line 5) runs from the airport to Piazzale Roma every 30 minutes (every hour after 8:10 PM), but you need a ticket (€0.80) before boarding, which can only be purchased at the airport tobacconist-newsstand, open daily 6:30 AM–9 PM. Luggage can be a hassle on the bus, which is usually crowded with local commuters. The trip takes 35–40 minutes.

By Taxi: A yellow taxi from the airport to Piazzale Roma costs about €30 and takes 15–20 minutes.

➤ CONTACTS: **ACTV** (contact Pronto Vela, ☎ 899/909090, WEB www.actv.it or www.velaspa.com). **Alilaguna** (☎ 041/5235775). **ATVO** (☎ 041/929500). **Taxis** (☎ 041/5237774). **Water taxis** (☎ 041/5415084).

DUTY-FREE SHOPPING

As of July 1999 duty-free shopping in airports was eliminated in Italy (and EU countries); you can still make in-flight duty-free purchases, however.

BEACHES

In the Veneto and Friuli regions, the tame landscape features sandy beaches with well-maintained facilities, catering mostly to crowds of locals and sunbathers from Austria and Germany. The lack of rocks and cliffs, and the shallowness of the sea, makes them ideal for families with small children. As you go from south to north, the most popular sea resorts in the area are Venice beaches on the Lido; Jesolo (40 km [25 mi] from Venice), famous for its vibrant nightlife in summer; Lignano Sabbiadoro, named after the "golden sand" that attracts more than 100,000 visitors a day (located a few miles from the mouth of the Tagliamento River in Friuli); and the historic town of

Grado, which makes a great day trip from Trieste. Inland, the shores of Lago di Garda bring together natural beauty with a low-key worldliness that includes discos, spas, and stylish restaurants; Torbole, to the north of Monte Baldo on the eastern shore, is a sailing and wind-surfing center.

For most Italians who live along the coast, going to the beach is more a part of the regular summer routine than a vacation activity: locals head to the nearest beach during the long Italian lunch break and for the evening *passeggiata* (stroll). In Italy a healthy suntan is still much sought after, although awareness of the dangers of long-term overexposure is spreading. Creams and sunblocks are available, but read the labels carefully to make sure you are getting the protection you desire, and don't underestimate the scorching power of the Italian sun. The "tanning" season begins in early May, when bathing suits by the major designers begin to appear in the windows of Italian shops, and the beach season starts in earnest in early June, with the opening of beaches run by concessionaires.

It is essential to distinguish between the private and public beaches. The former are free and open to the public but offer no services. Although on the most popular public beaches it's sometimes possible to buy sandwiches and soft drinks from kiosks or roaming vendors, as a general rule you shouldn't expect such comforts, let alone pay telephones, toilets, or showers. Private beaches charge admission and range from spartan (cold showers and portable toilets) to luxurious (with gardens, stylish bars, fish restaurants, and private guest huts). Admission policies and prices vary accordingly: although most establishments offer day passes that cost from €5.00 to €26.00 per person and include a chaise lounge and an umbrella, some of the more exclusive places cater only to patrons who pay by the week or month. Inquire at local tourist offices for details.

The summer season ends on September 15. During weekends, holidays and in August, most sea resorts and beaches tend to be very crowded, some posting no-vacancy signs by 10 AM, so an early start is essential. If in northern and central Italy sunbathing topless is common practice, in the south it could lead to undesired attention from local men. Nowhere in Italy, except in the rare nudist beach, is it common practice to walk around topless, and beach attire (bare chests and thighs) worn in town can still earn you a fine in some places.

BIKE TRAVEL

Italians are great bicycling enthusiasts—in the flatlands and historical centers of the Veneto region, locals often commute by bike, and they are proud of it. Those who enjoy touring have fine bicycling itineraries at their disposal throughout Italy. The Federazione Italiana Amici della Bicicletta (FIAB) will help you plan your itinerary. The Web site www.cycling.it contains an interesting selection of articles (in Italian) from the publication *La Bicicletta,* with detailed descriptions of itineraries across national parks and areas of natural beauty.

Given the country's hilly terrain, it is essential to have a good map with clearly marked indications of elevation, distances, and the various types of roads. An excellent map choice is the green regional series issued by the Italian Touring Club, available from major book stores. Road conditions are generally good throughout Italy, but, as you move along, it's always a good idea to ask local tourist information offices about cyclist-friendly routes. Especially in the smaller towns and villages, cyclists do not go unnoticed, and if you speak a little Italian you'll be likely to meet sympathetic native cyclists eager to give valuable tips about the local region.

Always park (and lock) your bike inside your hotel for the night. Keep in mind one small but potentially important matter: laundromats are rare in Italy and can be found only in the bigger cities.

➤ LOCAL RESOURCES: **FIAB** (✉ Viale Venezia 7, 30170 Mestre, ☎ FAX 041/ 938092, WEB www.fiab-onlus.it).

BIKES IN FLIGHT

Most airlines accommodate bikes as luggage, provided they are dismantled and boxed. Airlines sell bike boxes, which are often free at bike shops, for about $5 (it's at least $100 for bike bags). International travelers can sometimes substitute a bike for a piece of checked luggage at no charge; otherwise, the cost is about $100. Domestic and Canadian airlines charge $25–$50.

BOAT & FERRY TRAVEL

GONDOLAS

If you simply can't leave Venice without a gondola ride, the best time is in the late afternoon or early evening hours, when the Grand Canal isn't so heavily trafficked. Try to avoid low tide, when the odors of the canals are at their worst. It's best to start from a station on the Grand Canal, because the lagoon is usually choppy. Make it clear that you want to see the smaller canals, and **come to terms on the cost and duration of the ride before you start.** Gondoliers are supposed to charge a fixed minimum of about €65.00 for up to six passengers for 50 minutes. Before 8 AM and after 8 PM the rate increases to approximately €80.00. Bargaining may get you a better price.

TRAGHETTI

Few tourists know about the two-man gondolas that ferry people across the Grand Canal at various fixed points. They are the cheapest and shortest gondola ride in Venice and can save a lot of walking. The fare is €0.40, which you hand to the gondolier when you get on. Look for TRAGHETTO signs as you approach the following "stations": Dogana (from Punta della Dogana to Calle Vallaresso); Santa Maria del Giglio (from Calle Lanza, near the Chiesa della Salute, to Campo Santa Maria del Giglio); San Samuele (from Salizzada Ca' Malipiero, near Palazzo Grassi, to Calle del Traghetto off Campo San Barnaba); San Tomá (from Calle del Traghetto near Campo San Tomá to Calle del Traghetto near Campiello Nuovo o dei Morti); Rialto (from Fondamenta del Vin to Riva del Carbon); Santa Sofia (from the Pescheria in the Rialto market to Campo Santa Sofia near the Ca' d'Oro); and San Marcuola (from Campo San Marcuola to the Fontego dei Tedeschi). Note that only the San Tomá and Santa Sofia traghetti are operative any day of the week (except on major holidays) from about 7 AM to 7 PM. All the other traghetti have undependable schedules: they might run just in the morning, close on Sunday, or even suddenly shut down for lack of passengers or due to strong currents.

VAPORETTI

ACTV water buses run the length of the Grand Canal and circle the city. There are several lines, some of which connect Venice with the major and minor islands in the lagoon. The fare (which is subject to change) is €3.10 on all lines (€5.15 round-trip). A 24-hour tourist ticket costs €9.30, a three-day ticket €18.60, and a seven-day ticket €31; these tickets are especially worthwhile if you are planning to visit the islands, and they are also valid for buses in Mestre and on the Lido. Free timetables and maps are available at the ticket office at Piazzale Roma. They run every 10 or 20 minutes during the day, depending on the line. Timetables are also posted at every landing stage, and there is a ticket booth at each stop. After 9 PM, tickets are available on the boats, but you must immediately inform the controller that you need a ticket. For this reason, it may be useful to buy a *blocchetto* (book of tickets) in advance. The blocchetto called *carnet di dieci biglietti di corsa semplice*, with 10 tickets at €2.60 each, is a good deal, but don't throw away the last page of the book, which must be shown to the controller. If you have just one stop to go along or across the Grand Canal, or if you are going from San Zaccaria to the Isola di San Giorgio or from Sant'Elena to the Lido, ask for a traghetto (€1.55; round-trip €2.60). If you are traveling in a group of three, four, or five people you are eligible for the *biglietto family*—ask for details about different discount options at ticket booths. Be sure to **validate tickets in the time-stamp machines before getting on board,** or you will be subject to a fine. Below is a list of the most useful lines.

Line 1 is the Grand Canal local, making all stops but San Samuele and continuing via San Marco to the Lido. (It takes about 45 minutes from the train station to San Marco.)

Line 3 is the fast line connecting the Tronchetto with San Marco Giardinetti via the Grand Canal, stopping only at Ferrovia (train station), San Samuele, and Accademia. Note that it doesn't stop at Piazzale Roma and Rialto (to Piazzale Roma and Rialto from the Tronchetto see Line 82 below) and that it runs in a loop: from San Marco Giardinetti it goes back to the Tronchetto via the Canale della Giudecca (not via the Grand Canal). For a fast return via the Grand Canal see Line 4, below.

Line 4 is the fast line connecting San Marco Giardinetti with the Tronchetto via the Grand Canal, stopping only at Accademia, San Samuele, Rialto, Ferrovia (train station), and Piazzale Roma. Like Line 3, it runs in a loop: note that from the Tronchetto it makes a straight trip to San Marco Giardinetti via the Canale della Giudecca.

Line 12 connects the Fondamente Nuove with Murano (Faro stop only), Burano, and Torcello without stopping at the cemetery. (To the cemetery on Isola di San Michele see Line 41 and 42, below.)

Line 41 (or Circolare Antioraria) and **Line 42** (or Circolare Oraria) circle the town, following long loop routes in opposite directions: for example, take Line 42 clockwise from San Zaccaria to the Redentore, but Line 41 counterclockwise from the Redentore to San Zaccaria. As you go clockwise, convenient stops to the north include Ferrovia (train station), Guglie (near the Jewish Ghetto), Sant'Alvise (near the church of the same name), Fondamente Nove (where you can get connecting boats to Burano and Torcello), Cimitero (Isola di San Michele), and many stops in Murano. Stops to the south are Sant'Elena, Giardini (where the Biennale d'Arte takes place), Arsenale, San Zaccaria (near Piazza San

Marco), and three stops on the Giudecca (Zitelle, Redentore, and Sacca Fisola). Before getting on board, it's a good idea to confirm with the boat operator that you are going in the right direction.

Line 51 runs in a loop from the railway station to San Zaccaria via Piazzale Roma and Zattere and continues to the Lido. **Line 52** goes along the same route but in the opposite direction, so from the Lido it makes stops at Sant'Elena, the Giardini, San Zaccaria, Zattere, Santa Marta, Piazzale Roma, the train station, Guglie, Tre Archi (near the Chiesa di San Giobbe), Sant'Alvise, Orto (near the Chiesa della Madonna dell'Orto), Fondamente Nove, Ospedale, Celestia (near the Chiesa di San Francesco della Vigna), San Pietro di Castello, and back to the Lido.

Line DIR is the direct line from Piazzale Roma and Ferrovia to Murano (and back); there's no service on Sunday and holidays.

Line 61 goes direct from Piazzale Roma to the Lido via Zattere; note that it doesn't stop at San Zaccaria. **Line 62** follows the same route in the opposite direction.

Line 71 is the fast line from San Zaccaria to Murano, and from there it continues to the Tronchetto, stopping at the train station and Piazzale Roma. **Line 72** does exactly the same route as Line 71, but in the opposite direction.

Crowded **Line 82** travels the following route: San Zaccaria, San Giorgio, Giudecca, Zattere, Tronchetto, Piazzale Roma, the train station, Rialto, Accademia and Vallaresso (with fewer stops along the Grand Canal than Line 1), and back. There's no service on the tracts San Tomá–Vallaresso and Vallaresso–San Tomá (or Sant'Angelo) before 9 AM and after 9 PM. Note that from June to the first week of September Line 82 continues to the Lido.

The best way to go to the Lido from the center of town is by taking the large, three-floor *motonave* **(Line 6 and Line 14)**, which leaves from San Zaccaria every 20 minutes.

Vaporetto Lines

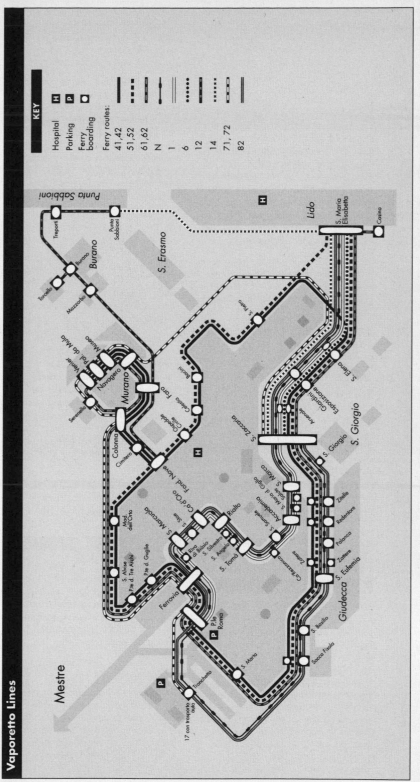

At night, there is only local **Line N,** with boats leaving every 20 minutes from the Lido to San Zaccaria and back, and from Rialto to Piazzale Roma and back. With less frequent departures, there are also boats leaving from the Lido which, after stopping at San Zaccaria (at the dock opposite the Hotel Danieli), continue to the Tronchetto via the Grand Canal and return to San Zaccaria (at the dock opposite the Hotel Jolanda) via the Giudecca, serving most stops along the route. Similarly, more Line N boats go from San Zaccaria (from the dock opposite the hotel Jolanda) to the Tronchetto via the Giudecca, then continue along the Grand Canal and all the way up to the Lido via San Zaccaria (dock opposite the hotel Danieli).

The **Servizio Notturno Laguna Nord** runs very limited night service from Fondamente Nove to Murano and Burano, and back.

➤ CONTACT: **ACTV** (contact Pronto Vela, ☎ 899/909090, 🕸 www.actv.it or www.velaspa.com).

WATER TAXIS

The stylish powerboat *motoscafi* (water taxis) are extremely expensive, and the fare system is as complex as Venice's layout. Plan on spending at least €45.00 for a short trip in town and €75.00 to or from the airport. Always agree on the fare before starting out, and beware of other additions such as hand luggage and late or early hours. Call **Cooperativa San Marco** for 24-hour service in town.

➤ CONTACTS: **Cooperativa San Marco** (☎ 041/5222303). **Water taxis to and from airport** (☎ 041/5235775).

BUS TRAVEL

Frequent ACTV buses leave from Piazzale Roma to Mestre and other destinations in the province, including Aeroporto Marco Polo (Line 5). Lines 1 and 7 stop in central Mestre, Line 4 and 4/ go past Corso del Popolo, and Line 2 goes to Mestre train station. Between midnight and 5 AM, buses run every 30 minutes, with line N 1/ serving Mestre's train station. Line N 2/ goes through Corso del Popolo. Tickets cost €0.80 (a book of 10 is €7.25) and are valid for 60 minutes after validation. Fares are expected to rise in 2002 or 2003.) Tickets are sold at the ACTV office in Piazzale Roma (daily 7:30 AM to 8 PM) and at tobacconists; at night you can buy them from coin-operated machines.

On the Lido, buses leave from the main vaporetto landing on Piazzale Santa Maria Elisabetta. Orange Line A goes to San Nicolò and back. Dark blue Line B goes to the Alberoni/Faro Rocchetta (Malamocco) and, in the opposite direction, to the Ospedale al Mare. Blue Line C serves long Via Sandro Gallo. Green Line V goes to Malamocco (Via Parri). Line 11 goes to Pellestrina.

Detailed information about routes and departure times is printed in the monthly *Venezia News,* and you can pick up free maps and schedules from the ACTV office. The ACTV staff speaks English, French, and Spanish. The lost-property office is open daily 7:30 AM–8 PM.

Bus networks in the Veneto and Friuli-Venezia Giulia are extensive, although bus travel in Italy is not as attractive an option as in other European countries. This is partly due to the comparatively low cost and convenience of train travel. However, in some areas buses can be faster and more direct than local trains, so it's a good idea to **compare bus and train schedules.**

➤ BUS INFORMATION: **ACTV** (☎ 041/ 5287886, 🕸 www.actv.it; lost property office, ✉ inside the ACTV office in Piazzale Roma, ☎ 041/2722179).

BUSINESS HOURS

BANKS & OFFICES

Banks are open weekdays 8:30 to 1:30 and 2:45 to 3:45. Venice's main post office, known as Fondaco dei Tedeschi, is open Monday to Saturday 8:15 to 7 for stamps and registered mail, until 6 for other operations.

GAS STATIONS

Gas stations are generally open Monday through Saturday from 7 to 7 with a break at lunch. Many stations have automatic self-service pumps that accept bills (some also take credit cards). Gas stations on autostrade are open 24 hours.

MUSEUMS & SIGHTS

In Venice, the group of 14 noteworthy churches belonging to the Chorus Association are open Monday through Saturday 10 to 5 and Sunday 1 to 5 (with minor variations for the churches of the Frari and of San Sebastiano). Other churches usually open early in the morning until noon or 12:30, when they close for three to four hours or more; they open again in the afternoon, closing about 7 PM or later. The Basilica di San Marco is open Monday to Saturday 9:45 to 4:30 and Sunday 1 to 4:30 from November to April, until 5:30 the rest of the year. Note that sightseeing in churches during religious services is discouraged. Services usually begin at 7 AM, noon, and 6:30 PM.

Museum hours vary and change with the seasons. Venice's major museums (Museo Correr, Palazzo Ducale, and the Gallerie dell'Accademia) are open daily, but try to avoid visiting during crowded weekends. Other museums are closed one day a week: always check ahead.

PHARMACIES

Pharmacies are open Monday to Friday 9 to 12:30 and 4 to 7:30 and Saturday 9 to 12:30. The names and addresses of pharmacies open 24 hours and during holidays are always posted on the door of each pharmacy; they are also published in the local newspaper *Gazzettino* and in the monthly *Venezia News*.

SHOPS

Most shops are open from 9:30 to 1 and from 3:30 or 4 to 7 or 7:30. In Venice, most clothing and tourist-oriented shops are open all day, Sunday included. Food shops stay open 8 to 1 and 5 to 7:30 and are closed Sunday and Wednesday afternoon (except for butchers, who are open only in the morning) and for part of August. Bars and pastry shops usually close one day a week. Barbers and hairdressers, with some exceptions, are closed Sunday and Monday.

CAMERAS & PHOTOGRAPHY

The *Kodak Guide to Shooting Great Travel Pictures* (available at bookstores everywhere) is loaded with tips.

➤ PHOTO HELP: Kodak Information Center (☎ 800/242–2424).

EQUIPMENT PRECAUTIONS

Don't pack film and equipment in checked luggage, where it is much more susceptible to damage. X-ray machines used to view checked luggage are becoming much more powerful and therefore are much more likely to ruin your film. Always **keep film and tape out of the sun.** Carry an extra supply of batteries, and **be prepared to turn on your camera or camcorder** to prove to security personnel that the device is real. Always **ask for hand inspection of film,** which becomes clouded after repeated exposure to airport X-ray machines, and **keep videotapes away from metal detectors.**

FILM & DEVELOPING

In Venice and most major cities you'll see scores of photo developing shops, many with service in one hour (or less). In smaller cities look for a shop with a Kodak sign outside its door. Although it's not expensive to develop film in Italy (around €6.00 per 36-exposure roll), film is considerably more expensive than in the United States (around €8.30 for a color 36-exposure roll), so it's a good idea to stock on film before you leave.

VIDEOS

While VHS videotapes and players are common, be forewarned that Italy, like other countries in Europe, uses a different video system than that used in the United States. This means that you won't be able to play the videotapes that you bring from home on Italian equipment, nor tapes purchased in Italy on an American VCR.

CAR RENTAL

Rates in Venice begin at €45.00 a day and €220.00 a week for an economy car with air-conditioning, a manual transmission, and mileage limited to 150 km (93 mi) a day. This includes the 20% IVA tax on car rentals. Most major American car-rental companies have offices or affiliates in Italy, but the rates are generally better if you make a reservation from abroad rather than from within Italy. In Italy, you can save up to 30% by renting your car on-line pretending you are still abroad. Weekend rates with limited mileage are usually good deals. Note that in Italy car-rental companies usually make it mandatory to purchase the collision-damage waiver, regardless of what coverage may be provided by your credit card.

➤ MAJOR AGENCIES: **Alamo** (☎ 800/522–9696; 020/8759–6200 in the U.K., WEB www.alamo.com). **Avis** (☎ 800/331–1084; 800/879–2847 in Canada; 02/9353–9000 in Australia; 09/525–1982 in New Zealand; 0870/606–0100 in the U.K., WEB www.avis.com). **Budget** (☎ 800/527–0700; 0870/156–5656 in the U.K., WEB www.budget.com). **Dollar** (☎ 800/800–6000; 0124/622–0111 in the U.K., where it's affiliated with Sixt; 02/9223–1444 in Australia, WEB www.dollar.com). **Hertz** (☎ 800/654–3001; 800/263–0600 in Canada; 020/8897–2072 in the U.K.; 02/9669–2444 in Australia; 09/256–8690 in New Zealand, WEB www.hertz.com). **National Car Rental** (☎ 800/227–7368; 020/8680–4800 in the U.K., WEB www.nationalcar.com).

CUTTING COSTS

To get the best deal, **book through a travel agent, who will shop around.** Do **look into wholesalers,** companies that do not own fleets but rent in bulk from those that do and often offer better rates than traditional car-rental operations. Payment must be made before you leave home.

➤ LOCAL AGENCIES: **Avis** (✉ Piazzale Roma, ☎ 041/5225825; ✉ Aeroporto Marco Polo, ☎ 041/5415030; 199/100133 countrywide, WEB www.avis.com). **Hertz** (✉ Piazzale Roma, ☎ 041/5284091; ✉ Aeroporto Marco Polo, ☎ 041/5416075; 199/112211 countrywide, WEB www.hertz.com). **Sixt Rent-a-Car** (✉ Aeroporto Marco Polo, ☎ 041/5415654, WEB www.sixt.it). **Thrifty** (✉ Aeroporto Marco Polo, ☎ 041/5416049, WEB www.italybycar.it).

➤ WHOLESALERS: **Auto Europe** (☎ 207/842–2000 or 800/223–5555, FAX 207/842–2222, WEB www.autoeurope.com). **DER Travel Services** (✉ 9501 W. Devon Ave., Rosemont, IL 60018,

☎ 800/782–2424, FAX 800/282–7474 for information; 800/860–9944 for brochures, WEB www.dertravel.com). **Europe by Car** (☎ 212/581–3040 or 800/223–1516, FAX 212/246–1458, WEB www.europebycar.com).

INSURANCE

When driving a rented car you are generally responsible for any damage to or loss of the vehicle. Before you rent, see what coverage your personal auto-insurance policy and credit cards provide.

Before you buy collision coverage, check your existing policies—you may already be covered. However, collision policies that car-rental companies sell for European rentals usually do not include stolen-vehicle coverage. Note that in Italy, all car-rental companies make you buy theft-protection policies (included in the price).

REQUIREMENTS & RESTRICTIONS

In Italy your own driver's license is acceptable. An International Driver's Permit is a good idea; it's available from the American or Canadian Automobile Association and, in the United Kingdom, from the Automobile Association or Royal Automobile Club. These international permits are universally recognized, and having one in your wallet may save you a problem with the local authorities. In Italy you must be 21 years of age to rent an economy or sub-compact car and at least 25 years of age to rent a bigger car. Upon rental, all companies require credit-card numbers as a warranty.

SURCHARGES

Before you pick up a car in one city and leave it in another, **ask about drop-off charges or one-way service fees,** which can be substantial. Note, too, that some rental agencies charge extra if you return the car before the time specified in your contract. To avoid a hefty refueling fee, **fill the tank just before you turn in the car,** but be aware that gas stations near the rental outlet may overcharge.

CAR TRAVEL

There is an extensive network of *autostrade* (toll highways), complemented by equally well maintained but free *superstrade* (expressways). All are clearly signposted and numbered. The ticket you are issued upon entering an autostrada must be returned when you exit and pay the toll; on some shorter autostrade, mainly connecting highways, the toll is paid upon entering. Viacard cards, on sale at many autostrada locations, make paying tolls easier and faster. A *raccordo* is a connecting expressway. *Strade statali* (state highways, denoted by *S* or *SS* numbers) may be single-lane roads, as are all secondary roads; directions and turnoffs are not always clearly marked. Venice is on the east–west A4 autostrada, which connects with Padua, Verona, Brescia, Milan, and Turin.

Automobil Club Italiano (ACI) gives travel tips and information in English about rules of the road, road conditions, and car insurance.

➤ CONTACT: **ACI** (☎ 06/49982389), open daily 8–8.

EMERGENCY SERVICES

Automobil Club Italiano (ACI) emergency service is available 24 hours a day by dialing 116 from any phone.

➤ CONTACT: **ACI emergency service** (☎ 116).

GASOLINE

Gas costs about €1.20 per liter.

PARKING

If you bring a car to Venice, you will have to pay for a garage or parking space. Warning: do not be waylaid by illegal touts, often wearing fake uniforms, who may try to flag you down as you approach Venice and offer to arrange parking and hotels; their activities have become a scandal in a city generally free of con men and criminals. Ignore them and continue on until you reach the automatic ticket machines.

Do not leave valuables in the car. There is a luggage storage office, open daily 8–8, next to the Pullman Bar on the ground floor of the municipal garage at Piazzale Roma. You can take your car to the Lido—the car ferry (Line 17) makes the half-hour trip about every 50 minutes from a landing at Tronchetto, but in summer there can be long lines. It costs €6.50 to €16.00, depending on the size of the car.

Parking at Autorimessa Comunale at Piazzale Roma costs €19.00 for 24 hours. The private Garage San Marco at Piazzale Roma costs €18.00 for 12 hours and €25.00 for 24 hours. To reach the privately run Tronchetto parking area, follow the signs to turn right before Piazzale Roma. Parking costs €15.50 for 24 hours. The AVA (☞ Lodging, *below*) has arranged a discount of 20% per day for hotel guests who use the Garage San Marco or the Tronchetto facilities. Ask for a voucher upon checking into your hotel and present it at the parking area when you pay. Only Garage San Marco accepts reservations. Vaporetto line 82 runs from Tronchetto to Piazzale Roma and Piazza San Marco and also goes on to the Lido in summer. (When there is thick fog or extreme tides, a bus runs to Piazzale Roma instead.) Avoid private boats—they are a rip-off.

In most cities, parking space is at a premium; historic town centers are closed to most traffic, and peripheral parking areas are usually full. Parking in an area signposted ZONA DISCO is allowed for limited periods (from 30 minutes to two hours or more—the limit is posted); if you don't have the cardboard disk to show what time you parked, you can use a piece of paper. The *parcometro*, the Italian version of metered parking, has been introduced in some major cities. It's advisable to **leave your car only in guarded parking areas.** Unofficial parking attendants can help you find a space but offer no guarantees. In major cities your car may be towed away if illegally parked.

➤ CONTACTS: **Autorimessa Comunale** (☎ 041/2727301). **Garage San Marco** (☎ 041/5232213). **Tronchetto** (☎ 041/5207555)

ROAD CONDITIONS

Autostrade are well maintained, as are most interregional highways. The condition of provincial (county) roads varies, but road maintenance at this level is generally good in Italy. Traffic is heaviest around cities in morning and late-afternoon commuter hours, and on weekends. Street and road signs are often challenging—a good map and patience are essential.

RULES OF THE ROAD

Driving is on the right, as in the United States. Regulations are largely as in Britain and the United States, except that the police have the power to levy on-the-spot fines. In most Italian towns the use of the horn is forbidden in certain, if not all, areas; a large sign, ZONA DI SILENZIO, indicates where. Italians drive fast and are impatient with those who don't. Speed limits are 130 kph (80 mph) on autostrade and 110 kph (70 mph) on state and provincial roads, unless otherwise marked. Fines for driving after drinking are heavy, with the additional possibility of six months' imprisonment.

CHILDREN IN VENICE & THE VENETO

Italians love children and are generally very tolerant and patient with them, but there are few amenities provided specifically for them. Some discounts do exist. Always **ask about a sconto bambino** (child's discount) before purchasing tickets. Children under a certain height (under 3 ft in Venice) ride free on trains, municipal buses, vaporetti, and trams. Children under 18 who are EU citizens are admitted free to state-run museums and galleries, and there are similar privileges in many municipal or private museums.

If you are renting a car, don't forget to **arrange for a car seat** when you reserve. For general advice about traveling with children, consult *Fodor's FYI: Travel with Your Baby* (available in bookstores everywhere).

FLYING

If your children are two or older, **ask about children's airfares.** As a general rule, infants under two not occupying a seat fly at greatly reduced fares or even for free. When booking, **confirm carry-on allowances** if you're traveling with infants. In general, for babies charged 10% of the adult fare you are allowed one carry-on bag and a collapsible stroller; if the flight is full, the stroller may have to be checked or you may be limited to less.

Experts agree that it's a good idea to use safety seats aloft for children weighing less than 40 pounds. Airlines set their own policies: U.S. carriers usually require that the child be ticketed, even if he or she is young enough to ride free, since the seats must be strapped into regular seats. Do **check your airline's policy about using safety seats during takeoff and landing.** And since safety seats are not allowed everywhere in the plane, get your seat assignments early.

When reserving, **request children's meals or a freestanding bassinet** if you need them. But note that bulkhead seats, where you must sit to use the bassinet, may lack an overhead bin or storage space on the floor.

FOOD

In restaurants and trattorias you may find a high chair or a cushion for the child to sit on, but rarely a children's menu. You can order a *mezza porzione* (half-portion) of any dish, or ask the waiter for a *porzione da bambino* (child's portion). Most restaurants will have no problem making simple dishes that might be more palatable to children, such as pasta *con olio e parmigiano* (pasta with olive oil and Parmesan), *pesce lesso* (steamed fish), *riso al burro* (boiled rice with butter), *verdura lessa* (boiled vegetables), *uova* (eggs), and so on.

LODGING

Almost always in Venetian hotel rooms an extra bed for children can be added, but it rarely comes free of charge. Expect to pay between 20% and 40% extra. Most hotels in Venice allow children under a certain age to stay in their parents' room at no extra charge, but others charge for them as extra adults; be sure to **find out the cutoff age for children's discounts.** The Luxury Collection of Sheraton Hotels has more than 20 properties in Italy, all of which welcome families. Notable is the Hotel Des Bains on the Lido in Venice, which is right on the beach and has a parklike area for children to enjoy.

➤ BEST CHOICES: **Hotel des Bains** (☎ 041/5265921). **Sheraton Hotels Luxury Collection** (☎ 800/221–2340 in the U.S.).

SIGHTS & ATTRACTIONS

Places that are especially appealing to children are indicated by a rubber-duckie icon (🦆) in the margin.

COMPUTERS ON THE ROAD

Getting on-line in Venice isn't difficult; Internet points and Internet cafés, sometimes open 24 hours a day, are becoming more and more common. Prices and special offers differ from place to place, so **spend some time to figure out the best deal.** This isn't always readily apparent: a place might charge higher rates, but because it belongs to a chain you won't be charged an initial flat fee again when you move to a different city with the same chain. Some hotels have in-room modem lines, but, as with phones, using the hotel's line is relatively expensive. **Always check modem rates before plugging in.** You may need an adapter for your computer for the European-style plugs. As always, if you are traveling with a laptop, carry a spare battery and an adapter. Never plug your computer into any socket before asking about surge protection. IBM sells a pea-size modem tester that plugs into a telephone jack to check if the line is safe to use.

➤ INTERNET CAFÉS: **Internet cafe net house** (✉ Campo Santo Stefano, 2967/2958 San Marco, Venice, ☎ 041/2771190, 🌐 www.nethouseportal.com). **Planet Internet** (✉ down the Ponte delle Guglie on Strada Nova, 1519 Cannaregio, Venice, ☎ 041/5244188, planetInternet@veniceone.it). **Thenetgate** (✉ Crosera San Pantalon, 3812/a Dorsoduro, Venice, ☎ 041/2440213, 🌐 www.thenetgate.it).

CONSUMER PROTECTION

Whenever shopping or buying travel services in the Veneto region, **pay with a major credit card,** if possible, so you can cancel payment or get reimbursed if there's a problem. If you're doing business with a particular company for the first time, **contact your local Better Business Bureau and the attorney general's offices** in your state and (for U.S. businesses) the company's home state as well. Have any complaints been filed? Finally, if you're buying a package or tour, always **consider travel insurance** that includes default coverage (☞ Insurance, *below*).

➤ BBB: **Council of Better Business Bureaus** (✉ 4200 Wilson Blvd., Suite 800, Arlington, VA 22203, ☎ 703/276–0100, FAX 703/525–8277, 🌐 www.bbb.org).

CUSTOMS & DUTIES

When shopping, **keep receipts** for all purchases. Upon reentering the country, **be ready to show customs officials what you've bought.** If you feel a duty is incorrect or object to the way your clearance was handled, note the inspector's badge number and ask to see a supervisor. If the problem isn't resolved, write to the appropriate authorities, beginning with the port director at your point of entry.

IN AUSTRALIA

Australian residents who are 18 or older may bring home $A400 worth of souvenirs and gifts (including jewelry), 250 cigarettes or 250 grams of tobacco, and 1,125 ml of alcohol (including wine, beer, and spirits). Residents under 18 may bring back $A200 worth of goods. Prohibited items include meat products. Seeds, plants, and fruits need to be declared upon arrival.

➤ INFORMATION: **Australian Customs Service** (Regional Director, ✉ Box 8, Sydney, NSW 2001, ☎ 02/9213–2000, FAX 02/9213–4000, 🌐 www.customs.gov.au).

IN CANADA

Canadian residents who have been out of Canada for at least seven days may bring home C$750 worth of goods duty-free. If you've been away fewer than seven days but more than 48 hours, the duty-free allowance drops to C$200; if your trip lasts 24–48 hours, the allowance is C$50. You may not pool allowances with family members. Goods claimed under the C$750 exemption may follow you by mail; those claimed under the lesser exemptions must accompany you. Alcohol and tobacco products may be included in the seven-day and 48-hour exemptions but not in the 24-hour exemption. If you meet the age requirements of the province or territory through which you reenter Canada, you may bring in, duty-free, 1.14 liters (40 imperial ounces) of wine or liquor *or* 24 12-ounce cans or bottles of beer or ale. If you are 19 or older you may bring in, duty-free, 200 cigarettes and 50 cigars. Check ahead of time with the Canada Customs Revenue Agency or the Department of Agriculture for policies regarding meat products, seeds, plants, and fruits.

You may send an unlimited number of gifts worth up to C$60 each duty-free to Canada. Label the package UNSOLICITED GIFT—VALUE UNDER $60. Alcohol and tobacco are excluded.

➤ INFORMATION: **Canada Customs Revenue Agency** (✉ 2265 St. Laurent Blvd. S, Ottawa, Ontario K1G 4K3,, ☎ 204/983–3500 or 506/636–5064; 800/461–9999 in Canada, WEB www.ccra-adrc.gc.ca).

IN NEW ZEALAND

Homeward-bound residents 17 or older may bring back $700 worth of souvenirs and gifts. Your duty-free allowance also includes 4.5 liters of wine or beer; one 1,125-ml bottle of spirits; and either 200 cigarettes, 250 grams of tobacco, 50 cigars, or a combination of the three up to 250 grams. Prohibited items include meat products, seeds, plants, and fruits.

➤ INFORMATION: **New Zealand Customs** (Custom House, ✉ 50 Anzac Ave., Box 29, Auckland, ☎ 09/300–5399, FAX 09/359–6730), WEB www.customs.govt.nz.

IN THE U.K.

If you are a U.K. resident and your journey was wholly within the European Union (EU), you won't have to pass through customs when you return to the United Kingdom. If you plan to bring back large quantities of alcohol or tobacco, check EU limits beforehand.

➤ INFORMATION: **HM Customs and Excise** (✉ St. Christopher House, Southwark, London SE1 OTE, ☎ 020/7928–3344, WEB www.hmce.gov.uk).

IN THE U.S.

U.S. residents who have been out of the country for at least 48 hours (and who have not used the $400 allowance or any part of it in the past 30 days) may bring home $400 worth of foreign goods duty-free.

U.S. residents 21 and older may bring back 1 liter of alcohol duty-free. In addition, regardless of your age, you are allowed 200 cigarettes and 100 non-Cuban cigars. Antiques, which the U.S. Customs Service defines as objects more than 100 years old, enter duty-free, as do original works of art done entirely by hand, including paintings, drawings, and sculptures.

You may also mail or ship packages home duty-free: up to $200 worth of goods for personal use, with a limit of one parcel per addressee per day (except alcohol or tobacco products or perfume worth more than $5); label the package PERSONAL USE and attach a list of its contents and their retail value. Do not label the package UNSOLICITED GIFT or your duty-free exemption will drop to $100. Mailed items do not affect your duty-free allowance on your return.

➤ INFORMATION: **U.S. Customs Service** (✉ 1300 Pennsylvania Ave. NW, Room 6.3D, Washington, DC 20229, WEB www.customs.gov; inquiries ☎ 202/354–1000; complaints c/o ✉ 1300 Pennsylvania Ave. NW, Room 5.4D, Washington, DC 20229; registration of equipment c/o Office of Passenger Programs, ☎ 202/927–0530).

IN VENICE & THE VENETO

Of goods obtained anywhere outside the EU the allowances are as follows: (1) 200 cigarettes or 100 cigarillos or 50 cigars or 250 grams of tobacco; (2) 2 liters of still table wine or 1 liter of spirits over 22% volume or 2 liters of spirits under 22% volume or 2 liters of fortified and sparkling wines; and (3) 50 ml of perfume and 250 ml of toilet water.

Of goods obtained (duty and tax paid) within another EU country, the allowances are as follows: (1) 800 cigarettes or 400 cigarillos or 400 cigars or 1 kilogram of tobacco; (2)

90 liters of still table wine plus (3) 10 liters of spirits over 22% volume plus 20 liters of spirits under 22% volume plus 60 liters of sparkling wines plus 110 liters of beer.

➤ INFORMATION: **Dogana Sezione Viaggiatori** (✉ Aeroporto Leonardo da Vinci, Fiumicino, 00054 Rome, ☎ 06/65954343). **Ministero delle Finanze, Direzione Centrale dei Servizi Doganali, Divisione I** (✉ Via Carucci 71, 00143 Rome, ☎ 06/ 50242117).

DINING

The restaurants we list in this guide are the cream of the crop in each price category. Unless otherwise noted, the restaurants listed in this guide are open daily for lunch and dinner.

A few pointers on Italian dining etiquette: Italians diners tend to know exactly how they want their food, so **don't be afraid to ask the waiter for what you want** (salt, extra Parmesan cheese, or olive oil on the side) or to have a dish prepared without ingredients you do not care for (for example, *senz'aglio, per favore*—without garlic, please). Although mineral water makes its way to almost every table, you can always order a carafe of tap water (*acqua di rubinetto* or *acqua semplice*) instead. Italians order their food first, then wine and beverages. Wiping your bowl clean with a (small) piece of bread is considered a sign of appreciation, not bad manners. Spaghetti should be eaten with a fork only; although a little help from a spoon will not horrify the locals the way cutting spaghetti into little pieces might. When you finish eating and are ready to have your plate cleared, rest your utensils together on your plate at about five o'clock. Order your espresso (Italians do not drink a cappuccino after dinner) after dessert, not with it. When you are ready for the check, ask for it: unless it's well past closing time, no waiter would dare put a bill on your table without your having asked first. Don't ask for a doggy bag.

MEALS & SPECIALTIES

What's the difference between a *ristorante* and a *trattoria*? Can you

order food at an *enoteca*? Can you go to a restaurant just for a snack, or order just a salad at a *pizzeria*? The following definitions should help.

Not too long ago, restaurants tended to be more elegant and expensive than trattorie and *osterie*, which served more traditional, home-style fare in an atmosphere to match. But the distinction has blurred considerably, and an osteria in the center of town might be far fancier (and pricier) than a ristorante across the street. In all these types of places, you are generally expected to order at least a two-course meal, such as a *primo* (first course) and a *secondo* (main course); an *antipasto* (starter) followed by either primo or secondo; or a secondo and a *dolce* (dessert). In an enoteca (wine bar) or pizzeria, it's not inappropriate to order just one dish. An enoteca menu is often limited to a selection of cheese, cured meats, pickles, salads, and desserts, but if there is a kitchen, you'll also find vegetable soups, pasta, meat, and fish preparations. Venetian *bacari* are something between an old-style osteria and a wine bar: here it's possible to grab a fast snack (*cicheto*) at the counter to be swallowed down with a glass of wine (*ombra*), or sit down for a fast meal. Most pizzerie don't offer just pizza, and although the other dishes on the menu are supposed to be starters, there's no harm in skipping the pizza. The typical pizzeria fare includes *affettati misti* (selection of cured pork), simple salads, and various kinds of *bruschetta* and *crostino* (similar to bruschetta, but baked). All pizzerie have fresh fruit, ice cream, and simple desserts.

Throughout the country, the handiest and least expensive places for a quick snack between sights are probably *bar, caffè,* and *pizza al taglio* spots. Most bars have a selection of *panini* (sandwiches, often to be warmed up on the griddle—*piastra*) and *tramezzini* (sandwiches served on un-toasted white bread triangles). In larger cities, bars also serve prepared salads, fruit salads, cold pasta dishes, and yogurt around lunchtime. Most bars offer beer and a variety of alcohol, but very few bars (except in Venice) sell wine by the glass. A caffè is like a bar but usually with more tables to sit down. Pizza at a caffè is to be avoided—it's usually frozen and reheated in a microwave oven. If you place your order at the counter, ask if you can sit down: some places charge extra for table service, while others do not. In a self-service bar and caffè, it's good manners to clean up your table before you leave. Note that in some places you have to pay before you place the order and be ready to show your *scontrino* (receipt) when you move to the counter. Pizza al taglio shops are easy. They sell pizza by weight: just point out which kind of pizza you want and how much. Very few pizza al taglio shops have places to sit down.

MEALTIMES

Breakfast is usually served from 7 to 10:30; lunch is served from 12:30 to 2:30; dinner from 7:30 to 10. Enoteche and bacari are open also in the morning and late afternoon for a snack at the counter. Most pizzerie open at 8 PM and close around midnight–1 AM or later in the summer and on weekends. Most bars and caffè are open nonstop from 7 AM until 8–9 PM, and a few stay open until midnight or so.

PAYING

Prices for goods and services in Italy include tax. Restaurant menu prices include service (*servizio*), unless indicated otherwise on the menu. It is customary to leave an additional small tip of a few euros in appreciation of good service. Tips are always given in cash directly to your waiter. Some restaurants still charge a separate "cover" charge per person, usually listed on the menu as *pane e coperto*. It should be a modest charge (from €1.00 to €2.50 per person, except at the most expensive restaurants). Some restaurants instead charge for bread, which should be brought to you (and paid for) only if you order it. Whenever in doubt, ask about the servizio and pane e coperto policy upon ordering to avoid unpleasant discussions about payment later. The price of grilled and baked fish dishes is often given by weight (before cooking), so the price you see on the menu is for 100 grams of fish, not for the whole dish. An average fish portion is about 350 grams.

RESERVATIONS & DRESS

Reservations are always a good idea in restaurants and trattorias, especially over weekends and holidays. We mention them only when they are essential or not accepted. Book as far ahead as you can, and reconfirm as soon as you arrive in town. Pizzerie and enoteche accept reservations only for large groups. We mention dress only when men are required to wear a jacket or a jacket and tie. But unless they are at a sea resort eating outdoors and are perfectly tanned, Italian men never wear shorts or running shoes in a restaurant—no matter how humble—or in an enoteca. Shorts are acceptable in pizzerie and side caffè. The same "rules" apply to ladies' casual shorts, running shoes, sandals, and clogs.

DISABILITIES & ACCESSIBILITY

Italy has only recently begun to provide facilities such as ramps, telephones, and rest rooms for people with disabilities; such things are still the exception, not the rule. Travelers' wheelchairs must be transported free of charge according to Italian law, but the logistics of getting a wheelchair on and off trains and buses can make this requirement irrelevant. Seats are reserved for people with disabilities on public transportation, but few buses have lifts for wheelchairs. High, narrow steps for boarding trains create additional problems. In many monuments and museums, even in some hotels and restaurants, architectural barriers make it difficult, if not impossible, for those with disabilities to gain access.

Contact the nearest Italian consulate about bringing a Seeing Eye dog into Italy; this requires an import license, a current certificate detailing the dog's inoculations, and a letter from your veterinarian certifying the dog's health. Local tourist information offices can provide a list of accessible hotels and addresses of Italian associations for travelers with disabilities.

The privately run Sanitrans has a fleet of water taxis with facilities for the disabled; it also has wheelchairs, crutches, and other mobility aides for rent.

➤ LOCAL RESOURCES: **Informahandicap** (✉ Viale Garibaldi 155 30174, Mestre, ☎ 041/5341700; closed Sun., Mon., Aug.). **Sanitrans** (☎ 041/ 5239977, FAX 041/5245357, WEB www. sanitrans.veniceone.com).

RESERVATIONS

When discussing accessibility with an operator or reservations agent, **ask hard questions.** Are there any stairs, inside *or* out? Are there grab bars next to the toilet *and* in the shower/ tub? How wide is the doorway to the room? To the bathroom? For the most extensive facilities meeting the latest legal specifications, **opt for newer accommodations.**

SIGHTS & ATTRACTIONS

Palazzo Ducale, the Basilica di San Marco, Gallerie dell'Accademia, Ca' Rezzonico, Palazzo Grassi, Galleria Franchetti inside the Ca' d'Oro, Ca' Mocenigo, and the Scuola di San Rocco have either lifts or ramps for wheelchairs. Most churches, including the Basilica di San Marco, have only one or two low steps to overcome.

TRANSPORTATION

In Venice, bridges, narrow *calli* (streets), and uneven access to vaporetto landings complicate matters. **Contact Informahandicap** for detailed information about routes for wheelchair users.

➤ COMPLAINTS: **Aviation Consumer Protection Division** (☞ Air Travel, *above*) for airline-related problems. **Civil Rights Office** (✉ U.S. Department of Transportation, Departmental Office of Civil Rights, S-30, 400 7th St. SW, Room 10215, Washington, DC 20590, ☎ 202/366–4648, FAX 202/366–9371, WEB www.dot.gov/ ost/docr/index.htm) for problems with surface transportation. **Disability Rights Section** (✉ U.S. Department of Justice, Civil Rights Division, Box 66738, Washington, DC 20035-6738, ☎ 202/514–0301 or 800/514–0301; 202/514–0383 TTY; 800/514–0383 TTY, FAX 202/307–1198, WEB www. usdoj.zgov/crt/ada/adahom1.htm) for general complaints.

TRAVEL AGENCIES

In the United States, the Americans with Disabilities Act requires that travel firms serve the needs of all travelers. Some agencies specialize in working with people with disabilities.

➤ TRAVELERS WITH MOBILITY PROBLEMS: **Access Adventures** (✉ 206 Chestnut Ridge Rd., Scottsville, NY 14624, ☎ 716/889–9096, dltravel@ prodigy.net), run by a former physical-rehabilitation counselor. **Care-Vacations** (✉ No. 5, 5110–50 Ave., Leduc, Alberta T9E 6V4, Canada, ☎ 780/986–6404 or 877/478– 7827, FAX 780/986–8332, WEB www. carevacations.com), for group tours and cruise vacations. **Flying Wheels Travel** (✉ 143 W. Bridge St., Box 382, Owatonna, MN 55060, ☎ 507/451– 5005 or 800/535–6790, FAX 507/451– 1685, WEB www.flyingwheelstravel. com).

DISCOUNTS & DEALS

Be a smart shopper and **compare all your options** before making decisions. A plane ticket bought with a promotional coupon from travel clubs, coupon books, and direct-mail offers or on the Internet may not be cheaper than the least expensive fare from a discount ticket agency. And always keep in mind that what you get is just as important as what you save.

DISCOUNT RESERVATIONS

To save money, **look into discount reservations services** with toll-free numbers, which use their buying power to get a better price on hotels, airline tickets, even car rentals. When booking a room, always **call the hotel's local toll-free number** (if one is available) rather than the central reservations number—you'll often get a better price. Always ask about special packages or corporate rates.

When shopping for the best deal on hotels and car rentals, **look for guaranteed exchange rates,** which protect you against a falling dollar. With your rate locked in, you won't pay more, even if the price goes up in the local currency.

➤ AIRLINE TICKETS: ☎ 800/AIR– 4LESS.

➤ HOTEL ROOMS: **Hotel Reservations Network** (☎ 800/964–6835, WEB www.hoteldiscount.com). **Players Express Vacations** (☎ 800/458–6161, WEB www.playersexpress.com). **Steigenberger Reservation Service** (☎ 800/223–5652, WEB www.srs-worldhotels.com). **Travel Interlink** (☎ 800/888–5898, WEB www.travelinterlink.com). **Turbotrip.com** (☎ 800/473–7829, WEB www.turbotrip.com).

PACKAGE DEALS

Don't confuse packages and guided tours. When you buy a package, you travel on your own, just as though you had planned the trip yourself. Fly-drive packages, which combine airfare and car rental, are often a good deal. In cities, ask the local visitors' bureau about hotel packages that include tickets to major museum exhibits or other special events. If you **buy a rail-drive pass,** you may save on train tickets and car rentals. All Eurail- and Europass holders get a discount on Eurostar fares through the Channel Tunnel.

ELECTRICITY

To use electric-powered equipment purchased in the United States or Canada, **bring a converter and adapter.** The electrical current in Italy is 220 volts, 50 cycles alternating current (AC); wall outlets take Continental-type plugs, with two round prongs.

If your appliances are dual-voltage, you'll need only an adapter. Don't use 110-volt outlets marked FOR SHAVERS ONLY for high-wattage appliances such as blow-dryers. Most laptops operate equally well on 110 and 220 volts and so require only an adapter.

EMBASSIES & CONSULATES

➤ AUSTRALIA: **Australian Consulate, Milan** (✉ Via Borgogna 2, ☎ 02/777041).

➤ CANADA: **Canadian Embassy, Rome** (✉ Via G.B de Rossi 27, ☎ 06/445981).

➤ NEW ZEALAND: **New Zealand Embassy, Rome** (✉ Via Zara 28, ☎ 06/4417171).

➤ UNITED KINGDOM: **U.K. Consulate, Venice** (✉ Campo della Carità, 1051 Dorsoduro, ☎ 041/5227207). **U.K. Consulate, Rome** (✉ Via Venti Settembre 80A, ☎ 06/4825441).

➤ UNITED STATES: **U.S. Consulate, Rome** (✉ Via Veneto 121, ☎ 06/46741).

EMERGENCIES

No matter where you are in Italy, **dial 113 for all emergencies,** or find someone, such as a concierge, to call for you, as not all 113 operators speak English. The Italian word to use to draw people's attention in an emergency is *aiuto* (meaning "help," pronounced ah-*you*-toh). *Pronto soccorso* means "first aid" and will get you an ambulance (*ambulanza*). If you just need a doctor, ask for *un medico.* (Most hotels will be able to refer you to a local doctor.) Don't forget to ask the doctor for *una ricevuta* (invoice) to show to your insurance company in order to get a reimbursement. Other useful Italian words to use in an emergency are *al fuoco* ("fire," pronounced ahl fuh-*woe*-co), and *Al ladro* ("Follow the thief," pronounced ahl *lah*-droh). In Venice, a backup in emergencies is Sanitrans, a private road and water ambulance service.

Italy has a national police force (*carabinieri*) as well as local police (*polizia*, also known as *questura*). Both are armed and have the power to investigate crimes and make arrests. Always report the loss of your passport to either the carabinieri or the police (in addition to your consulate or embassy). Local traffic police are known as *vigili* (though their official name is *Polizia Municipale*). They are responsible for, among other things, giving out parking tickets and clamping cars, so before you even consider parking the Italian way, make sure you are at least able to spot their white (in summer) or black uniforms. (Many are women.) Should you find yourself involved in a minor car accident in town, you should call the vigili. The country-wide toll-free number to call the carabinieri in an emergency is 112.

➤ EMERGENCY SERVICES: **Carabinieri** (militarized police; ☎ 112). **Fire** (☎ 115). **Italian Automobile Club** (☎ 116). **Medical emergency and ambu-**

lance (☎ 118; not yet operational in all areas; alternatively call ☎ 113). **Police** (☎ 113). **Sanitrans** (☎ 041/5239977, WEB www.sanitrans. veniceone.com). **Vigili** (Venice ☎ 041/2748111, Padua ☎ 049/8205111, Verona ☎ 045/8077111, Vicenza ☎ 0444/221111, Trieste ☎ 040/366111, Treviso ☎ 0422/6581, Udine ☎ 0432/271111).

➤ HOSPITAL: **Venice Hospital First Aid** (✉ Campo SS. Giovanni e Paolo, ☎ 041/5230000).

➤ 24-HOUR PHARMACIES: The weekly list of after-hours pharmacies is posted on the front of every pharmacy.

ENGLISH-LANGUAGE MEDIA

☞ *See* Specialty Shops *in* Chapter 6.

GAY & LESBIAN TRAVEL

Local gays and lesbians maintain a low profile in Venice and the Veneto. Favorite clubs and bars are usually mixed rather than exclusively homosexual.

➤ GAY- & LESBIAN-FRIENDLY TRAVEL AGENCIES: **Different Roads Travel** (✉ 8383 Wilshire Blvd., Suite 902, Beverly Hills, CA 90211, ☎ 323/651–5557 or 800/429–8747, FAX 323/651–3678, lgernert@tzell.com). **Kennedy Travel** (✉ 314 Jericho Turnpike, Floral Park, NY 11001, ☎ 516/352–4888 or 800/237–7433, FAX 516/354–8849, WEB www. kennedytravel.com). **Now Voyager** (✉ 4406 18th St., San Francisco, CA 94114, ☎ 415/626–1169 or 800/255–6951, FAX 415/626–8626, WEB www.nowvoyager.com). **Skylink Travel and Tour** (✉ 1006 Mendocino Ave., Santa Rosa, CA 95401, ☎ 707/546–9888 or 800/225–5759, FAX 707/546–9891, WEB www.skylinktravel. com), serving lesbian travelers.

GUIDEBOOKS

Plan well and you won't be sorry. Guidebooks are excellent tools—and you can take them with you. You may want to check out color-photo-illustrated *Fodor's Exploring Venice,* thorough on culture and history, and pocket-size *Citypack Venice,* which includes a foldout map. Both are available at on-line retailers and bookstores everywhere.

HEALTH

The Centers for Disease Control and Prevention (CDC) in Atlanta caution that most of southern Europe is in the "intermediate" range for risk of contacting traveler's diarrhea. Part of this risk may be attributed to an increased consumption of olive oil and wine, which can have a laxative effect on stomachs used to a different diet. The CDC also advises all international travelers to swim only in chlorinated swimming pools, unless they are absolutely certain the local beaches and freshwater lakes are not contaminated.

FOOD & DRINK

In 2001, mad cow disease had a significant impact on Italian dining habits. Although into the fall there were no reported cases of the disease in humans in Italy, and only two Italian cows were found infected, most Italians stopped eating beef altogether. In the early part of the year news stories regularly reported that butchers were being driven out of business. The beloved *bistecca alla fiorentina,* the thick T-bone steak cut from Tuscan beef, was banned by the European Union; restaurants famous for this specialty have switched to grilled pork. Other traditional dishes at least temporarily unavailable include *osso buco* (braised veal shank), oxtail, and offal specialties prepared throughout the country. *Vitello* (veal), *vitellone* (young beef), and *manzo* (beef) are considered safe to eat by both the Italian government and the European Union (these are cuts that don't come in touch with spinal marrow). Yet consumers tend to trust veal only. As a result, some restaurants have experimented with "alternative meats" such as *struzzo* (ostrich) and *canguro* (kangaroo). *Cavallo* (horse meat, which is sweet and lean), *buffalo* (buffalo, like beef but less tender), and *coniglio* (rabbit) can be found at many butchers. The price of lamb and pork has risen 20%, while the price of fish has remained stable.

As of the fall of 2001, hoof-and-mouth disease had yet to have an impact on the Italian table.

PESTS & OTHER HAZARDS

Mosquitoes are a problem in Venice. In many hotel rooms you'll find the *fornelletto antizanzare,* an electrical devise that uses mosquito-repellent tablets. Insert a fresh tablet in the metal slot and plug the fornelletto in the wall (ideally in the vicinity of an open window): it should warm up after one minute. Leave at least one window open while the fornelletto is on and wash your hands carefully after touching tablets. One tablet is good for one night.

HIKING & WALKING

The Dolomites have many good places to hike and an extensive network of trails. For detailed information **contact the CAI** (Club Alpino Italiano) headquarters, which can put you in contact with local offices. Local tourist information offices can also be helpful.

➤ HIKING ORGANIZATION: **CAI** (✉ via Petrella 19, 201124 Milan, ☎ 02/2057231, FAX 02/205723201).

HOLIDAYS

National holidays include New Year's Day (January 1); Epiphany (January 6); Easter Sunday and Monday (March 31 and April 1 in 2002, April 20 and 21 in 2003); Liberation Day (April 25); St. Mark's Day in Venice (April 25); Labor Day or May Day (May 1); Festa della Repubblica (June 2), Assumption of Mary, also known as Ferragosto (August 15); All Saints' Day (November 1); Immaculate Conception (December 8); Christmas Day and Boxing Day (December 25 and 26).

The feast days of patron saints are observed locally. Many businesses and shops may be closed in Venice on November 21 (Madonna della Salute).

INSURANCE

The most useful travel-insurance plan is a comprehensive policy that includes coverage for trip cancellation and interruption, default, trip delay, and medical expenses (with a waiver for preexisting conditions).

Without insurance you will lose all or most of your money if you cancel your trip, regardless of the reason.

Default insurance covers you if your tour operator, airline, or cruise line goes out of business. Trip-delay covers expenses that arise because of bad weather or mechanical delays. Study the fine print when comparing policies.

If you're traveling internationally, a key component of travel insurance is coverage for medical bills incurred if you get sick on the road. Such expenses are not generally covered by Medicare or private policies. U.K. residents can buy a travel-insurance policy valid for most vacations taken during the year in which it's purchased (but check preexisting-condition coverage). British and Australian citizens need extra medical coverage when traveling overseas.

Always **buy travel policies directly from the insurance company**; if you buy them from a cruise line, airline, or tour operator that goes out of business you probably will not be covered for the agency or operator's default, a major risk. Before making any purchase, **review your existing health and home-owner's policies** to find what they cover away from home.

➤ TRAVEL INSURERS: In the United States: **Access America** (✉ 6600 W. Broad St., Richmond, VA 23230, ☎ 800/284–8300, FAX 804/673–1491, WEB www.etravelprotection.com). **Travel Guard International** (✉ 1145 Clark St., Stevens Point, WI 54481, ☎ 715/345–0505 or 800/826–1300, FAX 800/955–8785, WEB www.travelguard.com).

➤ INSURANCE INFORMATION: In Australia: **Insurance Council of Australia** (✉ Level 3, 56 Pitt St., Sydney NSW 2000, ☎ 02/9253–5100, FAX 02/9253–5111, WEB www.ica.com.au). In Canada: **RBC Travel Insurance** (✉ 6880 Financial Dr., Mississauga, Ontario L5N 7Y5, ☎ 905/791–8700; 800/668–4342 in Canada, FAX 905/816–2498, WEB www.royalbank.com). In New Zealand: **Insurance Council of New Zealand** (✉ Level 7, 111–115 Customhouse Quay, Box 474, Wellington, ☎ 04/472–5230, FAX 04/473–3011, WEB www.icnz.org.nz). In the United Kingdom: **Association of British Insurers** (✉ 51–55 Gresham

St., London EC2V 7HQ, U.K., ☎ 020/7600–3333, FAX 020/7696–8999, WEB www.abi.org.uk).

LANGUAGE

In Venice, language is not a big problem. You can always find someone who speaks at least a little English. Remember that the Italian language is pronounced exactly as it is written. (Many Italians try to speak English the same way, enunciating every syllable, with disconcerting results.) You may run into a language barrier in the countryside, but a phrase book and close attention to the Italians' astonishing use of pantomime and expressive gestures will go a long way. Try to **master a few phrases for daily use**, and familiarize yourself with the terms you'll need to decipher signs and museum labels.

More than just a dialect, locally spoken *veneziano* is a real language with a rich history. All the official documents of the Republic, all commercial transactions, and even many diplomatic missions to foreign states were written or conducted in the Venetian language. Today you'll hear veneziano being spoken everywhere in Venice—on the streets, in shops, hospitals, even in the city hall. Restaurant menus are often written in Venetian, Italian, and English. Bacaro menus are written only in Venetian. The Italian word *ciao* meaning both "hi" and "see you" derives from the old Venetian greeting *sciavo* (literally "slave," pronounced without the "v").

LANGUAGES FOR TRAVELERS

A phrase book and language-tape set can help get you started. *Fodor's Italian for Travelers* (available at bookstores everywhere) is excellent.

LODGING

Lodging options are numerous, from hotels to short-term rentals in city or country.

The lodgings we list in this guide are the cream of the crop in each price category. We always list the facilities that are available—but we don't specify whether they cost extra: when pricing accommodations, always ask what's included and what costs extra.

Assume that hotels operate on the Continental Plan (CP, with a Continental breakfast daily) unless we specify that they use the European Plan (EP, with no meals), Modified American Plan (MAP, with breakfast and dinner daily) or the Full American Plan (FAP, with all meals). All hotels listed have private bath unless otherwise noted.

APARTMENT & VILLA RENTALS

If you want a home base that's roomy enough for a family and comes with cooking facilities, **consider a furnished rental**. These can save you money, especially if you're traveling with a group. Home-exchange directories sometimes list rentals as well as exchanges.

➤ INTERNATIONAL AGENTS: **At Home Abroad** (✉ 405 E. 56th St., Suite 6H, New York, NY 10022, ☎ 212/421–9165, FAX 212/752–1591, WEB www. athomeabroadinc.com). **Drawbridge to Europe** (✉ 98 Granite St., Ashland, OR 97520, ☎ 541/482–7778 or 888/268–1148, FAX 541/482–7779, WEB www.drawbridgetoeurope.com). **Hideaways International** (✉ 767 Islington St., Portsmouth, NH 03801, ☎ 603/430–4433 or 800/843–4433, FAX 603/430–4444, WEB www. hideaways.com; membership $129). **Hometours International** (✉ Box 11503, Knoxville, TN 37939, ☎ 865/ 690–8484 or 800/367–4668, WEB http://thor.he.net/~hometour/). **Interhome** (✉ 1990 N.E. 163rd St., Suite 110, N. Miami Beach, FL 33162, ☎ 305/940–2299 or 800/882–6864, FAX 305/940–2911, WEB www.interhome. com). **Villanet** (✉ 11556 1st Ave. NW, Seattle, WA 98177, ☎ 206/417–3444 or 800/964–1891, FAX 206/417–1832, WEB www.rentavilla.com). **Villas and Apartments Abroad** (✉ 1270 Avenue of the Americas, 15th floor, New York, NY 10020, ☎ 212/897–5045 or 800/433–3020, FAX 212/897–5039, WEB www.ideal-villas.com). **Villas International** (✉ 950 Northgate Dr., Suite 206, San Rafael, CA 94903, ☎ 415/499–9490 or 800/ 221–2260, FAX 415/499–9491, WEB www.villasintl.com).

➤ ITALY-ONLY AGENCIES: **Cuendet USA** (✉ 165 Chestnut St., Allendale, NJ 07041, ☎ 201/327–2333;

✉ Suzanne T. Pidduck, c/o Rentals in Italy, 1742 Calle Corva, Camarillo, CA 93010, ☎ 800/726–6702). **Vacanze in Italia** (✉ 22 Railroad St., Great Barrington, MA 01230, ☎ 413/528–6610 or 800/533–5405).

➤ IN THE U.K.: **CV Travel** (✉ 43 Cadogan St., London SW3 2PR, England, ☎ 020/7581–0851). **Magic of Italy** (✉ 227 Shepherds Bush Rd., London W6 7AS, England, ☎ 020/8748–7575).

FARM HOLIDAYS & AGRITOURISM

Rural accommodations in the *agriturismo* (agritourism) category are increasingly popular with both Italians and international tourists. You stay on a working farm or vineyard, often in stone farmhouses that accommodate a number of guests. Contact local APT tourist offices, or, once in Italy, buy a copy of *Agriturism,* which lists more than 1,600 farms. Although it's available in Italian only from major bookstores, pictures and the use of international symbols describing facilities make the guide a good tool to use.

➤ AGENCY: **Italy Farm Holidays** (✉ 547 Martling Ave., Tarrytown, NY 10591, ☎ 914/631–7880, 𝔽𝔸𝕏 914/631–8831).

HOME EXCHANGES

If you would like to exchange your home for someone else's, **join a home-exchange organization,** which will send you its updated listings of available exchanges for a year and will include your own listing in at least one of them. It's up to you to make specific arrangements.

➤ EXCHANGE CLUB: **HomeLink International** (✉ Box 47747, Tampa, FL 33647, ☎ 813/975–9825 or 800/638–3841, 𝔽𝔸𝕏 813/910–8144, 𝕎𝔼𝔹 www.homelink.org; $106 per year).

HOSTELS

No matter what your age, you can **save on lodging costs by staying at hostels.** In some 4,500 locations in more than 70 countries around the world, Hostelling International (HI), the umbrella group for a number of national youth-hostel associations, offers single-sex, dorm-style beds and,

at many hostels, rooms for couples and family accommodations. Membership in any HI national hostel association, open to travelers of all ages, allows you to stay in HI-affiliated hostels at member rates; one-year membership is about $25 for adults (C$26.75 in Canada, £9.30 in the United Kingdom, $30 in Australia, and $30 in New Zealand); hostels run about $10–$25 per night. Members have priority if the hostel is full; they're also eligible for discounts around the world, even on rail and bus travel in some countries.

➤ LOCAL HOSTELS: **Foresteria Valdese** (✉ 5170 Castello, off Campo Santa Maria Formosa, 30122, ☎ 041/5286797, 𝔽𝔸𝕏 041/2416238, 𝕎𝔼𝔹 www.doge.it/valdesi). **Istituto Canossiano** (✉ Ponte Piccolo 428, Giudecca, 30133 Venice, ☎ 041/5222157, for women only; no bookings, show up in the morning). **Ostello di Venezia** (✉ Fondamenta delle Zitelle 86, Giudecca, 30133 Venice, ☎ 041/5238211, 𝔽𝔸𝕏 041/5235689).

➤ ORGANIZATIONS: **Hostelling International—American Youth Hostels** (✉ 733 15th St. NW, Suite 840, Washington, DC 20005, ☎ 202/783–6161, 𝔽𝔸𝕏 202/783–6171, 𝕎𝔼𝔹 www.hiayh.org). **Hostelling International—Canada** (✉ 400–205 Catherine St., Ottawa, Ontario K2P 1C3, ☎ 613/237–7884; 800/663–5777 in Canada, 𝔽𝔸𝕏 613/237–7868, 𝕎𝔼𝔹 www.hostellingintl.ca). **Youth Hostel Association Australia** (✉ 10 Mallett St., Camperdown, NSW 2050, ☎ 02/9565–1699, 𝔽𝔸𝕏 02/9565–1325, 𝕎𝔼𝔹 www.yha.com.au). **Youth Hostel Association of England and Wales** (✉ Trevelyan House, 8 St. Stephen's Hill, St. Albans, Hertfordshire AL1 2DY, ☎ 0870/8708808, 𝔽𝔸𝕏 01727/844126, 𝕎𝔼𝔹 www.yha.org.uk). **Youth Hostels Association of New Zealand** (✉ Level 3, 193 Cashel St., Box 436, Christchurch, ☎ 03/379–9970, 𝔽𝔸𝕏 03/365–4476, 𝕎𝔼𝔹 www.yha.org.nz).

HOTELS

Italian hotels are classified from five-star (deluxe) to one-star (very basic hotels and small inns). Stars are assigned according to standards set by regional boards (there are 20 in Italy), but rates are set by each hotel. During slack periods, or when a hotel is not full, you can often negotiate a discounted rate. In the major cities, room rates are on a par with other European capitals: deluxe and four-star rates can be quite extravagant. In these categories, **ask for one of the better rooms,** since less desirable rooms—and there usually are some—don't give you what you're paying for. Except in deluxe and some four-star hotels, rooms may be very small by U.S standards.

In all hotels there is a rate card inside the door of your room, or inside the closet door; it tells you exactly what you will pay for that particular room (rates in the same hotel may vary according to the location and type of room). On this card, breakfast and any other optionals must be listed separately. Any discrepancy between the basic room rate and that charged on your bill is cause for complaint to the manager and to the local tourist office.

Although, by law, breakfast is supposed to be optional, most hotels quote room rates including breakfast. When you book a room, specifically **ask whether the rate includes breakfast** (*colazione*). You are under no obligation to take breakfast at your hotel, but in practice most hotels expect you to do so. The trick is to "offer" guests "complimentary" breakfast and have its cost built into the rate. However, it is encouraging to note that many of the hotels we recommend are offering generous buffet breakfasts instead of simple, even skimpy "Continental breakfasts." Remember, if the latter is the case, you can **eat for less at the nearest coffee bar.**

Hotels that we list as ($$) and ($)—moderate to inexpensively priced accommodations—may charge extra for optional air-conditioning. In older hotels the quality of the rooms may be very uneven; if you don't like the room you're given, request another. This applies to noise, too. Front rooms may be larger and have a view, but they also may have a lot of street noise. If you're a light sleeper, **request a quiet room when making reservations.** Rooms in lodgings listed in this guide have a shower and/or bath,

unless noted otherwise. Remember **to specify whether you care to have a bath or shower,** since not all rooms, especially in lodgings outside major cities, have both.

You can save considerably on hotel rooms in Venice during low season, especially November through March (except during Carnevale and from December 22 to January 6, which are both considered high-season periods). In July and August, prices are slightly lower than in the spring and autumn months. There are **AVA hotel-reservation service booths** at Piazzale Roma (open daily 9 AM–10 PM, commission fee €2.00), inside the Santa Lucia train station (open daily 8 AM–9 PM, commission fee €0.50), and at the Marco Polo airport (open daily 9 AM–10 PM, commission fee €2.00). You must show up in person to use these services. A deposit, which will be deducted from your hotel bill, is required to hold a room (€11,00–€47.00 per person; V and MC accepted). Alternatively, **Venezia Sì** offers free reservations over the phone Monday–Saturday 9–7.

➤ RESERVING A ROOM: **AVA** administration (Venetian Hoteliers Association, ✉ 3829 Cannaregio, ☎ 041/5228004). **AVA hotel-reservation service booths** (✉ Piazzale Roma, ☎ 041/5231397; ✉ Santa Lucia train station, ☎ 041/715288 and 041/715016; ✉ Marco Polo airport, ☎ 041/5415133). **Venezia Sì** (☎ 800/843006 in Italy, toll-free, Mon.–Sat. 9 AM–7 PM; 0039/0415222264 from abroad, FAX 0039/0415221242).

➤ TOLL-FREE NUMBERS: **Best Western** (☎ 800/528–1234, WEB www.best-western.com). **Choice** (☎ 800/221–2222, WEB www.choicehotels.com). **Comfort** (☎ 800/228–5150, WEB www.comfortinn.com). **Hilton** (☎ 800/445–8667, WEB www.hilton.com). **Holiday Inn** (☎ 800/465–4329, WEB www.basshotels.com). **Jolly** (☎ 800/247–1277 in New York state; 800/221–2626 elsewhere in U.S.; 800/237–0319 in Canada; 800/017703 in Italy). **Quality Inn** (☎ 800/228–5151, WEB www.qualityinn.com). **Sheraton** (☎ 800/325–3535, WEB www.starwoodhotels.com). **Sheraton/The Luxury Collection** ☎ 800/221–2340; 800/835035 toll-free in Italy,

WEB www.starwood.com). **Westin Hotels & Resorts** (☎ 800/228–3000, WEB www.westin.com).

MAIL & SHIPPING

The Italian mail system is notoriously slow. Allow up to 15 days for mail to and from the United States and Canada, about a week to and from the United Kingdom and within Italy. Posta Prioritaria and Postacelere are special-delivery services from the post office that guarantee delivery within 24 hours in Italy and 3–5 days abroad.

Venice's main post office is open Monday–Saturday 8:10–7.

➤ POST OFFICES: **Venice main post office** (✉ Fondaco dei Tedeschi, near Rialto Bridge on Salizzada Fontego dei Tedeschi, ☎ 041/5289257; 160 countrywide postal information).

OVERNIGHT SERVICES

Private courier companies make sending overnight mail internationally from major cities in Italy fairly easy. Most couriers have a morning deadline for fastest service (next day or two-day delivery).

For information on rates, drop-off points, or to schedule a pick-up, call the services' toll-free numbers.

➤ MAJOR SERVICES: **DHL** (☎ 800/ 345345), 24 hours a day. **Federal Express** (☎ 800/123800), weekdays 8 AM–7 PM. **SDA** (☎ 800/016027), weekdays 8:30 AM–7:30 PM and Saturday 8:30 AM–1:30 PM.

POSTAL RATES

Airmail postcards and letters (lightweight stationery) to the United States and Canada cost €0.70 for the first 20 grams; for heavier stationery, you should go to the post office. Always stick the blue airmail tag on your mail, or write "Airmail" in big, clear characters to the side of the address. Postcards and letters (for the first 20 grams) to the United Kingdom, as well as to any other EU country, including Italy, cost €0.40. You can buy stamps at tobacconists and from the *francobolli* window in all post offices.

Posta Prioritaria (stationery and small packages up to 2 kilograms) and the more expensive *Postacelere* (up to 20 kilograms) are special delivery services from the post office that guarantee delivery within 24 hours in Italy and three to five days abroad. Lightweight stationery sent as Posta Prioritaria to the United States and Canada costs €0.77 (for the first 20 grams, double that for parcels up to 100 grams); to the United Kingdom, Italy, and all other EU countries it costs €0.62. As regular stamps are not valid for this service, make sure you buy the special golden Posta Prioritaria stamps. Postacelere rates to the United States and Canada range between €23.75 (€15.50 to the United Kingdom and Europe) for parcels up to 500 grams (a little over a pound) and €185.00 (€76.50 to the United Kingdom and Europe) for packages weighing 20 kilograms.

All rates are subject to change in 2002 and 2003.

➤ CONTACTS: **Informazioni Poste Italiane** (☎ 160 for information in Italian about rates and local post offices' hours of operation; 800/ 009966 toll-free for information about Postacelere; WEB www.poste.it for information in Italian about postal codes, rates, and post offices' addresses and to trace packages sent as Postacelere).

RECEIVING MAIL

Correspondence can be addressed to you care of the Italian post office. Letters should be addressed to your name, "c/o Ufficio Postale Centrale," followed by "Fermo Posta" on the next line, and the name of the city (preceded by its postal code) on the next. You can **collect it at the central post office** by showing your passport or photo-bearing I.D. and paying a small fee. American Express also has a general-delivery service. There's no charge for cardholders, holders of American Express traveler's checks, or anyone who booked a vacation with American Express.

MONEY MATTERS

Venice is considered the most expensive city in Italy. Italy's prices are in line with those in the rest of Europe, with costs in its main cities comparable to those in other major capitals, such as Paris and London. The days when the country's high-quality attractions came with a comparatively low Mediterranean price tag are gone. With the cost of labor and social benefits rising and an economy weighed down by the public debt, Italy is therefore not a bargain, but there is an effort to hold the line on hotel and restaurant prices that had become inordinately high by U.S. standards. Depending on season and occupancy, you may be able to obtain unadvertised lower rates in hotels; always inquire.

In Venice, admission to Palazzo Ducale is €9.30, but the same ticket includes entrance to seven other museums, including Museo Correr. Admission to the Gallerie dell'Accademia is €6.20 (free for children under 12). A vaporetto ride costs €3.10, a 40-minute gondola ride about €45.00. An English-language newspaper is €1.50. An inexpensive hotel room for two, including breakfast, is about €80.00 in low season, nearly twice as much in the spring and fall months and during Carnevale. An inexpensive restaurant dinner is €30.00, with a simple pasta dish on the menu running about €8.00 and ½ liter carafe of house wine €3.00. A *bacaro* (wine bar) lunch is €15.00, including a glass of good wine. A Coca-Cola (standing) at a caffè is €1.90, a cup of coffee €0.80, and a pint of beer from a pub or pizzeria (at the table) €4.80.

Prices throughout this guide are given for adults. Substantially reduced fees are almost always available for children, students, and senior citizens. For information on taxes, *see* Taxes, *below.*

ATMS

Fairly common in city centers and in smaller towns as well as in airports and train stations, ATMs are the easiest way to get euros in Italy. Don't, however, count on finding ATMs in tiny villages and rural areas.

CREDIT CARDS

All over Italy, Visa and MasterCard are preferred to American Express, but in tourist areas American Express is usually accepted. While increasingly common, not all establishments and stores take credit cards, and some require a minimum expenditure. If you want to pay with a card in a small hotel, store, or restaurant, it's a good idea to make your intentions known early on.

Throughout this guide, the following abbreviations are used: AE, American Express; DC, Diners Club; MC, MasterCard; and V, Visa.

➤ REPORTING LOST CARDS: **American Express** (☎ 336/668–5110 international collect). **Diners Club** (☎ 702/797–5532 collect; 800/864034 toll-free in Italy). **MasterCard** (☎ 800/870866 toll-free in Italy). **Visa** (☎ 800/018548 toll-free in Italy).

CURRENCY

The new single European Union (EU) currency, the euro, replaced the Italian lira in January 2002. There are seven notes—5, 10, 20, 50, 100, 200, and 500 euros (practically impossible to change outside of banks)—and eight coins: 1 and 2 euros, plus 1, 2, 5, 10, 20, and 50 centimes, or cents, which are 100 to the euro. While notes are the same for all EU countries, coins have one side that has the value of the euro on it and the other side with each country's own unique national symbol.

CURRENCY EXCHANGE

For the most favorable rates, **change money through banks.** Although ATM transaction fees may be higher abroad than at home, ATM rates are excellent because they are based on wholesale rates offered only by major banks. You won't do as well at exchange booths in airports or rail and bus stations, in hotels, in restaurants, or in stores. To avoid lines at airport exchange booths, **get a bit of local currency before you leave home.**

At press time, the exchange rate was €1.10 to the U.S. dollar, €0.71 to the Canadian dollar, €1.59 to the pound sterling, €0.58 to the Australian dollar, and €0.48 to the New Zealand dollar.

➤ EXCHANGE SERVICES: **International Currency Express** (☎ 888/278–6628 for orders, WEB www.foreignmoney.com). **Thomas Cook Currency Services** (☎ 800/287–7362 for telephone

orders and retail locations,
WEB www.us.thomascook.com).

TRAVELER'S CHECKS

Do you need traveler's checks? It
depends on where you're headed. If
you're going to rural areas and small
towns, go with cash; traveler's checks
are best used in cities. Lost or stolen
checks can usually be replaced within
24 hours. To ensure a speedy refund,
buy your own traveler's checks—
don't let someone else pay for them:
irregularities like this can cause delays. The person who bought the
checks should make the call to request a refund.

OUTDOORS & SPORTS

Italians are sports lovers, and several
daily newspapers are devoted solely
to sports. *Calcio* (soccer) is fiercely
popular in Italy, and if you make the
effort to get tickets to a match, you
won't be denied fancy footwork and
raving fans. The climate makes it
almost impossible to resist the temptation to try a cannonball serve on the
red-clay tennis courts, sink a birdie
putt on a scenic green, or just hike up
a hill to savor the fresh air and views.
Come winter, skiers take to the resorts and slopes of the Apennines and
the Alps for world-class conditions.

PACKING

The weather is considerably milder in
the Veneto region than in the north
and central United States or Great
Britain. In summer, stick with clothing
that is as light as possible, although a
sweater may be necessary for cool
evenings, especially in the mountains,
even during the hot months. Brief
summer afternoon thunderstorms are
common, so an umbrella will come in
handy. But don't underestimate the
humid cold of a Venetian winter:
bring a heavy coat and a raincoat, lip
balm, gloves, hats, sturdy shoes, and
scarves. Central heating is usually
warm enough, so you will be able to
escape the cold when indoors, and
you should pack with that in mind as
well. In Venice, a pair of comfortable
walking shoes and sunglasses are a
must in any season.

Italians dress exceptionally well, but
Venetians prefer a more relaxed,
casual style than the more fashion-
conscious Romans, Florentines, and
Milanese; they often wear shorts in
summer and parkas in winter. Men
aren't required to wear ties or jackets
anywhere, except in some of the
grander hotel dining rooms and top-
level restaurants, but are expected to
look reasonably sharp—and they do.
Formal wear is the exception rather
than the rule at the opera nowadays,
though people in expensive seats
usually do get dressed up.

Dress codes for visiting a church (no
bare knees or shoulders) are actively
enforced at the Basilica di San Marco
and the churches that are part of the
Chorus group.

For sightseeing, **pack a pair of binocu-
lars**; they will help you get a good
look at painted ceilings and domes. If
you stay in budget hotels, **take your
own soap**; many such hotels do not
provide it or give guests only one tiny
bar per room.

In your carry-on luggage, **pack an
extra pair of eyeglasses or contact
lenses and enough of any medication**
you take to last the entire trip. You
may also ask your doctor to write a
spare prescription using the drug's
generic name, since brand names may
vary from country to country. In
luggage to be checked, **never pack
prescription drugs or valuables.** And
don't forget to carry with you the
addresses of offices that handle refunds of lost traveler's checks. Check
Fodor's How to Pack (available in
bookstores everywhere) for more tips.

To avoid customs and security delays,
carry medications in their original
packaging; don't carry on any sharp
objects, including knives of any size
or material, scissors, manicure tools,
and corkscrews, or anything else that
might arouse suspicion.

CHECKING LUGGAGE

You are allowed one carry-on bag
and one personal article, such as a
purse or a laptop computer. Make
sure that everything you carry aboard
will fit under the seat or in the overhead bin. Get to the gate early, so you
can board as soon as possible, before
the overhead bins fill up.

If you are flying internationally, note that baggage allowances may be determined not by piece but by weight—generally 88 pounds (40 kilograms) in first class, 66 pounds (30 kilograms) in business class, and 44 pounds (20 kilograms) in economy.

Airline liability for baggage is limited to $1,250 per person on flights within the United States. On international flights it amounts to $9.07 per pound or $20 per kilogram for checked baggage (roughly $640 per 70-pound bag) and $400 per passenger for unchecked baggage. You can buy additional coverage at check-in for about $10 per $1,000 of coverage, but it excludes a rather extensive list of items, shown on your airline ticket.

Before departure, **itemize your bags' contents** and their worth, and label the bags with your name, address, and phone number. (If you use your home address, cover it so potential thieves can't see it readily.) Inside each bag, **pack a copy of your itinerary.** At check-in, **make sure that each bag is correctly tagged** with the destination airport's three-letter code. If your bags arrive damaged or fail to arrive at all, file a written report with the airline before leaving the airport.

PASSPORTS & VISAS

When traveling internationally, **carry your passport** even if you don't need one (it's always the best form of ID) and **make two photocopies of the data page** (one for someone at home and another for you, carried separately from your passport). If you lose your passport, promptly call the nearest embassy or consulate and the local police.

ENTERING ITALY

AUSTRALIAN CITIZENS

Citizens of Australia need only a valid passport to enter Italy for stays of up to 90 days.

CANADIAN CITIZENS

You need only a valid passport to enter Italy for stays of up to 90 days.

NEW ZEALAND CITIZENS

Citizens of New Zealand need only a valid passport to enter Italy for stays of up to 90 days.

U.K. CITIZENS

Citizens of the United Kingdom need only a valid passport to enter Italy for an unlimited stay.

U.S. CITIZENS

All U.S. citizens, even infants, need only a valid passport to enter Italy for stays of up to 90 days.

PASSPORT OFFICES

The best time to apply for a passport or to renew is in fall and winter. Before any trip, check your passport's expiration date, and, if necessary, renew it as soon as possible.

➤ AUSTRALIAN CITIZENS: **Australian Passport Office** (☎ 131–232, WEB www.dfat.gov.au/passports).

➤ CANADIAN CITIZENS: **Passport Office** (☎ 819/994–3500; 800/567–6868 in Canada, WEB www.dfait-maeci.gc.ca/passport).

➤ NEW ZEALAND CITIZENS: **New Zealand Passport Office** (☎ 04/494–0700, WEB www.passports.govt.nz).

➤ U.K. CITIZENS: **London Passport Office** (☎ 0870/521–0410, WEB www.ukpa.gov.uk) for fees and documentation requirements and to request an emergency passport.

➤ U.S. CITIZENS: **National Passport Information Center** (☎ 900/225–5674; calls are 35¢ per minute for automated service, $1.05 per minute for operator service; WEB www.travel.state.gov/npicinfo.html).

REST ROOMS

Public rest rooms are rather rare in Italy, and the locals seem to make do with well-timed pit stops and rely on the local bar. While private businesses can refuse to make their toilets available to the passing public, most bars will allow you to use the rest room if you ask politely. Alternatively, it is not uncommon to pay for a little something—a few cents for a mineral water or espresso—in order to get access to the facilities. Standards of cleanliness and comfort vary greatly. In cities, restaurants, hotel halls, department stores like La Rinascente and Coin, and McDonald's restaurants tend to have the cleanest rest rooms. Pubs and bars rank among the worst. In general, it is in your interest always to carry tissues with you. There are bathrooms in all airports and train stations (in major train stations you'll find well-kept pay toilets for €0.25–€0.50) and in most museums. There are also bathrooms at highway rest stops and gas stations; a small tip to the cleaning person is always appreciated. There are no bathrooms in churches, post offices, public beaches, or subway stations. Aside from those in Venice, pay toilets scattered through the city center of Italian towns are the exception, not the rule. In Venice, pay toilets are well posted and strategically located along the main tourist routes: on Strada Nova, near the Ponte delle Guglie; at the feet of the Accademia Bridge, on the vaporetto stop side of the Grand Canal; and next to the tourist information office at the Giardinetti Reali, close to Piazza San Marco. The charge is €0.50.

SAFETY

Protect yourself against purse snatchers and pickpockets by wearing a money belt or a pouch on a string around your neck, keeping either concealed. If you carry a bag or camera, be absolutely sure it has straps; you should sling it across your body bandolier-style. Always **be astutely aware of stealthy pickpockets,** especially when in jam-packed city buses and Venice vaporetti, when making your way through train corridors, and when in busy piazzas.

WOMEN IN VENICE AND THE VENETO

The difficulties encountered by women traveling alone in Italy are often overstated. Younger women have to put up with much male attention, but it is rarely dangerous. Ignoring whistling and questions is the best way to get rid of unwanted attention.

SENIOR-CITIZEN TRAVEL

EU citizens over 60 are entitled to free admission to state museums, as well as to many other museums—always ask at the ticket office. Older travelers may be eligible for special fares on Alitalia.

To qualify for age-related discounts, **mention your senior-citizen status up front** when booking hotel reservations (not when checking out) and before you're seated in restaurants (not when paying the bill). When renting a car, ask about promotional car-rental discounts, which can be cheaper than senior-citizen rates.

➤ EDUCATIONAL PROGRAMS: **Elderhostel** (✉ 11 Ave. de Lafayette, Boston, MA 02111-1746, ☎ 877/426–8056, FAX 877/426–2166, WEB www.elderhostel.org).

SHOPPING

The notice PREZZI FISSI (fixed prices) means just that; in shops displaying this sign it's a waste of time to bargain unless you're buying a sizable quantity of goods or a particularly costly object. Always try to bargain, however, at outdoor markets (except food markets) and when buying from street vendors. For information on VAT refunds, *see* Taxes, *below.*

SIGHTSEEING TOURS

EXCURSION TOURS

Venice's Cooperativa San Marco organizes tours of the islands of Murano, Burano, and Torcello. The 3½-hour tours depart daily at 9:30 and 2:30 (October through March, daily at 2 PM) from the landing stage in front of the Giardini Reali, just off Piazza San Marco; they cost about €16.00. Though popular, the tours tend to be annoyingly commercial and emphasize glass-factory showrooms, pressuring you to buy, sometimes at higher prices than normal. You can do better taking the vaporetto and looking around on your own.

American Express runs several worthwhile excursions starting from Venice. A day trip to Padua goes by boat along the Brenta River, with stops at three Palladian villas, and a return to Venice by bus. The tours run three days a week from March to October and cost €62.00 per person (€88.00 with lunch); bookings need to be made the day before.

The Palladio Villa Tour (by minibus, maximum eight people), besides a visit to the Palladian villas, includes a walking tour of Vicenza (Wednesday only; €98.00 per person, optional lunch €10.50 per person).

The interesting Hills of the Veneto tour (by minibus, maximum 8 people) focuses on the little-known, picturesque hill towns of Marostica, Bassano del Grappa, and Asolo; with stops at Villa Barbaro at Maser and at a vineyard along the Strada del Prosecco for a prosecco wine tasting (Tuesday, Thursday, and weekends; €90.00 per person, optional lunch €13.00 per person.)

For a break from the heat of Venice, consider the Dolomiti Tour (by minibus, maximum eight people), with a loop itinerary through the stupendous scenery of the Dolomites; stops include Titian's birthplace, Pieve di Cadore; the Santa Caterina and Misurina lakes; the famous Cime di Lavaredo peaks; and Cortina d'Ampezzo (Monday and Friday; €93.00 per person includes packet lunch). For these last three tours it is essential to make reservations a couple of weeks in advance.

ORIENTATION TOURS

Two-hour walking tours of Venice's San Marco area can be booked through American Express. Its daily "Jewels of the Venetian Republic" tour (about €24.00) ends with a glassblowing demonstration. From April 25 to November 15, American Express also offers an afternoon walking tour that ends with a gondola ride (about €26.00).

SPECIAL-INTEREST TOURS

"Secret Itineraries" is a two-hour guided tour of the Palazzo Ducale's secret rooms. It takes you to the Doge's private apartments, up into the attic and the Piombi prisons, and through hidden passageways to the torture chambers, where prisoners were interrogated. It costs €12.40, plus the regular €9.30 palazzo admission. English-language tours are usually offered daily at 10:30. Reservations are mandatory.

The Gallerie dell'Accademia's Quadreria can be visited every Tuesday afternoon by reservation at no extra charge.

From June through August, free guided tours (some in English) of the Basilica di San Marco are offered by the Procuratoria; information is available in the atrium of the church (no tours Sunday).

Venicescapes, an Italian-American cultural association, conducts five "theme" itineraries. Tours are all private and can accommodate a maximum of six people. Reservations are necessary (book at least a couple of months ahead). Custom-designed itineraries are available on request.

➤ CONTACTS: **American Express** (⌂ Salizzada San Moisè 1471, San Marco, ☎ 041/5200844, FAX 041/5229937). **Cooperativa Guide Turistiche Autorizzate** (⌂ San Marco 750, near San Zulian, ☎ 041/5209038, FAX 041/5210762, guideve@tin.it). **Cooperativa San Marco** (⌂ just off San Marco, ☎ 041/5235775 or 041/2406736). **Gallerie dell'Accademia** (☎ 041/5222247). **Palazzo Ducale "Secret Itineraries"** (☎ 041/5224951). **Venicescapes** ⌂ Campo San Provolo 4954, Castello, 30122, ☎ FAX 041/5206361, WEB www.venicescapes.org).

SMOKING

To the dismay of many clean-air-loving travelers, Italians are unrepentant smokers. Although the number of smokers is dropping slowly each year, Italians are known for disregarding the many no-smoking laws that do exist but are seldom seriously enforced. If you ask someone to smoke elsewhere or not to smoke in no-smoking areas, don't expect him or her to respond or respect your request. By Italian law, restaurants and bars should be equipped with ventilation systems, but many restaurants seem not to comply adequately. Your best bet for finding as smoke-free an environment as possible is to stick to large establishments and, weather permitting, to eat outside. All FS trains have no-smoking cars; always specify when you make reservations.

STUDENTS IN VENICE & THE VENETO

Venice is a popular student destination, with several facilities (information, lodging) geared to students' needs. The "Rolling Venice" youth card (€2.50:), for those aged 14 to 29, includes handy guidebooks to the city and offers good discounts for

ACTV vaporetto passes and a few museums, as well as many hotels, restaurants, and shops. It is available all year round from the Assessorato alla Gioventù (open weekdays 9:30–1, Tuesday and Thursday 9:30–1 and 3–5); from the Associazione Italiana Alberghi per la Gioventù (open Monday–Saturday 8–2); and from the Centro Turistico Studentesco e Giovanile (CTS; open weekdays 9:30–1:30 and 3–7). From July through September, you can purchase it also at the Agenzia Transalpino inside the train station (daily 8–8). You must show your passport to qualify.

➤ CONTACTS: **Agenzia Transalpino** (✉ inside Santa Lucia train station, ☎ 041/5241334). **Assessorato alla Gioventù** (✉ Corte Contarini 1529, behind Piazza San Marco post office, ☎ 041/2747651). **Associazione Italiana Alberghi per la Gioventù** (✉ Calle Castelforte, near the Scuola di San Rocco, ☎ 041/5204414). **Centro Turistico Studentesco** (CTS; ✉ opposite Ca' Foscari University, 3252 Dorsoduro, Venezia, ☎ 041/5205660, WEB www.cts.it).

TRAVEL AGENCIES

To save money, **look into deals available through student-oriented travel agencies.** To qualify you'll need a bona fide student I.D. card. Members of international student groups are also eligible.

The Centro Turistico Studentesco (CTS) is a student and youth travel agency with offices in major Italian cities; CTS helps its clients find low-cost accommodations and bargain fares for travel in Italy and elsewhere. CTS is also the Rome representative for EuroTrain International.

➤ IDS & SERVICES: **Centro Turistico Studentesco** (CTS; ✉ opposite Ca' Foscari University, 3252 Dorsoduro, Venezia, ☎ 041/5205660, WEB www.cts.it).**Council Travel** (CIEE; ✉ 205 E. 42nd St., 15th floor, New York, NY 10017, ☎ 212/822–2700 or 888/268–6245, FAX 212/822–2699, WEB www.councilexchanges.org) for mail orders only, in the United States. **Travel Cuts** (✉ 187 College St., Toronto, Ontario M5T 1P7, Canada, ☎ 416/979–2406 or 800/667–2887 in Canada, FAX 416/979–8167, WEB www.travelcuts.com).

TAXES

VALUE-ADDED TAX

Value-added tax (VAT, or IVA in Italian) is 20% on clothing, wine, luxury goods, and most services. On all consumer goods it is already included in the amount shown on the price tag, whereas on services it may not be. IVA is always included in restaurant bills, and only a few five-star deluxe hotels treat IVA as a separate 10% item added to the bill at departure.

To **get a VAT refund,** when you are leaving Italy take the goods and the invoice to the customs office at the airport or other point of departure and have the invoice stamped. (If you return to the United States or Canada directly from Italy, go through the procedure at Italian customs; if your return is via any of the EU countries, for instance, via Britain, take the Italian goods and invoice to British customs.) Under Italy's VAT-refund system, a non-EU resident can obtain a refund of tax paid on consumer goods. Shop with your passport and ask the store for an invoice itemizing the article(s), price(s), and the amount of tax. Once back home—and within 90 days of the date of purchase—mail the stamped invoice to the store, which will send the VAT rebate to you. The VAT on services is not refundable.

Global Refund is a VAT refund service that makes getting your money back hassle-free. The service is available Europe-wide at 130,000 affiliated stores. In participating stores, **ask for the Global Refund refund form** (called a Shopping Cheque). Have it stamped like any customs form by customs officials when you leave the European Union (be ready to show customs officials what you've bought). Then take the form to one of the more than 700 Global Refund counters—located at every major airport and border crossing—and your money will be refunded on the spot in the form of cash, check, or a refund to your credit-card account (minus a small percentage for processing).

➤ VAT REFUNDS: **Global Refund** (✉ 99 Main St., Suite 307, Nyack, NY 10960, ☎ 800/566–9828, FAX

845/348–1549, WEB www.globalrefund. com).

TELEPHONES

CALLS WITHIN ITALY

For all calls within Italy—local and long distance—you must dial the area code (*prefisso*), which begins with a 0, such as 041 for Venice or 06 for Rome. If you are calling from a public phone you must deposit a coin or use a calling card to get a dial tone.

AREA & COUNTRY CODES

The country code for Italy is 39. Area codes (*prefissi*) for major cities in the Veneto region are as follows: Venice, 041; Verona, 045; Treviso, 0422; Padua, 049; Belluno, 0437; Vicenza, 0444; Rovigo, 0425. Note that in Italy, all calls, including local ones, must be preceded by the appropriate regional area code, zero included. Calls from abroad must be preceded by 39 and the regional area code, zero included. For example, a call from New York to Venice would be dialed as 011 + 39 + 041 + local phone number; from Venice to another number in Venice, dial 041 + local phone number; from Rome to Venice, 041 + local phone number. Country codes are 1 for the United States and Canada, 61 for Australia, 64 for New Zealand, and 44 for the United Kingdom.

CELL PHONES

In Italy you may hear the ring of a cell phone at almost any time and in almost any place. Most Italians are addicted to their *telefonini* ("small phones") and leave them on in restaurants, bars, cafés, museums, trains, and buses. There are three major companies selling many different kinds of rates and special deals: Tim, Omnitel, and Wind. You can easily find out about their offers in any cell phone store. In summer 2001, all cell phone prefissi dropped the zero. For example, from New York to a cell phone number in Italy, dial 011 + 338 (instead of 0338) + personal phone number; in Italy, dial 338 + personal number. If you receive a call on an Italian cell phone you won't be charged for it like you would be in the U.S.

DIRECTORY & OPERATOR ASSISTANCE

For general information in English, dial 176. To place international telephone calls via operator-assisted service, dial 170 or long-distance access numbers (☞ Long-Distance Services, *below*).

INTERNATIONAL CALLS

Since hotels tend to overcharge, sometimes exorbitantly, for long-distance and international calls, it is best to make such calls from public phones, using telephone cards (☞ Public Phones, *below*). You can **make collect calls from any phone by dialing 172-1011,** which will get you an English-speaking operator. Rates to the United States are lowest around the clock on Sunday and 10 PM to 8 AM (Italian time) on weekdays.

From major Italian cities, you can place a direct call to the United States by reversing the charges or using your phone credit-card number. When calling from pay telephones, insert a coin, which will be returned upon completion of your call. You automatically reach an operator in the country of destination and thereby avoid all language difficulties.

LONG-DISTANCE SERVICES

AT&T, MCI, and Sprint access codes make calling long distance relatively convenient, but you may find the local access number blocked in many hotel rooms. First ask the hotel operator to connect you. If the hotel operator balks, ask for an international operator, or dial the international operator yourself. One way to improve your odds of getting connected to your long-distance carrier is to travel with more than one company's calling card (a hotel may block Sprint, for example, but not MCI). If all else fails, call from a pay phone.

➤ ACCESS CODES: AT&T Direct (☎ 172–1011). MCI WorldPhone (☎ 172–1022). Sprint International Access (☎ 172–1877).

PHONE CARDS

Prepaid *carte telefoniche* (calling cards) are prevalent throughout Italy and more convenient than coins. You buy cards at post offices and tobacconists, most bars and news stalls, and vending machines inside airports and major train stations. Tear off the corner of the card and insert it in the slot. When you dial, its value appears in the window. After you hang up, the card is returned so you can use it until its value runs out.

PUBLIC PHONES

Some pay phones accept only coins, others only *carte telefoniche,* so be smart and always have both ready in your pockets (☞ Phone Cards, *above*).

TIME

Venice is 6 hours ahead of New York (so when it's one o'clock in New York it's seven o'clock in Venice). Venice is 1 hour ahead of London, 10 hours behind Sydney, and 12 hours behind Auckland. Italy keeps time using the 24-hour (or "military") method, which means that after 12 noon you continue counting the hours forward: 1 PM is 13:00, 2 PM is is 14:00, and so on.

TIPPING

The following guidelines apply to Venice, but Italians tip smaller amounts in smaller cities and towns. In restaurants, a service charge of about 12% usually appears as a separate item on your check. A few restaurants state on the menu that cover and service charge are included. Either way, it's customary to leave an additional 5% to 10% tip, depending on the quality of service and the number of servers involved. Tip checkroom attendants €0.50 per person, rest room attendants €0.20–€0.30 (more in expensive hotels and restaurants). At a hotel bar, tip €1.00 and up for a round or two of cocktails.

Italians tip taxi drivers only under exceptional circumstances. Railway and airport porters charge a fixed rate per bag. Tip an additional €0.50 per person, more if the porter is very helpful. On sightseeing tours, tip guides about €1.00–€2.00 per person for a half-day group tour, more if they are very good. In museums and other places of interest where admission is free, a contribution is expected (starting from €1.00).

In hotels, give the *portiere* (concierge) about 15% of the bill for services, or €10.00–€20.00 if he has been generally helpful. For two people in a double room in a moderately priced hotel, leave the chambermaid about €2.00–€3.00 per day and tip a minimum of €1.00 for valet or room service. Double those amounts in an expensive hotel. In expensive hotels, tip doormen €1.00 for calling a cab and a minimum of €2.00 for carrying bags to the check-in desk, bellhops €3.00–€4.00 for carrying your bags to the room.

TOURS & PACKAGES

Because everything is prearranged on a prepackaged tour or independent vacation, you spend less time planning—and often get it all at a good price.

BOOKING WITH AN AGENT

Travel agents are excellent resources. But it's a good idea to collect brochures from several agencies, as some agents' suggestions may be influenced by relationships with tour and package firms that reward them for volume sales. If you have a special interest, **find an agent with expertise in that area;** the American Society of Travel Agents (ASTA; ☞ Travel Agencies, *below*) has a database of specialists worldwide.

Make sure your travel agent knows the accommodations and other services of the place being recommended. Ask about the hotel's location, room size, beds, and whether it has a pool, room service, or programs for children, if you care about these. Has your agent been there in person or sent others whom you can contact?

Do some homework on your own, too: local tourism boards can provide information about lesser-known and small-niche operators, some of which may sell only direct.

BUYER BEWARE

Each year consumers are stranded or lose their money when tour operators—even large ones with excellent reputations—go out of business. So **check out the operator.** Ask several travel agents about its reputation, and try to **book with a company that has a consumer-protection program.** (Look for information in the company's brochure.) In the United States, members of the National Tour Association and the United States Tour Operators Association are required to set aside funds to cover your payments and travel arrangements in the event that the company defaults. It's also a good idea to choose a company that participates in the American Society of Travel Agents' Tour Operator Program (TOP); ASTA will act as mediator in any disputes between you and your tour operator.

Remember that the more your package or tour includes the better you can predict the ultimate cost of your vacation. Make sure you know exactly what is covered, and **beware of hidden costs.** Are taxes, tips, and transfers included? Entertainment and excursions? These can add up.

➤ TOUR-OPERATOR RECOMMENDATIONS: **American Society of Travel Agents** (☞ Travel Agencies, *below*). **National Tour Association** (NTA; ✉ 546 E. Main St., Lexington, KY 40508, ☎ 859/226–4444 or 800/682–8886, WEB www.ntaonline.com). **United States Tour Operators Association** (USTOA; ✉ 342 Madison Ave., Suite 1522, New York, NY 10173, ☎ 212/599–6599 or 800/468–7862, FAX 212/599–6744, WEB www.ustoa.com).

TRAIN TRAVEL

All Italian trains have first and second classes. On local trains the higher first-class fare gets you little more than a clean doily on the headrest of your seat, but on long-distance trains you get wider seats, more legroom, and better ventilation and lighting. At peak travel times, first-class train travel is worth the difference. It's a good idea to **always make seat reservations in advance,** for either class.

The fastest trains on the Ferrovie dello Stato (FS), the Italian state railways, are the Eurostar trains, operating on several main lines, including Rome–Milan; Rome–Venice and Rome–Udine via Florence and Bologna; and Milan–Venice via Verona, Vicenza, and Padua. Supplement is included in the fare; although seat reservations are mandatory only during weekends and holidays, they are always advisable. Ask for seats located away from the smoking car, as the poorly designed partitions are not smoke-proof. Some Eurostar trains (the ETR 460 trains) have little aisle and luggage space (though there is a space near the door where you can put large bags). To avoid having to squeeze through narrow aisles, board only at your car—look for the car number on the reservation ticket.

The next-fastest trains are the Intercity (IC) trains, for which you pay a supplement and for which seat reservations may be required and are always advisable. *Interregionale* trains usually make more stops and are a little slower. *Regionale* and *locale* trains are the slowest; many serve commuters.

There is refreshment service on most long-distance trains, with mobile carts and a cafeteria or dining car. Tap water on trains is not drinkable.

Venice has rail connections with every major city in Italy and Europe. Some trains do not terminate at Stazione Ferroviaria Santa Lucia, on the Grand Canal in the northwest of the city. Instead, they stop only at the Stazione Ferroviaria Venezia-Mestre, on the mainland. All trains traveling to and from Santa Lucia stop at Mestre; to get from Venezia-Mestre to Santa Lucia, or vice versa (a 10-minute trip), purchase a €1 ticket at the station booth and take the first available train (keeping in mind that there is a *supplemento*—extra charge—for traveling on Intercity and Eurocity and Eurostar trains). Before boarding, validate your ticket in the machine on the platform; otherwise, you could be subject to a hefty fine.

Traveling by night is inexpensive, but you should be vigilant about security: never leave your belongings unattended (even for a minute) and make sure the door of your compartment is well locked. More comfortable trains run on the longer routes (Sicily–Rome, Sicily–Milan, Sicily–Venice, Rome–Turin, Lecce–Milan); ask for the good-value T3, the Intercity Notte, and the Carrozza Comfort lines. The Vagone Letto Excelsior has private bathrooms, coffee machines, microwave ovens, refrigerators, and a suite with a double bed and a VCR.

CUTTING COSTS

To save money, **look into rail passes.** But be aware that if you don't plan to cover many miles you may come out ahead by buying individual tickets.

If Italy is your only destination in Europe, **consider purchasing an Italian Railpass,** which allows unlimited travel on the entire Italian Rail network. The Italy Flexi Rail Card allows a limited number of travel days within one month: 4 days of travel for $216 first class, $144 second class; 8 days for $312 first class, $202 second class; and 12 days for $389 first class, $259 second class. Passes for travel on consecutive days are also available: 8 days for $273 first class, $182 second class; 15 days for $341 first class, $228 second class; 21 days for $396 first class, $264 second class; and 30 days for $478 first class, $318 second class.

The Italian Kilometric Ticket (*biglietto chilometrico*) is valid for two months and can be used by as many as five people to travel a maximum of 20 journeys covering an overall distance of 3,000 km (1,800 mi). The price is €185.00 for first class and €112.00 for second class.

Once in Italy, **inquire about the Cartaverde (Green Card) if you're under 26** (€24.00 for one year), which entitles the holder to a 30% discount on first-class travel and a 20% discount on second-class tickets. Those under 26 should also inquire about discount travel fares under the Billet International Jeune (BIJ) and Euro Domino Junior plans. Also in Italy, you can **purchase the Carta d'Argento (Silver Card) if you're over 60** (€24.00 for one year), which allows a 30% discount on first-class rail travel and a 20% discount on second-class travel. **Biglietti per mini-gruppi** entitle parties of three to five people traveling together to a 30% discount on all tickets except during Easter holidays, July–August, October 27–November 5, and December–January 14. Finally, disabled travelers in need of assistance can acquire the **Carta Blu (Dark-blue**

Card) (€6.00 for five years), which entitles their companion to ride for free. For further information, check out the Ferrovie dello Stato (FS) Web site (www.fs-on-line.com).

Italy is one of 17 countries in which you can **use Eurailpasses,** which provide unlimited first-class travel in all of the participating countries. If you plan to rack up the miles, get a standard pass. Train travel is available for 15 days ($554), 21 days ($718), one month ($890), two months ($1,260), and three months ($1,558). You can also receive free or discounted fares on some ferry lines.

If your plans call for only limited train travel, **look into the Europass,** which costs less than a Eurailpass and allows train travel in France, Germany, Italy, Spain, and Switzerland within a two-month period ($348 for 5 days of travel; $368 6 days; $448 8 days; $528 10 days; and $728 15 days). Rail travel to Austria/Hungary, Portugal, Greece, and Benelux can be added for additional fees ($60 one country, $100 two countries). You can receive discounts for two or more people. Note that fares are subject to change.

In addition to standard Eurailpasses, **ask about special rail-pass plans.** Among these are the Eurail Youthpass (for those under age 26), Eurail Saverpass and Eurail Saver Flexipass (which give a discount for two or more people traveling together), Eurail Flexipass (which allows a certain number of travel days within a set period), and the EurailDrive Pass, which combines travel by train and rental car.

Whichever pass you choose, remember that you must **purchase your Eurailpass or Europass before you leave** for Europe.

Many travelers assume that rail passes guarantee them seats on the trains they wish to ride. Not so. You need to **book seats ahead even if you are using a rail pass.** Seat reservations are required on some European trains, particularly high-speed trains, and are a good idea on trains that may be crowded—particularly in summer on popular routes. You will also need a reservation if you purchase sleeping accommodations.

TICKETING

Trains can be very crowded; it is always a good idea to make a reservation. To avoid long lines at station windows, **buy tickets and make seat reservations up to two months in advance** at travel agencies displaying the FS emblem. Tickets can be purchased at the last minute, but seat reservations can be made at agencies (or the train station) up until about five hours before the train departs from its city of origin. For trains that require a reservation (all Eurostar and some Intercity), you may be able to get a seat assignment just before boarding the train; look for the conductor on the platform.

You must **date-stamp your ticket in the small yellow or red machines on the platform before you board.** Once stamped, your ticket is valid for 6 hours if your destination is within 200 km (124 mi) and for 24 hours for destinations beyond that. You can get on and off at will at stops in between for the duration of the ticket's validity. If you forget to stamp your ticket in the machine, or you didn't make it in time to buy the ticket, you must actively seek out a conductor and pay a €6.00 fine. Don't wait for the conductor to find out that you are without a valid ticket (unless the train is overcrowded and walking becomes impossible), as he might charge you a much heavier fine. You can buy train tickets for nearby destinations (within a 200-km [125-mi] range) at tobacconists and at ticket machines in stations.

➤ TRAIN INFORMATION/ITALIAN RAIL PASSES: **Ferrovie dello Stato** (FS; ☎ 147/888088 toll-free in Italy, WEB www.fs-on-line.com).

➤ EURAILPASSES: **CIT Rail** (✉ 9501 W. Devon Ave., Suite 502, Rosemont, IL 60018, ☎ 800/248–7245). **DER Travel Services** (✉ Box 1606, Des Plaines, IL 60017, ☎ 800/782–2424, FAX 800/282–7474). **Rail Europe** (✉ 226-230 Westchester Ave., White Plains, NY 10604, ☎ 914/682–5172 or 800/438–7245, WEB www.raileurope.com; ✉ 2087 Dundas E., Suite 105, Mississauga, Ontario L4X 1M2, ☎ 416/602–4195).

TRANSPORTATION

First-time visitors find that getting around Venice presents some unusual problems: the layout is complex; the waterborne transportation can be bewildering; the house-numbering system is baffling; many street names in the *sestieri* (six districts) of San Marco, Cannaregio, Castello, Dorsoduro, Santa Croce, and San Polo are duplicated; and often you must walk, whether you want to or not. It's essential to have a good map showing all street names and vaporetto routes; buy one at a newsstand. Signs are posted on many corners pointing you in the right direction for the nearest major landmark—San Marco, Rialto, Accademia, etc.—but don't count on finding such signs once you're deep into residential neighborhoods.

TRAVEL AGENCIES

A good travel agent puts your needs first. Look for an agency that has been in business at least five years, emphasizes customer service, and has someone on staff who specializes in your destination. In addition, **make sure the agency belongs to a professional trade organization.** The American Society of Travel Agents (ASTA)—the largest and most influential in the field, with more than 26,000 members in some 170 countries—maintains and enforces a strict code of ethics and will step in to help mediate any agent-client disputes if necessary. ASTA (whose motto is "Without a travel agent, you're on your own") also maintains a Web site that includes a directory of agents. (If a travel agency is also acting as your tour operator, *see* Buyer Beware *in* Tours & Packages, *above*.)

➤ AGENTS IN VENICE: **Albatravel** (✉ Calle dei Fabbri 4538, San Marco, ☎ 041/5210123, FAX 041/5200781). **American Express** (✉ Salizzada San Moisè 1471, San Marco, ☎ 041/5200844, FAX 041/5229937). **Gran Canal** (✉ Ponte del Ovo, near the Rialto Bridge, 4759 San Marco, ☎ 041/2712111, FAX 041/5223380).

➤ LOCAL AGENT REFERRALS: **American Society of Travel Agents** (ASTA; ✉ 1101 King St., Suite 200, Alexandria, VA 22314 ☎ 800/965–2782

24-hr hot line, FAX 703/739–7642, WEB www.astanet.com). **Association of British Travel Agents** (✉ 68–71 Newman St., London W1T 3AH, ☎ 020/7637–2444, FAX 020/7637–0713, WEB www.abtanet.com). **Association of Canadian Travel Agents** (✉ 130 Albert St., Suite 1705, Ottawa, Ontario K1P 5G4, ☎ 613/237–3657, FAX 613/237–7052, WEB www.acta.net). **Australian Federation of Travel Agents** (✉ Level 3, 309 Pitt St., Sydney NSW 2000, ☎ 02/9264–3299, FAX 02/9264–1085, WEB www.afta.com. au). **Travel Agents' Association of New Zealand** (✉ Level 5, Paxus House, 79 Boulcott St., Box 1888, Wellington 10033, ☎ 04/499–0104, FAX 04/499–0827, WEB www.taanz.org. nz).

VISITOR INFORMATION

➤ AT HOME: **Italian Government Tourist Board** (ENIT; WEB www. italiantourism.com; ✉ 630 5th Ave., New York, NY 10111, ☎ 212/245–4822, FAX 212/586–9249; ✉ 401 N. Michigan Ave., Chicago, IL 60611, ☎ 312/644–0990, FAX 312/644–3019; ✉ 12400 Wilshire Blvd., Suite 550, Los Angeles, CA 90025, ☎ 310/820–0098, FAX 310/820–6357; ✉ 1 Pl. Ville Marie, Ste 1914, Montréal, Québec H3B 3M9, ☎ 514/866–7667, FAX 514/392–1429; ✉ 1 Princes St., London W1R 8AY, ☎ 020/7408–1254, FAX 020/7493–6695).

➤ LOCAL TOURIST OFFICES: **Venice tourist offices** (✉ Santa Lucia train station, ☎ 041/5298727; ✉ San Marco 71/f, near the Museo Correr, ☎ no phone; ✉ Venice Pavillon, next to the ex-Giardinetti Reali, ☎ no phone; ✉ Venice Pavillon, c/o Garage Comunale, ☎ no phone; ✉ Gran Viale S. Maria Elisabetta 6/a, Lido, ☎ no phone. ☎ 041/5298711 for information by phone, weekdays 8:30–5; WEB www.turismovenezia.it).

Marostica (✉ Piazza Castello 1, 36063, ☎ 0424/72127. **Padua** (✉ Stazione Ferroviaria, 35100, ☎ 049/8752077, WEB www.padovanet.it/ apt). **Treviso** (✉ Piazzetta Monte di Pietà 8, 31100, ☎ 0422/547632, WEB www.sevenonline.it/tvapt). **Trieste** (✉ Riva III Novembre 9, 34100, ☎ 040/ 420182; ✉ inside the Eurostar lounge at train station, ☎ 040/3478312, WEB www.triestetourism.it). **Udine** (✉ Piazza Primo Maggio 7, 33100, ☎ 0432/295972). **Verona** (✉ Piazza Bra, 37100, ☎ 045/8068680; ✉ Stazione FS, ☎ 045/8000861, WEB www.verona-apt.net). **Vicenza** (✉ Piazza Matteotti 12, 36100, ☎ 0444/320854, WEB www.ascom.vi.it/ aptvicenza).

➤ U.S. GOVERNMENT ADVISORIES: **U.S. Department of State** (✉ Overseas Citizens Services Office, Room 4811 N.S., 2201 C St. NW, Washington, DC 20520, ☎ 202/647–5225 for interactive hot line, WEB http://travel. state.gov/travel/html); enclose a self-addressed, stamped, business-size envelope.

WEB SITES

Do check out the World Wide Web when planning your trip. You'll find everything from weather forecasts to virtual tours of famous cities. Be sure to **visit Fodors.com** (www.fodors.com), a complete travel-planning site. You can research prices and book plane tickets, hotel rooms, rental cars, vacation packages, and more. In addition, you can post your pressing questions in the Travel Talk section. Other planning tools include a currency converter and weather reports, and there are loads of links to travel resources.

➤ SUGGESTED WEB SITES: For Venice: www.elmoro.com, www. meetingvenice.it, www.aguestinvenice. com; for Italy: www.initaly.com, www. wel.it.

WHEN TO GO

The main tourist season in Venice runs from April to October and during Carnevale. For serious sightseers the best months are from fall to early spring. The so-called low season is cooler and inevitably rainier, but it has its rewards: less time waiting on lines; and close, hurried views of what you want to see; and substantial hotel discounts.

CLIMATE

Weather-wise, the best months for sightseeing are March, April, May, June, September, and October—generally pleasant and not too hot. The hottest months are July and

August, when the south wind called *scirocco* brings about sticky days in Venice. Brief afternoon thunderstorms are common (and welcome) in the whole Veneto region. Venetian winters are relatively mild but always include foggy days, some rainy spells, and the risk of *acqua alta* (high water, when portions of the city are flooded). Inland towns are generally colder in winter and hotter in summer than Venice but less humid.

VENICE

Jan.	42F	6C	May	70F	21C	Sept.	75F	24C
	33	1		56	13		61	16
Feb.	46F	8C	June	76F	25C	Oct.	65F	19C
	35	2		63	17		53	12
Mar.	53F	12C	July	81F	27C	Nov.	53F	12C
	41	5		66	19		44	7
Apr.	62F	17C	Aug.	80F	27C	Dec.	46F	8C
	49	10		65	19		37	3

FESTIVALS & SEASONAL EVENTS

➤ DEC. AND JAN.: Art movies from central and eastern Europe are shown at the **Alpe-Adria Film Festival** in Trieste.

➤ JAN. 6: For the **Regata delle Befane,** five champions from the historical Bucintoro rowing club get dressed as the witch of the Befana to race along the Grand Canal.

➤ 10–12 DAYS PRECEDING LENT: **Carnevale,** dating from the Middle Ages, is celebrated in Venice with plays, masked balls, concerts, and fireworks.

➤ 2ND SUN. OF MAR.: **Su Zo per i Ponti.** a long-distance running event, goes "up and down the bridges" of Venice.

➤ APR. 25: For the **Festa di San Marco** a solemn Mass is held in the Basilica di San Marco to honor the city's patron saint, and red roses are sold.

➤ APR. AND MAY: During the **spring concert season,** performances are staged every Sunday at the castle in Monselice.

➤ 1ST, 2ND, OR 3RD SUN. IN MAY: Crews bring their own boats for **La Vogalonga,** an amateur rowing race.

➤ MAY: A **Jazz Festival** featuring internationally renowned performers is staged at various venues in Vicenza.

➤ LAST SUN. IN MAY: The **Sagra delle Ciliege** (Cherry Festival) is held in the castle yard at Marostica.

➤ 6TH SUN. AFTER EASTER: On **Festa della Sensa** (Ascension Day) a procession of boats makes its way toward the Lido, and the mayor, doge for a day, throws a golden ring in the water to celebrate the wedding of Venice and the Adriatic.

➤ MAY AND JUNE: Vicenza's Teatro Olimpico hosts a **concert season.**

➤ JUNE: The **International Jazz Festival** takes place in Verona.

➤ 2ND WK OF JUNE: Arquà Petrarca's **Festa della Sacra Trinità** features local food and wine tastings, theater performances, and music.

➤ 3RD WK OF JUNE: **La Maciliana** is celebrated in Chioggia with medieval fun and games.

➤ 3RD WEEKEND OF JULY: On the day of the **Festa del Redentore** a fireworks display takes place above the Giudecca and a pontoon for pilgrims is built across the Canale della Giudecca.

➤ THIRD WK OF JULY: The **Sagra del Pesce** (Fish Festival) in Chioggia has fish tasting, music, poetry, and theater.

➤ JULY AND AUG.: The **Festival dell'-Opera** sees spectacular productions at Verona's Arena.

➤ JULY AND AUG.: A **Shakespeare Festival** is staged at the Teatro Romano in Verona.

➤ JULY AND AUG.: **I Concerti Scaligeri** are free concerts that take place in Verona's Piazza dei Signori.

➤ JULY AND AUG.: The **Festival Internazionale dell'Operetta** is held at various venues in Trieste.

➤ JULY AND AUG.: Bassano del Grappa's **Opera Estate Festival** includes classical and jazz music, dance, opera, cinema, and theater.

➤ LAST WK IN AUG.: **Le Nozze Carsiche** is a biennial festival reenacting 19th-century weddings at Monrupino, near Trieste.

➤ END OF AUG.–1ST WK OF SEPT.: **Biennale del Cinema,** Venice's international film festival, takes place on the Lido, where first runs of movies are shown in the Palazzo del Cinema.

➤ FIRST SUN. OF SEPT.: A procession of historic boats with crews in Renaissance costumes opens the **Regata Storica** rowing competition.

➤ SECOND WEEKEND IN SEPT.: The *partita a scacchi* is a giant chess game played out by humans in Marostica every other year (on even-numbered years).

➤ THIRD WEEKEND IN SEPT.: A *palio* (horse race) run by Roman chariots takes place in the streets of Asolo.

➤ THIRD SUN. IN SEPT.: A **palio** with nine competing districts is run in Montagnana.

➤ THIRD SUN. IN SEPT.: The **Giostra della Rocca** in Monselice relives medieval feasting games, climaxing with the *quintana* (medieval competition).

➤ SEPT.: The **Teatro Olimpico** in Vicenza hosts a classical drama season.

➤ FIRST WEEKEND IN OCT.: The **Dama Castellana** in Conegliano has a human chess match with processions, flag waving, and fireworks.

➤ LAST SUN. OF OCT.: The **Venice Marathon** begins in Stra and follows the Brenta River into Venice.

➤ NOV. 21: **Festa della Madonna della Salute** includes the traditional thanksgiving pilgrimage to the Chiesa della Madonna della Salute.

WORDS AND PHRASES

English	Italian	Pronunciation
Basics		
Yes/no	Sí/No	see/no
Please	Per favore	pear fa-**vo**-ray
Yes, please	Sí grazie	see **grah**-tsee-ay
Thank you	Grazie	**grah**-tsee-ay
You're welcome	Prego	**pray**-go
Excuse me, sorry	Scusi	**skoo**-zee
Sorry!	Mi dispiace!	mee dis-spee-**ah**-chay
Good morning/afternoon	Buon giorno	bwohn **jor**-no
Good evening	Buona sera	**bwoh**-na **say**-ra
Good bye	Arrivederci	a-ree-vah-**dare**-chee
Mr. (Sir)	Signore	see-**nyo**-ray
Mrs. (Ma'am)	Signora	see-**nyo**-ra
Miss	Signorina	see-nyo-**ree**-na
Pleased to meet you	Piacere	pee-ah-**chair**-ray
How are you?	Come sta?	**ko**-may **stah**
Very well, thanks	Bene, grazie	**ben**-ay **grah**-tsee-ay
And you?	E lei?	ay **lay**-ee
Hello (phone)	Pronto?	**proan**-to
Numbers		
one	uno	**oo**-no
two	due	**doo**-ay
three	tre	tray
four	quattro	**kwah**-tro
five	cinque	**cheen**-kway
six	sei	say
seven	sette	**set**-ay
eight	otto	**oh**-to
nine	nove	**no**-vay
ten	dieci	dee-**eh**-chee
eleven	undici	**oon**-dee-chee
twelve	dodici	**doe**-dee-chee
thirteen	tredici	**tray**-dee-chee
fourteen	quattordici	kwa-**tore**-dee-chee
fifteen	quindici	**kwin**-dee-chee
sixteen	sedici	**say**-dee-chee
seventeen	diciassette	dee-cha-**set**-ay

eighteen	diciotto	dee-**cho**-to
nineteen	diciannove	dee-cha-**no**-vay
twenty	venti	**vain**-tee
twenty-one	ventuno	vain-**too**-no
twenty-two	ventidue	vayn-tee-**doo**-ay
thirty	trenta	**train**-ta
forty	quaranta	kwa-**rahn**-ta
fifty	cinquanta	cheen-**kwahn**-ta
sixty	sessanta	seh-**sahn**-ta
seventy	settanta	seh-**tahn**-ta
eighty	ottanta	o-**tahn**-ta
ninety	novanta	no-**vahn**-ta
one hundred	cento	**chen**-to
ten thousand	diecimila	dee-eh-chee-**mee**-la
one hundred thousand	centomila	chen-to-mee-la

Useful Phrases

Do you speak English?	Parla inglese?	par-la een-glay-zay
I don't speak Italian	Non parlo italiano	non **par**-lo ee-tal-**yah**-no
I don't understand	Non capisco	non ka-**peess**-ko
Can you please repeat?	Può ripetere?	pwo ree-**pet**-ay-ray
Slowly!	Lentamente!	**len**-ta-men-tay
I don't know	Non lo so	noan lo **so**
I'm American/ British	Sono americano(a)	**so**-no a-may-ree-**kah**-no(a)
	Sono inglese	**so**-no een-**glay**-zay
What's your name?	Come si chiama?	**ko**-may see kee-**ah**-ma
My name is . . .	Mi chiamo . . .	mee kee-**ah**-mo
What time is it?	Che ore sono?	kay **o**-ray **so**-no
How?	Come?	**ko**-may
When?	Quando?	**kwan**-doe
Yesterday/today/ tomorrow	Ieri/oggi/domani	**yer**-ee/**o**-jee/ do-**mah**-nee
This morning/ afternoon	Stamattina/Oggi pomeriggio	sta-ma-**tee**-na/**o**-jee po-mer-**ee**-jo
Tonight	Stasera	sta-**ser**-a
What?	Che cosa?	kay **ko**-za
What is it?	Che cos'è?	kay ko-**zay**
Why?	Perché?	pear-**kay**
Who?	Chi?	kee
Where is . . .	Dov'è . . .	doe-**veh**
the bus stop?	la fermata dell'autobus?	la fer-**mah**-ta del ow-toe-**booss**
the train station?	la stazione?	la sta-tsee-**oh**-nay
the subway station?	la metropolitana?	la may-tro-po-lee-**tah**-na
the terminal?	il terminal?	eel ter-mee-**nahl**
the post office?	l'ufficio postale?	loo-**fee**-cho po-**stah**-lay

the bank?	la banca?	la **bahn**-ka
the . . . hotel?	l'hotel . . .?	lo-**tel**
the store?	il negozio?	ell nay-**go**-tsee-o
the cashier?	la cassa?	la **kah**-sa
the . . . museum?	il museo . . .?	eel moo-**zay**-o
the hospital?	l'ospedale?	lo-spay-**dah**-lay
the first aid station?	il pronto soccorso?	eel **pron**-to so-**kor**-so
the elevator?	l'ascensore?	la-shen-**so**-ray
a telephone?	un telefono?	oon tay-**lay**-fo-no
Where are the restrooms?	Dov'è il bagno?	do-**vay** eel **bahn**-yo
Here/there	Qui/là	kwee-la
Left/right	A sinistra/a destra	a see-**neess**-tra/ a **des**-tra
Straight ahead	Avanti dritto	a-**vahn**-tee **dree**-to
Is it near/far?	È vicino/lontano?	ay vee-**chee**-no/ lon-**tah**-no
I'd like . . .	Vorrei . . .	vo-**ray**
a room	una camera	**oo**-na **kah**-may-ra
the key	la chiave	la kee-**ah**-vay
a newspaper	un giornale	oon jor-**nah**-lay
a stamp	un francobollo	oon-frahn-ko-**bo**-lo
I'd like to buy . . .	Vorrei comprare . . .	vo-**ray** kom-**prah**-ray
a cigar	un sigaro	oon see-**gah**-ro
cigarettes	delle sigarette	day-lay see-ga-**ret**-ay
some matches	dei fiammiferi	day-ee fec-ah-**mea**-fer-ee
some soap	una saponetta	**oo**-na sa-po-**net**-a
a city plan	una pianta della città	**oo**-na **pyahn**-ta day-la chee-**tah**
a road map of . . .	una cara stradaleldi . . .	**oo**-na **cart**-a stra-**tah**-lay dee
a country map	una carta geografica	**oo**-na **cart**-a jay-o-**grah**-fee-ka
a magazine	una rivista	**oo**-na rec-**voess**-ta
envelopes	delle buste	day-lay **booss**-tay
writing paper	della carta da lettere	**day**-la **cart**-a da **let**-air-ay
a postcard	una cartolina	**oo**-na car-toe-**lee**-na
a guidebook	una guida turistica	**oo**-na **gwee**-da too-**reess**-tee-ka
How much is it?	Quanto costa?	**kwahn**-toe **coast**-a
It's expensive/cheap	È caro/economico	ay **car**-o/ay-ko-no-mee-ko
A little/a lot	Poco/tanto	**po**-ko-**tahn**-to
More/less	Più/meno	pee-**oo**/**may**-no
Enough/too (much)	Abbastanza/troppo	a-bas-**tahn**-sa/**tro**-po
I am sick	Sto male	sto **mah**-lay
Please call a doctor	Chiami un dottore	kee-**ah**-mee oon doe-**toe**-ray

Help!	Aiuto!	a-**yoo**-toe
Stop!	Alt!	ahlt
Fire!	Al fuoco!	ahl **fwo**-ko
Caution/Look out!	Attenzione!	a-ten-**syon**-ay

Dining Out

A bottle of . . .	Una bottiglia di . . .	**oo**-na bo-**tee**-lee-ah dee
A cup of . . .	Una tazza di . . .	**oo**-na **tah**-tsa dee
A glass of . . .	Un bicchiere di . . .	oon bee-key-**air**-ay dee
Bill/check	Il conto	eel **cone**-toe
Bread	Il pane	eel **pah**-nay
Breakfast	La prima colazione	la **pree**-ma ko-la-**tsee**-oh-nay
Cocktail/aperitif	L'aperitivo	la-pay-ree-**tee**-vo
Dinner	La cena	la **chen**-a
Fixed-price menu	Menù a prezzo fisso	may-**noo** a **pret**-so **fee**-so
Fork	La forchetta	la for-**ket**-a
I am diabetic	Ho il diabete	o eel dee-a-**bay**-tay
I am vegetarian	Sono vegetariano/a	**so**-no vay-jay-ta-ree-**ah**-no/a
I'd like . . .	Vorrei . . .	vo-**ray**
I'd like to order	Vorrei ordinare	vo-**ay** or-dee-**nah**-ray
Is service included?	Il servizio è incluso?	eel ser-**vee**-tzee-o ay een-**kloo**-zo
It's good/bad	È buono/cattivo	ay **bwo**-no/ka-tee-vo
It's hot/cold	È caldo/freddo	ay **kahl**-doe/**fred**-o
Knife	Il coltello	eel kol-**tel**-o
Lunch	Il pranzo	eel **prahnt**-so
Menu	Il menù	eel may-**noo**
Napkin	Il tovagliolo	eel toe-va-lee-**oh**-lo
Please give me . . .	Mi dia . . .	mee **dee**-a
Salt	Il sale	eel **sah**-lay
Spoon	Il cucchiaio	eel koo-kee-**ah**-yo
Sugar	Lo zucchero	lo **tsoo**-ker-o
Waiter/Waitress	Cameriere/cameriera	ka-mare-**yer**-ay/ka-mare-**yer**-a
Wine list	La lista dei vini	la **lee**-sta **day**-ee **vee**-nee

INDEX

NOTES

FODOR'S VENICE AND THE VENETO

EDITORS: Matthew Lombardi, David Cashion

Editorial Contributors: Robert Andrews, Robin S. Goldstein, Valerie Hamilton, Carla Lionello, Caragh Matthews Rockwood

Editorial Production: Stacey Kulig

Maps: David Lindroth, Inc., Mapping Specialists, cartographers; Rebecca Baer and Bob Blake, map editors

Design: Fabrizio La Rocca, creative director; Guido Caroti, art director; Jolie Novak, senior picture editor; Melanie Marin, photo editor

Cover Design: Pentagram

Production/Manufacturing: Robert B. Shields

Second Edition

ISBN 0–676–90213–8

ISSN 1527–4845

SPECIAL SALES

Fodor's Travel Publications are available at special discounts for bulk purchases for sales promotions or premiums. Special editions, including personalized covers, excerpts of existing guides, and corporate imprints, can be created in large quantities for special needs. For more information, contact your local bookseller or write to Special Markets, Fodor's Travel Publications, 280 Park Avenue, New York, NY 10017. Inquiries from Canada should be directed to your local Canadian bookseller or sent to Random House of Canada, Ltd., Marketing Department, 2775 Matheson Boulevard East, Mississauga, Ontario L4W 4P7. Inquiries from the United Kingdom should be sent to Fodor's Travel Publications, 20 Vauxhall Bridge Road, London SW1V 2SA, England.

PRINTED IN THE UNITED STATES OF AMERICA

10 9 8 7 6 5 4 3 2 1

IMPORTANT TIP

Although all prices, opening times, and other details are based on information supplied to us at press time, changes occur all the time in the travel world, and Fodor's cannot accept responsibility for facts that become outdated or for inadvertent errors or omissions. So **always confirm information when it matters,** especially if you're making a detour to visit a specific place.

PHOTOGRAPHY

Bob Krist, cover. (Rialto Bridge, Venice)

Tibor Bognar, 11D.

Bonotto Hotel Belvedere, 14B.

G. Carfagna & Associati: Gianluca Belei, 9I. Guiseppe Carfagna, 11C, 11E, 13B. Robert Palozzi, 9H.

Corbis: 2 top left, 2 top right, 2 bottom center, 2 bottom right, 3 top left, 3 top right, 3 center right, 3 bottom right, 14G. Paul Almasy, 13A. Bojan Brecelj, 8F. Elio Ciol, 13C, 14D. Eye Ubiquitous, 12A. Mark L. Stephenson, 6C. Vanni Archive, 8G. Nik Wheeler, 12B.

Gritti Palace, 14F.

Blaine Harrington III, 12C.

Houserstock: Jan Butchofsky-Houser, 7D.

The Image Bank: F. Reginato, 10A.

Bob Krist, 1.

Daniele Nalesso, 3 bottom left.

Richard T. Nowitz, 7E, 10B, 16.

PhotoDisc, 14E./

Andrea Pistolesi, 6B, 8 top left, 9J.

Mark Smith, 14C.

Stone: John Lamb, 4–5. Jeremy Walker, 6A.

Villa Cortine Palace Hotel, 2 bottom left, 14A.

ABOUT OUR WRITERS

The more you know before you go, the better your trip will be. Venice's most fascinating small museum (or its chicest boutique or coziest bacaro) could be just around the corner from your hotel, but if you don't know it's there, it might as well be on the other side of the globe. That's where this book comes in. It's a great step toward making sure your next trip lives up to your expectations. As you plan, check out the Web as well. Guidebooks have been helping smart travelers find the special places for years; the Web is one more tool. Whatever reference you consult, be savvy about what you read, and always consider the source. Images and language can be massaged to make places appear better than they are. And one traveler's quaint is another's grimy. Here at Fodor's, and at our on-line arm, Fodors.com, our focus is on providing you with information that's not only useful but accurate and on target. Every day Fodor's editors put enormous effort into getting things right, beginning with the search for the right contributors—people who have objective judgment, broad travel experience, and the writing ability to put their insights into words. There's no substitute for advice from a like-minded friend who has just come back from where you're going, but our writers, having seen all corners of Italy, are the next best thing. They're the kind of people you'd poll for tips yourself if you knew them.

After travel writing tours of duty covering Mexico, Spain, the southern United States, and Ecuador, **Robin Goldstein** changed Romance languages and headed to Italy. Though his family roots lie in the southern villages of Toritto and Cherchiara di Calabria, Robin wandered north to the more seasonal shores of the Riviera and the fertile soils of the Po Plain. Unfortunately, not even the thick fog rolling in off the Adriatic could obscure the sorry demise of his beloved Sampdoria soccer team. Nevertheless, Robin continues to cover northern Italy for Fodor's; he updated the Veneto and Friuli chapters of this guide.

Carla Lionello grew up in Venice, where she received a degree in English literature. In 1989 she traded Piazza San Marco for the Spanish Steps and moved to Rome, where she writes for food magazines and guidebooks. Carla also teaches Italian cooking workshops to culinary-inspired visitors. She still hasn't learned to drive, but that doesn't stop her from traveling all over Italy in search of endangered pastry. She shares the essence of her native city with you in chapters 1 through 6 and Smart Travel Tips.

Don't Forget to Write

We love feedback—positive and negative—and follow up on all suggestions. So contact the Venice editor at editors@fodors.com or c/o Fodor's, 280 Park Avenue, New York, NY 10017. Have a wonderful trip!

Karen Cure

Karen Cure
Editorial Director